Handbook of Episodic Memory

Handbook of Episodic Memory

Editor: Jonathan Gold

AMERICAN
MEDICAL PUBLISHERS
www.americanmedicalpublishers.com

AMERICAN
MEDICAL PUBLISHERS
www.americanmedicalpublishers.com

Cataloging-in-Publication Data

Handbook of episodic memory / edited by Jonathan Gold.
p. cm.
Includes bibliographical references and index.
ISBN 979-8-88740-145-4
1. Episodic memory. 2. Memory. 3. Psychiatry. I. Gold, Jonathan.
BF378.E65 H36 2023
153.13--dc23

© American Medical Publishers, 2023

American Medical Publishers,
41 Flatbush Avenue,
1st Floor, New York,
NY 11217, USA

ISBN 979-8-88740-145-4 (Hardback)

This book contains information obtained from authentic and highly regarded sources. Copyright for all individual chapters remain with the respective authors as indicated. All chapters are published with permission under the Creative Commons Attribution License or equivalent. A wide variety of references are listed. Permission and sources are indicated; for detailed attributions, please refer to the permissions page and list of contributors. Reasonable efforts have been made to publish reliable data and information, but the authors, editors and publisher cannot assume any responsibility for the validity of all materials or the consequences of their use.

Trademark Notice: Registered trademark of products or corporate names are used only for explanation and identification without intent to infringe.

Contents

Preface

Memory is the ability of the brain to encode, store, and recall data or information when needed. It is the long-term retention of information for the goal of influencing future action. Episodic memory is the memory of everyday events that can be explicitly stated or conjured. It is a compilation of prior personal experiences that occurred at certain periods and locations. Humans may also recall their exact impressions, feelings and thoughts during a given encounter. Episodic memory comprises a synopsis of sensory-perceptual-conceptual-affective processing. It is able to retain activation/inhibition patterns over a long period of time. The hippocampus which is part of the medial temporal lobe is essential for the formation of new episodic memories. New procedural memories can be developed without the medial temporal lobe, but they are unable to recollect the events that transpired at that time. Such selected concepts that redefine the study of episodic memory have been presented in this book. Those in search of information to further their knowledge will be greatly assisted by it.

This book unites the global concepts and researches in an organized manner for a comprehensive understanding of the subject. It is a ripe text for all researchers, students, scientists or anyone else who is interested in acquiring a better knowledge of this dynamic field.

I extend my sincere thanks to the contributors for such eloquent research chapters. Finally, I thank my family for being a source of support and help.

Editor

Competitive trace theory: A role for the hippocampus in contextual interference during retrieval

Michael A. Yassa* and Zachariah M. Reagh

Department of Psychological and Brain Sciences, Johns Hopkins University, Baltimore, MD, USA

Correspondence:
Michael A. Yassa, Department of Psychological and Brain Sciences, Johns Hopkins University, 3400 North Charles Street, Ames 216A, Baltimore, MD 21218, USA
e-mail: yassa@jhu.edu

Much controversy exists regarding the role of the hippocampus in retrieval. The two dominant and competing accounts have been the Standard Model of Systems Consolidation (SMSC) and Multiple Trace Theory (MTT), which specifically make opposing predictions as to the necessity of the hippocampus for retrieval of remote memories. Under SMSC, memories eventually become independent of the hippocampus as they become more reliant on cortical connectivity, and thus the hippocampus is not required for retrieval of remote memories, only recent ones. MTT on the other hand claims that the hippocampus is always required no matter the age of the memory. We argue that this dissociation may be too simplistic, and a continuum model may be better suited to address the role of the hippocampus in retrieval of remote memories. Such a model is presented here with the main function of the hippocampus during retrieval being "recontextualization," or the reconstruction of memory using overlapping traces. As memories get older, they are decontextualized due to competition among partially overlapping traces and become more semantic and reliant on neocortical storage. In this framework dubbed the Competitive Trace Theory (CTT), consolidation events that lead to the strengthening of memories enhance conceptual knowledge (semantic memory) at the expense of contextual details (episodic memory). As a result, remote memories are more likely to have a stronger semantic representation. At the same time, remote memories are also more likely to include illusory details. The CTT is a novel candidate model that may provide some resolution to the memory consolidation debate.

Keywords: systems consolidation, multiple trace theory, pattern separation, pattern completion, interference, episodic memory, semantic memory, competition

INTRODUCTION

Much evidence points to the significant role of the hippocampus in the encoding of new declarative memories (Milner et al., 1998; Squire, 2009). This small region of the brain possesses a unique architecture that allows it to rapidly encode experiences while minimizing interference. Virtually every model of learning ascribes this important function to the hippocampus, especially in the context of declarative memory (in contrast to habit or other procedural learning). However, the role of the hippocampus in retrieval (especially episodic retrieval) is still subject to debate. While there is certainly a neural architecture in the hippocampus capable of such contextual retrieval, for example, a recurrent collateral network in CA3 capable of autoassociation (Marr, 1971), as well as an abundance of evidence across species demonstrating the involvement of the hippocampus in contextual retrieval tasks (Eldridge et al., 2000; Ryan et al., 2001; Yonelinas et al., 2002, 2005; Holdstock et al., 2004; Daselaar et al., 2006; Diana et al., 2007; Wiltgen et al., 2010; Goshen et al., 2011) there is still an active debate about whether the hippocampus is required for retrieval of *remote* episodic memories.

SYSTEMS CONSOLIDATION VS. MULTIPLE TRACE THEORY

At present, two major theories make predictions relevant to this debate. The first is the Standard Model of Systems Consolidation (SMSC: Squire and Alvarez, 1995), a widely influential view in the field. The SMSC holds that the initial memory trace is encoded both in the hippocampus and in the cortex, though the cortex is itself unable to initially support the memory. Rather, the hippocampus is critical in early encoding stages. As a function of time, replay, and retrieval, the hippocampus "teaches" the cortex the memory trace such that the associative connectivity between the individual elements of the cortical memory increase in strength over time. After the memory has been consolidated, the hippocampus is no longer required for retrieval. This is based on the large body of evidence that synapses change much more rapidly and dynamically in the hippocampus than they do in cortex (Frankland and Bontempi, 2005). These ideas were first proposed by Marr (1971) and further elaborated by the widely influential Complementary Learning Systems (CLS) model of McClelland et al. (1995), which emphasizes the role of hippocampal-neocortical interactions in the formation and consolidation of memory. Thus, the SMSC predicts that the hippocampus is not required for the retrieval of remote memories, only recent ones that have not yet been fully consolidated.

The competing theory, known as Multiple Trace Theory (MTT), was proposed by Nadel and Moscovitch (1997) as an alternative to the standard model. Unlike the SMSC, MTT proposed that the hippocampus has an important role in the retrieval of all episodic memories, including remote ones. Similar to the SMSC, MTT also proposed that memories are encoded in hippocampal-neocortical networks, but that each reactivation resulted in a different trace in the hippocampus. Hippocampal-bound traces are presumed to be contextual and rich in spatial and temporal details, while cortical-bound traces are presumed to be semantic and largely context-free. Thus, retrieval of remote semantic memories does not require the hippocampus, however, retrieval of remote episodic memories always does, irrespective of the age of the memory.

Thus, at the heart of the debate is the role of the hippocampus in the retrieval of remote episodic memories. In fact, that has been the only reliably testable prediction for either theory thus far, although as discussed below, support for even this single prediction proved tenuous at best. First, it is important to recognize that both models were proposed to explain amnesia data from human and animal studies, and namely the nature of the retrograde amnesia (RA) gradient observed. While numerous studies have observed that the RA gradient was temporally graded, in many cases, the RA gradient was flat, and in some cases the degree of RA gradient depended on the size of the lesion (reviewed in Frankland and Bontempi, 2005). In addition to lesion data, data from functional magnetic resonance imaging (fMRI) has been brought to bear on this debate. For example, Nadel and Moscovitch (1997) have shown that medial temporal fMRI activity was equally predictive of recent and remote memory retrieval. However, a major criticism of these studies is that the hippocampus is involved in incidental and automatic encoding during retrieval tasks, which may obscure retrieval-related activity (Buckner et al., 2001; Haist et al., 2001; Stark and Okado, 2003). A recent survey of the evidence based on amnesia studies in rodents with partial and full hippocampal damage provides overwhelming support for flat RA gradients, which argues against the SMSC (cf. Sutherland et al., 2010). Importantly, however, these data also argue against one prediction of MTT, which is that *partial* hippocampal damage will lead to a temporal RA gradient. Thus, neither model can adequately account for lesion data in animals.

Two particularly compelling pieces of data are worth discussing here to further illustrate the complexity of this debate. Scoville and Milner (1957) initially reported that patient H. M. had a case of temporally graded RA. In fact, much of the subsequent work on RA was based on this initial finding. Much later, however, as it became clearer that neuropsychological testing procedures were not as refined in that era and that episodic memory could not have been tested fully. Corkin (2002) later asserted that "H. M. was unable to supply an episodic memory of his mother or his father – he could not narrate even one event that occurred at a specific time and place." She surmised that many of the remote memories H. M. was able to retrieve were indeed "semanticized." In contrast, patient E. P., another case of profound amnesia studied by Squire and colleagues, was able to demonstrate highly detailed spatial remote memories (Stefanacci et al., 2000), arguing against the notion of a flat episodic RA gradient. This is further complicated by the inconsistency of results across studies of different amnesic patients with partial medial temporal lobe or hippocampal damage, and the lack of detailed neuroanatomical quantification in many cases. Thus, evidence from amnesia as to the RA gradient is not entirely conclusive, and provides only partial and sometimes conflicting support for either of the major theories discussed above.

A recent study by Goshen et al. (2011) used optogenetic techniques to demonstrate that hippocampal CA1 neuron activation was necessary for the retrieval of several week old (i.e., remote) memories, providing evidence against the SMSC. However, they also showed that longer inhibition (matching the timescale of the more typical pharmacological inhibition) abolished this dependence on the hippocampus, weakening the account provided by MTT. While Goshen and colleagues suggested that there is compensation via other structures such as the anterior cingulate cortex, the data can be taken to suggest both MTT and SMSC may both be at work and that perhaps each offers elements of the true nature of memory consolidation. This recent work motivates and underscores the value of alternate proposals that attempt to harmonize between the two models.

THE HIPPOCAMPUS AS AN INDEX

Both accounts discussed above rely to an extent on the notion of hippocampal indexing. These ideas were initially presented by Teyler and DiScenna (1985), and were formally developed into the hippocampal memory indexing theory (Teyler and DiScenna, 1986). This theory has served as a critical component of our current understanding of hippocampal computations, and as such, it warrants discussion here (for review, see Teyler and Rudy, 2007).

The central aim of the hippocampal memory indexing theory is to explain the nature of hippocampal involvement in encoding and retrieving memory traces. Particularly, this was among the first attempts at explaining interactions between the hippocampus and neocortex during episodic memory computations. Though evidence had accumulated to underscore the importance of the hippocampus in many memory processes, two important realizations came to light. First, there appeared to be multiple neural networks capable of supporting memory (Sherry and Schacter, 1987). Second, the neocortex itself was found to be sufficient to support some aspects of memory (Squire et al., 1984). Tulving and Markowitsch (1998) went on to propose that episodic memory – that is, memory rich in associated contextual details – is especially dependent on the hippocampus. Indexing theory describes the involvement and ultimate fate of these contextual details.

According to this theory, when a memory trace is encoded, inputs from cortical sensory regions activate a relatively small population of hippocampal synapses. The hippocampus in turn activates a network of neocortical regions, and as the memory is consolidated, the connections between the hippocampus and neocortex are strengthened. Laying down hippocampal-neocortical connections in this manner creates a physical instantiation of the memory trace. Importantly, the hippocampus here plays a pivotal role in memory retrieval. Activation of a small subset of neocortical regions, part of a larger pattern comprising a consolidated memory trace, can signal the hippocampus to re-instantiate the full pattern despite partial or degraded input. In short, this provides an account for how certain aspects or contextual details of an event can lead to recall of other related details.

It deserves further emphasis that under this interpretation, the hippocampus does not store details about an event *per se*, but as the name of the theory implies, rather acts as an index. That is, as was described in Teyler and DiScenna's theory, the hippocampus is proposed to serve in coupling the activity of neocortical regions such that patterns of activity can induce recall of a given memory trace. To make this proposition as clear as possible, let us consider another description. If information is stored across the neocortex, we might imagine it as a library. Memories, much like library books, are often added, removed, or replaced. When reconstructing an experience, one may need to access information residing in different wings of the library. This is where the hippocampus, our trusty librarian, comes in. While it has not stored the wealth of knowledge contained in the library in a way that it can readily reproduce, it can point to the correct locations where this knowledge can be retrieved.

COMPETITIVE TRACE THEORY

We propose an alternative to the current theories of recent and remote memory that combines elements of SMSC and MTT largely within the framework of indexing theory. The account, which we will refer to as the competitive trace theory (CTT), is an integrated theory that attempts to explain phenomenological distinctions such as episodic vs. semantic, using neurocomputational proposals based on interference and associations.

CONSOLIDATION AND DECONTEXTUALIZATION

First, we will start with some operational definitions. The words "episodic" and "semantic" have been used abundantly in the memory literature to refer to memories that are rich in contextual detail and memories that are devoid of such details, respectively. However, there is an additional important distinction that should be considered here. That is the accuracy of such memory, which is often uncorrelated with the success of recollection (Gallo et al., 2001; Roediger et al., 2004; Kensinger and Schacter, 2007; Stahl and Klauer, 2008; Kim and Yassa, 2013). Thus, in the CTT framework, the word "episodic" will only be used to describe the phenomenological experience of contextual recollection and not in reference to the accuracy of the memory. Inherent in this assignment is the strong claim that these labels ("recollection" and "episodic") are only helpful insofar as they describe the experience and not describe the memory representation itself, which is far more dynamic and often contains illusory details.

The word "semantic," on the other hand, will be used to refer to the accurate knowledge that builds up over time and with much repetition. The use of these terms will become more defined as we describe the central tenets of the model, and we will maintain that their use is only helpful in relative terms and not absolutes (i.e., one memory can be *more episodic than* another, but should not be labeled as "episodic" absent a frame of reference). For now, it is important to bear in mind three crucial assumptions of CTT: (1) memories are most episodic *and* veridical at the moment they are first encoded, (2) with every subsequent reactivation, the memory can become less episodic, and accurate details can be replaced with illusory details, and (3) central features of experiences become simultaneously consolidated and decontextualized (lose associated details) over time.

How does this occur? We suggest that when a memory is reactivated by an internal or external cue, the hippocampus acts to re-instantiate the neural signature of the original memory trace. In doing so, the hippocampus effectively recombines the elements of the original memory trace. Critically, the central features of that memory trace are reactivated. However, unlike prior theories of episodic memory retrieval, we propose that this process potentially adds or subtracts individual contextual features. Given the reactivation of the central features of the memory trace, the new memory significantly overlaps with the original. However, some of the features are non-overlapping, which leads to a slightly altered version of the memory. This altered memory is now capable of being stored as a new memory trace and undergoes the same storage process as the original memory. This in some ways is reminiscent of MTT, but with several important distinctions. According to our proposal, these memories are not stored in parallel, but rather compete for representation in the neocortex. Also, MTT hypothesizes that the memory traces themselves are stored in the hippocampus and not in the neocortex (this is the logic behind the "larger lesions knock out older memories" effect (Nadel and Moscovitch, 1998). Neocortical traces, according to MTT, are overlapping only insofar as the encoding and retrieval contexts are overlapping, which allows for contextual retrieval driven by hippocampal or neocortical traces. CTT, on the other hand, hypothesizes that the hippocampus itself is not the site of trace storage but rather it links the individual components of a neocortical memory together such that it can be retrieved later by the hippocampus or by the neocortex directly. Furthermore, neocortical traces themselves become devoid of context with increasing reactivations.

Two distinct phenomena can occur here: consolidation and decontextualization. First, overlapping features in the memories should not compete for representation and thus are strengthened (i.e., consolidated) in a Hebbian fashion. As a result of repeated activations, these overlapping features have a higher likelihood of being retrieved with high fidelity. The increase in associative connectivity over time allows these personal semantic components of the memory to become hippocampus-independent. That is, the overlapping neocortical components of such a memory trace have become strengthened to the extent that the hippocampus is no longer necessary to couple their activity. Second, the non-overlapping features should compete with one another resulting in mutual inhibition in an anti-Hebbian fashion, and a reduced likelihood of any of such features being retrieved. In other words, memories become decontextualized.

It follows from the above that retrieval of remote memories appears episodic and contextual because of hippocampal reconstruction and re-encoding, rather than a reactivation of a veridical representation. Without the presence of the hippocampus during retrieval (as in amnesia), the only retrievable memory is the high fidelity semantic representation in the neocortex (see **Figure 1**). These highly semanticized memories, having been consolidated and reconsolidated, are likely to feature a core set of important facts but little contextual depth. Thus, CTT can be viewed as a harmonization of SMSC and MTT in which consolidation and hippocampal independence occurs for semantic components of experiences via a multiple trace mechanism, provided that the non-overlapping portions of these traces compete for representation.

The CTT model asserts that recent episodic memories and remote episodic memories, although they share phenomenological features such as the sense of recollection or mental time

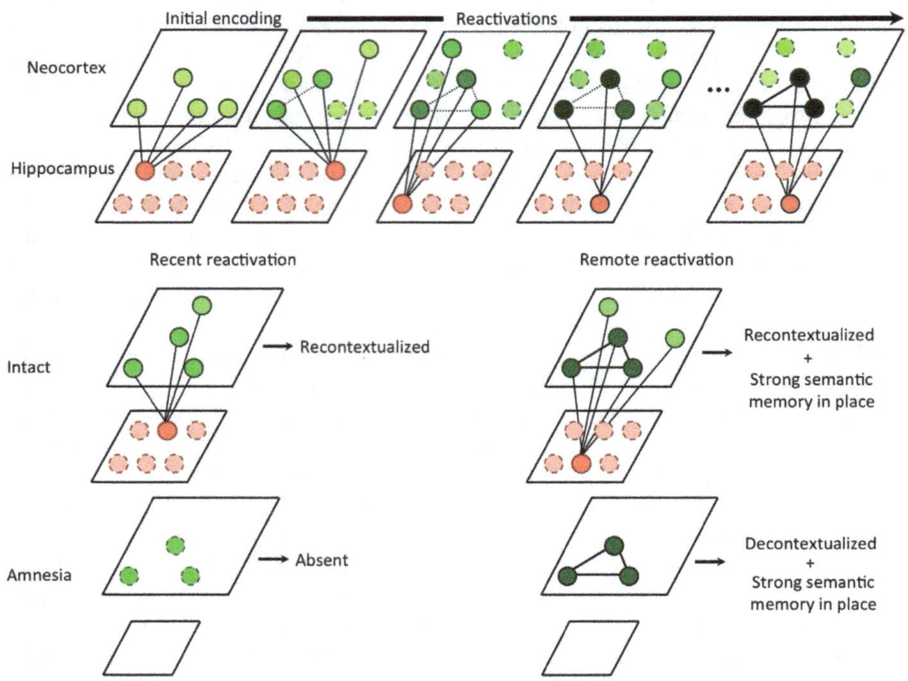

FIGURE 1 | Hippocampal competitive trace theory. Every time a memory is reactivated, the hippocampus encodes a partially overlapping trace that serves to compete with other similar traces from other reactivations in the neocortex. In the hippocampus, traces are non-overlapping due to pattern separation. In the neocortex, the overlapping features are strengthened (i.e., consolidated) while the non-overlapping features become decontextualized. During recent memory reactivation, an intact hippocampus is able to recontextualizes the memory, storing an additional trace. In amnesia, the recent memory cannot be retrieved in the absence of the hippocampus, since no features have yet been consolidated. During remote memory reactivation, an intact hippocampus continues to recontextualizes the memory, however, a strong consolidated semantic memory is in place due to a number of prior reactivations. In amnesia, the remote memory can be retrieved at least in part based on the semantic memory. Absent the hippocampus, recontextualization can no longer occur and additionally, the retrieval experience may be less contextual than that of an intact subject.

travel (Suddendorf and Corballis, 1997), possess underlying representations that could not be more different. A recent memory has no semantic components as those take time and repeated instances of remembering to build, but it is rich in accurate contextual detail. A remote memory, on the other hand, has a strong semantic component as a result of repeated retrieval events, but also contains degraded contextual information, or reconstructed contextual details that are often inaccurate.

Given these assumptions, we can redefine systems consolidation as the selective strengthening of the core content of the memory in neocortical circuits via hippocampal-neocortical interactions, coupled with a selective weakening of irrelevant and highly variable contextual details associated with each reactivation of the memory. It is important to note that the second condition of consolidation is most directly observable in hippocampal amnesia as the presence of the hippocampus in the intact brain gives the illusion of intact contextual detail, while in fact this experience is the direct result of mnemonic reconstruction and retrieval of illusory contextual details (**Figure 1**).

This raises the question of why the hippocampus continues to manufacture these illusory recollections, while a perfectly intact semantic memory is accessible in the neocortex. There are several potential answers. First, it is likely that contextual recollection, despite its inaccuracy, facilitates social interactions, and the sharing of experiences for the purpose of social bond formation. Second, reconstructing such details, which become influenced by cultural and other personal biases, may serve the important adaptive role of creating narratives that can influence others' behavior. Imagine, for example, how compelling reading someone's autobiography can be. Of course, another alternative is that there is no evolutionary advantage to recollection aside from facilitating the competition that is used to abstract memories so that massive amounts of information can be stored. In this sense, it may better facilitate learning and future adaptive behavior to incorporate illusory details into a memory than to simply forego details altogether, and the recollective experience may be nothing more than an epiphenomenon of an otherwise adaptive system.

THE RECONTEXTUALIZATION CONTINUUM

Figure 2 illustrates the episodic-semantic memory continuum (purely based on the retrieval experience, not taking into consideration the accuracy of memory). Given the slow cortical dynamics responsible for consolidation, this relationship is best represented as a continuum of decontextualization/recontextualization. In other words, the axis of this continuum is the degree of contextual detail (a function of reactivation events), which can be formally quantified. The hippocampus, at the very left of the continuum, is a context-encoding, associative device that simultaneously

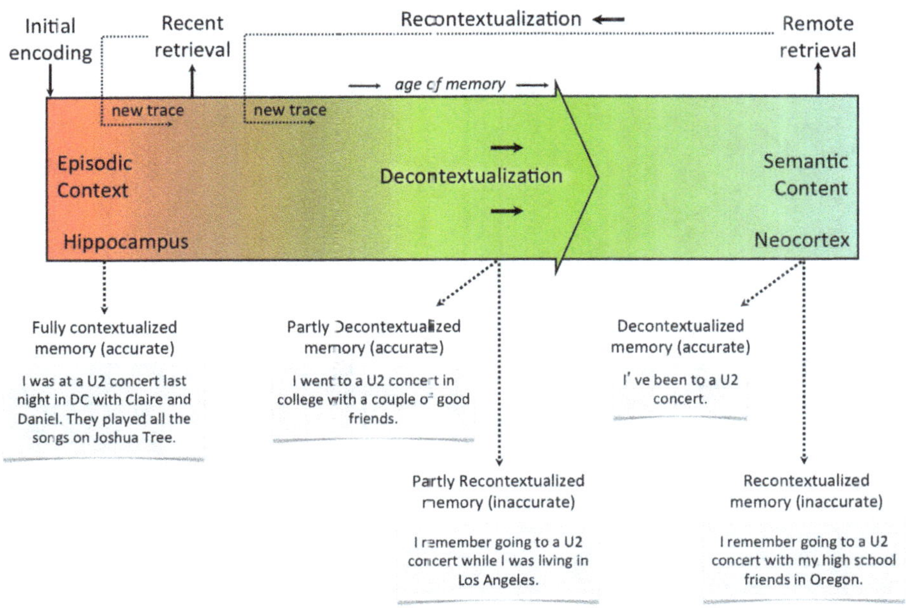

FIGURE 2 | The recontextualization continuum. Memories are most rich in episodic context the moment they are first encoded. With every subsequent reactivation (whether it's internally or externally cued), the memory becomes less episodic and more semantic (i.e., decontextualized). Every time a memory is retrieved, however, it can be recontextualized or re-encoded as a new trace with some overlapping features and some new ones. This means memories recalled from the distant past could either be decontextualized and accurate or recontextualized and inaccurate. Of course, neither accuracy or contextualization is a categorical assignment for the memory, but rather each memory can be described in terms of the accuracy of its details and the degree to which they are contextual (i.e., episodic).

strengthens some components of the memory and distorts others. The neocortex, at the very right of the continuum, is the final storage site of semantic memories that have been consolidated using slow cortical dynamics and trace interference over time. At the neocortical stage, recurrent and overlapping details have become relatively crystallized as the memory trace has been reconsolidated, but non-overlapping details are more transient and may be unique to a given recollective experience. That is, retrieval at any point in time results in a new trace that is stored as a slightly alternate version of the original memory. Retrieval at different points in this continuum is shown using examples. Altering contextual details may involve a large distortion (e.g., misremembering the city in which something occurred) or a very small one (e.g., misremembering which side of the sofa you were sitting on). Importantly, however, any deviation from the original representation is likely to correspond to a deviation from the initial neural representation of that memory trace. Even if a given retrieval event produces a memory trace that highly overlaps with the original memory, any amount of difference may be sufficient to induce competition.

Figure 3A is another demonstration of the change in contextual details over time that is predicted by CTT. Recent memories are high in accurate details, low in semantic content (which has not yet been consolidated), and low in inaccurate details, as the hippocampus has not yet had an opportunity to distort the memory owing to only a few replay/reactivation events. Remote memories, on the other hand, are low in accurate details, high in semantic content (which is now consolidated in the neocortex), and high in inaccurate details, as the hippocampus has had ample opportunity to distort the memory across numerous replay/reactivation events. The decline in accuracy of the memory follows the typical forgetting curve of Ebbinghaus (1885).

The increase in semantic strength is assumed to be monotonic and linear, although it is quite possible that it follows the same curvilinear pattern. Replay studies repeatedly demonstrate reactivation events in the short term (minutes, hours), with very few on the order of days (reviewed in Sutherland et al., 2010). Thus it is possible that most events leading to consolidation occur in the short term and the memory asymptotes quickly. However, in the absence of robust data for remote replay (exceeding several days), the exact pattern is difficult to infer. Importantly, CTT only makes assumptions about the slopes of these curves relative to one another and not about the exact shape of any particular curve.

To summarize, below are the central tenets of CTT:

1. Every time a memory is reactivated, the hippocampus recontextualizes the memory by re-encoding a similar but not identical memory trace that is stored using associative connectivity between the hippocampus and neocortex.
2. Memories are decontextualized over time by competitive interference among these similar but not identical multiple memory traces. This simultaneously leads to consolidation of semantic memory in the neocortex and loss of episodic details.
3. Veridical episodic details are only available in very recent memories. As memories get older, these details are replaced by recontextualized details stored by the hippocampus that give rise to illusory memories that become more prevalent as the

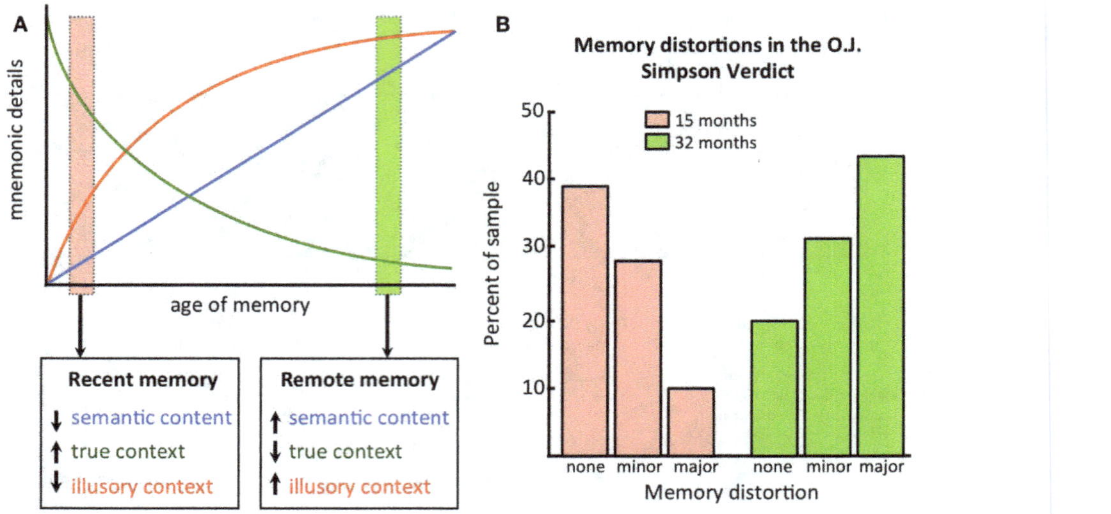

FIGURE 3 | Illusory details build up as memories get older. **(A)** A conceptual representation of how information content changes as a function of the age of the memory. Semantic content increases with consolidation, while true contextual details are replaced by illusory details; **(B)** An empirical demonstration of how illusory details increase as a function of time. See text for discussion. Data plotted based on values from Schmolck et al. (2000).

age of the memory increases. In other words, recent episodic and remote episodic memories vary in accuracy of details and strength of semantic content.

HARMONIZING CTT WITH PRE-EXISTING IDEAS

As we previously mentioned, CTT borrows elements from many existing theories and models. It is largely consistent with indexing theory (Teyler and DiScenna, 1986) and stresses the role of the hippocampus in encoding and binding the initial memory traces, and acting as an index during retrieval. Much like the CLS (McClelland et al., 1995) framework, CTT also assumes that the reactivation of hippocampal-neocortical traces strengthens the cortico-cortical traces leading to consolidation of memories. On the other hand, CTT also assumes that each reactivation of the memory results in a new trace and not just the reactivation of the old trace, which is consistent with MTT. Also consistent with the MTT proposal is the notion that the hippocampus is involved in the "reconstruction" rather than the "retrieval" of the memory. Nadel and Moscovitch (1998) also propose that reactivation of neocortical traces strengthens the links among multiple traces, which is the basis for building knowledge. This is further in agreement with CTT, however, we also suggest that the non-overlapping components of the traces compete with one another resulting in decontextualization in addition to consolidation.

We propose that the new hippocampal-neocortical traces formed are always partially but not completely overlapping with the original trace, resulting in competition for representation in the neocortex (this competition does not occur in the hippocampus due to pattern separation mechanisms discussed in detail below), leading to a selective strengthening of semantic information and weakening of contextual information. Thus, under CTT, the role of the hippocampus during retrieval is hypothesized to be the recontextualization of memories during retrieval to generate new competing traces. On the face of it, this may seem to be counterproductive at the level of the neocortex. As we will discuss below, we believe that this arises as a function of pattern separation computations necessary for episodic encoding. However, inducing competition may have a particular benefit in maintaining and retrieving memory traces. Namely, degradation of competing elements of a memory trace ensures that the important central features of that memory are not only preserved, but also strengthened.

The role of the hippocampus in recontextualization is also closely related to its role in mental imagery and imagining the future. Hassabis et al. (2007) demonstrated that this ability is impaired in hippocampal amnesic patients. They surmised that the hippocampus may contribute to the creation of new experiences by allowing disparate elements of prior memories to be bound in a spatial context. Addis and Schacter (2011) further extend this in a recent review of patient and neuroimaging findings to suggest that the hippocampus is also necessary for imagining the future and "episodic simulation." These roles in imagery are consistent with the notion of hippocampal recontextualization that we propose herein.

Our view is also largely consistent with the Distributed Reinstatement Theory of Sutherland et al. (2010) in which it is the frequency of replay/re-encoding episodes rather than the passage of time that leads to memories becoming independent of the hippocampus. Indeed, the central tenet of CTT is that reactivation events occurring as the age of the memory increases are the critical event in consolidation. While "age of memory" is plotted along the abscissa in the illustrations, it is used merely as a proxy that makes measurement feasible. Quantifying the number of reactivations, which is likely non-linear, is much less feasible. While one can pit these two alternatives (age of memory vs. number of reactivations) against each other in an experimental setup, only cued, not spontaneous, reactivation events can be assessed easily.

One potential possibility using advanced optogenetics techniques is to allow the hippocampus to engage in initial learning which could label the neurons involved using an immediate-early gene (e.g., Liu et al., 2012), then quantify reactivation events occurring within the labeled population only. Better yet, by silencing these neurons during specific time epochs, only circumscribed reactivations could be allowed. Thus, the effect of the passage of time vs. number of reactivations can be assessed directly.

The notion of competition for representation is not unique to memory by any means, and in fact seems to be a general principle of cortical operation. For example, it generally believed that in order for objects in the visual field to capture attention and be subjected to further neural processing they compete with one another for representation. Bottom-up and top-down influences can bias this competition by assigning priority to certain features or items but not others (Desimone and Duncan, 1995). A similar argument has been extended to the role of arousal in increasing the contrast between important and unimportant details in mnemonic representation (Mather and Sutherland, 2011). Thus, competition among memory *traces* (in contrast to competition among memory *systems*, which is widely accepted) is not an implausible idea, and in fact could be supported by very similar mechanisms to competition in other domains.

We further propose that the mechanisms involved in this competition arise as a result of hippocampal-neocortical dynamics and are particularly dependent on hippocampal processing. This harmonizes the model with the hippocampus's role in minimizing interference (i.e., pattern separation), a central tenet of the CLS. Below, we discuss this function in detail and suggest a potential mechanism by which it can facilitate cortical interference whilst minimizing hippocampal interference.

CONTRIBUTIONS OF PATTERN SEPARATION AND PATTERN COMPLETION

The hippocampus is capable of supporting rapid encoding of unique experiences by orthogonalizing incoming inputs such that interference is minimized, a function termed pattern separation, which is typically ascribed to the hippocampal dentate gyrus (DG) (Marr, 1971; Treves and Rolls, 1994; McClelland et al., 1995; O'Reilly and Norman, 2002; Norman and O'Reilly, 2003; Yassa and Stark, 2011). The hippocampus also has a well-recognized role in the formation of arbitrary associations using its recurrent collateral network in the CA3 subregion, a function termed pattern completion (Rolls, 2007). Recent evidence from animals (Nakazawa et al., 2003; Guzowski et al., 2004; Lee et al., 2004; Leutgeb et al., 2004, 2005, 2007; Vazdarjanova and Guzowski, 2004; Gold and Kesner, 2005; Kesner, 2007; McHugh et al., 2007) and humans (Bakker et al., 2008; Lacy et al., 2011) has provided strong support for the involvement of the hippocampus in these two important mnemonic computations. Though there is still some debate as to the precise nature of episodic memory, most in the field regard its core components as consisting of autobiographical details such as what occurred in addition to where and when. The capacity to orthogonalize overlapping input to create distinct memory traces, or to reinstate a particular memory trace based on partial or degraded input, are critical for encoding and remembering such details (Norman and O'Reilly, 2003; Norman, 2010). We suggest that pattern separation and pattern completion, provided they occur across different dimensions including space and time, are together necessary and sufficient to give rise to our episodic memory system with all of its richness, associativity, and flexibility (Yassa and Stark, 2011).

Given this deeper understanding of episodic memory mechanisms, it is important to discuss how the proposed CTT framework fits with these computations. First, let us make the case for pattern completion. This ability requires the reactivation of a previously stored representation when presented with a partial or a degraded cue. It is hypothesized to be a specific function of the CA3 region of the hippocampus due to recurrent collateral connectivity, which forms an autoassociative network and its innervation from the neocortex via the perforant path. This rapid retrieval is also balanced against new encoding in the CA3 region, which is subject to strong input by mossy fiber innervation from the DG granule cells (a pattern separation signal) (Treves and Rolls 1994). Thus, the CA3 region regulates the dynamic balance between pattern separation and pattern completion at least in the spatial domain. A similar role may exist for the CA1 region in temporal pattern separation and completion, though there is less existing data on this phenomenon (see Hunsaker and Kesner, 2013 for a comprehensive recent review).

We suggest that pattern completion in the hippocampus reactivates the neocortical trace and leads to a strengthening of the overlapping trace over time. A pattern completion mechanism is necessary for CTT and could in theory underlie the ability to strengthen representations over time in a Hebbian fashion (using a slow cortical dynamic). The decay in non-overlapping features of the memory due to competitive interference is likewise presumed to occur in anti-Hebbian fashion.

Next, we turn to pattern separation. An important tenet of CTT is that every time a memory is reactivated, re-encoding of the trace occurs. This re-encoding contains some of the reactivated features (the attractor state), in addition to some unique associations that attempt to orthogonalize, though incompletely, the current representation from past memories. According to CTT, pattern separation in the hippocampus (in particular, the DG) is the most important factor in re-encoding a slightly different version of the experience (i.e. recontextualization), which causes the subsequent competition among overlapping traces in the neocortex. This can be viewed as a side effect of an otherwise very adaptive process, which acts to minimize interference in the initial storage of information, but *leads to competitive interference* in the cortex over time as previous memories are reactivated. This is a much more dynamic view of pattern separation and attempts to examine its long-term not just short term effects. It is important to note that this type of interference is unlike the catastrophic interference that would occur if sequential learning occurred too rapidly. Cortical interference is much slower and thus is much more stable in terms of network dynamics. Given the above, CTT is not only consistent with the pattern separation/completion framework but in fact relies on these computations to formulate its predictions.

HARMONIZING CTT WITH EXISTING DATA

Competitive trace theory is generally consistent with, and offers explanations for, much of the existing episodic memory literature across species. While discussing every bit of evidence in the field is beyond the scope of this article, we present the case here using specific representative examples from behavioral studies of false memory and neuropsychological studies of amnesia in animals and humans.

BEHAVIORAL STUDIES OF FALSE MEMORY

To see the extent to which memory is non-veridical and is subject to constant updating, one need not look any further than the pioneering work of Bartlett (1932). Using the method of serial reproductions with material ranging from abstract drawings to stories such as "War of the Ghosts," Bartlett illustrated beautifully how memory can be altered every time it is retrieved. While this insightful work taught us about the impact of social bias on remembering, it also demonstrated unequivocally that memory is not veridical and is subject to constant change and reconstruction. Since Bartlett, research in false memory has enjoyed a rich tradition. Loftus (2005) has been investigating how humans adopt misinformation for over 30 years providing much of what we know about how false memories can be formed and how they can be extraordinarily rich in complexity and detail. False recall is also easily demonstrated by memory tasks such as the Deese–Roediger–McDermott (DRM) paradigm (Deese, 1959; Roediger and McDermott, 1995), and mnemonic discrimination tasks with similar lures (Yassa et al., 2011). Schacter discusses these memory "sins" as features of an adaptive memory system (Schacter, 1999). The frequency and abundance of these phenomena are consistent with the premise of recontextualization in CTT and suggest that reactivations lead to reconstructions of and updates to the initial memory.

Aside from the mere existence of false memory, for which there is extensive evidence within our field, CTT further proposes that the probability by which false memories are created are increased with repeated reactivations. Since reactivations are difficult to assess directly in humans unless they are induced using a cueing procedure, one can use the age of the memory as a proxy. We predict that the more time passing since initial encoding would be associated with increased tendency for false memories or distortions. In other words, the number of veridical details reported would decline with the age of the memory, while the number of illusory details would increase. There are many demonstrations of this effect, but we will discuss just two examples here.

The first example comes from a study by Schmolck et al. (2000) where college students were asked to recall the circumstances surrounding hearing about the verdict in the O. J. Simpson double murder trial after 3 days and were re-tested on their memories 15 or 32 months later. They found that as a function of a longer retention interval, the frequency of memory distortions increased (at 32 months, more than 40% of the recollections contained major distortions and only 29% were highly accurate). These results are shown in **Figure 3B**.

The second example comes from flashbulb memories. Brown and Kulik first described the flashbulb memory in 1977 as a vividly detailed memory of the circumstances surrounding an important emotional event, such as the assassination of John F. Kennedy (Brown and Kulik, 1977). Neisser (1982) wrote of his own flashbulb memory of the Japanese attack on Pearl Harbor on Sunday, December 7th, 1941. He recalled that he was listening to a baseball game on the radio. Many years later, it occurred to him that no baseball games are played in December (it was later suggested that it was actually a football game). It is now well accepted that although flashbulb memories are high in vividness, accuracy in many cases is low. A more recent study by Talarico and Rubin (2003) suggested that confidence in flashbulb memories increases while accuracy decreases over time. The investigators tested college students on their memory of first hearing about the September 11th terrorist attacks the day after the events occurred. Repeat testing occurred at 1, 6, or 32 weeks later. They found that the decline in accuracy for flashbulb memories was no different than everyday memories, however ratings of vividness and confidence did not decline for flashbulb memories. This report is also consistent with CTT's predictions, as the inclusion of fictitious details over time may give the illusion of accuracy and thus, recollection confidence (i.e., metamemory) remains high.

NEUROPSYCHOLOGICAL STUDIES OF HUMAN AMNESIA

While it is commonly agreed upon that cases of human amnesia suggest that remote retrograde memory is relatively intact, there is less agreement about whether the intact memories are rich enough in contextual detail to be deemed episodic or whether the recalled memories are more semantic in nature. SMSC asserts that those memories are truly episodic as they have become consolidated and become independent of the hippocampus long before hippocampal damage occurred. MTT, on the other hand, asserts that these memories are not entirely episodic because the hippocampus continues to be required for remote episodic memory recall.

As previously mentioned, Corkin characterized H. M.'s memories as "semanticized" or lacking in episodic detail, which is consistent with MTT. Other amnesia cases have demonstrated similar deficits in remote memories (Hirano and Noguchi, 1998; Moscovitch et al., 2000; Cipolotti et al., 2001). However, work by Squire and colleagues has strongly suggested that with more detailed neuropsychological investigations, the quality of retrieved remote memories in amnesia is similar to controls (Bayley et al., 2003; Kirwan et al., 2008). Squire and colleagues argue that the impairment in remote memory found in some cases of amnesia is secondary to non-MTL damage. In the absence of detailed neuroanatomical quantification, it is difficult to know whether this is truly the case. Another potential confound is the absence of corroboration to ensure the veracity of these memories (e.g., informant or diaries) in most if not all cases. Thus, it is not known whether the details retrieved are accurate or fictitious.

While the literature on remote memory in human amnesia is subject to much debate with respect to the episodic nature of such memories, CTT's predictions have much to do with the veracity of these memories. Similar to MTT, it hypothesizes that the hippocampus continues to be important for remote memories, but for entirely different reasons. During recall of remote memories, the hippocampus recontextualizes or updates the memory. In its absence, a strong personal semantic memory is available in the cortex and can be accessed directly. It is important to note here that MTT proposes that retrieval is dependent on the hippocampus because the hippocampus is required to reconstruct the memory of the episode within a spatial scaffold (Nadel and Moscovitch,

1998), thus a non-hippocampal memory would lack spatial context. CTT, on the other hand, proposes that any context (spatial or otherwise) can additionally be consolidated and strengthened to become independent of the hippocampus, as long as it is overlapping and not interfering with prior exposures. The critical difference between the two models is the explicit role assigned for overlap and interference in CTT.

Whether this personal semantic memory has associated contextual detail is not a categorical distinction but rather depends on the position of this memory on the contextualization continuum previously discussed. Thus, some memories may have more contextual details than others. The counterintuitive prediction of CTT here, however, is that amnesic patients will have remote memories that are more accurate than healthy controls, since the absence of a hippocampus prevents the recontextualization and reconstruction of those memories. While the data supporting this account are only circumstantial, autobiographical memory reports from patients like E. P. do suggest that autobiographical memories were less likely to be embellished or changed despite repeated recall in amnesia (Bayley et al., 2003).

Overall, the data from human amnesia cannot be used as strong support for CTT or any other model for recent vs. remote memory, given the disagreements about the (1) quality (e.g., richness, vividness, etc.) of the memories retrieved, (2) quantity of the memories retrieved, (3) accuracy of the memories retrieved, and (4) neuroanatomical characterization of medial temporal lobe damage. It is our hope, however, that the additional predictions afforded by CTT provide a platform for future studies with amnesic patients that may support or refute some of these basic ideas.

RODENT MODELS OF RETROGRADE AMNESIA

Most investigations of RA in the rodent hippocampus have been conducted using contextual fear conditioning. While several early examinations of recent vs. remote memories reported a temporal RA gradient (Kim and Fanselow, 1992; Maren et al., 1997; Anagnostaras et al., 1999), other studies have reported flat RA gradients (Lehmann et al., 2007; Sutherland et al., 2008). Investigations of RA in hippocampus lesioned rats in spatial navigation tasks have also reported generally flat RA gradients (Sutherland et al., 2001; Clark et al., 2005a,b; Martin et al., 2005). CTT predicts that the extent to which the hippocampus is critical for remote retrieval (i.e., whether there is a temporal or flat RA gradient) depends on (1) how much reactivation has occurred since the initial learning and (2) the nature of the retrieval task and whether it requires hippocampal recontextualization. The latter point is one deserving of further analysis. The ability of the hippocampus to engage in recontextualization should be a function of all of the other experiences it has encoded (these are the sources of interfering traces that can compete with the memory with each reactivation), thus factors such as rearing in rich vs. impoverished environments can significantly influence the results.

This is evidenced by phenomena such as immediate shock deficit (ISD: Fanselow, 1986) and the context pre-exposure effect (Fanselow, 1990), where a critical role of the hippocampus in learning about the environment in contextual fear conditioning is demonstrated. It is likely that the parameters of these phenomena (e.g., latency required for ISD or pre-exposure) are dependent on the animal's prior history. Most studies with rodents use individually housed rats in impoverished conditions, which results in the hippocampus operating under suboptimal conditions. We suggest that the hippocampus' ability to facilitate cortical interference by encoding recontextualized versions of the memories will depend on this prior history. In light of this, a re-examination of lesion studies in rodents and future studies using animals reared in enriched environments are required to fully test the predictions of CTT.

Several studies have shown that hippocampal learning can compete with learning in non-hippocampal systems (Maren et al., 1997; Frankland et al., 1998; Driscoll et al., 2005; Lehmann et al., 2006; Sutherland et al., 2006; Wiltgen et al., 2006), suggesting that different memory traces do compete for representational resources in the brain. In a recent demonstration, Sutherland and colleagues (Sparks et al., 2011) showed that a non-hippocampally acquired contextual fear memory (learned while hippocampus was temporarily inactivated) was susceptible to interference or competition from the hippocampus when it was subsequently reactivated. These findings are directly predicted by CTT and further demonstrate the impact of competition among hippocampal-neocortical memory traces. These data also offer an alternative account to demonstrations of anterograde amnesia following pre-training hippocampal inactivation (e.g., Bast et al., 2001). While it is possible that the inactivation prevented the animals from learning the task, another possibility is that the reactivation of the hippocampus after learning disrupted performance on test due to competition with memory traces formed outside the hippocampus.

The above data suggest that there is indeed interference and competition between hippocampal and neocortical memories. The CTT formalizes this competition and describes a potential mechanism (via hippocampal pattern separation) by which it can occur.

MEMORY UPDATING AND RECONSOLIDATION

It has been long known that retrieved memories are labile and can be disrupted. For example, Donald Lewis's seminal experiments in 1968 demonstrated that reactivated memories can be disrupted by electroconvulsive shock (Misanin et al., 1968). Based on this work, Lewis proposed that reactivating a memory brings it into an active state that is vulnerable to disruption by external agents (Lewis, 1979). In 2000, Nader et al. (2000a) demonstrated that a protein synthesis inhibitor (anisomycin) resulted in the disruption of a reactivated fear memory. The authors proposed a mechanism for this disruption they termed "reconsolidation," which essentially posits that reactivation results into two distinct events: an unbinding of the synapses representing the memory and a concurrent second round of protein synthesis to re-instantiate the memory. Protein synthesis inhibitors, they surmised, blocked the second event, thus disrupting the memory permanently (Nader et al., 2000b). Although initial reports were inconsistent across laboratories [e.g., memory loss was not always permanent (see Power et al., 2006)] and the widespread effects of protein synthesis inhibitors were seen as potential confounds (Rudy et al., 2006), more recent data has partly supported the notion that reconsolidation may occur under some conditions and may be at least one way in which memory updating can occur (Besnard et al., 2012).

Conceptually, CTT is consistent with both Lewis's *Active Trace Theory* and reconsolidation theory in that it puts great emphasis on memory reactivation as the critical event by which a memory can be updated. We also similarly suggest that intervening with the memory trace during retrieval can disrupt it. However, the exact mechanisms diverge. CTT's account is based on interference among competing memory traces and not a synaptic "resetting" *per se*. The extent to which spontaneous recovery can be observed (as in extinction procedures) will depend on the extent of the interference among the competing traces. If the competition results in suppression of much of the original memory, spontaneous recovery may not be observed.

More directly relevant to CTT, Monfils et al. (2009) recently suggested that preceding an extinction procedure with a single reactivation trial can disrupt fear memory. The same procedure has recently been applied to disrupt fear memories in humans (Schiller et al., 2010) and decrease cue-induced craving in human heroin users (Xue et al., 2012). While the results of this type of memory disruption have been interpreted in terms of reconsolidation, they do not necessarily speak to the underlying mechanism. We argue that results from retrieval-extinction procedures are more consistent with the CTT account, where retrieval is associated with a re-encoding of the memory, which only partially overlaps with the original memory and can compete with it for storage. In the retrieval-extinction procedure this process is greatly accelerated by providing the competing memory directly in the extinction trials.

It is likely that this update process happens all the time, however, there is typically no systematic attempt to extinguish behavior with competing memories in every day circumstances. This results in a subtle update that removes some features of the memory and adds others. In an experimental setting, however, where a competing memory is explicitly encoded to extinguish the fear behavior, it is much easier to observe a complete or near-complete ablation of the memory. Episodic memories in humans are also likely much richer than fear memories in animals thus a complete ablation would be more difficult to instantiate as the competition needs to occur repeatedly and over an extended period of time.

MAKING NEW PREDICTIONS BASED ON CTT

The CTT framework represents a plausible mechanism by which hippocampal-neocortical traces are established and updated. It makes a set of empirical predictions that can be tested directly in animals or humans. We highlight some of these predictions here, in hopes that they will be instigate such research in the future to attempt to support or refute CTT's core premises.

- The first prediction is the remote episodic memories should be less accurate than recent episodic memories. We discussed some evidence for this in studies of false memory as well as human amnesia, however the prediction needs to be tested more directly using veridical records of information. This prediction may also be tested using an animal model where the accuracy of the memory can be tested using a discrimination/generalization procedure. For example, Wiltgen and Silva (2007) provide supporting evidence for this by demonstrating that context generalization increases as a function of time, consistent with our proposal that more remote memories are less context-specific.
- The second prediction is that amnesia patients as well as rodents with hippocampal lesions should have more accurate remote semantic memories compared to healthy controls. This follows from the premise that having a hippocampus has the capacity to distort the memory every time it is recalled. Removing this brain region should also remove the capacity for distortion, leaving an intact semantic memory without associated illusory details.
- The third prediction is that whether a flat or graded RA curve is observed in rodent studies will depend on whether contextual information was repeatedly presented to the animal. If contextual information was presented more than once, some amount of this context will become semanticized, and thus hippocampal damage will lead to a flat RA gradient. However, if contextual information was presented only once, there isn't an opportunity for semantic information to build up, and hippocampus damage will lead to a graded RA. Controlled experiments with amnesic patients or lesioned animals can test this prediction. It is interesting to note here that flat or graded RA curves can be obtained also with cortical lesions. Cho and Kesner (1996) showed that a flat RA gradient could be obtained with parietal cortical lesions while a temporally graded RA could be obtained with entorhinal cortical lesions in a spatial discrimination task. Thus, the location of the lesion, as well as the degree of contextual repetition are both hypothesized to influence the temporal gradient of RA.
- The fourth prediction is that the fidelity of mnemonic representations should change with repeated reactivations in the hippocampus and the neocortex. The degree of overlap in representations from exposure to exposure should predict how strong the memory is in a subsequent test (i.e., should generate a generalizable representation), while the degree of stochasticity should predict how contextual the memory is. Furthermore, given the hippocampus' powerful capacity for orthogonalizing inputs, it may be the case that repetitions of identical study items may nonetheless induce competition as a result of varying external and internal contextual elements. This prediction can be tested using multivariate pattern classification techniques such as representational similarity analyses (Kriegeskorte et al., 2008) applied to fMRI or neurophysiological recording data.
- The fifth prediction is that there will be evidence for interference in the neocortex and not just the hippocampus, however, the timescale for neocortical trace interference will be much slower than the hippocampus and the mechanism will be more dependent on competitive inhibition via LTD-like mechanisms rather than pattern separation. This prediction may prove especially difficult to assess, though neurophysiological recordings and gene expression assays in animal models, or post-exposure representational similarity analyses via fMRI in humans may provide some insight. It is important to note here that LTD mechanisms are not hypothesized to be limited to the neocortex or to competitive inhibition *per se*. There is strong evidence that these mechanisms are also necessary for the acquisition of new memories in the hippocampus (Kemp and Manahan-Vaughan, 2004). Thus, this is likely a much more general mechanism, which could serve several purposes for our memory system.

CONCLUSION

The role of the hippocampus in retrieval has been subject to much debate. The two schools of thought on the topic, SMSC and MTT, have had divergent predictions and so far, it is still not clear which model best describes the empirical data. We propose an alternative model in the form of a continuum and hypothesize that the role of the hippocampus during retrieval is recontextualization of memories along this continuum. This process, in turn, facilitates competition and trace interference in the cortex such that that consolidated memory traces become semantic. Our model explains much of the current data and provides fodder for future research in the form of testable empirical predictions. It may prove helpful as we shift our focus from categorical assignments such as "episodic" and move toward a more computationally grounded, cross-species compatible, continuum approach to declarative memory.

ACKNOWLEDGMENTS

Michael A. Yassa is supported by grants from the National Institute on Aging (R01 AG034613; P50 AG05146), the Ossoff Award in Cognitive Disorders Research, and a Johns Hopkins University research fund. Zachariah M. Reagh is supported by a National Science Foundation Graduate Research Fellowship. Many of the ideas proposed here were discussed with colleagues at the annual meeting of the Center for Neurobiology of Learning and memory at the University of California, Irvine in 2012.

REFERENCES

Addis, D. R., and Schacter, D. L. (2011). The hippocampus and imagining the future: where do we stand? *Front. Hum. Neurosci.* 5:173. doi:10.3389/fnhum.2011.00173

Anagnostaras, S. G., Maren, S., and Fanselow, M. S. (1999). Temporally graded retrograde amnesia of contextual fear after hippocampal damage in rats: within-subjects examination. *J. Neurosci.* 19, 1106–1114.

Bakker, A., Kirwan, C. B., Miller, M., and Stark, C. E. L. (2008). Pattern separation in the human hippocampal CA3 and dentate gyrus. *Science* 319, 1640–1642. doi:10.1126/science.1152882

Bartlett, F. F. C. (1932). *Remembering: A Study in Experimental and Social Psychology.* Cambridge: Cambridge University Press.

Bast, T., Zhang, W.-N., and Feldon, J. (2001). The ventral hippocampus and fear conditioning in rats. *Exp. Brain Res.* 139, 39–52. doi:10.1007/s002210100746

Bayley, P. J., Hopkins, R. O., and Squire, L. R. (2003). Successful recollection of remote autobiographical memories by amnesic patients with medial temporal lobe lesions. *Neuron* 38, 135–144. doi:10.1016/S0896-6273(03)00156-9

Besnard, A., Caboche, J., and Laroche, S. (2012). Reconsolidation of memory: a decade of debate. *Prog. Neurobiol.* 99, 61–80. doi:10.1016/j.pneurobio.2012.07.002

Brown, R., and Kulik, J. (1977). Flashbulb memories. *Cognition* 5, 73–99. doi:10.1016/0010-0277(77)90018-X

Buckner, R. L., Wheeler, M. E., and Sheridan, M. A. (2001). Encoding processes during retrieval tasks. *J. Cogn. Neurosci.* 13, 406–415. doi:10.1162/08989290151137430

Cho, Y. H., and Kesner, R. P. (1996). Involvement of entorhinal cortex or parietal cortex in long-term spatial discrimination memory in rats retrograde amnesia. *Behav. Neurosci.* 110, 436–442. doi:10.1037/0735-7044.110.3.436

Cipolotti, L., Shallice, T., Chan, D., Fox, N., Scahill, R., Harrison, G., et al. (2001). Long-term retrograde amnesia ... the crucial role of the hippocampus. *Neuropsychologia* 39, 151–172. doi:10.1016/S0028-3932(00)00103-2

Clark, R. E., Broadbent, N. J., and Squire, L. R. (2005a). Hippocampus and remote spatial memory in rats. *Hippocampus* 15, 260–272. doi:10.1002/hipo.20056

Clark, R. E., Broadbent, N. J., and Squire, L. R. (2005b). Impaired remote spatial memory after hippocampal lesions despite extensive training beginning early in life. *Hippocampus* 15, 340–346. doi:10.1002/hipo.20076

Corkin, S. (2002). What's new with the amnesic patient H.M.? *Nat. Rev Neurosci.* 3, 153–160. doi:10.1038/nrn726

Daselaar, S. M., Fleck, M. S., and Cabeza, R. (2006). Triple dissociation in the medial temporal lobes: recollection, familiarity, and novelty. *J. Neurophysiol.* 96, 1902–1911. doi:10.1152/jn.01029.2005

Deese, J. (1959). On the prediction of occurrence of particular verbal intrusions in immediate recall. *J. Exp. Psychol.* 58, 17–22. doi:10.1037/h0046671

Desimone, R., and Duncan, J. (1995). Neural mechanisms of selective visual attention. *Annu. Rev. Neurosci.* 18, 193–222. doi:10.1146/annurev.ne.18.030195.001205

Diana, R. A., Yonelinas, A. P., and Ranganath, C. (2007). Imaging recollection and familiarity in the medial temporal lobe: a three-component model. *Trends Cogn. Sci. (Regul. Ed.)* 11, 379–386. doi:10.1016/j.tics.2007.08.001

Driscoll, I., Howard, S. R., Prusky, G. T., Rudy, J. W., and Sutherland, R. J. (2005). Seahorse wins all races: hippocampus participates in both linear and non-linear visual discrimination learning. *Behav. Brain Res.* 164, 29–35. doi:10.1016/j.bbr.2005.05.006

Ebbinghaus, H. (1885). *Memory. A Contribution to Experimental Psychology (Translated to English in 1913).* New York: Teachers College, Columbia University.

Eldridge, L. L., Knowlton, B. J., Furmanski, C. S., Bookheimer, S. Y., and Engel, S. A. (2000). Remembering episodes: a selective role for the hippocampus during retrieval. *Nat. Neurosci.* 3, 1149–1152. doi:10.1038/80671

Fanselow, M. S. (1986). Associative vs. topographical accounts of the immediate shock-freezing deficit in rats: implications for the response selection rules governing species-specific defensive reactions. *Learn. Motiv.* 17, 16–39. doi:10.1016/0023-9690(86)90018-4

Fanselow, M. S. (1990). Factors governing one-trial contextual conditioning. *Anim. Learn. Behav.* 18, 264–270. doi:10.3758/BF03205285

Frankland, P. W., and Bontempi, B. (2005). The organization of recent and remote memories. *Nat. Rev. Neurosci.* 6, 119–130. doi:10.1038/nrn1607

Frankland, P. W., Cestari, V., Filipkowski, R. K., McDonald, R. J., and Silva, A. J. (1998). The dorsal hippocampus is essential for context discrimination but not for contextual conditioning. *Behav. Neurosci.* 112, 863–874. doi:10.1037/0735-7044.112.4.863

Gallo, D. A., Roediger, H. L., and McDermott, K. B. (2001). Associative false recognition occurs without strategic criterion shifts. *Psychon. Bull. Rev.* 8, 579–586.

Gold, A. E., and Kesner, R. P. (2005). The role of the CA3 subregion of the dorsal hippocampus in spatial pattern completion in the rat. *Hippocampus* 15, 808–814. doi:10.1002/hipo.20103

Goshen, I., Brodsky, M., Prakash, R., Wallace, J., Gradinaru, V., Ramakrishnan, C., et al. (2011). Dynamics of Retrieval Strategies for Remote Memories. *Cell* 147, 678–689. doi:10.1016/j.cell.2011.09.033

Guzowski, J. F., Knierim, J. J., and Moser, E. I. (2004). Ensemble dynamics of hippocampal regions CA3 and CA1. *Neuron* 44, 581–584. doi:10.1016/j.neuron.2004.11.003

Haist, F., Bowden Gore, J., and Mao, H. (2001). Consolidation of human memory over decades revealed by functional magnetic resonance imaging. *Nat. Neurosci.* 4, 1139–1145. doi:10.1038/nn739

Hassabis, D., Kumaran, D., Vann, S. D., and Maguire, E. A. (2007). Patients with hippocampal amnesia cannot imagine new experiences. *Proc. Natl. Acad. Sci. U.S.A.* 104, 1726–1731. doi:10.1073/pnas.0610561104

Hirano, M., and Noguchi, K. (1998). Dissociation between specific personal episodes and other aspects of remote memory in a patient with hippocampal amnesia. *Percept. Mot. Skills* 87, 99–107. doi:10.2466/pms.1998.87.1.99

Holdstock, J. S., Mayes, A. R., Gong, Q. Y., Roberts, N., and Kapur, N. (2004). Item recognition is less impaired than recall and associative recognition in a patient with selective hippocampal damage. *Hippocampus* 15, 203–215. doi:10.1002/hipo.20046

Hunsaker, M. R., and Kesner, R. P. (2013). The operation of pattern separation and pattern completion processes associated with different attributes or domains of memory. *Neurosci. Biobehav. Rev.* 37, 36–58. doi:10.1016/j.neubiorev.2012.09.014

Kemp, A., and Manahan-Vaughan, D. (2004). Hippocampal long-term depression and long-term potentiation encode different aspects of novelty acquisition. *Proc. Natl. Acad. Sci. U.S.A.* 101, 8192–8197. doi:10.1073/pnas.0402650101

Kensinger, E. A., and Schacter, D. L. (2007). Remembering the specific visual details of presented objects: neuroimaging evidence for effects of emotion. *Neuropsychologia* 45, 2951–2962. doi:10.1016/j.neuropsychologia.2007.05.024

Kesner, R. P. (2007). Behavioral functions of the CA3 subregion of the hippocampus. *Learn. Mem.* 14, 771–781.

Kim, J., and Yassa, M. A. (2013). Assessing recollection and familiarity of similar lures in a behavioral pattern separation task. *Hippocampus* 23, 287–294. doi:10.1002/hipo.22087

Kim, J. J., and Fanselow, M. S. (1992). Modality-specific retrograde amnesia of fear. *Science* 256, 675–677. doi:10.1126/science.1585183

Kirwan, C. B., Bayley, P. J., Galván, V. V., and Squire, L. R. (2008). Detailed recollection of remote autobiographical memory after damage to the medial temporal lobe. *Proc. Natl. Acad. Sci. U.S.A.* 105, 2676–2680. doi:10.1073/pnas.0712155105

Kriegeskorte, N., Mur, M., and Bandettini, P. (2008). Representational similarity analysis – connecting the branches of systems neuroscience. *Front. Syst. Neurosci.* 2:4. doi:10.3389/neuro.06.004.2008

Lacy, J. W., Yassa, M. A., Stark, S. M., Muftuler, L. T., and Stark, C. E. L. (2011). Distinct pattern separation related transfer functions in human CA3/dentate and CA1 revealed using high-resolution fMRI and variable mnemonic similarity. *Learn. Mem.* 18, 15–18. doi:10.1101/lm.1971111

Lee, I., Yoganarasimha, D., Rao, G., and Knierim, J. J. (2004). Comparison of population coherence of place cells in hippocampal subfields CA1 and CA3. *Nature* 430, 456–459. doi:10.1038/nature02739

Lehmann, H., Lacanilao, S., and Sutherland, R. J. (2007). Complete or partial hippocampal damage produces equivalent retrograde amnesia for remote contextual fear memories. *Eur. J. Neurosci.* 25, 1278–1286. doi:10.1111/j.1460-9568.2007.05374.x

Lehmann, H., Lecluse, V., Houle, A., and Mumby, D. G. (2006). Retrograde amnesia following hippocampal lesions in the shock-probe conditioning test. *Hippocampus* 16, 379–387. doi:10.1002/hipo.20159

Leutgeb, J. K., Leutgeb, S., Moser, M.-B., and Moser, E. I. (2007). Pattern separation in the dentate gyrus and CA3 of the hippocampus. *Science* 315, 961–966. doi:10.1126/science.1135801

Leutgeb, J. K., Leutgeb, S., Treves, A., Meyer, R., Barnes, C. A., McNaughton, B. L., et al. (2005). Progressive transformation of hippocampal neuronal representations in "morphed" environments. *Neuron* 48, 345–358. doi:10.1016/j.neuron.2005.09.007

Leutgeb, S., Leutgeb, J. K., Treves, A., Moser, M.-B., and Moser, E. I. (2004). Distinct ensemble codes in hippocampal areas CA3 and CA1. *Science* 305, 1295–1298. doi:10.1126/science.1100265

Lewis, D. J. (1979). Psychobiology of active and inactive memory. *Psychol. Bull.* 86, 1054–1083. doi:10.1037/0033-2909.86.5.1054

Liu, X., Ramirez, S., Pang, P. T., Puryear, C. B., Govindarajan, A., Deisseroth, K., et al. (2012). Optogenetic stimulation of a hippocampal engram activates fear memory recall. *Nature* 484, 381–385. doi:10.1038/nature11028

Loftus, E. F. (2005). Planting misinformation in the human mind: a 30-year investigation of the malleability of memory. *Learn. Mem.* 12, 361–366.

Maren, S., Aharonov, G., and Fanselow, M. S. (1997). Neurotoxic lesions of the dorsal hippocampus and Pavlovian fear conditioning in rats. *Behav. Brain Res.* 88, 261–274. doi:10.1016/S0166-4328(97)00088-0

Marr, D. (1971). Simple memory: a theory for archicortex. *Philos. Trans. R. Soc. Lond. B Biol. Sci.* 262, 23–81. doi:10.1098/rstb.1971.0078

Martin, S. J., De Hoz, L., and Morris, R. G. M. (2005). Retrograde amnesia: neither partial nor complete hippocampal lesions in rats result in preferential sparing of remote spatial memory, even after reminding. *Neuropsychologia* 43, 609–624. doi:10.1016/j.neuropsychologia.2004.07.007

Mather, M., and Sutherland, M. R. (2011). Arousal-biased competition in perception and memory. *Perspect. Psychol. Sci.* 6, 114–133. doi:10.1177/1745691611400234

McClelland, J. L., McNaughton, B. L., and O'Reilly, R. C. (1995). Why there are complementary learning systems in the hippocampus and neocortex: insights from the successes and failures of connectionist models of learning and memory. *Psychol. Rev.* 102, 419–457. doi:10.1037/0033-295X.102.3.419

McHugh, T. J., Jones, M. W., Quinn, J. J., Balthasar, N., Coppari, R., Elmquist, J. K., et al. (2007). Dentate gyrus NMDA receptors mediate rapid pattern separation in the hippocampal network. *Science* 317, 94–99. doi:10.1126/science.1140263

Milner, B., Squire, L. R., and Kandel, E. R. (1998). Cognitive neuroscience and the study of memory. *Neuron* 20, 445–468. doi:10.1016/S0896-6273(00)80987-3

Misanin, J. R., Miller, R. R., and Lewis, D. J. (1968). Retrograde amnesia produced by electroconvulsive shock after reactivation of a consolidated memory trace. *Science* 160, 554–555. doi:10.1126/science.160.3827.554

Monfils, M.-H., Cowansage, K. K., Klann, E., and LeDoux, J. E. (2009). Extinction-reconsolidation boundaries: key to persistent attenuation of fear memories. *Science* 324, 951–955. doi:10.1126/science.1167975

Moscovitch, M., Yaschyshyn, T., Ziegler, M., and Nadel, L. (2000). "Remote episodic memory and retrograde amnesia: was Endel Tulving right all along?," in *Memory, Consciousness and the Brain: The Tallinn Conference*, ed. E. Tulving (Philadelphia, PA: Psychology Press/Taylor & Francis), 331–345.

Nadel, L., and Moscovitch, M. (1997). Memory consolidation, retrograde amnesia and the hippocampal complex. *Curr. Opin. Neurobiol.* 7, 217–227. doi:10.1016/S0959-4388(97)80010-4

Nadel, L., and Moscovitch, M. (1998). Hippocampal contributions to cortical plasticity. *Neuropharmacology* 37, 431–439. doi:10.1016/S0028-3908(98)00057-4

Nader, K., Schafe, G. E., and Le Doux, J. E. (2000a). Fear memories require protein synthesis in the amygdala for reconsolidation after retrieval. *Nature* 406, 722–726. doi:10.1038/35021052

Nader, K., Schafe, G. E., and LeDoux, J. E. (2000b). The labile nature of consolidation theory. *Nat. Rev. Neurosci.* 1, 216–219. doi:10.1038/35044580

Nakazawa, K., Sun, L. D., Quirk, M. C., Rondi-Reig, L., Wilson, M. A., and Tonegawa, S. (2003). Hippocampal CA3 NMDA receptors are crucial for memory acquisition of one-time experience. *Neuron* 38, 305–315. doi:10.1016/S0896-6273(03)00165-X

Neisser, U. (1982). "Snapshots or benchmarks?," in *Memory Observed*, ed. U. Neisser (New York: W. H. Freeman), 45.

Norman, K. A. (2010). How hippocampus and cortex contribute to recognition memory: revisiting the complementary learning systems model. *Hippocampus* 20, 1217–1227. doi:10.1002/hipo.20855

Norman, K. A., and O'Reilly, R. C. (2003). Modeling hippocampal and neocortical contributions to recognition memory: a complementary-learning-systems approach. *Psychol. Rev.* 110, 611–646. doi:10.1037/0033-295X.110.4.611

O'Reilly, R. C., and Norman, K. A. (2002). Hippocampal and neocortical contributions to memory: advances in the complementary learning systems framework. *Trends Cogn. Sci. (Regul. Ed.)* 6, 505–510. doi:10.1016/S1364-6613(02)02005-3

Power, A. E., Berlau, D. J., McGaugh, J. L., and Steward, O. (2006). Anisomycin infused into the hippocampus fails to block "reconsolidation" but impairs extinction: the role of re-exposure duration. *Learn. Mem.* 13, 27–34.

Roediger, H. L., and McDermott, K. B. (1995). Creating false memories: remembering words not presented in lists. *J. Exp. Psychol. Learn. Mem. Cogn.* 24, 803–814. doi:10.1037/0278-7393.21.4.803

Roediger, H. L., McDermott, K. B., Pisoni, D. B., and Gallo, D. A. (2004). Illusory recollection of voices. *Memory* 12, 586–602. doi:10.1080/09658210344000125

Rolls, E. T. (2007). An attractor network in the hippocampus: theory and neurophysiology. *Learn. Mem.* 14, 714–731.

Rudy, J. W., Biedenkapp, J. C., Moineau, J., and Bolding, K. (2006). Anisomycin and the reconsolidation hypothesis. *Learn. Mem.* 13, 1–3.

Ryan, L., Nadel, L., Keil, K., Putnam, K., Schnyer, D., Trouard, T., et al. (2001). Hippocampal complex and retrieval of recent and very remote autobiographical memories: evidence from functional magnetic resonance imaging in neurologically intact people. *Hippocampus* 11, 707–714. doi:10.1002/hipo.1086

Schacter, D. L. (1999). The seven sins of memory. Insights from psychology and cognitive neuroscience. *Am. Psychol.* 54, 182–203. doi:10.1037/0003-066X.54.3.182

Schiller, D., Monfils, M.-H., Raio, C. M., Johnson, D. C., Ledoux, J. E., and Phelps, E. A. (2010). Preventing the return of fear in humans using reconsolidation update mechanisms. *Nature* 463, 49–53. doi:10.1038/nature08637

Schmolck, H., Buffalo, E. A., and Squire, L. R. (2000). Memory distortions develop over time: recollections of the O.J. Simpson trial verdict after 15 and 32 months. *Psychol. Sci.* 11, 39–45. doi:10.1111/1467-9280.00212

Scoville, W. B., and Milner, B. (1957). Loss of recent memory after bilateral hippocampal lesions. *J. Neurol. Neurosurg. Psychiatr.* 20, 11–21. doi:10.1136/jnnp.20.1.11

Sherry, D. F., and Schacter, D. L. (1987). The evolution of multiple memory systems. *Psychol. Rev.* 94, 439–454. doi:10.1037/0033-295X.94.4.439

Sparks, F. T., Lehmann, H., and Sutherland, R. J. (2011). Between-systems memory interference during retrieval. *Eur. J. Neurosci.* 34, 780–786. doi:10.1111/j.1460-9568.2011.07796.x

Squire, L. R. (2009). The legacy of patient H.M. for neuroscience. *Neuron* 61, 6–9. doi:10.1016/j.neuron.2008.12.023

Squire, L. R., and Alvarez, P. (1995). Retrograde amnesia and memory consolidation: a neurobiological perspective. *Curr. Opin. Neurobiol.* 5, 169–177. doi:10.1016/0959-4388(95)80023-9

Squire, L. R., Cohen, N. J., and Zouzounis, J. A. (1984). Preserved memory in retrograde amnesia: sparing of a recently acquired skill. *Neuropsychologia* 22, 145–152. doi:10.1016/0028-3932(84)90057-5

Stahl, C., and Klauer, K. C. (2008). A simplified conjoint recognition paradigm for the measurement of gist and verbatim memory. *J. Exp. Psychol. Learn. Mem. Cogn.* 34, 570–586. doi:10.1037/0278-7393.34.3.570

Stark, C. E., and Okado, Y. (2003). Making memories without trying: medial temporal lobe activity associated with incidental memory formation during recognition. *J. Neurosci.* 23, 6748–6753.

Stefanacci, L., Buffalo, E. A., Schmolck, H., and Squire, L. R. (2000). Profound amnesia after damage to the medial temporal lobe: a neuroanatomical and neuropsychological profile of patient E. P. *J. Neurosci.* 20, 7024–7036.

Suddendorf, T., and Corballis, M. C. (1997). Mental time travel and the evolution of the human mind. *Genet. Soc. Gen. Psychol. Monogr.* 123, 133–167.

Sutherland, R. J., Lehmann, H., Spanswick, S. C., Sparks, F. T., and Melvin, N. R. (2006). Growth Points in Research on Memory and Hippocampus. *Can. J. Exp. Psychol.* 60, 166–174. doi:10.1037/cjep20060016

Sutherland, R. J., O'Brien, J., and Lehmann, H. (2008). Absence of systems consolidation of fear memories after dorsal, ventral, or complete hippocampal damage. *Hippocampus* 18, 710–718. doi:10.1002/hipo.20431

Sutherland, R. J., Sparks, F. T., and Lehmann, H. (2010). Hippocampus and retrograde amnesia in the rat model: a modest proposal for the situation of systems consolidation. *Neuropsychologia* 48, 2357–2369. doi:10.1016/j.neuropsychologia.2010.04.015

Sutherland, R. J., Weisend, M. P., Mumby, D., Astur, R. S., Hanlon, F. M., Koerner, A., et al. (2001). Retrograde amnesia after hippocampal damage: recent vs. remote memories in two tasks. *Hippocampus* 11, 27–42. doi:10.1002/1098-1063(2001)11:1<27::AID-HIPO1017>3.0.CO;2-4

Talarico, J. M., and Rubin, D. C. (2003). Confidence, not consistency, characterizes flashbulb memories. *Psychol. Sci.* 14, 455–461. doi:10.1111/1467-9280.02453

Teyler, T. J., and DiScenna, P. (1985). The role of hippocampus in memory: a hypothesis. *Neurosci. Biobehav. Rev.* 9, 377–389.

Teyler, T. J., and DiScenna, P. (1986). The hippocampal memory indexing theory. *Behav. Neurosci.* 100, 147–154. doi:10.1037/0735-7044.100.2.147

Teyler, T. J., and Rudy, J. W. (2007). The hippocampal indexing theory and episodic memory: updating the index. *Hippocampus* 1169, 1158–1169. doi:10.1002/hipo.20350

Treves, A., and Rolls, E. T. (1994). Computational analysis of the role of the hippocampus in memory. *Hippocampus* 4, 374–391. doi:10.1002/hipo.450040319

Tulving, E., and Markowitsch, H. J. (1998). Episodic and declarative memory: role of the hippocampus. *Hippocampus* 8, 198–204. doi:10.1002/(SICI)1098-1063(1998)8:3<198::AID-HIPO2>3.3.CO;2-J

Vazdarjanova, A., and Guzowski, J. F. (2004). Differences in hippocampal neuronal population responses to modifications of an environmental context: evidence for distinct, yet complementary, functions of CA3 and CA1 ensembles. *J. Neurosci.* 24, 6489–6496. doi:10.1523/JNEUROSCI.0350-04.2004

Wiltgen, B. J., Sanders, M. J., Anagnostaras, S. G., Sage, J. R., and Fanselow, M. S. (2006). Context fear learning in the absence of the hippocampus. *J. Neurosci.* 26, 5484–5491. doi:10.1523/JNEUROSCI.2685-05.2006

Wiltgen, B. J., and Silva, A. J. (2007). Memory for context becomes less specific with time. *Learn. Mem.* 14, 313–317.

Wiltgen, B. J., Zhou, M., Cai, Y., Balaji, J., Karlsson, M. G., Parivash, S. N., et al. (2010). The hippocampus plays a selective role in the retrieval of detailed contextual memories. *Curr. Biol.* 20, 1336–1344. doi:10.1016/j.cub.2010.06.068

Xue, Y.-X., Luo, Y.-X., Wu, P., Shi, H.-S., Xue, L.-F., Chen, C., et al. (2012). A memory retrieval-extinction procedure to prevent drug craving and relapse. *Science* 336, 241–245. doi:10.1126/science.1215070

Yassa, M. A., Lacy, J. W., Stark, S. M., Albert, M. S., Gallagher, M., and Stark, C. E. L. (2011). Pattern separation deficits associated with increased hippocampal CA3 and dentate gyrus activity in nondemented older adults. *Hippocampus* 21, 968–979. doi:10.1002/hipo.20808

Yassa, M. A., and Stark, C. E. L. (2011). Pattern separation in the hippocampus. *Trends Neurosci.* 34, 515–525. doi:10.1016/j.tins.2011.06.006

Yonelinas, A. P., Kroll, N. E. A., Quamme, J. R., Lazzara, M. M., Sauvé, M.-J., Widaman, K. F., et al. (2002). Effects of extensive temporal lobe damage or mild hypoxia on recollection and familiarity. *Nat. Neurosci.* 5, 1236–1241. doi:10.1038/nn961

Yonelinas, A. P., Otten, L. J., Shaw, K. N., and Rugg, M. D. (2005). Separating the brain regions involved in recollection and familiarity in recognition memory. *J. Neurosci.* 25, 3002–3008. doi:10.1523/JNEUROSCI.3295-04.2005

2

Orbitofrontal reality filtering

Armin Schnider*

Division of Neurorehabilitation, Department of Clinical Neurosciences, University Hospital, University of Geneva, Geneva, Switzerland

Correspondence:
Armin Schnider, Service de Neurorééducation, Hôpitaux Universitaires de Genève, Av. de Beau-Séjour 26, CH-1211 Geneva 14, Switzerland
e-mail: armin.schnider@hcuge.ch

Decades of research have deepened our understanding of how the brain forms memories and uses them to build our mental past and future. But how does it determine whether an evoked memory refers to the present and can be acted upon? The study of patients who confuse reality, as evident from confabulation and disorientation, has opened ways to explore this vital capacity. Results indicate that the brain recurs to a phylogenetically old faculty of the orbitofrontal cortex – extinction – and structures of the reward system to keep thought and behavior in phase with reality.

Keywords: orbitofrontal cortex, confabulations, reward system, reality monitoring, continuous recognition

INTRODUCTION

Since the early studies of patients who lost the ability to acquire new memories after damage to the hippocampal area (Scoville and Milner, 1957), the understanding of brain processes allowing the storage of information has been immensely refined (Squire and Wixted, 2011). Memories eventually become independent of the hippocampus, are stored and processed in distributed cortical areas (Squire and Wixted, 2011). Forging plans for the future appears to involve very much the same neural structures that are necessary to store information; building a mental future is very similar to constructing a personal past (Schacter et al., 2007). This raises the question of this review: how does the brain determine whether an upcoming thought pertains to "now"? How do we sense what our current duties are, what day it is, and what ideas we may currently act upon?

LOST SENSE OF REALITY

Brain damage may deprive humans of the ability to sense where they are and what their role is, while leaving other mental capacities intact. Hospitalized patients insisting on their obligation to organize a funeral or to resume military duties were already documented a century ago (Korsakoff, 1891; Kalberlah, 1904). A patient of ours, a retired psychiatrist hospitalized after rupture of aneurysm of the anterior communicating artery, was convinced that she was actually working as a psychiatrist at our clinic and repeatedly left therapy sessions in the conviction that she had to see patients (Schnider et al., 2005a; Schnider, 2008). A young lawyer, suffering from limbic encephalitis, desperately searched for her files, convinced that she was expected at court (Nahum et al., 2010). Both insisted on their resented reality although the hospital environment and therapy sessions should have indicated to them that they were not at work and that their ideas were wrong.

These patients had typical behaviorally spontaneous confabulation (Schnider, 2008), a syndrome first described by Korsakoff (1891) more than 100 years ago: the patients act according to false ideas that can mostly be traced back to real experiences (mostly habits), justify their actions with apparently invented stories (confabulations), are amnesic, and are disoriented regarding time, place, and their current situation.

The disorder was initially described in alcoholic, malnourished people suffering from the Wernicke–Korsakoff syndrome and in subjects having traumatic brain injury (Korsakoff, 1891; Bonhoeffer, 1901; Kalberlah, 1904). Nowadays, it is most frequently reported after rupture of an aneurysm of the anterior communicating artery, traumatic brain injury, or encephalitis (Schnider, 2008). The critical variable is not the type of brain damage, but the location: all hitherto described patients with circumscribed lesions – apart from dementia or a confusional state – had damage to the posterior medial orbitofrontal cortex or of brain regions directly connected with it (**Figure 1**) (Schnider et al., 1996b; Schnider and Ptak, 1999; Gilboa and Moscovitch, 2002; Schnider, 2008). Posterior lesion extension determines how much information the patients can store but is irrelevant for reality confusion as described above (Schnider, 2008). Hippocampal damage is often absent but may also be maximal (Schnider and Ptak, 1999; Nahum et al., 2010). Extremely severe amnesia and extended hippocampal damage do not protect against confabulation, as recently claimed (Dalla Barba and La Corte, 2013).

LIMBIC CONTROL OF MEMORY AND REALITY

These clinical observations alone reveal a fundamental organizing principle of the limbic system's contribution to memory control: while the posterior limbic system with the hippocampus is necessary for long-term encoding of memories (Squire et al., 2004), possibly also the retrieval of episodic details (Moscovitch et al., 2005), the anterior limbic system with the posterior medial orbitofrontal cortex is critical for the sense of whether an activated memory relates to the "now" or not. It signals when an activated memory does not pertain to ongoing reality (Schnider, 2008). It thus prevents behavior from being based on fantasies, that is, ideas that do not refer to the present.

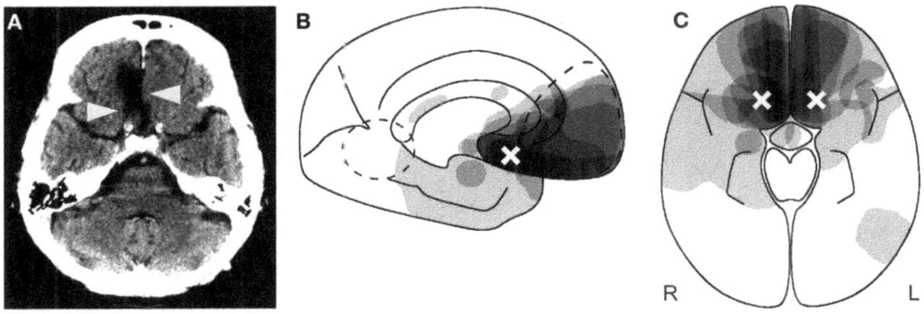

FIGURE 1 | Anatomy of reality filtering. **(A)** Typical orbitofrontal lesion causing reality confusion. In this case, the right gyrus rectus is destroyed (arrowheads) following rupture of an aneurysm of the anterior communicating artery. **(B,C)** Superimposition of the lesions of 14 patients who confused reality for weeks to months. **(B)** Sagittal cut; **(C)** axial cut. As indicated by the shades of gray, maximal lesion overlap was in the posterior medial orbitofrontal area. The white crosses indicate the area of peak activity in healthy subjects who performed a similar task as the one on which the reality-confusing patients failed. **(B,C)** Reproduced from Schnider (2008), with permission.

SENSE OF TIME

Reality-confusing patients also have a disturbed sense for the "now," the "perceived or psychological present," defined as the duration of an experiential process, suggested to take about 0.1–5 s (Fraisse, 1984). In comparison to non-confabulating amnesics and healthy controls, reality-confusing patients failed to discriminate short, temporally overlapping intervals in the range of 0.2–3 s (Schnider, 2000). Similar findings have been obtained in patients with damage of the basal ganglia or cerebellum (Ivry and Keele, 1989; Gibbon et al., 1997; Riesen and Schnider, 2001). These structures were also activated, together with dorsolateral prefrontal and parietal cortex, in functional magnetic resonance imaging (fMRI) of time estimation and reproduction (Bueti et al., 2008). Damage to these structures does not induce reality confusion. It might, therefore, be that the disturbed discrimination within the psychological present in reality-confusing patients either reflects an independent time function, not causally related to reality confusion, or that the posterior medial orbitofrontal cortex, which is difficult to discern in fMRI due to artifacts, holds a central role in the sense of the "now," but requires participation of association areas. The precise significance of the finding is as yet unclear.

EXPLORING THE SENSE OF REALITY

In any case, the temporal difficulty of reality-confusing patients transcends the perception of the present moment: they apparently fail to place themselves correctly in time and space. They act as obstinately on ideas that have no relation with the present as on ideas that refer to the present. How might one experimentally seize this intrusion of thoughts, which have no relation with the present, into their concept of reality and actions? We were lucky to develop a task, which tests the sense for memories' relation with the "now" and which has proved very reliable in separating reality-confusing patients from other amnesic subjects (Schnider et al., 1996a; Schnider and Ptak, 1999; Nahum et al., 2012). The task uses repeated runs of a continuous recognition test, in which subjects see a long series of pictures and have to indicate picture recurrences within the ongoing run (**Figure 2**). When subjects do such a task for the first time, they can recognize picture repetitions on the sole basis of familiarity (**Figure 2A**). Healthy subjects performing such a first run activated the hippocampal area (Schnider et al., 2000b).

As subjects repeat the task, always composed of the same picture series, familiarity alone is not sufficient anymore; all items look familiar. Thus, the recognition of a repetition within the ongoing run now requires the ability to sense whether a picture was previously seen within the ongoing run (the "present reality" of the ongoing run) or a previous run; it requires reality filtering (**Figure 2B**). Despite this requirement, healthy subjects perform the task intuitively, with no particular effort: reaction times are similar to the first run and errors (false positive responses) are very scarce (Schnider et al., 2002; Wahlen et al., 2011). Indeed, it has proved very difficult to develop a task version which lowered performance of healthy subjects (Schnider et al., 2010).

When healthy subjects performed repeated runs of this task, they had activation of the posterior medial orbitofrontal cortex, area 13 (**Figures 1B,C**) (Schnider et al., 2000b), which corresponds to the area of maximal damage in patients who confuse reality.

The task structurally resembles well-known source memory tasks requiring attribution of stimuli to previous task stages, such as, the exclusion condition of the process dissociation procedure (Jacoby, 1991), in that it has multiple runs. Despite this resemblance, the processes involved in such tasks are very different from ours: they require conscious, effortful monitoring (Jacoby, 1991), activate the dorsolateral prefrontal (rather than orbitofrontal) cortex (Rugg et al., 2003), and have no predictive value for the occurrence of behaviorally spontaneous confabulation (Johnson et al., 1997). Reality filtering is not about knowing to what episode in the past a memory refers but whether it pertains to present reality or not.

Our reality-filtering task, as easy as it may be for healthy subjects, proved an insurmountable challenge for reality-confusing patients, even at much longer intervals between the runs (30–60 min) than in healthy subjects (1 min). While healthy subjects and non-confabulating amnesics maintained performance over repeated runs, reality-confusing patients had a sharp increase of false positive responses: they believed increasingly more often that they had already seen pictures within the ongoing run, which in

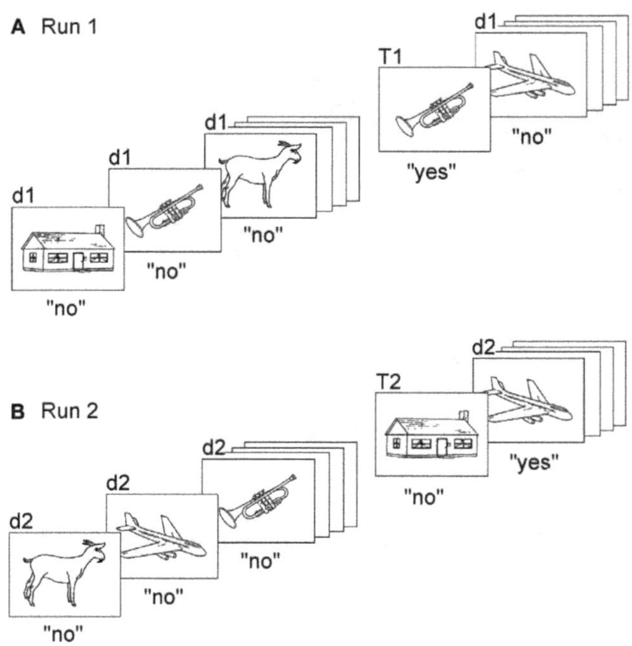

FIGURE 2 | Task to measure the sense of present reality. Subjects make two runs (or more) of a continuous recognition task, each run composed of the same set of pictures. Subjects have to indicate, in both runs, only repetitions within the ongoing run (original version: Schnider et al., 1996a). **(A)** The first run demands learning and recognition and can be solved on the basis of familiarity alone. **(B)** In the second run, all items are already familiar. The task now demands the ability to distinguish between memories that pertain to the ongoing run (repetitions within the run, T2) and memories that do not (d2; not previously presented within the run, albeit familiar from the first run). Confabulating patients had a steep increase of false positives in response to d2 stimuli. "d" denotes "distracters," i.e., pictures' first appearance within a run; "T" denotes targets, i.e., repeated pictures within the run. "d1" and "T1" are stimuli presented in the first run, "d2" and "T2" are stimuli of the second run. "Yes" and "no" indicate correct responses. Illustration reproduced from Schnider (2008), with permission.

reality appeared for the first time within the run (Schnider et al., 1996a; Schnider and Ptak, 1999; Nahum et al., 2012). This increase of false positives was also tightly associated with the degree of disorientation, that is, the number of false answers to questions about current time, place, or situation (Schnider et al., 1996b; Nahum et al., 2012). Recovery of the ability to sense that familiar items had not yet appeared within the ongoing run was individually predictive of the recovery of the sense of reality with cessation of confabulations and inappropriate acts and re-installment of correct orientation (Schnider et al., 2000a). The increase of false positives in reality-confusing patients indicates that orbitofrontal reality-filtering functions by exclusion: it signals when a memory does not relate to current reality.

PRECONSCIOUS REALITY FILTERING

The conviction that healthy subjects, but also reality-confusing patients hold in their concept of current reality – the present day, their current role and location, etc. – suggests that reality filtering is an early process, which precedes conscious control. Experimental evidence supports this notion. When healthy subjects performed a similar task while their brain activity was observed with electroencephalography, processing of new and repeated items in the first run, which requires learning and recognition, differed over posterior electrodes at around 400–600 ms (Schnider et al., 2002; Wahlen et al., 2011). By contrast, processing of new items in the second run, which requires reality filtering, induced a strikingly different electrocortical potential than all other stimuli of the first and second run: at 200–300 ms, they did not evoke a negative frontal potential common to all other stimuli. Thus, correct processing of the stimuli on which reality-confusing patients had failed (first presentations within the second run) differed from all other stimuli at an early stage, before processes of recognition set in. In other words, even before we recognize the precise content of an upcoming memory (thought), the orbitofrontal cortex has already decided whether it refers to ongoing reality or not.

Spatio-temporal analysis of the electrical activity over the whole brain indicated that the absence of the negative potential reflected the fact that new stimuli of the second run skipped a processing stage common to all other stimuli, which was characterized by a particularly extended neocortical, temporo-parietal area of synchronous activity (Schnider et al., 2002; Schnider, 2003; Wahlen et al., 2011), as indicated by source estimation (Michel et al., 2004). This suggests that, whenever a memory is activated that does not relate to reality (fantasy), neocortical synchronization is transiently inhibited at 200–300 ms (Schnider, 2003). Fantasies would thus assume a different electrocortical format than thoughts that pertain to ongoing reality and that have passed through the stage of extended neocortical activation (Schnider, 2008).

This sequence of processes – first reality filtering, then recognition and re-encoding of memories (thoughts), as depicted in **Figure 3A** – not only ensures that we distinguish between memories that pertain to ongoing reality and memories that do not, but also that we know tomorrow whether we have really experienced a situation today or only thought about it; as these thoughts (memories) are re-encoded, they are labeled as referring to reality or as a fantasy (Schnider, 2008). In reality-confusing patients (**Figure 3B**), memories that do not relate to reality are not filtered and thus assume the same format as memories relating to reality. Any upcoming thought, be it a memory of the past, a thought about the present, or a plan for the future, is sensed as if it referred to the present. Depending on the evoked memories, patients' behavior sometimes agrees, sometimes disagrees with reality. As far as the patients encode their own thoughts, they experience them as if they referred to reality and may, therefore, subsequently produce false statements about the past, present, or future. In agreement with this interpretation, confabulating patients may recall events that they have simply talked about, as if they had really experienced them (Schnider et al., 2005a).

Reality filtering is not limited to visual information: we observed similar orbitofrontal activation in functional imaging with visually presented verbal or non-verbal visual material (Treyer et al., 2003) as well as with auditorily presented words (Treyer et al., 2006). The process is precise: the electrocortical signal was much more distinct when stimuli between the runs were identical with, rather than only resembled previously presented ones (Wahlen et al., 2011). Thus, reality filtering seems to be challenged particularly when present reality is very similar to a past reality.

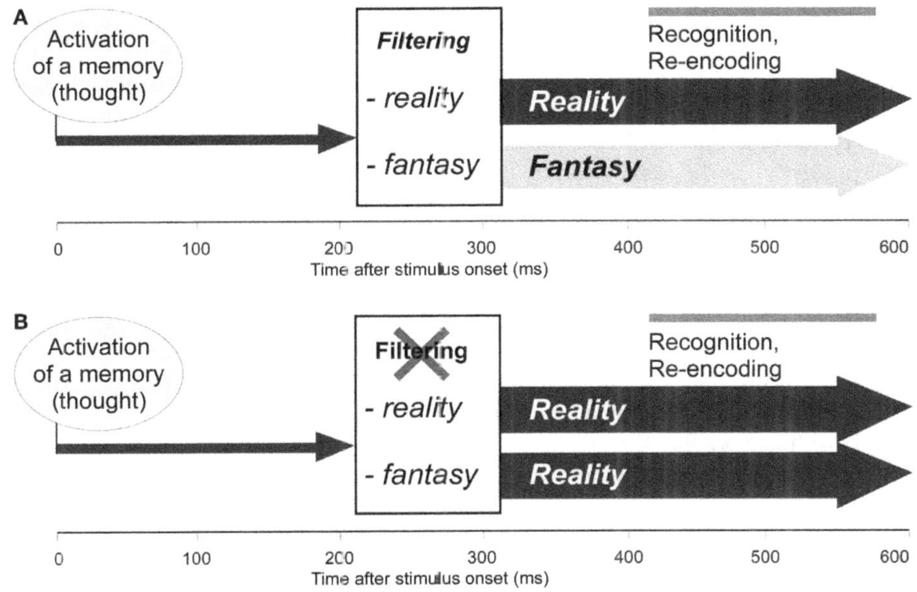

FIGURE 3 | Functional model of the orbitofrontal reality filter. (A) Normal function: 200–300 ms after activation of a memory (thought), reality filtering sets in, inhibiting extended neocortical activation when the upcoming memory does not relate to ongoing reality. At 400–600 ms, the activated memory (thought) is recognized and again encoded (Schnider et al., 2002; Wahlen et al., 2011). **(B)** Hypothetical dysfunction of reality filtering in reality-confusing patients: memories (thoughts) are normally activated, but are not checked regarding their relation with reality; all memories are activated, and later recognized and re-encoded, as if they related to ongoing reality. Adapted from Schnider (2008), with permission.

Finally, the process is distinct from other memory control mechanisms: to recognize that a stimulus only resembles, but is not identical with a previously seen stimulus (task described by Gilboa et al., 2006) also evokes an electrocortical signal at 200–300 ms but with inverse polarity than the one produced by reality filtering (Wahlen et al., 2011). That is, the recognition of a memory's concordance with the present (reality filtering) dissociates from the recognition of its concordance with the past (its content).

ORBITOFRONTAL CORTEX AND REALITY FILTERING

The posterior medial orbitofrontal cortex is a phylogenetically old and ontogenetically consistent structure (Chiavaras et al., 2001). One may, therefore, wonder what specific faculty enables it to assume the role of a reality filter. Reality-confusing patients fail to adapt to the fact that their anticipations never come true: the hospitalized psychiatrist did not find her expected patients, the lawyer did not find the colleagues and judges she expected to meet. Yet, both continued to act according to such anticipations – based on habits – as if they were still valid. This behavior is reminiscent of animals continuing to choose a conditioned stimulus, which was previously followed by reward, even after this association has proved to be no longer valid. The ability to learn from the fact that a stimulus is no longer followed by reward and to abandon a previously valid stimulus-outcome association is called extinction (Pavlov, 1927; Ouyang and Thomas, 2005). In non-human primates, lesions of the posterior medial orbitofrontal cortex, corresponding to area 13, induced a specific deficit of extinction, unlike damage to any other region of the prefrontal lobes (Butter, 1969). Single cell recordings showed that this area contains a particularly high density of neurons that specifically discharge when an expected reward fails to be delivered (Rosenkilde et al., 1981). Our hypothesis is that the brain uses this neural signal to label an upcoming memory as not pertaining to ongoing reality, that is, as a fantasy. The neurons producing this signal might be appropriately described as "reality neurons."

Clinical evidence supports this hypothesis: we asked a group of amnesic subjects to perform a reversal learning task, in which they had to predict which one of two faces would have a target stimulus on the nose (Nahum et al., 2009). Reality-confusing patients did not differ from other amnesics in their ability to learn the association, but they had significantly more difficulty in switching to the alternate face after trials indicating absence of the target stimulus. Over all patients, this difficulty, but not other cognitive measures, highly correlated with the degree of disorientation.

The data indicate that, rather than invoking high-level monitoring mechanisms, the brain uses a phylogenetically old capacity, already available to primitive creatures like aplysia (Hawkins et al., 2006) and drosophila (Schwaerzel et al., 2002), to keep thought and behavior in phase with reality: it uses the neural signal that also underlies behavioral extinction. So, evolution did not have to devise a separate mechanism to assure the behaviorally appropriate use of an ever-increasing stock of memories in higher species like humans.

REALITY CHECK AND REWARD SYSTEM

These results point to a hitherto unappreciated role of the orbitofrontal cortex and the reward system in reality filtering beyond processing the pleasure associated with outcomes. Indeed, orbitofrontal activity does not depend on the prospect of pleasure: the human orbitofrontal cortex is also activated when anticipating and monitoring neutral events devoid of any tangible reward value (Schnider et al., 2005b). In such a task, the non-occurrence of anticipated outcomes induced a distinct electrocortical signal, which occurred in the same period (200–300 ms) and with a similar configuration (frontal positivity) as the signal produced in reality filtering (Schnider et al., 2007). Indeed, it appears that, in humans, posterior orbitofrontal activity in response to the non-delivery of expected reward is driven much more by the need to adapt behavior than the sole absence of the reward; when there was no need to adapt behavior, absence of reward did not activate this area (Nahum et al., 2011). While these results do not question the role of the orbitofrontal cortex in hedonic processing (Kringelbach, 2005), decision-making, and optimizing behavior (Bechara et al., 1997; Wallis, 2007), they underscore that the orbitofrontal cortex contains the neural apparatus allowing it to function as a generic reality-filtering system, irrespective of whether reward is at stake or not.

The similarity between reality filtering and reward processing extends to transmitter systems. While select orbitofrontal neurons increase firing when an anticipated reward fails to occur (Rosenkilde et al., 1981; Thorpe et al., 1983), dopaminergic neurons in the nigro-striatal system transiently decrease their firing (Schultz et al., 1997; Schultz, 2007). A "hyper-dopaminergic" state would, accordingly, be expected to impair reality filtering. This is what we found (Schnider et al., 2010): when healthy subjects performed a very difficult version of our reality-filtering task under the influence of L-DOPA, which is transformed to dopamine in the brain, they produced specifically more false positive responses than when they received a dopamine antagonist (risperidone). Thus, reality filtering, similar to reward processing, is under dopaminergic modulation. Of note, a hyper-dopaminergic state has also been suspected to underlie schizophrenia, another disorder characterized by reality confusion (Howes and Kapur, 2009). Actively hallucinating schizophrenic patients failed in our reality-filtering task (Badcock et al., 2005). Pervasive confabulations were described in such patients in the nineteenth century (Kraepelin, 1887/88) before the advent of neuroleptics (dopamine antagonists) in the late 1940s. The implication of diverse dopamine sub-systems and other transmitter systems in reward and outcome processing is a topic of current research (Schultz and Dickinson, 2000; Bromberg-Martin et al., 2010); their role for reality filtering is entirely unknown.

Available data suggest a link between orbitofrontal activity and subcortical dopaminergic transmission. The orbitofrontal cortex projects onto dopaminergic neurons in the midbrain (Joel and Weiner, 2000), which, in turn, project onto, and modulate activity in frontal-subcortical loops that connect specific areas of the prefrontal lobes, including the orbitofrontal cortex, with themselves and other frontal areas (Alexander et al., 1986). By transiently inhibiting dopaminergic neurons, the orbitofrontal cortex might thus modulate activity in subcortical connections and convey the signal inhibiting neocortical synchronization when an upcoming memory does not relate to reality. In agreement with this, we observed activation of a loop connecting the orbitofrontal cortex with the striatum, substantia nigra, and the medial thalamus when healthy subjects performed a more sensitive version of the reality-filtering task containing different stimulus types (Treyer et al., 2003). This result, together with the pharmacological evidence, suggests that reality filtering not only relies on the same orbitofrontal signal, but also on the same circuitry as the one used to signal that an anticipated reward failed to occur. We surmise that reality filtering is a specific instance of "reward" processing: it refers to all types of outcomes, irrespective of hedonic value, and specifically processes the situation that anticipated events fail to happen.

COMPARISON WITH OTHER HYPOTHESES

Orbitofrontal reality filtering, as described in this review, does not yet have the status of a distinct, acknowledged brain function. Accordingly, there is no hypothesis to compare it with. By contrast, the two obvious disorders resulting from its dysfunction – disorientation and confabulation – have received the attention of cognitive models.

Disorientation has been linked to amnesia and perception: an uninterrupted flow of memories and correct perception of the environment would be necessary to maintain orientation in time and space (Kraepelin, 1909; Benton et al., 1964; High et al., 1990). Our data only partially support this notion: the severity of amnesia, as measured with a continuous recognition task, is only weakly associated with disorientation (Schnider et al., 1996b; Schnider, 2008). However, early authors also speculated that there might be a distinct function of orientation (Bleuler, 1923) and Jaspers (1973) separated "delusional disorientation" in patients with full consciousness as a distinct form. Deficient reality filtering might be the mechanism they thought of.

Confabulations have been the topic of diverse hypotheses. Most of them tried to explain confabulations as a verbal phenomenon, irrespective of inappropriate behavior or disorientation. The question at the center of these hypotheses was: "What makes patients tell incorrect stories and fabricate false responses to questions?" The question at the basis of our studies was: "why do the patients confuse reality?"

The first question refers to two forms of confabulation: (1) Intrusions in memory tests (simple provoked confabulations). These dissociate from all other forms of confabulation and are independent of reality confusion (Schnider et al., 1996a; Nahum et al., 2012). (2) Momentary confabulations (also called out-of-embarrassment confabulations) (Bonhoeffer, 1901; Van der Horst, 1932; Schnider, 2008) that patients produce in discussions or in response to questions. It is the most commonly reported form of confabulation. It need not be accompanied by disorientation. Only a relatively small proportion of patients who produce momentary confabulations have deficient reality filtering (Nahum et al., 2012).

The second question refers to two other forms: (3) behaviorally spontaneous confabulation, as defined above – the topic of this review. It can be conceived as a specific subform of momentary confabulations, namely, the form caused by reality confusion, as evident from inappropriate acts in accordance with the confabulations and disorientation. (4) Fantastic confabulations, which defy any sense of plausibility. These are rare and occur in severe confusion, dementia, or psychosis (Schnider, 2008).

Most hypotheses did not distinguish between forms of confabulations. Thus, they have differing significance for the explanation of behaviorally spontaneous confabulation and reality confusion. The most prominent hypotheses can be summarized as follows: (1) Confabulations emanate from a combination of amnesia with frontal executive failures. The hypothesis stems from the observation that executive functions may recover in parallel with the cessation of confabulations (Papagno and Baddeley, 1997; Nys et al., 2004) and that confabulations in cohorts of brain damaged patients are associated with executive dysfunction (Cunningham et al., 1997). However, patients with behaviorally spontaneous confabulation did not differ from similarly severe non-confabulating amnesics with regards to executive functions (Schnider et al., 1996a; Schnider and Ptak, 1999; Nahum et al., 2012). (2) Confabulations reflect a desire to fill gaps in memory or may compensate for the embarrassment of being unable to respond to questions (Flament, 1957; Conway and Tacci, 1996; Fotopoulou et al., 2008). This mechanism appears to account for a certain proportion of momentary confabulations, but was not associated with behaviorally spontaneous confabulation or disorientation (Schnider et al., 1996a; Nahum et al., 2012). Nonetheless, it may be that this mechanism explains the content of false ideas, possibly also the tendency to talk about them. If reality filtering fails, then patients not only talk about, but also act in accordance with these ideas. (3) Confabulations emanate from deficient monitoring of the source (spatial, temporal, personal context) of memories (Johnson and Raye, 1998). Insofar as this function has been defined by experimental procedures, which typically require effortful and conscious monitoring (see process dissociation procedure, above), it has failed to differentiate confabulating from non-confabulating patients (own unpublished data and Johnson et al., 1997). Conversely, reality filtering, which precedes the re-encoding of thoughts, is likely to be a prerequisite for later source monitoring. (4) Confabulations reflect insufficient monitoring of memories' content (Moscovitch and Melo, 1997; Gilboa et al., 2006). Confabulating patients who failed both in our reality-filtering task and a task requiring fine distinction between closely similar items were indeed described (Gilboa et al., 2006). We found that these two challenges evoked different cortical processes (Wahlen et al., 2011). It may be that in select patient groups, both processes may contribute to the occurrence and the content of confabulations. (5) Confabulations results from a deficient temporal tag of memories or reflect temporally displaced consciousness (Van der Horst, 1932; Talland, 1961; Dalla Barba, 2002; Dalla Barba and La Corte, 2013). The hypothesis is based on the observation that confabulations very often are rooted in patients' true experiences and falsely recombine elements of real events. While these authors never proposed a way to experimentally verify the hypothesis, the idea is entirely compatible with the concept of reality filtering, but with a twist: reality filtering only explains confabulations emanating from reality confusion and, therefore, only a certain proportion of confabulations.

LIMITATIONS OF THE TASK

The continuous recognition task used to test reality filtering, as predictive as it has been in clinical practice and as consistent imaging and electrophysiological results have been, has its limitations. First, it may fail to seize memory confusion in patients with extremely severe amnesia who fail to encode any information in the first run (Schnider et al., 1996a). Such patients still failed in the extinction task (Nahum et al., 2009; Schnider et al., 2013). Second, like any cognitive test, a subject's strategy may influence results. One of our patients was so skeptical about the difficulties of the second run that he rejected all items as being repetitions. When the task was repeated indicating that not only his correct rejections, but also his correct recognitions would be counted, the typical pattern of memory confusion became apparent (Ptak and Schnider, 1999). Third, in our studies, patients were matched according to the severity of amnesia. There are indications that, if patients are selected according to a single etiology, irrespective of the severity of cognitive deficits, the task may not be very predictive of reality confusion (Joray et al., 2004; Gilboa et al., 2006). Fourth, the most important limitation of the task is its specificity. As this review should make clear, it has been developed to measure reality confusion; it is not a predictor of all forms of confabulation. This limitation, of course, applies to the whole concept of orbitofrontal reality filtering.

PERSPECTIVES

A number of questions remain: what qualifies a real-world memory, composed of different modalities, as pertaining to reality? Is there a hierarchy of modalities, for example, with visual information, which is used in most experiments, prevailing over tactile information? Then, there are anatomical enigmas: first, virtually all patients confusing reality after an orbitofrontal lesion eventually regain the sense of reality, albeit sometimes only after many months (Schnider et al., 2000a, 2005a). This suggests that the neural apparatus ensuring reality filtering – presumably the outcome monitoring system – is redundantly organized or may undergo plastic changes after damage, similar to other systems. What brain areas and mechanism allow these patients to regain the sense of reality? Secondly, only a minority of people having a classic disease and orbitofrontal lesion actually suffer sustained reality confusion (Schnider, 2008); a typical lesion alone does not reliably predict the occurrence of reality confusion. Thus, do reality-confusing patients have the misfortune of concentrating their reality cells in the areas damaged by the common causes of behaviorally spontaneous confabulation? Is there a genetic predisposition for such an arrangement or for the ability to rapidly adapt thought to ongoing reality?

While some of these questions can be examined in humans, others need the precision of animal experimentation. The association between human reality filtering and the capacity to abandon previously valid anticipations suggests that extinction trials in reward tasks would be an appropriate animal model of human reality filtering. In contrast to extinction of fear memories (in which the animals gain access to a previously avoided stimulus) (LeDoux, 1996; Quirk et al., 2010) extinction of reward associations (in which the animals give up a previously rewarding association) has rarely been studied because such trials rapidly discourage the animals from participating. Experimentation would thus take longer. The investment may clearly be worth it: a better understanding of the processes underlying reality filtering might open new ways to treat diseases impairing the sense of reality.

ACKNOWLEDGMENTS

The work reported here was supported by Swiss National Science Foundation Grant No. 320030-132447. I thank Radek Ptak and Louis Nahum for helpful comments.

REFERENCES

Alexander, G. E., Delong, M. R., and Strick, P. L. (1986). Parallel organization of functionally segregated circuits linking basal ganglia and cortex. *Annu. Rev. Neurosci.* 9, 357–381. doi:10.1146/annurev.ne.09.030186.002041

Badcock, J. C., Waters, F. A., Maybery, M. T., and Michie, P. T. (2005). Auditory hallucinations: failure to inhibit irrelevant memories. *Cogn. Neuropsychiatry* 10, 125–136. doi:10.1080/13546800344000363

Bechara, A., Damasio, H., Tranel, D., and Damasio, A. R. (1997). Deciding advantageously before knowing the advantageous strategy. *Science* 275, 1293–1295. doi:10.1126/science.275.5304.1293

Benton, A. L., Van Allen, M. W., and Fogel, M. L. (1964). Temporal orientation in cerebral disease. *J. Nerv. Ment. Dis.* 139, 110–119. doi:10.1097/00005053-196408000-00003

Bleuler, E. (1923). *Lehrbuch der Psychiatrie.* Berlin: Julius Springer Verlag.

Bonhoeffer, K. (1901). *Die Akuten Geisteskrankheiten des Gewohnheitstrinkers. Eine klinische Studie.* Jena: Gustav Fischer.

Bromberg-Martin, E. S., Matsumoto, M., and Hikosaka, O. (2010). Dopamine in motivational control: rewarding, aversive, and alerting. *Neuron* 68, 815–834. doi:10.1016/j.neuron.2010.11.022

Bueti, D., Walsh, V., Frith, C., and Rees, G. (2008). Different brain circuits underlie motor and perceptual representations of temporal intervals. *J. Cogn. Neurosci.* 20, 204–214. doi:10.1162/jocn.2008.20017

Butter, C. M. (1969). Perseveration in extinction and in discrimination reversal tasks following selective frontal ablations in *Macaca mulatta. Physiol. Behav.* 4, 163–171. doi:10.1016/0031-9384(69)90075-4

Chiavaras, M. M., Legoualher, G., Evans, A., and Petrides, M. (2001). Three-dimensional probabilistic atlas of the human orbitofrontal sulci in standardized stereotaxic space. *Neuroimage* 13, 479–496. doi:10.1006/nimg.2000.0641

Conway, M. A., and Tacci, P. C. (1996). Motivated confabulation. *Neurocase* 2, 325–339. doi:10.1093/neucas/2.4.325-a

Cunningham, J. M., Pliskin, N. H., Cassisi, J. E., Tsang, B., and Rao, S. M. (1997). Relationship between confabulation and measures of memory and executive function. *J. Clin. Exp. Neuropsychol.* 19, 867–877. doi:10.1080/01688639708403767

Dalla Barba, G., and La Corte, V. (2013). The hippocampus, a time machine that makes errors. *Trends Cogn. Sci. (Regul. Ed.)* 17, 102–104. doi:10.1016/j.tics.2013.01.005

Dalla Barba, G. F. (2002). *Memory, Consciousness and Temporality.* Boston: Kluwer Academic Publishers.

Flament, J. (1957). La fabulation dans le syndrome de Korsakov d'étiologie traumatique. Considérations cliniques, psycho-pathologiques et neuro-pathologiques à propos d'une observation de fabulation à caractère mythopathique. *Acta Neurol. Belg.* 57, 119–161.

Fotopoulou, A., Conway, M. A., Tyrer, S., Birchall, D., Griffiths, P., and Solms, M. (2008). Is the content of confabulation positive? An experimental study. *Cortex* 44, 764–772. doi:10.1016/j.cortex.2007.03.001

Fraisse, P. (1984). Perception and estimation of time. *Annu. Rev. Psychol.* 35, 1–36. doi:10.1146/annurev.ps.35.020184.000245

Gibbon, J., Malapani, C., Dale, C. L., and Gallistel, C. (1997). Toward a neurobiology of temporal cognition: advances and challenges. *Curr. Opin. Neurobiol.* 7, 170–184. doi:10.1016/S0959-4388(97)80005-0

Gilboa, A., Alain, C., Stuss, D. T., Melo, B., Miller, S., and Moscovitch, M. (2006). Mechanisms of spontaneous confabulations: a strategic retrieval account. *Brain* 129, 1399–1414. doi:10.1093/brain/awl093

Gilboa, A., and Moscovitch, M. (2002). "The cognitive neuroscience of confabulation: a review and a model," in *The Handbook of Memory Disorders*, 2nd Edn, eds A. Baddeley, M. D. Kopelman, and B. Wilson (West Sussex: John Wiley & Sons), 315–342.

Hawkins, R. D., Clark, G. A., and Kandel, E. R. (2006). Operant conditioning of gill withdrawal in Aplysia. *J. Neurosci.* 26, 2443–2448. doi:10.1523/JNEUROSCI.3294-05.2006

High, W. M., Levin, H. S., and Gary, H. E. (1990). Recovery of orientation following closed head injury. *J. Clin. Exp. Neuropsychol.* 12, 703–714. doi:10.1080/01688639008401013

Howes, O. D., and Kapur, S. (2009). The dopamine hypothesis of schizophrenia: version III – the final common pathway. *Schizophr. Bull.* 35, 549–562. doi:10.1093/schbul/sbp006

Ivry, R. B., and Keele, S. W. (1989). Timing functions of the cerebellum. *J. Cogn. Neurosci.* 1, 136–152. doi:10.1162/jocn.1989.1.2.136

Jacoby, L. L. (1991). A process dissociation framework: separating automatic from intentional uses of memory. *J. Mem. Lang.* 30, 513–541. doi:10.1016/0749-596X(91)90025-F

Jaspers, K. (1973). *Allgemeine Psychopathologie.* Berlin: Springer-Verlag.

Joel, D., and Weiner, I. (2000). The connections of the dopaminergic system with the striatum in rats and primates: an analysis with respect to the functional and compartmental organization of the striatum. *Neuroscience* 96, 451–474. doi:10.1016/S0306-4522(99)00575-8

Johnson, M. K., O'Connor, M., and Cantor, J. (1997). Confabulation, memory deficits, and frontal dysfunction. *Brain Cogn.* 34, 189–206. doi:10.1006/brcg.1997.0873

Johnson, M. K., and Raye, C. L. (1998). False memories and confabulation. *Trends Cogn. Sci. (Regul. Ed.)* 2, 137–145. doi:10.1016/S1364-6613(98)01152-8

Joray, S., Herrmann, F., Mulligan, R., and Schnider, A. (2004). Mechanism of disorientation in Alzheimer's disease. *Eur. Neurol.* 52, 193–197. doi:10.1159/000082034

Kalberlah, F. (1904). Ueber die acute Commotionspsychose, zugleich ein Beitrag zur Aetiologie des Korsakow'schen Symptomenkomplexes. *Arch. Psychiatr. Nervenkr.* 38, 402–438. doi:10.1007/BF02173472

Korsakoff, S. S. (1891). Erinnerungstäuschungen (Pseudoreminiscenzen) bei polyneuritischer Psychose. *Allg. Z. Psychiatr. Psych. Med.* 47, 390–410.

Kraepelin, E. (1909). *Psychiatrie. Ein Lehrbuch für Studierende und Ärzte. I. Band, Allgemeine Psychiatrie.* Leipzig: Johann Ambrosius Barth Verlag.

Kraepelin, E. (1887/88). Ueber Erinnerungsfälschungen. *Arch. Psychiatr. Nervenkr.* 17, 830–843. doi:10.1007/BF02207467

Kringelbach, M. L. (2005). The human orbitofrontal cortex: linking reward to hedonic experience. *Nat. Rev. Neurosci.* 6, 691–702. doi:10.1038/nrn1747

LeDoux, J. (1996). *The Emotional Brain. The Mysterious Underpinnings of Emotional Life.* New York: Simon & Schuster.

Michel, C. M., Murray, M. M., Lantz, G., Gonzalez, S., Spinelli, L., and Grave De Peralta, R. (2004). EEG source imaging. *Clin. Neurophysiol.* 115, 2195–2222. doi:10.1016/j.clinph.2004.06.001

Moscovitch, M., and Melo, B. (1997). Strategic retrieval and the frontal lobes: evidence from confabulation and amnesia. *Neuropsychologia* 35, 1017–1034. doi:10.1016/S0028-3932(97)00028-6

Moscovitch, M., Rosenbaum, R. S., Gilboa, A., Addis, D. R., Westmacott, R., Grady, C., et al. (2005). Functional neuroanatomy of remote episodic, semantic and spatial memory: a unified account based on multiple trace theory. *J. Anat.* 207, 35–66. doi:10.1111/j.1469-7580.2005.00421.x

Nahum, L., Bouzerda-Wahlen, A., Guggisberg, A., Ptak, R., and Schnider, A. (2012). Forms of confabulation: dissociations and associations. *Neuropsychologia* 50, 2524–2534. doi:10.1016/j.neuropsychologia.2012.06.026

Nahum, L., Gabriel, D., and Schnider, A. (2011). Human processing of behaviorally relevant and irrelevant absence of expected rewards: a high-resolution ERP study. *PLoS ONE* 6:e16173. doi:10.1371/journal.pone.0016173

Nahum, L., Ptak, R., Leemann, B., Lalive, P., and Schnider, A. (2010). Behaviorally spontaneous confabulation in limbic encephalitis: the roles of strategic monitoring and reality filtering. *J. Int. Neuropsychol. Soc.* 16, 995–1005. doi:10.1017/S1355617710000780

Nahum, L., Ptak, R., Leemann, B., and Schnider, A. (2009). Disorientation, confabulation, and extinction capacity. Clues on how the brain creates reality. *Biol. Psychiatry* 65, 966–972. doi:10.1016/j.biopsych.2009.01.007

Nys, G. M., Van Zandvoort, M. J., Roks, G., Kappelle, L. J., De Kort, P. L., and De Haan, E. H. (2004). The role of executive functioning in spontaneous confabulation. *Cogn. Behav. Neurol.* 17, 213–218.

Ouyang, M., and Thomas, S. A. (2005). A requirement for memory retrieval during and after long-term extinction learning. *Proc. Natl. Acad. Sci. U.S.A.* 102, 9347–9352. doi:10.1073/pnas.0502315102

Papagno, C., and Baddeley, A. (1997). Confabulation in a dysexecutive patient: implication for models of retrieval. *Cortex* 33, 743–752. doi:10.1016/S0010-9452(08)70731-7

Pavlov, P. I. (1927). *Conditioned Reflexes: An Investigation of the Physiological Activity of the Cerebral Cortex*, trans. G. V. Anrep (London: Oxford University Press).

Ptak, R., and Schnider, A. (1999). Spontaneous confabulations after orbitofrontal damage: the role of temporal context confusion and self-monitoring. *Neurocase* 5, 243–250. doi:10.1080/13554799908402729

Quirk, G. J., Pare, D., Richardson, R., Herry, C., Monfils, M. H., Schiller, D., et al. (2010). Erasing fear memories with extinction training. *J. Neurosci.* 30, 14993–14997. doi:10.1523/JNEUROSCI.4268-10.2010

Riesen, J., and Schnider, A. (2001). Time estimation in Parkinson's disease: normal long term estimation despite impaired short duration discrimination. *J. Neurol.* 248, 27–35. doi:10.1007/s004150170266

Rosenkilde, C. E., Bauer, R. H., and Fuster, J. M. (1981). Single cell activity in ventral prefrontal cortex of behaving monkeys. *Brain Res.* 209, 375–394. doi:10.1016/0006-8993(81)90160-8

Rugg, M. D., Henson, R. N., and Robb, W. G. (2003). Neural correlates of retrieval processing in the prefrontal cortex during recognition and exclusion tasks. *Neuropsychologia* 41, 40–52. doi:10.1016/S0028-3932(02)00129-X

Schacter, D. L., Addis, D. R., and Buckner, R. L. (2007). Remembering the past to imagine the future: the prospective brain. *Nat. Rev. Neurosci.* 8, 657–661. doi:10.1038/nrn2213

Schnider, A. (2000). Spontaneous confabulations, disorientation, and the processing of 'now'. *Neuropsychologia* 38, 175–185. doi:10.1016/S0028-3932(99)00064-0

Schnider, A. (2003). Spontaneous confabulation and the adaptation of thought to ongoing reality. *Nat. Rev. Neurosci.* 4, 662–671. doi:10.1038/nrn1179

Schnider, A. (2008). *The Confabulating Mind. How the Brain Creates Reality*. Oxford: Oxford University Press.

Schnider, A., Bonvallat, J., Emond, H., and Leemann, B. (2005a). Reality confusion in spontaneous confabulation. *Neurology* 65, 1117–1119. doi:10.1212/01.wnl.0000178900.37611.8d

Schnider, A., Treyer, V., and Buck, A. (2005b). The human orbitofrontal cortex monitors outcomes even when no reward is at stake. *Neuropsychologia* 43, 316–323. doi:10.1016/j.neuropsychologia.2004.07.003

Schnider, A., Guggisberg, A., Nahum, L., Gabriel, D., and Morand, S. (2010). Dopaminergic modulation of rapid reality adaptation in thinking. *Neuroscience* 167, 583–587. doi:10.1016/j.neuroscience.2010.02.044

Schnider, A., Mohr, C., Morand, S., and Michel, C. M. (2007). Early cortical response to behaviorally relevant absence of anticipated outcomes: a human event-related potential study. *Neuroimage* 35, 1348–1355. doi:10.1016/j.neuroimage.2007.01.047

Schnider, A., Nahum, L., Pignat, J., Leemann, B., Lövblad, K., Wissmeyer, M., et al. (2013). Isolated prospective confabulation in Wernicke-Korsakoff syndrome: a case for reality filtering. *Neurocase* 19, 90–104. doi:10.1080/13554794.2011.654221

Schnider, A., and Ptak, R. (1999). Spontaneous confabulators fail to suppress currently irrelevant memory traces. *Nat. Neurosci.* 2, 677–681. doi:10.1038/10236

Schnider, A., Ptak, R., Von Däniken, C., and Remonda, L. (2000a). Recovery from spontaneous confabulations parallels recovery of temporal confusion in memory. *Neurology* 55, 74–83. doi:10.1212/WNL.55.1.74

Schnider, A., Treyer, V., and Buck, A. (2000b). Selection of currently relevant memories by the human posterior medial orbitofrontal cortex. *J. Neurosci.* 20, 5880–5884.

Schnider, A., Valenza, N., Morand, S., and Michel, C. M. (2002). Early cortical distinction between memories that pertain to ongoing reality and memories that don't. *Cereb. Cortex* 12, 54–61. doi:10.1093/cercor/12.1.54

Schnider, A., Von Däniken, C., and Gutbrod, K. (1996a). The mechanisms of spontaneous and provoked confabulations. *Brain* 119, 1365–1375. doi:10.1093/brain/119.4.1365

Schnider, A., Von Däniken, C., and Gutbrod, K. (1996b). Disorientation in amnesia. A confusion of memory traces. *Brain* 119, 1627–1632. doi:10.1093/brain/119.5.1627

Schultz, W. (2007). Multiple dopamine functions at different time courses. *Annu. Rev. Neurosci.* 30, 259–288. doi:10.1146/annurev.neuro.28.061604.135722

Schultz, W., Dayan, P., and Montague, P. R. (1997). A neural substrate of prediction and reward. *Science* 275, 1593–1599. doi:10.1126/science.275.5306.1593

Schultz, W., and Dickinson, A. (2000). Neuronal coding of prediction errors. *Annu. Rev. Neurosci.* 23, 473–500. doi:10.1146/annurev.neuro.23.1.473

Schwaerzel, M., Heisenberg, M., and Zars, T. (2002). Extinction antagonizes olfactory memory at the subcellular level. *Neuron* 35, 951–960. doi:10.1016/S0896-6273(02)00832-2

Scoville, W. B., and Milner, B. (1957). Loss of recent memory after bilateral hippocampal lesions. *J. Neurol. Neurosurg. Psychiatr.* 20, 11–21. doi:10.1136/jnnp.20.1.11

Squire, L. R., Stark, C. E., and Clark, R. E. (2004). The medial temporal lobe. *Annu. Rev. Neurosci.* 27, 279–306. doi:10.1146/annurev.neuro.27.070203.144130

Squire, L. R., and Wixted, J. T. (2011). The cognitive neuroscience of human memory since H.M. *Annu. Rev. Neurosci.* 34, 259–288. doi:10.1146/annurev-neuro-061010-113720

Talland, G. A. (1961). Confabulation in the Wernicke-Korsakoff syndrome. *J. Nerv. Ment. Dis.* 132, 361–381. doi:10.1097/00005053-196105000-00001

Thorpe, S. J., Rolls, E. T., and Maddison, S. (1983). The orbitofrontal cortex: neuronal activity in the behaving monkey. *Exp. Brain Res.* 49, 93–115. doi:10.1007/BF00235545

Treyer, V., Buck, A., and Schnider, A. (2003). Subcortical loop activation during selection of currently relevant memories. *J. Cogn. Neurosci.* 15, 610–618. doi:10.1162/089892903321662985

Treyer, V., Buck, A., and Schnider, A. (2006). Selection of currently relevant words: an auditory verbal memory study using positron emission tomography. *Neuroreport* 17, 323–327. doi:10.1097/01.wnr.0000199457.78670.44

Van der Horst, L. (1932). Über die Psychologie des Korsakowsyndroms. *Monatsschr. Psychiatr. Neurol.* 83, 65–84. doi:10.1159/000164016

Wahlen, A., Nahum, L., Gabriel, D., and Schnider, A. (2011). Fake or fantasy: rapid dissociation between strategic content monitoring and reality filtering in human memory. *Cereb. Cortex* 21, 2589–2598. doi:10.1093/cercor/bhr049

Wallis, J. D. (2007). Orbitofrontal cortex and its contribution to decision-making. *Annu. Rev. Neurosci.* 30, 31–56. doi:10.1146/annurev.neuro.30.051606.094334

3

The pivotal role of semantic memory in remembering the past and imagining the future

***Muireann Irish*[1,2,3]* *and Olivier Piguet*[2,3,4]**

[1] *School of Psychology, University of New South Wales, Sydney, NSW, Australia*
[2] *Neuroscience Research Australia, Randwick, NSW, Australia*
[3] *Australian Research Council Centre of Excellence in Cognition and its Disorders, Sydney, NSW, Australia*
[4] *School of Medical Sciences, University of New South Wales, Sydney, NSW, Australia*

Correspondence:
Muireann Irish, Neuroscience Research Australia, Barker Street, Randwick, Sydney, NSW 2031, Australia.
e-mail: m.irish@neura.edu.au

Episodic memory refers to a complex and multifaceted process which enables the retrieval of richly detailed evocative memories from the past. In contrast, semantic memory is conceptualized as the retrieval of general conceptual knowledge divested of a specific spatiotemporal context. The neural substrates of the episodic and semantic memory systems have been dissociated in healthy individuals during functional imaging studies, and in clinical cohorts, leading to the prevailing view that episodic and semantic memory represent functionally distinct systems subtended by discrete neurobiological substrates. Importantly, however, converging evidence focusing on widespread neural networks now points to significant overlap between those regions essential for retrieval of autobiographical memories, episodic learning, and semantic processing. Here we review recent advances in episodic memory research focusing on neurodegenerative populations which has proved revelatory for our understanding of the complex interplay between episodic and semantic memory. Whereas episodic memory research has traditionally focused on retrieval of autobiographical events from the past, we also include evidence from the recent paradigm shift in which episodic memory is viewed as an adaptive and constructive process which facilitates the imagining of possible events in the future. We examine the available evidence which converges to highlight the pivotal role of semantic memory in providing schemas and meaning whether one is engaged in autobiographical retrieval for the past, or indeed, is endeavoring to construct a plausible scenario of an event in the future. It therefore seems plausible to contend that semantic processing may underlie most, if not all, forms of episodic memory, irrespective of temporal condition.

Keywords: semantic dementia, autobiographical memory, future thinking, Alzheimer's disease, episodic memory, anterior temporal lobes, semantic memory

INTRODUCTION

One of the most fascinating aspects of human cognition is our ability to withdraw from the current moment and to mentally transport ourselves to another time, place, or perspective. Collectively, the abilities to remember the past via episodic autobiographical memory (ABM), or to imagine possible future events, represent important expressions of the human memory system (Tulving, 2002), potentially conferring a significant adaptive advantage in planning for the future (Suddendorf and Corballis, 2007; Klein, 2013). In recent years, episodic memory has been reconceptualized as not only the capacity for retrieval from our personal past, but also encompassing the ability to imagine and envisage possible future scenarios, leading to a constructivist view on how humans might achieve such sophisticated acts of cognition (Hassabis and Maguire, 2007; Schacter and Addis, 2007a). Neuroimaging studies have uncovered a widespread "core" network which subtends the successful retrieval of autobiographical memories from our past (Maguire, 2001; Svoboda et al., 2006; Cabeza and St. Jacques, 2007; Schacter et al., 2007). Importantly, this core network includes frontal and medial temporal regions, notably the hippocampus, lateral temporal, sensory association cortices, and more posterior parietal regions (Spreng et al., 2009), reflecting the multifaceted nature of this type of memory (see **Figure 1**). While considerable variation exists in the classification of episodic memory, in this article, we refer to the contents of episodic memory as "remembered experiences," or ABM (see Tulving and Szpunar, 2009). As will become evident, however, the contents of episodic memory invariably involve semantic representations.

In contrast to the largely evocative, spatiotemporally specific, and often emotionally charged, instances of episodic memories from the past sits the repository of all acquired atemporal knowledge of the world, semantic memory. Traditionally, the episodic/semantic distinction has served as a useful heuristic within the neuropsychological literature (Greenberg and Verfaellie, 2010), underscoring the importance of the medial temporal lobes, specifically the hippocampus, in the encoding and retrieval of episodic memories in contrast with the centrality of the anterior temporal lobes for the retrieval of semantic information. Similar to episodic memory, semantic memory is viewed as essential for many aspects of cognition, including language, reasoning,

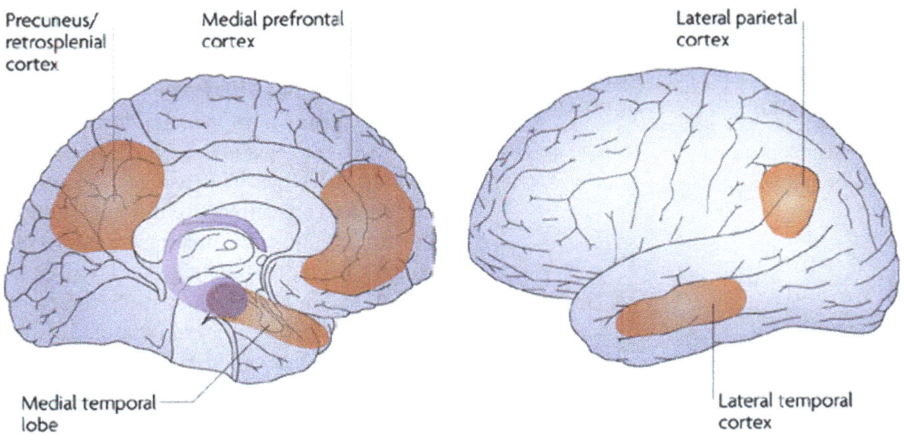

FIGURE 1 | Component structures of the core memory network consistently activated during autobiographical retrieval of the past and constructive simulation of the future. Notably, the lateral temporal cortex is implicated across past and future contexts, highlighting the central role for semantic memory in past and future oriented thought. Reprinted by permission from Macmillan Publishers Ltd., Schacter et al. (2007).

planning, problem-solving, and social interaction (Binder et al., 2009). In support of this position, neuroimaging studies have demonstrated significant activation in semantic processing regions in healthy individuals across a wide variety of cognitive abilities including distinguishing real from fictitious scenarios (Abraham et al., 2008a), positive counterfactual thinking (Van Hoeck et al., in press), as well as engaging in processes relevant for creativity (Vartanian, 2012). In contrast to the spatiotemporal specificity of episodic memory, semantic memory is derived from the abstraction of content from experiences, which is represented using modality-specific simulations whereby information relevant to a specific mode of experience is processed within the corresponding sensory, motor, or affective system (Binder and Desai, 2011). These representations are processed, therefore, in high level supramodal convergence zones in the brain including the inferior parietal cortex, the middle and inferior temporal gyri, and anterior portions of the fusiform gyrus (Patterson et al., 2007; Binder et al., 2009; Binder and Desai, 2011). Importantly, the semantic system recently identified in a meta-analysis of 120 functional neuroimaging studies exhibits striking overlap to the large-scale core ABM network (Maguire, 2001; Svoboda et al., 2006; Binder et al., 2009) prompting the observation that autobiographical memories necessarily contain a high level of semantic concepts (Binder et al., 2009), and that, by its nature, semantic representations are essential for a host of complex cognitive functions including remembering the past and imaging the future (Binder and Desai, 2011). These recent proposals resonate with mounting evidence from the neuroimaging literature demonstrating considerable overlap between episodic and semantic memory systems and the unclear boundaries that exist between these forms of memory (Burianova et al., 2010).

With the advent of sophisticated neuroimaging techniques, we have witnessed a shift in perspective from studying specific brain structures in isolation to the consideration of carefully orchestrated neural networks. Converging evidence now points to the role of large-scale neural networks in subtending complex cognitive processes, and the intriguing possibility that semantic processing may play a central role in all aspects of internal mentation.

THE STUDY OF NEURODEGENERATIVE DISORDERS

Neurodegenerative disorders offer a compelling view of the cognitive architecture of the brain when specific neural systems break down in a coordinated fashion (Irish et al., 2012c). In this review, we will focus on Alzheimer's disease (AD) and semantic dementia (SD) as lesion models for episodic and semantic memory processes, respectively, to demonstrate how these dementia syndromes illuminate our understanding of the complexity of the episodic memory system, and crucially, how episodic and semantic memory invariably interact during complex forms of past and future oriented thought.

Alzheimer's disease has long been heralded as a suitable lesion model for episodic memory processes, in light of the characteristic medial temporal lobe neural degeneration evident from a very early stage in the pathological process (Butters et al., 1987; Braak and Braak, 1991). Recent studies point to the preferential accumulation of amyloid deposits in specific nodes of the core ABM network in AD, most notably the posterior cingulate cortex and the anteromedial prefrontal cortex (Buckner et al., 2008). Clinically, AD patients typically present with an amnestic profile in which anterograde episodic memory difficulties concerning the encoding and retrieval of recent events are prominent (de Toledo-Morrell et al., 2000; McKhann et al., 2011). This disruption to episodic memory emerges as a consequence of the neuropathological process (neurofibrillary tangles and amyloid deposition), which affects the entorhinal cortex and hippocampus of the medial temporal lobes, and spreads to the neocortex (Ewers et al., 2011; Sperling et al., 2011). Importantly, such episodic memory deficits occur in the context of a relative sparing of semantic processing in the early stages of the disease (see **Table 1**).

The neurodegenerative disorder of SD represents the other side of the coin, in that the hallmark clinical feature of this disease concerns the progressive and amodal loss of semantic or general

Table 1 | Clinical characteristics of semantic dementia and Alzheimer's disease.

	Semantic dementia (SD)	Alzheimer's disease (AD)
Predominant brain atrophy	Lateral temporal Left > Right	Medial temporal Bilateral
Cognition[a]		
Executive function	Intact	+ – ++
Orientation	Intact	++
Recent episodic memory	Intact[b]	+++
Remote episodic memory	+++	+
Semantic knowledge	+++	±
Word comprehension	+++	±

[a]Functions are relatively intact in the early stages of the disease; [b]contingent on the nature of test materials used; +, mild deficits; ++, moderate deficits; +++, severe deficits; ±, variable deficits.

conceptual knowledge of the world (Hodges and Patterson, 2007). This loss of world knowledge occurs irrespective of modality and is theoretically attributable to the deterioration of a central amodal semantic hub (Rogers et al., 2004; Patterson et al., 2007; but, see Mesulam et al., 2013). On a neural level, SD is characterized by the progressive degeneration of the anterior temporal lobes (Hodges and Patterson, 2007), most severe on the ventral surface and including the perirhinal cortex, anterior fusiform gyrus (Whitwell et al., 2005; Mion et al., 2010), and typically lateralized to the left more than the right hemisphere. Importantly, volumetric MRI studies have confirmed that the degree of hippocampal atrophy in SD is equivalent, or greater, to that seen in disease-matched cases of AD, albeit in the context of much more severe temporal lobe atrophy (Chan et al., 2001; Galton et al., 2001). Of paramount importance in the current context, however, is the observation that despite profound semantic deficits, SD patients nevertheless display otherwise relatively preserved cognitive functions, including retrieval of recent episodic information, particularly when nonverbal tasks are employed (see **Table 1**; Bozeat et al., 2000; Crutch and Warrington, 2002; Hodges and Patterson, 2007).

In summary, the neurodegenerative disorders of AD and SD offer a unique opportunity to disentangle the interaction between the episodic and semantic memory systems. A theoretically important distinction is evident: while in AD we see the loss of episodic memory in the context of medial temporal lobe degeneration and relative preservation of semantic knowledge, in SD, the amodal deterioration of semantic memory occurs in the context of relatively preserved recent episodic memory. A range of interdependencies between episodic and semantic memory have recently been expounded (Greenberg and Verfaellie, 2010). Here, however, we will constrain our focus to explore how these dementia syndromes inform our understanding of two putative expressions of the episodic memory system, namely autobiographical retrieval of the past, and simulation of the future.

REMEMBERING THE PAST – AUTOBIOGRAPHICAL MEMORY

Perhaps the most important advances in understanding the interplay between episodic and semantic elements stem from the domain of ABM. The recollection of personal past memories from across our subjective timeline represents a powerful expression of the episodic memory system, requiring the retrieval of sensory-perceptual details, and emotional connotations, integrated within a specific spatiotemporal and personally relevant framework (Conway et al., 2004). Unsurprisingly, this complex endeavor is subtended by a distributed neural network involving the medial temporal lobes including the hippocampus and parahippocampal gyrus, the frontal poles, and more posterior regions including the posterior cingulate and parietal cortices, as well as the lateral temporal cortices (Maguire, 2001; Addis et al., 2004; Svoboda et al., 2006). It is noteworthy that across studies of ABM retrieval, activation of the lateral temporal cortices, regions known to be essential for semantic memory (Mion et al., 2010), is reliably observed (Spreng et al., 2009), suggesting a fundamental role for semantic processing underlying all forms of episodic past retrieval (see **Figure 1**).

PRESERVATION OF REMOTE ABMs IN ALZHEIMER'S DISEASE

The main structures implicated in ABM retrieval are those regions harboring significant atrophy in AD and SD. Importantly, our understanding of the neurocognitive mechanisms of ABM retrieval has been advanced from studying how the characteristic patterns of atrophy in AD and SD impact on the capacity for ABM retrieval. Little doubt exists regarding the prominent deficits in ABM typically seen in AD from early in the disease course. Irrespective of measure used, patients with AD demonstrate striking impairments, particularly on event or episodic subscales of these measures, in contrast with a relative preservation of personal semantics, at least in the early stages of the disease (Barnabe et al., 2012). A central debate in the ABM literature concerns the temporal profile of the episodic ABM deficit in AD, and specifically whether it conforms to Ribot's law (Ribot, 1881), in which memories from more distant time periods appear relatively intact. A number of early studies of ABM have demonstrated a disproportionate impairment of recent compared to remote episodic memories in AD (Kopelman et al., 1989; Greene et al., 1995; Graham and Hodges, 1997; Eustache et al., 2004; Irish et al., 2006, 2011b; Leyhe et al., 2009), which in turn has been interpreted in favor of a time-limited role of the hippocampus in long-term retrieval (Squire and Alvarez, 1995). The preservation of remote memories in AD, however, is of interest if we consider that older memories are more likely to undergo a process of semanticization (Cermak, 1984), leading to overgeneral memories that are divested of rich episodic re-experiencing (Irish et al., 2008, 2011b). The relative sparing of the lateral temporal cortices, and a reasonably intact capacity for reminiscence in remote epochs of one's life, in the early stages of AD accords with observations of reliance on gist memory in this syndrome (Gallo et al., 2006) and suggests that patients may overly depend on semantic representations of formerly episodic events. Similarly, patients with AD have been shown to lose access to sensory-perceptual details and appear particularly deficient in evoking specific self-referential visual imagery during ABM retrieval (Irish et al., 2011b). This loss of visual imagery may preclude the triggering of an emotional response (Kosslyn et al., 2001) and disrupts the overall re-experiencing of the retrieved event. A recent study has demonstrated that the capacity to generate complex visual imagery is compromised in AD, with the proposal that such deficits may impinge upon the envisaging of oneself across past and future contexts (Hussey et al., 2012). Thus, for AD patients, the retrieval of a past event occurs in the absence of vivid visual imagery, producing overgeneral and depersonalized or semanticized accounts of the formerly evocative event. These categories of events can be subsumed under Neisser's concept of "repisodes" (Neisser, 1981), Barsalou's "extended events" (Barsalou, 1988), or Conway's view of "general events" within the ABM system (Conway, 2001; Greenberg and Verfaellie, 2010). While Irish et al. (2011b) reported a loss of self-referential visual imagery during retrieval of specific episodic autobiographical memories, the ability of AD patients to visualize repeated or abstracted experiences remains to be established. This represents an interesting, but underexplored area of research that has obvious relevance for the constructs under consideration.

Recent studies, including a large study from our group, have failed to demonstrate temporal gradients during ABM retrieval in AD (Piolino et al., 2003; Irish et al., 2011a). Such conflicting results may reflect differences in probing and scoring of ABMs across experimental protocols (Barnabe et al., 2012). Importantly, the separation of internal "episodic," from external, or non-episodic, details using the Autobiographical Interview (AI; Levine et al., 2002) in the Irish et al. (2011a) study, serves to constrain the focus to purely episodic recall in AD. While this approach has proved extremely useful for studying strictly episodic components of ABM narratives, the resultant flat profiles in AD are also revelatory in this context. The disappearance of temporal gradients during ABM retrieval, following the parsing of semantic from episodic details, suggests that semantic knowledge represents a sizeable proportion of remote memory content in AD. This observation meshes well with the view that the episodic and semantic memory systems are invariably interlinked (Greenberg and Verfaellie, 2010), and that episodic memory requires binding of contextual elements within existing frameworks of conceptual knowledge (Reder et al., 2009). The characteristic loss of episodic memory, thus prompts the AD patient to sample intact semantic and gist-based knowledge to guide their retrieval effort, as this approach represents the most accessible and efficient route of access (Greenberg and Verfaellie, 2010; Szpunar, 2010a).

AUTOBIOGRAPHICAL MEMORY RETRIEVAL IN SEMANTIC DEMENTIA

The investigation of profiles of ABM in SD has elucidated the impact of progressive semantic memory deterioration on episodic memory retrieval. Studies of ABM in SD have yielded inconsistent results, with most pointing to the converse profile to that characteristically seen in AD, namely a reverse temporal gradient, or more accurately, a step function (Hodges and Graham, 2001). The step function describes the observation of relatively preserved recent period retrieval in contrast with impairments in the recollection of memories from more remote epochs (Graham and Hodges, 1997; Nestor et al., 2002; Piolino et al., 2003; Hou et al., 2005; Matuszewski et al., 2009; Irish et al., 2011a; see **Figure 2**). The precise underpinnings of relatively intact recent period retrieval in SD remain contentious. This effect has been interpreted as reflecting preserved anterograde processes and encoding and retrieval mechanisms (Adlam et al., 2009; Matuszewski et al., 2009). Further, it has been suggested that recent memories encompass more sensory-perceptual elements rather than overgeneral or semanticized information (Hodges and Graham, 2001; Nestor et al., 2002), with SD patients relying on such perceptual features for recent retrieval. The step function profiles of ABM in SD offer further insights into the possible semanticization of episodic memories with repeated rehearsal and the passing of time. The repeated recollection and rehearsal of remote memories allows for the abstraction of the gist of the episode without its accompanying sensory-perceptual details (Rosenbaum et al., 2001), resulting in a largely schematic account of the formerly evocative event. By this view, remote memory deficits in SD reflect a loss of semantic information that is integral to the memory trace (Westmacott et al., 2001). Interestingly, McKinnon et al. (2008) reported an elevation of external (non-episodic) details in concert with a reduction in internal (episodic) details during ABM retrieval in SD. This effect was interpreted as reflecting a relative sparing of generic autobiographical information as well as the provision of tangential details. Thus, while the deterioration of semantic knowledge impinges on the capacity for successful ABM retrieval in SD, semantic elements relevant to the retrieved event are often present within the patients' ABM narratives. Notably, the ability to retrieve personal semantic and overgeneral autobiographical information from their past appears relatively preserved in SD (Greenberg and Verfaellie, 2010).

It should be noted, however, that a number of studies have failed to replicate the step function during ABM retrieval in SD (Westmacott et al., 2001; Moss et al., 2003; McKinnon et al., 2006; Maguire et al., 2010a). Such inconsistencies in the literature may stem from the methods used to probe ABM retrieval. It is notable that these

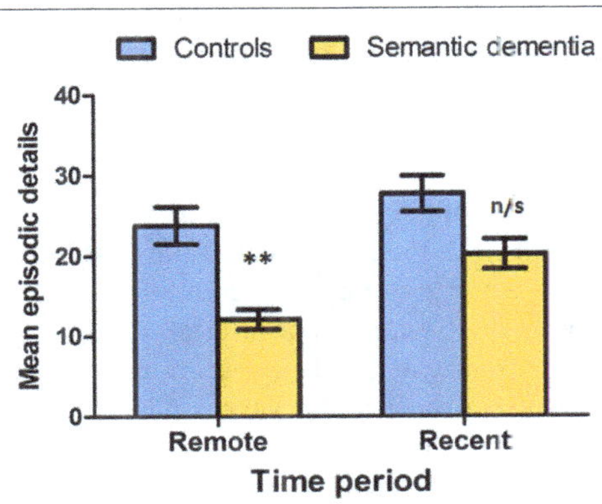

FIGURE 2 | Differential impairment of remote versus recent autobiographical memory in semantic dementia compared to healthy controls during free recall on the Autobiographical Interview (AI). Error bars represent standard error of the mean. $**P < 0.0001$; n/s, not significant. Data adapted from Irish et al. (2011a).

studies all used non-verbal stimuli, such as family photographs, to elicit ABMs. Importantly, the use of non-verbal stimuli in SD tends to produce a flat profile, with recent and remote memories recalled equally well (Westmacott et al., 2001; Moss et al., 2003; Maguire et al., 2010a; Greenberg et al., 2011). This finding resonates with the proposal that SD patients may harness perceptual features of such visual cues to bypass their profound verbal and language impairments, enabling them to access sensory-perceptual details at a higher level in the ABM system (Conway, 2001; Nestor et al., 2002). The accessibility of perceptual details represents a plausible mechanism underlying preserved recent memory, given that SD patients demonstrate an intact capacity to retrieve sensory-perceptual details during recent, but not remote, ABM retrieval (Irish et al., 2011a), and have been shown to perform normally on sensory-perceptual processing tasks, at least, when feature ambiguity is low (Barense et al., 2010). Critically, the salience of ABMs in SD following the provision of such non-verbal cues speaks to the nature of the interdependence between semantic memory and ABM. When SD patients attempt to retrieve a remote event during traditional verbally loaded ABM tasks, their ability to access relevant perceptual details is hampered by their severe semantic impairment, with the ABM search terminating at the level of non-specific episodes or repeated events in the ABM system (Conway, 2001). Evidence from the domain of ABM therefore underscores the proposition that semantic memories form the basic foundation necessary for retrieval of complex and detailed episodic memories (Greenberg and Verfaellie, 2010). Of note, the Serial-Parallel-Independent (SPI) model proposed by Tulving (1995) has long held that information first enters episodic memory via semantic memory. This model resonates with our view emphasizing the interdependence between these memory systems, and accords with studies demonstrating that impairment in the semantic framework adversely affects the acquisition of new episodic memories in the verbal modality (Ween et al., 1996; Graham et al., 2000). In concert with the progressive deterioration of semantic memory in SD, we see the gradual erosion of episodic ABMs (Maguire et al., 2010a). Collectively, these findings reinforce the view that ABMs necessarily contain, and may critically rely upon, abstracted, supramodal representations of perceptual experiences, which in turn support the sophisticated act of self-projection backwards in time to remember the past (Binder and Desai, 2011; Irish et al., 2012c).

The evidence reviewed here indicates that semantic concepts form an integral component of episodic autobiographical memories, and accords with the conceptualization of autobiographical and semantic memory as opposite ends of a contextual continuum (Kihlstrom, 1984; Burianova et al., 2010). Despite well documented differences in specificity, emotional valence, and contextual detail between these memory types, it is apparent that ABM retrieval relies heavily upon the integrity of semantic information, with the converse observation that semantic memory relies on contextual and episodic components also holding true (Gilboa, 2004; Burianova et al., 2010). Thus, evidence from the study of neurodegenerative conditions serves to reinforce the view that the retrieval of autobiographical memories invariably involves a "synergy between semantic memory and contextual information" (Greenberg and Verfaellie, 2010, p. 749).

IMAGINING THE FUTURE – FUTURE ORIENTED THOUGHT

The arena of future oriented thought has undergone a dramatic surge of research activity within the last few years, with growing evidence in favor of a link between remembering the past, imagining the future, and engaging in mental simulation processes (Addis et al., 2007; Hassabis and Maguire, 2007; Hassabis et al., 2007; Schacter et al., 2012). The capacity to imagine specific events in the future has been shown to rely on a number of important component processes including the retrieval of sensory-perceptual episodic details, specificity, fluency, and phenomenological elements such as introspective processes, and the apprehension of subjective time (D'Argembeau et al., 2010). Two prominent theories have been proposed regarding the process by which humans engage in imagining future events. The scene construction hypothesis contends that the capacity to mentally generate and maintain a complex scene within a coherent spatial context represents a critical process which underpins a wide range of constructive processes, such as remembering the past, imagining the future, as well as atemporal and hypothetical simulation (Hassabis and Maguire, 2007, 2009). In contrast, the constructive episodic simulation hypothesis (Schacter and Addis, 2007a,b) holds that the extraction of episodic details from past memories, and their flexible recombination, is fundamental to the successful generation of novel future scenarios. Notably, the discovery that the capacity to envisage future events relies on the same neural machinery as retrieval of autobiographical events from the past (Addis et al., 2007; Szpunar et al., 2007; reviewed by Verfaellie et al., 2012) has proved influential in the resulting conceptualization of future oriented thought. Demonstrations of comparable activity across past and future conditions in the medial temporal lobes, anteromedial prefrontal cortices, posterior cingulate and retrosplenial cortex, lateral parietal and temporal areas has led to the hypothesis that a common "core" network underlies these capacities (Schacter et al., 2007, 2012; see **Figure 1**). In turn, the largely overlapping neurobiological substrates of past and future modes of thinking have led to the proposition that the capacity to mentally project oneself forward in subjective time is intimately linked to the ability to remember the past (Addis et al., 2007). Unsurprisingly, a sizeable proportion of studies have focused on the episodic component of future oriented thought, with the effects evident even down to the nomenclature of this construct ("episodic future thinking," Atance and O'Neill, 2001; Klein, 2013) although an episodic-semantic neutral conceptualization has recently been proposed (Stocker, 2012). Under the constructive episodic simulation hypothesis, a fundamental feature of the episodic memory system is its inherent constructive flexibility, which permits the creation of novel events not previously experienced (Schacter and Addis, 2007a,b). Damage to the episodic memory system, therefore, is expected to preclude the ability to mentally simulate future events.

PARALLEL DEFICITS ACROSS PAST AND FUTURE CONTEXTS IN ALZHEIMER'S DISEASE

The detection of equivalent deficits across past and future conditions in a range of clinical conditions, including AD (Addis et al., 2009), Mild Cognitive Impairment (Gamboz et al., 2010), schizophrenia (D'Argembeau et al., 2008), and depression (Williams et al., 1996) has strengthened the putative relationship between autobiographical retrieval of the past and simulation of future events. In the study by Addis et al. (2009), patients with AD were found to exhibit marked difficulties in envisaging future events. Importantly these future thinking deficits correlated strongly with retrieval of past events. A recent study investigated the neural correlates of future thinking dysfunction in AD using voxel-based morphometry of structural MRI scans, and corroborated the close correspondence between episodic memory deficits and a compromised capacity for future thinking (Irish et al., 2012a). Crucially, parallel deficits across past and future contexts in AD were associated with disruption to key nodes of the core ABM network, notably the posterior cingulate cortex and the frontal poles. It seems likely that episodic memory dysfunction largely underpins the gross deficits exhibited by AD patients when they are attempting to envision their personal future. Accordingly, AD patients may rely on accessible abstracted semantic representations during future simulation, resulting in gist-based and overgeneral constructions. One area that remains underexplored to date concerns the potential role of scene construction processes as a contributory factor in future thinking dysfunction in AD. Irish et al. (2012a) documented that atrophy in the posterior cingulate cortex, and posterior parahippocampal gyrus correlated significantly with future thinking dysfunction in AD, regions which have been strongly implicated in the construction of spatially integrated scenes (Hassabis et al., 2007). Given the neural regions implicated in future thinking deficits in AD, it is therefore reasonable to assume that scene construction abilities will also be compromised in these patients. Thus, it remains unclear whether the prominent future thinking deficits observed in AD correspond to an impaired capacity for past retrieval, or difficulties with the construction of spatially coherent scenes, or perhaps, more likely, a confluence of multiple deficits arising from widespread neuronal damage to the core network.

THE ARRIVAL OF SEMANTIC MEMORY TO THE FUTURE THINKING LITERATURE

Greenberg and Verfaellie's (2010, p. 750) observation that "semantic memories are the basic material from which complex and detailed episodic memories are constructed" seems remarkably fitting when considered in relation to future oriented thinking. Research within the field of future thinking, however, has tended to eschew the possible contribution of semantic memory in favor of focusing on how future thinking may relate to the integrity of the episodic memory system (Klein, 2013). An early study of mental time travel in patient D.B. (Klein et al., 2002) served to reinforce the classic distinction between dissociable systems mediating episodic and semantic past and future thinking. Patient D.B. displayed profound deficits in his recollection of personal events from his past (episodic memory), which, in turn, impinged on his ability to project himself into the future. By contrast, D.B.'s semantic memory was largely preserved, enabling him to remember and to simulate events within the public, non-personal (semantic) domain (Klein et al., 2002). These findings served to reinforce previous views on the dissociation between episodic and semantic memory systems, and pointed toward distinct temporal divisions between what Klein (2013) termed "lived time" for the re-experiencing of the personal past, versus a "known time" in which semantic knowledge is drawn upon to enable temporal projection to the impersonal past.

Up until recently, the traditional heuristic of treating episodic and semantic memory as dissociable systems persisted into the future thinking domain. Klein (2013, p. 66) notes that as the relationship between episodic memory and future orientated thought has strengthened, researchers "simply may have overlooked the possibility that different types of memory contribute to future oriented temporal experience." A number of anomalies emerged within the literature, whereby experimental findings could not be adequately subsumed under models that exclusively emphasized the role of episodic memory in future oriented thought. In an fMRI study of past and future oriented thinking in personal (episodic) and non-personal (semantic) domains, Abraham et al. (2008b) reported functional dissociations between past and future, and between personal versus non-personal conditions. Importantly, significant engagement of semantic regions, including the inferior temporal gyrus and temporal poles, was observed irrespective of temporality or self-referential condition. Most notable is the observation that patients with developmental amnesia, as a consequence of hippocampal damage, displayed in some instances a preserved capacity to construct future experiences (Maguire et al., 2010b; Hurley et al., 2011; Mullally et al., 2012). Explanations for this relative preservation of future thinking abilities included the possibility that such patients could harness residual hippocampal function to support future projection (Maguire et al., 2010b; Mullally et al., 2012), but also the suggestion that semantic knowledge is an important facet of such imagined scenarios (Cooper et al., 2011; Hurley et al., 2011).

A COMPROMISED CAPACITY FOR FUTURE THINKING IN SEMANTIC DEMENTIA

While previous studies pointed to the possible contribution of semantic memory for future oriented thought, the first empirical demonstration that both episodic and semantic memory systems need to be functional to facilitate future thinking has emerged only recently. Duval et al. (2012) investigated the ability of patients with SD to form self-representations across past, present, and future contexts. While patients with SD demonstrated an intact capacity to retrieve recent self-representations, a striking impairment was observed when these patients envisaged their possible future selves. This deficit manifested in a marked inability to construct future self-images or to provide relevant contextual details to support their conception of their future selves (Duval et al., 2012). The authors concluded that personal semantic information therefore makes an important contribution to future oriented self-projection.

The asymmetric impairment of future with respect to past oriented thought was corroborated by another study that explicated the neural underpinnings of episodic and semantic future thinking impairments in SD (Irish et al., 2012a). Participants were required to remember three spatiotemporally specific events from the preceding year, and were asked to envisage three novel future events that might occur within the next year. Using the AI scoring procedure, a marked incapacity for future simulation was found in SD, despite their relatively intact retrieval of recent episodic events. Voxel-based morphometry analyses revealed that these striking future thinking deficits in SD robustly correlated with brain regions known to underpin semantic representations (Visser et al., 2010), namely the left anterior inferior temporal gyrus and the bilateral temporal poles (Irish et al., 2012a; see **Figure 3**). Crucially, these results suggest that the retrieval of past episodes alone is not sufficient for the successful simulation of future events (see also Hassabis and Maguire, 2007; Andelman et al., 2010) and that regions beyond the classic episodic memory system are implicated in complex cognitive endeavors of this kind (Binder et al., 2009; Irish et al., 2012c).

DIFFERENTIAL DISRUPTION OF CONTEXTUAL DETAILS DURING FUTURE THINKING IN SD

The specific vulnerability of future simulation in SD is noteworthy as it speaks to the complexity of this cognitive construct. Further, the findings from the SD literature challenge the prevailing view of future simulation, which to date has focused primarily on the role of the medial temporal lobe and episodic memory (Schacter and Addis, 2007a,b; Race et al., 2011). Given the relative preservation of recent episodic memory in SD, and the profound deficits observed when these patients attempt to envisage their futures, it has been suggested that certain types of details may be differentially disrupted as the patient attempts to move from past to future contexts (Irish et al., 2012a). While much of the research impetus to date has focused on the relationship between episodic memory and future simulation, the extent to which the content of imagined future scenarios reflects elements of episodic memories remains unclear (Szpunar, 2010a). A recent analysis of the types of contextual details reported during future simulation in SD has offered important insights into the component processes underlying the capacity for future oriented thought. Irish et al. (2012b) dissected the types of contextual details embedded within past and future narratives using the AI scoring protocol, and investigated the profiles of contextual details for internal (episodic) and external (non-episodic) subscales. The fine-grained analysis of contextual details in SD has previously pointed to the disruption of recent spatiotemporal and emotional internal details during autobiographical retrieval (Irish et al., 2011a), whereas external details have been shown to be uniquely elevated in this group (McKinnon et al., 2008). Importantly, Irish et al. (2012b) reported that SD patients' generation of internal event details (i.e., those details conveying the crux of the episode) showed an asymmetric profile (past > future effect), whereby recent past retrieval was within Control levels yet such details were profoundly impaired exclusively in the future condition. In contrast, SD patients demonstrated a future > past effect for external event details, that is, those details which are believed to reflect non-episodic, or semantic, information (Irish et al., 2012b).

The asymmetric decline of internal, and concurrent elevation of external, details during future simulation in SD mirrors that previously demonstrated in healthy aging for retrieval of past autobiographical memories (Levine et al., 2002), and simulation of future events (Gaesser et al., 2011) albeit to an exaggerated degree. Of significance here, however, is the observation that while internal event details can be readily extracted from the past in SD, and remain available during the process of simulation, the construction of a future event ultimately fails. This finding underscores previous observations that thinking about the future necessarily draws upon contributions from both episodic and semantic memory (D'Argembeau and Mathy, 2011; Klein, 2013). In parallel with the failure to utilize readily available episodic details from the past, is the observation that SD patients produce a preponderance of off-target information not directly relevant to the event being simulated. At first glance, the over-production of non-episodic content in a cohort typified by marked semantic deficits seems counterintuitive, however, Irish et al. (2012b) note that such external details, in fact, represent off-target retrieval from unrelated past episodes. Thus the information provided by the SD patients is largely episodic, albeit unrelated to the event being simulated.

These recent findings are important as they resonate with a review article which questioned whether the strict reliance on the

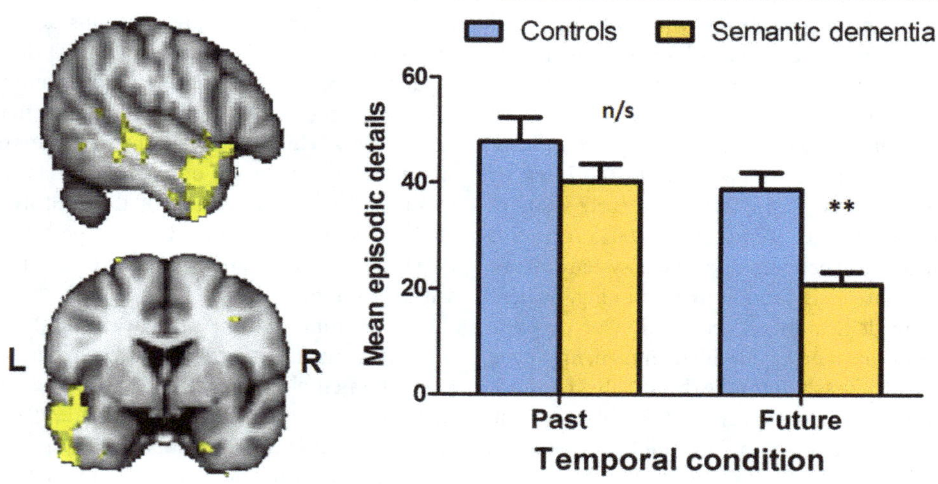

FIGURE 3 | Deficits in future thinking in semantic dementia are exclusively associated with gray matter intensity decrease in the left anterior temporal lobe, as revealed by voxel-based morphometry analyses. Clusters are significant at $P < 0.001$ and overlaid on the Montreal Neurological Institute standard brain. Error bars represent standard error of the mean. $^{**}P < 0.0001$; n/s, not significant. Figure adapted from Irish et al. (2012a).

contents of episodic memory represents the most efficient route to construct future scenarios (Szpunar, 2010a). By this view, Szpunar (2010a) reasons that the contribution of episodic and semantic elements during future simulation will invariably depend upon the accessibility of information that is relevant to the event of interest. Crucially, the content of any future simulation will reflect the information that is most readily accessible (Kahneman and Tversky, 1982; Szpunar, 2010a,b). Healthy individuals are likely to draw upon abstracted representations and such representations should, in general, be more accessible than specific one-off episodic representations (Szpunar, 2010a). In contrast, certain scenarios may exist in which episodic representations of specific events may represent the most efficient mode for future thinking. If we consider the findings from the SD patients in the Irish et al. (2012a,b) series, it becomes evident that the information most accessible to these patients is that of unique recent episodic occurrences and more general repeated events or "repisodes" in the absence of general conceptual semantic knowledge.

THE SEMANTIC SCAFFOLDING HYPOTHESIS

If episodic details represent the most accessible and efficient means for SD patients to construct a future scenario, why then are these details so vulnerable during future simulation? In line with current views emphasizing the importance of episodic and semantic contributions during future thinking, the findings from SD studies offer compelling evidence that the disintegration of the conceptual knowledge base adversely affects the ability to construct events in the future (Irish et al., 2012a). In this light, the recently proposed semantic scaffolding hypothesis is particularly pertinent, whereby semantic knowledge appears to provide a framework or scaffolding which facilitates past retrieval and future thinking (Greenberg and Verfaellie, 2010; Irish et al., 2012a). This semantic scaffolding hypothesis is relevant to the finding that a loss of semantic knowledge precludes the ability to simulate novel future events. In SD, the successful extraction of sensory-perceptual details from recent events occurs in the absence of the necessary conceptual framework to impart overall structure to the scenario (Irish et al., 2012b). If extraction of episodic details from the past represents the building blocks of future simulations, any attempt to construct a coherent scenario without the necessary scaffold or framework, results in the provision of a series of unrelated mini-events. Essentially, the episodic details cannot be integrated within the appropriate schema or abstracted representation from semantic memory. One further issue to disentangle, in this regard, is at which point in the simulation process semantic memory becomes pivotal? SD patients may not possess the relevant abstracted semantic representations to facilitate the construction of future events; however, a second possibility is that the loss of conceptual knowledge in SD also adversely impacts on the integrative mechanism necessary to bind episodic details into a coherent simulation. The final product of a successful future simulation likely comprises elements of various episodic and semantic details that are flexibly recombined to create an integrated and coherent representation of a specific future event (Szpunar, 2010a; Addis et al., 2011). It remains unknown, however, whether the amodal loss of semantic knowledge in SD precludes the recombination of episodic details from past retrieval into a coherent novel scenario, although this proposal represents an intriguing and plausible explanation for the elevation of unrelated event details in this group (Irish et al., 2012b). Further work is necessary to elucidate the precise mechanisms of detail recombination and, specifically, whether the reconfiguring of past details entails some form of semantic associative processing. It is possible that recombination may reflect a two-step process, in which firstly semantic associations between disparate details are made, drawing on abstracted representations that are accessible contingent on the specific task requirements, following which a process of integrative binding is required to flexibly recombine these details together into a coherent spatiotemporal framework. Determining the precise constituent elements of recombination within semantic frameworks represents an important line of enquiry for future research.

SEMANTIC KNOWLEDGE AND NOVELTY OF FUTURE SIMULATIONS

Semantic memory may be particularly important for the simulation of novel future events, in which no prior experience can be drawn upon from episodic memory. By its nature, semantic memory can be generalized to many different contexts (Mion et al., 2010), thus providing undifferentiated conceptual information that can be drawn upon to facilitate novel event construction (Binder and Desai, 2011; Irish et al., 2012a). The novelty of the simulated event becomes of paramount importance when we consider the profound difficulties experienced by patients with SD in envisioning events that have not occurred previously. Irish et al (2012a) found that 80% of future events described by SD patients represented events that had been previously experienced in their entirety. Simply put, the SD patients demonstrated a marked propensity to sample past episodes and to recapitulate these events into the future condition, despite explicit task instructions requiring them to generate novel events not previously experienced. The severe semantic impairment in SD, therefore, disrupts the capacity for novel event generation, manifesting in scenarios that have been recast from intact past memories (Irish et al., 2012b). Recasting of the past is an intriguing phenomenon in SD, and suggests that the construction of novel events critically relies on the harnessing and deployment of semantic knowledge. By this argument, events which occur within familiar and repeated spatiotemporal contexts may be more readily accessible in SD, as the patients can successfully retrieve prior instances within such familiar contexts (Graham et al., 1999; Irish et al., 2011a). It may be that the envisaging of novel scenarios, for which one has little to no prior episodic experience, heavily taxes the semantic memory system, requiring the individual to draw on general world knowledge to guide them in their constructive endeavor. In SD, however, the progressive deterioration of the semantic memory system renders such conceptual knowledge inaccessible, causing the patient to overly rely on previously encountered scenarios, and ultimately resulting in the recapitulation of past events into the future condition.

It has recently been suggested that the creation of a suitable "situation model" represents a crucial process to facilitate the retrieval of past, and simulation of future, events (Ranganath and Ritchey, 2012). The successful formation of a situation model is, in turn, posited to depend on the integrity of a posterior medial cortical system centered on the posterior parahippocampal cortex and retrosplenial cortex (Ranganath and Ritchey, 2012). This view corroborates previous fMRI studies of healthy individuals engaging in future simulation, in which the importance of posterior regions including the posterior cingulate cortex and parahippocampal cortex in the activation of well-known contextual settings has been emphasized (Szpunar et al., 2009). Notably, posterior brain regions remain relatively preserved until later in SD. These posterior regions offer a potential neuroanatomical signature for the harnessing of familiar contexts effect that is reliably demonstrated in future thinking studies in SD. Accordingly, SD patients draw upon the accessible situation model but cannot integrate or update this model to create a novel scenario, and inevitably recapitulate overgeneral or previously experienced events during future simulation. Further exploration of this recasting of familiar contexts effect in SD is clearly warranted, in particular how this phenomenon is related to the observation of an intact capacity to generate "repisodes" (Neisser, 1981) during ABM retrieval (Greenberg and Verfaellie, 2010). Likewise, an obvious outstanding area of research relates to whether the amodal loss of semantic knowledge in SD precludes the construction of spatially coherent scenes, in line with the scene construction theory advanced by Hassabis and Maguire (2007) and Hassabis et al. (2007). Unraveling the contribution of semantic memory to scene construction processes will be essential in clarifying the precise role of conceptual knowledge in memory and imagination.

CONCLUDING REMARKS

We conclude this review at an exciting juncture in episodic memory research. What has become evident is the incontrovertible extent to which episodic and semantic memory interact during complex forms of past and future oriented thinking, and the limitations of couching such endeavors within the traditional taxonomy of episodic and semantic memory as dissociable systems. The studying of complex cognitive processes in neurodegenerative conditions has proved critical for explicating how episodic and semantic elements may work in concert during autobiographical retrieval and future simulation, yet much remains to be elucidated. We suggest that concerted efforts are warranted to disentangle and elucidate the precise contributions of each memory system to constructive recollective and simulative endeavors, which in turn will illuminate our understanding of the episodic memory system of the brain.

ACKNOWLEDGMENTS

This research was supported by an Australian Research Council (ARC) Cross Program Support Scheme Grant from the ARC Centre of Excellence in Cognition and its Disorders (CE110001021) and an ARC Discovery Project grant (DP1093279). Muireann Irish is supported by an ARC Discovery Early Career Research Award (DE130100463). Olivier Piguet is supported by a National Health and Medical Research Council of Australia Career Development Fellowship (APP1022684).

REFERENCES

Abraham, A., von Cramon, D. Y., and Schubotz, R. I. (2008a). Meeting George Bush versus meeting Cinderella: the neural response when telling apart what is real from what is fictional in the context of our reality. *J. Cogn. Neurosci.* 20, 965–976.

Abraham, A., Schubotz, R. I., and von Cramon, D. Y. (2008b). Thinking about the future versus the past in personal and non-personal contexts. *Brain Res.* 1233, 106–119.

Addis, D. R., Cheng, T., Roberts, R. P., and Schacter, D. L. (2011). Hippocampal contributions to the episodic simulation of specific and general future events. *Hippocampus* 21, 1045–1052.

Addis, D. R., Moscovitch, M., Crawley, A. P., and McAndrews, M. P. (2004). Recollective qualities modulate hippocampal activation during autobiographical memory retrieval. *Hippocampus* 14, 752–762.

Addis, D. R., Sacchetti, D. C., Ally, B. A., Budson, A. E., and Schacter, D. L. (2009). Episodic simulation of future events is impaired in mild Alzheimer's disease. *Neuropsychologia* 47, 2660–2671.

Addis, D. R., Wong, A. T., and Schacter, D. L. (2007). Remembering the past and imagining the future: common and distinct neural substrates during event construction and elaboration. *Neuropsychologia* 45, 1363–1377.

Adlam, A., Patterson, K., and Hodges, J. R. (2009). "I remember it as if it were yesterday": memory for recent events in patients with semantic dementia. *Neuropsychologia* 47, 1344–1351.

Andelman, F., Hoofien, D., Goldberg, I., Aizenstein, O., and Neufeld, M. (2010). Bilateral hippocampal lesion and a selective impairment of the ability for mental time travel. *Neurocase* 16, 426–435.

Atance, C. M., and O'Neill, D. K. (2001). Episodic future thinking. *Trends Cogn. Sci. (Regul. Ed.)* 5, 533–539.

Barense, M. D., Rogers, T. T., Bussey, T. J., Saksida, L. M., and Graham, K. S. (2010). Influence of conceptual knowledge on visual object discrimination: insights from semantic dementia and MTL amnesia. *Cereb. Cortex* 20, 2568–2582.

Barnabe, A., Whitehead, V., Pilon, R., Arsenault-Lapierre, G., and Chertkow, H. (2012). Autobiographical memory in mild cognitive impairment and Alzheimer's disease: a comparison between the Levine and Kopelman interview methodologies. *Hippocampus* 22, 1809–1825.

Barsalou, L. W. (1988). "The content and organisation of autobiographical memories," in *Remembering Reconsidered: Ecological and Traditional Approaches to the Study of Memory*, eds U. Neisser, and E. Winograd (New York: Cambridge University Press), 193–243.

Binder, J. R., and Desai, R. H. (2011). The neurobiology of semantic memory. *Trends Cogn. Sci. (Regul. Ed.)* 15, 527–536.

Binder, J. R., Desai, R. H., Graves, W. W., and Conant, L. L. (2009). Where is the semantic system? A critical review and meta-analysis of 120 functional neuroimaging studies. *Cereb. Cortex* 19, 2767–2796.

Bozeat, S., Gregory, C. A., Ralph, M. A., and Hodges, J. R. (2000). Which neuropsychiatric and behavioural features distinguish frontal and temporal variants of frontotemporal dementia from Alzheimer's disease? *J. Neurol. Neurosurg. Psychiatr.* 69, 178–186.

Braak, H., and Braak, E. (1991). Neuropathological stageing of Alzheimer-related changes. *Acta Neuropathol.* 82, 239–249.

Buckner, R. L., Andrews-Hanna, J. R., and Schacter, D. L. (2008). The brain's default network: anatomy, function, and relevance to disease. *Ann. N. Y. Acad. Sci.* 1124, 1–38.

Burianova, H., McIntosh, A. R., and Grady, C. L. (2010). A common functional brain network for autobiographical, episodic, and semantic memory retrieval. *Neuroimage* 49, 865–874.

Butters, N., Granholm, E., Salmon, D. P., Grant, I., and Wolfe, J. (1987). Episodic and semantic memory: a comparison of amnesic and demented patients. *J. Clin. Exp. Neuropsychol.* 9, 479–497.

Cabeza, R., and St. Jacques, P. (2007). Functional neuroimaging of autobiographical memory. *Trends Cogn. Sci.* 11, 219–227.

Cermak, L. (1984). *The Episodic-Semantic Distinction in Amnesia.* New York: Guilford Press.

Chan, D., Fox, N., Scahill, R., Crum, W., Whitwell, J., Leschziner, G., et al. (2001). Patterns of temporal lobe atrophy in semantic dementia and Alzheimer's disease. *Ann. Neurol.* 49, 433–442.

Conway, M. A. (2001). Sensory–perceptual episodic memory and its context: autobiographical memory. *Philos. Trans. R. Soc. Lond. B Biol. Sci.* 356, 1375–1384.

Conway, M. A., Singer, J. A., and Tagini, A. (2004). The self and autobiographical memory: correspondence and coherence. *Soc. Cogn.* 22, 491–529.

Cooper, J. M., Vargha-Khadem, F., Gadian, D. G., and Maguire, E. A. (2011). The effect of hippocampal damage in children on recalling the past and imagining new experiences. *Neuropsychologia* 49, 1843–1850.

Crutch, S. J., and Warrington, E. K. (2002). Preserved calculation skills in a case of semantic dementia. *Cortex* 38, 389–399.

D'Argembeau, A., and Mathy, A. (2011). Tracking the construction of episodic future thoughts. *J. Exp. Psychol. Gen.* 140, 258–271.

D'Argembeau, A., Ortoleva, C., Jumentier, S., and Van der Linden, M. (2010). Component processes underlying future thinking. *Mem. Cognit.* 38, 809–819.

D'Argembeau, A., Raffard, S., and Van der Linden, M. (2008). Remembering the past and imagining the future in schizophrenia. *J. Abnorm. Psychol.* 117, 247.

de Toledo-Morrell, L., Dickerson, B., Sullivan, M. P., Spanovic, C., Wilson, R., and Bennett, D. A. (2000). Hemispheric differences in hippocampal volume predict verbal and spatial memory performance in patients with Alzheimer's disease. *Hippocampus* 10, 136–142.

Duval, C., Desgranges, B., De La Sayette, V., Belliard, S., Eustache, F., and Piolino, P. (2012). What happens to personal identity when semantic knowledge degrades? A study of the self and autobiographical memory in semantic dementia. *Neuropsychologia* 50, 254–265.

Eustache, F., Piolino, P., Giffard, B., Viader, F., De La Sayette, V., Baron, J. C., et al. (2004). "In the course of time": a PET study of the cerebral substrates of autobiographical amnesia in Alzheimer's disease. *Brain* 127, 1549–1560.

Ewers, M., Sperling, R. A., Klunk, W. E., Weiner, M. W., and Hampel, H. (2011). Neuroimaging markers for the prediction and early diagnosis of Alzheimer's disease dementia. *Trends Neurosci.* 34, 430–442.

Gaesser, B., Sacchetti, D. C., Addis, D. R., and Schacter, D. L. (2011). Characterizing age-related changes in remembering the past and imagining the future. *Psychol. Aging* 26, 80–84.

Gallo, D. A., Shahid, K. R., Olson, M. A., Solomon, T. M., Schacter, D. L., and Budson, A. E. (2006). Overdependence on degraded gist memory in Alzheimer's disease. *Neuropsychology* 20, 625–632.

Galton, C., Patterson, K., Graham, K., Lambon-Ralph, M., Williams, G., Antoun, N., et al. (2001). Differing patterns of temporal atrophy in Alzheimer's disease and semantic dementia. *Neurology* 57, 216–225.

Gamboz, N., De Vito, S., Brandimonte, M. A., Pappalardo, S., Galeone, F., Iavarone, A., et al. (2010). Episodic future thinking in amnesic mild cognitive impairment. *Neuropsychologia* 48, 2091–2097.

Gilboa, A. (2004). Autobiographical and episodic memory – one and the same? *Neuropsychologia* 42, 1336–1349.

Graham, K. S., and Hodges, J. R. (1997). Differentiating the roles of the hippocampal complex and the neocortex in long-term memory storage: evidence from the study of semantic dementia and Alzheimer's disease. *Neuropsychology* 11, 77–89.

Graham, K. S., Patterson, K., and Hodges, J. R. (1999). Episodic memory: new insights from the study of semantic dementia. *Curr. Opin. Neurobiol.* 9, 245–250.

Graham, K. S., Simons, J. S., Pratt, K. H., Patterson, K., and Hodges, J. R. (2000). Insights from semantic dementia on the relationship between episodic and semantic memory. *Neuropsychologia* 38, 313–324.

Greenberg, D. L., Ogar, J. M., Viskontas, I. V., Gorno Tempini, M. L., Miller, B., and Knowlton, B. J. (2011). Multimodal cuing of autobiographical memory in semantic dementia. *Neuropsychology* 25, 98–104.

Greenberg, D. L., and Verfaellie, M. (2010). Interdependence of episodic and semantic memory: evidence from neuropsychology. *J. Int. Neuropsychol. Soc.* 16, 748–753.

Greene, J., Hodges, J. R., and Baddeley, A. (1995). Autobiographical memory and executive function in early dementia of Alzheimer type. *Neuropsychologia* 33, 1647–1670.

Hassabis, D., Kumaran, D., and Maguire, E. A. (2007). Using imagination to understand the neural basis of episodic memory. *J. Neurosci.* 27, 14365–14374.

Hassabis, D., and Maguire, E. A. (2007). Deconstructing episodic memory with construction. *Trends Cogn. Sci. (Regul. Ed.)* 11, 299–306

Hassabis, D., and Maguire, E. A. (2009). The construction system of the brain. *Philos. Trans. R. Soc. Lond. B Biol. Sci.* 364, 1263–1271.

Hodges, J. R., and Graham, K. S. (2001). Episodic memory: insights from semantic dementia. *Philos. Trans. R. Soc. Lond. B Biol. Sci.* 356, 1423–1434.

Hodges, J. R., and Patterson, K. (2007). Semantic dementia: a unique clinicopathological syndrome. *Lancet Neurol.* 6, 1004–1014.

Hou, C., Miller, B., and Kramer, J. (2005). Patterns of autobiographical memory loss in dementia. *Int. J. Geriatr. Psychiatry* 20, 809–815.

Hurley, N. C., Maguire, E. A., and Vargha-Khadem, F. (2011). Patient HC with developmental amnesia can construct future scenarios. *Neuropsychologia* 49, 3620–3628.

Hussey, E. P., Smolinsky, J. G., Piryatinsky, I., Budson, A. E., and Ally, B. A. (2012). Using mental imagery to improve memory in patients with Alzheimer's disease. *Alzheimer Dis. Assoc. Disord.* 26, 124–134.

Irish, M., Addis, D. R., Hodges, J. R., and Piguet, O. (2012a). Considering the role of semantic memory in episodic future thinking: evidence from semantic dementia. *Brain* 135, 2178–2191.

Irish, M., Addis, D. R., Hodges, J. R., and Piguet, O. (2012b). Exploring the content and quality of episodic future simulations in semantic dementia. *Neuropsychologia* 50, 3488–3495.

Irish, M., Piguet, O., and Hodges, J. R. (2012c). Self-projection and the default network in frontotemporal dementia. *Nat. Rev. Neurol.* 8, 152–161.

Irish, M., Cunningham, C. J., Walsh, J. B., Coakley, D., Lawlor, B. A., Robertson, I. H., et al. (2006). Investigating the enhancing effect of music on autobiographical memory in mild Alzheimer's disease. *Dement. Geriatr. Cogn. Disord.* 22, 108–120.

Irish, M., Hornberger, M., Lah, S., Miller, L., Pengas, G., Nestor, P. J., et al. (2011a). Profiles of recent autobiographical memory retrieval in semantic dementia, behavioural-variant frontotemporal dementia, and Alzheimer's disease. *Neuropsychologia* 49, 2694–2702.

Irish, M., Lawlor, B. A., O'Mara, S. M., and Coen, R. F. (2011b). Impaired capacity for autonoetic reliving during autobiographical event recall in mild Alzheimer's disease. *Cortex* 47, 236–249.

Irish, M., Lawlor, B. A., O'Mara, S. M., and Coen, R. F. (2008). Assessment of behavioural markers of autonoetic consciousness during episodic autobiographical memory retrieval: a preliminary analysis. *Behav. Neurol.* 19, 3–6.

Kahneman, D., and Tversky, A. (1982). "The simulation heuristic," in *Judgment Under Uncertainty*, eds D. Kahneman, P. Slovic, and A. Tversky (Cambridge: Cambridge University Press), 201–208.

Kihlstrom, J. F. (1984). A fact is a fact is a fact [commentary]. *Behav. Brain Sci.* 7, 243–244.

Klein, S. B. (2013). The complex act of projecting oneself into the future. *Wiley Interdiscip. Rev. Cogn. Sci.* 4, 63–79.

Klein, S. B., Loftus, J., and Kihlstrom, J. F. (2002). Memory and temporal experience: the effects of episodic memory loss on an amnesic patient's ability to remember the past and imagine the future. *Soc. Cogn.* 20, 353–379.

Kopelman, M. D., Wilson, B. A., and Baddeley, A. D. (1989). The autobiographical memory interview: a new assessment of autobiographical and personal semantic memory in amnesic patients. *J. Clin. Exp. Neuropsychol.* 11, 724–744.

Kosslyn, S. M., Ganis, G., and Thompson, W. L. (2001). Neural foundations of imagery. *Nat. Rev. Neurosci* 2, 635–642.

Levine, B., Svoboda, E., Hay, J. F., Winocur, G., and Moscovitch, M. (2002). Aging and autobiographical memory: dissociating episodic from semantic retrieval. *Psychol. Aging* 17, 677–689.

Leyhe, T., Muller, S., Milian, M., Eschweiler, G. W., and Saur, R. (2009). Impairment of episodic and semantic autobiographical memory in patients with mild cognitive impairment and early Alzheimer's disease. *Neuropsychologia* 47, 2464–2469.

Maguire, E. A. (2001). Neuroimaging studies of autobiographical event memory. *Philos. Trans. R. Soc. Lond. B Biol. Sci.* 356, 1441–1451.

Maguire, E. A., Kumaran, D., Hassabis, D., and Kopelman, M. D. (2010a). Autobiographical memory in semantic dementia: a longitudinal fMRI study. *Neuropsychologia* 48, 123–136.

Maguire, E. A., Vargha-Khadem, F., and Hassabis, D. (2010b). Imagining fictitious and future experiences: evidence from developmental amnesia. *Neuropsychologia* 48, 3187–3192.

Matuszewski, V., Piolino, P., Belliard, S., De La Sayette, V., Laisney, M., Lalevée, C., et al. (2009). Patterns of autobiographical memory impairment according to disease severity in semantic dementia. *Cortex* 45, 456–472.

McKhann, G. M., Knopman, D. S., Chertkow, H., Hyman, B. T., Jack, C. R. Jr., Kawas, C. H., et al. (2011). The diagnosis of dementia due to Alzheimer's disease: recommendations from the National Institute on Aging-Alzheimer's Association workgroups on diagnostic guidelines for Alzheimer's disease. *Alzheimers Dement.* 7, 263–269.

McKinnon, M., Black, S., Miller, B., Moscovitch, M., and Levine, B. (2006). Autobiographical memory in semantic dementia: implications for theories of limbic-neocortical interaction in remote memory. *Neuropsychologia* 44, 2421–2429.

McKinnon, M., Nica, E., Sengdy, P., Kovacevic, N., Moscovitch, M., Freedman, M., et al. (2008). Autobiographical memory and patterns of brain atrophy in fronto-temporal lobar degeneration. *J. Cogn. Neurosci.* 20, 1839–1853.

Mesulam, M. M., Wieneke, C., Hurley, R., Rademaker, A., Thompson, C. K., Weintraub, S., et al. (2013). Words and objects at the tip of the left temporal lobe in primary progressive aphasia. *Brain* 136, 601–618.

Mion, M., Patterson, K., Acosta-Cabronero, J., Pengas, G., Izquierdo-Garcia, D., Hong, Y. T., et al. (2010). What the left and right anterior fusiform gyri tell us about semantic memory. *Brain* 133, 3256–3268.

Moss, H. E., Kopelman, M. D., Cappelletti, M., Davies Pde, M., and Jaldow, E. (2003). Lost for words or loss of memories? Autobiographical memory in semantic dementia. *Cogn. Neuropsychol.* 20, 703–732.

Mullally, S. L., Hassabis, D., and Maguire, E. A. (2012). Scene construction in amnesia: an FMRI study. *J. Neurosci.* 32, 5646–5653.

Neisser, U. (1981). John Dean's memory: a case study. *Cognition* 9, 1–22.

Nestor, P. J., Graham, K. S., Bozeat, S., Simons, J. S., and Hodges, J. R. (2002). Memory consolidation and the hippocampus: further evidence from studies of autobiographical memory in semantic dementia and frontal variant frontotemporal dementia. *Neuropsychologia* 40, 633–654.

Patterson, K., Nestor, P., and Rogers, T. (2007). Where do you know what you know? The representation of semantic knowledge in the human brain. *Nat. Rev. Neurosci.* 8, 976–987.

Piolino, P., Desgranges, B., Belliard, S., Matuszewski, V., Lalevee, C., De La Sayette, V., et al. (2003). Autobiographical memory and autonoetic consciousness: triple dissociation in neurodegenerative diseases. *Brain* 126, 2203–2219.

Race, E., Keane, M. M., and Verfaellie, M. (2011). Medial temporal lobe damage causes deficits in episodic memory and episodic future thinking not attributable to deficits in narrative construction. *J. Neurosci.* 31, 10262–10269.

Ranganath, C., and Ritchey, M. (2012). Two cortical systems for memory-guided behaviour. *Nat. Rev. Neurosci.* 13, 713–726.

Reder, L. M., Park, H., and Kieffaber, P. D. (2009). Memory systems do not divide on consciousness: reinterpreting memory in terms of activation and binding. *Psychol. Bull.* 135, 23–49.

Ribot, T. (1881). *Les maladies de la mémoire*. Paris: Germer Baillière.

Rogers, T. T., Lambon Ralph, M. A., Garrard, P., Bozeat, S., McClelland, J. L., Hodges, J. R., et al. (2004). Structure and deterioration of semantic memory: a neuropsychological and computational investigation. *Psychol. Rev.* 111, 205–235.

Rosenbaum, R. S., Winocur, G., and Moscovitch, M. (2001). New views on old memories: re-evaluating the role of the hippocampal complex. *Behav. Brain Res.* 127, 183–197.

Schacter, D. L., and Addis, D. R. (2007a). The cognitive neuroscience of constructive memory: remembering the past and imagining the future. *Philos. Trans. R. Soc. Lond. B Biol. Sci.* 362, 773–786.

Schacter, D. L., and Addis, D. R. (2007b). On the constructive episodic simulation of past and future events. *Behav. Brain Sci.* 30, 331–332.

Schacter, D. L., Addis, D. R., and Buckner, R. L. (2007). Remembering the past to imagine the future: the prospective brain. *Nat. Rev. Neurosci.* 8, 657–661.

Schacter, D. L., Addis, D. R., Hassabis, D., Martin, V. C., Spreng, R. N., and Szpunar, K. (2012). The future of memory: remembering, imagining, and the brain. *Neuron* 76, 677–694.

Sperling, R. A., Aisen, P. S., Beckett, L. A., Bennett, D. A., Craft, S., Fagan, A. M., et al. (2011). Toward defining the preclinical stages of Alzheimer's disease: recommendations from the National Institute on Aging-Alzheimer's Association workgroups on diagnostic guidelines for Alzheimer's disease. *Alzheimers Dement.* 7, 280–292.

Spreng, R. N., Mar, R. A., and Kim, A. S. (2009). The common neural basis of autobiographical memory, prospection, navigation, theory of mind, and the default mode: a quantitative meta-analysis. *J. Cogn. Neurosci.* 21, 489–510.

Squire, L., and Alvarez, P. (1995). Retrograde amnesia and memory consolidation: a neurobiological perspective. *Curr. Opin. Neurobiol.* 5, 169–177.

Stocker, K. (2012). The time machine in our mind. *Cogn. Sci.* 36, 385–420.

Suddendorf, T., and Corballis, M. (2007). The evolution of foresight: what is mental time travel, and is it unique to humans? *Behav. Brain Sci.* 30, 299–313.

Svoboda, E., McKinnon, M. C., and Levine, B. (2006). The functional neuroanatomy of autobiographical memory: a meta-analysis. *Neuropsychologia* 44, 2189–2208.

Szpunar, K. (2010a). Episodic future thought. *Perspect. Psychol. Sci.* 5, 142.

Szpunar, K. (2010b). Evidence for an implicit influence of memory on future thinking. *Mem. Cognit.* 38, 531–540.

Szpunar, K., Chan, J. C., and McDermott, K. B. (2009). Contextual processing in episodic future thought. *Cereb. Cortex* 19, 1539–1548.

Szpunar, K., Watson, J., and McDermott, K. B. (2007). Neural substrates of envisioning the future. *Proc. Natl. Acad. Sci. U.S.A.* 104, 642–647.

Tulving, E. T. (1995). "Organization of memory: quo vadis?" in *The Cognitive Neurosciences*, ed. M. S. Gazzaniga (Cambridge, MA: MIT Press), 839–847.

Tulving, E. T. (2002). Episodic memory: from mind to brain. *Annu. Rev. Psychol.* 53, 1–25.

Tulving, E. T., and Szpunar, K. (2009). Episodic memory. *Scholarpedia* 4, 3332.

Van Hoeck, N., Ma, N., Ampe, L., Baetens, K., Vandekerckhove, M., and Van Overwalle, F. (in press). Counterfactual thinking: an fMRI study on changing the past for a better future. *Soc. Cogn. Affect. Neurosci.* doi:10.1093/scan/nss031

Vartanian, O. (2012). Dissociable neural systems for analogy and metaphor: implications for the neuroscience of creativity. *Br. J. Psychol.* 103, 302–316.

Verfaellie, M., Race, E., and Keane, M. M. (2012). Medial temporal lobe contributions to future thinking: evidence from neuroimaging and amnesia. *Psychol. Belg.* 52, 77–94.

Visser, M., Embleton, K. V., Jefferies, E., Parker, G. J., and Ralph, M. A. (2010). The inferior, anterior temporal lobes and semantic memory clarified: novel evidence from distortion-corrected fMRI. *Neuropsychologia* 48, 1689–1696.

Ween, J. E., Verfaellie, M., and Alexander, M. P. (1996). Verbal memory function in mild aphasia. *Neurology* 47, 795–801.

Westmacott, R., Leach, L., Freedman, M., and Moscovitch, M. (2001). Different patterns of autobiographical memory loss in semantic dementia and medial temporal lobe amnesia: a challenge to consolidation theory. *Neurocase* 7, 37–55.

Whitwell, J. L., Josephs, K. A., Rossor, M. N., Stevens, J. M., Revesz, T., Holton, J. L., et al. (2005). Magnetic resonance imaging signatures of tissue pathology in frontotemporal dementia. *Arch. Neurol.* 62, 1402–1408.

Williams, J. M., Ellis, N. C., Tyers, C., Healy, H., Rose, G., and Macleod, A. K. (1996). The specificity of autobiographical memory and imageability of the future. *Mem. Cognit.* 24, 116–125.

4

Using voxel-based morphometry to examine the relationship between regional brain volumes and memory performance in amnestic mild cognitive impairment

Patric Meyer[1]*, Hanna Feldkamp[1], Michael Hoppstädter[1], Andrea V. King[1], Lutz Frölich[2], Michèle Wessa[3] and Herta Flor[1]

[1] *Department of Cognitive and Clinical Neuroscience, Central Institute of Mental Health, Medical Faculty Mannheim, Heidelberg University, Mannheim, Germany*
[2] *Division of Gerontopsychiatry, Central Institute of Mental Health, Medical Faculty Mannheim, Heidelberg University, Mannheim, Germany*
[3] *Section for Experimental Psychopathology and Neuroimaging, Department of General Psychiatry, Center for Psychosocial Medicine, Heidelberg University, Heidelberg, Germany*

Correspondence:
Patric Meyer, Department of Cognitive and Clinical Neuroscience, Central Institute of Mental Health. Medical Faculty Mannheim, Heidelberg University, Square J5, 68159 Mannheim, Germany
e-mail: patric.meyer@zi-mannheim.de

Alzheimer's disease (AD) is a slowly progressive neurodegenerative disorder, in which morphological alterations of brain tissue develop many years before the first neuropsychological and clinical changes occur. Among the first and most prominent symptoms are deficiencies of declarative memory functions. This stage of precursory symptoms to AD has been described as amnestic mild cognitive impairment (aMCI) and is discussed as a potential AD prodrome. As therapy in the later stages of AD has been shown to be of limited impact, aMCI would be the key target for early intervention. For that purpose a comprehensive neuropsychological and anatomical characterization of this group is necessary. Previous neuropsychological investigations identified tests which are highly sensitive in diagnosing aMCI and very early AD. However, the sensitivity of those neuropsychological tests to the particular structural neuropathology in aMCI remains to be specified. To this end, we investigated 25 patients with single-domain aMCI. All participants underwent extensive neuropsychological testing and anatomical scanning with structural magnetic resonance imaging. Voxel-based morphometry (VBM) was performed to identify brain regions that show a significant correlation between regional brain volume and behavioral measures of memory and executive functioning. We found that performance in a variety of mnemonic tests was directly related to the integrity of the medial temporal lobe cortex (MTLC). Moreover, impairment of memory sub-functions in aMCI might be detected earlier than overt structural damage. By this, these findings contribute to the identification of cerebral structures associated with memory deficits in aMCI.

Keywords: voxel-based morphometry, amnestic mild cognitive impairment, neuropsychological tests, medial temporal lobe, episodic memory, semantic memory

INTRODUCTION

Alzheimer's disease (AD) is a progressive neurodegenerative condition, in which neuropathological changes of brain tissue advance many years before the first clinically detectable neuropsychological alterations occur. The transitional phase in which first neuropsychological performance deficits become subjectively – and objectively – detectable but are not severe enough to be diagnosed as dementia has been labeled as mild cognitive impairment (MCI). Depending on the involvement of only one or of several cognitive domains (single-domain vs. multiple-domain MCI) and if one of the compromised functions is memory (amnestic vs. non-amnestic MCI), there are four possible subtypes of MCI (Petersen, 2004). As shown by the results of longitudinal studies, particularly the single-domain amnestic MCI (aMCI) subtype is related to an increased probability of converting to dementia whereby AD was the most prevalent demential outcome (Busse et al., 2006; Yaffe et al., 2006; Fischer et al., 2007). Hence, aMCI is rather considered to constitute a precursory phase of AD than the other subtypes. This makes a deeper investigation and understanding of aMCI-related memory impairments and their structural neural correlates a significant purpose for an early diagnosis of AD.

In the course of AD, neurofibrillary pathology, in the form of tangles made up of hyperphosphorylated tau, begins in the perirhinal cortex, and then spreads to the entorhinal cortex and the hippocampus proper (Braak and Braak, 1991). This observation is in agreement with numerous imaging studies that have found medial temporal lobe (MTL) atrophy in early AD as well as in aMCI (Pennanen et al., 2004).

Moreover, various studies have investigated the volume of the MTL with structural MRI scans in AD and MCI (aMCI or across subtypes) using manual tracing methods or voxel-based morphometry (VBM). AD patients showed significant neuronal atrophy in the MTL including the hippocampus (e.g., Karas et al., 2004; Barbeau et al., 2008; Pihlajamäki et al., 2009; Schmidt-Wilcke et al., 2009) whereas patients with MCI only displayed major neuronal loss in the medial temporal lobe cortex (MTLC) (Kordower et al., 2001).

In line with results on the contribution of myelin breakdown to AD pathology (Hyman et al., 1986; Wallin et al., 1989; Bartzokis, 2004), a further line of evidence suggests that alterations in white matter (WM) tracts which interconnect MTL structures occur before gray matter (GM) atrophy sets in and are also more severe in the preclinical phase of AD (De la Monte, 1989). Moreover, WM pathology was reported to be independent of regional cortical degeneration (Hyman et al., 1986; Delacourte et al., 1999; Kalus et al., 2006; Salat et al., 2010; Agosta et al., 2011).

Although significant neuropathological changes can be observed very early in the course of AD, it can be very difficult to diagnose aMCI since the associated cognitive deficits cannot easily be discriminated from the decline found in other cerebral disorders or in healthy aging (Petersen, 2004). However, while the memory deficits in AD are initially related to MTLC pathology, memory problems in healthy aging seem to be associated with the observed accelerated shrinkage of the hippocampus and prefrontal areas (Raz et al., 2005). In contrast, volume loss of the MTLC is minimal in healthy aging and only of a higher degree in very old age. Hence, neuropsychological tests that focus on cognitive functions relying on the integrity of the MTLC can provide an effective and sufficiently sensitive marker for an early diagnosis as those deficits should be different from deficits caused by healthy aging or other neurological or mental disorders. This may also promote early treatment allowing to slow down the progress of the disease by maintaining the patients' present cognitive level for a longer period of time.

In order to identify those neuropsychological tests which are most sensitive in diagnosing very early AD, Swainson et al. (2001) compared the performance of patients with mild AD, aMCI, major depression, and healthy controls on a range of tests including the CANTAB (Cambridge Neuropsychological Test Automated Battery). Scores on two CANTAB tests – paired associates learning (PAL) and delayed matching to sample (DMS) as well as performance on the Wechsler Memory Scale-Revised (WMS-R; Wechsler, 1987) logical memory recall task precisely classified participants to the AD or the control group. In addition, the CANTAB PAL and DMS test scores were correlated with the degree of global cognitive decline during an 8-month follow-up period. These same two tests together with logical memory recall, semantic naming, and a category fluency (CF) task were also sensitive to deficits in aMCI when compared to the control group. Also, Égerházi et al. (2007) used the CANTAB to examine the cognitive decline of patients with aMCI and AD and confirmed that especially performance on the PAL task is a very sensitive measure to detect early neuropathological symptoms that are related to AD. In another study, Fowler et al. (2002) showed that the decline in PAL and DMS performance within a 6-month interval predicts the progression from aMCI to AD within 2 years. The WMS-R subtest logical memory, which consists of two detailed stories that subjects have to freely recall and retell, was also shown to be very sensitive to early memory impairments. Rubin et al. (1998) reported that even at a time when clinical changes were not yet evident, older subjects who later converted to AD performed significantly poorer on this test than non-converters. However, the neural origin of the sensitivity of all these neuropsychological tests for aMCI and early AD remains to be specified. Moreover, the relationship between the extent of AD-related neuropathology in aMCI and the extent of mnemonic impairment is broadly unclear up to now.

A valuable source of information on the neural basis of this sensitivity can be provided by the investigation of the relationship between inter-individual differences in performance and differences in brain structure (Kanai and Rees, 2011). In order to relate the reported neuropsychological test impairments in aMCI and early AD to underlying morphological brain changes, we used VBM on structural neuroimaging data from subjects with single-domain aMCI. As neurofibrillary pathology in AD starts in the MTLC before reaching the hippocampus, we hypothesized that performance of those neuropsychological tests from the CANTAB and the Consortium to Establish a Registry for Alzheimer's Disease (CERAD-Plus, Morris et al., 1989) batteries which are sensitive to aMCI and early AD [Boston naming test (BNT), CF, DMS, PAL, and WMS-R logical memory recall] is mainly related to the integrity of this brain region. Only patients with aMCI were investigated in order to counteract artificially modified correlations caused by group differences in regional brain volume and memory performance.

MATERIALS AND METHODS

SAMPLE

Twenty-five individuals (mean age 67.96 years, SD 4.36, range 61–75, five female) who met criteria for single-domain aMCI (Petersen et al., 1999; Winblad et al., 2004) took part in the study. Participants were recruited from the Memory Clinic of the Central Institute of Mental Health. The study was approved by the ethics committee of the Medical Faculty Mannheim, University of Heidelberg and was conducted in accordance with the Declaration of Helsinki. All participants gave written informed consent prior to study start.

CLINICAL ASSESSMENT

All patients were diagnosed after medical and neurological examination, clinical history, scoring on the Mini-Mental State Examination (MMSE), and after neuropsychological assessment with tests assessing psychomotor speed, attention, verbal fluency, executive functions, orientation, constructional praxis, and episodic memory taken from the CERAD, the CANTAB, and the WMS-R. In addition, all participants were screened for mental disorders by the German version of the Structured Clinical Interview for DSM-IV (SCID I, Wittchen et al., 1997). All participants were German native speakers. **Table 1** provides demographic characteristics and performance in neuropsychological tests. Additionally, the patient form of the Patient Competency Rating Scale (PCRS, Prigatano et al., 1986) and the PCRS relative's form (both forms were taken from the German PCRS analog Marburger Kompetenz-Skala, MKS, Gauggel, 1998) were used as measures for ratings of impairment of daily functioning. Participants also underwent a structural MRI examination. Images were screened for probable exclusion criteria by an experienced neuroradiologist.

Participants were diagnosed as having aMCI if they fulfilled the following criteria (Petersen et al., 1999; Winblad et al., 2004): (1) concerns about memory decline, corroborated by a patient's relative, (2) objective memory impairment defined by performance at

Table 1 | Demographics of the patient sample and mean scores for neuropsychological tests (standard deviation in parentheses, SD).

Number of subjects	25			
Mean age (years)	67.96	(4.36)		
Female/male	5/20			
Mean years of education (years)	11.28	(2.92)		
	Raw score	(SD)	Standard score*	(SD)
ASSESSMENT OF CLINICAL/GLOBAL FUNCTIONING				
Hamilton rating scale for depression (HAMD)	0.76	(1.27)	n/a	n/a
General depression scale (ADS-L)	7.92	(5.80)	−0.68	(0.82)
State – trait anxiety inventory – trait (STAI-T): total score	31.04	(8.25)	−0.36	(1.00)
Competence rating scale (patient form): functional abilities	102.72	(11.42)	n/a	n/a
Competence rating scale (patient form): cognitive abilities	46.56	(7.98)	n/a	n/a
Competence rating scale (relative's form): functional abilities	107.46	(8.07)	n/a	n/a
Competence rating scale (relative's form): cognitive abilities	50.00	(5.91)	n/a	n/a
Mehrfachwahl-Wortschatz-Intelligenztest-B (IQ-score)	101.84	(12.12)	0.16	(0.82)
CERAD: MMSE	28.16	(1.18)	−0.57	(0.99)
CANTAB simple reaction time: mean correct latency	250.36	(32.03)	n/a	n/a
ASSESSMENT OF MNEMONIC FUNCTIONING				
CANTAB delayed matching to sample test: percent correct (all delays)	78.93	(9.01)	0.15	(0.86)
CANTAB delayed matching to sample test: percent correct (12000 ms)	70.8	(17.30)	−0.03	(1.23)
CANTAB delayed matching to sample test: percent correct (4000 ms)	83.2	(11.44)	0.25	(0.78)
CANTAB paired associates learning test: total errors (6 shapes, adjusted)	9.12	(7.88)	0.06	(0.81)
CANTAB pattern recognition memory test: percent correct (immediate recall)	92.33	(9.89)	n/a	n/a
CANTAB pattern recognition memory test: percent correct (delayed recall)	74.00	(17.89)	n/a	n/a
CERAD: Boston naming test	14.28	(1.17)	0.35	(1.05)
CERAD: category fluency	20.44	(5.29)	0.29	(0.99)
Logical memory immediate (WMS-R)	31.52	(29.01)	31.52[a]	(29.01)
Logical memory delayed (WMS-R)	31.88	(29.58)	31.88[a]	(29.58)
ASSESSMENT OF EXECUTIVE FUNCTIONING				
CANTAB stockings of Cambridge: problems solved in minimum moves	7.6	(1.75)	−0.07	(0.90)

**Standard scores are z-values if not specified differently by a superscript letter.*

[a]The standardized mean is indicated by a percentile rank.

n/a Standardized scores are not available for these tests.

CANTAB, Cambridge Neuropsychological Test Automated Battery; CERAD, Consortium to Establish a Registry for Alzheimer's Disease; MMSE, Mini-Mental State Examination; WMS-R, Wechsler Memory Scale-Revised.

or lower than 1.3 SDs below the mean value (i.e., under the tenth percentile) of an age- and education-matched reference population on one or more memory tests, (3) preserved general cognitive functioning defined by performance at least above 1.3 SDs below the mean on all other measures not assessing memory, (4) independence of functioning in everyday life as assessed with the PCRS, (5) not demented or suffering from conditions that also may cause memory impairments as evaluated by MRI examination, medical history, and structured clinical interviews.

All participants were required to have a negative history for neurological disorders (e.g., stroke, cerebral neoplasm, hemorrhage, inflammation, Parkinson's disease, vascular encephalopathy with increased WM lesions), medical disorders (e.g., diabetes, untreated vitamin deficiencies, disorders of the thyroid, anemia, sleep apnea, other significant concurrent physical illnesses), and mental disorders (e.g., affective disorders). Current drug intake of dopaminergic or serotonergic agents, beta-adrenergic blockers, or benzodiazepines was ruled out. Additionally, all participants had to have normal or corrected to normal visual acuity and contrast sensitivity and had to be free of metallic biomedical implants (exclusion for MRI).

NEUROPSYCHOLOGICAL TESTS

Boston naming test

A short version of the BNT (Kaplan et al., 1983) is included in the CERAD testing battery. Participants are presented with 15 black-and-white line drawings for confrontation naming. If naming is not successful, a semantic, and if required, a phonetic cue is presented. We used the number of spontaneously correctly named items as the critical measure for the regression analyses.

Category fluency

In the CF task, participants have to name as many animals as possible in 1 min. The total number of items named in this interval was used in the analyses.

Wechsler memory scale – revised, logical memory

The WMS subtest logical memory consists of two detailed, thematically independent stories (25 items per story), that participants have to recall freely immediately after hearing and after a delay of 30 min. For analysis, we used the total number of recalled items in the immediate and in the delayed version.

Delayed matching to sample

The DMS assesses forced-choice recognition memory for novel visual patterns. Participants are confronted with a complex visual pattern. After a delay, this pattern is presented together with three similar patterns. The task is to identify which of these samples matches the target. The outcome measure used for regression analyses was the percentage of correct answers at the 4000 ms delay.

Paired associates learning

In this test, boxes are presented on the screen and opened in randomized order. A pattern is enclosed in one or more of them. Afterward, one pattern at a time is shown in the middle of the screen and the participant's task is to indicate the box where the pattern was initially placed. In case of an error, the patterns are presented again. Test difficulty increases in terms of the number of tested patterns. We used the adjusted score of total errors at the six-pattern stage in reversed polarity for analyses. In the Swainson et al. (2001) study, this outcome measure was shown to differentiate patients with mild AD from non-demented controls with 98% accuracy.

Pattern recognition memory

This is a two alternatives forced-choice recognition test with abstract visual patterns. During a study phase, the participant is presented with a series of 12 visual patterns. In the recognition phase, the participant is required to choose between a pattern already seen and a new one. The percentage of correct responses was used for regression analysis.

Stockings of Cambridge

The stockings of Cambridge (SOC) is a spatial planning test where participants are confronted with two displays containing three colored balls. The task is to copy the pattern shown in the upper display by moving the balls in the lower display. As an expression of overall executive planning accuracy, we used the outcome measure which contains the frequency of having successfully completed a test problem in the minimum possible number of moves (Robbins et al., 1998).

IMAGE ACQUISITION AND ANALYSIS

Structural MRI was acquired with a 3 Tesla magnetic resonance scanner (Magnetom Trio, Siemens Medical Solutions, Erlangen, Germany). For each participant, a T1-weighted gradient echo MP-RAGE (Magnetization Prepared Rapid Gradient Echo) sequence (TR = 2300 ms, TE = 2.98 ms, flip angle 9°, FOV: 256 mm × 256 mm, voxel size: 1.0 mm × 1.0 mm × 1.1 mm, 160 sagittal slices) was acquired.

Voxel-based morphometry was applied to analyze correlations between neuropsychological test scores and GM and WM values. Contrary to manual tracing approaches, VBM permits to investigate the presence of structure-function relationships across the entire brain without *a priori* decisions about which structures to evaluate. This strategy allows to investigate if the critical tests were exclusively or especially sensitive to AD-related changes. Additionally, VBM is an automated, rater-independent method, and provides very reproducible results (Busatto et al., 2008). In contrast, the tracing procedure is dependent on unambiguous borders and anatomical landmarks and results are difficult to replicate between laboratories (Good et al., 2001). Data pre-processing and analysis were performed using SPM8[1] (Wellcome Department of Imaging Neuroscience, London, UK). Data pre-processing involved visual inspection of the T1-weighted images to control for imaging artifacts and the consecutive segmentation into GM, WM, and cerebrospinal fluid (CSF), building a customized template for GM and WM through an iteratively non-linear registration algorithm (DARTEL Toolbox for SPM8; Good et al., 2001; Ashburner, 2007) and a normalization of this template to the Montreal Neurological Institute template[2]. The Jacobian determinants resulting from the normalization procedure were used to obtain modulated VBM data preserving regional volumes. Individual GM and WM images were smoothed with an isotropic Gaussian kernel of 6 mm full-width at half-maximum before entering them into statistical analyses. Global volumes of GM, WM, and CSF were assessed from segmented images using the VBM8 toolbox for SPM8 (http://dbm.neuro.uni-jena.de/vbm8) and summed to generate an estimate for total intracranial volume (TIV). To correlate volumes and neuropsychological performance, separate test-wise regression analyses were calculated using raw scores of each test and GM and WM volumes, respectively. Age, gender, TIV as well as education were entered as covariates of no interest into all regression analyses. Results were considered significant if they consisted of at least 15 neighboring voxels that surpassed an uncorrected threshold of $p < 0.001$ (Forman et al., 1995). Given the poorer signal-to-noise ratio often observed in MTL regions due to susceptibility-related signal loss (e.g., Schacter and Wagner, 1999), a more liberal threshold of $p < 0.005$ was used for analyses within this region.

RESULTS

White matter regression analyses demonstrated various significant positive correlations with neuropsychological test scores from the CANTAB and CERAD batteries. Significant correlations with WM volume for tests from the visual memory domain [DMS, PAL, pattern recognition memory (PRM)] were widespread but accumulated in bilateral temporal lobes including parahippocampal WM. For WMS story recall, which reflects immediate and delayed verbal memory, significant correlations were found with WM volume in the bilateral parahippocampal gyri and the left precuneus. Semantic memory test scores (CF, BNT) and WM volume were significantly correlated in the left parahippocampal gyrus. Besides task and modality specific structure-function relationships along the entire parahippocampal gyrus, a high degree of overlap of the clusters from the independent VBM analyses was found in the vicinity of the left perirhinal cortex (see **Figure 1**; **Table 2**).

In contrast to the memory-dependent measures, performance scores of the SOC, reflecting executive functioning, revealed significant correlations with WM values localized in the left frontal lobe.

No coherent results were obtained in the regression analysis with regard to GM volumes.

---

[1] http://www.fil.ion.ucl.ac.uk/spm/software/spm8
[2] http://www.loni.ucla.edu/ICBM/ICBM_Databases.html

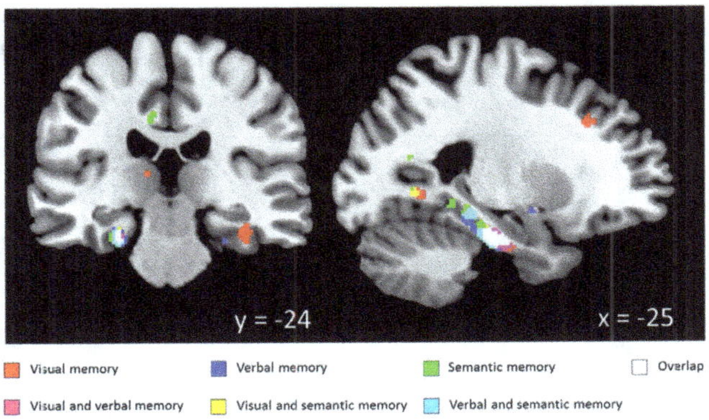

FIGURE 1 | Correlation between white matter volume and memory scores (coordinates in MNI space; thresholded at $p < 0.005$). *Visual memory*: paired associates learning, delayed matching to sample, pattern recognition memory; *Verbal memory*: Wechsler memory scale-revised, logical memory recall; *Semantic memory*: Boston naming test, category fluency.

DISCUSSION

The present study revealed the neural correlates of different cognitive sub-functions assessed by neuropsychological tests that are most commonly used for diagnosing aMCI and early AD. VBM analyses demonstrated that performance in a variety of mnemonic tests is directly related to the integrity of the MTLC in patients with single-domain aMCI. In more detail, performance in BNT, CF, PAL, DMS, PRM as well as WMS was mainly associated with reduced WM volume in the perirhinal and entorhinal region. Although no exact tract definition is possible using VBM-derived data, it is likely that the perforant path, which provides the major input route to the hippocampus as well as the cingulum bundle connecting the various components of the limbic system, are included in the reported MTLC WM clusters. In contrast, a significant association of measures of executive functioning and WM volume was found in the frontal lobe. Retrospectively, these tests were found to be sensitive to MCI and early AD in previous studies because they rely on the integrity of those brain structures which are specifically injured in these conditions. These findings are consistent with the specific pathology in the AD process (Hyman et al., 1986; Wallin et al., 1989; Bartzokis, 2004) and support the notion of a very early involvement of the MTLC during the disease process. Previous comparisons of MCI patients to healthy controls showed different forms of brain atrophy depending on the nature and state of the cognitive impairment (e.g., Whitwell et al., 2007). Interestingly, a cohort analysis revealed no decreases in GM and WM volumes in the MTL in our patients with aMCI. This might be due to the fact that they are at a very early stage of the disease process so that a subtle decline in regional GM and WM volume is not detectable yet, at least not when using VBM. Nevertheless, even in the absence of visible atrophy on MRI scans, the result of the regression analyses demonstrated a clear relationship between the mnemonic impairments and the integrity of the MTLC. This fits well to the results of a recent meta-analysis by Schmand et al. (2010) who concluded that memory impairment is a much more precise early predictor of AD than local brain atrophy. Recently, Leal and Yassa (2013) argued that the sensitivity of AD markers may vary as a function of how far patients are in the disease process with small changes in the perforant path being a much more salient feature than frank volume loss in the MTL in the early MCI phase. The authors concluded that in the absence of overt structural decline, functional markers are most important.

Contrary to our expectations, we could not observe a structure-function relationship with regard to GM. Similarly to the missing signs of clear MTLC atrophy in our patient sample, this might be caused by the very early state of the cognitive impairment. As mentioned above, alterations in WM tracts connecting MTL structures seem to occur before cortical degeneration starts and were also found to be partly independent of it (Delacourte et al., 1999; Kalus et al., 2006; Salat et al., 2010). In a postmortem investigation of very mild AD patients, Hyman et al. (1986) could demonstrate that cell loss in the MTLC causes a disconnection of the hippocampus from cortical inputs and that this disconnection was related to memory impairments. Recent diffusion tensor imaging and VBM studies confirmed that it is the MTLC WM that is affected most prominently in aMCI (Salat et al., 2010) and AD (Stoub et al., 2006) and that those alterations are related to later memory impairments (Salat et al., 2010). In addition, Zhuang et al. (2012) investigated retrospectively whether microstructural WM changes are already present in cognitively normal individuals without dementia who will later develop aMCI. At baseline, converters compared to non-converters showed substantial reductions in WM integrity in the MTLC whose degree was correlated with greater verbal episodic memory decline. In contrast, GM density was found not to be related to longitudinal episodic memory loss.

A considerable number of findings indicate that the involvement of the MTLC in binding seems both necessary and sufficient for the formation of semantic representations, i.e., semantic memories of events (e.g., Taylor et al., 2006). By binding associative or contextual information together with the semantic item representation, the hippocampus instead provides both necessary and sufficient conditions for the formation of episodic memories (e.g., Aggleton and Brown, 2006). However, due to this probable interruption of information flow between the different MTL structures, MTLC and hippocampus were not differently associated with semantic and episodic memory processes in our study. Although recall and cued recall tests normally rely more on the hippocampus (Golomb et al., 1994; Pohlack et al., 2013), performance in the WMS logical memory recall task or in the PAL were related to MTLC integrity in our sample. However, WM volume of different MTLC areas was differently associated with certain memory sub-functions with regard to laterality. Both PAL and DMS performance primarily correlated with WM volume in the area of the right parahippocampal gyrus while semantic memory as measured by CF and BNT was associated with left hemisphere WM volume.

Within this context, it is important to note that we did not identify the brain regions underlying the specific task-relevant cognitive processes *per se* as only participants in a pathological condition were investigated. Consequently, it is very likely that due to the probable disconnection of MTL structures, reorganization, or compensation processes are at work in aMCI patients.

Table 2 | Coordinates of peak value for clusters of white matter positively correlated with neuropsychological test performance.

Test score	Region	Hemisphere	Talairach coordinates			Cluster size	Peak *T*-value
			x	*y*	*z*	*k*	
DMS	Parahippocampal gyrus (uncus)	R	32	−4	−29	63	3.53*
	Temporal lobe (superior temporal gyrus)[a]	L	−45	−8	−7	78	4.47**
	Occipital lobe (Cuneus)[a]	L	−3	−83	25	60	4.39**
	Temporal lobe (middle temporal gyrus)	R	43	−45	6	45	3.93**
PAL	Parahippocampal gyrus	R	36	−26	−14	150	5.16**
	Frontal lobe (middle frontal gyrus)[a]	L	−38	17	25	39	4.46**
PRM	Parahippocampal gyrus	L	−23	−17	−17	87	5.11**
WMS_I	Parahippocampal gyrus	R	29	−23	−19	63	3.87*
	Parahippocampal gyrus	L	−26	−23	−21	177	5.71**
WMS_II	Temporal lobe (middle temporal gyrus)	L	−54	−7	−17	19	3.98*
	Parahippocampal gyrus	L	−23	−22	−19	119	4.56**
CF	Parahippocampal gyrus[a]	R	42	−21	−19	79	6.70**
BNT	Limbic lobe (uncus)	R	29	−4	−29	23	3.58*
	Parahippocampal gyrus	L	−24	−34	−5	45	3.46*
	Parahippocampal gyrus	L	−31	5	−30	51	6.19**
	Parahippocampal gyrus	L	−29	−18	−17	50	4.26**
	Temporal lobe (middle temporal gyrus)[a]	L	−27	−61	19	45	4.48**
	Temporal lobe (middle temporal gyrus)[a]	R	33	−55	22	24	4.26**
SOC	Frontal lobe (inferior frontal gyrus)[a]	L	−43	19	16	151	4.90**

**$p < 0.005$ uncorrected for multiple comparisons.*

***$p < 0.001$ uncorrected for multiple comparisons.*

[a]For peak voxel coordinates that have been identified by the Talairach Daemon as sub-gyral, the nearest labeled gyrus/nucleus within a distance of 5 mm is given in parentheses.

DMS, delayed matching to sample; PAL, paired associates learning; PRM, pattern recognition memory; WMS_I, Wechsler Memory Scale-Revised, logical memory immediate recall; WMS_II, Wechsler Memory Scale-Revised, logical memory delayed recall; CF, category fluency; BNT, Boston naming test; SOC, Stockings of Cambridge.

This precludes any clear inferences to intact cognitive processes in a normal healthy population. Here, we asked instead why specific neuropsychological tests have previously been found to be sensitive for aMCI and early AD.

Besides methodological differences, the position of our patients on a very early stage of the disease process may also account for different findings in the literature relating to the reported regression analyses (e.g., Schmidt-Wilcke et al., 2009). Chételat et al. (2003) found that deficits in both word list encoding and retrieval, were correlated with a decline in hippocampal GM in patients with single-domain aMCI. In contrast to our study, only GM density in patients diagnosed using a more conservative performance cut-off score (1.5 SDs instead of 1.3 SDs as in the present study) was used. This was also the case in a study by Barbeau et al. (2008) who reported that in aMCI patients with preserved recognition and impaired recall, GM density was reduced in frontal areas while aMCI patients with impaired recall and recognition memory showed reduced density in the right MTL and bilateral temporo-parietal regions. In addition, the diagnostic sensitivity of the tests applied in these investigations is so far unclear. A cohort analysis conducted by Schmidt-Wilcke et al. (2009) revealed bilateral decreases in GM density in the MTLs and the lateral temporal lobes when aMCI patients were compared to healthy controls. Additional regression analyses showed a significant positive association between immediate verbal recall and GM integrity in the left MTLC while delayed free recall correlated with GM density in the hippocampus proper. However, in this study also patients with multiple-domain aMCI were enrolled. This was also the case in a recent study by Barbeau et al. (2012) which demonstrated significant positive correlations between semantic memory scores and MTLC as well as anterior hippocampus GM density. However, as the kind of conversion of patients suffering from multiple-domain aMCI is less clear (Petersen, 2004; Fischer et al., 2007), these data are not directly comparable to the results of the present study that only incorporated patients with single-domain aMCI, who are probably located at a transitional stage toward the development of AD. Thus, the current results obtained in a more homogenous sample at a probable earlier time point in the disease process argue even more strongly in favor of the diagnostic value of the reported memory tests.

CONCLUSION

In a homogenous sample of patients with single-domain aMCI, we detected relationships between brain structure and mnemonic function in regions closely similar to previously established early morphological alterations in aMCI and AD even before those structural manifestations are detectable. By this, the present results suggest that performance in frequently used neuropsychological memory tests can predict the integrity of the cortical regions which are affected first by AD pathology such as the perirhinal cortex.

However, it should be kept in mind that this study also has some limitations. Due to the exploratory purpose of this study and the poorer signal-to-noise ratio often observed in MTL regions due to susceptibility-related signal loss, a more liberal threshold of $p < 0.005$ together with a cluster-threshold of at least 15 neighboring voxels was used for analyses within this region. When using FWE as correction, none of the results survived. Moreover, the present sample was diagnosed with the same tests that were used for regression analyses. In addition no control group was tested. Consequently, the observed correlations are not necessarily aMCI-specific. Nevertheless, they demonstrate why specific neuropsychological tests have previously been found to be sensitive for aMCI and early AD.

REFERENCES

Aggleton, J. P., and Brown, M. W. (2006). Interleaving brain systems for episodic and recognition memory. *Trends Cogn. Sci. (Regul. Ed.)* 10, 455–463. doi:10.1016/j.tics.2006.08.003

Agosta, F., Pievani, M., Sala, S., Geroldi, C., Galluzzi, S., Frisoni, G. B., et al. (2011). White matter damage in Alzheimer disease and its relationship to gray matter atrophy. *Radiology* 258, 853–863. doi:10.1148/radiol.10101284

Ashburner, J. (2007). A fast diffeomorphic image registration algorithm. *Neuroimage* 38, 95–113. doi:10.1016/j.neuroimage.2007.07.007

Barbeau, E., Didic, M., Joubert, S., Guedj, E., Koric, L., Felician, O. R., et al. (2012). Extent and neural basis of semantic memory impairment in mild cognitive impairment. *J. Alzheimers Dis.* 28, 823–837. doi:10.3233/JAD-2011-110989

Barbeau, E. J., Ranjeva, J. P., Didic, M., Confort-Gouny, S., Felician, O., Soulier, E., et al. (2008). Profile of memory impairment and gray matter loss in amnestic mild cognitive impairment. *Neuropsychologia* 46, 1009–1019. doi:10.1016/j.neuropsychologia.2007.11.019

Bartzokis, G. (2004). Age-related myelin breakdown: a developmental model of cognitive decline and Alzheimer's disease. *Neurobiol. Aging* 25, 5–18. doi:10.1016/j.neurobiolaging.2003.03.001

Braak, H., and Braak, E. (1991). Neuropathological stageing of Alzheimer-related changes. *Acta Neuropathol.* 82, 239–259. doi:10.1007/BF00308809

Busatto, G. F., Diniz, B. S., and Zanetti, M. V. (2008). Voxel-based morphometry in Alzheimer's disease. *Expert Rev. Neurother.* 8, 1691–1702. doi:10.1586/14737175.8.11.1691

Busse, A., Hensel, A., Gühne, U., Angermeyer, M. C., and Riedel-Heller, S. G. (2006). Mild cognitive impairment: long-term course of four clinical subtypes. *Neurology* 67, 2176–2185. doi:10.1212/01.wnl.0000249117.23318.e1

Chételat, G., Desgranges, B., de la Sayette, V., Viader, F., Berkouk, K., Landeau, B., et al. (2003). Dissociating atrophy and hypometabolism impact on episodic memory in mild cognitive impairment. *Brain* 126, 1955–1967. doi:10.1093/brain/awg196

De la Monte, S. M. (1989). Quantitation of cerebral atrophy in preclinical and end-stage Alzheimer's disease. *Ann. Neurol.* 25, 450–459. doi:10.1002/ana.410250506

Delacourte, A., David, J. F., Sergeant, N., Buée, L., Wattez, A., Vermersch, P., et al. (1999). The biochemical pathway of neurofibrillary degeneration in aging and Alzheimer's disease. *Neurology* 52, 1158–1165. doi:10.1212/WNL.52.6.1158

Égerházi, A., Berecz, R., Bartók, E., and Degrell, I. (2007). Automated neuropsychological test battery (CANTAB) in mild cognitive impairment and in Alzheimer's disease. *Prog. Neuropsychopharmacol. Biol. Psychiatry* 31, 746–751. doi:10.1016/j.pnpbp.2007.01.011

Fischer, P., Jungwirth, S., Zehetmayer, S., Weissgram, S., Hoenigschnabl, S., Gelpi, E., et al. (2007). Conversion from subtypes of mild cognitive impairment to Alzheimer dementia. *Neurology* 68, 288–291. doi:10.1212/01.wnl.0000252358.03285.9d

Forman, S. D., Cohen, J. D., Fitzgerald, M., Eddy, W. F., Mintun, M. A., and Noll, D. C. (1995). Improved assessment of significant activation in functional magnetic resonance imaging fMRI: use of a cluster-size threshold. *Magn. Reson. Med. Sci.* 33, 636–647. doi:10.1002/mrm.1910330508

Fowler, K. S., Saling, M. M., Conway, E. L., Semple, J. M., and Louis, W. J. (2002). Paired associate performance in the early detection of DAT. *J. Int. Neuropsychol. Soc.* 8, 58–71. doi:10.1017/S1355617702811067

Gauggel, S. (ed.) (1998). *Marburger Kompetenz-Skala (MKS).* Marburg: University of Marburg.

Golomb, J., Kluger, A., de Leon, M. J., Ferris, S. H., Convit, A., Mittelman, M. S., et al. (1994). Hippocampal formation size in normal human aging: a correlate of delayed secondary memory performance. *Learn. Mem.* 1, 45–54.

Good, C. D., Johnsrude, I. S., Ashburner, J., Henson, R. N. A., Friston, K. J., and Frackowiak, R. S. J. (2001). A voxel-based morphometric study of ageing in 465 normal adult human brains. *Neuroimage* 14, 21–36. doi:10.1006/nimg.2001.0857

Hyman, B. T., Van Hoesen, G. W., Kromer, L. J., and Damasio, A. R. (1986). Perforant pathway changes and the memory impairment of Alzheimer's disease. *Ann. Neurol.* 20, 472–481. doi:10.1002/ana.410200406

Kalus, P., Slotboom, J., Gallinat, J., Mahlberg, R., Cattapan-Ludewig, K., Wiest, R., et al. (2006). Examining the gateway to the limbic system with diffusion tensor imaging: the perforant pathway in dementia. *Neuroimage* 30, 713–720. doi:10.1016/j.neuroimage.2005.10.035

Kanai, R., and Rees, G. (2011). The structural basis of inter-individual differences in human behaviour and cognition. *Nat. Rev. Neurosci.* 12, 231–242. doi:10.1038/nrn3000

Kaplan, E., Goodglass, H., Weintraub, S., and Segal, O. (1983). *Boston Naming Test.* Philadelphia: Lea & Febiger.

Karas, G. B., Scheltens, P., Rombouts, S. A., Visser, P. J., van Schijndel, R. A., Fox, N. C., et al. (2004). Global and local gray matter loss in mild cognitive impairment and Alzheimer's disease. *Neuroimage* 23, 708–716. doi:10.1016/j.neuroimage.2004.07.006

Kordower, J. H., Chu, Y., Stebbins, G. T., DeKosky, S. T., Cochran, E. J., Bennett, D., et al. (2001). Loss and atrophy of layer II entorhinal cortex neurons in elderly people with mild cognitive impairment. *Ann. Neurol.* 49, 202–213. doi:10.1002/1531-8249(20010201)49:2<202::AID-ANA40>3.0.CO;2-3

Leal, S. L., and Yassa, M. A. (2013). Perturbations of neural circuitry in aging, mild cognitive impairment, and Alzheimer's disease. *Ageing Res. Rev.* doi:10.1016/j.arr.2013.01.006

Morris, J. C., Heyman, A., Mohs, R. C., Hughes, J. P., van Belle, G., Fillenbaum, G., et al. (1989). The Consortium to Establish a Registry for Alzheimer's Disease CERAD Part I clinical and neuropsychological assessment of Alzheimer's disease. *Neurology* 39, 1159–1165. doi:10.1212/WNL.39.9 1159

Pennanen, C., Kivipelto, M., Tuomainen, S., Hartikainen, P., Hänninen, T., Laakso, M. P., et al. (2004). Hippocampus and entorhinal cortex in mild cognitive impairment and early AD. *Neurobiol. Aging* 25, 303–310. doi:10.1016/S0197-4580(03)00084-8

Petersen, R. C. (2004). Mild cognitive impairment as a diagnostic entity. *J. Intern. Med.* 256, 183–194. doi:10.1111/j.1365-2796.2004.01388.x

Petersen, R. C., Smith, G. E., Waring, S. C., Ivnik, R. J., Tangalos, E. G., and Kokmen, E. (1999). Mild cognitive impairment: clinical characterization and outcome. *Arch. Neurol.* 56, 303–308. doi:10.1001/archneur.56.3.303

Pihlajamäki, M., Jauhiainen, A. M., and Soininen, H. (2009). Structural and functional MRI in mild cognitive impairment. *Curr. Alzheimer Res.* 6, 179–185. doi:10.2174/156720509787602898

Pohlack, S. T., Meyer, P., Cacciaglia, R., Liebscher, C., Ridder, S., and Flor, H. (2013). Bigger is better! Hippocampal volume and declarative memory performance in healthy young men. *Brain Struct. Funct.* doi:10.1007/s00429-012-0497-z

Prigatano, G. P., Fordyce, D. J., Zeiner, H. K., Roueche, J. R., Pepping, M., and Wood, B. C. (1986). *Neuropsychological Rehabilitation after Brain Injury.* Baltimore: John Hopkins University Press.

Raz, N., Lindenberger, U., Rodrigue, K. M., Kennedy, K. M., Head, D., Williamson, A., et al. (2005). Regional brain changes in aging healthy adults: general trends, individual differences and modifiers. *Cereb. Cortex* 15, 1676–1689. doi: 10.1093/cercor/bhi044

Robbins, T. W., James, M., Owen, A. M., Sahakian, B. J., Lawrence, A. D., McInnes, L., et al. (1998). A study of performance on tests from the CANTAB battery sensitive to frontal lobe dysfunction in a large sample of normal volunteers: implications for theories of executive functioning and cognitive aging. Cambridge Neuropsychological Test Automated Battery. *J. Int. Neuropsychol. Soc.* 4, 474–490.

Rubin, E. H., Storandt, M., Miller, J. P., Kinscherf, D. A., Grant, E. A., Morris, J. C., et al. (1998). A prospective study of cognitive function and onset of dementia in cognitively healthy elders. *Arch. Neurol.* 55, 395–401. doi:10.1001/archneur.55.3.395

Salat, D. H., Tuch, D. S., van der Kouwe, A. J., Greve, D. N., Pappu, V., Lee, S. Y., et al. (2010). White matter pathology isolates the hippocampal formation in Alzheimer's disease. *Neurobiol. Aging* 31, 244–256. doi: 10.1016/j.neurobiolaging.2008.03.013

Schacter, D. L., and Wagner, A. D. (1999). Medial temporal lobe activations in fMRI and PET studies of episodic encoding and retrieval. *Hippocampus* 9, 7–24. doi: 10.1002/(SICI)1098-1063(1999)9:1<7::AID-HIPO2>3.0.CO;2-K

Schmand, B., Huizenga, H. M., and van Gool, W. A. (2010). Meta-analysis of CSF and MRI biomarkers for detecting preclinical Alzheimer's disease. *Psychol. Med.* 40, 135–145. doi:10.1017/S0033291709991516

Schmidt-Wilcke, T., Poljansky, S., Hierlmeier, S., Hausner, J., and Ibach, B. (2009). Memory perdormance correlates with gray matter density in the ento-/perirhinal cortex and posterior hippocampus in patients with mild cognitive impairment and healthy controls – a voxel based morphometry study. *Neuroimage* 47, 1914–1920. doi: 10.1016/j.neuroimage.2009.04.092

Stoub, T. R., deToledo-Morrell, L., Stebbins, G. T., Leurgans, S., Bennett, D. A., and Shah, R. C. (2006). Hippocampal disconnection contributes to memory dysfunction in individuals at risk for Alzheimer's disease. *Proc. Natl. Acad. Sci. U.S.A.* 103, 10041–10045. doi: 10.1073/pnas.0603414103

Swainson, R., Hodges, J. R., Galton, C. J., Semple, J., Michael, A., Dunn, B. D., et al. (2001). Early detection and differential diagnosis of Alzheimer's disease and depression with neuropsychological tasks. *Dement. Geriatr. Cogn. Disord.* 12, 265–280. doi: 10.1159/000051269

Taylor, K. I., Moss, H. E., Stamatakis, E. A., and Tyler, L. K. (2006). Binding crossmodal object features in perirhinal cortex. *Proc. Natl. Acad. Sci. U.S.A.* 103, 8239–8244. doi:10.1073/pnas.0509704103

Wallin, A., Gottfries, C. G., Karlsson, I., and Svennerholm, L. (1989). Decreased myelin lipids in Alzheimer's disease and vascular dementia. *Acta Neurol. Scand.* 80, 319–323. doi:10.1111/j.1600-0404.1989.tb03886.x

Wechsler, D. (1987). *Wechsler Memory Scale-Revised.* New York: Harcourt Brace Jovanovich.

Whitwell, J. L., Petersen, R. C., Negash, S., Weigand, S. D., Kantarci, K., Ivnik, R. J., et al. (2007). Patterns of atrophy differ among specific subtypes of mild cognitive impairment. *Arch. Neurol.* 64, 1130–1138. doi:10.1001/archneur.64.8.1130

Winblad, B., Palmer, K., Kivipelto, M., Jelic, V., Fratiglioni, L., Wahlund, L. O., et al. (2004). Mild cognitive impairment – beyond controversies, towards a consensus: report of the International Working Group on Mild Cognitive Impairment. *J. Intern. Med.* 256, 240–246. doi:10.1111/j.1365-2796.2004.01380.x

Wittchen, H. U., Wunderlich, U., Gruschwitz, S., and Zaudig, M. (1997). *SKID-I. Strukturiertes Klinisches Interview für DSM-IV.* Göttingen: Hogrefe.

Yaffe, K., Petersen, R. C., Lindquist, K., Kramer, J., and Miller, B. (2006). Subtype of mild cognitive impairment and progression to dementia and death. *Dement. Geriatr. Cogn. Disord.* 22, 312–319. doi: 10.1159/000095427

Zhuang, L., Sachdev, P. S., Trollor, J. N., Kochan, N. A., Reppermund, S., Brodaty, H., et al. (2012). Microstructural white matter changes in cognitively normal individuals at risk of amnestic MCI. *Neurology* 79, 748–754. doi: 10.1212/WNL.0b013e3182661f4d

5

Integrating events across levels of consciousness

Katharina Henke[1,2]*, Thomas P. Reber[1,2] and Simone B. Duss[1,2]

[1] Division of Experimental Psychology and Neuropsychology, Department of Psychology, University of Bern, Bern, Switzerland
[2] Center for Cognition, Learning and Memory, University of Bern, Bern, Switzerland

***Correspondence:**
Katharina Henke, Department of Psychology, University of Bern, Muesmattstrasse 45, 3012 Bern, Switzerland
e-mail: henke@psy.unibe.ch

Our knowledge grows as we integrate events experienced at different points in time. We may or may not become aware of events, their integration, and their impact on our knowledge and decisions. But can we mentally integrate two events, if they are experienced at different time points and at different levels of consciousness? In this study, an event consisted of the presentation of two unrelated words. In the stream of events, half of events shared one component ("tree desk" ... "desk fish") to facilitate event integration. We manipulated the amount of time and trials that separated two corresponding events. The contents of one event were presented subliminally (invisible) and the contents of the corresponding overlapping event supraliminally (visible). Hence, event integration required the binding of contents between consciousness levels and between time points. At the final test of integration, participants judged whether two supraliminal test words ("tree fish") fit together semantically or not. Unbeknown to participants, half of test words were episodically related through an overlap ("desk"; experimental condition) and half were not (control condition). Participants judged episodically related test words to be closer semantically than unrelated test words. This subjective decrease in the semantic distance between test words was both independent of whether the invisible event was encoded first or second in order and independent of the number of trials and the time that separated two corresponding events. Hence, conscious and unconscious memories were mentally integrated into a linked mnemonic representation.

Keywords: episodic memory, unconscious, masking, subliminal, associations, flexibility, compositionality, memory systems

INTRODUCTION

No event equals another event. But events may share aspects such as a person or an item in the scene. Such commonalities between events help us to bridge events, to integrate information from events, and to make inferences that guide our choices in new situations. We are usually aware of the events that we experience. But the act of our mental integration of memories of several events and its impact on our choices and behaviors may escape our awareness. While most past experiments aimed at investigating memory for single, discrete events, there is mounting evidence that (conscious) memories of multiple events are integrated into networks, which form the basis of inference (Heckers et al., 2004; Preston et al., 2004; Smith and Squire, 2005; Shohamy and Wagner, 2008; Zeithamova and Preston, 2010; Zeithamova et al., 2012). In some experiments, integration and inference were unconscious but the encoding of events was conscious (Greene et al., 2001, 2006; Leo and Greene, 2008). In other experiments, all mental processes were unconscious, namely the processing of subliminal (invisible) events, their mental integration, and resulting inference as measured behaviorally in a test situation (Reber and Henke, 2012; Reber et al., 2012).

Neuroimaging studies in volunteers showed that the hippocampus, a brain structure that is crucial for episodic memory (Tulving, 2002; Squire, 2004), was activated when overlapping events (i.e., events with common components) were experienced and/or when inferences were made in the test situation (Heckers et al., 2004; Preston et al., 2004; Greene et al., 2006; Shohamy and Wagner, 2008; Zeithamova and Preston, 2010; Reber et al., 2012; Zeithamova et al., 2012). Importantly, the hippocampus assisted these mental operations even when they occurred outside conscious awareness (Reber et al., 2012).

A fundamental question concerns whether and how conscious and unconscious memories interact. We ask whether the mental integration of discrete events is possible if consciousness divides between events. This may happen if a first event is experienced consciously, while a second event is experienced unconsciously; or vice versa. We hypothesized that two discrete, overlapping events can be bridged through integration of memory traces across consciousness levels because evidence indicates that memories of unconsciously and consciously experienced events are laid down in the same memory system, namely the hippocampus and related cortices (Henke et al., 2003; Degonda et al., 2005; Reber et al., 2012). Hence interactions between conscious and unconscious memory traces in this study are thought to occur within the same memory system and not between different memory systems. Earlier reports of implicit-explicit interactions concerned psychologically and neuroanatomically separate memory systems that either cooperated or competed in the process of learning a material or a certain procedure (Wagner et al., 2000; Poldrack et al., 2001; Voermans et al., 2004; Moses et al., 2010). Here, we study implicit-explicit interactions within a single memory system, namely episodic memory or the medial temporal lobe memory system, whose output is either accessible or inaccessible to conscious awareness depending on the input – subliminal versus supraliminal. We expect conscious and unconscious memory representations to be integrated into a cohesive memory space that guides choices in a test situation.

An event was operationalized as the visual presentation of two unrelated words, such as "tree desk." In the case of "unconscious events," word pairs were presented subliminal, i.e., for 17 ms and flanked by pattern masks. In the case of "conscious events," word pairs were presented supraliminal (visible). Half of word pairs shared one word, e.g., "tree desk" and "desk fish," and were therefore overlapping (experimental condition). The other half of word pairs was non-overlapping because they shared no words (control condition) (**Figure 1**). To examine whether integration success is modulated by intervening time and trials, we varied the number of word pairs that intervened two overlapping word pairs by presenting 1, 5, 9, or 13 word pairs in-between. Of the two corresponding word pairs, the first was presented subliminal and the second supraliminal to half of participants, reversed for the other half of participants. We hypothesized that overlapping events would be integrated across consciousness levels irrespective of whether the first or the second event was processed consciously. Either way, a successful integration of word pairs across events and across consciousness levels presupposes that within-event associations be established. The test of integration was given 1 min following encoding. This test required participants to judge whether two supraliminal words fit together semantically or not. The two test words were either unrelated (control condition) or episodically related (e.g., "tree fish") through two distinct events ("tree desk"... "desk fish") that shared one word (experimental condition) (**Figure 1**). Words in test pairs of both conditions had been seen during encoding; one word with and the other word without consciousness. The only difference between conditions was the unconscious episodic link between test words. The mental integration of overlapping events was expected to change the speed of participants' decisions and/or the outcome

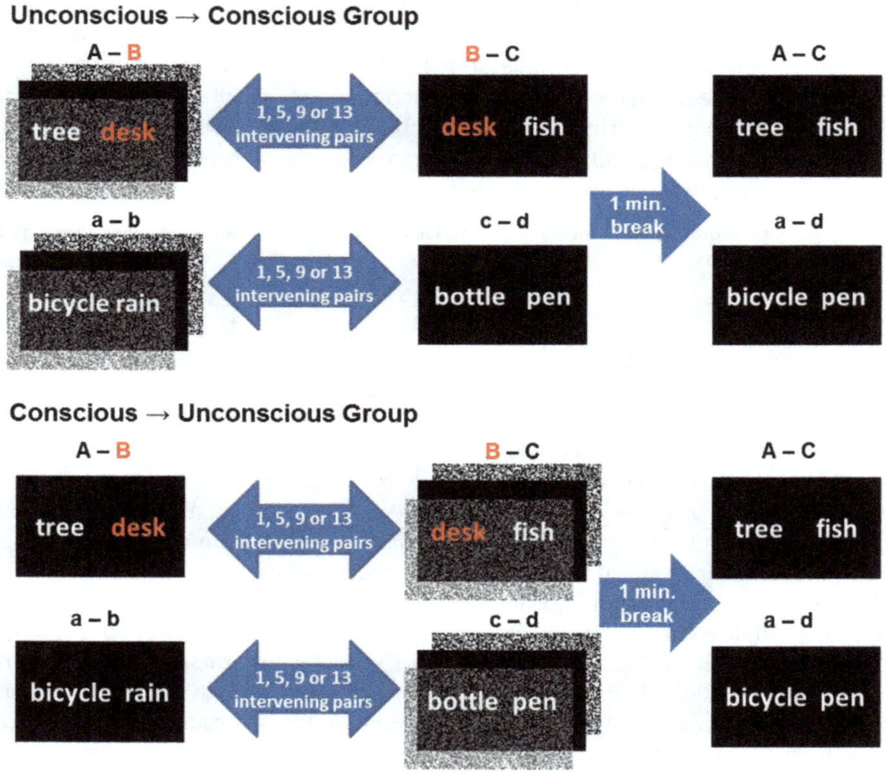

FIGURE 1 | Design. An event consisted of the presentation of two unrelated words. Participants experienced two overlapping (experimental condition; overlap indicated in red) or non-overlapping (control condition) encoding events. The temporal distance and amount of distraction given between two corresponding overlapping and non-overlapping events was varied in four levels with 1, 5, 9, or 13 word pairs presented in-between. Depending on the group assignment, either the first or the second encoding event was presented subliminal for unconscious encoding. The subliminal presentation mode is graphically illustrated by forward and backward pattern masks. We refer to overlapping word pairs presented in the experimental condition as A–B and B–C and to non-overlapping word pairs presented in the control condition as a–b, c–d. Words in test events were presented supraliminal. A and C words from the two encoding events were re-presented at test to induce the retrieval of the common counterpart (B) in the experimental condition. In the control condition, a and d words were re-presented at test, each of which could activate its respective counterpart (b or c), but no common counterpart. Hence retrieval words given in the control condition were not episodically related by a word that was part of both encoding events.

of their decisions at test (Reber and Henke, 2012; Reber et al., 2012).

MATERIALS AND METHODS

PARTICIPANTS

Sixty students participated in the study (age: 19–35 years, $M = 22.95$, SD = 3.10; 40 women; six left-handers). At the point of testing, all participants had already 12 years of education. Exclusion criteria were a native language other than German, suboptimal visual acuity, a history of neurological or psychiatric disorders, and the consumption of legal or illegal drugs. Participants were kept naïve regarding the study purpose and the presentation of subliminal stimuli. We misinformed participants initially that we investigated attention and word processing alone, but participants were fully debriefed following the main experiment. The study was approved by the local ethics committee.

MATERIALS AND DESIGN

The 384 German nouns of the main experiment were arranged to 192 semantically unrelated pairs that we presented to participants for conscious and unconscious encoding. These 192 word pairs were divided into two stimulus lists: one list was used for the experimental and the other for the control condition (96 word pairs per list/condition). Word overlaps were introduced in 48 couples of pairs (short hand: A–B, B–C; **Figure 1**) in list 1, which half of participants received for integrative encoding in their experimental condition. This half of participants received the 96 non-overlapping word pairs (short hand: a–b, c–d; **Figure 1**) of list 2 for non-integrative encoding in their control condition. The other half of participants received list 1 in the control condition and list 2 in the experimental condition. Accordingly, word overlaps were introduced in the 48 couples of pairs in list 2 for integrative encoding, while word pairs in list 1 were left non-overlapping. Importantly, all participants received the same word pairs for retrieval, counterbalanced between conditions. Hence, words in a given retrieval word pair were episodically related for half of participants (experimental condition) but unrelated for the other half of participants (control condition). Retrieval word pairs in both conditions consisted of the left-hand word of the first encoding word pair followed by the right-hand word of the corresponding second encoding word pair.

Stimuli of the experimental and the control condition were assigned to 12 sets that were used in 12 encoding-retrieval runs (**Figure 2**). Each run contained eight overlapping encoding word pairs in the experimental condition (A–B, B–C), eight non-overlapping encoding word pairs in the control condition (a–b, c–d), and four retrieval word pairs both in the experimental condition (A–C) and the control condition (a–d). The assignment of the 12 stimulus sets to runs was random. The practice run given before the main experiment was designed identical to the 12 experimental runs.

APPARATUS

The experiment took place in a dark room. A digital light processing (DLPTM) video beamer with a refresh rate of 60 Hertz projected the stimuli on a white screen positioned 2 m in front of the participant. The participant sat in a chair with his/her head fixated on a chin rest. The stimulated visual field spanned 10 (height) × 13 (width) degrees. For stimulus presentation we used the software Presentation ®(http://www.neurobs.com/). All responses were recorded with a standard computer mouse.

PROCEDURE

Encoding

The first encoding word pair was presented subliminal and the corresponding second word pair supraliminal for half of participants ("unconscious → conscious group") and vice versa for the other half of participants ("conscious → unconscious group") (see **Figure 2**). If word pairs appeared supraliminal (presentation duration: 3.5 s; inter-stimulus interval: 1 s), participants decided for each pair whether the two words fit together semantically or not (fit/don't fit task). This task invokes mental comparison processes that provide for incidental paired-associative semantic encoding of words. Because words in pairs were not closely associated semantically, participants were encouraged to relax their response criterion to arrive at about 50% fit responses. Participants were informed that closely related words such as "needle – yarn" would not be presented. Instead, word pairs such as "cow – grill" would be presented. Although such words are rather remote semantically, they may still elicit a "fit" answer because beef for example is a popular sort of meat for barbecues.

When word pairs were subliminal, participants perceived a flickering stream of pattern masks and simultaneously performed an attention task on images that were embedded in the sequence of subliminal words and pattern masks. We used the masking paradigm of our previous studies on subliminal encoding (Degonda et al., 2005; Duss et al., 2011; Reber and Henke, 2011, 2012; Reber et al., 2012; see "Subliminal Stimulus Presentation and Attention Task"). An instruction slide presented before the block of eight subliminal encoding pairs and the block of eight supraliminal encoding pairs prepared participants for their up-coming task (**Figure 2**). Time and trials between two corresponding word pairs were manipulated; we presented 1, 5, 9, or 13 word pairs in-between two corresponding encoding word pairs (**Figure 2**). Word pairs were randomly assigned to interval levels. Following encoding, participants took a 1-min break that served as a mini consolidation phase.

Retrieval

To test for relational integration, we presented four retrieval pairs in each condition. The order of these eight pairs was randomly generated for each participant and each run. Retrieval word pairs were presented in the same fashion (presentation duration: 3.5 s; inter-stimulus interval: 1 s) and with the same task (fit/don't fit task) as supraliminal encoding word pairs.

Subliminal stimulus presentation and attention task

We used the masking paradigm of our previous studies on subliminal encoding (Degonda et al., 2005; Duss et al., 2011; Reber and Henke, 2011, 2012; Reber et al., 2012). Each encoding word pair was flashed 12 times for 17 ms within a time window of 6 s that constituted one encoding trial. Word pairs were flanked by black and white dot pattern masks that were presented for 183 ms. In this

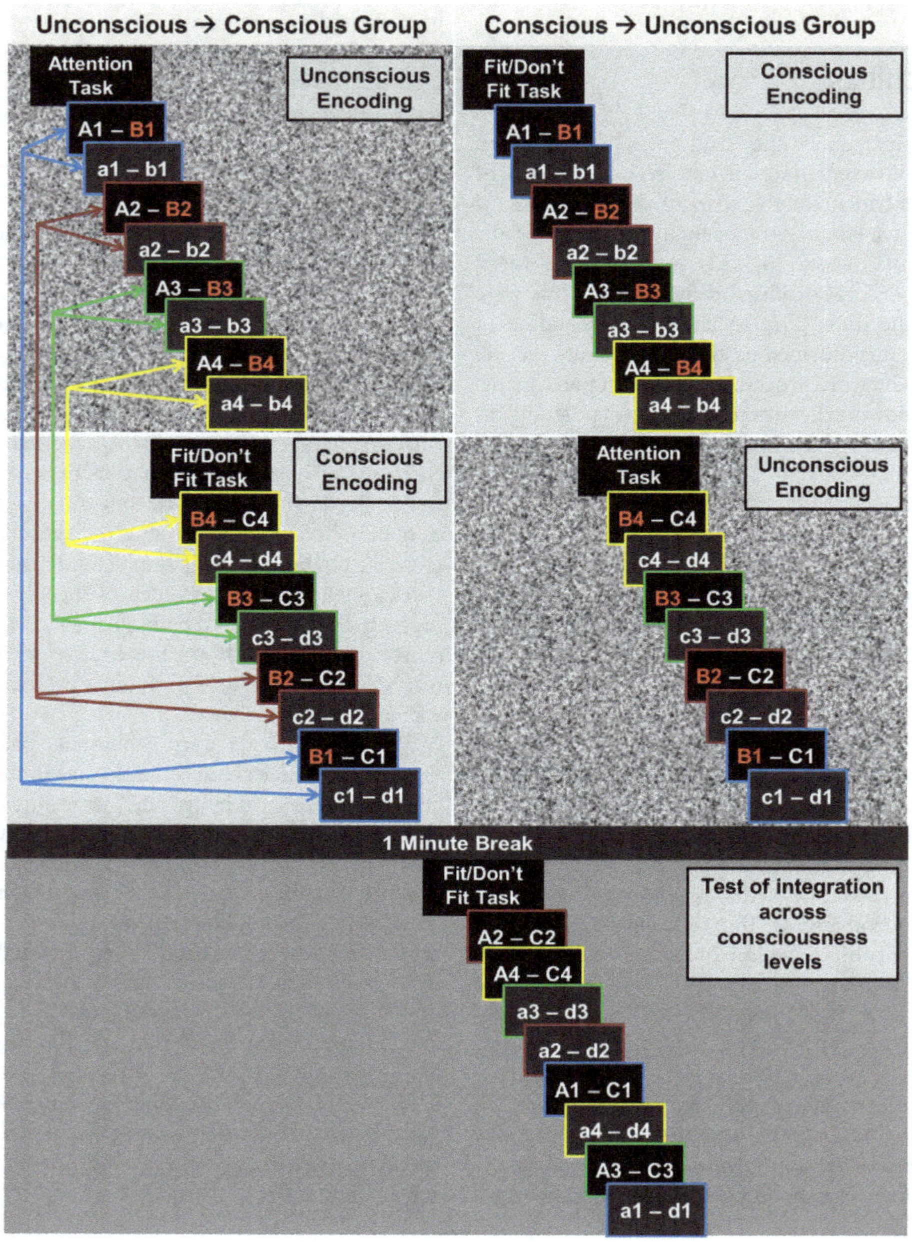

FIGURE 2 | Experimental procedure. The experiment consisted of 12 encoding-test runs. Here, we illustrate the procedure of one run. For the unconscious → conscious group (left-hand upper panel), the first encoding word pair (A–B and a–b) was presented subliminally (illustrated by the visual noise background) and the second, corresponding encoding word pair supraliminally (B–C and c–d). This order was reversed for the conscious → unconscious group of participants (right-hand upper panel). Corresponding encoding word pairs were overlapping in the experimental condition (A–**B**, **B**–C; overlaps depicted in red) and non-overlapping in the control condition (a–b, c–d). The distance between two corresponding encoding word pairs was varied fourfold with 1, 5, 9, or 13 intervening word pairs. The four distance levels are highlighted with color-coded arrows and color-coded image-frames. The same distances applied to the procedure in the conscious → unconscious group (arrows are omitted in right-hand panel). A break of 1 min separated encoding and test. Test trials of the experimental and the control condition were presented in random order and with supraliminal duration for participants in both groups. Both in supraliminal encoding and supraliminal test trials, participants decided whether the two words of a pair fit together semantically or not. During subliminal trials, participants performed an attention task.

stream of subliminal word pairs and pattern masks, we embedded an attention task for participants to stay focused and direct gaze at the screen center. The attention task required participants to fixate a repeatedly flashed central fixation cross and to indicate when the fixation cross was replaced by a horizontal or vertical line segment (push left or right key, respectively). The fixation cross was presented for 233 ms at a rate of one Hertz. The fixation cross was replaced only once by a line segment at a random time point within the 6-s time window that constituted a trial.

TEST OF AWARENESS

Following the main experiment, participants underwent a structured interview to find out whether they had noticed or suspected the presence of subliminal stimuli in the experiment. Next, participants were informed of subliminal word pairs in the experiment. Finally, they took an objective awareness test to assess their ability to consciously discern subliminal word pairs or fragments thereof. Participants were instructed to try to discern a subliminal word pair and to match it to a subsequently presented identical or different word pair on a trial-by-trial basis. While instructions in the main experiment were indirect not alluding to subliminal word pairs, instructions in the test of awareness were direct. Direct tests are predominantly sensitive to conscious rather than unconscious processes (Reingold and Merikle, 1988; Snodgrass and Shevrin, 2006) and therefore yield a measure of conscious access to subliminal stimuli. Indirect tests are predominantly sensitive to unconscious rather than conscious processes. We aimed at indirectly measured effects of unconscious processing with no directly measured effects of conscious word detection (Reingold and Merikle, 1988; Greenwald et al., 1995). The test of awareness was different for the two experimental groups because subliminal words (B words in B–C pairs) were primed by previously perceived supraliminal words (A–B pairs) in the conscious → unconscious group but not the unconscious → conscious group.

Test of awareness for the unconscious → conscious group

The test of awareness included 96 trials. Each trial consisted of the subliminal presentation of one word pair followed by the supraliminal presentation of either the same or a different word pair (**Figure 3**). The masking paradigm and psychophysical conditions applied in the main experiment were again applied in the test of awareness. Participants were instructed to attend to the subliminal presentation of a word pair, while doing the attention task, and then to indicate by button press whether the subsequently presented visible word pair corresponded to the subliminal word pair (target) or not (distractor). Supraliminal targets and distractors stayed on the screen till participants responded. The probability of targets was 50%.

Test of awareness for the conscious → unconscious group

This awareness test included 96 trials as well, but these trials were divided into six runs that each contained 16 subliminal-supraliminal test trials. As in this group's main experiment, each run started off with the supraliminal presentation of eight A–B word pairs for participants to decide whether words in a pair fit together or not (fit/don't fit task). This preactivation was followed by the 16 subliminal-supraliminal test trials. The presentation order of the 16 trials was randomized. Eight of the 16 trials contained subliminal pairs with a primed B word (B–C trials)

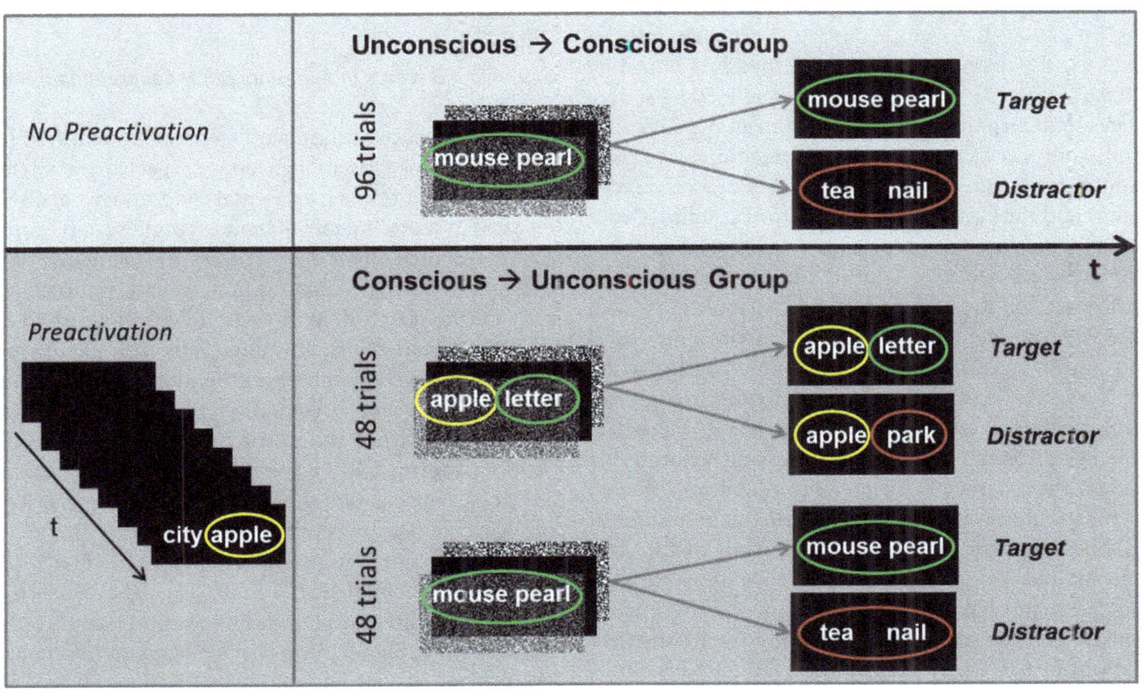

FIGURE 3 | Design of the test of awareness. Following the main experiment, participants took an objective awareness test to assess their ability to consciously discern subliminal word pairs or fragments thereof. Participants were instructed to try to discern a subliminal word pair and to match it to a subsequently presented identical (target) or different (distractor) word pair on a trial-by-trial basis. The test of awareness was different for the two experimental groups because subliminal words (B words in B–C pairs) were primed by previously perceived supraliminal words (A–B pairs) in the conscious → unconscious group (bottom panel) but not the unconscious → conscious group (top panel). *t*, time.

and eight trials contained subliminal pairs with unprimed words (**Figure 3**). Each of the subliminally presented word pairs was immediately followed by a supraliminal word pair (target or distractor) for participants to indicate by button press whether the visible word pair was identical to the subliminal word pair or not. In trials where subliminal word pairs were unprimed, targets were equal to subliminal words and distracters differed (as for the unconscious → conscious group). However, in trials where the first word in a subliminal pair was primed (e.g., apple), targets were equal to subliminal words, while distractors were composed of the same first word (e.g., apple) plus a second new word (e.g., park) (**Figure 3**). Hence, both targets and distractors contained the primed word (e.g., apple). This circumstance allowed us to test only for the perceptual processing of subliminal new words that were presented besides the primed words in pairs. Hence, with this procedure we could not test for a perceptual advantage of the primed words contained in subliminal pairs. Even if only the targets, but not the distractors, would contain a primed word (e.g., apple), participants' selections would still fail to indicate whether the subliminal processing of primed words is facilitated because the absence versus presence of a previously seen (during preactivation) and probably remembered word would skew selections in favor of targets.

STATISTICAL ANALYSES

For the analysis of performance accuracy at test, we computed the rate of each participant's fit responses to A–C pairs (experimental condition) and to a–d pairs (control condition) by dividing the total of fit responses by the respective total of given responses. The rate of fit responses was also computed for each encoding interval (1, 5, 9, or 13 word pairs between two corresponding encoding word pairs; see **Figure 2**). Trials with RTs below 500 ms were excluded. Rates of fit responses were analyzed in an ANOVA with the two within-subjects factors Condition (experimental versus control condition) and Encoding Interval (1, 5, 9, or 13 intervening word pairs) and the between-subjects factor Encoding Order (unconscious → conscious versus conscious → unconscious). For the analysis of reaction latency, RTs of fit and don't fit responses were z-transformed with respect to the RT distribution of each participant. RTs with z-values deviating more than 2 SDs from a participant's mean were excluded. We computed each participant's mean RT for A–C pairs (experimental condition) and a–d pairs (control condition) and per encoding interval. Mean RTs were analyzed in an ANOVA that included the same factors as the ANOVA used for the accuracy data (rate of fit responses).

We also computed mean RTs of fit and don't fit responses to supraliminal encoding word pairs. For participants of the conscious → unconscious group, supraliminal encoding word pairs were A–B and a–b word pairs. For participants of the unconscious → conscious group, supraliminal encoding word pairs were B–C and c–d word pairs. Differences in mean RT between conditions were tested for significance with a paired-samples t-test.

RESULTS

TEST OF AWARENESS: PERFORMANCE AT CHANCE LEVEL

As in the main experiment, trials with RTs below 500 ms were excluded from the analysis. Rates of correct answers (hits plus correct rejections) in the test of awareness deviated from chance performance (0.50) neither in the unconscious → conscious group [$M \pm \text{SE} = 0.51 \pm 0.01$; $t(29) = 0.969$, $p = 0.341$; 96 trials] nor the conscious → unconscious group [$M \pm \text{SE} = 0.50 \pm 0.01$; $t(29) = -0.407$, $p = 0.687$; 96 trials]. Discrimination performance in the latter group remained at chance level, when preactivation trials [$M \pm \text{SE} = 0.49 \pm 0.01$; $t(29) = -0.601$, $p = 0.553$] and trials without preactivation [$M \pm \text{SE} = 0.50 \pm 0.01$; $t(29) = 0.158$, $p = 0.876$] were analyzed separately.

Binomial tests computed for every participant revealed that two of the 60 participants yielded a relatively good discrimination performance that reached a probability of 10% or lower (one-tailed) to be obtained by chance alone. Furthermore, one participant reported to have consciously perceived subliminal letters during the main experiment. However, this person's performance in the test of awareness was at chance level. We decided to exclude these three participants from the analysis of the data from the main experiment. Accordingly, 28 participants remained in the unconscious → conscious group and 29 in the conscious → unconscious group.

CONSCIOUS AND UNCONSCIOUS ENCODING OF EVENTS

Good accuracy on the attention task

Performance accuracy on the attention task given during subliminal trials was good and did not differ between the two experimental groups [$t(37.956) = -0.982$, $p = 0.332$, adjusted degrees of freedom because equality of variances was not assumed]. The unconscious → conscious group yielded a hit rate of 0.88 ± 0.02 ($M \pm \text{SE}$) and the conscious → unconscious group of 0.90 ± 0.01 ($M \pm \text{SE}$).

Subliminal B words in A–B pairs primed supraliminal B words in B–C pairs

As a consequence of the encoding of subliminal A–B pairs in the unconscious → conscious group, we expected a facilitated processing (priming) in the experimental condition, where B words were repeated in supraliminal B–C pairs. A premise of B word priming is a compositional rather than unitized representation of B words in A–B and B–C pairs. A compositional mental representation allows both for the reactivation of each individual part in a representation (A; B) and the reactivation of the complete representation (A–B). A unitized mental representation, however, would require the repeated visual presentation of the complete initial word pair (A–B), not just the B word, to trigger a reactivation of the previously formed A–B representation. Our data spoke for a compositional representation of subliminal A–B pairs. Responses to supraliminal B–C pairs were faster ($M \pm \text{SE} = 2106 \pm 71$ ms) than responses to supraliminal c–d pairs ($M \pm \text{SE} = 2163 \pm 78$ ms) [$t(27) = 3.502$, $p = 0.002$, $r^2 = 0.312$]. The absence of a corresponding difference in the processing speed of supraliminal A–B ($M \pm \text{SE} = 2138 \pm 68$ ms) versus supraliminal a–b pairs ($M \pm \text{SE} = 2147 \pm 65$ ms) [$t(28) = 0.440$, $p = 0.663$] in the conscious → unconscious group substantiates the interpretation in terms of priming.

TEST PERFORMANCE: SUCCESSFUL INTEGRATION OF EVENTS

We computed an ANOVA with the two within-subjects factors Condition and Encoding Interval as well as the between-subjects factor Encoding Order. The dependent variable was the rate of fit responses given at test. This ANOVA yielded a significant main effect of Condition (**Figure 4**). Participants gave more fit responses to episodically related A–C pairs ($M \pm SE = 0.38 \pm 0.02$) versus unrelated a–d pairs ($M \pm SE = 0.36 \pm 0.02$), $F(1,55) = 5.310$, $p = 0.025$, $\eta^2_{partial} = 0.088$. This effect of Condition interacted neither with Encoding Interval [$F(3,165) = 0.011$, $p = 0.999$] nor with Encoding Order [$F(1,55) = 0.263$, $p = 0.610$]. There was no main effect of Encoding Interval [$F(3,165) = 0.234$, $p = 0.872$], no significant interaction of Encoding Interval with Encoding Order [$F(3,165) = 1.156$, $p = 0.328$], and no three-way interaction of Condition with Encoding Interval and Encoding Order [$F(3,165) = 0.379$, $p = 0.768$]. The means (±SE) of the rate of fit responses were almost identical between encoding intervals (1 pair, 5 pairs, 9 pairs, 13 pairs) both for the experimental condition ($M_{1pair} = 0.38 \pm 0.03$; $M_{5pairs} = 0.38 \pm 0.02$; $M_{9pairs} = 0.38 \pm 0.02$; $M_{13pairs} = 0.40 \pm 0.02$) and the control condition ($M_{1pair} = 0.36 \pm 0.02$; $M_{5pairs} = 0.36 \pm 0.02$; $M_{9pairs} = 0.36 \pm 0.02$; $M_{13pairs} = 0.37 \pm 0.03$). However, the between-subjects factor Encoding Order reached significance [$F(1,55) = 5.294$, $p = 0.025$, $\eta^2_{partial} = 0.088$]. A potential reason for this main effect might be the unconscious → conscious group's criterion for generating fit responses, which might be looser yielding more fit responses ($M \pm SE = 0.41 \pm 0.02$) than the conscious → unconscious group ($M \pm SE = 0.34 \pm 0.02$). In support of this interpretation, the unconscious → conscious group also generated more fit responses during supraliminal encoding (B–C and c–d pairs; $M \pm SE = 0.45 \pm 0.02$) than the conscious → unconscious group (A–B and a–b pairs; $M \pm SE = 0.36 \pm 0.02$) [$t(52.605) = 3.256$, $p = 0.002$, $r^2 = 0.167$, adjusted degrees of freedom because equality of variances was not assumed].

Reaction latencies at test were comparable between the experimental (A–C; $M \pm SE = 1942 \pm 46$ ms) and the control condition [a–d; $M \pm SE = 1952 \pm 45$ ms; $t(56) = 0.854$, $p = 0.397$]. This absence of an integration effect on reaction speed was also reflected in the non-significance of all results of an ANOVA that included the same factors as the ANOVA on the rates of fit responses (all $Fs < 2.469$, all $ps > 0.122$). Hence, the mental integration of events across levels of consciousness influenced the type but not the speed of responses given at test.

CONSCIOUS WORD DISCRIMINATION DID NOT ASSIST THE UNCONSCIOUS INTEGRATION OF EVENTS

Using the regression method described by Greenwald et al. (1995), we found that discrimination performance in the test of awareness [(hits + correct rejections) – (false alarms + misses)] was not significantly associated with the increase in the rate of fit responses given to episodically related versus unrelated test words [$B = -0.314 \pm 0.184$, $\beta = -0.224$, $t(55) = -1.705$, $p = 0.094$; $N = 57$]. However, the y-axis intercept in this regression was significantly larger than zero [intercept $= 0.023 \pm 0.010$, $t(55) = 2.309$, $p = 0.025$, $r^2 = 0.088$]. This indicates that the unconscious integration of events was significant, when discrimination performance in the test of awareness was zero (**Figure 4**).

DISCUSSION

We asked whether the mental integration of discontiguous events is possible if consciousness divides between events because one event is experienced consciously and the other unconsciously. An event was operationalized as the visual presentation of two unrelated words that were either presented supraliminal for conscious inspection or subliminal for unconscious processing. At the test

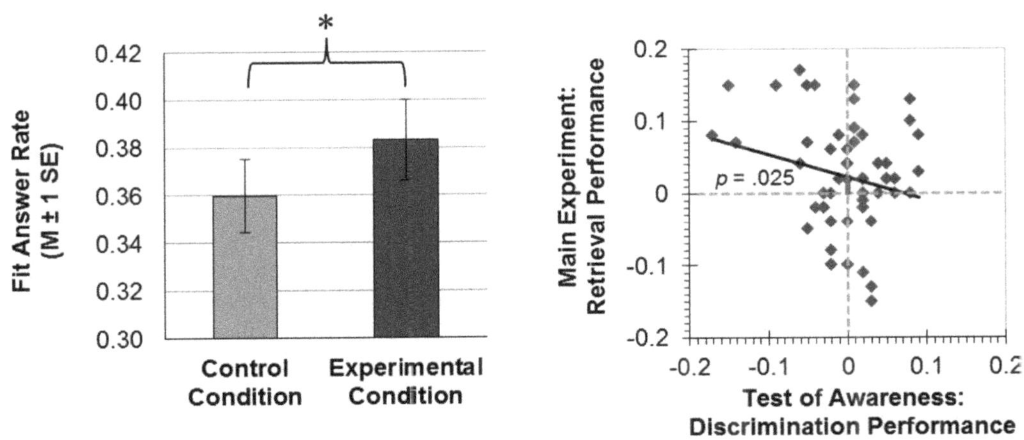

FIGURE 4 | Results. Left-hand panel: at the test of integration across consciousness levels, participants gave more fit answers in the experimental than the control condition (*$p < 0.05$; M, mean; SE, standard error of the mean). Subliminal and supraliminal encoding word pairs had shared a word in the experimental condition, which lent these word pairs to integration that manifested in biased semantic decisions at test (more fit responses). Right-hand panel: using the regression method of Greenwald et al. (1995), we regressed the discrimination performance in the test of awareness [(hits + correct rejections) – (false alarms + misses)] onto the rate of fit responses given to episodically related (experimental condition) minus unrelated (control condition) test words. The y-axis intercept was significantly greater than zero. This indicates that the integration of events across consciousness levels was significant, when conscious discrimination performance was zero.

of integration, we presented a word from the unconscious event besides a word from the corresponding conscious event in both the experimental and the control condition. These test words were semantically unrelated. But test words in the experimental condition were episodically related by a word (not present in the test trial) that had been the counterpart of each of the test words drawn from the two encoding events. Test words in the control condition were episodically unrelated. Episodically related versus unrelated test words were more often judged as closely related semantically. It thus appears that episodic associations intruded into judgments of semantic distance leading to more fit responses in the experimental versus the control condition. This effect is known from studies with supraliminal stimulus presentations: two unrelated words that had been presented in the same encoding context and were episodically (but not semantically) related, appeared closer semantically than words that had not been presented in the same encoding context; or they appeared equally close as words that were related semantically (McKoon and Ratcliff, 1979, 1986; Dosher and Rosedale, 1991; Patterson et al., 2009; Coane and Balota, 2011). This line of research suggests that connections between mental representations or between nods in the semantic network, which have been co-activated in the same encoding context, acquire a greater linkage strength leading to the impression of stronger conceptual relatedness. The co-occurrence of concepts in naturalistic events is indeed one way how the semantic system may be dynamically (re)organized throughout life (Coane and Balota, 2011). Although test words in the present experimental condition had not occurred in the same encoding context but in two different encoding contexts, they were linked by a third word that was presented in both encoding contexts. This mediated linkage between test words had apparently sufficed to decrease the perceived semantic distance between test words. Remarkably, this was possible with one of the two events processed outside consciousness.

Do these modifications in participants' semantic systems result from plastic chances in the neocortex alone or from additional plastic changes in the medial temporal lobe, particularly the hippocampus? The hippocampus is ordinarily assisting the rapid encoding of events by association formation between co-activated areas of the neocortex (Teyler and DiScenna, 1986; Treves and Rolls, 1994). Our task structure and results speak to a hippocampal role because encoding was rapid (one-trial) and memory representations must have been compositional and flexible (Cohen and Eichenbaum, 1993; Henke, 2010). There was no neuroimaging in the present study but earlier neuroimaging studies give a clue. Reber et al. (2012) used a similar design but presented all encoding events subliminally. There was hippocampal activation during the unconscious encoding of overlapping events and during judgments of semantic distance made on episodically related word pairs presented at test. Moreover, hippocampal activity measured during the encoding of overlapping subliminal events predicted judgments of semantic distance at test. The hippocampus was also activated in studies using supraliminal stimuli, either at the time when overlapping events were encoded or when inferences were made at test (Heckers et al., 2004; Preston et al., 2004; Greene et al., 2006; Shohamy and Wagner, 2008; Zeithamova and Preston, 2010; Zeithamova et al., 2012). Because the hippocampus played a role both in studies of inference that used supraliminal encoding events and in a study that used subliminal encoding events, we assume that the hippocampus is also engaged when encoding events were both conscious and unconscious. Increasing evidence suggests that the hippocampus engages in all tasks that require the rapid encoding of new, compositional, and flexible associations irrespective of the level of consciousness of stimulus processing (Henke, 2010).

The absence of an effect of time/stimuli between two overlapping encoding events on test performance replicates our previous result of the successful integration of two discrete subliminal events, which was also unaffected by intervening time/stimuli (Reber and Henke, 2012). The lack of a temporal distance effect in these two experiments is intriguing given previous evidence that temporal contiguity influences the retrieval from episodic memory (Temporal Context Model; Howard and Kahana, 1999; Howard et al., 2005). Core assumptions of the Temporal Context Model entail context-representations that change gradually over time and that act as retrieval cues for the items learned in the same contexts. Because items that are learned in close temporal proximity have similar contexts, they are more likely to be recalled (Howard and Kahana, 1999). If an encoding item is shown twice to boost learning, the context of its second presentation will resemble the context of its first presentation due to its presence at both moments in time. In our study, B words must have induced contiguity between the two overlapping encoding events A–B and B–C. The presence of B words in both encoding events may have rendered the two events more independent of their temporal (dis)contiguity (Howard et al., 2005). In other words, the configurational contiguity induced by the presence of B words in both overlapping events may have anchored and linked the two events to the extent of neutralizing potential adverse effects of temporal discontiguity (and interfering information) presented between overlapping events (Howard et al., 2005).

The current design does not allow pinning down the time point at which the integration of conscious and unconscious memories took place – at encoding or test. Either way, representations of unconscious events must have been solid and stable over time because test performance was not modulated by whether the unconscious event was preceding or following the corresponding conscious event. Hence, conscious and unconscious memory traces could be integrated independently of the order, in which the memory traces were formed. If integration of memory traces occurred at test, it may have been advantageous to encode the conscious event first because consciously acquired memories are stronger and decay not as rapidly as unconsciously acquired memories; after all, the time interval between the first event and the final test was as long as 170 s. Under the assumption that memories are integrated at retrieval, the lack of an order effect means that conscious and unconscious memories outlasted this time period equally well. If participants integrated memories already when the second encoding event was presented, the first memory trace had to outlast 7–72 s, which was certainly the case for both unconscious and conscious memories. The absence of an order effect additionally suggests that it was not easier to link an unconscious (weak) representation to a pre-existing conscious (strong) representation than vice versa. Hence, for these time intervals, the lack of an order effect suggests that unconscious memories were on a par with conscious memories regarding their endurance and flexibility.

We had hypothesized that conscious and unconscious memory representations could be integrated into a cohesive memory space assuming that the same memory system supports the encoding of subliminal and supraliminal events (Henke et al., 2003; Degonda et al., 2005; Reber et al., 2012). Yet, such harmonious interactions between explicit and implicit memory may not have been expected given past evidence of dissociations and competing interactions between implicit and explicit memory (Wagner et al., 2000; Poldrack et al., 2001). Such adverse interactions concerned separate memory systems (hippocampal interactions with other structures) that competed in the process of learning the same kind of material or procedure. Our study, however, concerned the encoding of distinct events by the same memory system that works at two different levels of intensity – conscious and unconscious. Furthermore, the information acquired in the first and the second overlapping event was neither identical nor conflicting (as in Degonda et al., 2005) but additive, which may have contributed to the smooth integration of information across consciousness levels.

Given that events can be encoded with and without consciousness by way of the hippocampus and related cortices (Henke et al., 2003; Degonda et al., 2005; Henke, 2010; Reber et al., 2012), the organization of consciously and unconsciously acquired information into a single, cohesive hippocampal memory space appears more economic than the organization of information in two discrete hippocampal memory spaces divided by consciousness. Linked episodic knowledge – conscious or unconscious – informs and guides us better through life than episodic knowledge segmented into levels of representation. Moreover, the level of representation of episodic knowledge is dynamic and shifts over time. A single hippocampal memory space maintains the stability and coherence of its organization when episodic memories shift from unconscious to conscious (Fischer et al., 2006; Drosopoulos et al., 2011; Yordanova et al., 2012) or from conscious to unconscious in the course of consolidation (Saletin et al., 2011).

ACKNOWLEDGMENTS

This research was supported by Grant 320000-114012 from the Swiss National Science Foundation to Katharina Henke.

REFERENCES

Coane, J. H., and Balota, D. A. (2011). Face (and nose) priming for book: the malleability of semantic memory. *Exp. Psychol.* 58, 62–70. doi:10.1027/1618-3169/a000068

Cohen, N. J., and Eichenbaum, H. (1993). *Memory, Amnesia, and the Hippocampal System.* Cambridge, MA: MIT Press.

Degonda, N., Mondadori, C. R. A., Bosshardt, S., Schmidt, C. F., Boesiger, P., Nitsch, R. M., et al. (2005). Implicit associative learning engages the hippocampus and interacts with explicit associative learning. *Neuron* 46, 505–520. doi:10.1016/j.neuron.2005.02.030

Dosher, B. A., and Rosedale, G. (1991). Judgments of semantic and episodic relatedness-common time-course and failure of segregation. *J. Mem. Lang.* 30, 125–160. doi:10.1016/0749-596X(91)90001-Z

Drosopoulos, S., Harrer, D., and Born, J. (2011). Sleep and awareness about presence of regularity speed the transition from implicit to explicit knowledge. *Biol. Psychol.* 86, 168–173. doi:10.1016/j.biopsycho.2010.11.005

Duss, S. B., Oggier, S., Reber, T. P., and Henke, K. (2011). Formation of semantic associations between subliminally presented face-word pairs. *Conscious. Cogn.* 20, 928–935. doi:10.1016/j.concog.2011.03.018

Fischer, S., Drosopoulos, S., Tsen, J., and Born, J. (2006). Implicit learning – explicit knowing: a role for sleep in memory system interaction. *J. Cogn. Neurosci.* 18, 311–319. doi:10.1162/jocn.2006.18.3.311

Greene, A. J., Gross, W. L., Elsinger, C. L., and Rao, S. M. (2006). An FMRI analysis of the human hippocampus: inference, context, and task awareness. *J. Cogn. Neurosci.* 18, 1156–1173. doi:10.1162/jocn.2006.18.7.1156

Greene, A. J., Spellman, B. A., Dusek, J. A., Eichenbaum, H. B., and Levy, W. B. (2001). Relational learning with and without awareness: transitive inference using nonverbal stimuli in humans. *Mem. Cogn.* 29, 893–902. doi:10.3758/BF03196418

Greenwald, A. G., Klinger, M. R., and Schuh, E. S. (1995). Activation by marginally perceptible ("subliminal") stimuli: dissociation of unconscious from conscious cognition. *J. Exp. Psychol. Gen.* 124, 22–42. doi:10.1037/0096-3445.124.1.22

Heckers, S., Zalesak, M., Weiss, A. P., Ditman, T., and Titone, D. (2004). Hippocampal activation during transitive inference in humans. *Hippocampus* 14, 153–162. doi:10.1002/hipo.10189

Henke, K. (2010). A model for memory systems based on processing modes rather than consciousness. *Nat. Rev. Neurosci.* 11, 523–532. doi:10.1038/nrn2850

Henke, K., Treyer, V., Nagy, E. T., Kneifel, S., Dürsteler, M., Nitsch, R. M., et al. (2003). Active hippocampus during nonconscious memories. *Conscious. Cogn.* 12, 31–48. doi:10.1016/S1053-8100(02)00006-5

Howard, M. W., Fotedar, M. S., Datey, A. V., and Hasselmo, M. E. (2005). The temporal context model in spatial navigation and relational learning: toward a common explanation of medial temporal lobe function across domains. *Psychol. Rev.* 112, 75–116. doi:10.1037/0033-295X.112.1.75

Howard, M. W., and Kahana, M. J. (1999). Contextual variability and serial position effects in free recall. *J. Exp. Psychol. Learn. Mem. Cogn.* 25, 923–941. doi:10.1037/0278-7393.25.4.923

Leo, P. D., and Greene, A. J. (2008). Is awareness necessary for true inference? *Mem. Cogn.* 36, 1079–1086. doi:10.3758/MC.36.6.1079

McKoon, G., and Ratcliff, R. (1979). Priming in episodic and semantic memory. *J. Verbal Learning Verbal Behav.* 18, 463–480. doi:10.1016/S0022-5371(79)90255-X

McKoon, G., and Ratcliff, R. (1986). Automatic activation of episodic information in a semantic memory task. *J. Exp. Psychol. Learn. Mem. Cogn.* 12, 108–115. doi:10.1037/0278-7393.12.1.108

Moses, S. N., Brown, T. M., Ryan, J. D., and McIntosh, A. R. (2010). Neural system interactions underlying human transitive inference. *Hippocampus* 20, 894–901. doi:10.1002/hipo.20735

Patterson, M. M., Light, L. L., Van Ocker, J. C., and Olfman, D. (2009). Discriminating semantic from episodic relatedness in young and older adults. *Neuropsychol. Dev. Cogn. B Aging Neuropsychol. Cogn.* 16, 535–562. doi:10.1080/13825580902866638

Poldrack, R. A., Clark, J., Paré-Blagoev, E. J., Shohamy, D., Creso Moyano, J., Myers, C., et al. (2001) Interactive memory systems in the human brain. *Nature* 414, 546–550 doi:10.1038/35107080

Preston, A. R., Shrager, Y., Dudukovic N. M., and Gabrieli, J. D. (2004) Hippocampal contribution to the novel use of relational information in declarative memory. *Hippocampus* 14, 148–152 doi:10.1002/hipo.20009

Reber, T. P., and Henke, K. (2011). Rapid formation and flexible expression of memories of subliminal word pairs. *Front. Psychol.* 2:343. doi:10.3389/fpsyg.2011.00343

Reber, T. P., and Henke, K. (2012). Integrating unseen events over time. *Conscious Cogn.* 21, 953–960. doi:10.1016/j.concog.2012.02.013

Reber, T. P., Luechinger, R., Boesiger, P., and Henke, K. (2012). Unconscious relational inference recruits the hippocampus. *J. Neurosci.* 32, 6138–6148. doi:10.1523/JNEUROSCI.5639-11.2012

Reingold, E. M., and Merikle, P. M. (1988). Using direct and indirect measures to study perception without awareness. *Percept. Psychophys.* 44, 563–575. doi:10.3758/BF03207490

Saletin, J. M., Goldstein, A. N., and Walker, M. P. (2011). The role of sleep in directed forgetting and remembering of human memories. *Cereb. Cortex* 21, 2534–2541. doi:10.1093/cercor/bhr034

Shohamy, D., and Wagner, A. D. (2008). Integrating memories in the human brain: hippocampal-midbrain encoding of overlapping events. *Neuron* 60, 378–389. doi:10.1016/j.neuron.2008.09.023

Smith, C., and Squire, L. R. (2005). Declarative memory, awareness, and transitive inference. *J. Neurosci.* 25, 10138–10146. doi:10.1523/JNEUROSCI.2731-05.2005

Snodgrass, M., and Shevrin, H. (2006). Unconscious inhibition and facilitation at the objective detection threshold: replicable and qualitatively different unconscious perceptual effects. *Cognition* 101, 43–79. doi:10.1016/j.cognition.2005.06.006

Squire, L. R. (2004). Memory systems of the brain: a brief history and current perspective. *Neurobiol. Learn. Mem.* 82, 171–177. doi:10.1016/j.nlm.2004.06.005

Teyler, T. J., and DiScenna, P. (1986). The hippocampus memory indexing theory. *Behav. Neurosci.* 100, 147–154. doi:10.1037/0735-7044.100.2.147

Treves, A., and Rolls, E. T. (1994). Computational analysis of the role of the hippocampus in memory. *Hippocampus* 4, 374–391. doi:10.1002/hipo.450040319

Tulving, E. (2002). Episodic memory: from mind to brain. *Annu. Rev. Psychol.* 53, 1–25. doi:10.1146/annurev.psych.53.100901.135114

Voermans, N. C., Petersson, K. M., Daudey, L., Weber, B., Van Spaendonck, K. P., Kremer, H. P., et al. (2004). Interaction between the human hippocampus and the caudate nucleus during route recognition. *Neuron* 43, 427–435. doi:10.1016/j.neuron.2004.07.009

Wagner, A. D., Maril, A., and Schacter, D. L. (2000). Interactions between forms of memory: when priming hinders new episodic learning. *J. Cogn. Neurosci.* 12(Suppl. 2), 52–60. doi:10.1162/089892900564064

Yordanova, J., Kolev, V., Wagner, U., Born, J., and Verleger, R. (2012). Increased alpha (8-12 Hz) activity during slow wave sleep as a marker for the transition from implicit knowledge to explicit insight. *J. Cogn. Neurosci.* 24, 119–132. doi:10.1162/jocn_a_00097

Zeithamova, D., Dominick, A. L., and Preston, A. R. (2012). Hippocampal and ventral medial prefrontal activation during retrieval-mediated learning supports novel inference. *Neuron* 75, 168–179. doi:10.1016/j.neuron.2012.05.010

Zeithamova, D., and Preston, A. R. (2010). Flexible memories: differential roles for medial temporal lobe and prefrontal cortex in cross-episode binding. *J. Neurosci.* 30, 14676–14684. doi:10.1523/JNEUROSCI.3250-10.2010

6

Hippocampal signatures of episodic memory: Evidence from single-unit recording studies

Amy L. Griffin* and Henry L. Hallock

Department of Psychology, University of Delaware, Newark, DE, USA

****Correspondence:***
Amy L. Griffin, Department of Psychology, University of Delaware, 108 Wolf Hall, Newark, DE 19716, USA.
e-mail: amygriff@psych.udel.edu

What hippocampal neural firing patterns signal memory and, more importantly, how is this memory code used by associated structures to translate a memory into a decision or action? Candidate hippocampal activity patterns will be discussed including (1) trajectory-specific firing of place cells with place fields on an overlapping segment of two (or more) distinct trajectories (2) prospective firing of hippocampal neurons that signal an upcoming event or action, and (3) place cell remapping to changes in environment and task. To date, there has not been compelling evidence for any of these activity patterns being the neural substrate of episodic memory. New findings suggest that learning and memory processes are emergent properties of interregional interactions and not localized within any one discrete brain region. Therefore, the next step in understanding how remapping and trajectory coding participate in memory coding may be to investigate how these activity patterns relate to activity in anatomically connected structures such as the prefrontal cortex.

Keywords: place cell remapping, trajectory coding, hippocampal-prefrontal synchrony, electrophysiology, dorsal hippocampus

INTRODUCTION

For decades scientists have been attempting to understand how memories are made, stored, and retrieved in the brain. Unraveling this problem is not only fascinating in its own right, but can lead to the development of treatments for a multitude of disorders and conditions that affect the ability to form and use memories in our day-to-day experiences. In recent years, the development of large-scale neural recording techniques has advanced our knowledge of neural underpinnings behind memory formation and retrieval. However, a challenge that remains in the field is the large degree of uncertainty in linking neural firing patterns with complex cognitive operations. For that reason, despite the many investigations of the neural correlates of memory, much ambiguity remains regarding which brain structures are involved and the nature of their involvement. An extensive body of literature has established the hippocampus as a critical brain structure in episodic memory. Hippocampal lesions (or disruption of hippocampal inputs) lead to performance impairments in tasks that rely on the encoding and retrieval of specific trajectories through a familiar environment. These tasks include the delayed spatial alternation task (Rawlins and Olton, 1982; Brito et al., 1983; Stanton et al., 1984; Aggleton et al., 1995; Czerniawski et al., 2009), the eight-arm radial maze (Olton et al., 1979), and the Morris water maze (Eichenbaum et al., 1990). Recording studies, in turn, are beginning to uncover the exact mechanisms utilized by the hippocampus to accomplish memory processing. The most direct way to study cellular mechanisms that support episodic memory is to record from populations of neurons while animals perform memory tasks. Candidate neural activity patterns that have been linked to episodic memory will be discussed in this review including (1) trajectory-specific firing of place cells with place fields on an overlapping segment of two (or more) distinct trajectories (2) prospective firing of hippocampal neurons (3) place cell remapping to changes in environment and task. Though these phenomena may indeed serve as a neural substrate for episodic memory, a complex process like episodic memory most likely relies on functional interactions among a network of brain regions. Therefore, developing an understanding of these hippocampal activity patterns in the broader context of network interactions could be a critical step in identifying the neural correlates of memory.

HIPPOCAMPAL INVOLVEMENT IN WORKING MEMORY AND SPATIAL COGNITION

Spatial working memory tasks have been an essential tool for developing rodent models of memory. However, during these tasks, there are presumably several processes at work: working memory, the temporary storage of information that is necessary for complex cognitive processes (Baddeley, 1992); spatial cognition, the development and use of a "cognitive map" of the environment (O'Keefe and Nadel, 1978) and episodic encoding and retrieval of specific trajectories through the environment (Hasselmo, 2009). In a typical working memory task, the spatial alternation task, rats are placed on an elevated T-maze and required to alternate between the left and right goal arms on each trial. The task relies on the rat's ability to remember which goal arm was visited on the previous trial in order to correctly select the opposite goal arm. There are two main versions of this task: continuous alternation, in which the rat alternatively visits the left and right goal arms in a "figure 8" pattern, and delayed alternation, in which the rat also alternates visits to the left and right goal arm, but pauses in the start box between trials. Because the insertion of the delay period necessitates remembrance of the previously rewarded goal location, the memory demand is theoretically greater for delayed version of the alternation task than for the continuous version. Accordingly, hippocampal lesions (or disruption of its inputs) lead to performance impairments in delayed alternation (Rawlins and Olton, 1982; Brito et al., 1983; Stanton et al., 1984; Ainge et al., 2007a; Czerniawski et al., 2009), but not continuous alternation (Ainge et al., 2007a). Although these studies have elucidated the brain regions that are necessary for memory, it is unclear if the results can be extrapolated to episodic memory in humans. In fact, episodic memory has been explicitly defined as having a "what" component, a "when" component, and a "where" component and as a process that is not present in animals other than humans (Tulving and Markowitsch, 1998). However, there is strong evidence that episodic memory is not a uniquely human phenomenon. Clayton and Dickinson (1999) have demonstrated that Western scrub jays can remember not only where a food cache was stored, but what type of food it was and how long ago it was cached. The type of memory that includes spatial, temporal information is often called "episodic-like" memory when applied to experimental animals. Fortin et al. (2002) demonstrated that "episodic-like" memory depends on the hippocampus by showing that rats with hippocampal lesions were unable to perform a sequential odor task. Rats were presented with a sequence of five odors and after a 3-min delay were presented with two of the odors and were required to identify which was presented earlier in the sequence. Rats with hippocampal lesions were impaired on this task, but importantly were not impaired on a probe recognition task in which they were required to discriminate between novel and familiar odors. Although this study demonstrated that rats could form hippocampus-dependent "what–when" representations, the "where" component was missing. Subsequent studies showed that rats (Ergorul and Eichenbaum, 2004) and mice (DeVito and Eichenbaum, 2010) were significantly impaired on tasks that required the integration of "what," "when," and "where" information following hippocampal damage. Together, these lesion studies have established the hippocampus as a critical brain region in many types of memory, including episodic memory. In order to examine the physiological properties that give rise to episodic memory, we must turn to studies that have recorded populations of hippocampal neurons in freely moving rats.

SPATIAL CODING IN HIPPOCAMPAL NEURONS

Hippocampal neurons known as place cells code spatial location by showing selective elevations in firing rate when the rat occupies specific locations in an environment (O'Keefe and Nadel, 1978). Although the discovery of hippocampal place cells was a significant advancement in the understanding of hippocampal physiology, it has been difficult to reconcile the human clinical findings that the hippocampus was critical for (non-spatial) episodic memory relative to the rodent findings, which suggested that the hippocampus was a "cognitive map" of the environment and thus participated solely in spatial processing. Additional research soon revealed that current spatial location was not the only factor that modified the behavior of place cells. McNaughton et al. (1983) found that the firing rate of a given place cell could be influenced by the direction in which a rat was heading when the rat passed through the neuron's place field. This place cell "directionality" was observed when rats moved through a radial arm maze, such that a given place cell would show a significantly different firing rate when the rat was headed toward the end of an arm (outbound journeys) than when the rat was headed toward the center of the maze (inbound journeys), and vice versa. This within-field directional coding provided early evidence that principal cells in the hippocampus could respond to an animal's previous and upcoming location in addition to its current location in an environment. However, place cell directionality only appeared under certain experimental conditions. When rats foraged for food in a circular or square open-field enclosure, the firing rates of place cells did not differ significantly as a function of the future or past position of the animal (Breese et al., 1989; Muller et al., 1994). Place cell directionality was again seen when rats performed a spatial navigation task in a radial arm maze, but not when rats performed a non-spatial odor discrimination task (Wiener et al., 1989). These results suggested that directional coding in the hippocampus only appears when an animal moves through a place field in a stereotyped manner, such as when an animal's trajectory through a place field is limited by the experimental apparatus in which testing is taking place.

Could the physical boundaries of an environment be the sole factor in determining whether place cell firing could be modified by an animal's direction? Markus et al. (1995) first recorded place cells while rats navigated through a radial arm maze, and then recorded place cells as rats foraged in an open cylinder. Predictably, the experimenters found that directional coding of place cells was observed in the radial arm maze, but not the open cylinder. However, when the task contingency in the open cylinder was altered so that the animals no longer foraged for randomly distributed food rewards, but were taught to run to the periphery of the cylinder toward reward zones that were sequentially baited, place cells began to display the same directionally modified properties that were observed in the radial arm maze. Thus, directional coding could be influenced by task strategy, even when the task was performed in an open-field environment.

PLACE CELL REMAPPING

Place cells are known to exhibit radical changes in firing properties with sometimes subtle changes in the features of an environment, a property known as "remapping" (for review Muller et al., 1996; Colgin et al., 2008). Operationally, remapping is defined as a change in firing rate and/or place field location in the "new" environment. These changes can manifest themselves in a number of ways: A place cell that ceases to fire; a previously silent place cell that begins to fire; or a place field that shifts to an entirely new location within the environment. The first demonstration of remapping was shown in a study by Muller and Kubie (1987). It was found that doubling the area of a circular or square enclosure caused a subset of place cells to remap. Similarly, in this same study, a population of hippocampal neurons was recorded while rats foraged in both circular and square environments. There was no relationship between the firing field locations in one enclosure and the field location in the other enclosure, suggesting that the hippocampal ensemble had a separate representation for each environment. Following this initial demonstration, Bostock et al. (1991) used a black or white cue card as a polarizing cue in an otherwise-identical recording chamber. The first time that the black card was replaced by the white card, few place cells changed. But, after alternating between the two cards several times, the place cells began to discriminate between the two "environments," with some cells shifting their place field location, some ceasing to fire in one environment and some showing "complex" or "global" remapping: changing in both location and shape. It was hypothesized that remapping allowed the rat to disambiguate similar environments; reducing interference by having populations of hippocampal neurons alter their firing correlates between conditions. This demonstration of remapping after experience with an environment was also seen in investigations of remapping between circular and square enclosures. Lever et al. (2002) recorded the same neurons in two separate enclosures that differed only in shape of the exterior walls: circular or square. As in the Bostock study, the first exposure to the changed environment did not induce a change in the place field locations or shape. However, the neurons began to discriminate between environments after multiple switches. Wills et al. (2005) morphed the recording enclosure gradually from a square to a circle in order to investigate further how hippocampal neurons differentiate between circular and square enclosures. Most hippocampal neurons showed remapping and the remapping was abrupt and consistent across simultaneously recorded cells, suggesting that the hippocampal network codes changes in the environment in a coherent manner. Importantly, it is not only sensory changes in the environment that can induce remapping. As described above, Markus et al. (1995) found that requiring the rat to switch from a foraging strategy to a goal-directed strategy in the same enclosure induced remapping. Similarly, Moita et al. (2004) showed remapping based on whether fear conditioning was performed in the environment.

Recent studies have shown place cell remapping in response to changes in task (in the absence of changes in the spatial layout of the environment). Ferbinteanu et al. (2011) showed that switching from a cue-guided strategy to a spatial strategy prompted place cell remapping. Importantly, the overt behavior of the rat was the same in the two different tasks; only the memory demand differed. Ainge et al. (2012) compared prospective coding across behaviorally identical tasks and showed no differences in the coding behavior of hippocampal neurons between the memory-guided and cue-guided conditions. Conversely, a recent study showed that a large percentage of hippocampal neurons remapped between continuous alternation and conditional discrimination tasks, a phenomenon that was termed "task remapping" (See **Figure 1**; Hallock and Griffin, 2013). When a delay was added to the alternation task, however, there was very little remapping between tasks, suggesting that the temporal structure of the task (discrete vs. continuous trials) was driving the place cell remapping rather than the memory demand of the task (Hallock and Griffin, 2013).

At this point, it is important to distinguish between the two types of remapping seen in hippocampal neural populations. Rate remapping, defined as a significant difference in place field firing rate without a change in place field location, was first reported in response to "local" changes in an environment: changing the wall color or shape of the recording enclosure within the same room (Leutgeb et al., 2005). In contrast, global remapping, defined as changes in place field locations and firing rate, is induced by either physically moving the rat between recording rooms as in Leutgeb et al. (2005) or by changing the recording environment substantially (e.g., Wills et al., 2005). Rate remapping theoretically allows the hippocampus to code different experiences that occur in the same location, whereas global remapping allows similar experiences to be distinguished based on where the experience took place (Leutgeb et al., 2005). The findings showing that place cells do not exclusively code spatial location have led many to speculate that remapping could be a mechanism for linking a spatial location (the "where") to events (the "what" and the "when") occurring in that location (Colgin et al., 2008). Formation of this "what-when-where" representation is a critical component of episodic memory.

TRAJECTORY CODING IN HIPPOCAMPAL NEURONS

Evidence for directional coding and remapping in the hippocampus added another chapter to the cognitive mapping theory of hippocampal function. Place cells could be tied to the current, past, or future spatial location. Directionally dependent firing in the hippocampus also added a possible clue of how hippocampal neurons participated in the formation, storage, and retrieval of contextually unique events that comprise episodic memories. Similar to the argument that place cell remapping could be a mechanism for linking the "where" with the "what" and the "when," the reasoning was that if place fields are present in one situation (e.g., the rat is moving in a particular direction) and absent in another situation, the neurons cannot exclusively be coding spatial location (Wood et al., 2000). It was tempting to speculate that the neurons could be coding memory on top of a place code. Since the pioneering studies on the amnesic patient H.M., who had undergone a surgical procedure to remove large portions of his medial temporal lobe in order to control seizure activity, it had been known that the hippocampus was critical for the formation of new episodic memories (Scoville and Milner, 1957). However, evidence from single-unit recording of hippocampal neurons in animals suggested that the primary role of the hippocampus was spatial processing (O'Keefe and Nadel, 1978). Although spatial mapping and episodic memory are not mutually exclusive, there are many aspects of memory that are non-spatial. Using a continuous non-matching to sample odor task, Wood et al. (1999) found that the majority of recorded hippocampal neurons (~85%) coded for non-spatial variables such as odor, trial type (match vs. non-match), approaching the stimulus cup, or a conjunctive coding of these non-spatial variables with location. These findings suggested that the hippocampus represents both spatial and non-spatial information related to memory. Subsequent studies by Frank et al. (2000) and Wood et al. (2000) began to tease apart the cognitive mapping and episodic memory functions of the hippocampus by recording from hippocampal neurons during tasks in which an animal was required to remember a previously visited location in order to successfully retrieve a reward on an upcoming trial. Wood et al. (2000) showed that when rats ran a continuous spatial alternation task in a T-maze, the majority of neurons with place fields on the stem of the maze showed a significantly higher firing rate during either left- or right-turn trials. Frank et al. (2000) added to this line of research by showing that place cell firing rate could be tied to both past and future location by recording

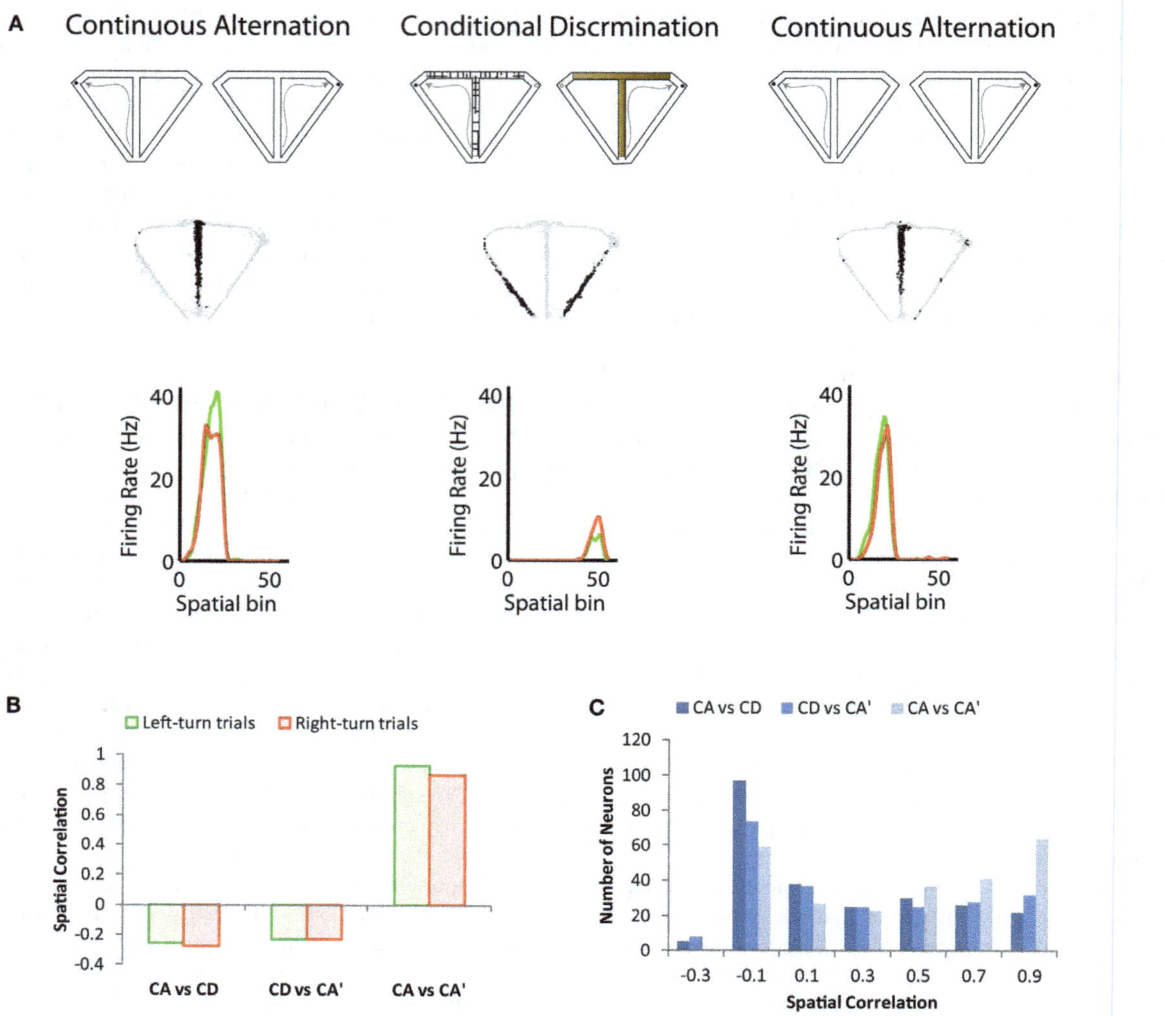

FIGURE 1 | Illustration of task remapping exhibited by dorsal CA1 hippocampal neurons. (A) The top panel is a schematic of the continuous alternation and conditional discrimination tasks. Rats were trained on both tasks prior to implantation of recording microdrives. Recoding sessions consisted of a set of continuous alternation trials, followed by a set of conditional discrimination trials, followed by a second set of continuous alternation trials. The middle panel shows the trajectory of the rat (gray) with superimposed spike locations (black) during the first set of continuous alternation trials (CA, left), a set of conditional discrimination trials (CD, middle), and second set of continuous alternation trials (CA', right). The neuron has a prominent place field on the central stem of the T-maze during both sets of continuous alternation trials, which remaps to the return arms of the T-maze during the set of conditional discrimination trials. The bottom panel shows the average firing rate for left (green) and right (red) trials across 5-cm spatial bins of the T-maze. Spatial bins 1–24 correspond to the central stem region of the maze; 25–26 to the choice point; 27–36 to the goal arm; and 37–55 to the return arm. The neuron does not exhibit trajectory coding as shown by the similar firing rate distributions on left- and right-turn trials. **(B)** Spatial correlation of bin firing rates across the continuous alternation and conditional discrimination tasks for the neuron shown in **(A)**. The spatial correlation is low between the conditional discrimination task and both sets of continuous alteration trials (CA vs. CD and CD vs. CA'), which indicates strong remapping. Conversely, the spatial correlation is high between the two sets of continuous alternation trials (CA vs. CA'). **(C)** Spatial correlation values across tasks for a population of recorded dorsal CA1 neurons. The population showed the same task remapping pattern as the neuron in **(A)**: high correlation values between sets of continuous alternation trials and low correlation values across the conditional discrimination and continuous alternation tasks. Data adapted from Hallock and Griffin (2013).

in a W-maze as rats alternated between the two outside arms via the central arm. This study revealed that firing rate was modulated both during inbound journeys through the central arm (indicative of retrospective coding), and outbound journeys (indicative of prospective coding).

Providing further evidence that hippocampal neurons could flexibly code for both future and past position, Ferbinteanu and Shapiro (2003) recorded from dorsal hippocampus while rats performed a spatial memory task in a plus maze, in which starting location and goal location could be varied. Neuronal firing rate was heavily modified by the trajectory of an animal, with neurons that fired on a start arm selectively signaling journeys to a specific goal arm, and neurons that fired on a goal arm selectively signaling journeys from a specific start arm. Hippocampal neurons display similar trajectory-dependent coding in a maze that has multiple choice points within a journey, as shown during recordings on a concatenated Y-maze (Ainge et al., 2007b). When a delay period is introduced between trials of the T-maze continuous alternation task, neurons cease to show trajectory-specific coding on the maze stem. Instead, neurons that fire during the delay period show firing rates that are modulated by the past or future location of the animal, indicating that trial-specific activity takes place at the location where memory coding that is necessary for contextual disambiguation is most likely to happen (Ainge et al., 2007a; Pastalkova et al., 2008). It has been theorized that this type of trajectory coding is a neural mechanism for memory processing, as hippocampal neurons can fire at different rates in a common location as a function of the animal's future or past position, and thus separate distinct events that occur in common spatial locations (Hasselmo and Eichenbaum, 2005; Smith and Mizumori, 2006; Griffin et al., 2007).

However, evidence from other experiments has challenged the idea that trajectory coding is important for distinguishing between events that contain common features. In one study, trajectory coding was not found as rats alternated continuously between arms of a Y-maze (Lenck-Santini et al., 2001). When rats are running on a circular track, trajectory coding is seen in larger proportion when local cues are present, indicating that levels of sensory input can influence bidirectional coding (Battaglia et al., 2004). Bower et al. (2005) showed that trajectory coding was not necessary for the successful performance of a task in which rats had to disambiguate between journeys that contained repeating elements that were common between different trajectories. Interestingly, trajectory coding did appear in this study, but only under certain circumstances; specifically, when removable barriers were introduced during training, and when rewards were withheld at intermediate steps and only given at the end of a trajectory. Further challenging the notion that trajectory coding is a hippocampal-dependent memory signal, trajectory coding appears in tasks that are not dependent on the integrity of the hippocampus (Wood et al., 2000; Lee et al., 2006; Ferbinteanu et al., 2011; Griffin et al., 2012). Trajectory coding is seen in equal proportion during a spatial task on a plus maze that is hippocampus-dependent, and a cue-approach task on a plus maze that is not hippocampus-dependent (Ferbinteanu et al., 2011). Trajectory coding is seen in a large proportion of hippocampal neurons during the continuous alternation task, which is not dependent on the functional integrity of the hippocampus (Wood et al., 2000; Lee et al., 2006; Griffin et al., 2012). Other studies have found that trajectory coding is not seen during a cue-approach task in a radial arm maze (Berke et al., 2009) and conditional discrimination tasks in T-mazes (Ainge et al., 2012; Griffin et al., 2012). These mixed results indicate that trajectory coding is not simply a mechanism for context-specific encoding in episodic memory, but is rather a complex phenomenon that is influenced by a variety of sensory and behavioral components of experiences.

More recent studies have begun to unravel the links between experience and trajectory coding by manipulating task, duration of exposure, and visual cues surrounding the recording environment. When rats switch from a well-known task strategy to a novel strategy in a W-maze, retrospective coding is seen before rats reach performance levels above chance on the novel task (Ji and Wilson, 2008). In agreement with this finding, Bahar and Shapiro (2012) found that when the goal arm was switched during a well-learned spatial task in a plus maze, prospective and retrospective trajectory coding stayed consistent even when animals were not yet able to perform the new variation of the task. In contrast, when the arrangement of visual cues in the recording room was significantly altered, trajectory coding disappeared and only returned when rats had oriented to the new environmental layout. Upon introduction to a circular track, hippocampal neurons show little directionally dependent variation in firing rate; as rats gain more experience on the track, trajectory coding develops over time (Navratilova et al., 2012). Finally, when rats are trained on both continuous alternation and conditional discrimination in a T-maze, trajectory coding on the maze stem is virtually absent when the rat switches between the two tasks, indicating that experience during task training has a large influence on whether or not trajectory coding will be observed (Hallock and Griffin, 2013). In this same study, prospective trajectory coding was seen when rats switched between delayed alternation and conditional discrimination tasks on the same T-maze. This prospective coding was only observed during the delay period of the delayed alternation task, suggesting that when a delay period is introduced that increases the hippocampal-dependent memory demand of a task, hippocampal neurons may be more likely to display trajectory coding, even when previous training experience would not otherwise favor its development.

The initial discovery that the firing rate of place cells was influenced by the rats' specific trajectory and thus by recent experiences led to speculation that this firing rate difference could be a "rate code" for episodic memory. However, this notion was challenged by the finding that trajectory coding was rarely observed in hippocampus-dependent tasks. After over a decade of research, the debate over whether trajectory coding represents a hippocampal memory signal or perhaps a broader phenomenon that encompasses training history and the structure of the task has not been resolved. More experiments will need to be completed in order to delineate the determining factors that produce trajectory coding during different tasks in different environments. It is clear, however, that both trajectory coding and remapping reflect coding mechanisms for distinguishing between tasks and environments. Remapping tends to occur with changes to the recording environment or task and trajectory coding is a specific type of remapping that occurs within a task when there are continuously overlapping paths toward different goal locations. In order to gain a true appreciation for the content of the information processed by the hippocampus, it may be fruitful to look outside of the hippocampus proper and explore the manner in which the contextual information is communicated to anatomically connected structures.

HIPPOCAMPAL–PREFRONTAL INTERACTIONS DURING MEMORY PROCESSING

Emerging evidence suggests that the neural signature of complex cognitive functions may not reside within an individual brain structure, but in the dynamic interactions that take place within system of related structures. Consistent with this notion, a functional imaging study in humans demonstrated selective activation of both the hippocampus and PFC during a memory task (Stern et al., 2001). The interactions between hippocampus and prefrontal cortex are of particular interest because (1) these structures have been shown to be coactive during memory tasks; (2) there are direct and indirect anatomical connections between them and (3) there is emerging evidence for hippocampal–prefrontal interactions during simple cognitive tasks. Disruption of hippocampus–mPFC interactions may result in failed transfer of spatial and contextual information processed by the hippocampus to the circuitry in mPFC responsible for decision making and goal-directed behavior (Colgin, 2011; Gordon, 2011). The mPFC is known to receive direct monosynaptic glutamatergic input from CA1 and subiculum of hippocampal formation (Ferino et al., 1987; Jay and Witter, 1991; Jay et al., 1992). From this pattern of connections, it is tempting to conclude that the functional interactions between the hippocampus and prefrontal cortex are an important component of complex behavior. Despite many demonstrations of individual contributions of hippocampus and mPFC to memory-guided behavior, the interactions between these two brain regions during complex tasks has not yet been well studied. One way to directly observe a functional interaction is to measure oscillatory synchrony, changes in activity patterns within a specific frequency range that occur simultaneously in disparate brain regions. Two measures of synchrony are *coherence*, a measure that reflects the strength of the temporal relationship between two oscillations and *entrainment*, a measure of the consistency with which action potentials from a neuron in one region occur on a particular phase of an oscillation in another region. In general, theta synchrony appears to be a mechanism used by the hippocampus to convey information to anatomically connected structures, including the mPFC (Siapas and Wilson, 1998; Hyman et al., 2005; Jones and Wilson, 2005; Siapas et al., 2005; Benchenane et al., 2010), as well as the amygdala (Seidenbecher et al., 2003; Popa et al., 2010) and the striatum (Berke et al., 2004; Tort et al., 2008). Hippocampal theta is one of the few sustained oscillations in the brain. It is a ~8 Hz oscillation dominating the hippocampal local field potential during exploration in the rodent (Buzsáki, 2002). Slow oscillations like the hippocampal theta rhythm are well-suited to coordinate interactions between disparate brain regions because the length of the theta cycle is sufficient to accommodate long conduction delays and even polysynaptic interactions. mPFC neurons exhibit strong entrainment to the hippocampal theta rhythm during exploration (Siapas and Wilson, 1998; Hyman et al., 2005) and spatial working memory (Jones and Wilson, 2005; Hyman et al., 2010;), suggesting a functional interaction between hippocampus and mPFC that may be especially important in situations in which demands on working memory are high. A recent study examined hippocampal–prefrontal interactions by performing lesions of the hippocampus and recording from mPFC neurons during a conditioned place preference task in which rats were required to wait in a goal zone before receiving food reward (Burton et al., 2009). Single mPFC neurons showed anticipatory activity during the wait time in the goal zone. Importantly, this activity was diminished in hippocampal-lesioned rats and this disruption was accompanied by impairments in task performance. This anticipatory activity may represent the expectation of forthcoming events. The disruption of this activity in hippocampal-lesioned rats suggests that hippocampal input may provide the mPFC with contextual information that is necessary for the selection of appropriate responses. A crucial next step in this line of research is to examine the link between trajectory coding, remapping, and hippocampal-prefrontal synchrony. It is reasonable to predict that hippocampal neurons that exhibit trajectory coding or remapping would be preferentially entrained to prefrontal activity when memory demand is high, confirming that the neural activity patterns that encode memories encompass a network of interconnected brain regions. Finally, the only way to address the issue of whether there is a causal link between neurophysiological phenomena and memory is to use multiple technical approaches. Therefore, a future direction in the area of memory research should be to combine techniques that measure neural activity patterns such as neurophysiology with inactivation techniques such as pharmacological inactivation of discrete brain regions (e.g., Brandon et al., 2011). The question of whether trajectory coding and remapping persist after disruption of the hippocampal-prefrontal circuit remains an open question.

CONCLUSION

Hippocampal place cell remapping has been demonstrated most commonly in open-field environments. In these environments, the rats are not required to perform any specific task to obtain food reward, but instead must forage for food pellets scattered across the floor. The fact that place cell remapping can be driven not only by changes in the layout of an environment, but also by experiences within that environment suggests that remapping could play a key role in the formation of an episodic memory by linking the "what" and the "when" with the "where." However, because studies that have reported global remapping have manipulated the sensory environment, the evidence so far suggests that remapping is the code for a context change; not an episode within that context. Rate remapping is more often associated with episodic memory in the literature. However, the evidence is simply insufficient at the stage to make statements about its role in episodic memory.

A number of investigations have recorded hippocampal neurons during memory task performance in apparatuses that restrict the rats' movement to a path or trajectory. These tasks include spatial alternation (both delayed and continuous), serial reversals, delayed non-match to position/place, complex sequence tasks, and visuospatial conditional discrimination. Reminiscent of the changes seen in place cell firing properties in response to sensory or cognitive information, some, but not all, of these studies have found that hippocampal neurons code specific trajectories. The most robust demonstrations of trajectory coding have been seen in continuous spatial alternation (Wood et al., 2000; Lee et al., 2006) and serial reversal tasks (Ferbinteanu and Shapiro, 2003).

Interestingly, some tasks that are known to depend on the hippocampus, such as delayed spatial alternation do not elicit robust trajectory coding (Ainge et al., 2007a; Griffin et al., 2012; Hallock and Griffin, 2013). This set of findings argues against the interpretation of trajectory coding being a memory signal used in task performance. Instead, trajectory coding may be a special case of remapping, in which the hippocampal network alternates between representing two or more different trajectories. The next step in understanding how remapping and trajectory coding participate in memory coding may be to look outside of the hippocampus in downstream structures such as the mPFC. By investigating mPFC–hippocampal interactions and synchrony during memory task performance and, most importantly, relating these interactions to trajectory coding and remapping of hippocampal neurons, we may finally uncover the meaning of these striking hippocampal firing patterns.

REFERENCES

Aggleton, J. P., Neave, N., Nagle, S., and Hunt, P. R. (1995). A comparison of the effects of anterior thalamic, mamillary body and fornix lesions on reinforced spatial alternation. *Behav. Brain Res.* 68, 91–101. doi:10.1016/0166-4328(94)00163-A

Ainge, J. A., van der Meer, M. A. A., Langston, R. F., and Wood, E. R. (2007a). Exploring the role of context-dependent hippocampal activity in spatial alternation behavior. *Hippocampus* 17, 988–1002. doi:10.1002/hipo.20301

Ainge, J. A., Tamosiunaite, M., Woergoetter, F., and Dudchenko, P. A. (2007b). Hippocampal CA1 place cells encode intended destination on a maze with multiple choice points. *J. Neurosci.* 27, 9769–9779. doi:10.1523/JNEUROSCI.2011-07.2007

Ainge, J. A., Tamosiunaite, M., Worgotter, F., and Dudchenko, P. A. (2012). Hippocampal place cells encode intended destination, and not a discriminative stimulus, in a conditional T-maze task. *Hippocampus* 22, 534–543. doi:10.1002/hipo.20919

Baddeley, A. (1992). Working memory. *Science* 255, 556–559. doi:10.1126/science.1736359

Bahar, A. S., and Shapiro, M. L. (2012). Remembering to learn: independent place and journey coding mechanisms contribute to memory transfer. *J. Neurosci.* 32, 2191–2203. doi:10.1523/JNEUROSCI.3998-11.2012

Battaglia, F. P., Sutherland, G. R., and McNaughton, B. L. (2004). Local sensory cues and place cell directionality: additional evidence of prospective coding in the hippocampus. *J. Neurosci.* 24, 4541–4550. doi:10.1523/JNEUROSCI.4896-03.2004

Benchenane, K., Peyrache, A., Khamassi, M., Tierney, P. L., Gioanni, Y., Battaglia, F. P., et al. (2010). Coherent theta oscillations and reorganization of spike timing in the hippocampal-prefrontal network upon learning. *Neuron* 66, 921–936. doi:10.1016/j.neuron.2010.05.013

Berke, J. D., Breck, J. T., and Eichenbaum, H. (2009). Striatal versus hippocampal representations during win-stay maze performance *J. Neurophysiol.* 101, 1575–1587 doi:10.1152/jn.91106.2008

Berke, J. D., Okatan, M., Skurski, J., and Eichenbaum, H. B. (2004) Oscillatory entrainment of striatal neurons in freely moving rats. *Neuron* 436, 883–896 doi:10.1016/j.neuron.2004.08.035

Bostock, E., Muller, R. U., and Kubie J. L. (1991). Experience-dependent modifications of hippocampal place cell firing. *Hippocampus* 1, 193–205. doi:10.1002/hipo.450010207

Bower, M. R., Euston, D. R., and McNaughton, B. L. (2005). Sequential-context-dependent hippocampal activity is not necessary to learn sequences with repeated elements. *J. Neurosci.* 25, 1313–1323. doi:10.1523/JNEUROSCI.2901-04.2005

Brandon, M. P., Bogaard, A. R., Libby, C. P., Connerney, M. A., Gupta, K., and Hasselmo, M. E. (2011). Reduction of theta rhythm dissociates grid cell spatial periodicity from directional tuning. *Science* 332, 595–599. doi:10.1126/science.1201652

Breese, C. R., Hampson, R. E., and Deadwyler, S. A. (1989). Hippocampal place cells: stereotypy and plasticity. *J. Neurosci.* 9, 1097–1111.

Brito, G. N., Davis, B. J., Stopp, L. C., and Stanton, M. E. (1983). Memory and the septo-hippocampal cholinergic system in the rat. *Psychopharmacology (Berl.)* 81, 315–320. doi:10.1007/BF00427569

Burton, B. G., Hok, V., Save, E., and Poucet, B. (2009). Lesion of the ventral and intermediate hippocampus abolishes anticipatory activity in the medial prefrontal cortex of the rat. *Behav. Brain Res.* 199, 222–234. doi:10.1016/j.bbr.2008.11.045

Buzsáki, G. (2002). Theta oscillations in the hippocampus. *Neuron* 33, 325–340. doi:10.1016/S0896-6273(02)00586-X

Clayton, N. S., and Dickinson, A. (1999). Scrub jays (Aphelocoma coerulescens) remember the relative time of caching as well as the location and content of their caches. *J. Comp. Psychol.* 113, 403–416. doi:10.1037/0735-7036.113.4.403

Colgin, L. L. (2011). Oscillations and hippocampal-prefrontal synchrony. *Curr. Opin. Neurobiol.* 21, 467–474. doi:10.1016/j.conb.2011.04.006

Colgin, L. L., Moser, E. I., and Moser, M. B. (2008). Understanding memory through hippocampal remapping. *Trends Neurosci.* 31, 469–477. doi:10.1016/j.tins.2008.06.008

Czerniawski, J., Yoon, T., and Otto, T. (2009). Dissociating space and trace in dorsal and ventral hippocampus. *Hippocampus* 19, 20–32. doi:10.1002/hipo.20469

DeVito, L. M., and Eichenbaum, H. (2010). Distinct contributions of the hippocampus and medial prefrontal cortex to the "what-where-when" components of episodic-like memory in mice. *Behav. Brain Res.* 215, 318–325. doi:10.1016/j.bbr.2009.09.014

Eichenbaum, H., Stewart, C., and Morris, R. G. (1990). Hippocampal representation in place learning. *J. Neurosci.* 10, 3531–3542.

Ergorul, C., and Eichenbaum, H. (2004). The hippocampus and memory for "what," "where," and "when". *Learn. Mem.* 11, 397–405. doi:10.1101/lm.73304

Ferbinteanu, J., and Shapiro, M. L. (2003). Prospective and retrospective memory coding in the hippocampus. *Neuron* 40, 1227–1239. doi:10.1016/S0896-6273(03)00752-9

Ferbinteanu, J., Shirvalkar, P., and Shapiro, M. L. (2011). Memory modulates journey-dependent coding in the rat hippocampus. *J. Neurosci.* 31, 9135–9146. doi:10.1523/JNEUROSCI.1241-11.2011

Ferino, F., Thierry, A. M., and Glowinski, J. (1987). Anatomical and electrophysiological evidence for a direct projection from Ammon's horn to the medial prefrontal cortex in the rat. *Exp. Brain Res.* 65, 421–426. doi:10.1007/BF00236315

Fortin, N. J., Agster, K. A., and Eichenbaum, H. (2002). Critical role of the hippocampus in memory for sequences of events. *Nat. Neurosci.* 5, 458–462.

Frank, L. M., Brown, E. N., and Wilson, M. (2000). Trajectory encoding in the hippocampus and entorhinal cortex. *Neuron* 27, 169–178. doi:10.1016/S0896-6273(00)00018-0

Gordon, J. A. (2011). Oscillations and hippocampal-prefrontal synchrony. *Curr. Opin. Neurobiol.* 21, 486–491. doi:10.1016/j.conb.2011.02.012

Griffin, A. L., Eichenbaum, H., and Hasselmo, M. E. (2007). Spatial representations of hippocampal CA1 neurons are modulated by behavioral context in a hippocampus-dependent memory task. *J. Neurosci.* 27, 2416–2423. doi:10.1523/JNEUROSCI.4083-06.2007

Griffin, A. L., Owens, C. B., Peters, G. J., Adelman, P. C., and Cline, K. M. (2012). Spatial representations in dorsal hippocampal neurons during a tactile-visual conditional discrimination task. *Hippocampus* 22, 299–308. doi:10.1002/hipo.20898

Hallock, H. L., and Griffin, A. L. (2013). Dynamic coding of dorsal hippocampal neurons between tasks that differ in structure and memory demand. *Hippocampus* 23, 169–186 doi:10.1002/hipo.22079

Hasselmo, M. E. (2009). A model of episodic memory: mental time travel along encoded trajectories using grid cells. *Neurobiol. Learn. Mem.* 92, 559–573 doi:10.1016/j.nlm.2009.07.005

Hasselmo, M. E., and Eichenbaum, H. (2005). Hippocampal mechanisms for the context-dependent retrieval of episodes *Neural Netw.* 18, 1172–1190 doi:10.1016/j.neunet.2005.08.007

Hyman, J. M., Zilli, E. A., Paley, A. M. and Hasselmo M. E. (2005). Medial prefrontal cortex cells show dynamic modulation with the hippocampal theta rhythm dependent on behavior. *Hippocampus* 15, 739–749 doi:10.1002/hipo.20106

Hyman, J. M., Zilli, E. A., Paley, A. M., and Hasselmo, M. E. (2010). Working memory performance correlates with prefrontal-hippocampal theta interactions but not with prefrontal neuron firing rates. *Front. Integr. Neurosci.* 4:2. doi:10.3389/neuro.07.002.2010

Jay, T. M., Thierry, A. M., Wiklund, L., and Glowinski J. (1992). Excitatory Amino Acid Pathway from the Hippocampus to the Prefrontal Cortex. Contribution of AMPA Receptors in Hippocampo-prefrontal Cortex Transmission. *Eur. J. Neurosci.* 4, 1285–1295. doi:10.1111/j.1460-9568.1992.tb00154.x

Jay, T. M., and Witter, M. P. (1991). Distribution of hippocampal CA1 and subicular efferents in the prefrontal cortex of the rat studied by means of anterograde transport of Phaseolus vulgaris-leucoagglutinin. *J. Comp. Neurol.* 313, 574–586. doi:10.1002/cne.903130404

Ji, D., and Wilson, M. A. (2008). Firing rate dynamics in the hippocampus induced by trajectory learning. *J. Neurosci.* 28, 4679–4689. doi:10.1523/JNEUROSCI.4597-07.2008

Jones, M. W., and Wilson, M. A. (2005). Theta rhythms coordinate hippocampal-prefrontal interactions in a spatial memory task. *PLoS Biol.* 3:e402. doi:10.1371/journal.pbio.0030402

Lee, I., Griffin, A. L., Zilli, E. A., Eichenbaum, H., and Hasselmo, M. E. (2006). Gradual translocation of spatial correlates of neuronal firing in the hippocampus toward prospective reward locations. *Neuron* 51, 639–650. doi:10.1016/j.neuron.2006.06.033

Lenck-Santini, P. P., Save, E., and Poucet, B. (2001). Place-cell firing does not depend on the direction of turn in a Y-maze alternation task. *Eur. J. Neurosci.* 13, 1055–1058. doi:10.1046/j.0953-816x.2001.01481.x

Leutgeb, S., Leutgeb, J. K., Barnes, C. A., Moser, E. I., McNaughton, B. L., and Moser, M. B. (2005). Independent codes for spatial and episodic memory in hippocampal neuronal ensembles. *Science* 309, 619–623. doi:10.1126/science.1114037

Lever, C., Wills, T., Cacucci, F., Burgess, N., and O'Keefe, J. (2002). Long-term plasticity in hippocampal place-cell representation of environmental geometry. *Nature* 416, 90–94. doi:10.1038/416090a

Markus, E. J., Qin, Y. L., Leonard, B., Skaggs, W. E., McNaughton, B. L., and Barnes, C. A. (1995). Interactions between location and task affect the spatial and directional firing of hippocampal neurons. *J. Neurosci.* 15, 7079–7094.

McNaughton, B. L., Barnes, C. A., and O'Keefe, J. (1983). The contributions of position, direction, and velocity to single unit activity in the hippocampus of freely-moving rats. *Exp. Brain Res.* 52, 41–49. doi:10.1007/BF00237147

Moita, M. A. P., Rosis, S., Zhou, Y., LeDoux, J. E., and Blair, H. T. (2004). Putting fear in its place: remapping of hippocampal place cells during fear conditioning. *J. Neurosci.* 24, 7015–7023. doi:10.1523/JNEUROSCI.5492-03.2004

Muller, R. U., Bostock, E., Taube, J. S., and Kubie, J. L. (1994). On the directional firing properties of hippocampal place cells. *J. Neurosci.* 14, 7235–7251.

Muller, R. U., and Kubie, J. L. (1987). The effects of changes in the environment on the spatial firing of hippocampal complex-spike cells. *J. Neurosci.* 7, 1951–1968.

Muller, R. U., Stead, M., and Pach, J. (1996). The hippocampus as a cognitive graph. *J. Gen. Physiol.* 107, 663–694. doi:10.1085/jgp.107.6.663

Navratilova, Z., Hoang, L. T., Schwindel, C. A., Tatsuno, M., and McNaughton, B. L. (2012). Experience-dependent firing rate remapping generates directional selectivity in hippocampal place cells. *Front. Neural Circuits* 6:6. doi:10.3389/fncir.2012.00006

O'Keefe, J., and Nadel, L. (1978). *The Hippocampus as a Cognitive Map.* Oxford: Oxford University Press.

Olton, D. S., Becker, J. T., and Handelmann, G. E. (1979). Hippocampus, space and memory. *Behav. Brain Sci.* 2, 313–365. doi:10.1017/S0140525X00062713

Pastalkova, E., Itskov, V., Amarasingham, A., and Buzsaki, G. (2008). Internally generated cell assembly sequences in the rat hippocampus. *Science* 321, 1322–1327. doi:10.1126/science.1159775

Popa, D., Duvarci, S., Popescu, A. T., Léna, C., and Paré, D. (2010). Coherent amygdalocortical theta promotes fear memory consolidation during paradoxical sleep. *Proc. Natl. Acad. Sci. U.S.A.* 107, 6516–6519. doi:10.1073/pnas.0913016107

Rawlins, J. N., and Olton, D. S. (1982). The septo-hippocampal system and cognitive mapping. *Behav. Brain Res.* 5, 331–358. doi:10.1016/0166-4328(82)90039-0

Scoville, W. B., and Milner, B. (1957). Loss of recent memory after bilateral hippocampal lesions. *J. Neurol. Neurosurg. Psychiatr.* 20, 11–21. doi:10.1136/jnnp.20.1.11

Seidenbecher, T., Laxmi, T. R., Stork, O., and Pape, H. C. (2003). Amygdalar and hippocampal theta rhythm synchronization during fear memory retrieval. *Science* 301, 846–850. doi:10.1126/science.1085818

Siapas, A. G., Lubenov, E. V., and Wilson, M. A. (2005). Prefrontal phase locking to hippocampal theta oscillations. *Neuron* 46, 141–151. doi:10.1016/j.neuron.2005.02.028

Siapas, A. G., and Wilson, M. A. (1998). Coordinated interactions between hippocampal ripples and cortical spindles during slow-wave sleep. *Neuron* 21, 1123–1128. doi:10.1016/S0896-6273(00)80629-7

Smith, D. M., and Mizumori, S. J. (2006). Learning-related development of context-specific neuronal responses to places and events: the hippocampal role in context processing. *J. Neurosci.* 26, 3154–3163. doi:10.1523/JNEUROSCI.3234-05.2006

Stanton, M. E., Thomas, G. J., and Brito, G. N. (1984). Posterodorsal septal lesions impair performance on both shift and stay working memory tasks. *Behav. Neurosci.* 98, 405–415. doi:10.1037/0735-7044.98.3.405

Stern, C. E., Sherman, S. J., Kirchhoff, B. A., and Hasselmo, M. E. (2001). Medial temporal and prefrontal contributions to working memory tasks with novel and familiar stimuli. *Hippocampus* 11, 337–346. doi:10.1002/hipo.1048.abs

Tort, A. B., Kramer, M. A., Thorn, C., Gibson, D. J., Kubota, Y., Graybiel, A. M., et al. (2008). Dynamic cross-frequency couplings of local field potential oscillations in rat striatum and hippocampus during performance of a T-maze task. *Proc. Natl. Acad. Sci. U.S.A.* 105, 20517–20522. doi:10.1073/pnas.0810524105

Tulving, E., and Markowitsch, H. J. (1998). Episodic and declarative memory: role of the hippocampus. *Hippocampus* 8, 198–204. doi:10.1002/(SICI)1098-1063(1998)8:3<198::AID-HIPO2>3.3.CO;2-J

Wiener, S. I., Paul, C. A., and Eichenbaum, H. (1989). Spatial and behavioral correlates of hippocampal neuronal activity. *J. Neurosci.* 9, 2737–2763.

Wills, T. J., Lever, C., Cacucci, F., Burgess, N., and O'Keefe, J. (2005). Attractor dynamics in the hippocampal representation of the local environment. *Science* 308, 873–876. doi:10.1126/science.1108905

Wood, E. R., Dudchenko, P. A., and Eichenbaum, H. (1999). The global record of memory in hippocampal neuronal activity. *Nature* 397, 613–616. doi:10.1038/17605

Wood, E. R., Dudchenko, P. A., Robitsek, R. J., and Eichenbaum, H. (2000). Hippocampal neurons encode information about different types of memory episodes occurring in the same location. *Neuron* 27, 623–633. doi:10.1016/S0896-6273(00)00071-4

7

A review of the neural and behavioral consequences for unitizing emotional and neutral information

Brendan D. Murray* and Elizabeth A. Kensinger

Department of Psychology, Boston College, Chestnut Hill, MA, USA

Correspondence:
Brendan D. Murray, Department of Psychology, Boston College, McGuinn Hall, Room 301, 140 Commonwealth Avenue, Chestnut Hill, MA 02467, USA.
e-mail: murrayds@bc.edu

A special type of association, called a "unitization," is formed when pieces of information are encoded as a single representation in memory (e.g., "shirt" and "blue" are encoded as a "blue shirt"; Graf and Schacter, 1989) and typically are later reactivated in memory as a single unit, allowing access to the features of multiple related stimuli at once (Bader et al. 2010; Diana et al., 2011). This review examines the neural processes supporting memory for unitizations and how the emotional content of the material may influence unitization. Although associative binding is typically reliant on hippocampal processes and supported by recollection, the first part of this review will present evidence to suggest that when two items are unitized into a single representation, memory for those bound items may be accomplished on the basis of familiarity and without reliance on the hippocampus. The second part of this review discusses how emotion may affect the processes that give rise to unitizations. Emotional information typically receives a mnemonic benefit over neutral information, but the literature is mixed on whether the presence of emotional information impedes or enhances the associative binding of neutral information (reviewed by Mather, 2007). It has been suggested that the way the emotional and neutral details are related together may be critical to whether the neutral details are enhanced or impeded (Mather, 2007; Mather and Sutherland, 2011). We focus on whether emotional arousal aids or inhibits the creation of a unitized representation, presenting preliminary data, and future directions to test empirically the effects of forming and retrieving emotional and neutral unitizations.

Keywords: emotion, associative memory, unitization, integration, medial temporal lobes

A key feature of human memory is the ability not only to remember discrete pieces of information but also to form novel associations between those pieces of information. Whether we are trying to identify the acquaintances who work at the same company or the specific combination of physical characteristics that indicate that a particular plant is poisonous, we frequently draw on memory for associations. A special type of association, called a "unitization," can be formed when the pieces are encoded as a single representation in memory (e.g., the item "shirt" and the color "blue" are encoded as a "blue shirt"; Wollen et al., 1972; Graf and Schacter, 1989; Yonelinas, 2002; Diana et al., 2008, 2011). As Graf and Schacter (1989) describe, unitization can happen in one of two ways: either the items are perceived as having some underlying perceptual structure that leads them to be perceived as a single unit, or their co-occurrence implies a relationship that leads them to be combined together due to their presentation in space and time. Unitizations can be beneficial because they are typically reactivated in memory as a single unit, allowing access to the features of multiple related stimuli at once.

THE CREATION AND RETRIEVAL OF UNITIZATIONS

In this first section, we will review some of the neuroanatomy relevant to the formation and retrieval of unitized representations. We will also describe patient and neuroimaging data that can elucidate how unitizations are mnemonically encoded, and later accessed, in memory.

ANATOMICAL ORGANIZATION OF THE MEDIAL TEMPORAL LOBES, AND ITS RELATION TO UNITIZATION

Hippocampus and surrounding cortices

The medial temporal lobes have been described as having a functionally hierarchical structure (Lavenex and Amaral, 2000; Montaldi and Mayes, 2010), consisting of the parahippocampal cortex (PHC), perirhinal (PrC), and entorhinal (EC) cortices, and the hippocampus proper. It is still debated whether these regions comprise a single system which enables declarative memory (e.g., Squire and Zola-Morgan, 1991; Squire et al., 2007) or contribute differentially to the encoding and retrieval of individual items and the relationships between those items (e.g., Cohen and Eichenbaum, 1993; Aggleton and Brown, 1999; Diana et al., 2007; Staresina and Davachi, 2008). Although coverage of this debate is outside the purview of this review, understanding of the proposed hierarchy is critical to discerning how unitized representations may be encoded and subsequently retrieved (Staresina and Davachi, 2006, 2008).

Briefly, the PrC and PHC have reciprocal connections with both unimodal (e.g., auditory and visual association areas) and multimodal association areas (e.g., posterior and anterior association areas; Lavenex and Amaral, 2000). PrC and PHC are believed to be the first site of integration of information from all sensory cortices, and data have suggested that there is functional specialization even at this first stage, with PrC primarily receiving object information from visual cortex and TE/TEO and PHC primarily receiving spatial information from the frontal and parietal cortices (Diana et al., 2007; Suzuki, 2010; also Bachevalier and Nemanic, 2008 for similar evidence from Rhesus macaques). As such, we can conceive of two possibilities for how the MTL may deal with unitized representations based on this differentiation. On the one hand, a to-be-unitized pair may be processed as a unitized object in regions within the dorsal or ventral visual processing stream (related to concepts of "object files" as originally conceived by Kahneman et al., 1992, and to the dual-system model of visual short-term memory proposed by Xu and Chun, 2006). This "pre-packaged" information could then be communicated to the PrC or PHC. On the other hand, the PrC may receive information about the separate to-be-unitized objects or object features and then begin the process of packaging them together – perceptually or mnemonically – into a single representation (e.g., Bussey et al., 2003; Bussey and Saksida, 2007; Kent and Brown, 2012) before passing on that information to the next regions in the hierarchy (see Cowell et al., 2010; Graham et al., 2010; Saksida and Bussey, 2010 for discussion of the role of the PRC in perception and memory for complex feature conjunctions).

Entorhinal cortex shares reciprocal connections with PrC and PHC, and it also receives direct inputs from multimodal association cortices. EC therefore receives input from all sensory modalities and is believed to play a greater role in the processing and integration of contextual information than of object information (Suzuki et al., 1997). EC does, however, receive object information from PrC and passes that information along to the hippocampus; most generally, the EC is considered to mediate much of the informational input to the hippocampus (Canto et al., 2008). Relative to other regions of MTL, less is known about the exact function of EC, but we can offer several possibilities. First, it is possible that because EC serves in this "gatekeeper" role of passing the hippocampus information from other brain regions (Hargreaves et al., 2005) – including PrC – that EC plays no direct role in the formation of unitizations. Instead, it may either pass pre-bound unitizations, formed in either the PrC or earlier regions of the ventral visual stream, to the hippocampus (if unitization happens before information reaches the hippocampus), or EC may pass information about individual objects or stimuli to the hippocampus, and unitization may take place within the hippocampus proper. Another alternative is that the EC itself is responsible for at least some processes relevant to forming unitizations, given its suggested role in contextual integration (Suzuki et al., 1997) and in subsequent correct recognition of verbal pairs (Jackson and Schacter, 2004). At present, these possibilities have not been distinguished, and so future research will be needed to explore the EC's role in memory for unitizations.

The hippocampus sits atop the anatomical hierarchy and receives well-integrated information from EC, PrC, and PHC (Mayes et al., 2007). The hippocampus projects this richly complex, integrated information back to cortical association areas, and this process – the feedback loop of information from cortical association areas, through MTL, and back to the cortex – is believed by some to be what produces the phenomenology of episodic memory (Squire, 1992). As we have alluded to, although it is clear that the hippocampus is essential for the formation of typical associations among stimuli (Aggleton and Brown, 1999; Eichenbaum et al., 2007), it is less clear whether the hippocampus is needed for the formation and retrieval of unitizations (Giovanello et al., 2006; Quamme et al., 2007). We will return to this debate in the next section of this review.

It is important to note that the interactions between these MTL regions may be complicated by the fact that these regions can have functional influences on one another without having direct anatomical connections (see also Damoiseaux and Greicius, 2009 for discussion). Lacy and Stark (2012) revealed that functional connectivity – the strength of correlation in activity among brain regions – was stronger among cortical regions of the MTL (PrC, EC, and PHC) than it was between these regions and the hippocampus. Conversely, hippocampal subfields had strong inter-field functional connectivity but little connectivity with the surrounding cortex. As such, it may not be sufficient to explore what each of these MTL regions contributes to unitized memory in isolation; rather, understanding the functional connections between these regions will likely be critical to understanding the genesis of unitized representations in the brain.

Amygdala

In reviewing how emotion may interact with the unitization process, we must also consider the role of the amygdala. The amygdala's role in the modulation of emotional memories – via its interaction with other MTL regions – has been well established (Gallagher and Chiba, 1996; Cahill and McGaugh, 1998; Kensinger and Schacter, 2006), and although its role has been investigated more thoroughly for memories that are fearful or aversive, it also plays a role in memories of pleasurable experiences (reviewed by LaBar, 2007). Animal research has demonstrated that the amygdala – particularly the lateral and basal nuclei – shares strong reciprocal connections with PrC, EC, and hippocampus, specifically in the subiculum and in subfield CA1 (Krettek and Price, 1977; Canteras and Swanson, 1992; Savander et al., 1997; Shi and Cassell, 1999; Pitkänen et al., 2000). Thus, there is substantial anatomical evidence indicating a reciprocal relationship between the amygdala and the anterior hippocampus as well as PrC. In addition, there is physiological and functional evidence of such a relationship. In rats, high frequency stimulation of the anterior hippocampus has been shown to produce long-term potentiation in the amygdala (Maren and Fanselow, 1985), and in patients, the amount of amygdala damage relates to the amount of hippocampal activity during an emotional memory task, and vice versa (Richardson et al., 2004). The amygdala also has robust connections to the visual cortex and regions along the ventral visual processing stream (Freese and Amaral, 2005; Duncan and Barrett, 2007). As such, there is an anatomical basis for predicting an interaction between the amygdala, PrC, and visual pathway, one that could influence the unitization process.

It has become clear that the amygdala does not act to enhance all aspects of a memory. Instead, the amygdala has selective effects on memory, enhancing some elements of a memory while having no beneficial impact – and sometimes even having an impairing effect – on other elements (reviewed by Kensinger, 2009; Mather and Sutherland, 2011). While not specifically discussing unitization, Mather (2007) described an "object-based framework" that is highly relevant to the process of unitization: when contextual details (such as color, temporal order, etc.) are viewed as being integral or intrinsic to the emotional stimulus, emotional arousal (likely via activation of the amygdala; see Kensinger et al., 2011 for evidence) enhances the binding of those details. This finding suggests that amygdala engagement can enhance the process of unitization.

Having reviewed the anatomical hierarchy within the medial temporal lobes, we now move to examine the empirical evidence for how these structures help produce episodic memory for items, their associations, and unitized representations. We begin with a brief discussion of a common way that memory for items and their associations is tested in the laboratory: through assessments of recognition memory. We focus on a model that argues that recognition memory can be supported by dissociable processes – recollection (including memory for episodic details) and familiarity (roughly akin to item familiarity; Atkinson and Juola, 1974; Yonelinas, 2002) – that have in turn been argued to map on specifically to the hippocampus and PrC, respectively (Aggleton and Brown, 1999; Diana et al., 2007; Bowles et al., 2010). Understanding how these regions and processes interact to produce an episodic memory is critical to understanding how the brain may encode, store, and retrieve unitized representations and how emotion may impact those processes.

MEMORY THROUGH RECOGNITION

Often in the laboratory, memory for the relationship between two items is tested through recognition. In a typical paradigm, participants will study lists of unrelated paired associates (e.g., two semantically unrelated words, face-name pairs, etc.) and then memory for pairs or for individual items can be tested as part of an "old/new" recognition test. Although there are still some disagreements even among those who propose a dual-process model of recognition comprising recollection and familiarity (e.g., Yonelinas, 1994, 2002; Wixted, 2007), what is generally agreed upon is that recollection typically refers to the recall of specific episodic detail that was associated with the test stimulus: for example, a participant sees a recognition cue and retrieves specific knowledge unique to the context in which that cue was initially encountered, such as what information it appeared in conjunction with, what information temporally preceded or followed it, what thought was triggered by the information's presentation, and so on (Montaldi and Mayes, 2010). Familiarity, on the other hand, is assumed to require no such access to episodic details. It is characterized by the knowledge that a particular test stimulus has been encountered previously – sometimes referred to as a "feeling of knowing" (Montaldi and Mayes, 2010) – but is not accompanied by retrieval of other contextual or otherwise associated details. Although there are alternative accounts to this "dual-process" model of memory (e.g., Squire et al., 2007), our goal in this review is not to adjudicate between the models. Rather, our review will follow from a wealth of research broadly demonstrating behavioral and neural dissociations between these processes.

UNITIZATION IN THE BRAIN

A plethora of studies have supported a dual-process view not only of recognition memory but also of the MTL system (see Eichenbaum et al., 1994; Brown and Aggleton, 2001 for initial proposals). This research has revealed that the hippocampus is involved in associative binding of an item to its episodic context while the PrC plays a more dominant role in the representation of single items (see Diana et al., 2007; Eichenbaum et al., 2007 for reviews). An important caveat, however, and the one that we describe next, is that this hippocampal binding, and associated recollection, may not be necessary in cases of unitization.

Patient and imaging data support the notion that unitized representations can be supported by PrC and recognized via familiarity. To examine whether familiarity could contribute to the recognition of unitized representations, Diana et al. (2011) asked participants to view items presented on either a red or green background, and they were instructed either to imagine the item in the color of the background (the high-unitization condition), or to remember independently what color of background the item was paired with (low-unitization). Behaviorally, familiarity-based judgments were significantly higher in the high- vs. low-unitization condition, while recollection-based judgments did not differ. ERP data showed that the ERP correlates of familiarity – the early, fronto-central positivity – were significantly more apparent in the high- vs. low-unitization condition, while unitization demands had no effect on the ERP correlates for recollection. As noted by Diana and colleagues, their data – taken together with data from other studies that also revealed enhanced ERP correlates of familiarity on tasks encouraging unitization (e.g., Ecker et al., 2007; Diana et al., 2008; Bader et al., 2010) – provide relatively strong support for the proposal that unitization enhances familiarity-based recognition.

Although unitization may enhance the ability to recognize item associations on the basis of familiarity, Pilgrim et al. (2012) revealed that this may come at a cost when recognizing the individual items within the pair. They asked participants to study lists of single items, as well as pairs of words studied using either a unitization strategy (i.e., using mental imagery of the two items interacting in some way) or a non-unitization strategy (i.e., imagining the two items separately). Participants were then given a recognition test of single items from both the item-only and unitization/non-unitization conditions. At retrieval, the authors observed a reduced frontal effect, typically associated with familiarity-based retrieval during recognition of items studied in the unitization condition relative to the item-only or non-unitization conditions. The authors interpret this result as suggesting that unitization limits familiarity-based access to items that have been combined into a unitized representation. Importantly, unitization did not affect overall item recognition accuracy: there was no difference in d', hit rate, or reaction time for items in those two conditions. Thus, unitization affected *how* the information was recognized (by familiarity or recollection) and not *whether* it was recognized. Although the authors describe this reduced familiarity signal as a potential "cost" of unitization, they note that it could alternatively be interpreted as a benefit of unitization: equivalent item recognition memory, in an equivalent amount of time, is produced without reliance on a familiarity signal. Regardless of the exact interpretation of these findings, the results of this study, along with those of Diana et al. (2008), suggest that the process of unitization may differentially affect the role of familiarity in recognizing the associations compared to the individual items, enhancing the influence of familiarity on the former while reducing its influence on the latter.

Further evidence to suggest that unitization creates an associative representation that can be retrieved by processes typically associated with item memory or familiarity has come from two sets of data sampling patients with MTL amnesia. Giovanello et al. (2006) first showed, in a group of non-amnestic individuals, that recognition of unitized associations relies more on familiarity than recognition of non-unitized associations. They then discovered that patients with amnesia were better at differentiating between studied and rearranged pairs if the pairs formed compound words (e.g., correctly responding "old" to the studied words "blackmail" and "jailbird," but "new" to the rearranged word "blackbird") than if the pairs formed novel associations (e.g., "surgeon-arrow"). For non-amnestic controls, there was no such difference between the two types of associations. These data are consistent with the proposal that unitized representations can be remembered on the basis of item memory or familiarity, processes more likely to be spared in amnesia than those related to associative binding or recollection.

Quamme et al. (2007) presented similar findings: the researchers tested five amnesic patients, two of whom had undergone a left unilateral temporal lobectomy, damaging the hippocampus as well as PrC and EC, and three of whom were believed to have lesions restricted to the hippocampus as a result of cerebral hypoxia following cardiac arrest. When given pairs of unrelated nouns to study, hypoxic patients with intact rhinal cortices later recognized the pairs more readily if the words had been combined into a compound word with a novel definition (e.g., "cloud-lawn" would be defined as, "A yard used for sky-gazing.") than if the words were presented in a sentence (e.g., "The ___ could be seen from the ___"). The two patients with temporal lobectomies, exhibiting damage to the rhinal cortices, did not show any such benefit from unitization.

These data offer compelling evidence that the hippocampus is not necessary for the encoding and retrieval of unitized representations, and they further suggest a role for the rhinal cortices in the formation of unitizations. Further evidence for a role of the PrC in unitization has come from studies using functional MRI. Using a paradigm similar to that of Quamme et al. (2007), Haskins et al. (2008) directly tested the hypothesis that PrC can support the encoding of unitized representations. Healthy participants were given pairs of semantically unrelated nouns (e.g., "steam tree") and were asked to rate how well the words fit into a given sentence frame (no unitization), or they were given a novel definition for the compound of the two words and asked to rate how well they thought the definition fit the compound (unitization). They were then shown test pairs that were either intact from study or rearranged and had to indicate whether the words had been studied together or not. The imaging data, along with behavioral data from participants' ROCs, indicated that left PrC was more active during compound than sentence trials, and that its activity at encoding was predictive of correct familiarity-based recognition judgments at test.

Staresina and Davachi (2006) also offer functional MRI evidence that the PrC can support the encoding of unitized item-color information. In their task, participants viewed the verbal label of an item (e.g., "elephant") on a colored background, and were asked to imagine the item in the color of the background (e.g., for a red background, imagine a red elephant) and decide if the representation could plausibly appear in the real world or not. Participants were then given a surprise test in which they had to indicate if items were old or new, and if they judged an item to be old, they had to indicate with what color the item had been presented. While they observed that bilateral hippocampal activity at encoding predicted subsequent associative recognition success, encoding activity in left PrC was also found to be predictive of success at retrieving both the words and also the word-color pairs. They suggested that the PrC was able to support associative recognition for the item and its corresponding color because the color and item information had been unitized at encoding.

To directly test their hypothesis, in a second study, Staresina and Davachi (2008) used a similar encoding task, but they also asked the participants to make one of two semantic decisions about the item (judging its pleasantness or its plausibility). This manipulation allowed the researchers to assess how MTL subregions contribute to memory for those different types of detail. Consistent with their previous results, they found that encoding activity in the left hippocampus and bilateral PrC predicted subsequent associative recognition for item-color pairings. In contrast, only the hippocampus and not PrC predicted successful retrieval of the item-context (i.e., encoding task) association. If we consider the color to be associated via a process of unitization but the encoding task to be associated through other means, then these data offered further evidence that PrC may indeed help to encode unitized associations but not other forms of associative learning.

While these three functional MRI studies indicate that PrC offers an important contribution to the formation of associative memory through unitization, they still cannot elucidate the specific role that PrC might play in the unitization process. That is, it still remains unclear from these data whether PrC is responsible for assembling unitizations – actually concatenating together the different object features into a single unit – or if it may receive already-unitized representations from other regions and PrC encodes that pre-assembled representation. To test this, Staresina and Davachi (2010) conducted a third study systematically varying the unitization demands at encoding to investigate how PrC would track with increasing unitization requirement. The hypothesis was that if PrC activity showed a variable relation based on the varying unitization demand, it would suggest that the PrC plays a role in actually putting together novel unitizations. In their study, participants viewed objects that were intact, fragmented into two parts, or fragmented into four parts, and participants were asked to imagine the whole item in the color of the background and to determine its real-world plausibility. By including three fragmentation conditions, the researchers were able to vary how much the item needed to be unitized to succeed at the encoding task. Participants were given the same recognition task from Staresina and Davachi (2006), described above. As in Staresina and Davachi (2006), PrC activation at encoding – this time, bilaterally – was predictive of subsequent item and associative recognition success; however, PrC activation was unaffected by level of fragmentation. Rather, regions throughout the ventral visual stream tracked with increasing unitization demand. These data suggest that while PrC can support the mnemonic encoding of unitized associations, the perceptual integration of a unitized representation may occur in earlier stages of processing.

The role of the PrC in unitization likely does not stop after encoding. Diana et al. (2010) asked participants to study nouns presented on a red or green background and to process the color either as an item feature – by imagining the item in that color – or as a contextual detail by imaging the item interacting with a stop sign (red) or dollar bill (green). Although control participants were able to retrieve the color information with equal probability, regardless of the encoding instructions, amnesic patients were more likely to retrieve the color information if it had been processed as an item feature rather than a contextual detail. fMRI results with healthy individuals revealed that PrC activity was associated with the retrieval of the color information if it had been studied as an item feature while PHC and hippocampal activity was associated with the retrieval of the color information if it had been studied as a contextual feature.

It is worth noting that domain in which information is presented and manipulated (e.g., whether the participant is creating a compound word or imagining the visual representation of an item) likely affects the neural processes that underlie successful unitization. Although to our knowledge, no study has directly contrasted the neural processes leading to integration by visual or verbal means, it seems plausible that tasks that require unitization of visual entities – such as those just described – would engage visual processing regions while tasks that achieve unitization through the creation of a new concept may engage semantic processing regions such as anterior temporal lobe (Lambon et al., 2010). Regardless of the domain in which the unitization occurs, however, one critical point remains true: it does not appear to be the case that hippocampal engagement is necessary for unitization to be successful.

The data reviewed in this section suggests three main conclusions: (1) Unitized associations can be remembered on the basis of familiarity and using processes typically associated with single item memory, but this effect of unitization may come at the cost of familiarity-based recognition of the individual components of the associated pair. (2) At an anatomical level, the data suggest that the hippocampus is not necessary for forming and encoding unitizations. Instead, PrC may play a role in the mnemonic encoding and retrieval of those unitizations, although (3) at encoding, PrC may, instead or in addition, receive already-unitized information from other brain regions and then work to store that unitized representation into long-term memory. In the section below, we outline the predictions that each of these findings makes with regard to the effect of emotion on memory for unitized representations.

EMOTION AND UNITIZATION

It has been well established that emotional information is handled differently in memory from non-emotional information, with emotional information typically receiving a mnemonic benefit (reviewed by Hamann, 2001; Kensinger, 2009). The emotionality of an experience is often characterized along two orthogonal dimensions: arousal (how exciting or calming an experience is) and valence (how pleasant or unpleasant; Russell, 1980). Because the bulk of research examining the effect of emotion on memory has focused on the dimension of arousal (Cahill et al., 1994; Cahill and McGaugh, 1995), and because arousal is thought to be the main factor that influences amygdala activity (Adolphs et al., 2001; Sharot and Phelps, 2004; Berntson et al., 2007), we will focus our review on the contributions of emotional arousal to emotional memory. It is important to note, however, that valence can influence associative memory as well (Pierce and Kensinger, 2011) and may interact with arousal to influence both the subjective qualities of a memory (Talarico and Rubin, 2003; Sharot and Phelps, 2004; Zimmerman and Kelley, 2010) and also the way that the amygdala interacts with visual and prefrontal processes (e.g., enhanced connectivity between amygdala and middle occipital gyrus and amygdala and inferior frontal gyrus during encoding of high-arousal negative items and low-arousal positive items; Mickley Steinmetz et al., 2010).

To date, there has been little research that specifically has examined the effect of arousal on unitization. There have, however been many studies that have more generally assessed the effect of arousal on recollection and familiarity, and on the associative binding of item features and contextual details. In the sections below, we review the research on the effects of arousal on memory that we believe can lead to informed predictions regarding the effects of arousal on unitization.

THE EFFECTS OF AROUSAL ON ASSOCIATIVE BINDING: IMPLICATIONS FOR UNITIZATION

Although the effects of arousal on associative binding initially seemed inconsistent – with arousal sometimes enhancing the binding of details (e.g., MacKay et al., 2004) and at other times having no effect, or impairing, such binding (e.g., Kensinger and Schacter, 2006; Bergmann et al., 2012; note that the latter examines interactions between both valence and arousal) – more recent accounts have proposed a unified framework for understanding the complex pattern. Mather (2007) proposed an "object-based" framework, with arousal enhancing the binding of information encoded as an item feature but not of information encoded as a contextual detail (see also Kensinger, 2007, 2009). This framework can account for much of the extant data, but there are some exceptions, when arousal does not enhance memory for intra-item features (Guillet and Arndt, 2009) and when it does enhance memory for inter-item binding (Pierce and Kensinger, 2011).

Recognizing the need to account for these contradictory patterns, Mather and Sutherland (2011) proposed the "Arousal-Biased Competition" (ABC) model, describing how arousal may bias resources toward the most conspicuous or goal-relevant stimuli. Thus, if a single item (e.g., a snake) gains priority, then arousal will enhance the binding of the features of that item (e.g., its color, form). But if the pairing of items takes on importance (e.g., the snake and its owner) then arousal will enhance the binding of that association. In other words, it is not the *type* of detail (item vs. contextual or intra- vs. inter-item associations) that predicts the effect of arousal but the *goal relevance* of the detail (see related discussion by Levine and Edelstein, 2009). Although it is always the case that goal-relevant information will be prioritized, according to ABC, arousal exaggerates this prioritization; thus, arousal will enhance the binding of goal-relevant features and will impair the binding of features that are not goal relevant.

In this context, the effect of arousal on associative binding will depend critically on the way the to-be-bound pieces of information are initially processed or perceived. On the one hand, because unitization requires that pieces of information be processed as a coherent whole, all features that are being bound into a unitized representation may be goal relevant. If true, then arousal may lead to a beneficial effect on the process of unitization. On the other hand, because arousing features can capture attention and become prioritized for processing, the presence of those arousing features may make it harder to attend to the other features present at the same time, thereby making the creation of a unitization harder to achieve. Each of these possibilities will be expanded upon in the next sections.

WHY AROUSAL MAY ENHANCE UNITIZATION

As described earlier, neuroimaging data (e.g., Staresina and Davachi, 2010) suggest that visual regions such as those within the ventral visual pathway can be responsible for the initial formation of unitized representations. Thus, unitizations may be created before the information reaches the MTL system. Separate literatures have revealed that activity in these visual regions can be modulated by the arousing content of information. Neuroimaging studies have shown that participants tend to exhibit greater activity in visual cortex and ventral visual stream when viewing emotional vs. non-emotional images (Vuilleumier et al., 2001, 2004; Compton, 2003; Mather et al., 2006), likely because of modulation of visual processing by the amygdala. These data suggest that processing of emotional items within the visual cortex may be prioritized, leading these items to be attended to before neutral items (Öhman and Mineka, 2001; Öhman et al., 2001), to hold attention longer (LaBar et al., 2000; Nummenmaa et al., 2006; Knight et al., 2007), and to be associated with greater encoding activity in visual regions than non-emotional items (Bradley et al., 2003; Mather et al., 2006).

Putting these literatures together: if visual regions such as those along the ventral visual pathway are responsible for the initial formation of unitized representations, the presence of arousal could facilitate activation within those regions, enabling the rapid creation of a unitization. In addition, these literatures may suggest that unitizations containing an arousing component would require less cognitive effort to create than unitizations that contain only neutral information. Because arousing information benefits from prioritized processing, it may be more rapidly and easily integrated unitized. On the other hand, neutral information – which is not privy to such prioritization – may require more cognitive effort to successfully unitize.

Several investigations have demonstrated that when non-emotional information is encoded as a feature of an emotional item, memory for the relationship between the emotional and non-emotional information is enhanced. For example, two recent studies (Mather and Nesmith, 2008; Nashiro and Mather, 2010) demonstrated that when participants passively viewed non-emotional and emotionally arousing pictures at different locations on a computer screen, their memory for the location of emotionally arousing pictures was significantly better than their memory for the location of non-emotional pictures. Mather and Nesmith (2008), in particular, offer evidence for the above points about emotional information being integrated with relatively little cognitive effort: In Experiment 4 of that investigation, the authors varied the amount of time participants had to view pictures (relative to the amount of study time provided in the first three experiments) to determine if location memory tracked with the amount of time participants had to view pictures. The authors found that memory for the location of pictures was independent of how long the pictures were presented. Moreover, it was shown that picture-location conjunction memory for non-emotional pictures was not impaired when those pictures were presented at the same time as emotional pictures, even when encoding time was limited. From this evidence, the authors conclude that arousing pictures did not capture attention for any extended period of time (or else picture-location memory for concurrent non-emotional pictures would be impaired), suggesting that picture-location binding for arousing pictures must happen quickly and with relatively little effort.

Another recent behavioral study (Guillet and Arndt, 2009) demonstrated that inter-item memory could be enhanced by arousal, as well. Mnemonic binding of verbal pairs was enhanced if one of the target words was arousing (i.e., a "taboo" word). Memory for the association between the taboo word and a neutral word was enhanced relative to when the neutral word was paired with another neutral word, or paired with a negative non-arousing word. Though these data offer evidence that arousal may enhance the formation of inter-item associations, it is important to note that relatively little is known about what makes taboo words – and their associations – memorable. Madan et al. (2012), for example, demonstrated that arousal is only one dimension that separates taboo words from other emotional high-arousal and emotional low-arousal words. Those authors used multidimensional scaling for several dimensions of normed ratings (e.g., "familiarity," "offensiveness," "imageability") of neutral, emotional, and taboo words to show that arousal alone does not clearly differentiate taboo words from other emotional words; rather, some undetermined combination of other stimulus characteristics is likely to better differentiate those stimuli. Therefore, it is unclear whether it is the arousing nature of taboo words that leads them to be better associated in Guillet and Arndt (2009), or if some other set of characteristics – like offensiveness or "tabooness" that may be separate from arousal – is driving those effects. Moreover, Madan et al. (2012) demonstrate that across a number of pair types – with pairs containing only taboo, only moderately arousing negative, only neutral, or any combination thereof – the presence of emotional arousal only ever improved item memory, and never improved association memory.

WHY AROUSAL MAY IMPAIR UNITIZATION

The prior discussion of goal relevance highlights an important caveat regarding the beneficial effect of arousal on unitization: Participants would need to find all of the to-be-unitized components to be goal relevant in order for arousal to facilitate their unitization. This goal relevance would likely be achieved in a task that directed participants to integrate the various features, as the task instructions would make both items relevant. But if integration is not emphasized, arousal may instead impair the unitization by focusing perceptual and cognitive resources only on the arousing feature, thereby preventing unitization with the other features.

If attention is directed to the arousing information and not distributed to all elements of the to-be-unitized set, the unitization may fail.

Arousing information can capture visual attention and can be processed in a prioritized fashion. Studies that record participants' eye gaze patterns while they view either arrays of emotional and non-emotional stimuli or complex visual scenes have shown that participants initially saccade to emotional information more quickly, and they saccade more frequently to the emotional information than to neutral information (LaBar et al., 2000; Öhman and Mineka, 2001; Öhman et al., 2001; Mather and Knight, 2006; Knight et al., 2007). In studies that require participants to detect two or more target items in a rapidly presented stream of stimulus items, a phenomenon known as the "attentional blink" is typically observed: participants readily detect the first target item in the rapid stream, but often miss the subsequent target item (e.g., Chun and Potter, 1995). The presumption is that attentional resources are directed toward detecting the first target item, resulting in the second item being missed. However, when the second target item is emotionally arousing, the attentional blink effect is attenuated. Despite presumably depleted attentional resources, participants can still detect the emotional second target item (Anderson and Phelps, 2001; Keil and Ihssen, 2004; Anderson, 2005). These findings suggest that when attentional resources are limited, emotionally arousing items are preferentially processed over neutral items.

This prioritized processing of the arousing information can result in poor processing of temporally- or spatially-proximate information (e.g., Easterbrook, 1959). These factors can combine to create instances in which the arousing elements of an event (e.g., a smashed car) are remembered at the expense of the surrounding, non-emotional details (e.g., details of the street on which the accident occurred; see reviews by Buchanan and Adolphs, 2002; Reisberg and Heuer, 2004; Levine and Edelstein, 2009). Indeed, in laboratory studies using complex visual scenes as encoding stimuli, a "trade-off" in memory is often observed: participants exhibit better memory for emotional than non-emotional items that appeared in the scenes, and their memory for the background details is better when those backgrounds are presented with neutral rather than emotional items (e.g., Kensinger et al., 2005). Neurally this trade-off is associated with increased activity in the middle temporal gyrus, among other regions (Waring and Kensinger, 2011). This region within the ventral visual stream is more active during the encoding of scenes for which the emotional item is subsequently remembered and the background forgotten than for scenes in which both the item and background are remembered, suggesting that visual resources may be preferentially processing the emotional information at the expense of the non-emotional information.

These findings may relate to the process of unitization for an emotional and a non-emotional feature. If sensory-processing regions preferentially process the emotional features over the non-emotional feature, the success of the unitization could be compromised. By giving preference to the emotional information the unitization may not equitably represent both the emotional and non-emotional components. Instead, the unitization may be dominated by the emotional information, or the unitization may fail altogether because processing resources are focused on the emotional information to the exclusion of the non-emotional details.

Further evidence that emotion may impair the formation of unitizations – particularly in the case of negative emotional information – comes from a study by Okada et al. (2011). In that study, participants were asked to learn novel pairs consisting of neutral faces paired with positive, negative, or neutral words while undergoing an fMRI scan. The researchers found a strong negative correlation between left amygdala activity during the encoding of negative pairs and subsequent memory performance, suggesting that amygdala activation at encoding may disrupt the formation of negative associations. It is important to note, though, that the opposite effect was observed for positive face-name pairs: increases in amygdala activation were related to better subsequent memory for those pairs, suggesting that the effect of arousal may depend on the valence of the information to be remembered.

THE MNEMONIC INFLUENCES OF AROUSAL: IMPLICATIONS FOR UNITIZATION

One of the most-often replicated effects of arousal on memory is the creation of a subjectively vivid memory (Phelps and Sharot, 2008; Sharot and Yonelinas, 2008; Zimmerman and Kelley, 2010). The beneficial effects of arousal on memory are often detected on tasks that assess not only recognition rates but also the subjective qualities of a memory. For instance, even when recognition rates do not differ between arousing and neutral stimuli, participants are often still more likely to say that they vividly recollect emotional items (Ochsner, 2000; Talarico and Rubin, 2003; Sharot et al., 2004). Although this effect may sometimes reflect a biased endorsement of emotional memories (Windmann et al., 2002; Dougal and Rotello, 2007), sometimes it seems to correspond with an improved ability to remember at least some features of an arousing item's presentation (Neisser and Harsch, 1992; Kensinger and Corkin, 2003; see review by Mather, 2007). By contrast, arousal often does not enhance the familiarity of items, and when it does, it often seems to do so for both studied and non-studied items alike, increasing both correct and incorrect endorsements and having little effect on memory discriminability (e.g., Sharot et al., 2004).

Consider that one of the predominant reasons why there is a mnemonic benefit for unitizations may be because of their ability to be recognized on the basis of familiarity (Diana et al., 2008, 2011; but see Mickes et al., 2010). If so, then the literature just reviewed may suggest that the relative benefit of unitization would be less for emotional associations than for neutral associations. That is, arousal may enhance processes that are connected to the recollection of information more than those connected to the familiarity of information, while unitizations may do the opposite.

At a neural level, it is less clear whether there is a distinction between the memory regions most influenced by arousal and those implicated in unitization. Certainly, much emphasis has been placed on the ability for arousal to modulate *hippocampal* function, via connections between the amygdala and the hippocampus. The initial studies examining the effect of arousal on memory consolidation focused on interactions between the amygdala and hippocampus proper (reviewed by McGaugh, 2004) and subsequent neuroimaging studies in humans have followed suit (reviewed by Phelps, 2004), often focusing on the correlations or co-activations between the amygdala and the hippocampus during the formation or retrieval of an emotional memory (e.g., Dolcos et al., 2004; Kensinger and Corkin, 2004). Yet the amygdala also shares strong reciprocal connections with the PrC (Pitkänen et al., 2000; Kajiwara et al., 2003). A recent study revealed that stimulation of the amygdala could lead to induction of synaptic plasticity (i.e., long-term potentiation) within the PrC (Perugini et al., 2012), demonstrating a functional connection between the two regions. Thus, the finding that unitizations rely less on the hippocampus and more on the PrC makes no strong prediction with regard to the effect of emotion on unitization. The reciprocal connections between the amygdala and the PrC appear to be sufficiently strong to enable arousal-driven modulation, though of course it remains an open question whether such modulation would occur during the encoding or retrieval of unitizations.

As noted earlier, if unitizations rely on processes within the ventral visual processing stream, the amygdala activation that occurs during the experience of arousal would be likely to modulate processing within that stream (Anderson, 2005; Vuilleumier, 2005). There is ample evidence that the amygdala sends strong back-projections to regions through the sensory cortices (Amaral and Price, 1984; Iwai and Yukie, 1987; Morris et al., 1998), and this prioritized processing may facilitate the creation of a unitization. Thus, arousal could enhance the process of unitization either through modulation of medial temporal-lobe processes or through modulation of earlier sensory processes.

THE EFFECTS OF AROUSAL ON UNITIZATION: PRELIMINARY EVIDENCE

We Murray and Kensinger (2012) conducted a study to examine the effect of arousal on associative binding when unitization is encouraged. We asked participants to study pairs of words and to either maintain separate mental images of the items (non-integrated) or to create an integrated, interactive mental image of the two items (integrated), a task similar to that described in Pilgrim et al. (2012). Some pairs contained an emotional and a neutral word, and other pairs contained two neutral words. Each study pair was displayed for 2, 4, or 6 s, and after each pair participants were asked to report the vividness of the two individual images (non-integrated) or one unified image (integrated) they were able to generate.

Participants consistently rated their imagery success as being high for emotional pairs, regardless of the length of the encoding trial, but they reported little success in generating images for neutral pairs during short (2-s) encoding trials. These results are consistent with the prediction that arousal would facilitate the process of unitization: When arousal was present, participants were able to create an image that integrated two distinct items, even with little time to do so.

Participants were then given a surprise cued recall test in which they were given a single studied word and asked to provide its paired counterpart. Because this was an associative task, we unsurprisingly found that pairs studied in the integration condition were better recalled than those studied in the non-integration condition. Conversely, on an item recognition test, performance was better in the non-integrated condition than in the integrated one. This finding is generally consistent with evidence presented earlier, suggesting that although the formation of unitizations can enhance memory for associations, this unitization sometimes comes at the cost of gaining access to the individual item representations (Pilgrim et al., 2012).

The twist, however, was that the integration benefit was disproportionately *greater* for neutral pairs than for pairs containing an emotion word. Although participants had an easier time generating the integrated images for the emotional pairs, they showed *less* of a mnemonic benefit from integration of those pairs. At the broadest level, these data suggest that *forming* unitizations – actually assembling together the different perceptual and semantic features – and *remembering* those unitizations in long-term memory could be differentially affected by arousal. It is interesting to note that this distinction parallels one noted by Zimmerman and Kelley (2010); they reported that participants gave higher judgments-of-learning to emotional pairs than to neutral ones but actually remembered the emotional pairs less well. When reviewing this study, Madan et al. (2012) suggested that the participants may have applied less effort when forming associations of those emotional items, an explanation that is also consistent with our data. It may be the case that if information is more easily unitized – perhaps via processes implemented in visual processing regions – the mnemonic storage of that unitization is less effortful and therefore less durable.

FUTURE DIRECTIONS AND CONCLUSION

FUTURE DIRECTIONS

The research we have reviewed suggests the importance of distinguishing the effects of arousal on the initial process of forming unitizations from the process of storing those unitizations over the long term. Future research would do well to examine whether – if these processes were distinguished, perhaps using methods similar to Staresina and Davachi (2010) – arousal would have different effects on these two general types of processes.

It is also possible that the presence of arousal may lead to a shift from conceptual to perceptual binding processes in creating unitizations (see Graf and Schacter, 1989 for discussion of the contribution of these different processes). In discussing the neural architecture that may underlie encoding of emotional and non-emotional unitization, we have offered that emotional unitizations may be supported by interactions between the amygdala, ventral visual stream, and PrC, suggesting that such unitizations may rely on more perceptual linkages (e.g., what a poisonous plant looks like). Non-emotional unitizations, by contrast, may more often be supported by conceptual processes, perhaps requiring stimulus elaboration to effectively concatenate (e.g., realizing that the blanket, watermelon, and basket go together as a picnic). Although further empirical testing of this hypothesis is required, a first set of neuroimaging data (Murray and Kensinger, 2013) is consistent with this hypothesis, with successful integration of emotional pairs resulting in disproportionate activation within visual regions and successful integration of neutral pairs resulting in greater activation within prefrontal regions. Moreover, amygdala activity during negative integration was negatively correlated with activity in prefrontal and MTL regions, suggesting that amygdala engagement may disrupt prefrontal and MTL processes, consistent with the finding of Okada et al. (2011).

Emotional arousal, then, may shift unitization processes away from more conceptual ones implemented by prefrontal engagement and toward more perceptual ones implemented within visual regions. These different types of processes (perceptual vs. conceptual) may have differential downstream effects on subsequent memory for the unitizations. Conceptual elaboration may be a slower, more laborious process, but it may lead to a more deeply encoded, and more durable, representation. By contrast, perceptual integrations may happen rapidly, but be less durable over time. In other words, there may be a levels-of-processing effect (Craik and Lockhart, 1972), leading to a stronger and more durable memory trace for unitizations formed using prefrontal and MTL processes than for unitizations formed with disproportionate use of visual processes.

It would be informative for future research to examine how arousal affects the durability of unitizations. On the one hand, if the main effect of arousal relates to the way in which unitizations are initially formed, and if the processes creating unitizations for arousing items are less effortful and less "deep," then it might be expected that the decay rate for emotional unitizations would be faster than for neutral unitizations. On the other hand, however, the consolidation hypothesis (Müller and Pilzecker, 1900), suggests that after information is initially encoded it remains in a fragile state before being solidified into memory (see review by McGaugh, 2000). The consolidation process is relatively slow, and one proposed reason is to give any associated emotional response sufficient time to influence the consolidation process (McGaugh, 2000; Phelps, 2004). Indeed, there is robust evidence that arousal often enhances the consolidation of information, such that the beneficial effects of arousal are more likely to be apparent after longer delays than after shorter ones. This pattern of results has been shown not only in assessments of item memory (Sharot and Phelps, 2004) but also in tests of associative memory (Pierce and Kensinger, 2011; however, see Szpunar et al., 2012 for evidence that memory for details of imagined future autobiographical events is better for positive and negative than neutral events after a 10-min delay, but better for positive and *neutral* than negative events after a 24-h delay). Thus, it is possible that even if emotional unitizations are less "deep" and are maintained less well over relatively short delays (e.g., 30 min), they may have a shallower forgetting curve than neutral unitizations, making them more durable over longer delays. Adjudicating between these alternatives – by assessing memory for unitizations after multiple delays, or by disrupting consolidation through a retroactive interference task – would appear to be important for determining whether arousal primarily exerts its effects on unitization through processes that occur as the unitization is initially formed or whether the effects continue as that unitization is stored.

As we have noted earlier, the neural processes that underlie the formation and retrieval of unitizations are likely to depend in some way on the verbal or visual demands of the unitization. Although verbal unitizations (e.g., novel compound words; Giovanello et al., 2006; Quamme et al., 2007; Haskins et al., 2008) and visual unitizations (e.g., assembling a fragmented item and imagining it in a specified color; Staresina and Davachi, 2010) share some similarity – that is, they can be performed without reliance on hippocampal processing – no study has directly contrasted the neural correlates supporting their creation or retrieval. Emotion may also affect the unitization process differently, depending on the modality of processing. The amygdala can influence both visual processing (Vuilleumier et al., 2001, 2004; Compton, 2003; Mather et al., 2006) and semantic processing (Skipper et al., 2011), but the extent to which those influences differ for visual and verbal unitization – or on tasks that require some combination thereof (e.g., Staresina and Davachi, 2006, 2008; Murray and Kensinger, 2012) – is currently unknown. Therefore, we believe a fruitful future investigation would employ both verbal and visual unitization of emotional and non-emotional information, in an attempt to elucidate the similarities and differences between those two domains.

One area that we have not discussed to this point is how unitization processes may be utilized in the creation of autobiographical memories. Current theories of autobiographical retrieval suggest that it is a reconstructive process (see reviews by Conway, 1996; Holland and Kensinger, 2010) in which memories of our past are reconstructed at retrieval from our stores of autobiographical knowledge. This reconstructive nature imparts flexibility on retrieval from events in our past: the same event may be described differently at different time points. Autobiographical details also can be intentionally recombined into past events that did not occur, or into simulated, plausible future events. In one fMRI study, Addis et al. (2009) asked participants to report details of autobiographical events (i.e., the "who," "what," and "where") during a pre-scan session, and then directed those participants to imagine novel past and future events that consisted of recombined details from participants' actual memories. For example, if the participant reported memories of "Jess buying a lottery ticket at a convenience store," "Eating chicken fajitas with Cathy at Border's Café," and "Buying a flat screen TV with John at Best Buy" the participant may be asked to imagine a novel past or future event that involved "John," "Border's Café," and "lottery ticket." One could conceive of this process as being similar to unitization in that participants must take previously unrelated details and combine them into a single representation. A key difference however, is that in these tasks participants are asked to generate a representation of a new *event*, localized in time and space. To our knowledge, no tasks of unitization require this type of temporal or spatial localization of the representation. Perhaps because of this key difference, in the studies by Addis et al. (2009), this imaginative generation was shown to recruit activity in bilateral hippocampus, as well as activity in anterior prefrontal cortex and angular gyrus. These results suggest that whereas unitization of two words or items into a new representation may be accomplished in the absence of hippocampal processing (e.g., Giovanello et al., 2006; Staresina and Davachi, 2010), when new representations are created as *events* anchored in time and space, this may require the hippocampus.

CONCLUSIONS

The literature reviewed here suggests that unitized associations can be formed and retrieved using dissociable processes from those used to support memory for other associative memories. Unitized associations can be remembered on the basis of familiarity and in the absence of hippocampal function. Their formation appears to be supported by some combination of processing within sensory-processing regions and within the rhinal cortex, although additional research is needed to further specify the involvement of these regions.

At least within a laboratory setting, when unitization is the specified goal, arousal appears to enhance the ability to form an integrated representation; this representation can be formed with high success even when under time pressure. Yet arousal does not enhance the ability to remember that unitized representation over the long-term, revealing a distinction between facilitated *formation* of a unitization and facilitated *retention* of that unitization. Further research will be needed to elucidate the reasons for these distinctions, but we suggest that arousal may facilitate the formation of unitizations via perceptual processing, whereas unitization for neutral items may be more likely to recruit conceptual processes implemented within prefrontal and MTL regions.

ACKNOWLEDGMENTS

This work was supported by grant MH080833 from the National Institute of Mental Health (awarded to Elizabeth A. Kensinger).

REFERENCES

Addis, D. R., Pan, L., Vu, M. A., Laiser, N., and Schacter, D. L. (2009). Constructive episodic simulation of the future and the past: distinct subsystems of a core brain network mediate imaging and remembering. *Neuropsychologia* 47, 2222–2238.

Adolphs, R., Denburg, N. L., and Tranel, D. (2001). The amygdala's role in long-term declarative memory for gist and detail. *Behav. Neurosci.* 115, 983–992.

Aggleton, J. P., and Brown, M. W. (1999). Episodic memory, amnesia, and the hippocampal-anterior thalamic axis. *Behav. Brain Sci.* 3, 425–444.

Amaral, D. G., and Price, J. L. (1984). Amygdalo-cortical projections in the monkey (*Macaca fascicularis*). *J. Comp. Neurol.* 230, 465–496.

Anderson, A. K. (2005). Affective influences on the attentional dynamics supporting awareness. *J. Exp. Psychol. Gen.* 134, 258–281.

Anderson, A. K., and Phelps, E. A. (2001). Lesions of the human amygdala impair enhanced perception of emotionally salient events. *Nature* 411, 305–309.

Atkinson, R. C., and Juola, J. F. (1974). "Search and decision processes in recognition memory," in *Contemporary Developments in Mathematical Psychology: Vol. 1. Learning, Memory & Thinking*, eds D. H. Krantz, R. C. Atkinson, R. D. Luce, and P. Suppes (San Francisco: Freeman Press), 243–293.

Bachevalier, J., and Nemanic, S. (2008). Spatial memory in monkeys as measured with the visual paired-comparison task: effects of selective hippocampal, perirhinal and areas TH/TF lesions. *Hippocampus* 18, 64–80.

Bader, R., Mecklinger, A., Hoppstädter, M., and Meyer, P. (2010). Recognition memory for one-trial-unitized word pairs: evidence from event-related potentials. *Neuroimage* 50, 772–781.

Bergmann, H. C., Rijpkema, M., Fernández, G., and Kessels, R. P. C. (2012). The effects of valence and arousal on associative working memory and long-term memory. *PLoS ONE* 7:e52616. doi:10.1371/journal.pone.0052616

Berntson, G. G., Bechara, A., Damasio, H., Tranel, D., and Cacioppo, J. T. (2007). Amygdala contribution to selective dimensions of emotion. *Soc. Cogn. Affect. Neurosci.* 2, 123–129.

Bowles, B., Crupi, C., Pigott, S., Parrent, A., Wiebe, S., Janzen, L., et al. (2010). Double dissociation of selective recollection and familiarity impairments following two different surgical treatments for temporal-lobe epilepsy. *Neuropsychologia* 48, 2640–2647.

Bradley, M. M., Sabatinelli, D., Lang, P. J., Fitzsimmons, J. R., King, W., and Desal, P. (2003). Activation of the visual cortex in motivated attention. *Behav. Neurosci.* 117, 369–380.

Brown, C. M., and Aggleton, J. P. (2001). Recognition memory: what are the roles of the perirhinal cortex and hippocampus? *Nat. Rev. Neurosci.* 2, 51–61.

Buchanan, T. W., and Adolphs, R. (2002). "The role of the human amygdala in emotional modulation of long-term declarative memory," in *Emotional Cognition: From Brain to Behavior*, eds S. Moore and M. Oaksford (Amsterdam: John Benjamins Publishing), 9–34.

Bussey, T. J., and Saksida, L. M. (2007). Memory, perception, and the ventral visual-perirhinal-hippocampal stream: thinking outside of the boxes. *Hippocampus* 17, 898–908.

Bussey, T. J., Saksida, L. M., and Murray, E. A. (2003). Impairments in visual discrimination after perirhinal cortex lesions: testing "declarative" vs. "perceptual-mnemonic" views of perirhinal cortex function. *Eur. J. Neurosci.* 17, 649–660.

Cahill, L., and McGaugh, J. L. (1995). A novel demonstration of enhanced memory associated with emotional arousal. *Conscious. Cogn.* 4, 410–421.

Cahill, L., and McGaugh, J. L. (1998). "Modulation of memory storage," in *Findings and Current Opinion in Cognitive Neuroscience*, eds L. R. Squire and S. M. Kosslyn (Cambridge: MIT Press), 85–90.

Cahill, L., Prins, B., Weber, M., and McGaugh, J. L. (1994). Adrenergic activation and memory for emotional events. *Nature* 371, 702–704.

Canteras, N. S., and Swanson, L. W. (1992). Projections of the ventral subiculum to the amygdala, septum, and hypothalamus: a PHAL anterograde tract-tracing study in the rat. *J. Comp. Neurol.* 8, 180–194.

Canto, C. B., Wouterlood, F. G., and Witter, M. P. (2008). What does the anatomical organization of the entorhinal cortex tell us?. *Neural Plast.* 2008, 1–18. doi:10.1155/2008/381243

Chun, M. M., and Potter, M. C. (1995). A two-stage model for multiple target detection in rapid serial visual presentation. *J. Exp. Psychol. Hum. Percept. Perform.* 21, 109–127.

Cohen, N. J., and Eichenbaum, H. (1993). *Memory, Amnesia, and the Hippocampal System.* Cambridge, MA: MIT Press.

Compton, R. J. (2003). The interface between emotion and attention: a review of evidence from psychology and neuroscience. *Behav. Cogn. Neurosci. Rev.* 2, 115–129.

Conway, M. A. (1996). "Autobiographical knowledge and autobiographical memories," in *Remembering Our Past: Studies in Autobiographical Memory*, ed. D. C. Rubin (Cambridge: Cambridge University Press), 67–93.

Cowell, R. A., Bussey, T. J., and Saksida, L. M. (2010). Components of recognition memory: dissociable cognitive processes or just differences in representational complexity? *Hippocampus* 20, 1245–1262.

Craik, F., and Lockhart, R. S. (1972). Levels of processing: a framework for memory research. *J. Verbal Learn. Verbal Behav.* 11, 671–684.

Damoiseaux, J. S., and Greicius, M. D. (2009). Greater than the sum of its parts: a review of studies combining structural connectivity and resting-state functional connectivity. *Brain Struct. Funct.* 213, 525–533.

Diana, R. A., Van den Boom, W., Yonelinas, A. P., and Ranganath, C. (2011). ERP correlates of source memory: unitized source information increases familiarity-based retrieval. *Brain Res.* 1367, 278–286.

Diana, R. A., Yonelinas, A. P., and Ranganath, C. (2007). Imaging recollection and familiarity in the medial temporal lobe: a three-component model. *Trends Cogn. Sci. (Regul. Ed.)* 12, 379–386.

Diana, R. A., Yonelinas, A. P., and Ranganath, C. (2008). The effects of unitization on familiarity-based source memory: testing a behavioral prediction derived from neuroimaging data. *J. Exp. Psychol. Learn. Mem. Cogn.* 34, 730–740.

Diana, R. A., Yonelinas, A. P., and Ranganath, C. (2010). Medial temporal lobe activity during source retrieval reflects information type, not memory strength. *J. Cogn. Neurosci.* 22, 1808–1818.

Dolcos, F., LaBar, K. S., and Cabeza, R. (2004). Interaction between the amygdala and the medial temporal lobe memory system predicts better memory for emotional events. *Neuron* 42, 855–863.

Dougal, S., and Rotello, C. M. (2007). "Remembering" emotional words is based on response bias, not recollection. *Psychon. Bull. Rev.* 66, 183–201.

Duncan, S., and Barrett, L. F. (2007). The role of the amygdala in visual awareness. *Trends Cogn. Sci. (Regul. Ed.)* 11, 190–192.

Easterbrook, J. A. (1959). The effect of emotion on cue utilization and the organization of behavior. *Psychol. Rev.* 66, 183–201.

Ecker, U. K. H., Zimmer, H. D., and Groh-Bordin, C. (2007). Color and context: an ERP study on intrinsic and extrinsic feature binding in episodic memory. *Mem. Cognit.* 35, 1483–1501.

Eichenbaum, H., Otto, T., and Cohen, N. J. (1994). Two functional components of the hippocampal memory system. *Behav. Brain Sci.* 17, 449–517.

Eichenbaum, H., Yonelinas, A. P., and Ranganath, C. (2007). The medial temporal lobe and recognition memory. *Annu. Rev. Neurosci.* 30, 123–152.

Freese, J. L., and Amaral, D. G. (2005). The organization of projections from the amygdala to visual cortical areas TE and V1 in the macaque monkey. *J. Comp. Neurol.* 486, 295–317.

Gallagher, M., and Chiba, A. A. (1996). The amygdala and emotion. *Curr. Opin. Neurobiol.* 6, 221–227.

Giovanello, K. S., Keane, M. M., and Verfaellie, M. (2006). The contribution of familiarity to associative memory in amnesia. *Neuropsychologia* 44, 1859–1865.

Graf, P., and Schacter, D. L. (1989). Unitization and grouping mediate dissociations in memory for new associations. *J. Exp. Psychol.* 15, 930–940.

Graham, K. S., Barense, M. D., and Lee, A. C. (2010). Going beyond LTM in the MTL: a synthesis of neuropsychological and neuroimaging findings on the role of the medial temporal lobe in memory and perception. *Neuropsychologia* 48, 831–853.

Guillet, R., and Arndt, J. (2009). Taboo words: the effect of emotion on memory for peripheral information. *Mem. Cognit.* 37, 866–879.

Hamann, S. (2001). Cognitive and neural mechanisms of emotional memory. *Trends Cogn. Sci. (Regul. Ed.)* 5, 394–400.

Hargreaves, E. L., Rao, G., Lee, I., and Knierim, J. J. (2005). Major dissociation between medial and lateral entorhinal input to dorsal hippocampus. *Science* 308, 1792–1794.

Haskins, A. L., Yonelinas, A. P., Quamme, J. R., and Ranganath, C. (2008). Perirhinal cortex supports encoding and familiarity-based recognition of novel associations. *Neuron* 59, 554–560.

Holland, A. C., and Kensinger, E. A. (2010). Emotion and autobiographical memory. *Phys. Life Rev.* 7, 88–131.

Iwai, E., and Yukie, M. (1987). Amygdalofugal and amygdalopetal connections with modality-specific visual cortical areas in macaques (*Macaca fuscata, M. mulatta,* and *M. fascicularis*). *J. Comp. Neurol.* 261, 362–387.

Jackson, O. III, and Schacter, D. L. (2004). Encoding activity in anterior medial temporal lobe supports subsequent associative recognition. *Neuroimage* 21, 456–462.

Kahneman, D., Treisman, A., and Gibbs, B. J. (1992). The reviewing of object files: object-specific integration of information. *Cogn. Psychol.* 24, 175–219.

Kajiwara, R., Takashima, I., Mimura, Y., and Iijima, T. (2003). Amygdala input promotes spread of excitatory neural activity from perirhinal cortex to the entorhinal-hippocampal circuit. *J. Neurophysiol.* 89, 2176–2184.

Keil, A., and Ihssen, N. (2004). Identification facilitation for emotionally arousing verbs during the attentional blink. *Emotion* 4, 23–35.

Kensinger, E. A. (2007). Negative emotion enhances memory accuracy behavioral and neuroimaging evidence. *Curr. Dir. Psychol. Sci.* 16 213–218.

Kensinger, E. A. (2009). Remembering the details: effects of emotion. *Emot. Rev.* 1, 99–113.

Kensinger, E. A., Addis, D. R., and Atapattu, R. K. (2011). Amygdala activity at encoding corresponds with memory vividness and with memory for select episodic details. *Neuropsychologia* 49, 663–673.

Kensinger, E. A., and Corkin, S. (2003). Memory enhancement for emotional words: are emotional words more vividly remembered than neutral words? *Mem. Cognit.* 31, 1169–1180.

Kensinger, E. A., and Corkin, S. (2004). Two routes to emotional memory: distinct neural processes for valence and arousal. *Proc. Natl. Acad. Sci. U.S.A.* 101, 3110–3115.

Kensinger, E. A., Geoff-Eaton, R. J., and Schacter, D. L. (2005). Memory for specific visual details can be enhanced by negative arousing content. *J. Mem. Lang.* 54, 99–112.

Kensinger, E. A., and Schacter, D. L. (2006). Amygdala activity is associated with the successful encoding of item, but not source, information for positive and negative stimuli. *J. Neurosci.* 26, 2564–2570.

Kent, B. A., and Brown, T. H. (2012). Dual functions of the perirhinal cortex in fear conditioning. *Hippocampus* 22, 2068–2079.

Knight, M., Seymour, T. L., Gaunt, J. T., Baker, C., Nesmith, K., and Mather, M. (2007). Aging and goal-directed emotional attention: distraction reverses emotional biases. *Emotion* 7, 705–714.

Krettek, J. E., and Price, J. L. (1977). Projections from the amygdaloid complex and adjacent olfactory structures to the entorhinal cortex and to the subiculum in the rat and cat. *J. Comp. Neurol.* 172, 723–752.

LaBar, K. S. (2007). Beyond fear emotional memory mechanisms in the human brain. *Curr. Dir. Psychol. Sci.* 16, 172–177.

LaBar, K. S., Mesulam, M., Gitelman, D. R., and Weintraub, S. (2000). Emotional curiosity: modulation of visuospatial attention by arousal is preserved in aging and early-stage Alzheimer's disease. *Neuropsychologia* 38, 1734–1740.

Lacy, J. W., and Stark, C. E. (2012). Intrinsic functional connectivity of the human medial temporal lobe suggests a distinction between adjacent MTL cortices and hippocampus. *Hippocampus* 22, 2290–2302.

Lambon, R. M. A., Sage, K., Jones, R. W., and Mayberry, E. J. (2010). Coherent concepts are computed in the anterior temporal lobes. *Proc. Natl. Acad. Sci. U.S.A.* 107, 2717–2722.

Lavenex, P., and Amaral, D. G. (2000). Hippocampal-neocortical interaction: a hierarchy of associativity. *Hippocampus* 10, 420–430.

Levine, L. J., and Edelstein, R. S. (2009). Emotion and memory narrowing: a review and goal-relevance approach. *Cogn. Emot.* 23, 833–875.

MacKay, D. G., Shafto, M., Taylor, J. K., Marian, D. E., Abrams, L., and Dyer, J. R. (2004). Relations between emotion, memory and attention: evidence from taboo Stroop, lexical decision, and immediate memory tasks. *Mem. Cognit.* 32, 474–488.

Madan, C. R., Caplan, J. B., Lau, C. S. M., and Fujiwara, E. (2012). Emotional arousal does not enhance association-memory. *J. Mem. Lang.* 66, 695–716.

Maren, S., and Fanselow, M. S. (1985). Synaptic plasticity in the basolateral amygdala induced by hippocampal formation stimulation *in vivo*. *J. Neurosci.* 15, 7548–7564.

Mather, M. (2007). Emotional arousal and memory binding: an object-based framework. *Perspect. Psychol. Sci.* 2, 33–52.

Mather, M., and Knight, M. R. (2006). Angry faces get noticed quickly: threat detection is not impaired among older adults. *J. Gerontol. B Psychol. Sci. Soc. Sci* 61, 54–57.

Mather, M., Mitchell, K. J., Raye, C. L., Novak, D. L., Greene, E. J., and Johnson, M. K. (2006). Emotional arousal can impair feature binding in working memory. *J. Cogn. Neurosci.* 18, 614–625.

Mather, M., and Nesmith, K. (2008). Arousal-enhanced location memory for pictures. *J. Mem. Lang.* 58, 449–464.

Mather, M., and Sutherland, M. R. (2011). Arousal-biased competition in perception and memory. *Perspect. Psychol. Sci.* 6, 114–133.

Mayes, A., Montaldi, D., and Migo, E. (2007). Associative memory and the medial temporal lobes. *Trends Cogn. Sci. (Regul. Ed.)* 11, 126–135.

McGaugh, J. (2000). Memory – a century of consolidation. *Science* 287, 248–251.

McGaugh, J. (2004). The amygdala modulates the consolidation of memories and emotionally arousing experiences. *Annu. Rev. Neurosci.* 27, 1–28.

Mickes, L., Johnson, E., and Wixted, J. T. (2010). Continuous recollection vs. unitized familiarity in associative recognition. *J. Exp. Psychol. Learn. Mem. Cogn.* 35, 843–863.

Mickley Steinmetz, K. R., Addis, D. R., and Kensinger, E. A. (2010). The effect of arousal on the emotional memory network depends on valence. *Neuroimage* 53, 318–324.

Montaldi, D., and Mayes, A. R. (2010). The role of recollection and familiarity in the functional differentiation of the medial temporal lobes. *Hippocampus* 20, 1291–1314.

Morris, J. S., Friston, K. J., Büchel, C., Frith, C. D., Young, A. W., Calder, A. J., et al. (1998). A neuromodulatory role for the human amygdala in processing emotional facial expressions *Brain* 121, 47–57.

Müller, G. E., and Pilzecker, A (1900). Experimentelle Beiträge zur Lehre vom Gedächtnis. *Z. Psychol Ergänzungsband* 1, 1–300.

Murray, B. D., and Kensinger, E. A (2012). The effects of emotion and encoding strategy on associative memory. *Mem. Cognit.* 40 1056–1069.

Murray, B. D., and Kensinger, E. A. (2013). "Mental integration of emotional and non-emotional verbal pairs is supported by dissociable neural regions at encoding and retrieval," in *Poster Presented at the Cognitive Neuroscience Society Annual Meeting* San Francisco, CA.

Nashiro, K., and Mather, M. (2010). How arousal affects older and younger adults' memory binding. *Exp. Aging Res.* 37, 108–128.

Neisser, U., and Harsch, N. (1992). "Phantom flashbulbs: false recollections of hearing the news about challenger," in *Affect and Accuracy in Recall: Studies of "Flashbulb" Memories*, eds E. Winograd and U. Neisser (New York: Cambridge University Press), 9–31.

Nummenmaa, L., Hyönä, J., and Calvo, M. G. (2006). Eye movement assessment of selective attentional capture by emotional pictures. *Emotion* 6, 257–268.

Ochsner, K. N. (2000). Are affective events richly "remembered" or simply familiar? The experience and process of recognizing feelings past. *J. Exp. Psychol. Gen.* 129, 242–261.

Öhman, A., Flykt, A., and Esteves, F. (2001). Emotion drives attention: detecting the snake in the grass. *J. Exp. Psychol. Gen.* 130, 466–478.

Öhman, A., and Mineka, S. (2001). Fear, phobias, and preparedness: toward and evolved module of fear and fear learning. *Psychol. Rev.* 108, 483–522.

Okada, G., Okamoto, Y., Kunisato, Y., Aoyama, S., Nishiyama, Y., Yoshimura, S., et al. (2011). The effect of negative and positive emotionality on associative memory: an fMRI study. *PLoS ONE* 6:e24862. doi:10.1371/journal.pone.0024862

Perugini, A., Laing, M., Berretta, N., Aicardi, G., and Bashir, Z. I. (2012). Synaptic plasticity from amygdala to perirhinal cortex: a possible mechanism for emotional enhancement of visual recognition memory? *Eur. J. Neurosci.* 36, 1–7.

Phelps, E. A. (2004). Human emotion and memory: interactions of the amygdala and hippocampal complex. *Curr. Opin. Neurobiol.* 14, 198–202.

Phelps, E. A., and Sharot, T. (2008). How (and why) emotion enhances the subjective sense of recollection. *Curr. Dir. Psychol. Sci.* 17, 147–152.

Pierce, B. H., and Kensinger, E. A. (2011). Effects of emotion on associative recognition: valence and retention interval matter. *Emotion* 11, 139–144.

Pilgrim, L. K., Murray, J. G., and Donaldson, D. I. (2012). Characterizing episodic memory retrieval: electrophysiological evidence for diminished familiarity following unitization. *J. Cogn. Neurosci.* 24, 1671–1681.

Pitkänen, A., Pikkarainen, M., Nurminen, N., and Ylinen, A. (2000). Reciprocal connections between the amygdala and the hippocampal formation, perirhinal cortex, and postrhinal cortex in rat: a review. *Ann. N. Y. Acad. Sci.* 911, 369–391.

Quamme, J. R., Yonelinas, A. P., and Norman, K. A. (2007). Effect of unitization on associative recognition in amnesia. *Hippocampus* 17, 192–200.

Reisberg, D., and Heuer, F. (2004). "Memory for emotional events," in *Memory and Emotion*, eds D. Reisberg and P. Hertel (New York: Oxford University Press), 3–41.

Richardson, M. P., Strange, B. A., and Dolan, R. J. (2004). Encoding of emotional memories depends on amygdala and hippocampus and their interactions. *Nat. Neurosci.* 7, 278–285.

Russell, J. A. (1980). A circumplex model of affect. *J. Pers. Soc. Psychol.* 39, 1161–1178.

Saksida, L. M., and Bussey, T. J. (2010). The representational-hierarchical view of amnesia: translation from animal to human. *Neuropsychologia* 48, 2370–2384.

Savander, V., LeDoux, J. E., and Pitkänen, A. (1997). Interamygdaloid projections of the basal and accessory basal nuclei of the rat amygdaloid complex. *Neuroscience* 76, 725–735.

Sharot, T., Delgado, M. R., and Phelps, E. A. (2004). How emotion enhances the feeling of remembering. *Nat. Neurosci.* 7, 1376–1380.

Sharot, T., and Phelps, E. A. (2004). How arousal modulates memory: disentangling the effects of attention and retention. *Cogn. Affect. Behav. Neurosci.* 4, 294–306.

Sharot, T., and Yonelinas, A. P. (2008). Differential time-dependent effects of emotion on recollective experience and memory for contextual information. *Cognition* 106, 538–547.

Shi, C. J., and Cassell, M. D. (1999). Perirhinal cortex projections to the amygdaloid complex and hippocampal formation in the rat. *J. Comp. Neurol.* 406, 299–328.

Skipper, L. M., Ross, L. A., and Olson, I. R. (2011). Sensory and semantic category subdivisions within the anterior temporal lobes. *Neuropsychologia* 49, 3419–3429.

Squire, L. R. (1992). Declarative and nondeclarative memory: multiple brain systems supporting learning and memory. *J. Cogn. Neurosci.* 4, 232–243.

Squire, L. R., Wixted, J. T., and Clark, R. E. (2007). Recognition memory and the medial temporal lobe: a new perspective. *Nat. Rev. Neurosci.* 8, 872–883.

Squire, L. R., and Zola-Morgan, S. (1991). The medial temporal lobe memory system. *Science* 253, 1380–1386.

Staresina, B. P., and Davachi, L. (2006). Differential encoding mechanisms for subsequent associative recognition and free recall. *J. Neurosci.* 26, 9162–9172.

Staresina, B. P., and Davachi, L. (2008). Selective and shared contributions of the hippocampus and perirhinal cortex to episodic item and associative encoding. *J. Cogn. Neurosci.* 20, 1478–1489.

Staresina, B. P., and Davachi, L. (2010). Object unitization and associative memory formation are supported by distinct brain regions. *J. Neurosci.* 30, 9890–9897.

Suzuki, W. A. (2010). Untangling memory from perception in the medial temporal lobe. *Trends Cogn. Sci. (Regul. Ed.)* 14, 195–200.

Suzuki, W. A., Miller, E. K., and Desimone, R. (1997). Object and place memory in the macaque entorhinal cortex. *J. Neurophysiol.* 78, 1062–1081.

Szpunar, K. K., Addis, D. R., and Schacter, D. L. (2012). Memory for emotional simulations: remembering a rosy future. *Psychol. Sci.* 23, 24–29.

Talarico, J. M., and Rubin, D. C. (2003). Confidence, not consistency, characterizes flashbulb memories. *Psychol. Sci.* 14, 455–461.

Vuilleumier, P. (2005). How brains beware: neural mechanisms of emotional attention. *Trends Cogn. Sci.* 9, 585–594.

Vuilleumier, P., Armony, J. L., Driver, J., and Dolan, R. J. (2001). Effects of attention and emotion on face processing in the human brain: an event-related fMRI study. *Neuron* 30, 829–841.

Vuilleumier, P., Richardson, M. P., Armony, J. L., Driver, J., and Dolan, R. J. (2004). Distant influences of amygdala lesion on visual cortical activation during emotional face processing. *Nat. Neurosci.* 7, 1271–1278.

Waring, J. D., and Kensinger, E. A. (2011). How emotion leads to selective memory: neuroimaging evidence. *Neuropsychologia* 49, 1831–1842.

Windmann, S., Urbach, T. P., and Kutas, M. (2002). Cognitive and neural mechanisms of decision biases in recognition memory. *Cereb. Cortex* 12, 808–817.

Wixted, J. T. (2007). Dual-process theory and signal-detection theory of recognition memory. *Psychol. Rev.* 114, 152–176.

Wollen, K. A., Webber, A., and Lowry, D. H. (1972). Bizarreness versus interaction of mental images as determinants of learning. *Cogn. Psychol.* 3, 518–523.

Xu, Y., and Chun, M. M. (2006). Dissociable neural mechanisms supporting visual sort-term memory for objects. *Nature* 440, 91–95.

Yonelinas, A. P. (1994). Receiver-operating characteristics in recognition memory: evidence for dual-process model. *J. Exp. Psychol. Learn. Mem. Cogn.* 20, 1341–1354.

Yonelinas, A. P. (2002). The nature of recollection and familiarity: a review of 30 years of research. *J. Mem. Lang.* 46, 441–517.

Zimmerman, C. A., and Kelley, C. M. (2010). "I'll remember this!" Effects of emotionality on memory predictions versus memory performance. *J. Mem. Lang.* 62, 240–253.

8

Context prediction analysis and episodic memory

Sheri J. Y. Mizumori *

Laboratory of Neural Systems, Decision Science, Learning and Memory, Department of Psychology, University of Washington, Seattle, WA, USA

***Correspondence:**
Sheri J. Y. Mizumori, Laboratory of Neural Systems, Decision Science, Learning and Memory, Department of Psychology, University of Washington, Box 351525, Seattle, WA 98195-1525, USA
e-mail. mizumori@uw.edu

Events that happen at a particular place and time come to define our episodic memories. Extensive experimental and clinical research illustrate that the hippocampus is central to the processing of episodic memories, and this is in large part due to its analysis of context information according to spatial and temporal references. In this way, hippocampus defines ones expectations for a given context as well as detects errors in predicted contextual features. The detection of context prediction errors is hypothesized to distinguished events into meaningful epochs that come to be recalled as separate episodic memories. The nature of the spatial and temporal context information processed by hippocampus is described, as is a hypothesis that the apparently self-regulatory nature of hippocampal context processing may ultimately be mediated by natural homeostatic operations and plasticity. Context prediction errors by hippocampus are suggested to be valued by the midbrain dopamine system, the output of which is ultimately fed back to hippocampus to update memory-driven context expectations for future events. Thus, multiple network functions (both within and outside hippocampus) combine to result in adaptive episodic memories.

Keywords: hippocampus, prediction errors, prefrontal cortex, dopamine, striatum, memory, decision making

INTRODUCTION

Events are typically defined by the situations that are associated with significant outcomes. Each situation, or context, is multifaceted in that it includes not only the external sensory environment, but also our intrinsic motivational and emotional state, as well as social considerations. Thus it should not be surprising that the cells of the hippocampus, long thought to mediate episodic or event-based memories (e.g., O'Keefe and Nadel, 1978; Tulving, 2002), have been found to represent a variety of context-defining information. The challenge has been, however, to understand how these hippocampal representations of context-specific information are used to generate episodic memories. The following discusses the view that hippocampus represents context information in order to determine whether the expected contextual features match those currently being experienced. The identification of mismatches (termed *context prediction errors*) may lead to a cascading series of assessments through connected brain regions that could ultimately alter future decisions and update memories.

SPATIAL CONTEXT-DEPENDENCY OF HIPPOCAMPAL NEURAL CODES

It is generally accepted that hippocampus processes contextual information (e.g., Hirsh, 1974; Myers and Gluck, 1994; Anagnostaras et al., 2001; Maren, 2001; Fanselow and Poulos, 2005; Bouton et al., 2006). There are numerous demonstrations in which conditioned responses to contextual stimuli are eliminated with hippocampal damage while responses to discrete conditioned stimuli are unaffected (e.g., Kim and Fanselow, 1992; Phillips and LeDoux, 1992, 1994). Also, animals with hippocampal or entorhinal cortical damage do not show the normal decrement in conditioned responding after a shift in context (Penick and Solomon, 1991; Freeman et al., 1996a,b). The hippocampus of freely behaving animals is predisposed to represent context information within a spatial framework: during unrestrained navigation, hippocampal neurons fire selectively as animals traverse restricted areas of their environment, referred to as *place fields* (O'Keefe and Dostrovsky, 1971). As decades of research have shown (summarized in Mizumori, 2008), place fields are dynamic and integrated representations of multiple types of context-defining information. For example, changing any modality of cues, the motivational state, or the behaviors needed to perform the task result in alterations of place field properties, a process commonly referred to as *remapping*.

The readiness of place fields to remap is evident when changes are made to the visual environment (e.g., Ranck, 1973; O'Keefe, 1976; Olton et al., 1978; Muller and Kubie, 1987), such as its geometric features (e.g., Gothard et al., 1996; O'Keefe and Burgess, 1996; Wiener, 1996). Other sensory inputs also bias place field activity, including olfactory (Save et al., 2000), auditory (O'Keefe and Conway, 1978; McEchron and Disterhoft, 1999), and somatosensory information (Young et al., 1994). Thus, an extensive literature (Mizumori, 2008) verifies that hippocampal pyramidal neurons process multimodal sensory input. Hippocampal place fields are also sensitive to changes in a task's reward structure (Smith and Mizumori, 2006b; Wikenheiser and Redish, 2011). Smith and Mizumori (2006b) explicitly tested this idea by training rats to distinguish Context A from Context B according to where reward was expected to be found. The motivational, sensory, and behavioral requirements of task performance were purposely held constant across the two contexts so that changes in place fields could be attributed to the recall of a different memory. Place fields remapped at the beginning of trials in Context B, a time when there is heightened uncertainty about the context conditions. In a similar experiment, Wikenheiser and Redish

(2011) demonstrated that changes in reward contingency can modulate the trial-to-trial variability of hippocampal place cell activity, again suggesting that uncertainty can drive place field remapping. Finally, the relative contributions of sensory, motivation (including reward), or response information to a given place field vary with task demands, and this is evidenced by findings across many laboratories that place fields change when rats use identical information to solve tasks according to different mnemonic strategies (e.g., Ferbinteanu and Shapiro, 2003; Mizumori et al., 2004; Eschenko and Mizumori, 2007).

In sum, it is clear that place fields can come to represent different types of sensory, behavioral, and intrinsic information that have strong spatial and contextual (i.e., experience-dependent) features, thereby validating the term *spatial context* when referring to the informational content of place fields (Nadel et al., 1985; Mizumori et al., 1999, 2000; Jeffery et al., 2004). If this information indeed underlies the effective use and generation of episodic memories, Nadel (2008) has argued that the neural representations that define a familiar context must be relatively stable and predictable, maintaining their relationship to each other, until prediction errors are detected. This pattern of place field responses has indeed been documented in the literature. Stable place fields, then, can be said to reflect *the integration of stable background sensory information, internal state or motivational information, as well as response or behavioral outcome expectancies within a spatial framework as a function of time.*

To the extent that different cognitive strategies are mediated by different underlying memories, one network pattern of activated place cells is thought to reflect one memory, and a different pattern of activated place cells corresponds to a different memory (e.g., Samsonovich and McNaughton, 1997). When one refers to place field remapping, then, implicit is the notion that each map (or collection of activated place cells) is driven by a different memory.

SPATIAL CONTEXT DISCRIMINATION AND PREDICTION

As striking as location-selective firing is to even the naive observer, equally impressive is the fact that the otherwise stable place fields readily remap when most any feature of the spatial context changes. This sensitivity to changes in context has led many to suggest that a fundamental operation of the hippocampus is to detect changes in contextual information so that animals can discriminate contexts (e.g., Smith and Mizumori, 2006a,b). The ability to distinguish contexts likely relies on computations that are often attributed to hippocampus, including those that underlie the flexible use of conjunctive, sequential, relational, and spatial algorithms (e.g., O'Keefe and Nadel, 1978; Foster et al., 1987; Eichenbaum et al., 1999; Wood et al., 2000; Eichenbaum and Cohen, 2001; O'Reilly and Rudy, 2001; Fortin et al., 2002). The latter, in turn, are thought to be supported by various forms of pattern separation and pattern completion neurocomputations (Mizumori et al., 2004, 2007b; Penner and Mizumori, 2012a,b).

A *Context Discrimination Hypothesis* (CDH) postulates that single hippocampal neuronal representations of context provide multidimensional data to population-based network computations that ultimately determine whether expected contextual features of a situation have changed (e.g., Mizumori et al., 1999, 2000, 2007a; Smith and Mizumori, 2006a,b; Mizumori, 2008). Initial suggestive evidence of this interpretation of hippocampal network function was the repeated observation that upon less than complete changes in a familiar context, many but not all place fields remap (e.g., Tanila et al., 1997; Mizumori et al., 1999; Brown and Skaggs, 2002; Knierim, 2002; Lee et al., 2004). The place fields that remained in the face of changes in a familiar context were considered to represent the stable or expected contextual features. The place fields that changed, then, could be thought of as representing current context information. The existence of these two types of place field responses gave rise to the notion that hippocampus compares expected and experienced context features (Mizumori et al., 1999). This idea begs the question, then, why does hippocampus represent both expected (learned) and current context information? These hippocampal spatial context representations (O'Keefe and Nadel, 1978; Nadel and Wilner, 1980; Nadel and Payne, 2002) may contribute to a match-mismatch type of analysis that evaluates the present context according to how similar it is to the context that an animal expects to encounter based on past experiences (e.g., Gray, 1982; Vinogradova, 1995; Mizumori et al., 1999, 2000; Gray, 2000; Lisman and Otmakhova, 2001; Hasselmo et al., 2002; Anderson and Jeffery, 2003; Jeffery et al., 2004; Hasselmo, 2005b; Smith and Mizumori, 2006a,b; Manns et al., 2007a; Nadel, 2008). Detected mismatches may be signaled by a change in the pattern of input from hippocampus or possibly by a specific input pattern. This question remains to be answered. Nevertheless, mismatch signals can be used to identify novel situations and to distinguish different contexts, functions that are necessary to define significant events or episodes. Mismatch signals also may engage neural mechanisms that determine the value of the mismatch so that existing memories can be updated and/or new memories can be formed. When context match signals are generated, the effect could be to strengthen currently active memory networks located elsewhere in the brain (e.g., neocortex). In this way, hippocampus may play different mnemonic roles depending on whether or not contexts actually change.

In support of the CDH, disconnecting hippocampus by fornix lesions impairs context discrimination (Smith et al., 2004), and hippocampal lesions reduce animals' ability to respond to changes in a familiar environment (Good and Honey, 1991; Save et al., 1992a,b). Spatial novelty detection corresponds to selective elevation of the immediate early gene c-*fos* in hippocampus, and not in surrounding parahippocampal cortical regions (Jenkins et al., 2004). Also, as described above, hippocampal neurons show significantly altered firing patterns when rats experience spatial or non-spatial changes in a familiar environment (O'Keefe, 1976; Muller and Kubie, 1987; Wood et al., 1999; Fyhn et al., 2002; Ferbinteanu and Shapiro, 2003; Moita et al., 2004; Yeshenko et al., 2004; Leutgeb et al., 2005a,b; Puryear et al., 2006; Smith and Mizumori, 2006b; Eschenko and Mizumori, 2007). As an example, Smith and Mizumori (2006b) showed that hippocampal neurons develop context-specific responses only when rats were required to discriminate contexts. Discriminating neural responses were not observed when rats were allowed to randomly forage for the same amount of time. Further, Manns et al. (2007b) demonstrated that relative to match trials in an odor cue or object recognition task, CA1 neurons preferentially discharged when animals experienced a non-match situation in these same tasks. Also consistent with the CDH, neuroimaging studies of human performance shows that hippocampus becomes differentially active during match and mismatch trials (Kumaran and Maguire, 2007; Kuhl et al., 2010; Chen et al., 2011; Dickerson et al., 2011; Foerde and Shohamy, 2011; Duncan et al., 2012a,b).

The detection of changes in context is fundamentally important for the continual selection of appropriate behaviors that optimize performance and learning in a variety of tasks (e.g., navigation-based learning, instrumental conditioning, or classical conditioning). Context discrimination engages and prepares cellular mechanisms for rapid and new learning at potentially important times (Paulsen and Moser, 1998), as it is generally known that novelty detection increases attention and exploratory behaviors in a variety of tasks. Interestingly, hippocampal cell firing tends to occur during the "encoding phase" of the ongoing theta rhythm (Hasselmo, 2005a), which is increased during exploratory and investigatory behaviors (Vanderwolf, 1969). Thus, detection of a non-match situation can change the relationship between cell discharge and the local theta rhythm such that encoding functions are enhanced. Detection of matches, on the other hand, does not cause changes in the hippocampal neural activity profile, resulting in efferent messages that continue to retrieve/utilize the currently active memory network that recently drove the execution of successful responses. Context discrimination, then, can be viewed as being critical for the formation of new episodic memories because it leads to the separation in time and space one meaningful event from the next. Such division of memories could facilitate long-term information storage according to memory schemas (Tse et al., 2007; Bethus et al., 2010).

Since hippocampus seems particularly sensitive to changes in the expected (i.e., experience-dependent) context-defining features of a situation, its mismatch signals can be considered to reflect errors in predicted encounters with contextual features, or *context prediction errors.* Indeed, it has been shown that the greater the change in familiar context information, the more place fields remap (e.g., Leutgeb et al., 2005a). It should be noted, however, that when hippocampal cells respond differently to two contexts, it may be because they receive different afferent signals when animals experience different contexts. A second possibility is that the hippocampus receives input from memories stores that define context expectations, and this is actively compared within hippocampus to different input that defines the current context. The simultaneous presence of both familiar and new context information in hippocampus supports the latter possibility. In either case, however, transmission of a context prediction error signal from hippocampus may inform distal brain areas that a change in the context has occurred. Upon receipt of the context prediction error message, efferent midbrain-striatal structures may respond with changes in excitation or inhibition that reflect preparations for, or actual evaluation of, the subjective value of the context prediction error signal (e.g., Mizumori et al., 2004; Lisman and Grace, 2005; Humphries and Prescott, 2010; Penner and Mizumori, 2012a). On the other hand, a hippocampal signal indicating that there was no prediction error may enable plasticity mechanisms that ultimately allow new information to be incorporated into existing memory schemas (e.g., Mizumori et al., 2007a,b; Tse et al., 2007; Bethus et al., 2010). Thus, hippocampal context analyses become critical for the formation of new episodic memories not only because prediction signals provide a mechanism that separates in time and space one meaningful event from the next, but also because the outcome of the prediction error computation engages appropriate neuroplasticity mechanisms in efferent structures that promote subsequent adaptive decisions and memory.

The midbrain dopaminergic system is part of a neural network that assesses the value of behavioral outcomes. Reward-induced excitation of dopamine neurons scales to the magnitude of expected and encountered rewards regardless of the task demands (Schultz et al., 1997; Puryear et al., 2010; Jo et al., 2013): encounters with large rewards are accompanied by larger amplitude phasic dopamine responses than encounters with small amounts of reward. In addition, dopamine cells respond to unexpected reward absences by decreasing their firing rates (Schultz et al., 1997; Puryear et al., 2010). The reduction in firing when rewards are unexpectedly absent is greater if the expectation was for a large, and not small, reward. Further, these reward responses are context-dependent in a manner similar to what is observed for hippocampal place fields (Puryear et al., 2010), a result consistent with the view that hippocampal information guides reward value assessment systems of the brain (e.g., Mizumori et al., 2004; Lisman and Grace, 2005; Puryear et al., 2010) such that the significance of context prediction error messages can be determined (e.g., Penner and Mizumori, 2012a,b). The outcome of the value determination may ultimately come to bias future behavioral responding so that desired goals are more likely to be achieved (see review in Penner and Mizumori, 2012b).

CONTEXT-DEPENDENT TEMPORAL INFORMATION PROCESSING AND EPISODIC MEMORY

Different episodic memories contain information within unique spatial and temporal domains (Tulving, 2002). While there is growing clarity regarding how and why hippocampal neurons represent spatial context information (e.g., Knierim et al., 2006; McNaughton et al., 2006; Penner and Mizumori, 2012a,b; Pilly and Grossberg, 2012; Buzsaki and Moser, 2013), the mechanisms by which spatial context-defined events are distinguished temporally in the service of episodic memory functions remains unclear. However, current evidence support the hypothesis that hippocampus contains an organization structure that permits grouping of information into a number of different time scales (e.g., as reviewed in Buzsaki, 2006; Lisman and Redish, 2009; Grossberg and Pilly, 2013), that are relevant for comparing expected and experienced context information, and thus for episodic memory.

The activity of single neurons and neural networks naturally oscillate within hippocampus and across the brain according to a range of frequencies from low (e.g., 2–4 Hz) to high (e.g., 80 Hz) (Buzsaki, 2006). Oscillatory activity reflects alternating periods of synchronous neural firing: synchronous activity is associated with greater synaptic plasticity and stronger coupling amongst cells of an ensemble, while desynchronous periods are associated with less plasticity and weak signal strength (Hasselmo et al., 2002; Hasselmo, 2005a; Buzsaki, 2006). Thus, inherent in oscillatory neural activity is the ability to segregate on a (very short) time scale the processing of event-related information. In fact, the precise temporal alignment of place cell firing relative to the phase of the ongoing (theta) rhythm processes as animals move through the cell's place field (referred to as *phase precession*; O'Keefe and Recce, 1993) suggests the possibility that *context-dependent changes in place cell activity alters the state of synaptic plasticity in hippocampus according to experience.* By extension, then, an important impact of altered contextual features is the corresponding change in the nature and/or efficiency of information read into and passed on from hippocampus. Importantly, hippocampal oscillations may enable more temporally precise context representations, and therefore episodic memory. This in turn may enable more precise detection of unexpected context information.

Hippocampal circuits are also observed to synchronize their activity at frequencies greater than the theta frequency. Of particular interest is the gamma band (30–80 Hz) which has been observed in many sensory and motor areas of cortex, hippocampus, parietal cortex, and striatum (e.g., Leung and Yim, 1993; Brosch et al., 2002; Csicsvari et al., 2003; Berke et al., 2004; Bauer et al., 2006; Hoogenboom et al., 2006; Womelsdorf et al., 2006). Orchestration of both excitatory and inhibitory networks within each structure underlies the generation of synchronized gamma oscillations (e.g., Whittington et al., 1995; Vida et al., 2006). Although the functional importance of gamma oscillations remains debated, information carried by the cells that participate in a gamma-burst is effectively accentuated against a background of disorganized neural activity. Therefore, it has been suggested that gamma-bursts represent a fundamental mechanism by which information becomes segmented, filtered, or highlighted within a structure, as well as a mechanisms by which to coordinate information across structures (Buzsaki, 2006). Theta and gamma have many common physiological and behavioral relationships, suggesting that they are components of a coordinated and larger scale oscillatory network. For example, similar to theta rhythms, single unit responses that are recorded simultaneously with gamma oscillations have been found to have specific phase relationships to the gamma rhythm, and both theta and gamma are at least in part regulated by dopamine (e.g., Berke, 2009; van der Meer and Redish, 2009; Kalenscher et al., 2010). Therefore, changes in context that induce remapping (i.e., that altered the constellation of activated neurons), likely change patterns of gamma activity that are characteristic of a familiar context. Since gamma oscillations may effectively select salient information that ultimately impacts decisions, learning, and behavioral responses (e.g., van der Meer and Redish, 2009; Kalenscher et al., 2010), it is predicted that changes in gamma oscillatory patterns are likely to alter future decisions and learning. Further, gamma-bursts should become more predictable as learning takes place within a given context. *The relationship between place fields and the overriding theta and gamma rhythms is then an important mechanism by which spatially organized context information becomes temporally organized as animals experience an environment* (Buzsaki, 2006; Buzsaki and Moser, 2013). Specifically, this type of temporal relationship may confer a high level of temporal alignment (and hence accuracy) between expected and experienced context information, and this in turn should increase the accuracy of their comparison.

Since multiple brain areas demonstrate rhythmic neural activity, neural oscillations are likely a fundamental mechanism for coordinating neural activity across the brain in the service of adaptive decisions, learning, and memory (e.g., Buzsaki, 2006; Fries, 2009; Monaco et al., 2011; Penner and Mizumori, 2012b). Numerous laboratories have now reported that synchronous neural activity (in particular coherence of the theta rhythm) can be detected within and between memory-related brain structures such as the hippocampus, striatum, or prefrontal cortex (Tabuchi et al., 2000; Engel et al., 2001; Fell et al., 2001; Varela et al., 2001; Siapas et al., 2005; DeCoteau et al., 2007a; Womelsdorf et al., 2007). For example, hippocampal theta activity can become synchronized with place cell firing, resulting in coordinated timing of spatial coding (O'Keefe and Recce, 1993; Gengler et al., 2005). Also, theta oscillations within the striatum can become entrained to the hippocampal theta rhythm (Berke et al., 2004; DeCoteau et al., 2007a). Stimulating the striatum can induce hippocampal theta activity (Sabatino et al., 1985) and increases high frequency theta power, which is thought to be important for sensorimotor integration (Hallworth and Bland, 2004). Also, hippocampal and striatal activity theta activity become increasingly coherent during goal-directed navigation (Allers et al., 2002; DeCoteau et al., 2007a). When neural activity is disrupted in the striatum via D2 receptor antagonism, striatal modulation of high frequency hippocampal theta activity is also disrupted. The result is that motor and spatial/contextual information is not integrated, and task performance is impaired (Gengler et al., 2005).

Particularly intriguing is a finding common to both hippocampus and striatum, and that is that synchronous activity occurs in specific task-relevant ways (e.g., Hyman et al., 2005; Jones and Wilson, 2005) particularly during times when rats are said to be engaged in decision making (e.g., Benchenane et al., 2010). For example, striatal theta is modified over the course of learning on an egocentric T-maze task, increasing in coherence as the rat chooses and initiates turn behavior (DeCoteau et al., 2007a,b). Rats that learn the task develop an antiphase relationship between hippocampal and striatal theta oscillations, while rats that do not learn the task also do not show this type of theta relationship. This coherence has also been observed during striatal-dependent classical conditioning (Kropf and Kuschinsky, 1993). Coherent theta oscillations across distant brain structures can be enhanced with application of dopamine (Benchenane et al., 2010). Dopamine, then, may play a crucial role in coordinating ensemble activity across brain areas during times of decision making during navigation. Functionally, this type of control by dopamine suggests that information about the saliency of reward may determine which brain systems become synchronized (and desynchronized). This in turn guides the nature and type of information that is used to update memories and to determine future responses.

Task demands, then, seem to dictate the nature of neural synchrony across distal brain structures, and this synchrony may take the form of comodulation of existing theta and gamma rhythms as well as the generation of an additional rhythm. The latter was illustrated in a recent study by Fujisawa and Buzsaki (2011). They demonstrated that the existence of very low frequency (4 Hz) entrainment of local field potentials, e.g., the 7–12 Hz theta oscillation, that emerges only during phases of a maze task when rats made decisions (i.e., in the stem of a T-Maze). During decision periods, the 4 Hz rhythm was phase locked to theta oscillations in both the prefrontal cortex and VTA. Some of the individual prefrontal and VTA neurons were also phase locked to hippocampal theta oscillation at this time. Importantly the 4 Hz rhythm was present only during a decision making period when theta oscillations were also present. The findings of this study suggest that a 4 Hz rhythm may coordinate activity in distal brains structures specifically as animals make decisions during goal-directed navigation.

Assuming that "orchestrating" rhythms such as the 4 Hz rhythm also incorporate hippocampal neural activity, place field remapping is expected to have effects that extend well beyond hippocampal computations. When an expected context changes, evidence shows that place fields change by either increasing or decreasing firing rates and/or changes in their spatial specificity and reliability. This period of place field change corresponds to the period of uncertainty that is generated with by the context change. Therefore, as uncertainty decreases, place fields become more stable, and this in turn should result in the generation of more stable comodulation of specific frequencies of EEG across brain structures.

To fully understand the role of the hippocampus in episodic memory requires an understanding of how hippocampus relates event-specific details to particular temporal features of a task. Recently many (Manns et al., 2007b; Pastalkova et al., 2008; Gill et al., 2011; McDonald et al., 2011; Kraus et al., 2013) have suggest the existence of "time cells" in addition to place cells in hippocampus. These studies demonstrate that the timing of cell firing by a subpopulation of hippocampal neurons is not directly related to spatial or behavioral metrics such as distance, location, or running speed but rather they appear tuned to the timing of task-relevant events. Another challenge for future research is to better define how hippocampal context prediction error signals are interpreted and valued by neural systems responsible for decisions based on the most recent context analysis, and ultimately, by neural systems that update memories (Lisman and Grace, 2005; Penner and Mizumori, 2012a,b). The midbrain dopaminergic system is likely involved in this assessment process since dopamine neurons are not only known to respond to changes in the learned value of rewards, and to cues that predict future rewards (Schultz et al., 1997), but also they respond to changes in reward values in a context-dependent manner when rats perform a hippocampal-dependent task (Puryear et al., 2010).

Dopamine neural responses to the expectation of rewards seem to be regulated at least in part by prefrontal cortex (Jo et al., 2013), suggesting that the prefrontal cortex may relay to dopamine neurons information based on stored memories about past consequences of behavior. Penner and Mizumori (2012b) recently reviewed an extensive literature that describes how dopamine cell responses to hippocampal-based context information can come to regulate subsequent choices and response selection as information is processed through iterative striatal-to-cortex information loops (Haber et al., 2000). The result of this sequence of striatal-cortical processing is the determination of the degree to which expected behavioral outcomes occurred, and the updating of long-term memory. The latter, in turn, updates the definition of expected context features that cortex subsequently provides hippocampus (Penner and Mizumori, 2012a,b; Mizumori and Jo, 2013). Indeed Martig and Mizumori (2011) have shown that inactivation of the VTA results in unstable hippocampal place fields and behavioral errors when rats perform a hippocampal-dependent spatial task. Since the outcome assessment by VTA impacts the subsequent stability of hippocampal neural codes and behavioral accuracy on a spatial working memory task, it is likely that hippocampus and the VTA-striatal circuitry comprise key components of an adaptive loop of neural processing that allows organisms to continuously update memories and memory representations according to the outcomes of choices made within circumscribed epochs of time.

HOMEOSTATIC REGULATION OF NEURAL SIGNALS OF PREDICTION ERRORS

An emerging view is that the brain has evolved in large part to allow organisms to accurately predict the outcomes of events and behaviors (e.g., Llinas and Roy, 2009; Buzsaki, 2013; Buzsaki and Moser, 2013; Mizumori and Jo, 2013). More specifically, it has been suggested that organisms have been able to adapt to environments and societies of increasing complexity because brains evolved more complex neural circuitry that support the ability to make dynamic and conditional decisions and predictions These neural ensembles evolved to retain information over times of varying scales depending on the desired goal. Different brain areas are known to generate and retain sequences of information, and this ability can be accounted for by state-dependent changes in network dynamics (Mauk and Buonomano, 2004), internally generated oscillatory activity (Pastalkova et al., 2008), and/or dedicated "time cells" (Kraus et al., 2013). Thus, many elemental features of prediction analyses seem to be intrinsic, or self-generated. This property is likely very important for it may provide a mechanism by which prediction analyses can occur automatically so that organisms naturally seek control of the outcomes to their behaviors. What, then, might be the mechanism of a self-generated, and thus auto-regulated, brain prediction system? It is suggested here that such a mechanism may to some extent mirror principles of self-regulation at synaptic and neural circuit levels (e.g., Turrigiano, 1999, 2008, 2011; Marder and Prinz, 2003; Turrigiano and Nelson, 2004; Marder and Goaillard, 2006; Shetty et al., 2012; Mizumori and Jo, 2013).

Marder and Goaillard (2006) suggested that homeostatic neuroplasticity may be nested: calcium sensors may monitor neural firing rates, then up or down regulate the availability of glutamate receptors to ramp up or down firing rates toward an optimal firing rate set point. Groups of neurons or neural networks may sense changes in firing collectively to regulate experience-dependently population activity levels and patterns of activation. In this way homeostatic plasticity enables groups of neural circuits to find a balance between flexible and stable processing as needed to learn from experiences, and to be responsive to future changed inputs. The details of how networks of cells or their connections engage in homeostatic regulation remain to be discovered. Nevertheless, it is worth noting that homeostatic regulation at the neural systems level is clearly evident from studies of brain development, as well as from studies of reactive or compensatory neuroplasticity mechanisms that occur in response to experience (e.g., sensorimotor learning; Froemke et al., 2007) or brain injury (e.g., brain trauma or addiction; Robinson and Kolb, 2004; Nudo,

2011). While specific homeostatic neural plasticity mechanisms have not been used to account for complex learning, current theories of reinforcement- and context-based learning and memory commonly rely on the autoregulation of feedback loops.

A homeostatic framework could apply to the autoregulation of prediction analyses, which in turn will impact regulation of future decisions and memories. Such a framework includes *variables* that are monitored by *sensors* and then regulated by *controllers*, and thus it likely involves multiple, interactive, and hierarchically organized (auto-regulated) information loops analogous to what was described by Buzsaki (2013). At the cellular or synaptic levels, homeostatic plasticity mechanisms (Turrigiano et al., 1998; Marder and Goaillard, 2006; Turrigiano, 2011) may regulate cell excitability around a neural activity *set point* such that neurons retain maximal responsivity to future inputs. This process enables neurons to achieve a balance between synaptic stability and flexibility. Changes in calcium flux appear to be an important part of the sensing system that determines the current level of firing. It is hypothesized here that a prediction error, or mismatch signal, may result in higher or lower firing rates, at which time *controller* mechanisms should be engaged to bring the firing rates back to set point levels. Indeed reward prediction errors are illustrated by transient and significant reduced or elevated neural firing depending on the valence of the error (Schultz et al., 1997). Future research should focus on understanding the enabling and restorative mechanisms of prediction error signals. Of particular interest are mechanisms by which cortical memory may impact the threshold for signaling prediction errors. One cortical area of interest is the prefrontal cortex given (a) its intrinsic recurrent circuitry and detailed excitatory and inhibitory extrinsic connections (as reviewed in Arnsten et al., 2012) with both hippocampal/temporal lobe and reward valuation systems, and (b) given its role in attention and working memory (e.g., Fuster, 2006, 2008, 2009). That is, prefrontal cortex may orchestrate and coordinate the level of neural excitability in different prediction error brain areas according to homeostatic principles and in this way, bias the nature of the outputs of connected brain areas according to experience and recent outcomes of decisions. Prefrontal cortex also has strong functional connections with other cortical memory areas (e.g., parietal and temporal cortex), and is thus strategically positioned to influence long-term memory updating based on prediction error analyses. In this way the most recent memories can be fed forward to hippocampus for future context evaluation.

Although it is reasonable to assume that the prefrontal cortex controls or biases neural signaling in distal prediction brain regions, it should be noted that other sources of control of cell excitability may arise via direct interconnections amongst the multiple prediction detection areas of the brain. For example, a prediction error signal from the hippocampus could be transmitted to midbrain-striatal neurons along pathways that do not necessarily include the prefrontal cortex. Indirect support for this idea come from observations that conditions that produce error messages in the hippocampus change reward responses of dopamine neurons (Puryear et al., 2010; Jo et al., 2013), phasic theta comodulation is observed between hippocampus and striatum (DeCoteau et al., 2007a) during decision tasks, and comodulation of neural activity has been reported between prefrontal cortex and parietal cortex (Diwadkar et al., 2000). However, the identification of such correlations does not necessarily mean that this is the source of the comodulation or neural synchrony. Finding the source of neural regulation remains a challenge for the general field of systems neuroscience, one that may soon have answers with continued development of new methodologies such as optogenetic analyses.

In sum, homeostatic regulatory processes may contribute to the automatic and continuous self-regulatory nature of prediction error analysis, and ultimately decision making and episodic memory. Such a naturally adaptive mechanism optimizes the contribution of different types of prediction error signals to future decisions and actions according to the pattern of recent successes and failures in prediction.

ACKNOWLEDGMENTS

This work was supported by NIH grant MH58755. The author is most grateful for the significant research and theoretical contributions of numerous outstanding students over many years, most recently Wambura Fobbs, Yong Sang Jo, Sujean Oh, Marsha Penner, and Valerie Tryon.

REFERENCES

Allers, K. A., Ruskin, D. N., Bergstrom, D. A., Freeman, L. E., Ghazi, L. J., Tierney, P. L., et al. (2002). Multisecond periodicities in basal ganglia firing rates correlate with theta bursts in transcortical and hippocampal EEG. *J. Neurophysiol.* 87, 1118–1122.

Anagnostaras, S. G., Gale, G. D., and Fanselow, M. S. (2001). Hippocampus and contextual fear conditioning: recent controversies and advances. *Hippocampus* 11, 8–17. doi:10.1002/1098-1063(2001)11:1<8::AID-HIPO1015>3.3.CO;2-Z

Anderson, M. I., and Jeffery, K. J. (2003). Heterogeneous modulation of place cell firing by changes in context. *J. Neurosci.* 23, 8827–8835.

Arnsten, A. F. T., Wang, M. J., and Paspalas, C. D. (2012). Neuromodulation of thought: flexibilities and vulnerabilities in prefrontal cortical network synapses. *Neuron* 76, 223–239. doi:10.1016/j.neuron.2012.08.038

Bauer, M., Oostenveld, R., Peeters, M., and Fries, P. (2006). Tactile spatial attention enhances gamma-band activity in somatosensory cortex and reduces low-frequency activity in parieto-occipital areas. *J. Neurosci.* 26, 490–501. doi:10.1523/JNEUROSCI.5228-04.2006

Benchenane, K., Peyrache, A., Khamassi, M., Tierney, P. L., Gioanni, Y., Battaglia, F. P., et al. (2010). Coherent theta oscillations and reorganization of spike timing in the hippocampal-prefrontal network upon learning. *Neuron* 66, 921–936. doi:10.1016/j.neuron.2010.05.013

Berke, J. D. (2009). Fast oscillations in cortical-striatal networks switch frequency following rewarding events and stimulant drugs. *Eur. J. Neurosci.* 30, 848–859. doi:10.1111/j.1460-9568.2009.06843.x

Berke, J. D., Okatan, M., Skurski, J., and Eichenbaum, H. B. (2004). Oscillatory entrainment of striatal neurons in freely moving rats. *Neuron* 43, 883–896. doi:10.1016/j.neuron.2004.08.035

Bethus, I., Tse, D., and Morris, R. G. (2010). Dopamine and memory: modulation of the persistence of memory for novel hippocampal NMDA receptor-dependent paired associates. *J. Neurosci.* 30, 1610–1618. doi:10.1523/JNEUROSCI.2721-09.2010

Bouton, M. E., Westbrook, R. F., Corcoran, K. A., and Maren, S. (2006). Contextual and temporal modulation of extinction: behavioral and biological mechanisms. *Biol. Psychiat.* 60, 352–360. doi:10.1016/j.biopsych.2005.12.015

Brosch, M., Budinger, E., and Scheich, H. (2002). Stimulus-related gamma oscillations in primate auditory cortex. *J. Neurophysiol.* 87, 2715–2725.

Brown, J. E., and Skaggs, W. E. (2002). Concordant and discordant coding of spatial location in populations of hippocampal CA1 pyramidal cells. *J. Neurophysiol.* 88, 1605–1613.

Buzsaki, G. (2006). *Rhythms of the Brain.* New York: Oxford Press.

Buzsaki, G. (2013). Time, space and memory. *Nature* 497, 568–569. doi:10.1038/497568a

Buzsaki, G., and Moser, E. I. (2013). Memory, navigation and theta rhythm in the hippocampal-entorhinal system. *Nat. Neurosci.* 16, 130–138. doi:10.1038/nn.3304

Chen, J., Olsen, R. K., Preston, A. R., Glover, G. H., and Wagner, A. D. (2011). Associative retrieval processes in the human medial temporal lobe: hippocampal retrieval success and CA1 mismatch detection. *Learn. Mem.* 18, 523–528. doi: 10.1101/lm.2135211

Csicsvari, J., Jamieson, B., Wise, K. D., and Buzsaki, G. (2003). Mechanisms of gamma oscillations in the hippocampus of the behaving rat. *Neuron* 37, 311–322. doi:10.1016/S0896-6273(02)01169-8

DeCoteau, W. E., Thorn, C., Gibson, D. J., Courtemanche, R., Mitra, P., Kubota, Y., et al. (2007a). Learning-related coordination of striatal and hippocampal theta rhythms during acquisition of a procedural maze task. *Proc. Natl. Acad. Sci. U.S.A.* 104, 5644–5649. doi:10.1073/pnas.0700818104

DeCoteau, W. E., Thorn, C., Gibson, D. J., Courtemanche, R., Mitra, P., Kubota, Y., et al. (2007b). Oscillations of local field potentials in the rat dorsal striatum during spontaneous and instructed behaviors. *J. Neurophysiol.* 97, 3800–3805. doi:10.1152/jn.00108.2007

Dickerson, K. C., Li, J., and Delgado, M. R. (2011). Parallel contributions of distinct human memory systems during probabilistic learning. *Neuroimage* 55, 266–276. doi:10.1016/j.neuroimage.2010.10.080

Diwadkar, V. A., Carpenter, P. A., and Just, M. A. (2000). Collaborative activity between parietal and dorso-lateral prefrontal cortex in dynamic spatial working memory revealed by fMRI. *Neuroimage* 12, 85–99. doi:10.1006/nimg.2000.0586

Duncan, K., Ketz, N., Inati, S. J., and Davachi, L. (2012a). Evidence for area CA1 as a match/mismatch detector: a high-resolution fMRI study of the human hippocampus. *Hippocampus* 22, 389–398. doi:10.1002/hipo.20933

Duncan, K., Sadanand, A., and Davachi, L. (2012b). Memory's penumbra: episodic memory decisions induce lingering mnemonic biases. *Science* 337, 485–487. doi:10.1126/science.1221936

Eichenbaum, H., and Cohen, N. J. (2001). *From Conditioning to Conscious Recollection: Memory Systems of the Brain.* New York: Oxford University Press.

Eichenbaum, H., Dudchenko, P., Wood, E., Shapiro, M., and Tanila, H. (1999). The hippocampus, memory, and place cells: is it spatial memory or a memory space? *Neuron* 23, 184–188.

Engel, A. K., Fries, P., and Singer, W. (2001). Dynamic predictions: oscillations and synchrony in top-down processing. *Nat. Rev. Neurosci.* 2, 704–716. doi:10.1038/35094565

Eschenko, O., and Mizumori, S. J. (2007). Memory influences on hippocampal and striatal neural codes: effects of a shift between task rules. *Neurobiol. Learn Mem.* 87, 495–509. doi:10.1016/j.nlm.2006.09.008

Fanselow, M. S., and Poulos, A. M. (2005). The neuroscience of mammalian associative learning. *Annu. Rev. Psychol.* 56, 207–234. doi:10.1146/annurev.psych.56.091103.070213

Fell, J., Klaver, P., Lehnertz, K., Grunwald, T., Schaller, C., Elger, C. E., et al. (2001). Human memory formation is accompanied by rhinal-hippocampal coupling and decoupling. *Nat. Neurosci.* 4, 1259–1264. doi:10.1038/nn759

Ferbinteanu, J., and Shapiro, M. L. (2003). Prospective and retrospective memory coding in the hippocampus. *Neuron* 40, 1227–1239. doi:10.1016/S0896-6273(03)00752-9

Foerde, K., and Shohamy, D. (2011). Feedback timing modulates brain systems for learning in humans. *J. Neurosci.* 31, 13157–13167. doi:10.1523/JNEUROSCI.2701-11.2011

Fortin, N. J., Agster, K. L., and Eichenbaum, H. B. (2002). Critical role of the hippocampus in memory for sequences of events. *Nat Neurosci.* 5, 458–462.

Foster, T. C., Christian, E. P., Hampson, R. E., Campbell, K. A., and Deadwyler, S. A. (1987). Sequential dependencies regulate sensory evoked responses of single units in the rat hippocampus. *Brain Res.* 408, 86–96. doi:10.1016/0006-8993(87)90361-1

Freeman, J. H. Jr., Cuppernell, C., Flannery, K., and Gabriel, M. (1996a). Context-specific multi-site cingulate cortical, limbic thalamic, and hippocampal neuronal activity during concurrent discriminative approach and avoidance training in rabbits. *J. Neurosci.* 16, 1538–1549.

Freeman, J. H. Jr., Cuppernell, C., Flannery, K., and Gabriel, M. (1996b). Limbic thalamic, cingulate cortical and hippocampal neuronal correlates of discriminative approach learning in rabbits. *Behav. Brain Res.* 80, 123–136. doi:10.1016/0166-4328(96)00027-7

Fries, P. (2009). Neuronal gamma-band synchronization as a fundamental process in cortical computation. *Annu. Rev. Neurosci.* 32, 209–224. doi:10.1146/annurev.neuro.051508.135603

Froemke, R. C., Merzenich, M. M., and Schreiner, C. E. (2007). A synaptic memory trace for cortical receptive field plasticity. *Nature* 450, 425–429. doi:10.1038/nature06289

Fujisawa, S., and Buzsaki, G. (2011). A 4 Hz oscillation adaptively synchronizes prefrontal, VTA, and hippocampal activities. *Neuron* 72, 153–165. doi:10.1016/j.neuron.2011.08.018

Fuster, J. M. (2006). The cognit: A network model of cortical representation. *Int. J. Psychophysiol.* 60, 125–132. doi:10.1016/j.ijpsycho.2005.12.015

Fuster, J. M. (2008). *The Prefrontal Cortex, Fourth Edition.* London: Academic Press.

Fuster, J. M. (2009). Cortex and memory: emergence of a new paradigm. *J. Cog. Neurosci.* 21, 2047–2072. doi:10.1162/jocn.2009.21280

Fyhn, M., Molden, S., Hollup, S., Moser, M. B., and Moser, E. (2002). Hippocampal neurons responding to first-time dislocation of a target object. *Neuron* 35, 555–566. doi:10.1016/S0896-6273(02)00784-5

Gengler, S., Mallot, H. A., and Holscher, C. (2005). Inactivation of the rat dorsal striatum impairs performance in spatial tasks and alters hippocampal theta in the freely moving rat. *Behav. Brain Res.* 164, 73–82. doi:10.1016/j.bbr.2005.06.009

Gill, P. R., Mizumori, S. J. Y., and Smith, D. M. (2011). Hippocampal episode fields develop with learning. *Hippocampus* 21, 1240–1249. doi:10.1002/hipo.20832

Good, M., and Honey, R. C. (1991). Conditioning and contextual retrieval in hippocampal rats. *Behav. Neurosci.* 105, 499–509. doi:10.1037/0735-7044.105.4.499

Gothard, K. M., Skaggs, W. E., Moore, K. M., and Mcnaughton, B. L. (1996). Binding of hippocampal CA1 neural activity to multiple reference frames in a landmark-based navigation task. *J. Neurosci.* 16, 823–835.

Gray, J. A. (1982). *The Neuropsychology of Anxiety: An Enquiry into the Functions of the Septo-Hippocamal System.* Oxford: Oxford University Press.

Gray, J. A. (2000). *The Neuropsychology of Anxiety: An Enquiry into the Functions of the Septo-Hippocamal System,* 2nd Edn. Oxford: Oxford University Press.

Grossberg, S., and Pilly, P. K. (2013). How entorhinal grid cells may learn multiple spatial scales from a dorsoventral gradient of cell response rates in a self-organizing map. *PLoS Comput. Biol.* 8:e1002648. doi:10.1371/journal.pcbi.1002648

Haber, S. N., Fudge, J. L., and McFarland, N. R. (2000). Striatonigrostriatal pathways in primates form an ascending spiral from the shell to the dorsolateral striatum. *J. Neurosci.* 20, 2369–2382.

Hallworth, N. E. and Bland, B. H. (2004). Basal ganglia – hippocampal interactions support the role of the hippocampal formation in sensorimotor integration. *Exp. Neurol.* 188, 430–443. doi:10.1016/j.expneurol.2004.04.014

Hasselmo, M. E. (2005a). What is the function of hippocampal theta rhythm? – Linking behavioral data to phasic properties of field potential and unit recording data. *Hippocampus* 15, 936–949. doi:10.1002/hipo.20116

Hasselmo, M. E. (2005b). The role of hippocampal regions CA3 and CA1 in matching entorhinal input with retrieval of associations between objects and context: theoretical comment on Lee etal. (2005). *Behav. Neurosci.* 119, 342–345. doi:10.1037/0735-7044.119.1.342

Hasselmo, M. E., Hay, J., Ilyn, M., and Gorchetchnikov, A. (2002). Neuromodulation, theta rhythm and rat spatial navigation. *Neural Netw.* 15, 689–707. doi:10.1016/S0893-6080(02)00057-6

Hirsh, R. (1974). The hippocampus and contextual retrieval of information from memory: a theory. *Behav. Biol.* 12, 421–444. doi:10.1016/S0091-6773(74)92231-7

Hoogenboom, N., Schoffelen, J. M. Oostenveld, R., Parkes, L. M., and Fries, P. (2006). Localizing human visual gamma-band activity in frequency, time and space. *Neuroimage* 29, 764–773. doi:10.1016/j.neuroimage.2005.08.043

Humphries, M. D., and Prescott, T. J. (2010). The ventral basal ganglia, a selection mechanism at the crossroads of space, strategy, and reward. *Prog. Neurobiol.* 90, 385–417. doi:10.1016/j.pneurobio.2009.11.003

Hyman, J. M., Zilli, E. A., Paley, A. M., and Hasselmo, M. E. (2005). Medial prefrontal cortex cells show dynamic modulation with the hippocampal theta rhythm dependent on behavior.

Hippocampus 15, 739–749. doi:10.1002/hipo.20106

Jeffery, K. J., Anderson, M. I., Hayman, R., and Chakraborty, S. (2004). A proposed architecture for the neural representation of spatial context. *Neurosci. Biobehav. Rev* 28, 201–218. doi:10.1016/j.neubiorev.2003.12.002

Jenkins, T. A., Amin, E., Pearce, J. M., Brown, M. W., and Aggleton, J. P. (2004). Novel spatial arrangements of familiar visual stimuli promote activity in the rat hippocampal formation but not the parahippocampal cortices: a c-fos expression study. *Neuroscience* 124, 43–52. doi:10.1016/j.neuroscience.2003.11.024

Jo, Y. S., Lee, J., and Mizumori, S. J. Y. (2013). Effects of prefrontal cortical inactivation on neural activity in the ventral tegmental area. *J. Neurosci.* 33, 8159–8171. doi:10.1523/JNEUROSCI.0118-13.2013

Jones, M. W., and Wilson, M. A. (2005). Theta rhythms coordinate hippocampal-prefrontal interactions in a spatial memory task. *PLoS Biol.* 3:e402. doi:10.1371/journal.pbio.0030402

Kalenscher, T., Lansink, C. S., Lankelma, J. V., and Pennartz, C. M. (2010). Reward-associated gamma oscillations in ventral striatum are regionally differentiated and modulate local firing activity. *J. Neurophysiol.* 103, 1658–1672. doi:10.1152/jn.00432.2009

Kim, J. J., and Fanselow, M. S. (1992). Modality-specific retrograde amnesia of fear. *Science* 256, 675–677. doi:10.1126/science.1585183

Knierim, J. J. (2002). Dynamic interactions between local surface cues, distal landmarks, and intrinsic circuitry in hippocampal place cells. *J. Neurosci.* 22, 6254–6264.

Knierim, J. J., Lee, I., and Hargreaves, E. L. (2006). Hippocampal place cells: parallel input streams, subregional processing and implications for episodic memory. *Hippocampus* 16, 755–764. doi:10.1002/hipo.20203

Kraus, B. J., Robinson, R. J. II, White, J. A., Eichenbaum, H., and Hasselmo, M. E. (2013). Hippocampal "time cells": time versus path integration. *Neuron* 78, 1–12. doi:10.1016/j.neuron.2013.04.015

Kropf, W., and Kuschinsky, K. (1993). Conditioned effects of apomorphine are manifest in regional EEG of rats both in hippocampus and in striatum. *Naunyn Schmiedebergs Arch. Pharmacol.* 347, 487–493. doi:10.1007/BF00166740

Kuhl, B. A., Shah, A. T., DuBrow, S., and Wagner, A. D. (2010). Resistance to forgetting associated with hippocampus-mediated reactivation during new learning. *Nat. Neurosci.* 13, 501–506. doi:10.1038/nn.2498

Kumaran, D., and Maguire, E. A. (2007). Match-mismatch processes underlie human hippocampal responses to associative novelty. *J. Neurosci.* 27, 8517–8524. doi:10.1523/JNEUROSCI.1677-07.2007

Lee, I., Yognarasimha, D., Rao, G., and Knierim, J. J. (2004). Comparison of population coherence of place cells in hippocampal subfields CA1 and CA3. *Nature* 430, 456–459. doi:10.1038/nature02739

Leung, L. S., and Yim, C. Y. (1993). Rhythmic delta-frequency activities in the nucleus accumbens of anesthetized and freely moving rats. *Can. J. Physiol. Pharmacol.* 71, 311–320. doi:10.1139/y93-049

Leutgeb, J. K., Leutgeb, S., Treves, A., Meyer, R., Barnes, C. A., McNaughton, B. L., et al. (2005a). Progressive transformation of hippocampal neuronal representations in "morphed" environments. *Neuron* 48, 345–358. doi:10.1016/j.neuron.2005.09.007

Leutgeb, S., Leutgeb, J. K., Barnes, C. A., Moser, E. I., McNaughton, B. L., and Moser, M. B. (2005b). Independent codes for spatial and episodic memory in hippocampal neuronal ensembles. *Science* 309, 619–623. doi:10.1126/science.1114037

Lisman, J. E., and Grace, A. A. (2005). The hippocampal-VTA loop: controlling the entry of information into long-term memory. *Neuron* 46, 703–713. doi:10.1016/j.neuron.2005.05.002

Lisman, J. E., and Otmakhova, N. A. (2001). Storage, recall, and novelty detection of sequences by the hippocampus: elaborating on the SOCRATIC model to account for normal and aberrant effects of dopamine. *Hippocampus* 11, 551–568. doi:10.1002/hipo.1071

Lisman, J. E., and Redish, A. D. (2009). Prediction, sequences and the hippocampus. *Philos. Trans R. Soc. Lond. B Biol. Sci.* 364, 1193–1201. doi:10.1098/rstb.2008.0316

Llinas, R. R., and Roy, S. (2009). The 'predictive imperative' as the basis for self-awareness. *Phil. Trans. R. Soc. Lond. B Biol. Sci.* 364, 1301–1307. doi:10.1098/rstb.2008.0309

McDonald, C. J., Lepage, K. Q., Eden, U. T., and Eichenbaum, H. (2011). Hippocampal "time cells" bridge the gap in memory for discontiguous events. *Neuron* 71, 737–749. doi:10.1016/j.neuron.2011.07.012

Manns, J. R., Howard, M. W., and Eichenbaum, H. (2007a). Gradual changes in hippocampal activity support remembering the order of events. *Neuron* 56, 530–540. doi:10.1016/j.neuron.2007.08.017

Manns, J. R., Zilli, E. A., Ong, K. C., Hasselmo, M. E., and Eichenbaum, H. (2007b). Hippocampal CA1 spiking during encoding and retrieval: Relation to theta phase. *Neurobiol. Learn. Mem.* 87, 9–20. doi:10.1016/j.nlm.2006.05.007

Marder, E., and Goaillard, J. M. (2006). Variability, compensation and homeostasis in neuron and network function. *Nat. Rev. Neurosci.* 7, 563–574. doi:10.1038/nrn1949

Marder, E., and Prinz, A. A. (2003). Current compensation in neuronal homeostasis. *Neuron* 37, 2–4. doi:10.1016/S0896-6273(02)01173-X

Maren, S. (2001). Neurobiology of Pavlovian fear conditioning. *Ann. Rev. Neurosci.* 24, 897–931. doi:10.1146/annurev.neuro.24.1.897

Martig, A. K., and Mizumori, S. J. (2011). Ventral tegmental area disruption selectively affects CA1/CA2 but not CA3 place fields during a differential reward working memory task. *Hippocampus* 21, 172–184. doi:10.1002/hipo.20734

Mauk, M. D., and Buonomano, D. V. (2004). The neural basis of temporal processing. *Annu. Rev. Neurosci.* 27, 307–340. doi:10.1146/annurev.neuro.27.070203.144247

McEchron, M. C., and Disterhoft, J. F. (1999). Hippocampal encoding of non-spatial trace conditioning. *Hippocampus* 9, 385–396. doi:10.1002/(SICI)1098-1063(1999)9:4<385::AID-HIPO5>3.0.CO;2-K

McNaughton, B. L., Battaglia, F. P., Jensen, O., Moser, E. I., and Moser, M.-B. (2006). Path integration and the neural basis of the 'cognitive map'. *Nat. Rev. Neurosci.* 7, 663–678. doi:10.1038/nrn1932

Mizumori, S. J. Y., Cooper, B. G., Leutgeb, S., and Pratt, W. E. (2000). A neural systems analysis of adaptive navigation. *Mol. Neurobiol.* 21, 57–82. doi:10.1385/MN:21:1-2:057

Mizumori, S. J. Y. (ed.) (2008). *A Context for Hippocampal Place Cells During Learning.* New York: Oxford University Press.

Mizumori, S. J. Y., and Jo, Y. S. (2013). Homeostatic regulation of memory systems and adaptive decisions. *Hippocampus.* doi:10.1002/hipo.22176

Mizumori, S. J. Y., Ragozzino, K. E., Cooper, B. G., and Leutgeb, S. (1999). Hippocampal representational organization and spatial context. *Hippocampus* 9, 444–451. doi:10.1002/(SICI)1098-1063(1999)9:4<444::AID-HIPO10>3.3.CO;2-Q

Mizumori, S. J. Y., Smith, D. M., and Puryear, C. B. (2007a). Hippocampal and neocortical interactions during context discrimination: electrophysiological evidence from the rat. *Hippocampus* 17, 851–862. doi:10.1002/hipo.20317

Mizumori, S. J. Y., Smith, D. M., and Puryear, C. B. (2007b). "Mnemonic contributions of hippocampal place cells," in *Neurobiology of Learning and Memory*, eds J. L. Martinez Jr. and R. P. Kesner (New York: Academic Press), 155–190.

Mizumori, S. J. Y., Yeshenko, O., Gill, K. M., and Davis, D. M. (2004). Parallel processing across neural systems: implications for a multiple memory system hypothesis. *Neurobiol. Learn. Mem.* 82, 278–298. doi:10.1016/j.nlm.2004.07.007

Moita, M. A., Rosis, S., Zhou, Y., LeDoux, J. E., and Blair, H. T. (2004). Putting fear in its place: Remapping of hippocampal place cells during fear conditioning. *J. Neurosci.* 24, 7015–7023. doi:10.1523/JNEUROSCI.5492-03.2004

Monaco, J. D., Knierim, J. J., and Zhang, K. (2011). Sensory feedback, error correction, and remapping in a multiple oscillator model of place-cell activity. *Front. Comput. Neurosci.* 5:1–17. doi:10.3389/fncom.2011.00039

Muller, R. U., and Kubie, J. L. (1987). The effects of changes in the environment on the spatial firing of hippocampal complex-spike cells. *J. Neurosci.* 7, 1951–1968.

Myers, C. E., and Gluck, M. (1994). Context, conditioning, and hippocampal representation in animal learning. *Behav. Neurosci.* 108, 835–847. doi:10.1037/0735-7044.108.5.835

Nadel, L. (2008). "The hippocampus and context revisited," in *Hippocampal Place Fields: Relevance to Learning and Memory*, ed. S. J. Y. Mizumori (New York: Oxford University Press), 3–15.

Nadel, L., and Payne, J. D. (2002). "The hippocampus, way finding and episodic memory," in *The Neural Basis of Navigation: Evidence from Single Cell Recording*, ed. P. E. Sharp (Norwell, MA: Kluwer Academic Publisher), 235–248.

Nadel, L., Willner, J., and Kurz, E. M. (1985). "Cognitive maps and environmental context," in *Context and Learning*, eds P. Balsam, and A. Tomie (Hillside, NJ: Erlbaum), 385–406.

Nadel, L., and Wilner, J. (1980). Context and conditioning: a place for space. *Physiol. Psychol.* 8, 218–228.

Nudo, R. J. (2011). Neural bases of recovery after brain injury. *J. Commun. Disord.* 44, 515–520. doi:10.1016/j.jcomdis.2011.04.004

O'Keefe, J. (1976). Place units in the hippocampus of the freely moving rat. *Exp. Neurol.* 51, 78–109. doi:10.1016/0014-4886(76)90055-8

O'Keefe, J., and Burgess, N. (1996). Geometric determinants of the place fields of hippocampal neurons. *Nature* 381, 425–428. doi:10.1038/381425a0

O'Keefe, J., and Conway, D. H. (1978). Hippocampal place units in the freely moving rat: why they fire where they fire. *Exp. Brain Res.* 31, 573–590. doi:10.1007/BF00239813

O'Keefe, J., and Dostrovsky, J. (1971). The hippocampus as a spatial map. Preliminary evidence from unit activity in the freely-moving rat. *Brain Res.* 34, 171–175. doi:10.1016/0006-8993(71)90358-1

O'Keefe, J., and Nadel, L. (1978). *The Hippocampus as a Cognitive Map.* Oxford: Oxford University Press.

O'Keefe, J., and Recce, M. L. (1993). Phase relationship between hippocampal place units and the EEG theta rhythm. *Hippocampus* 3, 317–330. doi:10.1002/hipo.450030307

Olton, D. S., Branch, M., and Best, P. J. (1978). Spatial correlates of hippocampal unit activity. *Exp. Neurol.* 58, 387–409. doi:10.1016/0014-4886(78)90096-1

O'Reilly, R. C., and Rudy, J. W. (2001). Conjunctive representations in learning and memory: Principles of cortical and hippocampal function. *Psychol. Rev.* 108, 311–345. doi:10.1037/0033-295X.108.2.311

Pastalkova, E., Itskov, V., Amarasingham, A., and Buzsaki, G. (2008). Internally generated cell assembly sequences in the rat hippocampus. *Science* 321, 1322–1327. doi:10.1126/science.1159775

Paulsen, O., and Moser, E. I. (1998). A model of hippocampal memory encoding and retrieval: GABAergic control of synaptic plasticity. *Trends Neurosci.* 21, 273–278. doi:10.1016/S0166-2236(97)01205-8

Penick, S., and Solomon, P. R. (1991). Hippocampus, context, and conditioning. *Behav. Neurosci.* 105, 611–617. doi:10.1037/0735-7044.105.5.611

Penner, M. R., and Mizumori, S. J. Y. (2012a). Age-associated changes in the hippocampal-ventral striatum-ventral tegmental loop that impact learning, prediction and context discrimination *Front. Aging Neurosci.* 4:1–12 doi:10.3389/fnagi.2012.00022

Penner, M. R., and Mizumori, S. J Y. (2012b). Neural systems analysis of decision making during goal-directed navigation. *Prog. Neurobiol.* 96, 96–135. doi:10.1016/j pneurobio.2011.08.010

Phillips, R. G., and LeDoux, J. E. (1992). Differential contribution of amygdala and hippocampus to cued and contextual fear conditioning. *Behav. Neurosci.* 106, 274–285. doi:10.1037/0735-7044.106.2.274

Phillips, R. G., and LeDoux, J. E. (1994). Lesions of the dorsal hippocampal formation interfere with background but not foreground contextual fear conditioning. *Learn Mem.* 1, 34–44. doi:10.1101/lm.1.1.34

Pilly, P. K., and Grossberg, S. (2012). How do spatial learning and memory occur in the brain? Coordinated learning of entorhinal grid cells and hippocampal place cells. *J. Cogn. Neurosci.* 24, 1031–1054. doi:10.1162/jocn_a_00200

Puryear, C. B., Kim, M. J., and Mizumori, S. J. Y. (2010). Conjunctive encoding of movement and reward by ventral tegmental area neurons in the freely navigating rodent. *Behav. Neurosci.* 124, 234–247. doi:10.1037/a0018865

Puryear, C. B., King, M., and Mizumori, S. J. Y. (2006). Specific changes in hippocampal spatial codes predict spatial working memory performance. *Behav. Brain Res.* 169, 168–175. doi:10.1016/j.bbr.2005.12.007

Ranck, J. B. Jr. (1973). Studies on single neurons in dorsal hippocampal formation and septum in unrestrained rats. I. Behavioral correlates and firing repertoires. *Exp. Neurol.* 41, 461–531. doi:10.1016/0014-4886(73)90290-2

Robinson, T. E., and Kolb, B. (2004). Structural plasticity associated with exposure to drugs of abuse. *Neuropharmacology* 47(Suppl. 1), 33–46. doi:10.1016/j.neuropharm.2004.06.025

Sabatino, M., Ferraro, G., Liberti, G., Vella, N., and La Grutta V. (1985). Striatal and septal influence on hippocampal theta and spikes in the cat. *Neurosci. Lett.* 61, 55–59. doi:10.1016/0304-3940(85)90400-8

Samsonovich, A., and McNaughton, B. L. (1997). Path integration and cognitive mapping in a continuous attractor neural network model. *J. Neurosci.* 17, 5900–5920.

Save, E., Buhot, M. C., Foreman, N., and Thinus-Blanc, C. (1992a). Exploratory activity and response to a spatial change in rats with hippocampal or posterior parietal cortical lesions. *Behav. Brain Res.* 47, 113–127. doi:10.1016/S0166-4328(05)80118-4

Save, E., Poucet, B., Foreman, N., and Buhot, M. C. (1992b). Object exploration and reactions to spatial and nonspatial changes in hooded rats following damage to parietal cortex or hippocampal formation. *Behav. Neurosci.* 106, 447–456. doi:10.1037/0735-7044.106.3.447

Save, E., Nerad, L., and Poucet, B. (2000). Contribution of multiple sensory information to place field stability in hippocampal place cells. *Hippocampus* 10, 64–76. doi:10.1002/(SICI)1098-1063(2000)10:1<64::AID-HIPO7>3.0.CO;2-Y

Schultz, W., Dayan, P., and Montague, P. R. (1997). A neural substrate of prediction and reward. *Science* 275, 1593–1599. doi:10.1126/science.275.5306.1593

Shetty, P. K., Galeffi, F., and Turner, D. A. (2012). Cellular links between neuronal activity and energy homeostasis. *Front. Pharmacol.* 3:1–14. doi:10.3389/fphar.2012.00043

Siapas, A. G., Lubenov, E. V., and Wilson, M. A. (2005). Prefrontal phase locking to hippocampal theta oscillations. *Neuron* 46, 141–151. doi:10.1016/j.neuron.2005.02.028

Smith, D. M., and Mizumori, S. J. (2006a). Hippocampal place cells, context, and episodic memory. *Hippocampus* 16, 716–729. doi:10.1002/hipo.20208

Smith, D. M., and Mizumori, S. J. (2006b). Learning-related development of context-specific neuronal responses to places and events: the hippocampal role in context processing. *J. Neurosci.* 26, 3154–3163. doi:10.1523/JNEUROSCI.3234-05.2006

Smith, D. M., Wakeman, D., Patel, J., and Gabriel, M. (2004). Fornix lesions impair context-related cingulothalamic neuronal patterns and concurrent discrimination learning. *Behav. Neurosci.* 118, 1225–1239. doi:10.1037/0735-7044.118.6.1225

Tabuchi, E. T., Mulder, A. B., and Wiener, S. I. (2000). Position and behavioral modulation of synchronization of hippocampal and accumbens neuronal discharges in freely moving rats. *Hippocampus* 10, 717–728. doi:10.1002/1098-1063(2000)10:6<717::AID-HIPO1009>3.0.CO;2-3

Tanila, H., Shapiro, M. K., and Eichenbaum, H. (1997). Discordance of spatial representation in ensembles of hippocampal place cells. *Hippocampus* 7, 613–623. doi:10.1002/(SICI)1098-1063(1997)7:6<613::AID-HIPO4>3.3.CO;2-#

Tse, D., Langston, R. F., Kakeyama, M., Bethus, I., Spooner, P. A., Wood, E. R., et al. (2007). Schemas and memory consolidation. *Science* 316, 76–82. doi:10.1126/science.1135935

Tulving, E. (2002). Episodic memory: from mind to brain. *Ann. Rev. Psychol.* 53, 1–25. doi:10.1146/annurev.psych.53.100901.135114

Turrigiano, G. G. (1999). Homeostatic plasticity in neuronal networks: the more things change, the more they stay the same. *Trends Neurosci.* 22, 221–227. doi:10.1016/S0166-2236(98)01341-1

Turrigiano, G. G (2008). The self-tuning neuron: synaptic scaling of excitatory synapses. *Cell* 135, 422–435. doi:10.1016/j.cell.2008.10.008

Turrigiano, G. G. (2011). Homeostatic synaptic plasticity: Local and global mechanisms for stabilizing neuronal function. *Cold Spring Harb. Perspect. Biol.* 4, a005736. doi:10.1101/cshperspect.a005736

Turrigiano, G. G., Leslie, K. R., Desai, N. S., Rutherford, L. C., and Nelson, S. B. (1998). Activity-dependent scaling of quantal amplitude in neocortical neurons. *Nature* 391, 892–896. doi:10.1038/36103

Turrigiano, G. G., and Nelson, S. B. (2004). Homeostatic plasticity in the developing nervous system. *Nat. Rev. Neurosci* 5, 97–107. doi:10.1038/nrn1327

van der Meer, M. A., and Redish, A. D. (2009). Low and high gamma oscillations in rat ventral striatum have distinct relationships to behavior, reward, and spiking activity on a learned spatial decision task. *Front. Integr. Neurosci.* 3:9. doi:10.3389/neuro.07.009.2009

Vanderwolf, C. H. (1969). Hippocampal electrical activity and voluntary movement in the rat. *Electroencephalogr. Clin. Neurophysiol.* 26, 407–418. doi:10.1016/0013-4694(69)90092-3

Varela, F., Lachaux, J. P., Rodriguez, E., and Martinerie, J. (2001). The brain web: phase synchronization and large-scale integration. *Nat. Rev. Neurosci.* 2, 229–239. doi:10.1038/35067550

Vida, I., Bartos, M., and Jonas, P. (2006). Shunting inhibition improves robustness of gamma oscillations in hippocampal interneuron networks by homogenizing firing rates. *Neuron* 49, 107–117. doi:10.1016/j.neuron.2005.11.036

Vinogradova, O. S. (1995). Expression, control, and probably functional significance of the neuronal theta-rhythm. *Prog. Neurobiol.* 45, 523–583. doi:10.1016/0301-0082(94)00051-I

Whittington, M. A., Traub, R. D., and Jefferys, J. G. (1995). Synchronized oscillations in interneuron networks driven by metabotropic glutamate receptor activation. *Nature* 373, 612–615. doi:10.1038/373612a0

Wiener, S. I. (1996). Spatial, behavioral and sensory correlates of hippocampal CA1 complex spike cell activity: implications for information processing functions. *Prog. Neurobiol.* 49, 335–361. doi:10.1016/0301-0082(96)00019-6

Wikenheiser, A. M., and Redish, A. D. (2011). Changes in reward contingency modulate the trial-to-trial variability of hippocampal place cells. *J. Neurophysiol.* 106, 589–598. doi:10.1152/jn.00091.2011

Womelsdorf, T., Fries, P., Mitra, P. P., and Desimone, R. (2006). Gamma-band synchronization in visual cortex predicts speed of change detection. *Nature* 439, 733–736. doi:10.1038/nature04258

Womelsdorf, T., Schoffelen, J. M., Oostenveld, R., Singer, W., Desimone, R., Engel, A. K., et al. (2007). Modulation of neuronal interactions through neuronal synchronization. *Science* 316, 1609–1612. doi:10.1126/science.1139597

Wood, E. R., Dudchenko, P. A., and Eichenbaum, H. (1999). The global record of memory in hippocampal neural activity. *Nature* 397, 613–616. doi:10.1038/17605

Wood, E. R., Dudchenko, P. A., Robitsek, R. J., and Eichenbaum, H. (2000). Hippocampal neurons encode information about different types of memory episodes occurring in the same location. *Neuron* 27, 623–633. doi:10.1016/S0896-6273(00)00071-4

Yeshenko, O., Guazzelli, A., and Mizumori, S. J. (2004). Context-dependent reorganization of spatial and movement representations by simultaneously recorded hippocampal and striatal neurons during performance of allocentric and egocentric tasks. *Behav. Neurosci.* 118, 751–769. doi:10.1037/0735-7044.118.4.751

Young, B. J., Fox, G. D., and Eichenbaum, H. (1994). Correlates of hippocampal complex-spike cell activity in rats performing a nonspatial radial maze task. *J. Neurosci.* 14, 6553–6563.

Directed forgetting in post-traumatic-stress-disorder: A study of refugee immigrants in Germany

Michaela Baumann[1], Bastian Zwissler[1,2], Inga Schalinski[1,3], Martina Ruf-Leuschner[1,3], Maggie Schauer[1,3] and Johanna Kissler[1,4]*

[1] *Department of Psychology, University of Konstanz, Konstanz, Germany*
[2] *Department of Psychiatry, University of Tuebingen, Tuebingen, Germany*
[3] *Center of Excellence for Psychotraumatology, University of Konstanz, Konstanz, Germany*
[4] *Department of Psychology, University of Bielefeld, Bielefeld, Germany*

***Correspondence:**
Johanna Kissler, Department of Psychology, University of Bielefeld, Box 10 01 31, D-33501 Bielefeld, Germany
e-mail: johanna.kissler@uni-bielefeld.de

People with post-traumatic stress disorder (PTSD) often suffer from memory disturbances. In particular, previous studies suggest that PTSD patients perform atypically on tests of directed forgetting, which may be mediated by an altered emotional appraisal of the presented material. Also, a special role of dissociative symptoms in traumatized individuals' memory performance has been suggested. Here, we investigate these issues in traumatized immigrants in Germany. In an item-method directed forgetting task, pictures were presented individually, each followed by an instruction to either remember or forget it. Later, recognition memory was tested for all pictures, regardless of initial instruction. Overall, the PTSD group's discrimination accuracy was lower than the control group's, as PTSD participants produced fewer hits and more false alarms, but the groups did not differ in directed forgetting itself. Moreover, the more negatively participants evaluated the stimuli, the less they were able to discriminate old from new items. Participants with higher dissociation scores were particularly poor at recognizing to-be-forgotten items. Results confirm PTSD patients' general discrimination deficits, but provide no evidence for a distinct directed forgetting pattern in PTSD. Furthermore, data indicate that, in general, more negatively perceived items are discriminated with less accuracy than more positively appraised ones. Results are discussed in the larger context of emotion and stress-related modulations of episodic memory, with particular focus on the role of dissociative symptoms.

Keywords: directed forgetting, post-traumatic stress disorder, emotion, dissociation

INTRODUCTION

Post-traumatic stress disorder (PTSD) is a possible aftereffect of extremely traumatic life experiences, that is, events which threaten one's own or others' lives or physical integrity and to which the individual reacts with intense feelings of fear or helplessness (APA, 1994). The disorder is characterized by symptoms of re-experiencing, avoidance/emotional numbing, and heightened arousal, persisting for a month at minimum.

Memory disturbances are a core feature of PTSD (for a review, see McNally, 2006). They can alternate between recurrent, intrusive recollections, and an inability to recall autobiographical information, including the traumatic experience, a paradox reflected in the diagnostic criteria (APA, 1994). On laboratory tasks, memory deficits in PTSD become apparent as a reduced ability to recall recently studied items in explicit tests and as an increased tendency to produce false memories in free recall (see Brewin et al., 2007) and old–new recognition tests (Bremner et al., 2000; Zoellner et al., 2000; Goodman et al., 2011).

The directed forgetting paradigm (DF; for an overview, see Johnson, 1994) is well-suited to explore cognitive abnormalities in PTSD. It can be used to test for the capability to selectively remember relevant and to forget irrelevant information and to distinguish presented items from similar, but never presented material. In DF tasks, participants are shown items and instructed to remember some of them but forget others. Later, memory is tested for both remember (R) and forget (F) items. Usually, participants are able to reproduce more R- than F-items – the DF effect. Conversely, false memories are typically higher in the F than in the R condition (e.g., Kimball and Bjork, 2002; Zwissler et al., 2011, 2012). In item-method DF, where each single item is followed by an instruction to either remember or forget it, the DF effect is generally attributed to selective encoding, since participants can stop encoding items immediately after receiving F instructions and can selectively rehearse after R instructions. In item-method DF, effects are seen on both free recall and recognition tasks.

Several studies have addressed modulations of item-method DF in clinical populations (for a review, see Geraerts and McNally, 2008). In particular, the hypothesis has been examined that traumatized individuals [particularly survivors of childhood sexual abuse (CSA)] use an avoidant or dissociative encoding style and are therefore better able to disengage from threatening events resulting in particularly poor encoding of emotionally negative F-items and larger DF effects (Terr, 1994). However, subsequent studies with traumatized participants in general or PTSD patients were inconsistent (see Geraerts and McNally, 2008).

For instance, Cloitre et al. (1996) found a larger recall advantage for R- versus F-items in individuals with borderline personality disorder and parental abuse histories, relative to borderline personality disorder without abuse histories or healthy controls. However, in a subsequent study, participants with borderline personality disorder, unlike controls, exhibited superior recall for negative F words, providing no evidence for participants' avoidant encoding of threatening information (Korfine and Hooley, 2000).

McNally and his colleagues investigated in several DF studies whether individuals with repressed, recovered, or continuous memories of CSA performed differently from participants without a history of CSA (e.g., McNally et al., 1998, 2001, 2004). Under the avoidant encoding hypothesis, CSA survivors, particularly those who claimed to have forgotten their abuse (i.e., participants with repressed or recovered memories), should forget more trauma-related words than participants with continuous memories or those without a history of CSA. Yet overall, participants reporting repressed or recovered memories of CSA did not differ from the other groups in DF performance, providing no evidence for avoidant encoding.

Zoellner et al. (2003) investigated DF in PTSD patients and healthy controls under the assumption that the current mood state affects DF patterns. They induced either a dissociative or a serene mood in PTSD patients and controls before the DF task. Although a standard DF effect occurred in the serenity condition, contrary to predictions this effect was completely absent in the dissociation condition, suggesting that, if anything, the dissociative state reduced rather than increased directed forgetting. Moreover, the PTSD and control groups recalled comparable numbers of threat-related items (a finding similar to McNally et al., 1998). Thus, the study neither provided evidence for avoidant nor for intrusive encoding of threatening information in PTSD. DePrince and Freyd (2001, 2004) argued that dissociation may facilitate DF performance under divided attention, in particular. Indeed, in a pre-selected student population, high-dissociative students recalled fewer trauma-related and more neutral items under divided attention conditions than did low-dissociative students. However, replications by other authors failed (McNally et al., 2005; Devilly et al., 2007; but see DePrince et al., 2007; Devilly and Ciorciari, 2007 for critical discussions).

Some evidence that traumatized individuals may indeed be better at forgetting particularly threatening material and that dissociative symptoms may play a special role comes from studies on participants with acute stress disorder (ASD; Moulds and Bryant, 2002, 2005): ASD patients recalled fewer trauma-related F words compared to controls and trauma-exposed participants without ASD. The authors suspected a modulatory role of dissociative symptoms, which are essential for the diagnosis of ASD but not PTSD. According to Moulds and Bryant, these might have caused superior forgetting in the ASD group.

So far, the evidence on DF patterns in traumatized individuals is very heterogeneous. Regarding the impact of emotional stimuli, one theory posits that traumatized individuals are superior at forgetting in general and at forgetting emotional or threatening information in particular. However, some of the above cited studies point to reduced DF, especially for emotional material. Similarly, Zwissler et al. (2012) found, in an item-method DF study on Ugandan civil war victims with and without PTSD, a DF effect in the control but not in the PTSD group. Furthermore, PTSD participants produced more false alarms than controls and rated the stimuli as significantly more arousing than Non-PTSD participants. Higher arousal ratings were associated with a reduced DF effect, suggesting that the attenuation of DF in PTSD was mediated by increased subjective arousal, in line with the finding that healthy participants in general have reduced DF for emotional information on recognition tasks (Hauswald et al., 2011; Zwissler et al., 2011).

Still, a role for a dissociative processing style resulting in more DF has been identified by some studies (Terr, 1994; DePrince and Freyd, 2001, 2004; Moulds and Bryant, 2002, 2005). Moreover, recently hyper-aroused and dissociative PTSD sub-types have been suggested. These sub-types are supposed to differ in their physiologic and psychological response patterns to trauma reminders, the dissociative sub-type being characterized by emotional numbing, in particular (Schauer and Elbert, 2010). If so, different admixtures of these sub-types in different memory experiments may have contributed to the inconsistent results in PTSD.

Overall, emotional content of the stimuli (e.g., valence and arousal), the trauma relevance of the stimuli, as well as the patients' dissociative symptoms have been suggested to affect DF in PTSD, but so far no study has considered these factors simultaneously. The present study investigates the DF performance of asylum seekers with and without PTSD in Germany, specifically examining dissociative symptoms and subjective stimulus appraisal as possible mediating factors. Because of their frequent exposure to traumatic events during war and political persecution, PTSD prevalence rates of up to 40% have been reported for asylum seekers (Gäbel et al., 2006; see also Lindert et al., 2008). However, the cognitive consequences of this fact are largely unexplored. We addressed DF patterns in this population in a language-free pictorial task, followed by arousal and valence ratings of the stimuli. Group differences in overall recognition memory (hits, false alarms, discrimination accuracy, response bias) and directed forgetting were investigated and the relationship between DF, participants' dissociation scores and stimulus appraisals were examined.

MATERIALS AND METHODS

PARTICIPANTS

Twenty-five migrants and refugees took part in the study, 12 being diagnosed with PTSD and 13 serving as controls.

For the PTSD group, individuals currently investigated or treated at the University of Konstanz Outpatient Clinic for Refugees (*Psychologische Forschungs- und Modellambulanz für Flüchtlinge*) were invited to participate. They all met DSM-IV criteria for PTSD (APA, 1994), as previously assessed with the Clinician-Administered PTSD Scale (CAPS; Blake et al., 1995) in the course of standard diagnostic procedures at the outpatient department. The PTSD group consisted of eight women and four men. Five participants were from African countries, three from Turkey, two from Kosovo, and one each from Iran and Iraq. On average, they were 32.3 years old ($SD = 9.28$) and had received 7.67 years of education ($SD = 5.50$).

The control group was partly recruited at the outpatient clinic (controls or interpreters of previous studies; $n = 6$) and partly through information and language courses for migrants ($n = 7$). All were screened for PTSD using the Post-traumatic Diagnostic Scale (PDS; Foa et al., 1997), and none of them met DSM-IV criteria (APA, 1994). Efforts were made to match the control group to the PTSD group: the controls had migrated from countries similar to the PTSD group's (five were from African countries, two from Iran, and one from Iraq, Turkey, Russia, Belarus, Romania, and Hungary, respectively) and neither differed significantly from the PTSD group in age [$M = 34.5$, SD $= 11.2$; $t(23) = 0.53$, $p = 0.60$[1]] nor in gender distribution [10 women versus three men; $L\chi^2$ (1) $= 0.33$, $p = 0.67$]. However, they had received formal education approximately 7 years longer than had the PTSD group [$M = 14.9$, SD $= 3.19$; $t(17) = 3.97$, $p = 0.001$].

STIMULI, DESIGN, AND PROCEDURES

After giving informed consent, participants were administered the Dissociative Experiences Scale (DES; Bernstein and Putnam, 1986). The DES is a self-assessment questionnaire measuring dissociative phenomena like amnesia, absorption, and alienation. Its 28 items describe experiences such as, "Some people have the experience of finding new things among their belongings that they do not remember buying" and, "Some people have the experience of feeling that other people, objects, and the world around them are not real." For each experience, participants rate the frequency of occurrence on a scale from 0 to 100, and the mean of these item scores constitutes the DES score. The DES possesses good reliability and validity (e.g., Frischholz et al., 1990; Dubester and Braun, 1995). For participants who neither spoke German nor English fluently, interpreters translated during the whole session.

Completion of the DES was followed by the DF task. Here, two sets of 28 complex photographs served as stimuli. The pictures showed scenes of daily life, such as landscapes, vehicles, or people (see **Figure 1** for examples). The sets were paired such that every picture in one set had a similar counterpart in the other set. In the learning phase, the 28 pictures of one set were presented on a computer screen in random order for 4000 ms each. Every picture was followed by a 2000 ms instruction indicating whether participants should memorize the picture (instruction "MMM" for the German word "merken") or forget it ("VVV" for "vergessen"). Then, a fixation cross appeared for 2000 ms before the next photograph was presented. After the learning phase, participants worked on "Tangram" puzzles for 5 min as a distracter task. In the ensuing recognition phase, the 28 pictures of the learning set were presented randomly intermixed with the 28 photographs of the second set, which served as lures. Each picture was shown for 1000 ms and participants made old–new decisions by pressing the right (for *old*) or left (for *new*) mouse button within a time limit of 4000 ms. Participants were informed that new pictures could look quite similar to old ones, and, importantly, that their old–new decisions should be independent of the original instructions associated with the pictures (i.e., participants were supposed to chose *old* if they recognized pictures regardless of whether they had been designated as R or F).

FIGURE 1 | Three exemplary pairs of used target and distracter pictures illustrating the range of emotional intensity and valence covered by the stimuli as well as target – distracter similarity.

Afterward, participants rated each of the 56 photographs on the dimensions valence, arousal, and trauma relevance: they indicated on nine-point scales whether they found a picture pleasant or unpleasant (valence), arousing or quiet (arousal), and whether it reminded them of their own traumatic experiences (trauma relevance). Controls were additionally screened for PTSD with the PDS at the end of the session before they – like PTSD participants – received a compensation of 20 €.

STATISTICAL ANALYSIS

Statistical calculations were carried out with SPSS Version 17.0. In a first step, recognition data were statistically analyzed by means of mixed-model ANOVAs with response type and instruction as within factors (hits R, hits F, false alarms R, false alarms F) and group as between factor (PTSD versus control). Effects are reported as significant at $p < 0.05$. In a second step, group differences in picture appraisals and dissociative symptoms were assessed and their correlative relationship explored. Finally, the influence of picture appraisals and dissociative symptoms on memory performance was addressed by entering mean valence, arousal, and trauma relevance ratings as well as DES scores individually into the ANOVA model as covariates. Furthermore, targeted analyses investigated the linear relationships between recognition accuracy for F and R items and valence, arousal, trauma relevance as well as dissociative symptoms.

RESULTS

RECOGNITION MEMORY AND DIRECTED FORGETTING

Table 1 presents mean hit and false alarm rates in the R and F conditions for the sample as a whole as well as for the two subgroups. Participants were included in the analyses if the number of pictures they designated as old was within one standard deviation around the mean of pictures designated as old across participants ($M = 28.9$, SD $= 7.31$; resulting in $n = 20$[2]). For hits,

[1]Before comparing means, equality of variances was examined using Levene's test. For unequal variances, corrected t-values and degrees of freedom are presented.

[2]For the five excluded participants (four PTSD patients and one control), it has to be assumed that instructions were not understood. For example, one participant designated 53 of the 56 pictures in the recognition test as old (when in fact 28 were old); including these extreme "overestimators" would have inflated false alarm rates. Another participant, on the contrary, designated only 13 pictures as old; here, the

Table 1 | Mean hit and false alarm rates in the R and F conditions for the whole sample as well as separately for the PTSD and control group.

	Hits R (SD)	Hits F (SD)	False alarms R (SD)	False alarms F (SD)
Overall ($n=20$)	0.77 (0.17)	0.77 (0.18)	0.23 (0.17)	0.30 (0.17)
PTSD ($n=8$)	0.70 (0.19)	0.65 (0.20)	0.30 (0.20)	0.39 (0.14)
Control ($n=12$)	0.82 (0.15)	0.85 (0.12)	0.18 (0.13)	0.24 (0.17)

a significant main effect of group [$F(1, 18)=6.14, p=0.023$] indicated that the control group produced more hits than the PTSD group. Regarding false alarms, there was a significant main effect of instruction [$F(1, 18)=7.05, p=0.016$], that is, participants produced more false alarms for F than R items and an effect of group [$F(1, 18)=4.23, p=0.054$], indicating that PTSD participants produced more false alarms than controls.

Next, hits and false alarms were considered contemporaneously, differentiating between discrimination accuracy (Pr = hits − false alarms) and response bias [Br = false alarms/(1–Pr)]. In terms of discrimination accuracy, a trend-level effect for instruction was observed [$F(1, 18)=3.99, p=0.061$; see **Figure 2**]: participants tended to show better discrimination accuracy for R than for F-items, that is, a DF effect. Moreover, the control group's discrimination accuracy was higher than PTSD group's, as demonstrated by a main effect of group [$F(1, 18)=6.27, p=0.022$]. There was no significant interaction of instruction and group [$F(1, 18)=1.95, p=0.18$]. Although PTSD patients and controls did not differ significantly in DF performance, visual inspection suggests that the DF effect was mainly carried by the PTSD group. For recognition bias, no significant main effects or interactions were found and the two groups did not differ significantly in that measure [$F(1, 18)=0.46, p=0.51$].

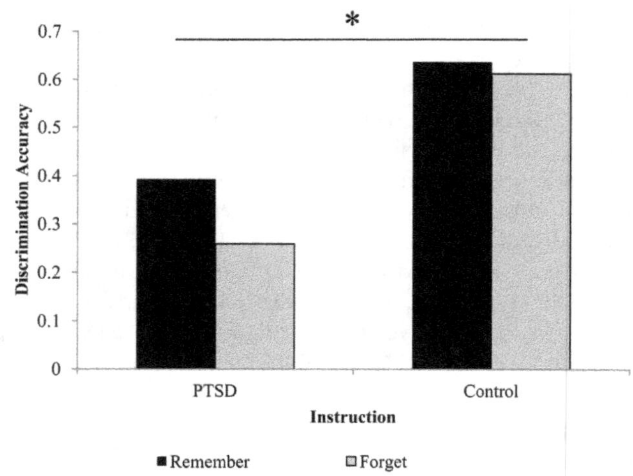

FIGURE 2 | Discrimination accuracy for the remember (R) and forget (F) conditions in the PTSD and control group illustrating both the group difference in recognition accuracy and the directed forgetting pattern.

PICTURE APPRAISAL AND DISSOCIATIVE SYMPTOMS

Overall, participants rated the pictures on the respective nine-point scales as somewhat negative ($M=3.70$, SD = 0.81), of average arousal ($M=5.30$, SD = 1.29), and not very trauma relevant ($M=3.56$, SD = 1.79). Comparing the two groups, there was a trend for the PTSD group to rate the pictures as more negative than the control group [dimension of valence; $t(18)=1.94, p=0.068$]. The ratings regarding the other dimensions were similar for the two groups, neither differing in arousal [$t(18)=1.24, p=0.23$] nor in trauma relevance [$t(18)=-0.61, p=0.55$].

Considering dissociation, the PTSD group had a mean DES score of 32.6 (SD = 7.32), which was much higher than the control group's [$M=11.3$, SD = 11.7, $t(18)=4.55, p<0.001$]. For two participants, the DES could not be administered. These participants' DES scores were therefore substituted by their scores on a similar dissociation questionnaire[3]. Overall, dissociation scores were negatively correlated with ratings of picture arousal ($r=-0.44, p=0.05$) and in tendency also valence ($r=-40, p=0.08$) and the relationship between valence and arousal ratings was well described by a linear relationship [$r=-0.61, p<0.01$; $r^2=0.37, F(1, 18)=10.56, p<0.01$] indicating that on average the more negative pictures were not rated as arousing but more positive pictures were rated as also more arousing. The linear relationship between valence and arousal observed in this sample is illustrated in **Figure 3**.

RECOGNITION MEMORY, PICTURE APPRAISAL, AND DISSOCIATIVE SYMPTOMS

ANCOVA revealed that discrimination accuracy differed depending on the perceived valence of the pictures [$F(1, 17)=6.65, p=0.020$]. Pearson correlations indicated a significant positive association between mean picture valence and discrimination accuracy ($r=0.59, p=0.007$ for R items; $r=0.61, p=0.004$ for F-items). As demonstrated in **Figure 4**, the more positive an individual rated the pictures, the higher the discrimination accuracy score. The two groups contributed similarly to this effect: in the PTSD group, the relationship between Pr and valence was $r=0.56, p=0.15$ for F-items and $r=0.63, p=0.09$ for R-items. In the control group it was $r=0.53, p=0.08$ for F-items and $r=0.46, p=0.13$ for R-items.

Adding mean arousal or trauma relevance ratings, or DES scores as covariates yielded no significant main effects. However, targeted correlation analyses revealed a trend for a positive relationship between DF magnitude ($Pr_R - Pr_F$) and DES scores ($r=0.43, p=0.061$), the numerical value of which was higher in the PTSD ($r=0.60$) than control group ($r=0.18$, both n.s.).

inclusion of these "underestimators" would have reduced hit rates artificially, without shedding more light on the difference between R- and F-items, which was the main research question in this study.

[3]This questionnaire called *Current Dissociation* was developed in the outpatient center and, similarly to the DES, asks for the occurrence of typical dissociative symptoms like blurred vision, out-of-body experiences, etc., in daily life. Since answers are rated on four-point scales, the mentioned two patients' test scores were transformed into a percentage rate (points reached/points possible) to ensure comparability with DES scores.

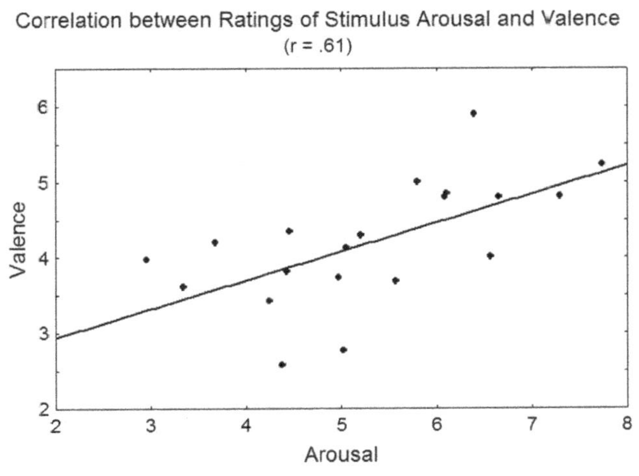

FIGURE 3 | Relationship between valence and arousal ratings in the present sample.

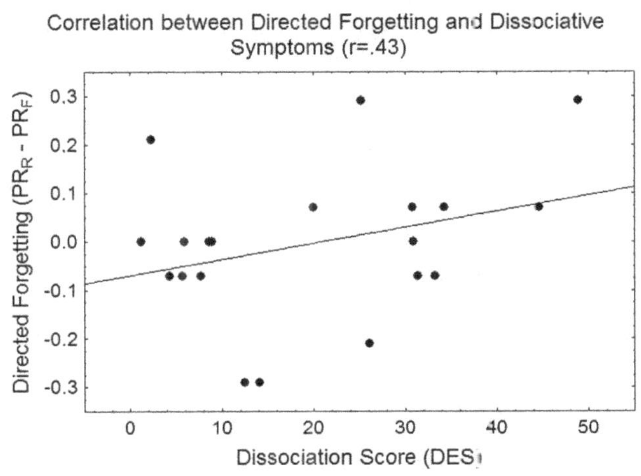

FIGURE 5 | Illustration of the linear correlation between the magnitude of DF (in terms of recognition accuracy Pr) and scores on the dissociative experience scale (DES).

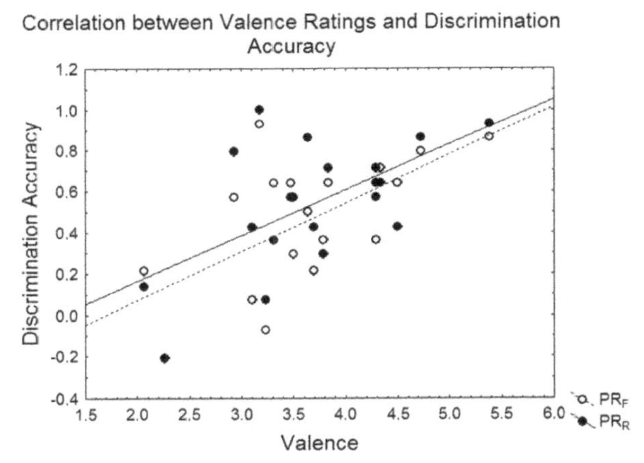

FIGURE 4 | Illustration of the linear correlation between mean valence ratings and discrimination accuracy (Pr). For valence ratings, higher numbers indicate more positive ratings.

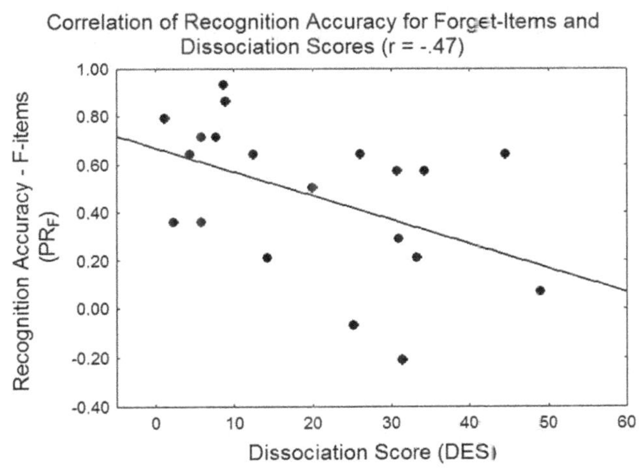

FIGURE 6 | Illustration of the linear correlation between recognition accuracy for to-be-forgotten items and dissociation scores.

In particular, DES scores were negatively correlated with Pr_F, the classification accuracy for F-items ($r = -0.47$, $p < 0.05$), indicating reduced recognition accuracy for F-items, but not R-items ($r = -0.23$, $p = 0.33$) in people with higher DES scores. **Figure 5** displays the overall relationship between directed forgetting and dissociation scores and **Figure 6** specifically illustrates the relationship between recognition accuracy for F-items and dissociation scores.

DISCUSSION

This study investigated item-method DF in a culturally heterogeneous group of traumatized refugees with PTSD, focusing on the role of possible mediating factors such as dissociative symptoms and stimulus appraisal. To this end, an item-method DF task with complex pictorial stimuli was used. Participants' dissociative symptoms and subjective appraisals of stimulus valence, arousal, and trauma relevance were assessed, and these variables' relationship to DF patterns was investigated.

Overall, controls produced more hits than PTSD patients, whereas PTSD patients produced more false alarms than controls, resulting in worse discrimination accuracy in the PTSD group. Consistent with typical DF patterns in recognition memory designs, across groups more false alarms were generated for F-lures than for R lures. Also, the more positively a picture was evaluated, the better it was discriminated. Moreover, participants with more dissociative symptoms had worse recognition of to-be-forgotten pictures and rated the pictures as less arousing and in tendency also more negative.

In the following, we will discuss these results in relation to extant literature and consider further suggestions emerging from this study: the higher false alarm rate in the PTSD group is consistent with previous reports of higher susceptibility to false memories in traumatized individuals (Bremner et al., 2000; Zoellner et al., 2000; Goodman et al., 2011). Considering hits and false alarms together, the control group's discrimination accuracy was higher than the PTSD group's, reflecting PTSD patients' memory impairment (e.g., Jelinek et al., 2006; McNally, 2006; Brewin et al., 2007) and extending this finding to a ethnically diverse population of immigrant refugees.

The directed forgetting instruction affected memory performance in that a significantly higher number of false alarms for F than R items (Kimball and Bjork, 2002; Zwissler et al., 2011, 2012) and a trend toward higher discrimination accuracy for R- than F-items were found. However, the two groups did not differ significantly in DF performance and if anything, the DF effect appeared to be carried more by the PTSD than by the control group. Several factors might explain this pattern: first, statistical power may have been insufficient as in between-group designs, 26 participants are considered necessary even for large effect sizes, given an α-level of 0.05, to achieve a statistical power of 0.8 (Cohen, 1992). For medium and small effect sizes, 64 and 393 participants would be needed, respectively, clearly many more than took part in the present study and produced useable data. Second, to avoid floor effects in the patient group, this study contained relatively few items and item presentation (4000 ms) was longer than in our previous experiments (Hauswald and Kissler, 2008; Hauswald et al., 2011; Zwissler et al., 2012). This may have fostered encoding of both R- *and* F-items in the non-memory impaired control group, thereby reducing DF. Studies that found a reduction of DF effects with increasing item-cue intervals, support this explanation (Wetzel and Hunt, 1977; Hourihan and Taylor, 2006).

The near ceiling results in the control group could also be attributable to the use of pictorial material. Although several studies (Hauswald and Kissler, 2008; Hauswald et al., 2011; Nowicka et al., 2011; Zwissler et al., 2011, 2012) have found robust DF effects using complex pictures, effects tend to be smaller than those typically found for words (Quinlan et al., 2010). However, pictorial stimuli allow for investigation of culturally and linguistically heterogeneous groups. In the present sample there was no single language all participants spoke.

Regarding the influence of stimulus appraisal on memory, valence ratings were significantly correlated with discrimination accuracy: the more positively the picture set was evaluated, the more accurately the pictures were discriminated. This result fits well with a study on intentional forgetting in children with PTSD that found significantly higher recognition accuracy for positive than negative words (Yang et al., 2010). In the present study PTSD patients tended to rate the pictures more negatively than did controls, which might contribute to their impaired discrimination accuracy. In general, memory for emotionally negative pictures is based more on gist than on detail (Adolphs et al., 2001), but the present design required encoding of details for successful discrimination.

The present study does not indicate that PTSD patients as such have larger DF effects, which is in line with other researchers' failure to observe differences between traumatized participants and controls (e.g., McNally et al., 1998, 2001, 2004). However, participants with higher dissociation scores had lower discrimination accuracies specifically for to-be-forgotten items. Indeed, under the avoidant encoding hypothesis individuals with high dissociation scores should be superior forgetters and thus show reduced memory for F-items. This pattern could be taken as tentative support for a special role of dissociative symptoms in directed forgetting. However, given the small sample and the controversy in the literature (cf. Cloitre et al., 1996; DePrince and Freyd, 2001, 2004; McNally et al., 2001, 2004), this finding needs extension and replication. Participants with higher dissociation scores also rated the stimuli as less arousing and somewhat more negative. This is in line with emotional numbing in dissociation (Frewen and Lanius, 2006) and could also account for the unusual linear relationship between valence and arousal found in the present data. Whereas typically both more negative and more positive stimuli are rated as more arousing, here, this held only for positive stimuli.

PTSD patients have been suggested to differ according to their physiologic and psychological response patterns to trauma reminders, resulting in hyper-aroused and dissociative sub-types (Schauer and Elbert, 2010) and the present results point to possible mnemonic consequences. Also, Moulds and Bryant (2002, 2005) founder larger DF effects in ASD, whose diagnosis requires high-dissociative symptom scores. Although challenging to conduct, a comparison of two large groups of PTSD patients who differ solely in their dissociative versus hyperarousal symptoms would provide a crucial test.

The previous finding of reduced DF for more arousing stimuli, concomitant with higher arousal ratings in PTSD, was not replicated in this study (Zwissler et al., 2012). Whereas several studies found a reduction of item-method DF for arousing stimuli in healthy participants (Yang et al., 2010; Hauswald et al., 2011; Nowicka et al., 2011; Zwissler et al., 2011, 2012), so far no study has systematically assessed the influence of valence and arousal on item-method DF across a wide range of arousal levels in large groups of PTSD patients. As suggested by the present data, emotional appraisal may vary with clinically relevant symptoms such as dissociation. Moreover, potential cultural variations in emotional appraisal are virtually unexplored. Future studies, using a broader range of stimuli, can shed more light on the relationship between valence, arousal, and DF in PTSD. In order to avoid clinical complications such as flashbacks or dissociative fainting during the experiment, the present experiment only used stimuli that were of relatively moderate valence and arousal, limiting statistical power to detect an effect on memory performance. This restriction probably also reduced our ability to identify any influence of "trauma relevance" on our data. Although participants perceived some variation of emotional content in the stimuli, they did not find them particularly representative of their own, often quite atrocious, experiences.

Taken together, results demonstrate reduced discrimination accuracy in PTSD patients, resulting from fewer hits and more false alarms. Data also reveal worse discrimination accuracy for more negatively evaluated stimuli. Participants with more dissociative symptoms exhibited altered stimulus appraisal, rating the stimuli as less emotionally intense. Importantly, individuals with high dissociation scores may indeed be better at directed forgetting. However, this last finding needs further scrutiny in a larger study, although large samples are difficult to obtain in this population. Traumatized patients typically have many problems related to their trauma, traumatized immigrants in particular also have many problems related to social and cultural factors, which, as such reduce their motivation to take part in scientific studies as well as reduce data quality and interpretability.

Despite these limitations, research on underprivileged samples that receive little attention from scientists and health-care providers, such as refugees with PTSD, is important for science and practice: systematic investigation will reveal typical cognitive phenomena and facilitate their scientific explanation. Identification of functional problems can aid the development of effective treatments. In refugees and migrants from war-torn societies, extremely traumatic experiences and resulting psychological impairments are quite frequent (Gäbel et al., 2006; Kinzie, 2006). Their investigation is essential to understand the characteristics, impairments, and needs of refugees and migrants in order to eventually provide help. The current study took one step toward this goal.

ACKNOWLEDGMENTS

Research was supported by the German Research Foundation (DFG KI1286/1-2). We also gratefully acknowledge support for the Article Processing Charge by the Deutsche Forschungsgemeinschaft and the Open Access Publication Funds of Bielefeld University Library.

REFERENCES

Adolphs, R., Denburg, N. L., and Tranel, D. (2001). The amygdala's role in long-term declarative memory for gist and detail. *Behav. Neurosci.* 115, 983–992. doi:10.1037/0735-7044.115.5.983

APA. (1994). *Diagnostic and Statistical Manual of Mental Disorders*, 4th Edn. Arlington, VA: American Psychiatric Publishing, Inc.

Bernstein, E. M., and Putnam, F. W. (1986). Development, reliability, and validity of a dissociation scale. *J. Nerv. Ment. Dis.* 174, 727–735. doi:10.1097/00005053-198612000-00004

Blake, D. D., Weathers, F. W., Nagy, L. M., and Kaloupek, D. G. (1995). The development of a Clinician-Administered PTSD Scale. *J. Trauma Stress* 8, 75–90. doi:10.1002/jts.2490080106

Bremner, J. D., Shobe, K. K., and Kihlstrom, J. F. (2000). False memories in women with self-reported childhood sexual abuse: an empirical study. *Psychol. Sci.* 11, 333–337. doi:10.1111/1467-9280.00266

Brewin, C. R., Kleiner, J. S., Vasterling, J. J., and Field, A. P. (2007). Memory for emotionally neutral information in posttraumatic stress disorder: a meta-analytic investigation. *J. Abnorm. Psychol.* 116, 448–463. doi:10.1037/0021-843x.116.3.448

Cloitre, M., Cancienne, J., Brodsky, B., Dulit, R., and Perry, S. W. (1996). Memory performance among women with parental abuse histories: enhanced directed forgetting or directed remembering? *J. Abnorm. Psychol.* 105, 204–211. doi:10.1037/0021-843x.105.2.204

Cohen, J. (1992). A power primer. *Psychol. Bull.* 112, 155–159. doi:10.1037/0033-2909.112.1.155

DePrince, A. P., and Freyd, J. J. (2001). Memory and dissociative tendencies: the roles of attentional context and word meaning in a directed forgetting task. *J. Trauma Dissociation* 2, 67–82. doi:10.1300/J229v02n02_06

DePrince, A. P., and Freyd, J. J. (2004). Forgetting trauma stimuli. *Psychol. Sci.* 15, 488–492. doi:10.1111/j.0956-7976.2004.00706.x

DePrince, A. P., Freyd, J. J., and Malle, B. F. (2007). A replication by another name: a response to Devilly et al. (2007). *Psychol. Sci.* 18, 218–219. doi:10.1111/j.1467-9280.2007.01876.x

Devilly, G. J., and Ciorciari, J. (2007). Conclusions in science when theory and data collide. *Psychol. Sci.* 18, 220–221. doi:10.1111/j.1467-9280.2007.01877.x

Devilly, G. J., Ciorciari, J. Piesse, A., Sherwell, S., Zammit, S., Cook, F., et al. (2007). Dissociative tendencies and memory performance on directed-forgetting tasks. *Psychol. Sci.* 18, 212–217. doi:10.1111/j.1467-9280.2007.01875.x

Dubester, K. A., and Braun, B. G. (1995). Psychometric properties of the Dissociative Experiences Scale. *J. Nerv. Ment. Dis.* 183, 231–235. doi:10.1097/00005053-199504000-00008

Foa, E. B., Cashman, L., Jaycox, L., and Perry, K. (1997). The validation of a self-report measure of posttraumatic stress disorder: the Posttraumatic Diagnostic Scale. *Psychol. Assess.* 9, 445–451. doi:10.1037/1040-3590.9.4.445

Frewen, P. A., and Lanius, R. A. (2006). Toward a psychobiology of posttraumatic self-dysregulation: reexperiencing, hyperarousal, dissociation, and emotional numbing. *Ann. N. Y. Acad. Sci.* 1071, 110–124. doi:10.1196/annals.1364.010

Frischholz, E. J., Braun, B. G., Sachs, R. G., and Hopkins, L. (1990). The dissociative experiences scale: further replication and validation. *Dissociation* 3, 151–153.

Gäbel, U., Ruf, M., Schauer, M., Odenwald, M., and Neuner, F. (2006). Prävalenz der Posttraumatischen Belastungsstörung (PTSD) und Möglichkeiten der Ermittlung in der Asylverfahrenspraxis. *Z. Klin. Psychol. Psychother.* 35, 12–20. doi:10.1026/1616-3443.35.1.12

Geraerts, E., and McNally, R. J. (2008). Forgetting unwanted memories: directed forgetting and thought suppression methods. *Acta Psychol. (Amst.)* 127, 614–622. doi:10.1016/j.actpsy.2007.11.003

Goodman, G. S., Ogle, C. M., Block, S. D., Harris, L. S., Larson, R. P., Augusti, E.-M., et al. (2011). False memory for trauma-related Deese-Roediger-McDermott lists in adolescents and adults with histories of child sexual abuse. *Dev. Psychopathol.* 23, 423–428. doi:10.1017/s0954579411000150

Hauswald, A., and Kissler, J. (2008). Directed forgetting of complex pictures in an item method paradigm. *Memory* 16, 797–809. doi:10.1080/09658210802169087

Hauswald, A., Schulz, H., Iordanov, T., and Kissler, J. (2011). ERP dynamics underlying successful directed forgetting of neutral but not negative pictures. *Soc. Cogn. Affect. Neurosci.* 6, 450–459. doi:10.1093/scan/nsq061

Hourihan, K. L., and Taylor, T. L. (2006). Cease remembering: control processes in directed forgetting. *J. Exp. Psychol. Hum. Percept. Perform.* 32, 1354–1365. doi:10.1037/0096-1523.32.6.1354

Jelinek, L., Jacobsen, D., Kellner, M., Larbig, F., Biesold, K.-H., Barre, K., et al. (2006). Verbal and nonverbal memory functioning in posttraumatic stress disorder (PTSD). *J. Clin. Exp. Neuropsychol.* 28, 940–948. doi:10.1080/13803390591004347

Johnson, H. M. (1994). Processes of successful intentional forgetting. *Psychol. Bull.* 116, 274–292. doi:10.1037/0033-2909.116.2.274

Kimball, D. R., and Bjork, R. A. (2002). Influences of intentional and unintentional forgetting on false memories. *J. Exp. Psychol. Gen.* 131, 116–130. doi:10.1037/0096-3445.131.1.116

Kinzie, J. D. (2006). Immigrants and refugees: the psychiatric perspective. *Transcult. Psychiatry* 43, 577–591. doi:10.1177/1363461506070782

Korfine, L., and Hooley, J. M. (2000). Directed forgetting of emotional stimuli in borderline personality disorder. *J. Abnorm. Psychol.* 109, 214–221. doi:10.1037/0021-843x.109.2.214

Lindert, J., Brähler, E., Wittig, U., Mielck, A., and Priebe, S. (2008) Depressivität, Angst und Posttraumatische Belastungsstörung bei Arbeitsmigranten, Asylbewerbern und Flüchtlingen – Systematische Übersichtsarbeit zu Originalstudien. *Psychother. Psychosom. Med. Psychol.* 58, 109–122. doi:10.1055/s-2003-1067358

McNally, R. J. (2006). Cognitive abnormalities in post-traumatic stress disorder. *Trends Cogn. Sci. (Regul. Ed.)* 10, 271–277. doi:10.1016/j.tics.2006.04.007

McNally, R. J., Clancy, S. A., Barrett, H. M., and Parker H. A. (2004). Inhibiting retrieval of trauma cues in adults reporting histories of childhood sexual abuse. *Cogn. Emot.* 18, 479–493. doi:10.1080/02699930341000400

McNally, R. J., Clancy, S. A., and Schacter, D. L. (2001). Directed forgetting of trauma cues in adults reporting repressed or recovered memories of childhood sexual abuse. *J. Abnorm. Psychol.* 110, 151–156. doi:10.1037/0021-843x.110.1.151

McNally, R. J., Metzger, L. J., Lasko, N. B., Clancy, S. A., and Pitman, R. K. (1998). Directed forgetting of trauma cues in adult survivors of childhood sexual abuse with and without posttraumatic stress disorder. *J. Abnorm. Psychol.* 107, 596–601. doi:10.1037/0021-843x.107.4.596

McNally, R. J., Ristuccia, C. S., and Perlman, C. A. (2005). Forgetting of trauma cues in adults reporting continuous or recovered memories of childhood sexual abuse. *Psychol. Sci.* 16, 336–340. doi:10.1111/j.0956-7976.2005.01536.x

Moulds, M. L., and Bryant, R. A. (2002). Directed forgetting in acute stress disorder. *J. Abnorm. Psychol.* 111, 175–179. doi:10.1037/0021-843x.111.1.175

Moulds, M. L., and Bryant, R. A. (2005). An investigation of retrieval inhibition in acute stress disorder. *J. Trauma Stress* 18, 233–236. doi:10.1002/jts.20022

Nowicka, A., Marchewka, A., Jednorog, K., Tacikowski, P., and Brechmann, A. (2011). Forgetting of emotional information is hard: an fMRI study of directed forgetting. *Cereb. Cortex* 21, 539–549. doi:10.1093/cercor/bhq117

Quinlan, C. K., Taylor, T. L., and Fawcett, J. M. (2010). Directed forgetting: comparing pictures and words. *Can. J. Exp. Psychol.* 64, 41–46. doi:10.1037/a0016569

Schauer, M., and Elbert, T. (2010). Dissociation following traumatic stress: etiology and treatment. *Z. Psychol.* 218, 109–127. doi:10.1027/0044-3409/a000018

Terr, L. (1994). *Unchained Memories: True Stories of Traumatic Memories, Lost and Found.* New York, NY: Basic Books.

Wetzel, C. D., and Hunt, R. E. (1977). Cue delay and the role of rehearsal in directed forgetting. *J. Exp. Psychol. Hum. Learn. Mem.* 3, 233–245. doi:10.1037/0278-7393.3.2.233

Yang, H.-B., Wang, Y.-Y., Bai, X.-J., Wen, Y.-X., and Chen, Z.-Y. (2010). Influence of emotional state on intentional forgetting of PTSD children after earthquake. *Chin. J. Clin. Psychol.* 18, 600–603.

Zoellner, L. A., Foa, E. B., Brigidi, B. D., and Przeworski, A. (2000). Are trauma victims susceptible to "false memories"? *J. Abnorm. Psychol.* 109, 517–524. doi:10.1037/0021-843x.109.3.517

Zoellner, L. A., Sacks, M. B., and Foa, E. B. (2003). Directed forgetting following mood induction in chronic posttraumatic stress disorder patients. *J. Abnorm. Psychol.* 112, 508–514. doi:10.1037/0021-843x.112.3.508

Zwissler, B., Hauswald, A., Koessler, S., Ertl, V., Pfeiffer, A., Wöhrmann, C., et al. (2012). Memory control in post-traumatic stress disorder: evidence from item method directed forgetting in civil war victims in Northern Uganda. *Psychol. Med.* 42, 1283–1291. doi:10.1017/S0033291711002273

Zwissler, B., Koessler, S., Engler, H., Schedlowski, M., and Kissler, J. (2011). Acute psycho-social stress does not disrupt item-method directed forgetting, emotional stimulus content does. *Neurobiol. Learn. Mem.* 95, 346–354. doi:10.1016/j.nlm

10

Aging-related episodic memory decline: Are emotions the key?

Kiyoka Kinugawa[1,2,3†], Sophie Schumm[3†], Monica Pollina[1,2,3], Marion Depre[1,2,3], Carolin Jungbluth[4], Mohamed Doulazmi[1,2], Claude Sebban[1,2,3], Armin Zlomuzica[5], Reinhard Pietrowsky[4], Bettina Pause[4], Jean Mariani[1,2,3] and Ekrem Dere[1,2,3]*

[1] Neurobiologie des Processus Adaptatifs, UMR 7102, Université Pierre et Marie Curie, Paris 6, Paris, France
[2] CNRS, UMR 7102, Paris, France
[3] Institut de la longévité, AP-HP Hôpital Charles Foix, Ivry-sur-Seine, Paris, France
[4] Institute of Experimental Psychology, University of Düsseldorf, Düsseldorf, Germany
[5] Center for the Study and Treatment of Mental Health, Ruhr-Universität Bochum, Bochum, Germany

***Correspondence:**
Ekrem Dere, Neurobiologie des Processus Adaptatifs, UMR 7102, Université Pierre et Marie Curie, Paris 6, 9 quai St. Bernard, Paris F-75005, France.
e-mail: ekrem.dere@snv.jussieu.fr

† These authors equally contributed to this work.

Episodic memory refers to the recollection of personal experiences that contain information on what has happened and also where and when these events took place. Episodic memory function is extremely sensitive to cerebral aging and neurodegenerative diseases. We examined episodic memory performance with a novel test in young ($N = 17$, age: 21–45), middle-aged ($N = 16$, age: 48–62) and aged but otherwise healthy participants ($N = 8$, age: 71–83) along with measurements of trait and state anxiety. As expected we found significantly impaired episodic memory performance in the aged group as compared to the young group. The aged group also showed impaired working memory performance as well as significantly decreased levels of trait anxiety. No significant correlation between the total episodic memory and trait or state anxiety scores was found. The present results show an age-dependent episodic memory decline along with lower trait anxiety in the aged group. Yet, it still remains to be determined whether this difference in anxiety is related to the impaired episodic memory performance in the aged group.

Keywords: aging, anxiety, episodic memory, depression, working memory

INTRODUCTION

Episodic memory refers to the conscious recollection of a personal experience that contains information on what has happened and also where and when it happened (Tulving, 1983). Remembering a personal experience might also be accompanied by the remembrance of specific perceptions, emotions, and thoughts one had during a particular experience (Tulving, 2002). Episodic memory deficits are observed after medial temporal lobe injury (Nyberg et al., 1996) which includes important memory structures such as the hippocampus (Burgess et al., 2002) and amygdala (Markowitsch and Staniloiu, 2011) but also after lesions to the frontal cortex (Kirchhoff et al., 2000) and diencephalic structures, such as the mediodorsal thalamus and the mammillary bodies (Tsivilis et al., 2008; Wolff et al., 2008).

Episodic memory function is also extremely sensitive to cerebral aging (Shing et al., 2010; Nyberg et al., 2012), neurodegenerative (Williams-Gray et al., 2006; Dubois et al., 2007), and psychiatric diseases (Dere et al., 2010). Cross-sectional studies have indicated that the age-dependent decline in episodic memory function starts as early as at the age of 30 (Park et al., 2002), while longitudinal studies propose a later onset between ages 65 and 70 years (Rönnlund et al., 2005). Age-dependent memory decline seems to be paralleled by volume reductions in brain structures important for memory performance, including the medial temporal lobe (Persson et al., 2006), the hippocampus (Rajah et al., 2010), and the prefrontal cortex (Van Petten et al., 2004). Although, it is well known that the amygdala, besides its prominent role in the generation of emotions, is also involved in memory consolidation after fear conditioning (LeDoux, 2007) and emotional events (McIntyre et al., 2003; McGaugh, 2004), its role during age-dependent memory decline has attracted surprisingly fewer research activity.

The role of emotions in the decline of episodic memory function that is seen in the course of physiological aging is still poorly understood. Although emotions are not necessarily an integral component of episodic memory, emotional arousal, or psychosocial stress induced in the laboratory during the encoding of episodic information can facilitate episodic memory consolidation into long-term memory (Wolf, 2012).

It has been also proposed that emotions might be a trigger for episodic memory formation (Libkuman et al., 2004; Dere et al., 2010; Kensinger et al., 2011), play a role in the binding of different features of an event into an integrated episodic memory (Nashiro and Mather, 2011), mediate the self-relevant aspect of an episodic memory (Wheeler et al., 1997) and might also determine their durability in a way that strong emotional activation leads to long-durable episodic memories, while weak emotional activation leads only to short-durable episodic memories (Dere et al., 2010). In line with this proposition it has been found that emotions improve the ability of aged individuals to retrieve more details of an event as well as its context (Kensinger, 2009). There is also evidence suggesting that the processing of emotional stimuli and the physiological arousal mediated by the autonomic system in response to emotionally negative stimuli is compromised in aged individuals (Kaszniak and Menchola, 2012). In this study, we investigated the possibility that aging-induced episodic memory decline might be due to changes in emotionality e.g., in terms of the response to stimuli that have been associated with an emotionally arousing context story.

In order to test the emotionality hypothesis of aging-induced episodic memory impairments, we measured episodic memory in young, middle-aged, and aged participants with a novel paradigm which measures memory for different stimuli, the temporal order of their presentation as well as the spatial locations where they have been presented. This test also measures the ability to establish new episodic memories. We further assessed trait and state anxiety in the 3 groups in order to determine if impairments in episodic memory performance are indeed correlated with decreased levels of trait and/or state anxiety.

Given that depressive symptoms are common in the aged population and are associated with cognitive impairments including working memory deficits (Bornstein et al., 1991; Nebes et al., 2000) we additionally probed whether aging-induced episodic memory decline would be associated with impairments in working memory or depressive symptoms.

MATERIALS AND METHODS

PARTICIPANTS

Forty-one healthy adult volunteers (♀ = 22, ♂ = 19) participated in this study. The participants were recruited from University Pierre and Marie Curie Paris 6 students and employees and among healthy relatives of patients attending the geriatric hospital Charles Foix in Ivry-Sur-Seine, France. The participants were aged between 21 and 83 years. They were divided into three groups of young ($N = 17$, mean: 26.76 ± 1.69, age range: 21–45), middle-aged ($N = 16$, mean: 55.31 ± 1.06, age range: 48–62) and aged participants ($N = 8$, mean: 79.13 ± 1.33, age range: 71–83).

None of the participants reported a psychiatric record, history of vascular, psychiatric, neurological, motor or oncologic disease, psychopharmacologic or hormonal therapy or any other health issue that would prohibit their testing. All participants had a corrected to normal vision and audition.

The groups were comparable regarding their socio-demographic and educational background. The study was conducted in accordance with the declaration of Helsinki. Written informed consent was obtained from all participants. All experimental procedures have been approved by the local ethical committee of the University Pierre and Marie Curie Paris 6.

EXPERIMENTAL DESIGN

In a reverse translational approach by Pause et al. (2010) the rationale and principles of the episodic-like memory test for rodents (Dere et al., 2005a,b; Kart-Teke et al., 2006) have been adapted to humans. We developed a paradigm that measures the spatio-temporal memory for emotional and neutral pictures presented on an eight-quadrant computer-screen task (Pause et al., 2010). This test has been further developed to be applicable to aged individuals and patient populations.

General procedure

The total experiment including the presentation of general information about the experiment, the completion of the participant questionnaire, the neuropsychological testing as well as the episodic memory test had a total duration of approximately 2.5 h. However, the net time of testing was approximately 65 min. The participants received 3 pauses of 2 × 20 min and 1 × 45 min in the course of the 2.5 h total duration in order to minimize possible effects of tiredness and fatigue on test performance in the older individuals. **Figure 1** gives overview of the different phases of the experiment, their sequence, and the approximate duration of each test.

First the participant was informed about the general procedure of the experiment without providing an explicit statement that he or she is participating in a memory experiment or had to retain the information presented during the course of the experiment. It is important to note that no explicit information about the purpose of the test was given. Instead the participants were informed that "The aim of this study is to investigate the effects of imagination on visual perception and attention." Thereafter, the participants were asked to complete a standard participant questionnaire including questions about the current and past health status, current and past medication, history of mental diseases, etc. After that the participants working memory for series of numbers was tested using a subtest of the WAIS-R. Immediately thereafter the participants performed the episodic memory test consisting of 3 slide presentations followed by an episodic memory test as described in detail below. Immediately after the third slide presentation, the participants were asked to complete the state anxiety subtest of the STAI (Spielberger et al., 1970). Finally, after the participants had completed the episodic memory test, the Goldberg trait anxiety, and depression scale was performed (Goldberg et al., 1988).

THE EPISODIC MEMORY TEST

This test is based on the "what, where, and when" paradigm (Clayton and Dickinson, 1999; Dere et al., 2005a) that allows to measure the core elements (content, temporal, and spatial context of an unique event) of episodic memory. The present test is designed to measure integrated memories for "what, where, and when" operationalized as "stimulus-position-trial" associations. The test does not allow the assessment of the individual components of episodic memory in terms of content, spatial, and temporal order memory.

Each participant received 3 presentation trials using the Presentation® software Version 12 (Neurobehavioral Systems, CA, USA) and an episodic memory test (recall of 27 different stimulus-position-trial associations). The 3 trials were embedded into a context story (see below) with emotional content. This context story was divided into 3 parts according to the 3 trials. Each part of the context story was narrated by the experimenter to the participant immediately before the presentation of the corresponding presentation trial. Each presentation trial

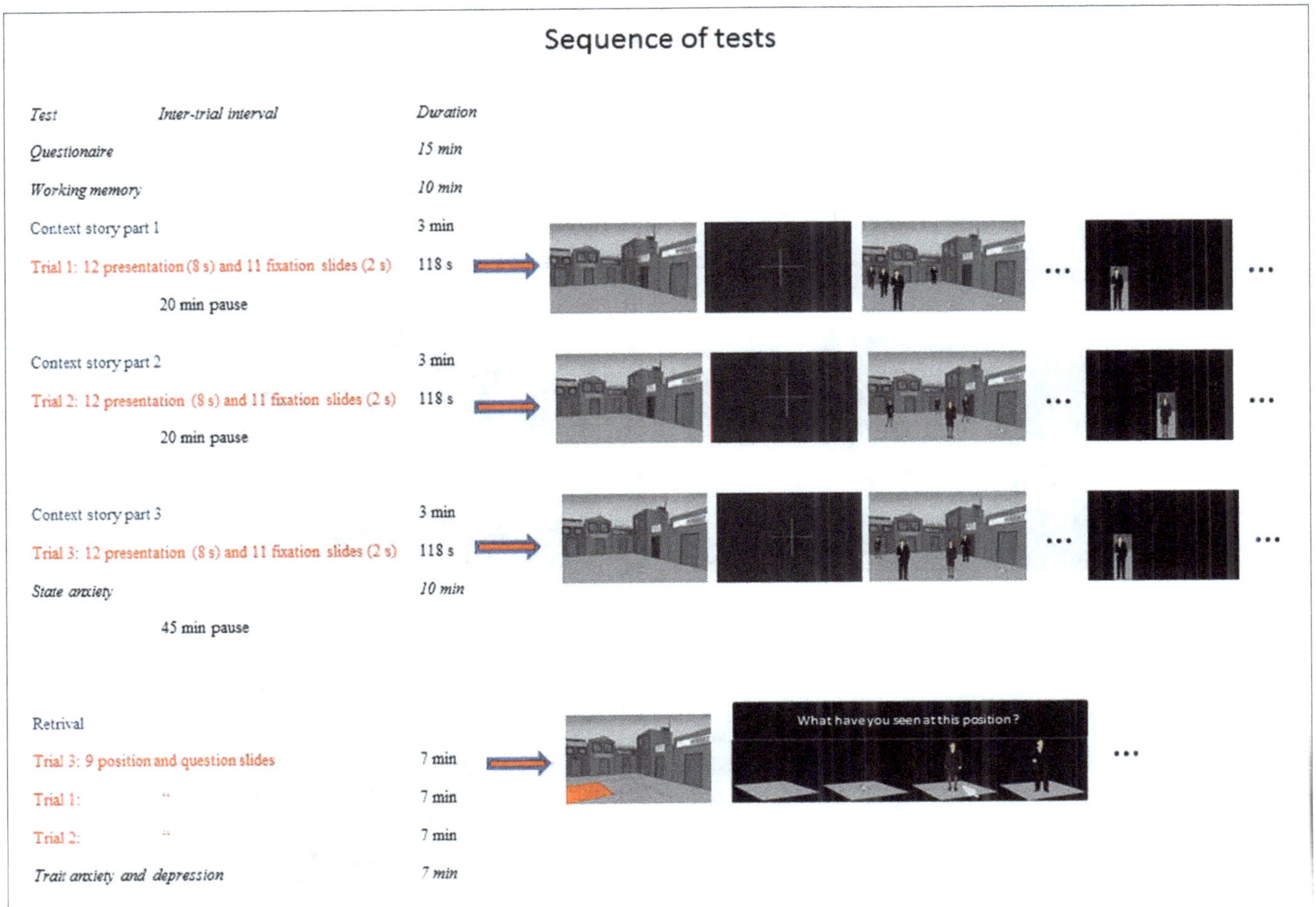

FIGURE 1 | Experimental design. Overview of the experimental design, the order of tests applied, presentation times of the slides, and the approximate duration of each experimental phase.

consisted of 12 slides. Each slide was presented for 8 s and was followed by the presentation of a fixation cross for 2 s. The first slide showed a background scene with an empty place surrounded by shops (**Figure 2A**). This place was virtually divided into a 3 × 3 matrix with 9 different positions for the presentation of stimuli (**Figure 3C**). The center position was not used for the presentation of stimuli. The second slide consisted of the same background scene including 4 context story-relevant and 4 context story non-relevant stimuli presented within the 3 × 3 matrix (**Figure 2B**). Context story-relevant stimuli were drawings of 4 men wearing suits and having slightly different postures (**Figure 2B**). Stimuli not relevant to the context story consisted of drawings of 4 pigeons (**Figure 2B**). During the slides 3–10 each stimuli position was presented individually for 8 s while the reminder of the background scene including the other stimuli were darkened (**Figures 2C,D**). Each slide was followed by the presentation of a gray slide for 2 s showing a plus-shaped fixation cross at the center. This slide ensured the saccadic resetting of the participants view back to the center of the slide before the next individual position was presented. Slide 11 again presented the complete scene including context story-relevant and non-relevant stimuli. This slide was followed by the presentation of the background scene without stimuli. After a delay of 20 min the second presentation trial was performed. This was identical to the first trial, except that drawings of women were presented instead of men (**Figures 2E,F**). Two of the context story-relevant stimuli (women) were presented at positions already used during the first trial for the placement of context story-relevant stimuli (men), while the remaining 2 context story relevant stimuli were placed at positions which contained context story non-relevant stimuli (pigeons).

After another delay of 20 min the participants viewed the third presentation trial (**Figure 3A**). The third trial was identical to the first 2 presentation trials except that the 4 context story-relevant stimuli consisted of 2 men (in the following referred to as "old" stimuli with respect to the temporal order of the 2 previous trials) and 2 women "recent" stimuli. Additionally one "old" and one "recent" stimuli were presented at a position which was not used for the placement of context story-relevant stimuli during their initial presentation. Thus one "old" and one "recent" stimuli had been displaced to a "novel" position. These stimuli

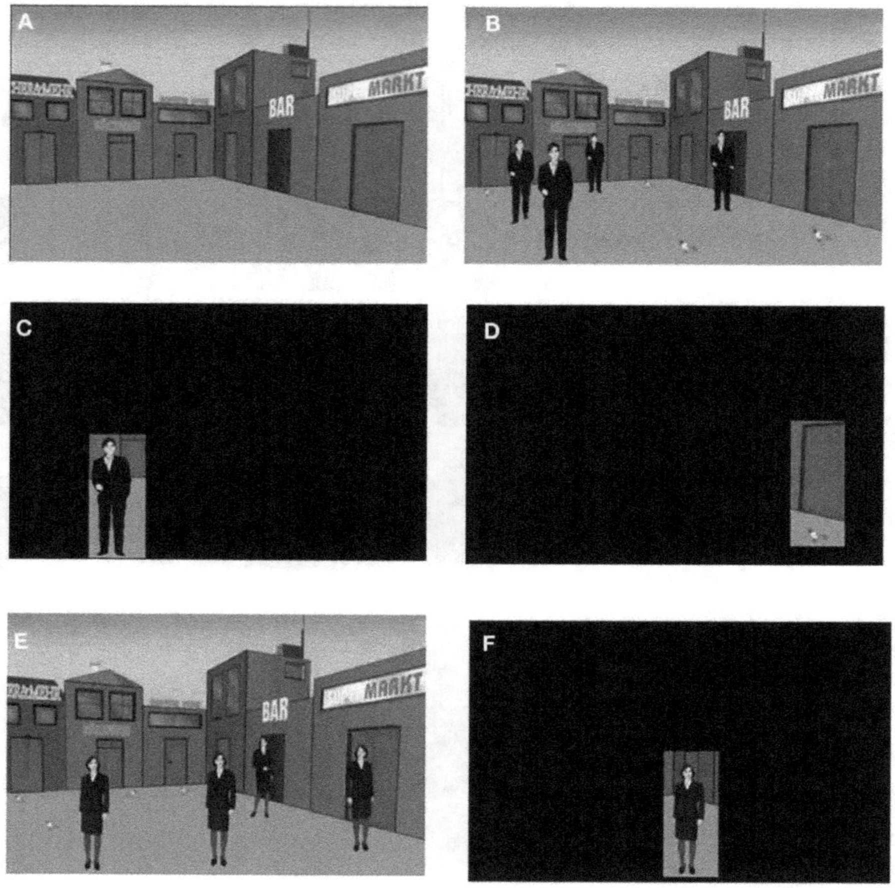

FIGURE 2 | The episodic memory test: presentation trials 1 and 2. Each presentation trial is composed of a series of 12 slides. Each slide is presented for 8 s and is followed by the presentation of a fixation cross for 2 s. Schematic drawings of men (presentation trial 1) or woman (presentation trial 2) are used as context story-relevant stimuli while pigeons are used as context story-non relevant stimuli. **(A)** The first slide of each presentation trial shows the background scene without context story-relevant and non-relevant stimuli. **(B)** Presentation of the 8 positions with 4 men as context story-relevant stimuli on the second slide of trial 1. **(C)** Example for the presentation of a single man-position stimulus during the presentation of the slides 3–10 on trial 1. **(D)** Example for the presentation of a single pigeon-position stimulus during the presentation of the slides 3–10 on trials 1 or 2. **(E)** Presentation of the 8 positions with 4 women as context story-relevant stimuli on the second slide of trial 1. **(F)** Example for the presentation of a single women-position stimulus during the presentation of the slides 3–10 on trial 2.

were referred to as "old displaced" and "recent displaced" stimuli (**Figure 3B**).

Sixty minutes after the third trial the episodic memory test was performed. Here, the participants were asked to recall each of the 27 stimulus-position-trial associations that have been formed during the 3 presentation trials. The sequence of memory tests for the 3 presentation trials was 3-1-2. First the 9 stimulus-position-trial associations of trial 3 were tested, followed by the tests for trials 1 and finally 2. During the test the participant was presented with the background scene without context story-relevant or non-relevant stimuli. The place was divided into a matrix of 9 positions.

Each episodic memory test for individual trials (1, 2, or 3) consisted of 18 slides. Each individual position, marked with red color, was presented for 2 s (**Figure 3C**). Thereafter, a slide appeared asking whether the participant remembered to have seen an empty place, a pigeon, a woman, or a man at this position during that particular trial. On the bottom of this slide the 4 choice options were presented as images. The participant could select the right answer by clicking on the corresponding stimuli (**Figure 3D**). The slide was presented until the participant made a decision. The responses of the participant were automatically recorded and transferred to an Excel® output file. Please note that this procedure allowed the measurement of a memory for what, where, and when in terms of stimulus-position-trial associations with a minimum of verbal requirements allowing the testing of patients with impairments in speech production.

CONTEXT STORY

The context story was divided into 3 parts which were narrated by the experimenter before each presentation trial and had an emotionally arousing content. Before the experimenter narrated each

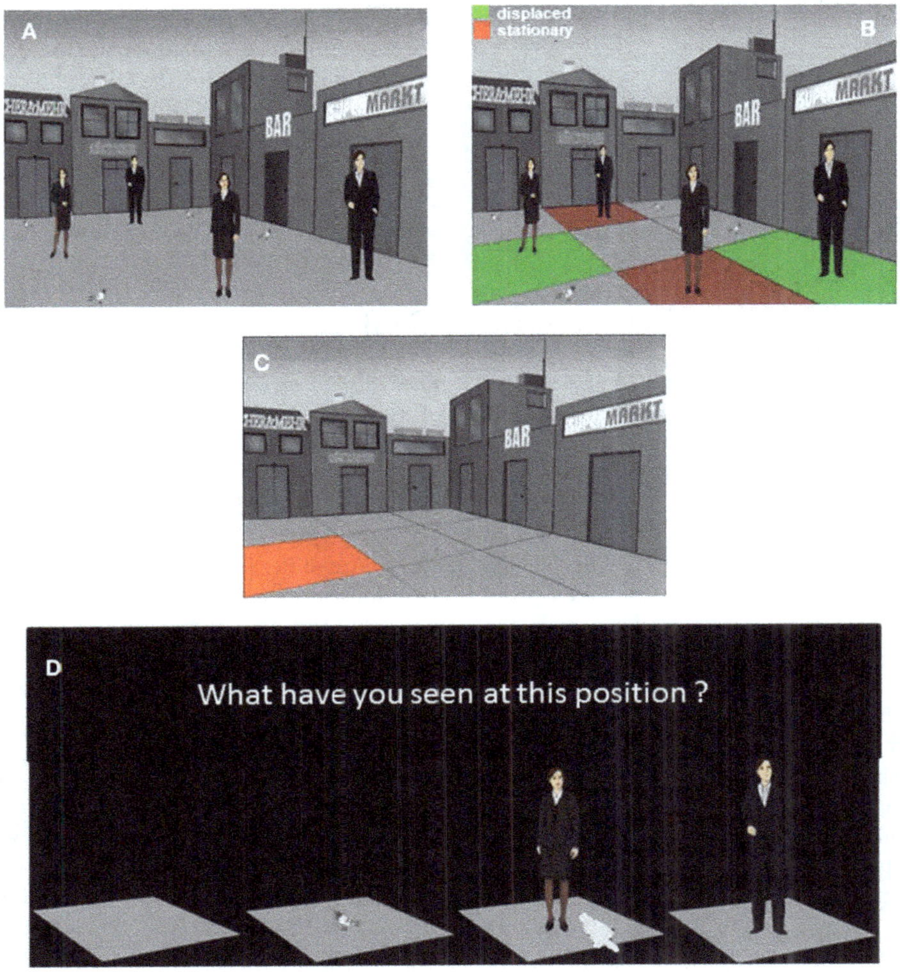

FIGURE 3 | The episodic memory test: presentation trial 3 and test trial. **(A)** Presentation trial 3 where human stimuli from trial 1 and 2 are presented together. Depicted are the 4 positions with human stimuli as context story-relevant stimuli and the 4 position with context story non-relevant stimuli. **(B)** One "old" man and one "recent" woman stimuli were displaced to an unfamiliar position not used during the corresponding presentation trials 1 or 2. Additionally, one "old" man and one "recent" woman stimuli were presented at familiar positions already used during the corresponding presentation trials 1 or 2. The red and green coloring of the quadrants with human stimuli was made for representational purposes and has not been presented to the participants. **(C)** Episodic memory test where participants have to remember the stimulus-position-trial associations formed during the 3 presentation trials. First the positions for the test trial were probed; thereafter the ones for the first trial and finally the ones for the second trial were tested. There were 27 questions in total. On the test trial only the background scene was presented without stimuli. The scene was divided into 9 quadrants. Each of the 9 quadrants was colored and presented individually. **(D)** Thereafter, a slide with the question "What have you seen on this position" and the corresponding response alternatives was presented. The participant was asked to select via mouse click the stimulus which he or she was remembering to be presented on that particular position during a particular presentation trial.

part of the context story the participant was asked to "Please try to imagine the situation."

Part 1

"Please try to imagine the following situation. You are in a foreign town for 3 days. On the first day you take a walk and reach a small place with little shops and pigeons. You see 4 men in black suits. You recognize these men. You remember to have seen their faces before. They are members of a terrorist group, who had recently attempted to commit a poison gas attack to prevent a political conference. You feel that your heart is beating faster. This attack had been prevented at the very latest moment. If it had been successful, there would have been hundreds of victims. You are quite sure that these men belong to this terrorist group. You now feel cold. You now have goose bumps. You are wondering why these men are here and what they have in mind. You are scared and you think about the cruel and unscrupulous crimes that have been committed by these men in the past.

Then the experimenter asked whether the participant had been able to imagine the situation: "Can you imagine the situation? In the following I will show you the close-ups of the place with the 4 terrorists. When viewing the close-ups please try to imagine what other crimes these people might have committed in the past."

Part 2

"Please try to imagine the following situation." This is your second day in the foreign town. During a walk you revisit the place with the small shops and the pigeons. This time you encounter 4 women. Again you are sure that you have seen these women before. There was a report on a group of women who have planned a bomb attack to the city hall in the local news this morning. You begin to sweat. This assault could only be stopped seconds before the detonation of the bomb. You are sure that these women are the terrorists who have planned and initiated this assault. Your heart beats faster and your palms are cold. You wonder why these women are here right now. You are scared and you think about the brutal and bloody crimes these women might have committed in the past.

"Can you imagine this situation? In the following I will show you the close-ups of the place with the 4 terrorists. When viewing the close-ups please try to imagine what other crimes these people have committed in the past."

Part 3

"Please try to imagine the following situation". This is your third day in the town. During a walk you revisit the place with the small shops and the pigeons. This time you see 2 men and 2 woman. You are sure that you have seen these men and woman on the previous occasions. You are breathing faster. You remember to have seen these people in the morning news. It was said that yesterday evening these people have committed an assault to the central station. You remember the pictures of the destruction and the injured victims you saw this morning in the news. While realizing that you are now very close to these dangerous people you are getting horrified. You are feeling sick and your hands are shivering. You feel insecure and you think about the brutal and bloody crimes these people might have committed in the past.

"Can you imagine this situation? In the following I will show you the close-ups of the place with the 4 terrorists. When viewing the close-ups please try to imagine what terrible consequences the attack to the central station might have for the injured innocents."

STATISTICAL PROCEDURES

Statistical analysis was performed with the program SigmaStat 3.1® (Sysstat Software Inc.). All variables have been initially analyzed with the Kolmogorov–Smirnov test to know whether the data varies significantly from the pattern expected if the data was drawn from a population with a normal distribution. Furthermore, the Levene test was performed to probe the homogeneity of variances across groups. Variables that failed the Kolmogorov–Smirnov or the Levene test were analyzed with nonparametric statistics using the Kruskal–Wallis one-way analysis of variance on ranks and Mann–Whitney rank sum tests for pair-wise multiple comparisons. Variables that passed the normality test were analyzed by means of One-Way ANOVA's and Holm–Sidak and Student *t*-tests for pair-wise multiple comparisons. Correlations between the state and trait anxiety measures and the different episodic memory measures (total score, human stimuli score, pigeon stimuli score, and the scores for the trials 1–3) were performed using both Pearson pair-wise and Spearman-rank correlation procedures in dependence of the distribution of the variables. All *P*-values given are two-tailed, and are considered to be significant when $P < 0.05$ or in the case of the Holm–Sidak tests when the *P*-value obtained was lower than the adjusted *P*-level of significance.

RESULTS

EPISODIC MEMORY PERFORMANCE

Total episodic memory score

In this experiment we investigated whether a novel test of episodic memory is suited to detect age-related decrements in episodic memory performance by testing 3 different age groups consisting of young [21–45], middle-aged [48–62], and aged [71–83] healthy adult participants. In order to know whether the groups differ in terms of episodic memory performance we calculated a total episodic memory score that could vary between 0 and 27 correctly remembered stimulus-position-trial associations.

As expected a One-Way ANOVA revealed that the performance of the 3 groups was indeed significantly different from each other (Kolmogorov–Smirnov test: $P > 0.05$, Levene test $P > 0.05$; ANOVA: $F_{(2, 38)} = 7.785$, $P = 0.001$, **Figure 4A**). In order to know which groups performed significantly different from each other, we computed *post-hoc* tests using the Holm–Sidak method. We found that the young group had significantly higher episodic memory scores as compared to both the middle ($T = 2.675$; $P = 0.011$, significant at the critical *P*-level of $P = 0.025$) and aged groups ($T = 3.72$; $P < 0.001$, significant at the critical *P*-level of $P = 0.017$). The latter two groups performed not significantly different from each other ($P > 0.05$).

This result suggest that episodic memory performance is significantly better in young individuals aged between 21 and 45 years as compared to individuals aged between 48 and 62 or older participants.

Episodic memory performance for individual presentation trials

We also analyzed whether the groups would differ regarding their episodic memory scores for the three presentation trials. We expected that the episodic memory performance for trial 1 would be significantly different between the groups because the delay between episodic memory encoding and the recollection of the episodic memory formed was longest >2 h for the first trial as compared to the second and third trials. As predicted, we found that the 3 age groups differed significantly regarding the number of correctly remembered stimulus-position associations for trial 1 (Kolmogorov–Smirnov test: $P > 0.05$, Levene test: $P > 0.05$; ANOVA: $F_{(2, 38)} = 7.056$, $P = 0.002$; **Figure 4B**).

Pair-wise *post-hoc* Holm–Sidak tests revealed that the performance of the aged group during the retrieval of the information for trial 1 was significantly worse as compared to both the young ($T = 3.756$; $P = 0.000578$, significant at the critical *P*-level

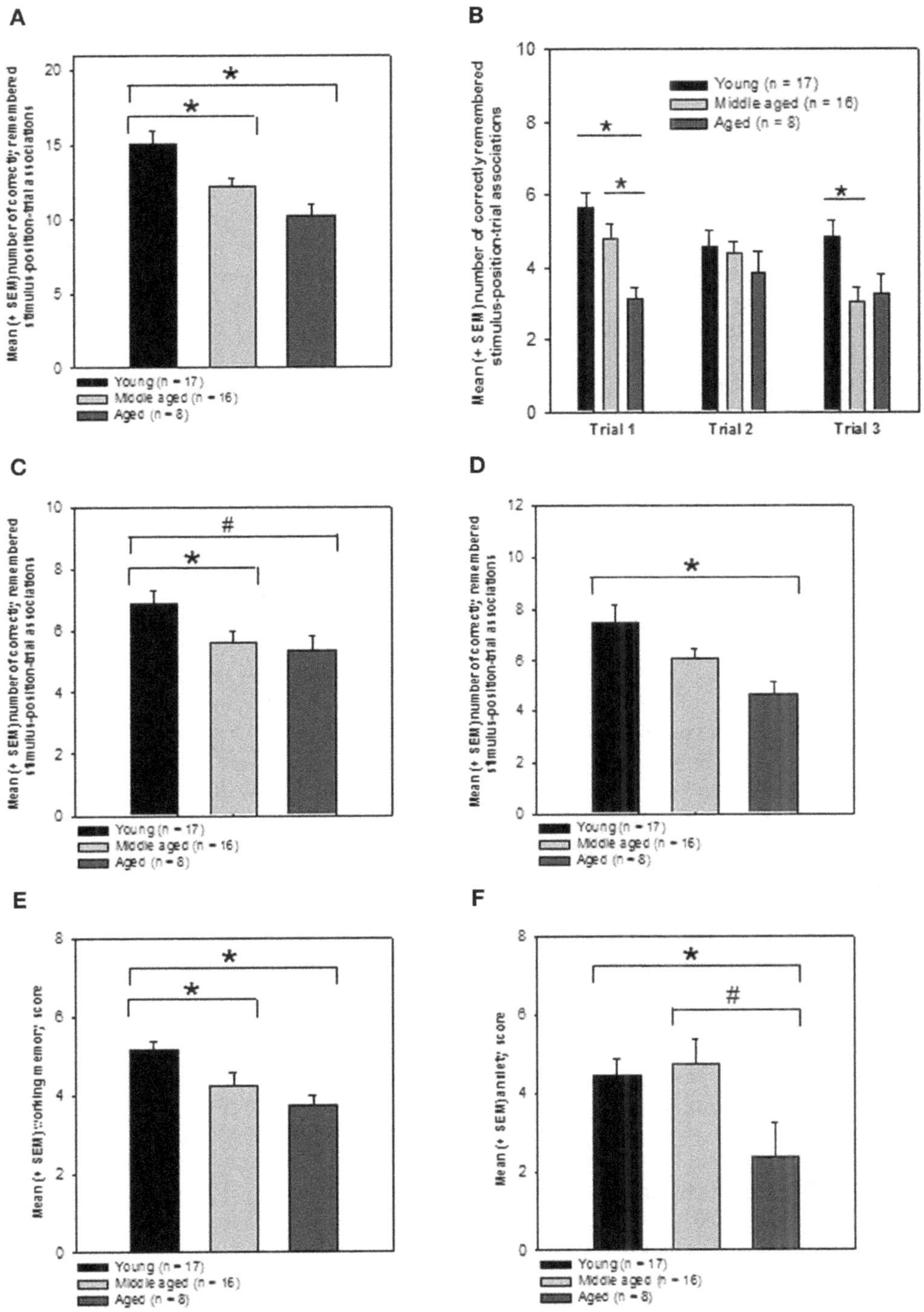

FIGURE 4 | Effects of aging on episodic memory performance, working memory, and emotionality. (A) Total episodic memory score. Bars represent mean and SEM number of correctly remembered stimulus-position-trial associations for indicated groups. $^*P \leq 0.05$, Holm–Sidak test. **(B)** Performance on individual presentation trials. Bars represent mean and SEM number of correctly remembered stimulus-position associations for indicated trials. $^*P \leq 0.05$, Holm–Sidak test. **(C)** Context story relevant stimulus-position-trial performance. Bars represent mean and SEM total number of correctly remembered human-position-trial associations for indicated groups. $^*P \leq 0.05$, $^{\#}0.05 < P < 0.1$, Mann–Whitney rank sum test. **(D)** Context story non-relevant stimulus-position-trial performance. Bars represent mean and SEM total number of correctly remembered pigeon-position-trial associations for indicated groups. $^*P \leq 0.05$, Holm–Sidak test. **(E)** Working memory performance. Bars represent mean and SEM working memory scores for indicated groups. $^*P \leq 0.05$, Mann–Whitney rank sum test. **(F)** Trait anxiety. Bars represent mean and SEM Goldberg anxiety scale scores. $^*P \leq 0.05$, $^{\#}0.05 < P < 0.1$, Student *t*-tests. Graphical presentation of the data: all data obtained with the episodic memory test and the neuropsychological tests were graphically presented as means ± SEM.

of $P = 0.017$) and middle-aged group ($T = 2.489$; $P = 0.0173$, significant at the critical P-level of $P = 0.025$). No significant difference was obtained for the comparison between the young and middle-aged group ($P > 0.05$).

While no significant difference between the groups was evident for the stimulus-position associations established on trial 2 (Kolmogorov–Smirnov test: $P > 0.05$, Levene test $P < 0.05$; Kruskal–Wallis One-Way analysis of variance on ranks: $P > 0.05$; **Figure 4B**), the groups performed significantly different when probed for the stimulus-position associations generated on trial 3 (Kolmogorov–Smirnov test: $P > 0.05$; Levene test: $P > 0.05$; ANOVA: $F_{(2, 38)} = 4.863$, $P = 0.013$).

The pair-wise *post-hoc* Holm–Sidak tests indicated a significant difference between the young and middle-aged group ($T = 2.933$; $P = 0.0057$, significant at the critical P-level of $P = 0.017$) but not for the remaining 2 comparisons ($Ps > 0.05$).

This result suggests that age-related changes in episodic memory performance are reflected by trial 1 and 3 performance. The inability of the second trial to discriminate between the groups might be due to processes of pro- and retroactive interference where the sequential acquisition of learning material has a detrimental effect on the subsequent retrieval process (Brophy et al., 2009). The susceptibility to pro- and retroactive interference might be possibly age-independent.

Episodic memory for context-story relevant vs. non-relevant stimuli

Next we analyzed whether the groups might show significant differences in the ability to establish and remember human-position-trial or pigeon-position-trial associations. We expected that the groups would differ significantly for the human context-relevant stimuli but possibly not for the context non-relevant pigeon stimuli.

A One-Way ANOVA on ranks revealed a trend toward a significant difference between the 3 groups regarding the human-position-trial associations (Kolmogorov–Smirnov test: $P > 0.05$, Levene test: $P < 0.05$; Kruskal–Wallis One-Way analysis of variance on ranks: $H = 5.345$, degrees of freedom: 2, $P = 0.069$, **Figure 4C**). Mann–Whitney rank sum tests for pair-wise comparisons revealed that the young group remembered the human-position-trial combinations significantly better as compared to the middle ($T = 216.5$, $P = 0.047$) group, while there was only a trend for a difference between the young and the aged group ($T = 74.5$, $P = 0.091$). The middle and aged groups performed not significantly different from each other ($P > 0.05$).

Contrarily to our hypothesis, the groups also differed significantly regarding their ability to remember the context-story non-relevant pigeon-position-trial combinations (Kolmogorov–Smirnov test: $P > 0.05$; Levene test $P > 0.05$, ANOVA: $F_{(2, 38)} = 4.986$, $P = 0.012$, **Figure 4D**). Pair-wise *post-hoc* Holm–Sidak tests for the pigeon-position-trial associations showed that the aged group remembered a significantly fewer number of pigeon-position-trial associations relative to the young group ($T = 3.075$; $P = 0.00389$, significant at the critical P-level of $P = 0.017$). There was no significant difference between the young and middle-aged group ($P > 0.05$) or the middle-aged and aged group ($P > 0.05$). Although statistically not significant, the aged group showed slightly better memory performances in the human-position-trial associations compared to the pigeon-position trial condition.

WITHIN-GROUP COMPARISONS OF THE EPISODIC MEMORY FOR CONTEXT-STORY RELEVANT vs. NON-RELEVANT STIMULI

Next we analyzed whether the performance of single groups was significantly different for human vs. pigeon-position-trial associations. However, none of the 3 groups showed a significant difference between the episodic memory for context-story relevant stimuli in comparison to the non-relevant stimuli (all $Ps > 0.05$).

NEUROPSYCHOLOGICAL AND PSYCHOLOGICAL ASSESSMENT

Working memory

In order to know whether the expected aging-related differences in episodic memory performance are at least in part due to changes in working memory performance we also measured this capacity in the three groups. A One-Way ANOVA on ranks revealed that the working memory performance of the 3 groups was indeed significantly different from each other (Kolmogorov–Smirnov test: $P < 0.05$; Levene test: $P > 0.05$; Kruskal–Wallis One-Way analysis of variance on ranks: $H = 13.997$, degrees of freedom: 2, $P < 0.001$, **Figure 4E**). In order to know which groups performed significantly different from each other, we computed Mann–Whitney rank sum tests for pair-wise comparisons. We found that the young group had significantly higher working memory scores as compared to both the middle ($T = 197.5$, $P = 0.008$) and aged groups ($T = 48$, $P = 0.001$). The latter two groups performed not significantly different from each other ($P > 0.05$).

Depressive symptoms

It is known that the incidence of major depression is increased in aged individuals and that depressive episodes are associated with memory impairments. We therefore tested whether possible differences in episodic memory performance between the 3 groups might be explained by differences in depressive symptoms. There were no significant differences between the groups on the Goldberg depression scale ($P > 0.05$).

Anxiety

We have hypothesized that age-related decline in episodic memory performance might be related to hypo-emotionality or changes in the processing of emotionally-valenced stimuli. Therefore, we also tested whether possible group-differences in episodic memory performance might be explained by differences in trait or state (experimental context-induced) anxiety.

Trait anxiety

A One-Way ANOVA indicated a trend for a difference between the groups in the Goldberg scale subtest measuring trait anxiety (Kolmogorov–Smirnov test: $P > 0.05$, Levene test $P > 0.05$;

ANOVA: $F_{(2, 37)} = 2.781$, $P = 0.075$, **Figure 4F**). Pair-wise comparisons by means of Student t-tests revealed that the aged group showed significantly lower trait anxiety scores as compared to the young group (Kolmogorov–Smirnov test: $P > 0.05$; Levene test $P > 0.05$; $T = 2.236$, degrees of freedom: 22, $P = 0.036$), but only a trend for a difference as compared to the middle-aged group (Kolmogorov–Smirnov test: $P > 0.05$, Levene test $P > 0.05$; $T = 2.016$, degrees of freedom: 22, $P = 0.056$). No significant difference was found for the comparison between the young and middle-aged group ($P > 0.05$).

State anxiety

The comparison of the STAI state anxiety reference values reported for patients with phobia or anxiety disorders (*F40/F41*) mean: 42.7 ± 11.5 (Laux et al., 1981) with the mean scores of our 3 age groups: young: 50.59 ± 0.68, middle aged: 52.25 ± and aged: 51.0 ± 2.67 indicates that the context story in combination with the slide presentations has induced an level of emotional arousal in the participants that is similar to the one that has been measured in clinical populations. However, there was no significant difference between groups in the state anxiety test ($P > 0.05$). This result suggest that the experimental context induced similar levels of emotional activation respectively anxiety in the 3 groups.

Correlations

We also performed Pearson and Spearman rank correlations including data from all participants between different measures of episodic memory performance and state and trait anxiety scores. There was only one significant correlation between the state anxiety scores and the episodic memory scores for the pigeon-position-trial associations ($R_{(38)} = 0.322$, $P = 0.049$) all other correlations obtained failed to reach the level of statistical significance. We also calculated single group correlations for the significant correlation found between state anxiety and pigeon-position-trial associations, but did not found significant correlations between the two variables in any group (all $Ps > 0.05$). The highest correlation found was $R_{(16)} = 0.431$ with a P-value of 0.095 in the middle aged group.

DISCUSSION

SUMMARY

In the present study, we hypothesized that episodic memory deficits will be associated with changes in trait and/or state anxiety in the aged but also in the middle-aged group. The results presented above suggest that our novel test of episodic memory that measures the core components of an episodic memory (event, spatial, and temporal information) and in addition probes the ability to form new episodic memories is suited to detect age-related impairments in episodic memory performance. The episodic memory deficits observed in the aged group were observed along with lower anxiety scores measured with the Goldberg anxiety scale. However, no significant correlation between episodic memory and trait or state anxiety scores were found.

EPISODIC MEMORY PERFORMANCE ON INDIVIDUAL PRESENTATION TRIALS

It is well known that aging affects episodic memory function more severely than other types of memory including semantic memory (Levine et al., 2002). It has been proposed that this difference is possibly mediated by changes in the processing of emotionally-competent stimuli (Allen et al., 2005; Kensinger, 2009). We found that the young group was able to remember a higher number of stimulus-position-trial associations (out of 27 associations to be remembered) as compared to both the middle-aged and aged groups. Age-dependent effects were most prominent when the recall of the information for trial 1 was tested. Here, the aged group performed inferior to both the young and middle-aged groups. These results suggest that the aged group failed to consolidate the trial 1 information (that had been acquired more than 2 h before the test) into long-term memory.

CONTEXT STORY RELEVANT AND NON-RELEVANT STIMULUS-POSITION-TRIAL PERFORMANCE

We hypothesized that context story-relevant stimuli (men and woman) might be generally better remembered as context story non-relevant stimuli and therefore would be much better suited to identify age-dependent impairments in episodic memory performance. However, the present results suggest that this was not the case. In fact there was no significant difference between the memory of the context story-relevant vs. non-relevant stimuli even in the young group. We found that both types of stimuli were suited to detect age-dependent changes in episodic memory performance. As expected the young group showed better performance for context story-relevant stimuli as compared to the other groups. Interestingly, the aged group showed impaired context story non-relevant recall of pigeon-position-trial associations as compared to the young group. The aged group also showed slightly better (although statistically not significant) memory performance in the context-story relevant human-position-trial associations condition as compared to the pigeon-position-trial associations condition. These results suggest the presence of an impairment in the possibly incidental or non-intentional encoding of information that is not directly relevant to the context-story in the aged group (Naveh-Benjamin et al., 2009). It seems that the limited attention and memory capacities of aged individuals do not permit the allocation of additional processing resources to attend to and encode context-story non-relevant stimuli. Another possible explanation of this deficit might be that the episodic memories encoded by aged individuals generally contain less event details and context-specific information In fact there is evidence for limited information processing capacities in aged individuals as well as changes in the management and allocation of processing resources in learning situations (Craik and Byrd, 1982).

Interestingly we found a significant correlation between the state anxiety scores and the episodic memory scores for the pigeon-position-trial associations. Given that the old group showed lower trait anxiety scores and impaired episodic memory for pigeon-position-trial associations, it is tempting to speculate that incidental or non-intentional encoding of context-story non-relevant information depends on the level of trait anxiety.

AGING-DEPENDENT EFFECTS OF WORKING MEMORY ON THE ENCODING OF EPISODIC INFORMATION

It is known that working memory mediated by the dorsolateral prefrontal cortex plays a role in the encoding and retrieval of long-term memories including episodic memory (Lee et al., 2000; Cabeza et al., 2002; Blumenfeld and Ranganath, 2006). Thus, we also investigated whether age-related differences in episodic memory performance might be explained by changes in working memory performance. We found that working memory performance is impaired in the middle-aged and aged groups as compared to the young group. It is possible that these working memory deficits might be related to an impairment at the encoding stage of episodic memory formation (Unsworth et al., 2011) in the middle-aged and aged groups in the course of the presentation of the 3 trials.

DEPRESSIVE SYMPTOMS AND EPISODIC MEMORY

It is known that the incidence of depressive symptoms that also include episodic memory impairments are increased in the aged population (Airaksinen et al., 2004, 2007; Potter and Steffens, 2007). In geriatric settings cognitive symptoms that are associated with a depressive disorder are often misinterpreted as dementia (Ouldred and Bryant, 2008). Therefore, we tested whether the middle-aged and aged group might exhibit an increase in depressive symptoms. However, this was not the case so that the differences in episodic memory performance observed between the young and the older groups are unlikely to be due to a depressive condition in the middle-aged and/or aged group.

AGING-RELATED IMPAIRMENTS IN EPISODIC MEMORY AND CHANGES IN EMOTIONALITY

It is well known that emotionally arousing events are more likely to be encoded into long-term memory as compared to neutral events (Cahill and McGaugh, 1998). Furthermore, it has been hypothesized that emotional activation might be a prerequisite for episodic memory formation (Dere et al., 2010). In the present study, we asked whether aging-related episodic memory decline might be associated with changes in state or trait anxiety. Trait anxiety reflects a general personality trait to exhibit anxiety-related behavior at the cognitive (e.g., worrying) and/or behavioral level (e.g., avoidance of anticipated fear-inducing situations) that might be affected by aging. Trait anxiety is relatively stable across time while state anxiety shows large fluctuations and depends on the current context.

We found lower anxiety scores in the aged group as compared to the young and middle-aged group. This change in the trait anxiety levels in the aged group might be associated with a reduced emotional activation by the experimental situation or by the context story. Given that there were no significant correlations between total episodic memory and trait or state anxiety scores, it still remains to be determined whether this difference in anxiety is indeed related to the impaired episodic memory performance in the aged group. In future studies, we will measure physiological correlates of emotional activation such as the blood pressure and the galvanic skin reaction in the aged population to test the above proposed relationship between decreased anxiety and impairments in episodic memory in healthy aged individuals.

There is evidence that older individuals exhibit a decreased functional connectivity between the amygdala and the hippocampus (St Jacques et al., 2009). Episodic memory impairments in the elderly might be related to a diminished emotional modulation of declarative memory formation implemented by the amygdala-hippocampus axis (McGaugh et al., 1996; Tulving and Markowitsch, 1998; Dere et al., 2010). This hypothesis might be tested by combining our novel test of episodic memory with hippocampal-amygdala EEG coherence measurements and neuroimaging methods such as functional MRI.

Novel tests of episodic memory and limitations of the present task

Recently novel episodic memory tasks have been designed that are based on paradigms that have been originally developed to study episodic-like memory in animals (Clayton and Dickinson, 1999; Dere et al., 2005a). These tasks are either based on the "what, where, and when" (Pause et al., 2010; Holland and Smulders, 2011) or "what, where, which" (Easton et al., 2012) principles. Pause et al. (2010) followed a reverse translational approach and adapted the episodic-like memory test for rodents (Dere et al., 2005a) to humans and devised a computer-based test. However, this test requiring the active exploration of the computer screen using a keyboard might be too complicated to be run with older individuals. Others have probed episodic memory based on the "what, where, and when" paradigm by asking participants to hide different coin types (what) in different locations (where) on two separate occasions (when) (Holland and Smulders, 2011). These authors conclude that paradigms based on the "what, where, and when" paradigm might be indeed reliable tests of episodic memory function. Another approach to translate findings from animal research into tests of human episodic memory was based on the "what, where, and which" paradigm (Easton et al., 2012). Here, it has been proposed that tasks using contextual information to discriminate events could only be accurately performed using recollection, not familiarity, while tasks using temporal information to discriminate events might be solved using either recollection or familiarity (Easton et al., 2012). It thus remains to be determined whether tasks based on the "what, where, and when" paradigm rely more on recollection vs. familiarity-based memory performance.

In order to fully explore the strengths and limits of the novel episodic memory test described here, follow-up studies should be performed in which recollection vs. familiarity-based memory performance is assessed, sample sizes are increased and in which direct physiological measurements of emotional activation during task performance are correlated with the episodic memory scores obtained.

ACKNOWLEDGMENTS

This study was supported by funds from the Deutsche Forschungsgemeinschaft (grant no.: DFG-DE-1149/6-1) and the Centre National de la Recherché Scientifique (Action Interdisciplinaire CNRS: Vieillissement) to Ekrem Dere.

REFERENCES

Airaksinen, E., Larsson, M., Lundberg, I., and Forsell, Y. (2004). Cognitive functions in depressive disorders: evidence from a population-based study. *Psychol. Med.* 34, 83–91.

Airaksinen, E., Wahlin, A., Forsell, Y., and Larsson, M. (2007). Low episodic memory performance as a premorbid marker of depression: evidence from a 3-year follow-up. *Acta Psychiatr. Scand.* 115, 458–465.

Allen, P. A., Kaut, K. P., Lord, R. G., Hall, R. J., Grabbe, J. W., and Bowie, T. (2005). An emotional mediation theory of differential age effects in episodic and semantic memories. *Exp. Aging Res.* 31, 355–391.

Blumenfeld, R. S., and Ranganath, C. (2006). Dorsolateral prefrontal cortex promotes long-term memory formation through its role in working memory organization. *J. Neurosci.* 26, 916–925.

Bornstein, R., Baker, G., and Douglass, A. (1991). Depression andmemoryin major depression disorder. *J. Neuropsychiatry Clin. Neurosci.* 3, 78–80.

Brophy, L. M., Jackson, M., and Crowe, S. F. (2009). Interference effects on commonly used memory tasks. *Arch. Clin. Neuropsychol.* 24, 105–112.

Burgess, N., Maguire, E. A., and O'Keefe, J. (2002). The human hippocampus and spatial and episodic memory. *Neuron* 35, 625–641.

Cabeza, R., Dolcos, F., Graham, R., and Nyberg, L. (2002). Similarities and differences in the neural correlates of episodic memory retrieval and working memory. *Neuroimage* 16, 317–330.

Cahill, L., and McGaugh, J. L. (1998). Mechanisms of emotional arousal and lasting declarative memory. *Trends Neurosci.* 21, 294–299.

Clayton, N. S., and Dickinson, A. (1999). Episodic-like memory during cache recovery by scrub jays. *Nature* 395, 272–274.

Craik, F. I. M., and Byrd, M. (1982). *Aging and Cognitive Deficits: The Role of Attentional Processes.* New York, NY: Plenum Press.

Dere, E., Huston, J. P., and De Souza Silva, M. A. (2005a). Integrated memory for objects, places and temporal order: evidence for episodic-like memory in mice. *Neurobiol. Learn. Mem.* 84, 214–221.

Dere, E., Huston, J. P., and De Souza Silva, M. A. (2005b). Protocol: episodic-like memory in mice: simultaneous assessment of object, place and temporal order memory. *Brain Res. Brain Res. Protoc.* 16, 10–19.

Dere, E., Pause, B., and Pietrowsky, R. (2010). Emotion and episodic memory in neuropsychiatric disorders. *Behav. Brain Res.* 215, 162–171.

Dubois, B., Feldman, H. H., Jacova, C., Dekosky, S. T., Barberger-Gateau, P., Cummings, J., et al. (2007). Research criteria for the diagnosis of Alzheimer's disease: revising the NINCDS-ADRDA criteria. *Lancet Neurol.* 6, 734–746.

Easton, A., Webster, L. A., and Eacott, M. J. (2012). The episodic nature of episodic-like memories. *Learn. Mem.* 19, 146–150.

Goldberg, D., Bridges, K., Duncan-Jones, P., and Grayson, D. (1988). Detecting anxiety and depression in general medical settings. *BMJ* 297, 897–899.

Holland, S. M., and Smulders, T. V. (2011). Do humans use episodic memory to solve a What-Where-When memory task? *Anim. Cogn.* 14, 95–102.

Kart-Teke, E., De Souza Silva, M. A., Huston, J. P., and Dere, E. (2006). Wistar rats show episodic-like memory for unique experiences. *Neurobiol. Learn. Mem.* 85, 173–182.

Kaszniak, A. W., and Menchola, M. (2012). Behavioral neuroscience of emotion in aging. *Curr. Top. Behav. Neurosci.* 10, 51–66.

Kensinger, E. A. (2009). How emotion affects older adults' memories for event details. *Memory* 17, 208–219.

Kensinger, E. A., Addis, D. R., and Atapattu, R. K. (2011). Amygdala activity at encoding corresponds with memory vividness and with memory for select episodic details. *Neuropsychologia* 49, 663–673.

Kirchhoff, B. A., Wagner, A. D., Maril, A., and Stern, C. E. (2000). Prefrontal-temporal circuitry for episodic encoding and subsequent memory. *J. Neurosci.* 20, 6173–6180

Laux, L., Glanzmann, P., Schaffner P., and Spielberger, C. D. (1981) *Das State-Trait-Angstinventar. Theoretische Grundlagen und Handanweisung.* Weinheim: Beltz Test GmbH.

LeDoux, J. (2007). The amygdala. *Curr. Biol.* 17, R868–R874.

Lee, A. C., Robbins, T. W., and Owen, A M. (2000). Episodic memory meets working memory in the frontal lobe: functional neuroimaging studies of encoding and retrieval. *Crit. Rev. Neurobiol.* 14, 165–197.

Levine, B., Svoboda, E., Hay, J. F., Winocur, G., and Moscovitch, M. (2002). Aging and autobiographical memory: dissociating episodic from semantic retrieval, *Psychol. Aging* 17, 677–689.

Libkuman, T. M., Stabler, C. L., and Otani, H. (2004). Arousal, valence, and memory for detail. *Memory* 12, 237–247.

Markowitsch, H. J., and Staniloiu, A. (2011). Amygdala in action: relaying biological and social significance to autobiographical memory. *Neuropsychologia* 49, 718–733.

McGaugh, J. L. (2004). The amygdala modulates the consolidation of memories of emotionally arousing experiences. *Annu. Rev. Neurosci.* 27, 1–28.

McGaugh, J. L., Cahill, L., and Roozendaal, B. (1996). Involvement of the amygdala in memory storage: interaction with other brain systems. *Proc. Natl. Acad. Sci. U.S.A.* 93, 13508–13514.

McIntyre, C. K., Power, A. E., Roozendaal, B., and McGaugh, J. L. (2003). Role of the basolateral amygdala in memory consolidation. *Ann. N.Y. Acad. Sci.* 985, 273–293.

Nashiro, K., and Mather, M. (2011). How arousal affects younger and older adults' memory binding. *Exp. Aging Res.* 37, 108–128.

Naveh-Benjamin, M., Shing, Y. L., Kilb, A., Werkle-Bergner, M., Lindenberger, U., and Li, S. C. (2009). Adult age differences in memory for name-face associations: the effects of intentional and incidental learning. *Memory* 17, 220–232.

Nebes, R. D., Butters, M. A., Mulsant, B. H., Pollock, B. G., Zmuda, M. D., Houck, P. R., et al. (2000). Decreased working memory and processing speed mediate cognitive impairment in geriatric depression. *Psychol. Med.* 30, 679–691.

Nyberg, L., Lövdén, M., Riklund, K., Lindenberger, U., and Bäckman, L. (2012). Memory aging and brain maintenance. *Trends Cogn. Sci.* 16, 292–305.

Nyberg, L., McIntosh, A. R., Houle, S., Nilsson, L. G., and Tulving, E. (1996). Activation of medial temporal structures during episodic memory retrieval. *Nature* 380, 715–717.

Ouldred, E., and Bryant, C. (2008). Dementia care. Part 1: guidance and the assessment process. *Br. J. Nurs.* 17, 138–145.

Park, D. C., Lautenschlager, G., Hedden, T., Davidson, N. S., Smith, A. D., and Smith, P. K. (2002). Models of visuospatial and verbal memory across the adult life span. *Psychol. Aging* 17, 299–320.

Pause, B., Jungbluth, C., Adolph, D., Pietrowsky, R., and Dere, E. (2010). Induction and measurement of episodic memories in healthy adults. *J. Neurosci. Methods* 189, 88–96.

Persson, J., Nyberg, L., Lind, J., Larsson, A., Nilsson, L. G., Ingvar, M., et al. (2006). Structure-function correlates of cognitive decline in aging. *Cereb. Cortex* 16, 907–915.

Potter, G. G., and Steffens, D. C. (2007). Contribution of depression to cognitive impairment and dementia in older adults. *Neurologist* 13, 105–117.

Rajah, M. N., Kromas, M., Han, J. E., and Pruessner, J. C. (2010). Group differences in anterior hippocampal volume and in the retrieval of spatial and temporal context memory in healthy young versus older adults. *Neuropsychologia* 48, 4020–4030.

Rönnlund, M., Nyberg, L., Bäckman, L., and Nilsson, L. G. (2005). Stability, growth, and decline in adult life span development of declarative memory: cross-sectional and longitudinal data from a population-based study. *Psychol. Aging* 20, 3–18.

Shing, Y. L., Werkle-Bergner, M., Brehmer, Y., Müller, V., Li, S. C., and Lindenberger, U. (2010). Episodic memory across the lifespan: the contributions of associative and strategic components. *Neurosci. Biobehav. Rev.* 34, 1080–1091.

Spielberger, C. D., Gorsuch, F. L., and Lushene, R. E. (1970). *Manual for the State-Trait Anxiety Inventory.* Palo Alto, CA: Consulting Psychologists Press.

St Jacques, P. L., Dolcos, F., and Cabeza, R. (2009). Effects of aging on functional connectivity of the amygdala for subsequent memory of negative pictures: a network analysis of functional magnetic resonance imaging data. *Psychol. Sci.* 20, 74–84.

Tsivilis, D., Vann, S. D., Denby, C., Roberts, N., Mayes, A. R., Montaldi, D., et al. (2008). A disproportionate role for the fornix and mammillary bodies in recall versus recognition memory. *Nat. Neurosci.* 11, 834–842.

Tulving, E. (1983). *Elements of Episodic Memory.* London: Oxford University Press.

Tulving, E. (2002). Episodic memory: from mind to brain. *Annu. Rev. Psychol.* 53, 1–25.

Tulving, E., and Markowitsch, H. J. (1998). Episodic and declarative memory: role of the hippocampus. *Hippocampus* 8, 198–204.

Unsworth, N., Brewer, G. A., and Spillers, G. J. (2011). Variation in working memory capacity and episodic memory: examining the importance of encoding specificity. *Psychon. Bull. Rev.* 18, 1113–1118.

Van Petten, C., Plante, E., Davidson, P. S., Kuo, T. Y., Bajuscak, L., and Glisky, E. L. (2004). Memory and executive function in older adults: relationships with temporal and prefrontal gray matter volumes and white matter hyperintensities. *Neuropsychologia* 42, 1313–1335.

Wheeler, M. A., Stuss, D. T., and Tulving, E. (1997). Toward a theory of episodic memory: the frontal lobes and autonoetic consciousness. *Psychol. Bull.* 121, 331–354.

Williams-Gray, C. H., Foltynie, T., Lewis, S. J., and Barker, R. A. (2006). Cognitive deficits and psychosis in Parkinson's disease: a review of pathophysiology and therapeutic options. *CNS Drugs* 20, 477–505.

Wolf, O. T. (2012). Immediate recall influences the effects of pre-encoding stress on emotional episodic long-term memory consolidation in healthy young men. *Stress* 15, 272–280.

Wolff, M., Loukavenko, E. A., Will, B. E., and Dalrymple-Alford, J. C. (2008). The extended hippocampal-diencephalic memory system: enriched housing promotes recovery of the flexible use of spatial representations after anterior thalamic lesions. *Hippocampus* 18, 996–1007.

11

Don't be too strict with yourself! Rigid negative self-representation in healthy subjects mimics the neurocognitive profile of depression for autobiographical memory

Marco Sperduti [1,2]****, Pénélope Martinelli*** [1,2]***, Sandrine Kalenzaga*** [1,2]***, Anne-Dominique Devauchelle*** [3]***, Stéphanie Lion*** [3]***, Caroline Malherbe*** [3]***, Thierry Gallarda*** [2,4]***, Isabelle Amado*** [2,4]***, Marie-Odile Krebs*** [2,4]***, Catherine Oppenheim*** [3] ***and Pascale Piolino*** [1,2,5]

[1] *Laboratoire Mémoire et Cognition, Institut de Psychologie, Université Paris Descartes, Boulogne-Billancourt, France*
[2] *INSERM U894, Centre de Psychiatrie et Neurosciences, Université Paris Descartes, Paris, France*
[3] *INSERM U894, Service d'Imagerie, Université Paris Descartes Sorbonne Paris Cité, Paris, France*
[4] *Faculté de Médecine, Centre Hospitalier Sainte-Anne, Service Hospitalier Universitaire, Université Paris Descartes, Paris, France*
[5] *Institut Universitaire de France, Paris, France*

***Correspondence:**
Marco Sperduti, UMR S894, Laboratoire Mémoire et Cognition, Centre de Psychiatrie et Neurosciences, Université Paris Descartes, 2 ter rue d'Alesia, 75014 Paris, France.
e-mail: marcosperduti@yahoo.it

Autobiographical memory (AM) comprises representation of both specific (episodic) and generic (semantic) personal information. Depression is characterized by a shift from episodic to semantic AM retrieval. According to theoretical models, this process ("overgeneralization"), would be linked to reduced executive resources. Moreover, "overgeneral" memories, accompanied by a negativity bias in depression, lead to a pervasive negative self-representation. As executive functions and AM specificity are also closely intricate among "non-clinical" populations, "overgeneral" memories could result in depressive emotional responses. Consequently, our hypothesis was that the neurocognitive profile of healthy subjects showing a rigid negative self-image would mimic that of patients. Executive functions and self-image were measured and brain activity was recorded, by means of fMRI, during episodic AMs retrieval in young healthy subjects. The results show an inverse correlation, that is, a more rigid and negative self-image produces lower performances in both executive and specific memories. Moreover, higher negative self-image is associated with decreased activity in the left ventro-lateral prefrontal and in the anterior cingulate cortex, repeatedly shown to exhibit altered functioning in depression. Activity in these regions, on the contrary, positively correlates with executive and memory performances, in line with their role in executive functions and AM retrieval. These findings suggest that rigid negative self-image could represent a marker or a vulnerability trait of depression by being linked to reduced executive function efficiency and episodic AM decline. These results are encouraging for psychotherapeutic approaches aimed at cognitive flexibility in depression and other psychiatric disorders.

Keywords: autobiographical memory, depression, executive functions, self, neuroimaging, anterior cingulate cortex, ventro-lateral prefrontal cortex

INTRODUCTION

Autobiographical memory (AM) is the "long term" memory system involved in the retention and retrieval of personal past events. A distinction between episodic AM (EAM) and semantic AM (SAM) has been proposed by several authors (Conway and Pleydell-Pearce, 2000; Conway, 2001; Tulving, 2002; Piolino et al., 2009; Klein and Gangi, 2010). The former refers to memory for unique events situated in time and space and recollected with phenomenological details and a sense of remembering, whereas the latter concerns decontextualized extended or repeated events and self-knowledge such as the name of one's acquaintances.

Autobiographical memory is impaired in a number of psychiatric disorders including post-traumatic stress disorder (McNally et al., 1994), schizophrenia (Riutort et al., 2003; Harrison and Fowler, 2004; Iqbal et al., 2004), and depression (Brittlebank et al., 1993; Kuyken and Dalgleish, 1995; Brewin et al., 1999; Wessel et al., 2001; Watson et al., 2013). The common pattern of AM impairment in these pathological states is characterized by a specific EAM deficit: patients recalling preferentially "overgeneral" memories (i.e., repeated and extended events) rather than unique episodes with a precise spatio-temporal context.

In depression the "overgenerality" characterizing AM retrieval is accompanied by a particular difficulty in recollecting details, even in the context of specific event retrieval (Lemogne et al., 2006). Interestingly, this lack of specificity has predictive value for the course of depression (Brittlebank et al., 1993; Peeters et al.,

2002; Raes et al., 2006; Hermans et al., 2008). Moreover, there is a large body of evidence showing that "overgeneral" AM is not simply a symptom of depression but can be regarded as a trait marker or vulnerability factor for this disease (Williams et al., 2007). Indeed, even in "non-clinical" populations, reduced memory specificity predicts increased emotional reactivity to stressful events (Mackinger et al., 2000; Gibbs and Rude, 2004; Van Minnen et al., 2005; Bryant et al., 2007; for a review, see Raes et al., 2007).

According to the Self-Memory System model (SMS, Conway and Pleydell-Pearce, 2000; Conway, 2005), specific memories are generally accessed through a hierarchical search starting from general events. This process engages executive functions in order to select relevant information and concurrently inhibit competing information. This theoretical model has been supported by numerous studies reporting that the ability to retrieve specific memories is linked to executive processes such as cognitive flexibility, inhibition, updating, shifting, and working memory (Baddeley and Wilson, 1986; Winthorpe and Rabbitt, 1988; Fivush and Nelson, 2004; Matuszewski et al., 2006; Piolino et al., 2007a,b, 2010; Addis et al., 2008; Raes et al., 2010; Ros et al., 2010; Coste et al., 2011).

Thus, "overgeneral" memories may arise when insufficient executive resources cause the premature break of the memory search at higher hierarchical levels. For instance, reduced AM specificity has been shown to be associated with poor performance in verbal fluency in controls (Williams and Dritschel, 1992) and in participants with eating disorders (Dalgleish et al., 2007). In the same vein, Heeren et al. (2009) have reported a parallel improvement of verbal fluency and AM specificity following a mindfulness training. Verbal fluency is sometimes considered as a measure of cognitive flexibility (Heeren et al., 2009), and more generally as a broad measure of executive control (Rosen and Engle, 1997).

Depressed patients show deficits in several executive functions including inhibition (Linville, 1996; MacQueen et al., 2000; Markela-Lerenc et al., 2006; Gohier et al., 2009) and cognitive flexibility (Naismith et al., 2003; Airaksinen et al., 2004; Meiran et al., 2010). Flexibility difficulties have emerged to be among the most prominent cognitive impairment in depression (Austin et al., 2001). Consequently, executive deficits are a central feature of a number of theoretical models of the depressive pathology (Hasher and Zacks, 1979; Ellis and Ashbrook, 1988; Hertel and Rude, 1991; Barrett et al., 2004). Thus, based on Conway and Pleydell-Pearce's (2000) proposition, the Capture and Rumination, Functional Avoidance, and eXecutive control model (CaR-FAX model, Williams et al., 2007) proposes that "overgeneralization" in depression may result from executive impairment, that leads to difficulty in inhibiting inappropriate (i.e., "overgeneral") memories. Recently, however, Watson et al. (2013) did not find any relationship between verbal fluency and memory specificity in depressed patients.

Nevertheless, contrasting results have been reported concerning the role of executive deficit in depression, with some studies reporting a normalization of performance after recovery from recurrent depression (Beblo et al., 1999; Neu et al., 2001), whereas others reported a persistent impairment after remission (Beats et al., 1996; Reischies and Neu, 2000). Biringer et al. (2005) have shown no significant difference between recovered patients and controls on a composite score measuring global executive functioning, although, in the same group, semantic fluency performance was still below that of the controls. Such results could depend on the particular process tested, it has been proposed that executive deficits may be a risk factor for emotional disorders (Nolen-Hoeksema and Watkins, 2011), particularly for depression (Ingram et al., 2008).

Theoretical considerations (James, 1890; Conway and Pleydell-Pearce, 2000; Gardiner, 2001), as well as behavioral ones (Rogers et al., 1977; Symons and Johnson, 1997) along with neuroimaging findings (Fletcher et al., 1996; Konishi et al., 2000; McDermott et al., 2000; Donaldson et al., 2001; Northoff and Bernpohl, 2004; Henson et al., 2005; Buckner et al., 2008; Sajonz et al., 2010; for reviews, see Cavanna and Trimble, 2006; Legrand and Ruby, 2009) suggest that AM and self-referential processing are intrinsically related. The relationship between self-concept and AM has been illustrated by a recent neuroimaging study reporting a correlation between the degree of certainty in self-evaluation and activity in dorso-medial prefrontal cortex (MPFC) (D'Argembeau et al., 2012). The authors proposed that this correlation may reflect the engagement of processes involved in the retrieval, integration, and evaluation of self-related information allowing the construction of a coherent self-image.

Thus, the categorical nature of "overgeneral" memories may contribute to other forms of "overgeneral" thinking found in depressed patients such as global negative self-judgment and "overgeneralization" in self-evaluation. Indeed, recurrent retrieval of "overgeneral" memories leads to categorical self-descriptors ("I am always boring") resulting in a retrieval style closely linked to rumination (Watkins and Teasdale, 2001; Raes et al., 2006; Debeer et al., 2011). Thus, depressed patients' cognition is characterized by negative schemas and a self-focus generating and maintaining a depressed mood and a pessimistic view of the self, the world, and the future (Beck, 1976, 2008; Beck et al., 1979). This negative bias has been associated with executive control impairments (Lo and Allen, 2011; De Lissnyder et al., in press), such as difficulties in inhibiting the processing of negative information (Joormann, 2004; Goeleven et al., 2006; see Gotlib and Joormann, 2010 for review). Such cognitive biases, in particular recurrent negative self-evaluations, are known to be predictive of future depressive symptoms (Carver, 1988; Dent and Teasdale, 1988). Accordingly, Mongrain (1990) demonstrated that high rates of dysfunctional attitudes, characterized by rigid content regarding self-worth leading to poor self-esteem (Mirabel-Sarron et al., 2001), are predictive of subsequent depressive symptoms (Beck, 1967; Beck et al., 1979; Segal and Ingram, 1994).

Cognitive theories posit that information processing and memory retrieval style may constitute a risk factor for the occurrence of depressive episodes. Thus, cognitive dysfunction may be an endophenotype for depression (Hasler et al., 2004). In particular, negative self-schemas (Ingram and Siegle, 2002) and self-evaluations (Carver, 1988; Dent and Teasdale, 1988) as well as rigid attitudes regarding self-judgment (Beck, 1967; Beck et al., 1979; Segal and Ingram, 1994) are known to represent vulnerability factors for depression.

Thus, we hypothesize that a rigid negative self-image in a "non-clinical" population would mimic the neurocognitive profile of depressed patients. To test our hypothesis, we assessed the subjective self-representation of 20 healthy subjects using a standard evaluation. Moreover, we measured different executive functions with standard neuropsychological tests. Then we asked participants to recall specific AMs while recording their brain activity by means of fMRI.

According to the existing literature (Joiner, 2000; Hammen, 2005; O'Brien et al., 2006; Evraire and Dozois, 2011; Morley and Moran, 2011; for review, see Sowislo and Orth, 2012), we expected to find that subjects showing higher negative self-image should show decreased scores on executive functions and, in turn, in the specificity of AMs. Regarding neuroimaging data, we expected to replicate previous findings on AM retrieval reporting activities in a widespread network encompassing fronto-parietal areas, cortical midline regions, and medial temporal structures (for a recent meta-analysis see Martinelli et al., 2012). Moreover, we predicted a significant correlation between the extent of the crystallized negative self-image and the activity in regions frequently reported as dysfunctional in depression (Brody et al., 1999; Mayberg et al., 1999; Drevets and Price, 2005; Murrough et al., 2011), in particular in lateral prefrontal cortex and anterior cingulate cortex (ACC), which are also linked to executive functions and memory retrieval (Ochsner et al., 2004; Kringelbach and Rolls, 2004; Ochsner and Gross, 2005; Niendam et al., 2012).

MATERIALS AND METHODS

PARTICIPANTS

Twenty healthy young volunteers (25–44 years old, mean = 29.2 ± 5.55, 10 women) all right-handed (according to the Edinburgh Handedness Inventory; Oldfield, 1971) and native French speakers participated to the study. All participants gave their informed written consent as required by the local ethic committee (CPP Ile de France 3 n°2687). Exclusion criteria included presence of history of alcohol or substance abuse, head trauma, major diseases affecting brain functions, neuropsychiatric disorders such as clinical depression (tested with the Mini-International Neuropsychiatric Interview, Sheehan et al., 1998). Moreover, all participants were under the cutoff score on the French version of the Beck Depression Inventory (BDI-21, Beck et al., 1988; Bouvard and Cottraux, 1996, cutoff score >14; mean = 2.65 ± 2.53).

SELF-CONCEPT ASSESSMENT

Each subject fulfilled the Tennessee Self-Concept Scale (TSCS, Fitts and Warren, 1996: French version Duval et al., 2007). This scale assesses the multidimensionality of the self over six domains (family, personal, social, moral, physical, academic), and contains 82 descriptive statements (e.g., "I am an honest person") that have to be rated on a five-point scale (always false, mostly false, partly false/partly true, mostly true, always true) according to how well they match the participant's personality. Two standard scores were computed: (1) the degree of certainty (TSCS-C) (for a comparable method, see Addis and Tippett, 2004; Naylor and Clare, 2008) was measured through the amount of responses rated "1" (always false) or "5" (always true) and reflects "the degree of certainty about the way one sees oneself, thus reflecting the extent to which a definite sense of identity is expressed" (Naylor and Clare, 2008, p. 595). A more definite sense of self has been shown to reflect a less nuanced and a more crystallized and rigid self-concept (Klein and Gangi, 2010; Martinelli et al., 2013; Picard et al., in press); (2) the total score of the TSCS (TSCS-V) that reflects the global valence of the self (i.e., direction of the self, Addis and Tippett, 2004) and adds up the separate TSCS scores of identity, satisfaction, and behavior. High scores indicate a positive self-concept and higher self-esteem. Finally, a "negative crystallization score" (NCS) was computed by dividing the degree of certainty by the total score (each score being previously transformed into z score), so the higher the NCS score the more the self-concept was crystallized and negative.

NEUROPSYCHOLOGICAL MEASURES

In order to characterize executive and working memory functions, we administered to the participants the following standard tests: the running span (Morris and Jones, 1990; Quinette et al., 2003; total score), the Stroop test (Stroop, 1935; interference score), and trail making test (Reitan, 1958, TMT B-A) to assess updating, inhibition, and shifting functions respectively (Miyake et al., 2000); verbal fluencies (Cardebat et al., 1990, sum of animal and letter P fluency), and digit and visuo-spatial spans (sum of backward and forward spans, Wechsler, 2000) to assess cognitive control and working memory functions. All scores were scaled in the same direction, so that higher scores reflect better performance.

NEUROIMAGING PROCEDURE

Pre-scanning interview

In the pre-scanning interview, exclusion and inclusion criteria were verified by means of a clinical examination and psychometric tests. Then the TSCS and neuropsychological tests were administered to participants. In addition, subjects completed the Taste and Interest Questionnaire (TIQ) that was employed to create personal cues to trigger AM retrieval in the scanning session. The aim of this questionnaire was to collect information in order to create personalized cues for each participant without directly asking for descriptions of past memories to avoid re-encoding memories (Viard et al., 2010; Addis et al., 2011). Participants were informed that the purpose of the questionnaire was to obtain a description of their personality based on information about their main life interests. They had no prior knowledge of the aim of the fMRI task, preventing the possibility for participants of searching for memories linked to their taste and interests between the two sessions. The questionnaire concerned their personal lives from their birth to 5 years ago. It consists of a list of 220 interests including leisure, food, drink, transport, places where they lived, holidays, jobs, studies. For each item, the participants had to answer whether it was personally pertinent or not, rated by 1 and 0 respectively. When an item was pertinent, they had to rate how important (from 0 to 10) and frequent (Frequent/Rare) the activity or interest had been in their life. An activity or interest was used as a cue for episodic AM retrieval if it was pertinent, important (>5), and rare. Twenty-four cues were created for each subject. Examples of activity assessed in the TIQ and the procedure to create cues is illustrated in the **Table A1** in Appendix.

Episodic autobiographical memory task

The participants were first invited to take part in a training session before the fMRI scanning. Participants received detailed explanations on the nature of the task and participated in a brief simulation of the experiment on a laptop. They were instructed to recall EAMs elicited by the cues and to press a button when a memory was recalled. EAMs were defined as memories of a single event that occurred at a specific time and place, of short duration, lasting less than 24 h. Participants were instructed to mentally relive personal episodes prompted by cues and to recollect affective and perceptual details (such as time, location, perceptions, feelings, scenery, and people present in the scene) (e.g.: "a unique memory linked to a trip in Italy"). After instructions, participants were trained on three trials with the experimenter providing feedback concerning the pertinence of the responses. The cues used for training were different from those used during the scanning session.

Scanning session

During fMRI recording, cues were visually presented in white font on a black background projected on a screen viewed by means of a mirror incorporated into the head-coil. E-Prime software (Psychology Software Tools, Inc., Pittsburgh, PA, USA) in combination with an Integrated Functional Imaging System (IFIS) was used for the presentation and timing of stimuli and collection of responses. Responses were made on an MR-compatible two-buttons box. Participants completed four functional scans in a single session. Each functional scan was composed of six items. Each trial lasted 26 s with the following time-course: the cue was presented for 5 s, followed by a white cross at the center of the screen for 19 s, then the cross turned red for 3 s informing the participants of the end of the present trial and the arrival of the next one. Participants were instructed to press a button as soon as they accessed a memory.

Post scan interview

Participants were asked to recall again each EAM retrieved in the scanner in order to check that memories met minimal criteria of specificity (single events, situated in time and place, lasting less than 24 h, e.g., "the day of the visit of the exhibition 'The man on the moon' in the Palace of Tokyo museum in Paris, in August 2009"). The subsequent analyses were performed only on memories that met all the above mentioned criteria.

Episodic AMs were rated for specificity on standard scales (Levine et al., 2002; Piolino et al., 2009). More precisely, the presence of specific spatial and temporal details, and other contextual and phenomenological details in each evocation was noted (one point by type of detail, max. 4; e.g., "I remember my visit in the Palace of Tokyo as if I was still there, being together with Chiara in a room of the exhibition in the first floor in the dark to see the TV reports and talking with other visitors. . ., it was 6:00 p.m., after then we settled down in the restaurant of the outdoor museum in front of the Seine. . ."). We computed for each participant a global ratio of specificity (EPI score) totaling up the sum of spatio-temporal, other contextual and phenomenological details, divided by the number of EAM.

fMRI METHOD

MRI data acquisition

All data were acquired with a 3 T scanner (MR 750, General Electric Healthcare, Little Chalfont, UK). The anatomical scan used an inversion recovery 3-D T1-weighted gradient-echo sequence images (TE = 4.3 ms, TR = 11.2 ms, TI = 400 ms, matrix = 384 × 384, slice thickness = 1.2 mm). Functional images were acquired using a gradient-echo echoplanar (EPI) sequence (TE = 30 ms, TR = 2000 ms, flip angle = 90°, matrix = 64 × 64, slice thickness = 3 mm, 42 contiguous sections). The first four volumes of each functional run were discarded in order to allow longitudinal magnetization to approach equilibrium.

Pre-processing of fMRI data

All data were processed using SPM5 software (Statistical Parametric Mapping 5, Welcome Dept. Cognitive Neurology, UK; www.fil.ion.ucl.ac.uk/spm). Standard pre-processing procedures were applied to MRI data. EPI volumes were corrected for slice timing, realigned to the first image, co-registered with the high-resolution T_1-weighted image and normalized into the Montreal Neurological Institute (MNI) template. Finally, the normalized EPI volumes were smoothed using an isotropic Gaussian kernel filter of 5 mm full-width half-maximum.

First level analysis of fMRI data

Only correct trials were used for the subsequent analyses. A trial was considered as correct if (1) the participant had pressed the button during the trial (indicating retrieval) and (2) the description of the memory during the debriefing corresponded to EAM (see above). Memory retrieval (i.e., access or strategic research phase) was modeled by convolving the time period between cue presentation and subjects' response with the hemodynamic response function (HRF). For each subject, General Linear Model was used to estimate the parameters of interest. Parameters of movement were also included in the model as regressors of no interest. A whole brain t-test was computed to estimate the contrast of interest for each subject: EAM vs. rest. Then, contrasts for each individual were used for second-level analyses.

Second-level analysis of fMRI data

We computed a whole brain t-test using first level contrasts for each subject. An activation map resulting from this analysis was then used to mask subsequent correlation analysis. The rationale of this choice was that we were only interested in correlations in areas showing a significant activation. Threshold for the whole brain t-test was fixed at $p < 0.01$ corrected for multiple comparison using the false discovery rate (FDR) with an extended threshold of $k = 20$.

Correlations

We computed correlations between signal change in regions showing a significant activity at the group level and the NCS using the multiple regression model in SPM in which we entered contrast images as well as the NCS for each subject as a covariate. The threshold for this analysis was fixed at $p < 0.01$ (uncorrected) with an extended threshold of $k = 10$. Then we extracted percentage signal change of clusters showing a significant correlation using Marsbar toolbox (Brett et al., 2002) and calculated correlations between signal change and the executive and EAM scores outside SPM using STATISTICA7©.

RESULTS

BEHAVIORAL RESULTS

Participants showed a high percentage of correct trials (CR, mean 87.85 ± 7.70) and a rapid response time (RT, mean 2.28 ± 0.94 s). NCS correlated negatively with inhibition, verbal fluency, and working memory performances. A trend for a negative correlation between NCS and the episodic score was found ($r = -0.44$, $p = 0.054$). Interestingly, the two basic scores of the TSCS, certainty (TSCS-C) and valence (TSCS-V) of self-concept, did not singularly correlate with executive functions and the episodic score. The episodic score correlated positively with performance on executive functions, namely inhibition, shifting (TMT B-A), verbal fluency, and working memory. For detailed results see **Table 1**.

fMRI RESULTS

Activation during EAM retrieval

We reported activations in several clusters encompassing lateral (mainly on the left side) and medial frontal regions and posterior medial regions. In particular we found activations in cortical midline structures comprising MPFC, ACC, posterior cingulate (PCC), and precuneus. Moreover insula, cerebellum, inferior parietal, and occipital regions as well as lateral and medial temporal regions comprising the hippocampus were found (**Figure 1**). The list of local activation maxima is reported on **Table 2**.

Correlation between brain activations, neuropsychological, and EAM scores

We observed negative correlations between the NCS and the dorsal ACC (dACC) and the ventro-lateral prefrontal cortex (vLPFC) in the left side (**Figure 2**). See **Table 3** for peaks coordinates. A positive correlation was reported between verbal fluency and both regions, whereas only the dACC showed a significant correlation with inhibition performance. Moreover, for correlations between activity in these regions and the other scores of interest we found a positive correlation with episodic scores. The basic scores of the TSCS did not show significant correlations with the other variables. For detailed results see **Table 4**.

A series of partial correlations (Bravais–Pearson) were calculated between the NCS, the episodic score, and activity in the dACC and vLPFC, separately controlling for inhibition, fluency,

Table 1 | Correlations between self-concept, episodic and neuropsychological scores.

	NCS	TSCS-C	TSCS-V	EPI	FLU	INHIB	TMT B-A	R-SPAN	WM	CR	RT
NCS		0.040	−0.365	−0.438	**−0.626**	**−0.582**	−0.271	−0.203	**−0.449**	0.149	0.011
p		0.869	0.114	0.054	**0.003**	**0.007**	0.248	0.391	**0.047**	0.532	0.965
TSCS-C	0.040		**0.748**	−0.118	−0.227	−0.051	0.120	0.114	−0.058	0.086	−0.321
p	0.869		**0.000**	0.622	0.337	0.832	0.613	0.632	0.809	0.719	0.168
TSCS-V	−0.365	**0.748**		0.040	0.207	0.194	0.202	0.369	0.346	−0.020	−0.094
p	0.114	**0.000**		0.867	0.381	0.412	0.394	0.110	0.135	0.934	0.692
EPI	−0.438	−0.118	0.040		**0.523**	**0.545**	**0.451**	0.411	**0.668**	0.363	0.076
p	0.054	0.622	0.867		**0.018**	**0.013**	**0.046**	0.072	**0.001**	0.115	0.750
FLU	**−0.626**	−0.227	0.207	**0.523**		**0.478**	**0.536**	**0.492**	**0.596**	0.264	−0.008
p	**0.003**	0.337	0.381	**0.018**		**0.033**	**0.015**	**0.027**	**0.006**	0.260	0.975
INHIB	**−0.582**	−0.051	0.194	**0.545**	**0.478**		−0.275	**0.498**	**0.581**	−0.074	0.088
p	**0.007**	0.832	0.412	**0.013**	**0.033**		0.241	**0.025**	**0.007**	0.755	0.712
TMT B-A	−0.271	0.120	0.202	**0.451**	**0.536**	−0.275		0.429	0.417	**0.460**	−0.209
p	0.248	0.613	0.394	**0.046**	**0.015**	0.241		0.059	0.068	**0.041**	0.377
R-SPAN	−0.203	0.114	0.369	0.411	**0.492**	**0.498**	0.429		**0.689**	0.100	0.174
p	0.391	0.632	0.110	0.072	**0.027**	**0.025**	0.059		**0.001**	0.677	0.462
WM	**−0.449**	−0.058	0.346	**0.668**	**0.596**	**0.581**	0.417	**0.689**		0.134	0.435
p	**0.047**	0.809	0.135	**0.001**	**0.006**	**0.007**	0.068	**0.001**		0.573	0.055
CR	0.149	0.086	−0.020	0.363	0.264	−0.074	**0.460**	0.100	0.134		−0.189
p	0.532	0.719	0.934	0.115	0.260	0.755	**0.041**	0.677	0.573		0.425
RT	0.011	−0.321	−0.094	0.076	−0.008	0.088	−0.209	0.174	0.435	−0.189	
p	0.965	0.168	0.692	0.750	0.975	0.712	0.377	0.462	0.055	0.425	

NCS, negative crystallization score; TSCS-C, TSCS, certainty score; TSCS-V, TSCS, valence score; EPI, episodic score of EAM; FLU, verbal fluency score; INHIB, interference score Stroop, inhibition; TMTB-A, trail making test B-A score, shifting; R-SPAN, running span, updating; WM, working memory score, digit and visuo-spatial spans; CR, correct responses; RT, response time. Correlations written in bold font are significant ($p < 0.05$ to $p < 0.001$).

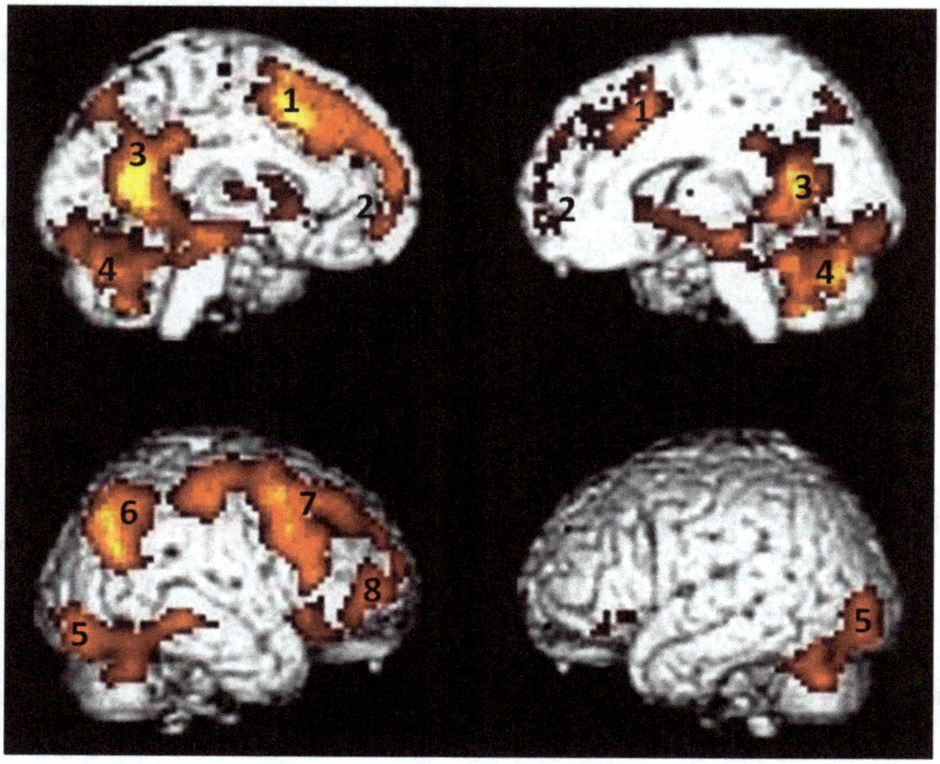

FIGURE 1 | Areas showing activity during retrieval of episodic autobiographical memory. (1) Dorsal anterior cingulate cortex (dACC), (2) medial prefrontal cortex (MPFC), (3) posterior cingulate cortex/precuneus (PCC/precuneus), (4) cerebellum, (5) occipital cortex, (6) posterior parietal cortex (PPC), (7) dorso-lateral prefrontal cortex (dLPFC), (8) ventro-lateral prefrontal cortex (vLPFC). Results are superimposed to a single subject rendering and are significant at a threshold of $p < 0.01$ corrected for multiple comparison using the false discovery rate (FDR) with an extended threshold of $k = 20$.

and working memory scores. When controlling for inhibition, fluency, or working memory performance the correlation between NCS and the episodic score disappeared. Moreover, when controlling for the fluency score, the correlations between the NCS and the vLPFC, and between the episodic score and the same region become marginally significant. See **Table 5** for detailed results.

DISCUSSION

In the present study we assessed, through standard tests, self-concept, executive functions' profile as well as brain activations during an EAM retrieval task in a group of young healthy subjects. In line with our hypotheses we reported that participants with a rigid negative self-representation tend to retrieve less detailed memories and show poorer performance on executive scores, in particular on inhibition, verbal fluency, and working memory. Interestingly, the valence and the certainty of self-representation taken alone did not seem to be linked either with executive functions, or with EAM performance. This result suggests that a negative self-representation accompanied by a flexible cognitive style would not necessarily lead to "depressive-like" cognitive functioning, and that a rigid self schema would not be inadaptative if not centered on negative content (see Martinelli et al., 2012). Moreover, two regions that were activated in the access or strategic research phase of EAM retrieval, the dACC and the left vLPFC, showed a negative correlation with the NCS, a positive correlation with verbal fluency, and a positive correlation with the episodic scores. Finally, only activity in dACC correlated significantly with inhibition.

Our results are coherent with models of AM retrieval assigning a central role to executive functions in the hierarchical search of episodic details (Baddeley and Wilson, 1986; Conway and Fthenaki, 2000; Conway and Pleydell-Pearce, 2000). Moreover, the negative correlation between executive and the NCS scores is in agreement with previous proposals of executive dysfunction as a trait marker or risk factor for depression (Hasler et al., 2004). Overall, our results suggest that executive functions could have a central role in both inefficient search mechanisms during EAM retrieval and in the construction of a rigid or schematic self-representation, concerning, above all, negative content. Of particular interest is the fact that the marginally significant correlation we found between the NCS and episodic details was removed when controlling for executive functions. Thus, executive functions may mediate the relationship between the NCS and low episodic score. This is in line with the CaRFAX model that assigns a central role to executive deficits in reduced AM specificity in depression (Williams et al., 2007). Also, our neuroimaging results indicated that activity

Table 2 | List of regions activated during memory retrieval.

Lobe	Labels	BA	*t*	MNI		
				x	*y*	*z*
Frontal	ACC	32	13.91	−6	15	45
	Mid. front.	6	11.81	−39	9	54
	Prec. gyr.	4	8.36	−36	−27	54
	SMA	6	8.04	−6	18	63
	Mid. front.	8	7.81	−24	27	51
	vLPFC	44	7.71	−51	12	36
	dLPFC	9	7.59	−18	36	45
	vLPFC	45	6.53	−54	24	15
	dLPFC	9	6.37	−9	54	36
	vMPFC	11	6.34	−9	60	−6
	Mid. front.	10	6.26	−33	48	12
	Mid. CC	23	6.09	0	−36	33
	Prec. gyr.	6	5.98	−33	−18	63
	vLPFC	47	5.59	−36	45	3
	vLPFC	47	4.61	30	27	0
Parietal	PCC	23	12.28	−6	−57	18
	Pre. cun.	7	11.53	6	−57	−48
	Inf. par.	7	10.37	−36	−72	42
	Ang. gyr.	39	9.98	−48	−69	30
	Inf. par.	40	8.72	−39	−33	48
	Sup. par.	7	7.54	−30	−69	51
	Postc. gyr.	3	7.31	−45	−27	51
Temporal	Fus. gyr.	37	10.3	−27	−36	−18
	Fus. gyr.	37	8.43	30	−57	−27
	Inf. temp.	20	6.56	−54	−39	−12
	Hipp.		5.54	−21	−13	−15
	pHipp.		4.94	24	−13	−21
Occipital	Calcarine	17	13.48	−9	−60	12
	Lingual gyr.	17	12.18	12	−54	9
	Calcarine	18	8.55	9	−72	−30
	Inf. occ.	19	8.01	−39	−87	−6
	Inf. occ.	18	6.29	−30	−90	−6
	Inf. occ.	19	6.21	39	−75	−18
Other	Cerebellum		6.65	0	−66	−30
	Insula		5.95	−30	24	−3

BA, Brodmann area; ACC, anterior cingulate cortex; Mid. front., middle frontal gyrus; Prec. gyr., precentral gyrus; SMA, supplementary motor area; vLPFC, ventro-lateral prefrontal cortex; dLPFC, dorso-lateral prefrontal cortex; vMPFC, ventro-medial prefrontal cortex; Mid. CC, middle cingulate cortex; PCC, posterior cingulate cortex; Pre. cun., precuneus; Inf. par., inferior parietal gyrus; Ang. gyr., angular gyrus; Sup. par., superior parietal gyrus; Postc. gyr., postcentral gyrus; Fus. gyr., fusiform gyrus; Inf. temp., inferior temporal gyrus; Hipp., hippocampus; pHipp, parahippocampus; Lingual gyr., lingual gyrus; Inf. occ., inferior occipital gyrus.

in dACC and vLPFC that were engaged in EAM retrieval, negatively correlated with the NCS and, in turn, positively correlated with executive functions and episodic details, suggesting shared neurocognitive processes.

The ACC has been divided into a dorsal "cognitive" and a rostral "emotional" component (Bush et al., 1998; Whalen et al., 1998; Etkin et al., 2006). The dACC is commonly reported to be recruited during tasks eliciting cognitive control, conflict resolution, and error monitoring (Bush et al., 2000; Beckmann et al., 2009). It has been found to be activated, together with other fronto-parietal regions, across diverse executive functions such as flexibility, inhibition, shifting, and working memory (Hedden and Gabrieli, 2010; Niendam et al., 2012). Regarding inhibition specifically, the positive correlation we found between dACC activity and the interference score corroborates previous findings reporting specific activity in the dACC during Stroop tasks (Bush et al., 1998). Moreover, ACC activity elicited during a Stroop task has been shown to be lower after a negative mood induction (Nixon et al., 2012).

Thus, dACC can be seen as supporting superordinate cognitive control processes (Niendam et al., 2012). This is in line with its role in EAM retrieval and with the pattern of correlations reported in the present study. Indeed, as mentioned above, during memory search, executive functions are supposed to be recruited to select relevant information and concurrently inhibit competing information.

Moreover, in healthy subjects, the dACC is known to exert an inhibitory influence over the limbic system that is devoted to emotional processing (Bush et al., 2000; Shafritz et al., 2006). In individuals with depression, hypo-activation in dACC is assumed to disrupt this inhibitory control leading to the attentional bias for negative information (Greicius et al., 2007). Indeed, in a task requiring participants to disengage attention from negative irrelevant material, depressed patients showed increased activity of the dACC, suggesting a greater cognitive and neural resources requirement during controlled emotional processing (Foland-Ross et al., 2013). Thus, the lower activity of dACC in subjects with greater NCS scores and the concurrent positive correlation between its activity and the inhibition score seems to mimic the neural profile associated with impaired emotional control in depression. This assumption appears quite relevant considering that the Stroop task has been shown to activate the dACC in healthy controls but not in subjects with mood-disorders (George et al., 1997).

Convincing evidence suggests that lateral prefrontal cortex is involved in high-order control processes regulating cognition and behavior (Miller, 2000; Miller et al., 2002; Petrides, 2005). Within prefrontal cortex, a dorso-ventral functional specialization has been proposed. The dorso-lateral prefrontal cortex would be engaged in on-line monitoring and manipulation of information in working memory, whereas the vLPFC would underpin active selection, comparison, and judgment of information held in short and long term memory (Petrides, 1995, 2002, 2005). Concerning memory retrieval, the same author reported that vLPFC, corresponding to BA 45 and 47, would be essential when active strategic retrieval of memories is at stake, but not during automatic retrieval. More recently, Badre and Wagner (2007) proposed a further subdivision of the vLPFC into the anterior vLPFC, corresponding to BA 47, and the mid-vLPFC, composed by BA 45. They reported evidence for a two-process account of controlled memory retrieval mechanisms implemented in the vLPFC with the anterior portion engaged in strategic processes and top down facilitation

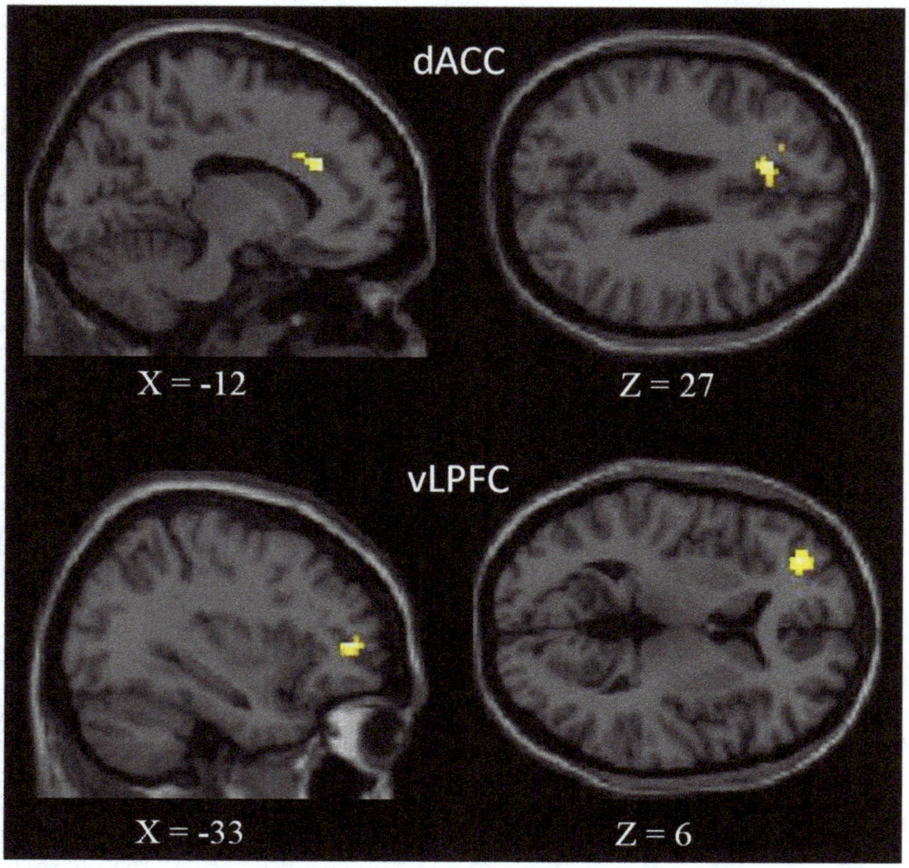

FIGURE 2 | Areas showing negative correlation with the NCS. In the upper part of figure, the dorsal anterior cingulate cortex (dACC), and in the bottom, the ventro-lateral prefrontal cortex (vLPFC). Results are superimposed to a single subject T1-weighted image normalized to the MNI stereotaxic space. Results are significant at a threshold of $p < 0.01$ (uncorrected) with an extended threshold of $k = 10$.

of relevant information and the mid-vLPFC that would be especially in charge of post retrieval selection of relevant information between competing representations. This account of the anterior vLPFC involvement in effortful strategic memory retrieval fits well with its activation in our task and the correlation found with performance on verbal fluency tasks.

Besides its strategic role in memory retrieval, vLPFC is also known to modulate emotional responses of the amygdala through an attentional biasing mechanism (Wager et al., 2008). Moreover, vLPFC is frequently altered in depression at both the functional (Brody et al., 1999; Mayberg et al., 1999) and structural levels (mainly BA 47, Drevets and Price, 2005). These changes may participate in explaining the depression-related negative bias. Indeed, there is evidence of attenuated neural response in the vLPFC of depressed patients when responding to targets that were preceded by sad distracters (Wang et al., 2008; Dichter et al., 2009). Moreover, rumination on bad feelings and past experiences is maintained in depressed patients by an impaired cognitive control mechanism associated with the hypoactivation of the left prefrontal regions, in particular of the vLPFC (Ochsner et al., 2004; Ray et al., 2005; Gotlib and Hamilton, 2008).

Table 3 | List of regions showing a correlation with the CNS.

Lobe	Labels	BA	*t*	MNI		
				x	*y*	*z*
Frontal	vLPFC	47	4.24	−33	45	6
	dACC	32	3.76	−12	27	27

BA, Brodmann area; dACC, dorsal anterior cingulate cortex; vLPFC, ventro-lateral prefrontal cortex.

Based on the aforementioned literature on abnormalities in emotional processing in depression, Murrough et al. (2011) proposed a model suggesting that depression-related functional changes are characterized by an imbalance between the cognitive control, implemented in the PFC, and the emotional system, based on limbic structures. In other words, the under-activity of the former regions is thought to mediate executive impairment and to contribute to explaining the failure of cognitive control on emotion in depression.

Interestingly, Beevers et al. (2010) reported that patients with a mild to moderate depression experienced difficulty recruiting

Table 4 | Correlations between brain activity self-concept, episodic and neuropsychological scores.

	NCS	TSCS-C	TSCS-V	EPI	FLU	INHIB	TMT B-A	R-SPAN	WM
dACC	**−0.717**	−0.001	0.153	**0.630**	**0.504**	**0.587**	0.285	0.114	0.330
p	**0.000**	0.996	0.520	**0.003**	**0.024**	**0.007**	0.224	0.634	0.155
vLPFC	**−0.632**	0.156	0.233	**0.591**	**0.538**	0.311	0.332	0.127	0.333
p	**0.003**	0.511	0.324	**0.006**	**0.015**	0.182	0.152	0.593	0.151

NCS, negative crystallization score; TSCS-C, TSCS, certainty score; TSCS-V, TSCS, valence score; EPI, episodic score of EAM; FLU, verbal fluency score; INHIB, interference score Stroop, inhibition; TMTB-A, trail making test B-A score, shifting; R-SPAN, running span, updating; WM, working memory score, digit and visuo-spatial spans: dACC, dorsal anterior cingulate cortex; vLPFC, ventro-lateral prefrontal cortex. Correlations written in bold font are significant (p < 0.05 to p < 0.001).

Table 5 | Partial correlations between brain activity, self-concept, and episodic score, controlling for executive functions performances.

	NCS	EPI	dACC	vLPFC
INHIB				
NCS		−0.18	**−0.57**	**−0.58**
p		0.469	**0.011**	**0.009**
EPI	−0.18		**0.46**	**0.53**
p	0.469		**0.049**	**0.020**
dACC	**−0.57**	**0.46**		**0.77**
p	**0.011**	**0.049**		**0.000**
vLPFC	**−0.58**	**0.53**	**0.77**	
p	**0.009**	**0.020**	**0.000**	
FLU				
NCS		−0.17	**−0.60**	−0.45
p		0.499	**0.007**	0.053
EPI	−0.17		**0.50**	0.43
p	0.499		**0.030**	0.066
dACC	**−0.60**	**0.50**		**0.70**
p	**0.007**	**0.030**		**0.001**
vLPFC	−0.45	0.43	**0.70**	
p	0.053	0.066	**0.001**	
WM				
NCS		−0.21	**−0.67**	**−0.57**
p		0.395	**0.002**	**0.010**
EPI	−0.21		**0.58**	**0.52**
p	0.395		**0.009**	**0.021**
dACC	**−0.67**	**0.58**		**0.75**
p	**0.002**	**0.009**		**0.000**
vLPFC	**−0.57**	**0.52**	**0.75**	
p	**0.010**	**0.021**	**0.000**	

NCS, negative crystallization score; EPI, episodic score of EAM; INHIB, interference score Stroop, inhibition; FLU, verbal fluency score; WM, working memory score; dACC, dorsal anterior cingulate cortex; vLPFC, ventro-lateral prefrontal cortex. Correlations written in bold font are significant (p < 0.05 to p < 0.001).

regions involved in cognitive control, notably vLPFC, when processing emotional information, whereas activity of cerebral regions that typically subserve emotional experience *per se*, such as amygdala and orbital PFC, were not associated with depressive symptoms. The authors concluded that more severe forms of depression may be necessary before neural activity in these emotional processing regions would be attained (Siegle et al., 2007; Hamilton and Gotlib, 2008).

In summary, according to the aforementioned literature, we propose that the neurocognitive profile of people with a negative crystallized self-representation would mimic that of mildly to moderately depressed patients. In particular, the negative rigid self-representation might result from diminished executive functions resources that, in turn, could affect EAM. This cognitive-profile pattern would be expressed at the neural level as an inefficient recruitment of prefrontal regions normally involved in cognitive control.

Our findings could have a potential impact on research on neurocognitive markers of depression and are encouraging for a psychotherapeutic approach promoting cognitive flexibility, such as novel cognitive behavioral therapies integrating mindfulness practices. Indeed, mindfulness meditation has been shown to produce structural and functional changes in the lateral PFC and in the ACC (Chiesa and Serretti, 2010; Tang et al., 2012), and to improve autobiographical specificity in formerly depressed patients (Williams et al., 2000) and in healthy subjects (Heeren et al., 2009). Moreover, in the latter study improved AM was correlated with enhanced executive functions.

In conclusion, we showed in healthy young participants, that the degree of crystallized negative self-representation mimics the cognitive profile reported in depression concerning executive functions and AM, and that this pattern could be mediated by an inefficient recruitment of prefrontal structures involved in cognitive control of emotional response.

ACKNOWLEDGMENTS

The present study was supported by the National Hospital Clinical Research Program (PHRC NEMAUVI) allotted to Thierry Gallarda and Pascale Piolino, the Institut Universitaire de France (postdoc funding for Marco Sperduti and Sandrine Kalenzaga) and the Ministry of Higher Education and Research of France (Ph.D. funding of Pénélope Martinelli). We thank all volunteers for their participation in this study and the clinical and neuroimaging staff of the Center of Psychiatry and Neuroscience at Sainte Anne Hospital, especially Marion Delhommeau and Adèle Anssens. We would like greatly to thank Angela Carpenter and Todd Lubart for the language corrections of the manuscript.

REFERENCES

Addis, D. R., Roberts, R. P., and Schacter, D. L. (2011). Age-related neural changes in autobiographical remembering and imagining. *Neuropsychologia* 49, 3656–3669.

Addis, D. R., and Tippett, L. J. (2004). Memory of myself: autobiographical memory and identity in Alzheimer's disease. *Memory* 12, 56–74.

Addis, D. R., Wong, A. T., and Schacter, D. L. (2008). Age-related changes in the episodic simulation of future events. *Psychol. Sci.* 19, 33–41.

Airaksinen, E., Larsson, M., Lundberg, I., and Forsell, Y. (2004). Cognitive functions in depressive disorders: evidence from a population-based study. *Psychol. Med.* 34, 83–91.

Austin, M. P., Mitchell, P., and Goodwin, G. M. (2001). Cognitive deficits in depression: possible implications for functional neuropathology. *Br. J. Psychiatry* 178, 200–206.

Baddeley, A. D., and Wilson, B. (1986). "Amnesia, autobiographical memory and confabulation," in *Autobiographical Memory*, ed. D. C. Rubin (Cambridge: Cambridge University Press), 225–252.

Badre, D., and Wagner, A. D. (2007). Left ventrolateral prefrontal cortex and the cognitive control of memory. *Neuropsychologia* 45, 2883–2901.

Barrett, L. F., Tugade, M. M., and Engle, R. W. (2004). Individual differences in working memory capacity and dual process theories of the mind. *Psychol. Bull.* 130, 553–573.

Beats, B., Sahakian, B., and Levy, R. (1996). Cognitive performance in tests sensitive to frontal lobe dysfunction in the elderly depressed. *Psychol. Med.* 26, 591–603.

Beblo, T., Baumann, B., Bogerts, B., Wallesch, C. W., and Herrmann, M. (1999). Neuropsychological correlates of major depression: a short term follow-up. *Cogn. Neuropsychiatry* 4, 333–341.

Beck, A. T. (1967). *Depression: Clinical, Experimental, and Theoretical Aspects*. New York: Hoeber.

Beck, A. T. (1976). *Cognitive Therapy and the Emotional Disorders*. New York: Penguin Books.

Beck, A. T. (2008). The evolution of the cognitive model of depression and its neurobiological correlates. *Am. J. Psychiatry* 165, 969–977.

Beck, A. T., Rush, A. J., Shaw, B. F., and Emery, G. (1979). *Cognitive Therapy of Depression*. New York: Guilford.

Beck, A. T., Steer, R. A., and Garbin, M. G. J. (1988). Psychometric properties of the Beck Depression Inventory twenty-five years of evaluation. *Clin. Psychol. Rev.* 8, 77–100.

Beckmann, M., Johansen-Berg, H., and Rushworth, M. F. (2009). Connectivity-based parcellation of human cingulate cortex and its relation to functional specialization. *J. Neurosci.* 29, 1175–1190.

Beevers, C. G., Clasen, P., Stice, E., and Schnyer, D. (2010). Depression symptoms and cognitive control of emotion cues: a functional magnetic resonance imaging study. *Neuroscience* 167, 97–103.

Biringer, E., Lundervold, A., Stordal, K., Mykletun, A., Egeland, J., Bottlender, R., et al. (2005). Executive function improvement upon remission of recurrent unipolar depression. *Eur. Arch. Psychiatry Clin. Neurosci.* 255, 373–380.

Bouvard, M., and Cottraux, J. (1996). *Protocoles et échelles d'évaluation en psychiatrie et en psychologie*. Paris: Masson.

Brett, M., Anton, J. L., Valbregue, R., and Poline, J. B. (2002). *8th International Conference on Functional Mapping of the Human Brain, June 2-6*, Sendai. Available at: CD-ROM in NeuroImage. 16. Region of interest analysis using an SPM toolbox [abstract].

Brewin, C. R., Reynolds, M., and Tata, P. (1999). Autobiographical memory processes and the course of depression. *J. Abnorm. Psychol.* 108, 511–517.

Brittlebank, A. D., Scott, J., Williams, J. M. G., and Ferrier, I. N. (1993). Autobiographical memory in depression: state or trait marker? *Br. J. Psychiatry* 162, 118–121.

Brody, A. L., Saxena, S., Silverman, D. H., Alborzian, S., Fairbanks, L. A., Phelps, M. E., et al. (1999). Brain metabolic changes in major depressive disorder from pre- to post-treatment with paroxetine. *Psych. Res.* 91, 127–139.

Bryant, R. A., Sutherland, K., and Guthrie, R. M. (2007). Impaired specific autobiographical memory as a risk factor for posttraumatic stress after trauma. *J. Abnorm. Psychol.* 116, 837–841.

Buckner, R. L., Andrews-Hanna, J. R., and Schacter, D. L. (2008). The brain's default network: anatomy, function, and relevance to disease. *Ann. N. Y. Acad. Sci.* 1124, 1–38.

Bush, G., Luu, P., and Posner, M. I. (2000). Cognitive and emotional influences in anterior cingulate cortex. *Trends Cogn. Sci. (Regul. Ed.)* 4, 215–222.

Bush, G., Whalen, P. J., Rosen, B. R., Jenike, M. A., McInerney, S. C., and Rauch, S. L. (1998). The counting Stroop: an interference task specialized for functional neuroimaging – validation study with functional MRI. *Hum. Brain Mapp.* 6, 270–282.

Cardebat, D., Doyon, B., Puel, M., Goulet, P., and Joanette, Y. (1990). Formal and semantic lexical evocation in normal subjects. Performance and dynamics of production as a function of sex, age and educational level. *Acta Neurol. Belg.* 90, 207–217.

Carver, C. S. (1988). Generalization, adverse events, and development of depressive symptoms. *J. Pers.* 66, 607–619.

Cavanna, A. E., and Trimble, M. R. (2006). The precuneus: a review of its functional anatomy and behavioural correlates. *Brain* 129, 564–583.

Chiesa, A., and Serretti, A. A. (2010). Systematic review of neurobiological and clinical features of mindfulness meditations. *Psychol. Med.* 40, 1239–1252.

Conway, M. A. (2001). Sensory-perceptual episodic memory and its context: autobiographical memory. *Philos. Trans. R. Soc. Lond. B Biol. Sci.* 356, 1375–1384.

Conway, M. A. (2005). Memory and the self. *J. Mem. Lang.* 53, 594–628.

Conway, M. A., and Fthenaki, A. (2000). "Disruption and loss of autobiographical memory," in *Handbook of Neuropsychology*, 2nd Edn, Vol. 2, eds F. Boller and J. Grafman (Amsterdam: Elsevier), 281–312.

Conway, M. A., and Pleydell-Pearce, C. W. (2000). The construction of autobiographical memories in the self-memory system. *Psychol. Rev.* 107, 261–288.

Coste, C., Agar, N., Petit Four, A. L., Quinette, P., Guillery, B., Azouvi, P., et al. (2011). Relationship between executive fonctions and short-term feature binding in retrograde autobiographical memory in severe traumatic brain injury. *Cortex* 47, 771–786.

Dalgleish, T., Williams, J. M. G., Golden, A. M. J., Perkins, N., Barrett, L. F., Barnard, P. J., et al. (2007). Reduced specificity of autobiographical memory and depression: the role of executive processes. *J. Exp. Psychol. Gen.* 136, 23–42.

D'Argembeau, A., Jedidi, H., Balteau, E., Bahri, M., Phillips, C., and Salmon, E. (2012). Valuing one's self: medial prefrontal involvement in epistemic and emotive investments in self-views. *Cereb. Cortex* 22, 659–667.

De Lissnyder, E., Koster, E. H. W., and De Raedt, R. (in press). Emotional interference in working memory is related to rumination. *Cogn. Ther. Res.*

Debeer, E., Raes, F., Mark, J., Williams, G., and Hermans, D. (2011). Context-dependent activation of reduced autobiographical memory specificity as an avoidant coping style. *Emotion* 11, 1500–1506.

Dent, J., and Teasdale, J. D. (1988). Negative cognition and the persistence of depression. *J. Abnorm. Psychol.* 97, 29–34.

Dichter, G. S., Felder, J. N., and Smoski, M. J. (2009). Affective context interferes with cognitive control in unipolar depression: an fMRI investigation. *J. Affect. Disord.* 14, 131–142.

Donaldson, D. I., Petersen, S. E., Ollinger, J. M., and Buckner, R. L. (2001). Dissociating state and item components of recognition memory using fMRI. *Neuroimage* 13, 129–142.

Drevets, W. C., and Price, J. L. (2005). "Neuroimaging and neuropathological studies of mood disorders," in *Biology of Depression: From Novel Insights to Therapeutic Strategies*, ed. J. W. M. Licinio (Weinheim: Wiley-VCH Verlag GmbH & Co.,).

Duval, C., Eustache, F., and Piolino, P. (2007). Multidimensional self, autobiographical memory and aging. *Psychol. Neuropsychiatr. Vieil.* 5, 179–192.

Ellis, H. C., and Ashbrook, P. W. (1988). "Resource allocation model of the effects of depressed mood states on memory," in *Affect, Cognition, and Social Behaviour*, ed. J. Forgas (Toronto, ON: Hogrefe), 25–43.

Etkin, A., Egner, T., Peraza, D. M., Kandel, E. R., and Hirsch, J. (2006). Resolving emotional conflict: a role for the rostral anterior cingulate cortex in modulating activity in the amygdala. *Neuron* 51, 871–882.

Evraire, L. E., and Dozois, D. J. A. (2011). An integrative model of excessive reassurance seeking and negative feedback seeking in the development and maintenance of depression. *Clin. Psychol. Rev.* 31, 1291–1303.

Fitts, W., and Warren, W. (1996). *Tennessee Self-Concept Scale Manual (Second Edition)*. Los Angeles: Western Psychological Services.

Fivush, R., and Nelson, K. (2004). Culture and language in the emergence of autobiographical memory. *Psychol. Sci.* 15, 573–577.

Fletcher, P. C., Shallice, T., Frith, C. D., Frackowiak, R. S., and Dolan,

R. J. (1996). Brain activity during memory retrieval. The influence of imagery and semantic cueing. *Brain* 119, 1587–1596.

Foland-Ross, L. C., Hamilton, J. P., Joormann, J., Berman, M. G., Jonides, J., and Gotlib, I. H. (2013). The neural basis of difficulties disengaging from negative irrelevant material in major depression. *Psychol. Sci.* 24, 334–344.

Gardiner, J. M. (2001). Episodic memory and autonoetic consciousness: a first-person approach. *Philos. Trans. R. Soc. Lond. B Biol. Sci.* 356, 1351–1361.

George, M. S. E. C., Ketter, T. A., Parekh, P. I., Rosinsky, N., Ring, H., Pazzaglia, P. J., et al. (1997). Blunted left cingulate activation in mood disorder subjects during a response interference task (the Stroop). *J. Neuropsychiatry Clin. Neurosci.* 9, 55–63.

Gibbs, B. R., and Rude, S. S. (2004). Overgeneral autobiographical memory as depression vulnerability. *Cogn. Ther. Res.* 28, 511–526.

Goeleven, E., De Raedt, R., Baert, S., and Koster, E. H. W. (2006). Deficient inhibition of emotional information in depression. *J. Affect. Disord.* 93, 149–157.

Gohier, B., Ferracci, L., Surguladze, S. A., Lawrence, E., El-Hage, W., Kefi, M. Z., et al. (2009). Cognitive inhibition and working memory in unipolar depression. *J. Affect. Disord.* 116, 100–105.

Gotlib, I. H., and Hamilton, J. P. (2008). Neuroimaging and depression: current status and unresolved issues. *Curr. Dir. Psychol. Sci.* 17, 159–163.

Gotlib, I. H., and Joormann, J. (2010). Cognition and depression: current status and future directions. *Annu. Rev. Clin. Psychol.* 6, 285–312.

Greicius, M. D., Flores, B. H., Menon, V., Glover, G. H., Solvason, H. B., Kenna, H., et al. (2007). Resting-state functional connectivity in major depression: abnormally increased contributions from subgenual cingulate cortex and thalamus. *Biol. Psychiatry* 62, 429–437.

Hamilton, J. P., and Gotlib, I. H. (2008). Neural substrates of increased memory sensitivity for negative stimuli in major depression. *Biol. Psychiatry* 63, 1155–1162.

Hammen, C. (2005). Stress and depression. *Annu. Rev. Clin. Psychol.* 1, 293–319.

Harrison, C. L., and Fowler, D. (2004). Negative symptoms, trauma, and autobiographical memory: an investigation of individuals recovering from psychosis. *J. Nerv. Ment. Dis.* 192, 745–753.

Hasher, L., and Zacks, R. T. (1979). Automatic and effortful processes in memory. *J. Exp. Psychol. Gen.* 108, 356–388.

Hasler, G., Drevets, W. C., Manji, H. K., and Charney, D. S. (2004). Discovering endophenotypes for major depression. *Neuropsychopharmacology* 29, 1765–1781.

Hedden, T., and Gabrieli, J. D. (2010). Shared and selective neural correlates of inhibition, facilitation, and shifting processes during executive control. *Neuroimage* 51, 421–431.

Heeren, A., Van Broeck, N., and Philippot, P. (2009). The effects of mindfulness on executive processes and autobiographical memory specificity. *Behav. Res. Ther.* 47, 403–409

Henson, R. N., Hornberger, M., and Rugg, M. D. (2005). Further dissociating the processes involved in recognition memory: an FMRI study. *J. Cogn. Neurosci.* 17, 1058–1073.

Hermans, D., Vandromme, H., Debeer, E., Raes, F., Demyttenaere, K., Brunfaut, E., et al. (2008). Overgeneral autobiographical memory predicts diagnostic status in depression. *Behav. Res. Ther.* 46, 668–677.

Hertel, P. T., and Rude, S. (1991) Depressive deficits in memory focusing attention improves subsequent recall. *J. Exp. Psychol. Gen.* 120 301–309.

Ingram, R. E., and Siegle, G. J. (2002) "Methodological issues in depression research: not your father's oldsmobile," in *Handbook of Depression*, 3rd Edn, eds I. Gotlib and C. Hammen (New York: Guilford Press).

Ingram, R. E., Steidtmann, D. K., and Bistricky, S. L. (2008). "Information processing: attention and memory," in *Risk Factors in Depression*, eds K. S. Dobson and D. J. A. Dozois (San Diego, CA: Academic Press), 145–169.

Iqbal, Z., Birchwood, M., Hemsley, D., Jackson, C., and Morris, E. (2004). Autobiographical memory and post-psychotic depression in first episode psychosis. *Br. J. Clin. Psychol.* 43, 97–104.

James, W. (1890). *Principles of Psychology*. Chicago: University of Chicago Press.

Joiner, T. E., Jr. (2000). Depression's vicious scree: self-propagating and erosive processes in depression chronicity. *Clin. Psychol. Sci. Pr.* 7, 203–218.

Joormann, J. (2004). Attentional bias in dysphoria: the role of inhibitory processes. *Cogn. Emot.* 18, 125–147.

Klein, S. B., and Gangi, C. E. (2010). The multiplicity of self: neuropsychological evidence and its implications for the self as a construct in psychological research. *Ann. N. Y. Acad. Sci.* 1191, 1–15.

Konishi, S., Wheeler, M. E., Donaldson, D. I., and Buckner, R. L. (2000). Neural correlates of episodic retrieval success. *Neuroimage* 12, 276–286.

Kringelbach, M. L., and Rolls, E. T. (2004). The functional neuroanatomy of the human orbitofrontal cortex: evidence from neuroimaging and neuropsychology. *Prog. Neurobiol.* 72, 341–372.

Kuyken, W., and Dalgleish, T. (1995). Autobiographical memory and depression. *Br. J. Clin. Psychol.* 33, 89–92.

Legrand, D., and Ruby, P. (2009). What is self-specific? Theoretical investigation and critical review of neuroimaging results. *Psychol. Rev.* 116, 252–282.

Lemogne, C., Piolino, P., Friszer, S., Claret, A., Girault, N., Jouvent, R., et al. (2006). Episodic autobiographical memory in depression: specificity, autonoetic consciousness and self-perspective. *Conscious. Cogn.* 15, 258–268.

Levine, B., Cabeza, R., McIntosh, A. R., Black, S. E., Grady, C. L., and Stuss, D. T. (2002). Functional reorganisation of memory after traumatic brain injury: a study with H(2)(15)0 positron emission tomography. *J. Neurol. Neurosurg. Psychiatr.* 73, 173–181.

Linville, P. (1996). "Attention inhibition: does it underlie ruminative thought?," in *Ruminative Thoughts. Advances in Social Cognition*, Vol. 9, ed. R. S. Wyer Jr. (Mahwah, NJ: Lawrence Erlbaum), 121–133.

Lo, B. C. Y., and Allen, N. B. (2011). Affective bias in internal attention shifting among depressed youth. *Psychiatry Res.* 187, 125–129.

Mackinger, H. F., Loschin, G. G., and Leibetseder, M. M. (2000). Prediction of postnatal affective changes by autobiographical memories. *Eur. Psychol.* 5, 52–61.

MacQueen, G. M., Tipper, S. P., Young, L. T., Joffe, R. T., and Levitt, A. J. (2000). Impaired distractor inhibition on a selective attention task in unmedicated, depressed subjects. *Psychol. Med.* 30, 557–564.

Markela-Lerenc, J., Kaiser, S., Fiedler, P., Weisbrod, M., and Mundt, C. (2006). Stroop performance in depressive patients: a preliminary report. *J. Affect. Disord.* 94, 261–267.

Martinelli, P., Anssens, A., Sperduti, M., and Piolino, P. (2013). The influence of normal aging and Alzheimer's disease in autobiographical memory highly related to the self. *Neuropsychology* 27, 69–78.

Martinelli, P., Sperduti, M., and Piolino, P. (2012). Neural substrates of the self-memory system: new insights from a meta-analysis. *Hum. Brain Mapp.* doi:10.1002/hbm.22008

Matuszewski, V., Piolino, P., de la Sayette, V., Lalevée, C., Pèlerin, A., Dupuy, B., et al. (2006). Retrieval mechanisms for autobiographical memories: insights from the frontal variant of frontotemporal dementia. *Neuropsychologia* 44, 2386–2397.

Mayberg, H. S., Liotti, M., Brannan, S. K., McGinnis S., Mahurin, R. K., Jerabek, P. A., et al. (1999). Reciprocal limbic-cortical function and negative mood: converging PET findings in depression and normal sadness. *Am. J. Psychiatr.* 156, 675–682.

McDermott, K. B., Jones, T. C., Petersen, S. E., Lageman, S. K., and Roediger, H. L. (2000). Retrieval success is accompanied by enhanced activation in anterior prefrontal cortex during recognition memory: an event-related fMRI study. *J. Cogn. Neurosci.* 12, 965–976.

McNally, R. J., Litz, B. T., Prassas, A., Shin, L. N., and Weathers, F. (1994). Emotional priming and autobiographical memory in posttraumatic stress disorder. *Cogn. Emot.* 8, 351–368.

Meiran, N., Diamond, G. M., Todor, D., and Nemtes, B. (2010). Cognitive rigidity in unipolar depression and obsessive compulsive disorder: examination of task switching, Stroop, working memory updating and post-conflict adaptation. *Psychiatry Res.* 185, 149–156.

Miller, E. K. (2000). The prefrontal cortex and cognitive control. *Nat. Rev Neurosci.* 1, 59–65.

Miller, E. K., Freedman, D. J., and Wallis J. D. (2002). The prefrontal cortex categories, concepts and cognition *Philos. Trans. R. Soc. Lond. B Biol Sci.* 357, 1123–1136.

Mirabel-Sarron, C., Vera, L., and Samuel-Lajeunesse, B. (2001). Estime de soi et dépression. *Ann. Méd-Psychol.* 159, 144–148.

Miyake, A., Friedman, N. P., Emerson, M. J., Witzki, A. H., and Howerter, A. (2000). The unity and diversity of executive functions and their contribution to complex "frontal lobe" tasks: a latent variable analysis. *Cogn. Psychol.* 41, 49–100.

Mongrain, M. (1990). "Motivational aspects of vulnerable personality styles," in *Presentation at the Graduate Student Colloquium of the D.O. Hebb lecture series* (Montreal: McGill).

Morley, T. E., and Moran, G. (2011). The origins of cognitive vulnerability in early childhood: mechanisms linking early attachment to later depression. *Clin. Psychol. Rev.* 31, 1071–1082.

Morris, N., and Jones, D. M. (1990). Habituation to irrelevant speech: effects on a visual short-term memory task. *Percept. Psychophys.* 47, 291–297.

Murrough, J. W., Iacoviello, B., Neumeister, A., Charney, D. S., and Iosifescu, D. V. (2011). Cognitive dysfunction in depression: neurocircuitry and new therapeutic strategies. *Neurobiol. Learn. Mem.* 96, 553–563.

Naismith, S. L., Hickie, I. B., Turner, K., Little, C. L., Winter, V., Ward, P. B., et al. (2003). Neuropsychological performance in patients with depression is associated with clinical, etiological and genetic risk factors. *J. Clin. Exp. Neuropsychol.* 25, 866–877.

Naylor, E., and Clare, L. (2008). Awareness of memory functioning, autobiographical memory and identity in early-stage dementia. *Neuropsychol. Rehabil.* 18, 590–606.

Neu, P., Kiesslinger, U., Schlattmann, P., and Reischies, F. (2001). Time-related cognitive deficiency in four different types of depression. *Psychiatry Res.* 103, 237–247.

Niendam, T. A., Laird, A. R., Ray, K. L., Dean, Y. M., Glahn, D. C., and Carter, C. S. (2012). Meta-analytic evidence for a superordinate cognitive control network subserving diverse executive functions. *Cogn. Affect. Behav. Neurosci.* 12, 241–268.

Nixon, E., Liddle, P. F., Nixon, N. L., and Liotti, M. (2012). On the interaction between sad mood and cognitive control: the effect of induced sadness on electrophysiological modulations underlying Stroop conflict processing. *Int. J. Psychophysiol.* doi:10.1016/j.ijpsycho.2012.11.014

Nolen-Hoeksema, S., and Watkins, E. R. (2011). A heuristic for developing transdiagnostic models of psychopathology: explaining multifinality and divergent trajectories. *Perspect. Psychol. Sci.* 6, 589–609.

Northoff, G., and Bermpohl, F. (2004). Cortical midline structures and the self. *Trends Cogn. Sci.* 8, 102–107.

O'Brien, E. J., Bartoletti, M., and Leitzel, J. D. (2006). "Self-esteem, psychopathology, and psychotherapy," in *Self-esteem Issues and Answers: A Sourcebook of Current Perspectives*, ed. M. H. Kernis (New York: Psychology Press), 306–315.

Ochsner, K. N., and Gross, J. J. (2005). The cognitive control of emotion. *Trends Cogn. Sci.* 9, 242–249.

Ochsner, K. N., Ray, R. D., Cooper, J. C., Robertson, E. R., Chopra, S., Gabrieli, J. D., et al. (2004). For better or for worse: neural systems supporting the cognitive downand up-regulation of negative emotion. *NeuroImage* 23, 483–499.

Oldfield, R. C. (1971). The assessment and analysis of handedness: the Edinburgh inventory. *Neuropsychologia* 9, 97–113.

Peeters, F., Wessel, L., Merckelbach, H., and Boon-Vermeeren, M. (2002). Autobiographical memory specificity and the course of major depressive disorder. *Compr. Psychiatry* 43, 344–350.

Petrides, M. (1995). Functional organization of the human frontal cortex for mnemonic processing. Evidence from neuroimaging studies. *Ann. N. Y. Acad. Sci.* 769, 85–96.

Petrides, M. (2002). The mid-ventrolateral prefrontal cortex and active mnemonic retrieval. *Neurobiol. Learn. Mem.* 78, 528–538.

Petrides, M. (2005). Lateral prefrontal cortex: architectonic and functional organization. *Philos. Trans. R. Soc. Lond. B Biol. Sci.* 360, 781–795.

Picard, L., Mayor-Dubois, C., Meader, F., Kalenzaga, S., Duval, C., Abram, M., et al. (in press). Functional independence within the self-memory system: new insights from two cases of developmental amnesia. *Cortex.*

Piolino, P., Chételat, G., Matuszewski, V., Landeau, B., De La Sayette, V., Eustache, F., et al. (2007a). In search of autobiographical memories: a PET study in frontotemporal dementia. *Neuropsychologia* 45, 2730–2743.

Piolino, P., Desgranges, B., Manning, L., North, P., Jokic, F., and Eustache, F. (2007b). Autobiographical memory, the sense of recollection and executive functions after severe closed head injury. *Cortex* 2, 176–195.

Piolino, P., Coste, C., Martinelli, P., Macé, A. M., Quinette, P., Guillery-Gerard, B., et al. (2010). Reduced specificity of autobiographical memory and aging: do the executive and feature binding functions of working memory have a role? *Neuropsychologia* 48, 429–440.

Piolino, P., Desgranges, B., and Eustache, F. (2009). Episodic autobiographical memories over the course of time: cognitive, neuropsychological and neuroimaging findings. *Neuropsychologia* 47, 2314–2329.

Quinette, P., Guillery, B., Desgranges, B., de la Sayette, V., Viader, F., and Eustache, F. (2003). Working memory and executive functions in transient global amnesia. *Brain* 126, 1917–1934.

Raes, F., Hermans, D., Williams, J. M. G., and Eelen, P. (2006). Reduced autobiographical memory specificity and affect regulation. *Cogn. Emot.* 20, 402–429.

Raes, F., Hermans, D., Williams, J. M. G., and Eelen, P. (2007). A sentence completion procedure as an alternative to the autobiographical memory test for assessing overgeneral memory in non-clinical populations. *Memory* 15, 495–507.

Raes, F., Verstraeten, K., Bijttebier, P., Vasey, M. W., and Dalgleish, T. (2010). Inhibitory control mediates the relationship between depressed mood and overgeneral memory recall in children. *J. Clin. Child Adolesc. Psychol.* 39, 276–281.

Ray, R. D., Ochsner, K. N., Cooper, J. C., Robertson, E. R., Gabrieli, J. D. E., and Gross, J. J. (2005). Individual differences in trait rumination and the neural systems supporting cognitive reappraisal. *Cogn. Affect. Behav. Neurosci.* 5, 156–168.

Reischies, F., and Neu, P. (2000). Comorbidity of mild cognitive disorder and depression – a neuropsychological analysis. *Eur. Arch. Psychiatry Clin. Neurosci.* 4, 186–193.

Reitan, R. (1958). Validity of the Trail Making Test as an indication of organic brain damage. *Percept. Mot. Skills* 8, 271–276.

Riutort, M., Cuervo, C., Danion, J. M., Peretti, C. S., and Salame, P. (2003). Reduced levels of specific autobiographical memories in schizophrenia. *Psychiatry Res.* 117, 35–45.

Rogers, T. B., Kuiper, N. A., and Kirker, W. S. (1977). Self-reference and the encoding of personal information. *J. Pers. Soc. Psychol.* 35, 677–688.

Ros, L., Latorre, J. M., and Serrano, J. P. (2010). Working memory capacity and overgeneral autobiographical memory in young and older adults. *Neuropsychol. Dev. Cogn. B Aging Neuropsychol. Cogn.* 17, 89–107.

Rosen, V. M., and Engle, R. W. (1997). The role of working memory capacity in retrieval. *J. Exp. Psychol. Gen.* 126, 211–227.

Sajonz, B., Kahnt, T., Margulies, D. S., Park, S. Q., Wittmann, A., and Stoy, M. (2010). Delineating self-referential processing from episodic memory retrieval: common and dissociable networks. *Neuroimage* 50, 1606–1617.

Segal, Z. V., and Ingram, R. E. (1994). Priming and construct activation in test of cognitive vulnerability to unipolar depression. *Clin. Psychol. Rev.* 14, 663–695.

Shafritz, K. M., Collins, S. H., and Blumberg, H. P. (2006). The interaction of emotional and cognitive neural systems in emotionally guided response inhibition. *Neuroimage* 31, 468–475.

Sheehan, D. V., Lecrubier, Y., Sheehan, K. H., Amorim, P., Janavs, J., Weiller, E., et al. (1998). The Mini-International Neuropsychiatric Interview (M.I.N.I.): the development and validation of a structured diagnostic psychiatric interview for DSM-IV and ICD-10. *J. Clin. Psychiatry* 59, 22–33.

Siegle, G. J., Thompson, W., Carter, C. S., Steinhauer, S. R., and Thase, M. E. (2007). Increased amygdala and decreased dorsolateral prefrontal BOLD responses in unipolar depression: related and independent features. *Biol. Psychiatry* 61, 198–209.

Sowislo, J. F., and Orth, U. (2012). Does low self-esteem predict depression and anxiety? a meta-analysis of longitudinal studies. *Psychol. Bull.* 139, 213–240.

Stroop, J. R. (1935). Studies of interference in serial verbal reactions. *J. Exp. Psychol.* 18, 643–662.

Symons, C. S., and Johnson, B. T. (1997). The self-reference effect in memory: a meta-analysis. *Psychol. Bull.* 121, 371–394.

Tang, Y. Y., Lu, Q., Fan, M., Yang, Y., and Posner, M. I. (2012). Mechanisms of white matter changes induced by meditation. *Proc. Natl. Acad. Sci. U.S.A.* 109, 10570–10574.

Tulving, E. (2002). Episodic memory: from mind to brain. *Annu. Rev. Psychol.* 53, 1–25.

Van Minnen, A., Wessel, I., Verhaak, C., and Smeenk, J. (2005). The relationship between autobiographical memory specificity and depressed mood following a stressful life event: a prospective study. *Br. J. Clin. Psychol.* 44, 405–415.

Viard, A., Lebreton, K., Chételat, G., Desgranges, B., Landeau, B., Young, A., et al. (2010). Patterns of hippocampal – neocortical interactions in the retrieval of episodic autobiographical memories across the entire life-span of aged adults. *Hippocampus* 20, 153–165.

Wager, T. D., Davidson, M. L., Hughes, B. L., Lindquist, M. A., and Ochsner, K. N. (2008). Prefrontal-subcortical pathways mediating successful emotion regulation. *Neuron* 59, 1037–1050.

Wang, L., LaBar, K. S., Smoski, M., Rosenthal, M. Z., Dolcos, F., Lynch, T. R., et al. (2008). Prefrontal mechanisms for executive control over emotional distraction are altered in major depression. *Psychiatry Res.* 163, 143–155.

Watkins, E., and Teasdale, J. D. (2001). Rumination and overgeneral memory in depression: effects of self-focus and analytic thinking. *J. Abnorm. Psychol.* 110, 353–357.

Watson, L. A., Bertsen, D., Kuyken, W., and Watkins, E. R. (2013). Involuntary and voluntary autobiographical memory specificity as a function of depression. *J. Behav. Ther. Exp. Psychiatry* 44, 7–13.

Wechsler, D. (2000). *Wechsler Adults Intelligence Scale, 3rd Edn*, Paris: Les Editions du Centre de Psychologie Appliquée.

Wessel, I., Meeren, M., Peeters, F., Arntz, A., and Merckelbach, H (2001). Correlates of autobiographical memory specificity: the role of depression, anxiety and childhood trauma. *Behav. Res. Ther.* 39, 409–421.

Whalen, P. J., Bush, G., McNally, R. J.,Wilhelm, S., McInerney, S. C, Jenike, M. A., et al. (1998). The emotional counting Stroop paradigm: a functional magnetic resonance imaging probe of the anterior cingulate affective division. *Biol. Psychiatry* 44, 1219–1228.

Williams, J. M., Teasdale, J. D., Segal, Z. V., and Soulsby, J. (2000). Mindfulness-based cognitive therapy reduces overgeneral autobiographical memory in formerly depressed patients. *J. Abnorm. Psychol.* 109, 150–155.

Williams, J. M. G., Barnhofer, T., Crane, C., Hermans, D., Raes, F., Watkins, E., et al. (2007). Autobiographical memory specificity and emotional disorder. *Psychol. Bull.* 113, 122–148.

Williams, J. M. G., and Dritschel, B. (1992). "Categoric and extended autobiographical memories," in *Theoretical Perspectives on Autobiographical Memory*, eds M. A. Conway, D. C. Rubin, H. Spinnler, and W. A. Wagenaar (Dordrecht: Kluwer Academic), 391–410.

Winthorpe, C., and Rabbitt, P. A. (1988). "Working memory capacity, IQ, age, and the ability to recount autobiographical events," in *Practical Aspects of Memory: Current Research and Issues II*, eds M. M. Gruneberg, P. E. Morris, and R. N. Sykes (Chichester: Wiley), 175–179.

12

Retrieval, monitoring and control processes: A 7 Tesla fMRI approach to memory accuracy

Uda-Mareke Risius[1], Angelica Staniloiu[1], Martina Piefke[1,2], Stefan Maderwald[3], Frank P. Schulte[3,4], Matthias Brand[3,4] and Hans J. Markowitsch[1,5,6]*

[1] *Physiological Psychology, University of Bielefeld, Bielefeld, Germany*
[2] *Neurobiology and Behavioral Genetics, University Witten-Herdecke, Witten, Germany*
[3] *Erwin L. Hahn Institute for Magnetic Resonance Imaging, Essen, Germany*
[4] *General Psychology: Cognition, University of Duisburg-Essen, Duisburg, Germany*
[5] *Institute for Advanced Science, Delmenhorst, Germany*
[6] *Center of Excellence Cognitive Interaction Technology, University of Bielefeld, Bielefeld, Germany*

Correspondence:
Hans J. Markowitsch, Physiological Psychology, University of Bielefeld, Universitätsstr. 25, 33615 Bielefeld, Germany.
e-mail: hjmarkowitsch@uni-bielefeld.de

Memory research has been guided by two powerful metaphors: the storehouse (computer) and the correspondence metaphor. The latter emphasizes the dependability of retrieved mnemonic information and draws upon ideas about the state dependency and reconstructive character of episodic memory. We used a new movie to unveil the neural correlates connected with retrieval, monitoring, and control processes, and memory accuracy (MAC), according to the paradigm of Koriat and Goldsmith (1996a,b). During functional magnetic resonance imaging, subjects performed a memory task which required (after an initial learning phase) rating true and false statements [retrieval phase (RP)], making confidence judgments in the respective statement [monitoring phase (MP)], and deciding for either venturing (volunteering) the respective answer or withholding the response [control phase (CP)]. Imaging data pointed to common and unique neural correlates. Activations in brain regions related to RP and MAC were observed in the precuneus, middle temporal gyrus, and left hippocampus. MP was associated with activation in the left anterior and posterior cingulate cortex along with bilateral medial temporal regions. If an answer was volunteered (as opposed to being withheld) during the CP, temporal, and frontal as well as middle and posterior cingulate areas and the precuneus revealed activations. Increased bilateral hippocampal activity was found during withholding compared to volunteering answers. The left caudate activation detected during withholding compared to venturing an answer supports the involvement of the left caudate in inhibiting unwanted responses. Contrary to expectations, we did not evidence prefrontal activations during withholding (as opposed to volunteering) answers. This may reflect our design specifications, but alternative interpretations are put forth.

Keywords: memory confidence, memory retrieval, monitoring, movie, real-life events

INTRODUCTION

When considering the contribution of subject-controlled processes to memory performance, it is important to distinguish between two different properties of memory: quantity and accuracy (Klatzky and Erdelyi, 1985). Koriat and Goldsmith (1994, 1996a) and Herrmann et al. (1996) have shown that these two features have received rather different emphasis in current research practices. With the quantity-oriented and accuracy-oriented approaches to memory, two fundamentally different ways of thinking about memory have been introduced. These ways map onto the distinction between two memory metaphors, the storehouse (where memory is seen as a storehouse garnering items for a later retrieval and is therefore defined in terms of the number of items that can be recovered; Gruneberg and Morris, 1978; Roediger, 1980; Markowitsch, 1994, 2008) and the correspondence metaphor (that construes memory in terms of its capability to faithfully represent past events, rather than just in terms of the quantity of items that are remembered and therefore are remaining in store) (Koriat and Goldsmith, 1996b).

According to Koriat and Goldsmith (1996b), experimental, laboratory memory research is preponderantly quantity-oriented, while in everyday-life the importance of the accuracy-oriented framework is underscored. A common example that illustrates the difference between the two approaches pertains to eyewitness reports: according to the quantity-oriented approach it would be important how much information about an offender can be retrieved, while the accuracy-oriented framework concerns the question whether essential information (e.g., the facial features of an offender) can be remembered. Moreover accuracy measures assess executive components of memory control by evaluating the correctness of retrieved information, and whether certain information would be reported if someone had for example to act as a witness in court (Kelley and Sahakyan, 2003).

The paradigm of Koriat and Goldsmith enables a separated evaluation of quantity and accuracy. Memory quantity performance is defined as the input-bound percentage of statements that were correctly answered (e.g., conditional on the number of input items), whereas memory accuracy (MAC) performance is formalized as the output-bound percentage of statements that were correct (e.g., conditional on the number of output items). The output-bound accuracy measures uniquely reflect the dependability of the reported information, that is, the extent to which each reported item can be counted on to be correct (Goldsmith et al., 2002). MAC performance is tied to the individual competence of controlling the correctness of given answers and deciding to volunteer correct answers and withhold incorrect answers, respectively (see **Figure 1**).

The paradigm of Koriat and Goldsmith entails three different phases of recall in which different monitoring processes proceed. In the retrieval phase (RP) subjects are presented with a set of memory questions and are requested to answer each of them, even if they have to guess. However, this phase is executed under forced recall conditions and quantity as well as accuracy performance is equalized in the RP.

In the monitoring phase (MP) the monitoring process is activated, hence subjects are required to rate their confidence of whether the retrieved item is correct or not (0–100%). In the control phase (CP) subjects are free to decide whether to bet on the correctness of their answer or not (volunteering or withholding). The control mechanism operates by establishing a confidence threshold (response criterion) on the monitoring output: if the assessed probability of being correct passes the threshold, the answer is volunteered; otherwise the answer is withheld. The setting of the threshold is sensitive to the gain for giving a correct answer relative to the cost of delivering an incorrect response.

The impact of monitoring and control on (free-report) memory performance has been proven to depend on several elements, such as the monitoring effectiveness, the control sensitivity, and the response criterion setting (Koriat and Goldsmith, 1996b). The extent to which the assessed probabilities successfully discern correct from wrong candidate answers and weighing the relative payoffs for accuracy and quantity for coming up with an optimal criterion level are captured by the construct of monitoring effectiveness.

The control sensitivity is the degree to which volunteering or withholding of answers is in fact susceptible to the monitoring output response. The (report) criterion setting reveals the probability level that is appointed (set) in consonance with the incentive to be accurate (and contending demands for quantity and accuracy). The criterion setting or report control policy can be gaged as "the cut-off on each participant's assessed-probability-correct ratings that best predicts his or her actual volunteering-withholding decisions in the free-report phase" (Halamish et al., 2012, p. 2). These three factors strongly influence quantity and accuracy of memory performance and therefore their investigation is warranted when examining MAC (Goldsmith et al., 2002).

The aim of the current study is to implement the model of the strategic regulation of MAC and memory quantity performance by Koriat and Goldsmith into a functional magnetic resonance imaging (fMRI) design, in order to disentangle the neural correlates connected with the three main processes: retrieval, monitoring, and control and, additionally unravel the brain areas related to MAC performance. For the purpose of approximating real-life conditions, we used in the present study a short film with emotional material. During the scanning procedure, subjects had to respond to veridical and incorrect statements pertaining to the content of the movie. This format shares a similitude to the study

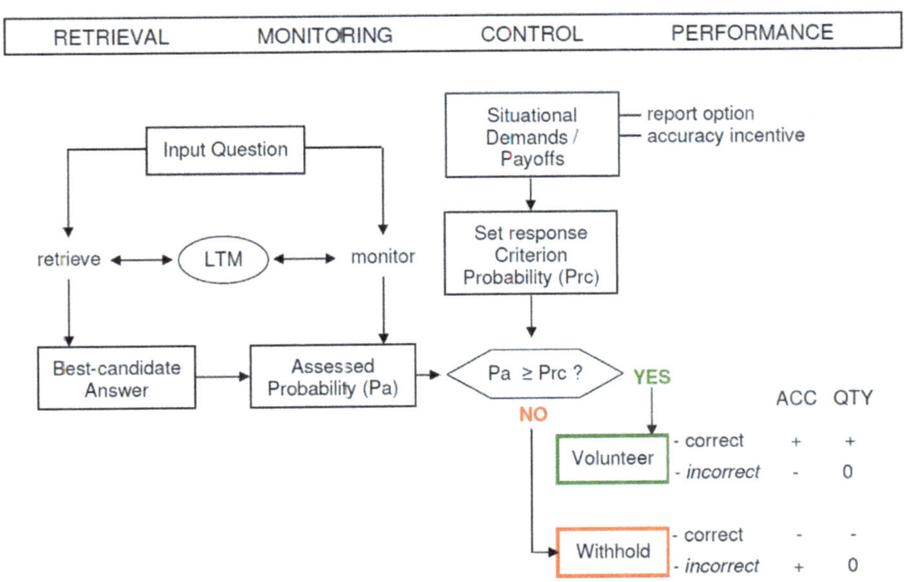

FIGURE 1 | A schematic model of the strategic regulation of memory accuracy and memory quantity performance. Performance effects are signified by plus (+ = increase), minus (− = decrease), and zero (0 = no effect). LTM, long-term memory; ACC, accuracy; QTY, quantity; Pa, assessed probability; Prc, response criterion probability (modified from Koriat and Goldsmith, 1996b).

of Mendelsohn et al. (2010): during the videotape audiovisual material was presented, while the fMRI-scanning phase contained only written statements. These statements had not been presented previously and therefore it is assumed that they "could not be answered properly without mentally reconstructing studied material" (Mendelsohn et al., 2010, p. 1). By employing this design we had the goal to come close to eyewitness testimony circumstances, where the testifiers might have watched a criminal event and subsequently, when they appear in court, they have to respond verbally.

MATERIALS AND METHODS

PARTICIPANTS

Twenty-nine subjects [14 male (mean age = 26, SD = 2.8, min = 22, max = 31 years), 15 female (mean age = 24.13, SD = 3.4, min = 20, max = 30 years)] without prior history of psychiatric conditions (including gambling problems) or neurological diseases (as determined by thorough screening) and with normal or corrected to normal vision participated in the experiment. The study was approved by the local ethics committee. Female and male subjects did not significantly differ with respect to their mean age (female versus male, $T = 0.55$, $p = 0.592$). All participants (mean age = 25, SD = 3.2, min = 20, max = 31 years) were right-handed, as assessed by the Edinburgh inventory (Oldfield, 1971), and native speakers of German. Participants were recruited from the University of Bielefeld community. Written consent for taking part in the study and publication of study's data in an anonymized form was obtained from all the participants. The participants received course credits or 20 Euros (plus the bonus they gained for correctly volunteering during the scanning procedure).

Neuropsychological tests

Participants underwent neuropsychological testing including standard assessments of intelligence, working memory, long-term explicit memory, visuo-constructive abilities, executive functioning, and attention. Intelligence was evaluated with the LPS (Leistungsprüfsystem)-4 (Horn, 1983), handedness, with the Edinburgh Handedness Inventory (Oldfield, 1971) and attention and concentration, with the d2-Test (Brickenkamp and Zillmer, 1998), the Trail Making Test A (Lezak, 1995), and the forward digit span subtest of the Wechsler-Memory Scale-Revised (Härting et al., 2000). Anterograde explicit memory was tested with the Verbal Learning and Memory Test (Helmstaedter et al., 2001) and the Rey–Osterrieth Complex Figure (Lezak, 1995) and working memory was evaluated with the backward digit span subtest of the Wechsler-Memory Scale-Revised (Härting et al., 2000). Executive functions and decision-making were examined with the Game of Dice task (Brand et al., 2005; Brand and Markowitsch, 2010) and the Trail Making Test B (Lezak, 1995). Trail Making Test B served also for testing cognitive flexibility. Verbal fluency tasks (animal words and words starting with the letters F, A, and S) (Lezak, 1995) were given to test word fluency as well as executive functions. In order to aid the exclusion of subjects with personality or psychiatric problems, three scales were given to the participants for self administration, such as the Beck Depression Inventory (BDI; Beck et al., 1995), the Freiburg Personality Inventory (FPI; Fahrenberg et al., 2001), and the Brief Symptom Inventory (BSI; Derogatis, 1993).

STIMULI

Videotape

A short film named "The New Cat," with an approximate duration of 6 min and emotional material appropriate for students was shown on a computer screen that was 13″ in size. For a consistent and sufficing volume external boxes were used. The film was shown about 2 h prior to the scanning phase. This film by Ziv Shachar (originally entitled "GATO-NOVO") was identified as being an adequate stimulus material for the research project "The assessment of eyewitness memory: a multi componential, correspondence oriented approach" by research colleagues from Haifa University (Koriat et al., 2000), who obtained the rights to utilize it for research purposes and who used it for behavioral, but not for neuroimaging experiments within the common project financed by the European Commission (De Mulder et al., 2010). (The design resembles that of Pansky and Tenenboim, 2011, though in that study a 6.5 min slide show had been used instead of a film). The soundtrack of the film (originally in Hebrew) was translated to German and English, respectively, to allow its use by the German and English research EU partners. The film has a good range of scenic details, well suited for the fMRI procedure. The movie is about a young adult man who is fond of dogs, but has problems with keeping them in the house, because they make dirt. He decides to have a cat as a pet, but he gets shortly in trouble with this, because he treats the cat like he would treat a dog. After only 1 day, the cat jumps from the window sill and is run over by a car driven by a young woman. Later the young woman and the main character fall in love with each other and they bury together the cat. The pair then moves to live together; the woman gives a dog as a present to the young man. None of the participants in the study indicated having seen the video before. Furthermore subjects were not communicated that their memory of the movie would be probed later ("incidental" encoding condition).

Statements

About 180 statements concerning the story of the film were constructed, of which one half concerned true details and the other half contained incorrect details of the film. Moreover, all true and all false statements were consistently related to different categories, like content, perception, and action. The formulated statements were short (with a range between 5 and 10 words in the German language version), in order to improve their readability on the screen inside the scanner. We attempted to have approximately similar numbers of items for the different categories and also to match the statements with respect to difficulty or complexity (see Appendix).

Experimental tasks

The tasks used during event-related fMRI procedure required the subjects to evaluate correct and incorrect statements from the videotape they saw before. In sum 180 statements appeared on a computer screen in a random order. Each statement had to be assessed with respect to its quality as being true or false (RP). This was followed by a confidence rating offering the options of three increments, namely 100% confidence, 75% confidence, and 50% confidence (MP). For further analyses we decided to differentiate between high (100%) and low confidence (combining 50 and 75%). In the next step, subjects had to decide whether to volunteer (bet) or withhold the answer (CP). Volunteering consisted of expressing the will to bet on the correctness of the given answer. An explicit bonus system of moderate incentive was implemented to motivate accurate responding. All participants were recompensed according to the number of bonus points. If a correct answer was volunteered one bonus point could be earned; if an incorrect answer was volunteered, one bonus point could be lost. When deciding for withholding the response, no bonus points were granted or deducted, irrespective of the correctness of the answer. For the baseline a fixation cross was presented to complete the foregone sequence and draw attention to the next sequence (see **Figure 2**).

During the fMRI measurement, subjects made their choices using three fingers of their right hand (index finger, middle finger, and ring finger) on a three button response device. Random jitter was included to prevent correlation of event regressors. For this, statements were presented between 3 and 5 s, and the confidence retrieval, the question for volunteering/withholding as well as the fixation cross were illustrated between 2 and 3 s. The whole run took about 43 min. In order to prevent head movements throughout the scan, the experiment was divided into two consecutive scans, each containing one half of the statements. Each run lasted an average of 17 min. For stimulus presentation and response collection, the software Presentation 9.0[1] (Neurobehavioral Systems, Albany, CA, USA) was used. During the fMRI experiment, the stimulus display was back-projected onto a screen mounted on a custom head coil.

Pre-scanning procedure

In order to get familiarized with the experimental set-up, subjects took part in a presentation of neutral statements adapted for utilization inside the scanner. Some of these 45 statements were

[1] http://www.neurobs.com

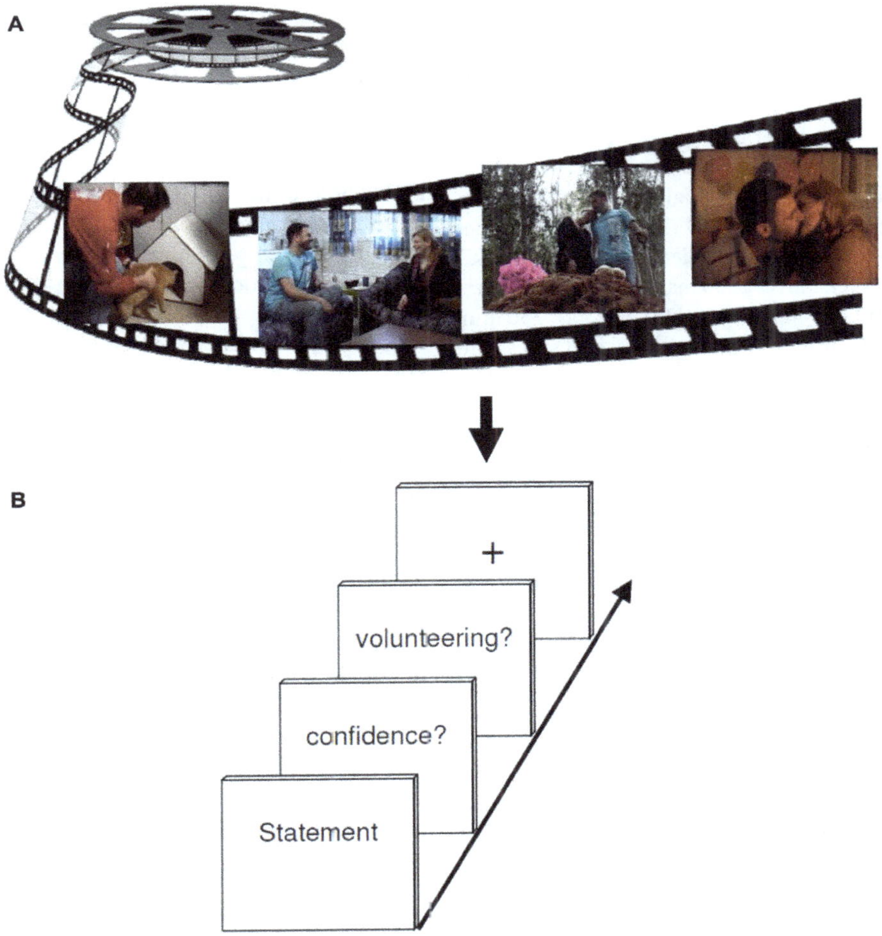

FIGURE 2 | Experimental design. (A) The encoding session consisted of watching a 6 min emotional film in a quiet room. **(B)** About 2 h later, participants performed a test session while undergoing an fMRI brain scan. Each retrieval task trial included either a correct or incorrect statement regarding events in the movie, to which subjects had to responded either "yes" (true) or "no" (false) (RETRIEVAL phase). Subsequently, participants had to rate their confidence (MONITORING phase) about the foregoing response (high versus low secureness) and had to decide either to volunteer or to withhold their answer (CONTROL phase).

true and some of them were false, e.g., "elephants have thick skin." Subjects completed the pre-testing-learning phase on the same PC the videotape was shown earlier and used the numbers "1" "2" and "3" of the PC keyboard. It was important that subjects deliberated on the statements, in order to get used to the available time slot. The instruction was similar to the fMRI-scanning procedure. The goal of the pre-scanning procedure was to make sure that subjects internalize the instruction and automated button-pushing, in order to secure an accurate scanning procedure. All participants reached the required cut-off value, which was saved in a txt file and therefore made available for an evaluation. For stimulus presentation and response collection, the software Presentation 9.0 (Neurobehavioral Systems, Albany, CA, USA; see text footnote 1) was utilized.

MR technical parameters

Functional MR images were acquired on a Siemens Magnetom Investigational Device 7T syngo MR B15 with echo planar imaging (EPI) capability. Head motion was restricted using expandable foam pads that surrounded the head. Stimuli were presented on a screen. Multislice T2*-weighted echo planar images were achieved from a gradient-echo sequence with the following parameters: repetition time (TR) = 3000 ms, echo time (TE) = 29 ms, field of view (FOV) = 230 mm, flip angle = 76°, slice thickness = 4 mm. About 30 axial slices were oriented in the plane of the anterior-posterior commissure and covered the whole brain. For each subject, additional high-resolution anatomical images were acquired using the 3D T1-weighted magnetization prepared, rapid acquisition gradient echo (MP-RAGE) sequence with the parameters: TR = 2300 ms, TE = 3.93 ms, inversion time (TI) = 1100 ms, flip angle = 12°, FOV = 256 × 256 mm, matrix size = 1.0 mm × 1.0 mm × 1.0 mm, 160 sagittal slices with a thickness of 1 mm (Poser and Norris, 2009; Poser et al., 2010).

Image processing and data analysis

Functional volumes were analyzed with SPM5[2] (Wellcome Department of Imaging Neuroscience, London, UK) implemented in MATLAB 7 (The Mathworks Inc., Natick, MA, USA). The images were realigned, normalized into the Montreal Neurological Institute (MNI) coordinate space and smoothed with a 5 mm × 5 mm × 5 mm Gaussian kernel (full width half maximum).

Parameter estimates of the resulting general linear model were calculated for each subject and each voxel. For population inference, a second level analysis was performed, using the contrast estimates for the simple effect of each experimental condition.

Differential contrasts of interest were calculated according to the experimental factors RP (correct answer versus incorrect answer, and vice versa), MP (high confidence versus low confidence, and vice versa), and CP (volunteering versus withholding, and vice versa) as well as RP versus MP (and vice versa), RP versus CP (and vice versa), and MP versus CP (and vice versa) to assess differential modulation of the BOLD signal induced by each factor. To detect only MAC (without an overlap to quality) according to the model of Koriat and Goldsmith (see **Figure 1**) the factor MAC was calculated: MAC+ (withholding an incorrect answer leads to an increase in MAC) versus MAC− (volunteering an incorrect answer leads to a decrease in MAC) (and vice versa).

The statistical threshold for within- and between-group comparisons was set to $p < 0.001$, corrected for multiple comparisons at the cluster level. This threshold was required due to the combination of a high Tesla Scanner and a rather complex experimental design.

Localization of activations

SPM_T maps resulting from the group analysis were superimposed onto a group mean MR image which was calculated from the normalized anatomical T1-images of each subject (see above). Standard stereotactic coordinates of voxels showing local maximum activation were determined within areas of significant relative changes in neural activity associated with different experimental conditions. Maxima were anatomically localized and labeled with an anatomical SPM5 toolbox, namely AAL, which refers to the Automated Anatomical Labeling map which is a three-dimensional map containing 116 brain regions coregistered to standard MNI space. MNI coordinates refers to a standard brain imaging coordinate system developed by the MNI (Tzourio-Mazoyer et al., 2002).

RESULTS

BEHAVIORAL DATA

Neuropsychological testing

Individual neuropsychological data were within the range of reference population norms for all tests which were administered.

Responding behavior during scanning

For the differential contrasts defined in the fMRI experiment T-tests for paired samples were executed to analyze subjects' response behavior. T-tests revealed that subjects responded to the statements mainly correctly (RP: correct answer versus incorrect answer, $T = 23.59$, $p < 0.001$). During retrieval process, different responding pattern can be distinguished: (A) to assume a true statement (hit), (B) to decline a true statement (miss), (C) to decline a false statement (correct rejection), and (D) to assume a false statement (false alarm). Correct responding is therefore defined as either correct rejection or hit, in contrast to incorrect responding that represents either false alarm or miss. The results of the present study show that when a statement was answered correctly this was a consequence of correct rejection significantly more often than it was resulting from a hit (correct rejection versus hit, $T = 6.56$, $p < 0.001$). When a statement was answered incorrectly this was because of a miss significantly more often than it was due to a false alarm (miss versus false alarm, $T = 8.57$, $p < 0.001$).

No significant difference can be reported for the confidence rating of the statements (MP: high confidence versus low confidence, $T = -1.43$, $p = 0.16$). Moreover, the analyses reveal that subjects rather volunteered an answer instead of withholding it (CP: volunteering versus withholding, $T = 2.1$, $p < 0.05$). Participants show respectively a significant increase in MAC (MAC+ versus MAC−, $T = 9.18$, $p < 0.001$). Data are displayed in **Figure 3**.

[2]http://www.fil.ion.ucl.ac.uk/spm

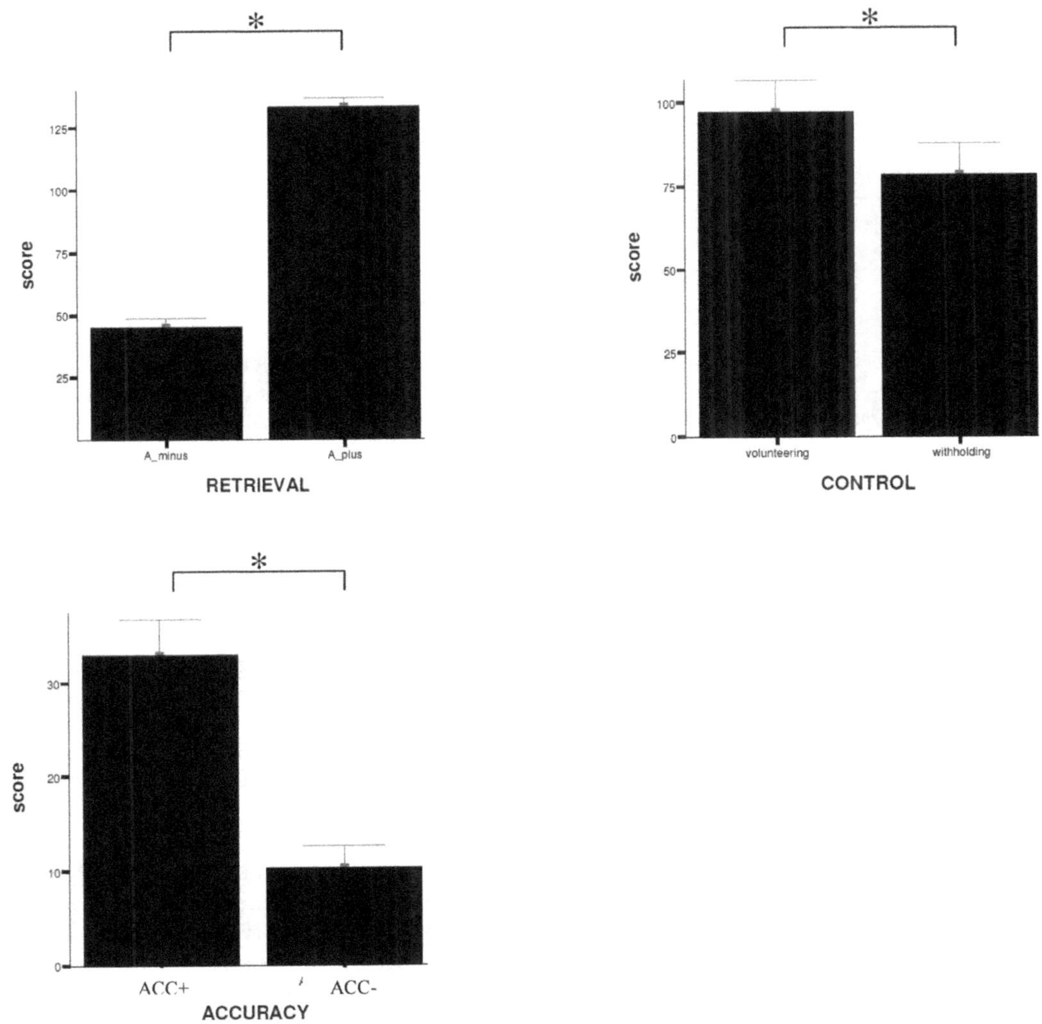

FIGURE 3 | Behavioral data. Comparison of mean ratings (±SD) given by the subjects on items during scanning procedure for the different experimental conditions, RETRIEVAL, CONTROL, and ACCURACY. W+, volunteering; W−, withholding; SD, standard deviation; *trend of statistical significance ($p < 0.05$, uncorrected). A_ minus = incorrect answering; A_ plus = correct answering.

fMRI DATA

Retrieval process (correct versus incorrect responding)

The main effect of the correct relative to incorrect (A+ > A−) answers revealed significant differential bilateral activations of the precuneus and activations of the left hippocampus, the left insula, left middle temporal gyrus (MTG), and right lingual gyrus ($p < 0.001$, uncorrected). The reverse contrast (A− > A+) did not show any differential activation. Data are displayed in **Table 1** and **Figure 4**.

Monitoring process (high confidence versus low confidence)

Areas of significant differential activation revealed by high confidence relative to low confidence (S+ > S−) ratings were located bilaterally in the fusiform gyrus and the left lingual gyrus and the left parahippocampal gyrus ($p < 0.001$, uncorrected) (**Table 2A**; **Figure 5A**). The reverse contrast (S− > S+) demonstrated, amongst others, bilateral activation of the hippocampus, the angular gyrus, precentral gyrus, lingual, middle occipital, inferior parietal and postcentral gyri, putamen, Rolandic operculum different temporal and frontal and occipital regions, the left precuneus, and the right insula ($p < 0.05$, False Discovery Rate-FDR corrected); at $p < 0.05$, Family Wise Error (FWE) corrected the left precuneus was activated. See **Table 2B** and **Figure 5B** for detailed information.

Control process (volunteering versus withholding)

Volunteering relative to withholding (W+ > W−) produced bilateral activations of temporal, frontal, and cingulate regions, namely of the MTG, the superior temporal pole, the left middle frontal and left inferior frontal cortex (pars opercularis), the left precuneus and the right posterior cingulate cortex ($p < 0.001$, uncorrected) (see **Table 3A**; **Figure 6A**). The reverse contrast, namely, withholding (W− > W+), revealed bilateral activation of the hippocampus, the left caudate nucleus, the left Heschl region, and the left postcentral

Table 1 | Group activations for the contrast between correct versus incorrect answers (RP), $p < 0.001$, uncorrected.

Anatomical region	Side	MNI coordinates**		
		x	*y*	*z*
CORRECT > INCORRECT				
Precuneus	L	−14	−48	40
	R	14	−16	36
Hippocampus	L	−20	−36	0
Insula	L	−36	−32	22
Lingual gyrus	R	10	−40	2
Middle temporal gyrus	L	−42	−50	8

Brain regions within the boundaries of the AAL atlas.*

**AAL refers to the Automated Anatomical Labeling map which is a three-dimensional map containing 116 brain regions co-registered to standard MNI space.*

***MNI coordinates refers to a standard brain imaging coordinate system developed by the Montreal Neurological Institute.*

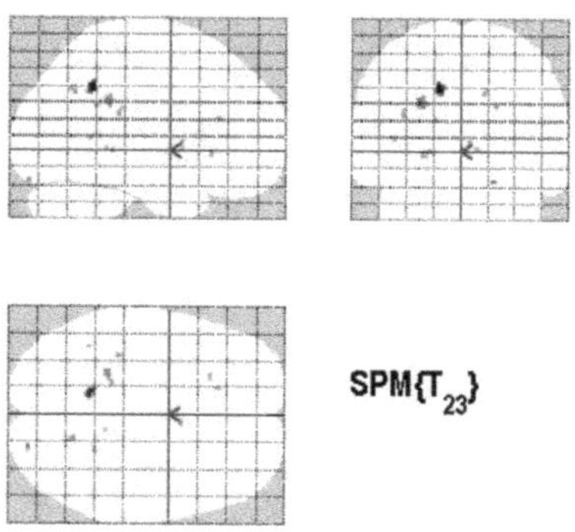

FIGURE 4 | Group activations for the contrast between correct versus incorrect answers (RETRIEVAL). Activations are superimposed on the anatomical group mean image (see Materials and Methods), depicting statistically significant relative increases in neural activity at $p < 0.001$, uncorrected. See **Table 1** for the exact MNI coordinates.

gyrus ($p < 0.001$, uncorrected). Data are presented in **Table 3B** and **Figure 6B**.

Monitoring versus retrieval process

The main effect of monitoring relative to retrieval revealed significant differential bilateral activations of the inferior occipital gyrus, precuneus, MTG, left middle cingulate cortex, left anterior and posterior cingulate cortex, left middle and superior frontal gyri ($p < 0.001$, uncorrected) (**Table 4**; **Figure 7**). The reverse contrast, retrieval (relative to monitoring), did not reach statistical significant activation.

Control versus retrieval

Areas of significant differential activation revealed by control relative to retrieval were located in the left middle frontal gyrus, left MTG, right fusiform gyrus, right putamen, right Rolandic operculum, and the right superior temporal gyrus (STG) ($p < 0.001$, uncorrected) (See **Table 5**; **Figure 8**). Again, the reverse contrast, retrieval (relative to control) did not show any differential activation.

Monitoring versus control process

The main effect of monitoring relative to control consisted of significant activations of the right STG ($p < 0.001$, uncorrected) (See **Table 6**; **Figure 9**). Due to the fact that only one region reached statistical significance this contrast will not be discussed here. The reverse contrast, control (relative to monitoring), did not reveal any significant activation.

Memory accuracy (MAC+ versus MAC−)

There are different ways of defining MAC; in the present study the manner of conceptualizing MAC was influenced by the paradigm put forth by Koriat and Goldsmith (1996a,b). MAC was defined as withholding an *incorrect* answer, whereas memory inaccuracy was related to volunteering an *incorrect answer* (See **Figure 10**). The main effect of high MAC relative to low MAC revealed significant differential bilateral activations of the STG, the supramarginal gyrus, left hippocampus, left Heschl region, the right superior temporal pole, MTG, and the right precuneus ($p < 0.001$, uncorrected), depicted in **Table 7A** and **Figure 11A**. The reverse contrast, low accuracy (relative to high accuracy), revealed activation only of the left hemisphere, namely the insula and the superior frontal gyrus ($p < 0.001$, uncorrected), illustrated in **Table 7B** and **Figure 11B**.

DISCUSSION

The current study had the goal of unveiling the neural mechanisms connected with retrieval, monitoring, and control processes according to the memory paradigm of Koriat and Goldsmith (1996b) and, furthermore of identifying the neural underpinnings of MAC. Below we discuss the responses of selected regions that were predicted on grounds of previous findings.

RETRIEVAL PROCESS (CORRECT VERSUS INCORRECT RESPONDING)

The factor RP (retrieval; correct versus incorrect responding) induced a significant effect in the behavioral rating during the scanning procedure: subjects gave more correct than incorrect answers, however, this was in general a consequence of correct rejection (instead of a hit). One could argue that these behavioral results resemble a distinctiveness heuristic (Schacter et al., 1999; Gallo et al., 2008; Koriat et al., 2008; McDonough and Gallo, 2012). Gallo (2011) noted that, when participants expect distinctive memories, they seem to be biased to avoid false alarms rather than enhancing true memory decisions (hits). When incorrect answers were given in our study, this resulted basically from a miss (instead of a false alarm). This finding indicates that subjects were able to correctly discriminate between correct and incorrect answers and moreover responded rather cautiously, avoiding risky decisions. Incidentally, no participant showed a tendency for risk-taking behavior on the Game of Dice task (Brand et al., 2005; Brand and Markowitsch, 2010).

When responding correctly instead of giving false (incorrect) answers brain activation was found mainly in areas that are agreed upon to be involved in mnemonic processing. In consonance

Table 2 | Group activations for the contrast between high versus low confidence (MP), $p < 0.001$, uncorrected.

Anatomical region	Side	MNI coordinates		
		x	*y*	*z*
(A) HIGH CONFIDENCE > LOW CONFIDENCE				
Fusiform gyrus	R	34	−48	−4
	L	−34	−50	−10
Parahippocampal area	L	−28	−42	−6
Lingual gyrus	L	−32	−48	−2
(B) LOW CONFIDENCE > HIGH CONFIDENCE				
Precuneus	L	−8	−50	36
	L	−2	−58	30
	L	−2	−64	24
Cuneus	L	−2	−80	28
	R	12	−98	10
Middle temporal gyrus	L	−44	−52	4
	L	−52	−62	4
	L	−52	−42	10
	R	56	−62	2
	R	54	−68	14
	R	62	−54	12
	R	52	−52	10
	R	60	−50	0
	R	58	−36	−8
Superior temporal pole	L	−44	22	−18
	L	−54	12	−8
Superior temporal gyrus	R	62	−50	20
	L	−60	−30	22
	L	−52	−34	10
	R	38	−32	12
	R	56	−44	20
Inferior temporal gyrus	R	58	−60	−6
Fusiform gyrus	L	−32	−24	−26
Insula	R	40	0	0
	R	44	18	0
	R	36	−12	22
	R	36	−18	4
Middle occipital gyrus	R	52	−68	26
	R	30	−72	22
	R	38	−72	16
	R	36	−84	30
	L	−24	−86	10
	L	−32	−88	14
Superior occipital gyrus	L	−14	−84	22
Inferior occipital gyrus	R	30	−86	−16
Parahippocampal area	L	−22	−26	−20
Hippocampus	R	24	−20	−16
	L	−30	−6	−26
Putamen	L	−22	12	0
	L	−30	2	−2
	R	22	14	−2
Inferior frontal gyrus pars opercularis	L	−52	12	6
	L	−34	24	−12
	L	−52	14	20
	L	−58	12	16
Inferior frontal gyrus pars triangularis	L	−44	40	0
	L	−46	32	16
Superior frontal gyrus medial	L	2	36	38
Superior frontal gyrus	L	−24	54	6
Middle frontal gyrus	L	−38	24	40
Supramarginal gyrus	L	−48	−44	34
	L	−56	−52	34
	L	−52	−30	24
Postcentral gyrus	R	−40	−32	10
Lingual gyrus	L	−14	−56	−10
	L	−16	−68	−6
	R	14	−60	−8
Precentral gyrus	R	54	−4	40
	L	−42	−2	30
Postcentral gyrus	L	−46	−12	38
	R	58	−22	42
	R	54	−16	40
Posterior cingulate cortex	L	−6	−44	8
Middle cingulate cortex	R	6	−16	34
	R	10	−30	32
Calcarine sulcus	L	−12	−80	12
	L	−14	−66	4
	L	−14	−72	8
Inferior parietal gyrus	L	−54	−48	50
	L	−46	−58	46
	L	−42	−56	48
	R	32	−42	52
	R	58	−48	40
Rolandic operculum	R	50	−18	12
	R	52	−10	18
	R	46	−12	20
	L	−60	−6	12
Angular gyrus	R	56	−48	30
	R	50	−66	40
	L	−46	−58	34
Paracentral lobule	R	16	−42	50

(Continued)

Brain regions within the boundaries of the AAL atlas.*

with other previous studies, we evidenced activation of the left hippocampus during correct responding (in contrast to incorrect answering). In particular, our finding supports the results of a relatively recent study of Mendelsohn et al. (2010) analyzing differential BOLD responses as a function of correctness in the left hippocampus. In this study, young adults saw a documentary movie. A week later they had to accept or reject factual or fictitious verbal statements about the movie while undergoing functional MRI.

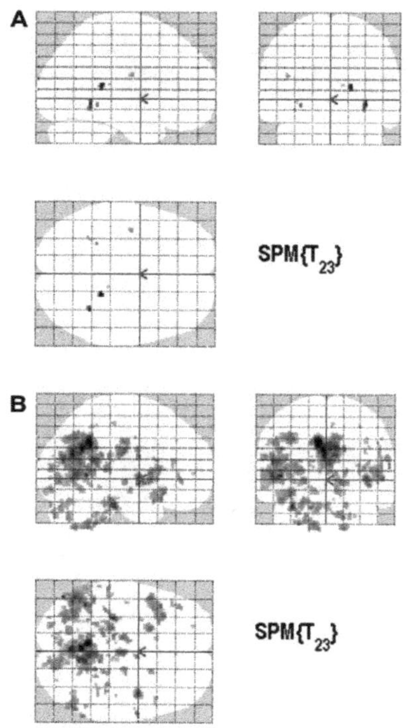

FIGURE 5 | (A) Group activations for the contrast between high versus low secureness (MONITORING). Activations are superimposed on the anatomical group mean image (see Materials and Methods), depicting statistically significant relative increases in neural activity at $p < 0.001$, uncorrected. See **Table 2A** for the exact MNI coordinates. **(B)** Group activations for the contrast between low versus high secureness (MONITORING). Activations are superimposed on the anatomical group mean image (see Materials and Methods), depicting statistically significant relative increases in neural activity at $p < 0.001$, uncorrected. See **Table 2B** for the exact MNI coordinates.

Table 3 | (A,B) Group activations for the contrast between volunteering versus withholding (CP), $p < 0.001$, uncorrected.

Anatomical region	Side	MNI coordinates		
		x	*y*	*z*
(A) VOLUNTEERING > WITHHOLDING				
Superior temporal pole	R	44	20	−24
	L	−48	10	−22
Middle temporal gyrus	R	50	0	−26
	L	−52	−46	12
Posterior cingulate cortex	R	6	−38	10
Middle cingulate cortex	R	12	−40	48
Middle frontal gyrus	L	−22	48	26
Inferior frontal gyrus pars opercularis	L	−36	12	14
Precuneus	L	−10	−44	46
(B) WITHHOLDING > VOLUNTEERING				
Heschl region	L	−44	−14	6
Hippocampus	L	−28	−18	−16
	R	28	−16	−22
Caudate nucleus	L	−14	−8	18
Postcentral gyrus	L	−54	−10	24

Brain regions within the boundaries of the AAL atlas.*

The laterality of hippocampus activations during recall and the degree to which hippocampus subserves recollection versus recognition are however topics of ongoing debate (Gilboa et al., 2004, 2006; Addis et al., 2012). Some authors concluded that hippocampus selectively supports recollection, whereas others proposed that hippocampus is equally implicated in familiarity and recollection (Wixted and Squire, 2011; Markowitsch and Staniloiu, 2012). Wixted and Squire (2011) put forth the idea that when Remember and Know judgments are equated for strength at high level, hippocampal activity is elevated to a similar degree for Remember and Know judgments. A recent study however provided findings consistent with the view that hippocampus offers selective support for recollection and fails to respond to adjustments in familiarity strength and does not sustain strength-matched familiarity, which is sustained by perirhinal cortex (Kafkas and Montaldi, 2012). And another new investigation sets the foundation for a compromise, by showing that both dual-process and strength theories are partly correct (Hayes et al., 2011). Ross et al. (2009) proposed that the hippocampus may play a role in disambiguation, which is in sequence organization during recollection. Rutishauser et al. (2008), using single unit recordings, observed that spike activity in hippocampus correlated positively with successful recall of previously perceived stimuli.

With respect to laterality, the left hippocampus was related to verbal memory tasks (Frisk and Milner, 1990). It was also found to facilitate general coherence of an episode or a scene and play a role in self projection of oneself in comparison to another. Additionally it was linked to context dependant recall of episodic information and vividness of details (Viard et al., 2012). The age of participants can also affect the laterality, with older people showing greater right hippocampus activation or bihemispheric activation during recall of episodic information than younger people (Oddo et al., 2010).

An interesting finding however comes from a recent review that showed that specific cues (verbal) associated to *strictly* episodic events elicited higher left (posterior) hippocampal activation than episodic events triggered by specific cues (Oddo et al., 2010; but see also Addis et al., 2012; Viard et al., 2012). This report lends support to the idea that the left hippocampal activation during correct answering in our study might have reflected a cued recollection experience. Similarly to Mendelsohn et al. (2010), we could argue that the statements presented during the fMRI-scanning acted as verbal cues for mentally recasting and recollecting the material presented in the film. On the other hand, several authors that looked at the hippocampus and processing of novel information (Tulving et al., 1994), found that the left hippocampus was activated during conditions that contained novel information (verbal or pictorial) (Poppenk et al., 2008; Hashimoto et al., 2012). These results are interesting in the light of our behavioral findings; as mentioned above, when participants answered a statement correctly, this was much more frequently the consequence of a correct rejection than of a hit. According to this line of

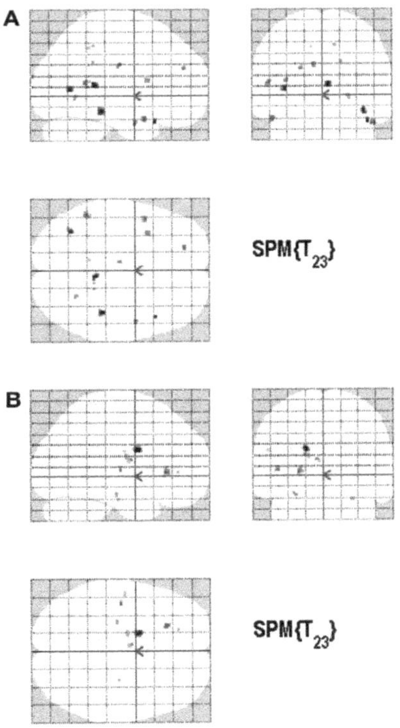

FIGURE 6 | (A) Group activations for the contrast between volunteering versus withholding (CONTROL). Activations are superimposed on the anatomical group mean image (see Materials and Methods), depicting statistically significant relative increases in neural activity at $p < 0.001$, uncorrected. See **Table 3A** for the exact MNI coordinates. **(B)** Group activations for the contrast between withholding versus volunteering (CONTROL). Activations are superimposed on the anatomical group mean image (see Materials and Methods), depicting statistically significant relative increases in neural activity at $p < 0.001$, uncorrected. See **Table 3B** for the exact MNI coordinates.

Table 4 | Group activations for the contrast between MP versus RP, $p < 0.001$, uncorrected.

Anatomical region	Side	MNI coordinates		
		x	*y*	*z*
MP > RP				
Precuneus	R	6	−52	20
	R	12	−58	24
	L	−6	−54	8
Middle cingulate cortex	L	−12	−50	36
	L	0	−32	36
Posterior cingulate cortex	L	−6	−36	30
Anterior cingulate gyrus	L	0	40	10
	L	−2	38	12
Inferior occipital gyrus	L	−34	−86	−8
	R	36	−80	−4
Middle occipital gyrus	R	40	−76	2
Middle frontal gyrus	L	−34	44	16
Superior frontal gyrus medial	L	−2	56	22
Middle temporal gyrus	L	−48	−70	18
	L	−40	−54	12
	R	50	−72	2
	R	50	−50	4

Brain regions within the boundaries of the AAL atlas.*

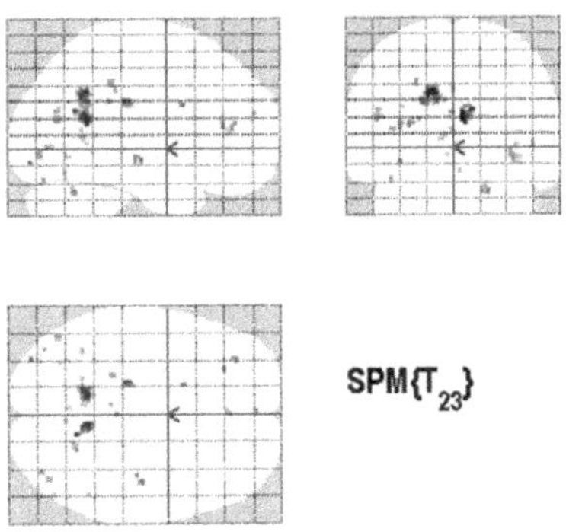

FIGURE 7 | Group activations for the contrast between MONITORING versus RETRIEVAL. Activations are superimposed on the anatomical group mean image (see Materials and Methods), depicting statistically significant relative increases in neural activity at $p < 0.001$, uncorrected. See **Table 4** for the exact MNI coordinates.

thought, the left hippocampal activation during correct answers may alternatively (or additionally) reflect a correct rejection of novel, unstudied material (Düzel et al., 2003). One could speculate that the activation of the hippocampus may have indicated the detection/encoding of novel material (Düzel et al., 2003; Friedman et al., 2011). Alternatively, the observed activation might have signified a recollection rejection strategy, which is a plausible strategy in this population with intact working memory capacity (Koriat et al., 2008; Leding, 2012).

In our study, we also found activation in the lingual gyrus, an area that was described to be more active for correct than for incorrect (lag) judgments (Greve et al., 2010). The lingual gyrus was described as being part of the default-mode network and has been implicated in the generation of visual mental images, visual details of actual past events and "image content that is accessed via verbal materials" (Greve et al., 2010, p. 7103). Leshikar et al. (2012) reported task-selective memory effects for visual imagery (a monotonic increase in activity according to vividness) in the left precuneus as well as left occipital and right lingual gyri. In a functional imaging study by Gilboa et al. (2004) context-rich memories were associated with increased activity in right precuneus and bilateral lingual gyrus independently of remoteness. Addis et al. (2009) identified activations of lingual gyrus (and other posterior visual areas) during recall of actual past events as well as during construction (imagination) of past or future episodes; however, the activation was higher during the first condition in comparison to the last two conditions. The higher activation of the lingual gyrus during the recall (recollection) of actual past events was interpreted as being in line with the sensory reactivation or reinstatement hypothesis (Nyberg et al., 2000; Wheeler et al., 2000; Schacter and Loftus, 2013).

Table 5 | Group activations for the contrast between CP versus RP, $p < 0.001$, uncorrected.

Anatomical region	Side	MNI coordinates		
		x	*y*	*z*
CP > RP				
Middle temporal gyrus	L	−42	−68	20
	L	−52	−46	8
Superior temporal gyrus	R	42	−34	12
Middle frontal gyrus	L	−32	44	16
Fusiform gyrus	R	34	−50	−4
Rolandic operculum	R	40	−32	18
Putamen	R	28	−16	4

Brain regions within the boundaries of the AAL atlas.*

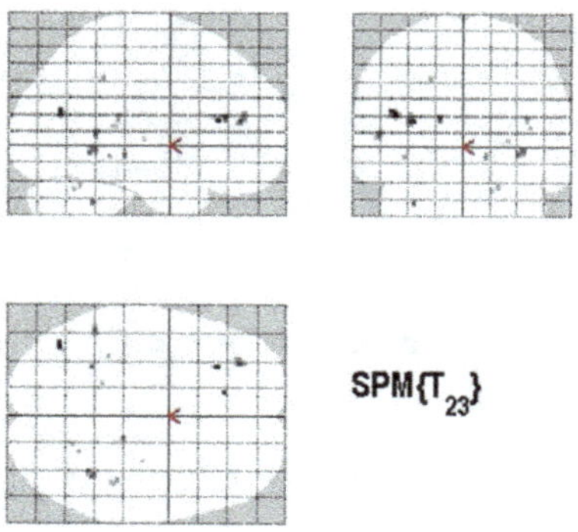

FIGURE 8 | Group activations for the contrast between CONTROL versus RETRIEVAL. Activations are superimposed on the anatomical group mean image (see Materials and Methods), depicting statistically significant relative increases in neural activity at $p < 0.001$, uncorrected. See **Table 5** for the exact MNI coordinates.

Table 6 | Group activations for the contrast between MP versus CP, $p < 0.001$, uncorrected.

Anatomical region	Side	MNI coordinates		
		x	*y*	*z*
MP > CP				
Superior temporal gyrus	R	46	−4	−14

Brain regions within the boundaries of the AAL atlas.*

Another interesting result yielded by our study concerns the bilateral activation of the precuneus in combination with the hippocampus. This result is related to the finding of hippocampal connectivity to the left precuneus in a recollection network (in contrast to familiarity) (Dörfel et al., 2009). Increased activity of precuneus was demonstrated for recollected items relative to misses, correct rejections, and strong familiarity (Kafkas and Montaldi, 2012). In a recent analysis, Kim (2013) showed that default-mode network areas, including the left precuneus,

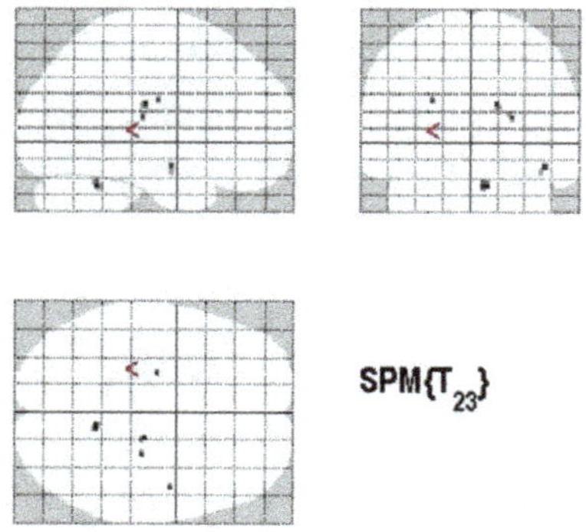

FIGURE 9 | Group activations for the contrast between MONITORING versus CONTROL. Activations are superimposed on the anatomical group mean image (see Materials and Methods), depicting statistically significant relative increases in neural activity at $p < 0.001$, uncorrected. See **Table 6** for the exact MNI coordinates.

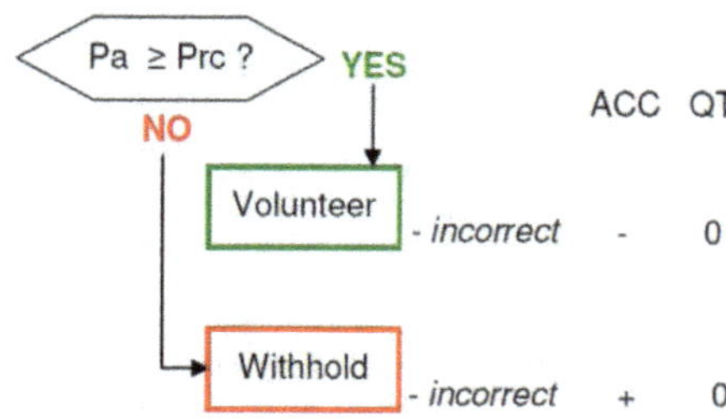

FIGURE 10 | Memory accuracy and inaccuracy according to the memory paradigm (cf. Figure 1 for abbreviations).

exhibited greater old/new (hit more than correct rejection) effects during a source-retrieval testing paradigm than during an item-retrieval task. This was interpreted as reflecting an enhanced ecphoric processing during the first testing paradigm (Kim, 2013). Addis et al. (2009) demonstrated via fMRI precuneus activations during both recollection of actual past events and construction of past or future events; however the construction-related tasks were accompanied by "greater percent signal change" in precuneus in comparison to the recollection-task. A PET study that investigated the neural correlates of true autobiographical memories and fictitious autobiographical memories found that fictitious autobiographical memories were associated with higher activations in the (left) precuneus than true autobiographical memories (Markowitsch et al., 2000). Cavanna and Trimble (2006) advanced the idea that there may be a functional dissociation within the precuneus; in particular, they proposed that the posterior precuneus may be associated with successful retrieval attempts, while the more anterior portion may be engaged in the retrieval mode via mental imaging. Memory-related imagery was in fact associated with significant activations of the anterior precuneus bilaterally in a seminal study, using positron emission tomography, conducted by Fletcher et al. (1995). In a recent fMRI study, Huijbers et al. (2011) however found the ventral precuneus to be associated with successful retrieval, but with unsuccessful imagery performance

Table 7 | (A,B) Group activations for the contrast between MAC+ versus MAC− (memory accuracy), $p < 0.001$, uncorrected.

Anatomical region	Side	MNI coordinates		
		x	*y*	*z*
(A) MAC+ > MAC−				
Superior temporal gyrus	L	−52	−28	12
	L	−60	−30	14
	R	62	−22	12
Superior temporal pole	R	52	4	−2
Middle temporal gyrus	R	48	−38	4
Hippocampus	L	−24	−40	0
Supramarginal gyrus	R	58	−38	32
	R	56	−36	34
	L	−62	−24	16
Heschl region	L	−32	−28	6
Precuneus	R	12	−42	46
(B) MAC− > MAC+				
Superior frontal gyrus medial	L	2	50	22
	L	0	46	32
	L	−8	60	8
Superior frontal gyrus	L	−14	60	8
Insula	L	−36	26	4

Brain regions within the boundaries of the AAL atlas.*

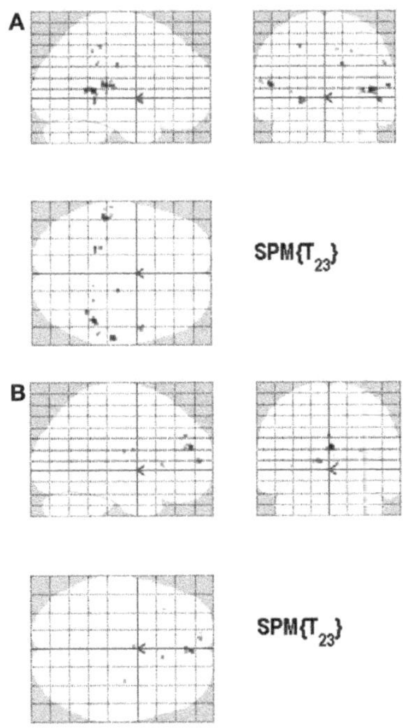

FIGURE 11 | (A) Group activations for the contrast between ACC+ versus ACC− (ACCURACY). Activations are superimposed on the anatomical group mean image (see Materials and Methods), depicting statistically significant relative increases in neural activity at $p < 0.001$, uncorrected. See **Table 7A** for the exact MNI coordinates. **(B)** Group activations for the contrast between ACC− versus ACC+ (ACCURACY). Activations are superimposed on the anatomical group mean image (see Materials and Methods), depicting statistically significant relative increases in neural activity at $p < 0.001$, uncorrected. See **Table 7B** for the exact MNI coordinates.

(including auditory imagery performance). The authors subsequently speculated that the activation of ventral precuneus during unsuccessful imagery may have reflected the processes of generation and comparison of alternative mental representations. The recruitment of precuneus areas during the generation and mental inspection and matching of alternative representations (Markowitsch et al., 2000; Kühnel et al., 2008; Hirshhorn et al., 2012) may offer an explanatory avenue for observed activations of precuneus regions not only during the RP (correct versus incorrect answering), but also during the MP (low confidence judgments versus high confidence judgments) of our study. In the latter case, it could be argued that the activation of the precuneus reflected the use of conscious visual imagery strategies, in an attempt to facilitate retrieval (Fletcher et al., 1996; Cavanna, 2007; Koriat et al., 2008; Desseilles et al., 2011).

The left MTG was found to be connected with memory recollection (Fink et al., 1996; Kroll et al., 1997; Markowitsch et al., 2000; Botzung et al., 2008; LePort et al., 2012) and essentially in the comparison between misses and correct rejections (Takahashi et al., 2008), which is reflected in the behavioral data insofar as the contrast correct versus incorrect responses was represented by correct rejections versus misses. This is supported by the importance of the medial temporal lobe in consolidation and retrieval of recently learned items (Cabeza and Nyberg, 2000; Sybirska et al., 2000; Frankland and Bontempi, 2005; Botzung et al., 2008). The observed activation of the insular cortex may reflect the posited contribution of the insula (especially of its anterodorsal part) to attentional processes, speech production, and memory recall (Manes et al., 1999; Nieuwenhuys, 2012).

Based on the current results we conjecture that a network of memory-related regions, including the hippocampus, the precuneus, areas within the posterior visual cortices (lingual gyrus), and other areas within the MTG, subserves correct (in contrast to incorrect) answering in the RP, at least at delays of around 2 h.

The contrast incorrect answering versus correct answering did not yield any significant results in our study. It can therefore be speculated that incorrect answering is not supported by a distinct neural net, but it is widely sustained by the same reconstructive approaches that support the correct answering. Incidentally, a study that investigated the neural correlates of false in comparison to true memories and vice versa via both functional connectivity analysis and direct contrasts, failed to identify any brain region displaying more activity during false versus true remembering (recollection) in direct contrasts; however, differences among the two conditions were suggested by connectivity analysis (Dennis et al., 2012).

MONITORING PROCESS (HIGH CONFIDENCE VERSUS LOW CONFIDENCE)

The factor MP (monitoring; high confidence versus low confidence) revealed no significant effect in the behavioral rating during the scanning procedure; hence there are no statistically significant differences between responses given with high confidence and responses given with low confidence. Imaging data draw a different picture: When contrasting high subjective confidence (defined here as absolute sureness) against low confidence, activation was particularly located in the fusiform gyrus (bilaterally), the left lingual gyrus, and the left parahippocampal area (Botzung et al., 2010). One might therefore argue that absolute sureness about a given answer was to a prevailing degree elicited by the accessibility (fluency) of rich visual details during the mental recasting or recollection of episodic-like material (Wheeler et al., 2000; Greenberg and Rubin, 2003; Greenberg, 2004; Kensinger and Schacter, 2006; Daselaar et al., 2008; Addis et al., 2009; Chua et al., 2012). Greenberg (2004) remarked that "when people retrieve visual images" (p. 367) they tend to be more confident in the veracity of their memories. The activation of the fusiform gyrus has been related to the visual processing of faces (but also objects and words) and that of the parahippocampal region to place perception (Kanwisher, 2010; Hofstetter et al., 2012), processing of scenes and landmarks (Piefke et al., 2003, 2005; Sharot et al., 2007), fine grained spatial judgments (Hirshhorn et al., 2012), and reinstating of visual context to facilitate successful retrieval (Hayes et al., 2007). Furthermore, it is worth mentioning that parahippocampus and ultimately hippocampus receive a diverse gamut of synthesized sensory-specific in addition to multimodal cortical information (Nieuwenhuys et al., 2008). Faces, objects, and places were of course frequently present in the movie and consequently a common subject of the questionnaire. Incidentally, confidence effects were related to parahippocampus in a recent study by Hayes et al. (2011). In this study, in the source, but not item memory task the high versus low confidence contrast induced activation in the right hippocampus, extending to parahippocampal cortex. Furthermore left parahippocampal activations were elicited for high confidence judgments versus low confidence judgments in an fMRI study that used a modified version of the Deese-Roediger-McDermott (DRM) (Roediger III and McDermott, 1995) paradigm (Moritz et al., 2006).

In our study, the reverse contrast (low confidence versus high confidence judgments) revealed activations within the same regions and in addition a broad pattern of diffuse frontal, temporal, parietal, occipital, and limbic activation. Interestingly, other recent fMRI-studies also reported brain regions common to high and low confidence recognition, indicating the contribution of these regions to both high and low confidence recognition activity (Kim and Cabeza, 2009; Hayes et al., 2011). The recruitment of the same brain regions by both high and low confidence ratings may be due to several factors, such as a division of labor (a functional dissociation or heterogeneity) among various parts of these regions (Hofstetter et al., 2012). The widespread activation of brain regions accompanying low confidence ratings may be interpreted as reflecting processes of increased and effortful allocation of attention, executive control, searching, mental inspection, matching, and self monitoring resources.

Significant neural activity was found in our analysis in the posterior and middle cingulate cortex for low confidence judgments. This finding partly overlaps with the results of Hayes et al. (2011). In their study the posterior cingulate cortex was activated during high confidence judgments, while the middle portion of the cingulate cortex was activated during low confidence judgments. Differentiated activations within cingulate regions, concerning comparisons of high versus low confidence judgments, were also described by Chua et al. (2006). The modulation of posterior cingulate cortex by confidence judgments could be related to its converging position within the default-mode network, which enables it to integrate mnemonic information with aspects derived from internally oriented mentation, such as self-referential (e.g., self monitoring), emotional, and social information (Kim, 2013; Chua, 2012). The middle cingulate cortex has been assigned functions in response selection or decision, such deliberating in a volatile environment (Chiu et al., 2008; Frith and Frith, 2008). Huijbers et al. (2011) advanced the idea that the midcingulate cortex, supramarginal gyrus, and precuneus areas contribute to the mental inspection of competing/alternative mental representations, which may explain the activations of these areas in the low confidence condition versus high confidence condition of our study.

Henson et al. (1999) performed an event-based functional MRI study, during which they asked volunteers to make one of three judgments to each presented word during recognition. Subjects had to judge whether they recollected seeing it during study (R judgments), whether they experienced a feeling of familiarity in the absence of recollection (K judgments), or whether they did not remember seeing it during study (N judgments). The R and N judgments can be assumed to be analogical to the high and low confidence rating in this study. Henson et al. (1999) found increases for N judgments (in contrast to R judgments) in the middle and superior frontal gyrus, insula, amygdala, precuneus, inferior parietal gyrus, and MTG. Except for the amygdala exactly the same areas were found to be activated in the current study when participants rated statements with low confidence (as opposed to high confidence). It is actually easy to imagine that subjects rated a statement with low confidence when they did not remember the accordant item. With respect to amygdala some studies proposed that increased activation may be associated with increased vividness, intensity of emotional judgments and self-relevance of memory, and memory confidence (for a review see Markowitsch and Staniloiu, 2011a). In our study we did not detect amygdala activation in association with either contrast during confidence ratings. The lack of amygdala activation (Vuilleumier et al., 2004) may reflect the process of habituation, such as in blocked fMRI designs (Greenberg et al., 2005; Daselaar et al., 2008). Another interpretation could be that the modulation of amygdala by confidence judgments may vary as a function of valence (Botzung et al., 2010).

Our data suggest that confidence ratings in general modulate temporal and occipital areas, which participate to gathering and integrating information (evidence) from various perceptual/sensory areas (Kim and Cabeza, 2009; Huijbers et al., 2010). These areas may show different modulations in relationship to valence, arousal, and novelty of mnemonic information and task characteristics. Furthermore, the relation between confidence and emotional intensity may vary as a matter of valence (Botzung et al., 2010). For positively valenced visual material (movie shots) associated with high confidence, Botzung et al. (2010) found increased activity was found in the medial temporal lobe as well as in the insula.

On the other side, specific frontal regions [inferior frontal gyrus (IFG), superior and middle frontal gyrus, paracentral lobule, precentral gyrus] were associated with low confidence in comparison to high confidence judgments, in our study, possibly reflecting executive control processes (Kim and Cabeza, 2009). The activation of the left IFG was connected to the deployment of controlled retrieval operations (Oztekin et al., 2009), especially when remembering is more difficult (Kim and Cabeza, 2009). Incidentally, the left IFG was detected to be activated in response to cues that elicit a strong need for selection among competing representations (Zhang et al., 2004; Moss et al., 2005). Furthermore higher activity at IFG was found to be correlated with higher risk aversion (Christopoulos et al., 2009) and the left IFG was attributed an essential role for suppressing prepotent, but inappropriate answers (Swick et al., 2008). One could speculate that the presence of competing mental representations may be conducive to a higher risk aversion, which may get translated into avoiding the 100% confidence option. When choosing the 50% confidence option subjects made no strong commitment and there was no risk.

Further activation during low confidence judgments was found in our study in the superior frontal gyrus being related to Brodmann area (BA) 10, which is assumed to play a role in strategic processes involved in memory retrieval and higher cognitive function (Burgess et al., 2007). This result again emphasizes the role of executive control processes in decision-making under uncertainty. We assume that when subjects are uncertain about a memory engram they invest more effort in retrieval of mnemonic information, which requires higher cognitive functions and is correlated with a rather ambivalent activation pattern compared to high confidence.

Some authors identified a laterality-confidence effect within frontal cortex. Right ventrolateral prefrontal regions were more active during low versus high confidence for both item and source memory tasks, supporting a role of this area in the processing of weak memories (Hayes et al., 2011). In the same study, several left prefrontal cortex regions showed greater activity for source than for item memory, independent of confidence.

When using a statistical height threshold of $p < 0.05$, FWE corrected for multiple comparisons only the left precuneus was activated in our study during low confidence versus high confidence ratings, a finding that mirrors results of other authors (Kim and Cabeza, 2009). Previous fMRI-studies have demonstrated that the precuneus (and posterior cingulate areas) show greater activity during recollection-based judgments (Henson et al., 1999; Wagner et al., 2005). In the study of Botzung et al. (2010) emotional intensity modulated the activity of the precuneus; furthermore, Sharot et al. (2007) found that precuneus activation correlated with the personal relevance during memory retrieval. In an elegant fMRI study that looked at the spatio-temporal dynamics of episodic-autobiographical memory, Daselaar et al. (2008) found that precuneus activation occurred at the elaboration phase of retrieval, after a specific memory had already been selected. Some authors connected the precuneus to gathering and integrating sensory details during watching movie sequences from silent films (Hasson et al., 2008). The precuneus was described as being part of the retrieval success network and was portrayed as being a sensory evidence accumulator (Huijbers et al., 2010).

In contrast to the view that holds the precuneus as being part of the retrieval success network, a recent study provided evidence that precuneus might be more implicated in retrieval confidence (decision-related retrieval processes) than successful episodic retrieval (Huijbers et al., 2010). The role of the precuneus in decision-making under uncertainty had also been suggested by Paulus et al. (2001), who asserted that both "STG and precuneus have been associated with sub processes that are consistent with the maintenance of strategies in the presence of uncertainty" (p. 97).

In conclusion, many more and differential brain areas were activated in our study when contrasting low against high confidence, a difference we attribute to greater monitoring demands and allocation of cognitive resources when confidence judgments are made under uncertainty.

CONTROL PROCESS (VOLUNTEERING VERSUS WITHHOLDING)

The factor CP (control; volunteering versus withholding) induced a significant effect in the behavioral rating during the scanning procedure: subjects rather volunteered an answer instead of withholding it, which is understandable due to the fact that each correctly volunteered answer was rewarded with a bonus, while volunteering an incorrect response led to a loss of one bonus point (moderate incentive). When no answer was provided (volunteered), no penalty or reward was instituted (no bonus points were gained or lost). The imaging data revealed differential activation for volunteering and withholding, suggesting that the two forms of behavior engage at least partially distinct sets of cognitive processes. If an answer was volunteered, particularly temporal and frontal as well as middle and posterior cingulate areas and the precuneus revealed activation. These data suggest that activation for volunteering is very similar to the neural correlates of monitoring (in contrast to retrieval). The findings are not surprising as they point to a relationship between memory confidence and answer volunteering (Koriat et al., 2008). Confidence judgments are assumed to be based on the strengths of the underlying memory trace. Also vivid remembering leads to making a high confidence decision. Volunteering an answer however might be even more influenced by perceived vividness of remembering due to the accompanying situational demands and payoffs (Belli et al., 1994; Yonelinas, 1994; Busey et al., 2000; Bradfield et al., 2002; Shaw and Zerr, 2003).

In contrast, when the answer was withheld, activations in parietal and temporal regions and also in the left caudate nucleus were identified. This may come as a surprise, because due to the task demands which were assumed to be connected with control processes like executive functioning, rather frontal and prefrontal brain activity would have been expected to reveal activation (Hedden and Gabrieli, 2010). The relevant brain areas for response inhibition which we anticipated to be related to withholding an answer include the ventrolateral PFC, mainly in the right hemisphere often in conjunction with a more extensive fronto-striato-parietal network (Garavan et al., 1999; Konishi et al., 1999; Aron et al., 2004; Walther et al., 2010; Ghahremani et al., 2012).

In our study we found during answer withholding a substantial activation in areas that play a differential role in memory retrieval

(Takahashi et al., 2008; Hoscheidt et al., 2010). This might suggest that subjects were more concentrated on the reconstruction or re-retrieval of the appropriate memory instead of response selection/inhibition (Robbins, 2007). This may have been caused by the design specification, because subjects had only very short time to answer. There might have been an overlap with the retrieval process especially when someone was not sure about the memory. We subsequently observed bilateral hippocampus activation, which speaks in favor of a great allocation of resources toward mentally reconstructing and generating internal memory details or contextual details that can be used as a retrieval cue (Koriat et al., 2008).

Caudate nuclei activity was found to be modulated by performance-feedback, including monetary rewards, with greater activation being observed during high confidence recollective experiences (Kim, 2013). However, in our study the identification of increased activation in the left caudate during withholding of answering might be congruent with new data showing the involvement of the left caudate in the inhibition of unwanted responses (Badgaiyan and Wack, 2011).

The meaning of activation of the left Heschl gyrus during withholding answers is unclear. It may reflect cognitive strategies or attempts at mental reconstruction (Zarnhofer et al., 2012). Imagining speech in third person was among other associated with left sided activation in STG and left postcentral gyrus (Shergill et al., 2001). During a visual imagery task Stokes et al. (2009) found activation of the superior temporal sulcus/Heschl's gyrus, but they speculated that it may have reflected the existence of auditory cues. Huijbers et al. (2011) however found overlapping activations in auditory cortex/ STG for auditory perception, retrieval, and imagery. The left postcentral gyrus activity was reported in one study in association with both novelty detection activity and encoding failure activity (Kim et al., 2010).

MONITORING PROCESS VERSUS RETRIEVAL PROCESS

The contrast between monitoring and retrieval resulted in temporal, occipital, parietal, and frontal brain activation, and moreover bilateral activation of the precuneus and differential left cingulate cortex areas. While during the RP subjects rated each statement as correct or incorrect, the MP was defined as a confidence judgment. During the confidence judgment, subjects monitored their recognition decision, and made an explicit subjective judgment about their previous memory performance. It is common sense to make the assumption that both processes (RP and MP) are related, although experience shows that there are instances where subjective confidence and objective correctness of memory answers divert (Simons et al., 2010). As Chua et al. (2009) expounded, confidence judgments are considered to be based on the strength and/or quality of the underlying memory trace, ease of retrieval, and also on study specific heuristics and test conditions, and ultimately on participants' general mnemonic abilities (Belli et al., 1994; Yonelinas, 1994; Busey et al., 2000; Bradfield et al., 2002; Shaw and Zerr, 2003). The functional imaging study conducted by Moritz et al. (2006) reported an increase in confidence at recognition associated with bilateral activation in the anterior and posterior cingulate cortex along with medial temporal regions. In comparison to recognition judgments, confidence judgments induced higher activations in various regions (such as superior frontal, dorsomedial frontal, orbitofrontal, and lateral parietal cortices), including areas involved in self-referential processing and internal mentation (such as medial prefrontal cortex) in an fMRI study conducted by Chua et al. (2006). Our own results reveal that, when contrasting confidence judgments to retrieval, activations are detected in areas involved in generation and inspection of mental imagery (e.g., precuneus, middle frontal gyrus, middle cingulate gyrus, supramarginal gyrus; Huijbers et al., 2011; Hirshhorn et al., 2012), monitoring and detecting conflict [e.g., anterior cingulate cortex (Acc)], post-retrieval monitoring and verification (prefrontal areas), decision and response selection under uncertainty (e.g., middle cingulate cortex, Frith and Frith, 2008), cognitive dissonance (e.g., Acc; van Veen et al., 2009), self appraisal (e.g., medial prefrontal cortex areas, Ries et al., 2012), and motivation and emotional processing (e.g., Acc). Activation of the Acc may support the relationship between monitoring processes and executive functions, given that the dorsal part of the Acc is connected with the prefrontal cortex, which plays a crucial role in executive functioning. Incidentally, Fan et al. (2005) described a kind of executive control network that showed activation of the anterior cingulate along with other brain areas.

The reverse contrast (RP versus CP) did not yield any statistically significant difference in our study. One may conclude from this that, even though monitoring and retrieval processes are strongly connected with each other, the former is characterized by a higher demand for cognitive performance and an additional allocation of resources toward internal reflection, inspection, verification, and comparison of alternatives and self-referential processing (Chua, 2012).

CONTROL PROCESS VERSUS RETRIEVAL PROCESS

According to our results, the CP (in contrast to retrieval) revealed (amongst others) the same neural activation as monitoring (in contrast to retrieval), namely the left MTG and the middle frontal gyrus. The left MTG was found to be activated during episodic-autobiographical memory retrieval (Markowitsch et al., 2000), but also during a variety of semantic tasks (for a review, see Svoboda et al., 2006). The MTG is indeed portrayed as an information convergence hub, as it integrates auditory and visual information (Visser et al., 2012). The left MTG is considered to be a crucial node of the conceptual network and has been attributed roles in word-picture matching, mapping concepts to words, and semantic task decision. Its recruitment during retrieval of old episodic memories was conjectured to support the idea of multimodal representation of episodic memory (Fink et al., 1996), on one hand and the more complex and effortful process of ecphorizing, on the other hand (Markowitsch et al., 2000). As mentioned above the left MTG was found to be activated during correct answering versus incorrect responding during the RP (Takahashi et al., 2008), which is in line with its involvement in the monitoring and CP, however the outcome of both processes is based on recognition decision (Chua et al., 2009).

MEMORY ACCURACY

The factor MAC (high MAC versus low MAC) induced differential brain activation for both contrasts. High MAC was here defined as withholding an incorrect answer in contrast to volunteering an incorrect answer. The present neural activation related to MAC (in contrast to inaccuracy) again confirms our previous assumption of a network of memory-related areas including the hippocampus, the precuneus, and the MTG being related to correct (in contrast to incorrect) memory retrieval hence these areas showed activation. The important role of the medial temporal lobe (including the parahippocampal gyrus) in memory performance and, particularly in non-verbal memory, has been known since the mid-1950s (Scoville and Milner, 2000; Frankland and Bontempi, 2005).

The reverse contrast, low MAC (in contrast to high MAC), was defined as volunteering incorrect answers. Interestingly, only the left superior frontal gyrus and the left insula demonstrated neural activation during low MAC in comparison to the high MAC condition. Mohr and colleagues investigated the role of the insula, concluding that this region was consistently associated with risky behavior (Weller et al., 2009; Mohr et al., 2010). Moreover the insula was found to be predominantly active in the presence of potential losses (Mohr et al., 2010). Insular activations were also reported in relationships to unexpected outcomes and errors (Klein et al., 2013). Low accuracy was defined in our study as volunteering an incorrect answer. If an answer rated with a confidence less that 100 percent were ventured, subjects would experience a homeostatic and visceral change in the face of potential losses, which would lead to insula activations. This would be in accordance with our experimental design hence participants knew that incorrect decisions would result in a loss of bonus and moreover therewith tended to a risky decision. Early studies had shown that people are loss aversive; however newer data pointed to a reduction (or even reversal of loss aversion) if people anticipate gains and losses and the anticipated loss is small (Harinck et al., 2007). The activation of the left superior frontal gyrus was detected in an imaging study when contrasting conceptual false to conceptual true information (Garoff-Eaton et al., 2007). In another study, activations of superior frontal gyri were reported to signify loss aversion when making decisions under risk (Tom et al., 2007; Xu et al., 2009). In our study the left superior frontal gyrus was also modulated when contrasting low confidence with high confidence ratings. It is therefore possible that uncertainty and inaccuracy belong to related processes.

CONCLUSION

In a 7 Tesla fMRI study that adopted the paradigm developed by Koriat and Goldsmith (1996a,b) and used complex, emotional, naturalistic, and culturally appropriate material at encoding (the movie "The New Cat"), we have provided evidence for common and unique neural correlates underlying the processes of memory retrieval, monitoring and control, and MAC performance in a group of healthy young adults. The participants were well matched for educational background and neuropsychological performance and equally distributed with respect to sex. The administration of the memory queries about the movie, which took place after a period of interference of about 2 h, tried to approximate the real-life situations related to eyewitness testimony. The 2-h period between seeing the short movie and being tested in the scanner was completely filled by neuropsychological testing and pre-scanning procedure; therefore the participants had no possibility to recapitulate details or to talk about the film. Furthermore, as it was mentioned above the participants were not informed that their memory of the movie would be probed later – a condition that again tried to approximate real-life eyewitness testimony circumstances.

As expected, the correct answering versus incorrect responding in the RP was accompanied by increased activation in hippocampus (Habib and Nyberg, 2008). The material used for incidental encoding involved complex multisensory information and it is known that information coming from all sensory modalities is transmitted to the hippocampal formation. In our study, we found a left lateralization of hippocampal engagement; this finding is relevant given data supporting the involvement of the left hippocampus during the retrieval of strict episodic memories in response to a specific cue.

Strict episodic memories are characterized by increased vividness, perceptual details, emotional engagement, self-relevance, and autonoetic consciousness (Markowitsch and Staniloiu, 2011b, 2012). The latter entails mental time traveling and reliving of the contextual details from the time of the encoding.

An alternative explanation is that the left hippocampal activation during correct answers (in comparison to incorrect answers) may have indicated a correct rejection of novel, unstudied material (either the detection/encoding of new material or a recollection rejection strategy). In our study, subjects gave more correct than incorrect answers, however, this was in general a consequence of correct rejection (instead of a hit) (McDonough and Gallo, 2012). The left hippocampus was also modulated in our study during the contrast high MAC versus low MAC.

One can assume from the results related to monitoring processes that temporal areas are involved in confidence ratings in general, whereas particular frontal regions are associated with low confidence judgments. The activation of the parahippocampal gyrus during confidence memory ratings is congruent with data showing that, similarly to hippocampus, parahippocampus receives a large gamut of sensory-specific and multimodal cortical information. The parahippocampus has been involved in retrieving non-verbal material and other authors evidenced its activation in relation to confidence memory judgments (Hayes et al., 2011) The finding of a significant positive association between left precuneus activation and the contrast low confidence versus high confidence judgments is consistent with other reports pointing to the recruitment of precuneus areas during post-retrieval monitoring processes (Huijbers et al., 2010).

In our study, answer volunteering seemed to be subject to increased monitoring processes, in contrast to answer withholding. These monitoring processes (suggested by activations in prefrontal, cingulate, and parietal cortices) may be modulated by the amount of potential gain relative to loss.

The increased bilateral hippocampal activation associated with withholding answers may reflect the posited role of hippocampus in disambiguation, mental construction, prospection, and future-minded choices (Ross et al., 2009; Peters and Büchel, 2010). As withholding of information may represent low memory confidence and/or reduced memory vividness, there may be a need for inter-hemispheric engagement of hippocampal formation, in order to generate and bind together pieces of information that are sensorially varied and complex (Botzung et al., 2010).

The caudate nuclei, which are part of the reward system, are assumed to support satisfaction linked to target detection (especially in relationship to hits) (Kim, 2013), monetary gain, and acquisition of good reputation (Izuma et al., 2008). In our study, we only found a left caudate activation during withholding of answering, but we interpreted this differently, namely by relating it to the involvement of the left caudate in the inhibition of unwanted responses (Badgaiyan and Wack, 2011).

The present study has a number of limitations; therefore its results cannot be generalized to the complex eyewitness situations. The short emotional movie only established a bridge between old laboratory memory testing and real-life situations, by inducing a controlled experience, with elements of real-life events (Mendelsohn et al., 2010). In real life, a much more variable mismatch between encoding situations and conditions at the time of memory testing might exist. The delay between learning and testing was about 2 h in our study. In eyewitness testimony situations, variable delays might be encountered. The observed neural correlates associated with some of the processes described above might not hold true at longer testing delays (Schacter and Loftus, 2013). A higher degree of homogeneity characterized the population investigated in our study, which obviously is not the case in eyewitness cases. Furthermore, we used a modest incentive during the CP of our study, whereas higher incentives may be involved in eyewitness testimony settings.

Despite its limitations, the present study demonstrates that dissociation between the retrieval, monitoring, and control processes described by the paradigm of Koriat and Goldsmith is realizable at the neurobiological level. We found a network of memory-related regions, including the hippocampus, the precuneus, and the MTG playing a crucial role in correct memory retrieval (correct answering during the RP) and MAC. Moreover, we show evidence for the fact that volunteering may be connected with monitoring processes hence both seem to be based on the strengths of the accordant memory trace. Our results reveal a strong relationship between monitoring and retrieval processes, whereas monitoring is defined by a higher demand for cognitive performance.

Beyond that, monitoring and control processes have in common that their outcome is based on a recognition decision which reflects their strong connection to memory retrieval – this relation seems to be mediated by activation of the medial temporal gyrus.

ACKNOWLEDGMENTS

We wish to thank our colleagues in the MR and Cognitive Neurology groups at the Erwin L. Hahn Institute for Magnetic Resonance Imaging, Essen, Germany for their support and helpful advice. Moreover we are grateful to all the participants who took part in this study. We thank our colleagues A. Koriat, M. Goldsmith and A. Pansky from Haifa University for giving us the movie used in the present study. This research was supported by grants of the EC (CN: 043460) and the Center of Cognitive Interaction Technology (CITEC) of the University of Bielefeld.

REFERENCES

Addis, D. R., Knapp, K., Roberts, R. P., and Schacter, D. L. (2012). Routes to the past: neural substrates of direct and generative autobiographical memory retrieval. *Neuroimage* 59, 2908–2922.

Addis, D. R., Pan, L., Vu, M. A., Laiser, N., and Schacter, D. L. (2009). Constructive episodic simulation of the future and the past: distinct subsystems of a core brain network mediate imagining and remembering. *Neuropsychologia* 47, 2222–2238.

Aron, A. R., Robbins, T. W., and Poldrack, R. A. (2004). Inhibition and the right inferior frontal cortex. *Trends Cogn. Sci. (Regul. Ed.)* 8, 170–177.

Badgaiyan, R. D., and Wack, D. (2011). Evidence of dopaminergic processing of executive inhibition. *PLoS ONE* 6:e28075. doi:10.1371/journal.pone.0028075

Beck, A. T., Steer, R. A., and Hautzinger, M. (1995). *Beck-Depressions-Inventar (BDI)*. Bern: Hans Huber.

Belli, R. F., Lindsay, D. S., Gales, M. S., and McCarthy, T. T. (1994). Memory impairment and source misattribution in postevent misinformation experiments with short retention intervals. *Mem. Cognit.* 22, 40–54.

Botzung, A., Denkova, E., Ciuciu, P., Scheiber, C., and Manning, L. (2008). The neural bases of the constructive nature of autobiographical memories studied with a self-paced fMRI design. *Memory* 16, 351–363.

Botzung, A., Rubin, D. C., Miles, A., Cabeza, R., and LaBar, K. S. (2010). Mental hoop diaries: emotional memories of a college basketball game in rival fans. *J. Neurosci.* 30, 2130–2137.

Bradfield, A. L., Wells, G. L., and Olson, E. A. (2002). The damaging effect of confirming feedback on the relation between eyewitness certainty and identification accuracy. *Mem. Cognit.* 87, 112–120.

Brand, M., Fujiwara, E., Borsutzky, S., Kalbe, E., Kessler, J., and Markowitsch, H. J. (2005). Decision-making deficits of Korsakoff patients in a new gambling task with explicit rules: associations with executive functions. *Neuropsychology* 19, 267–277.

Brand, M., and Markowitsch, H. J. (2010). Mechanisms contributing to decision-making difficulties in late adulthood: theoretical approaches, speculations and empirical evidence. *Gerontology* 56, 435–440.

Brickenkamp, R., and Zillmer, E. (1998). *The d2 Test of Attention*. Seattle, WA: Hogrefe and Huber.

Burgess, P. W., Gilbert, S. J., and Dumontheil, I. (2007). Function and localization within rostral prefrontal cortex (area 10). *Philos. Trans. R. Soc. Lond. B Biol. Sci.* 362, 887–899.

Busey, T. A., Tunnicliff, J., Loftus, G. R., and Loftus, E. F. (2000). Accounts of the confidence-accuracy relation in recognition memory. *Psychon. Bull. Rev.* 7, 26–48.

Cabeza, R., and Nyberg, L. (2000). Neural bases of learning and memory: functional neuroimaging evidence. *Curr. Opin. Neurol.* 13, 415–421.

Cavanna, A. E. (2007). The precuneus and consciousness. *CNS Spectr.* 12, 545–552.

Cavanna, A. E., and Trimble, M. R. (2006). The precuneus: a review of its functional anatomy and behavioural correlates. *Brain* 129, 564–583.

Chiu, P. H., Kavali, M. A., Kishida, K. T., Tomlin, D., Klinger, L. G., Klinger, M. R., et al. (2008). Self responses along cingulate cortex reveal quantitative neural phenotype for high-functioning autism. *Neuron* 57, 463–473.

Christopoulos, G. I., Tobler, P. N., Bossaerts, P., Dolan, R. J., and Schultz, W. (2009). Neural correlates of value, risk, and risk aversion contributing to decision making under risk. *J. Neurosci.* 29, 12574–12583.

Chua, E. F. (2012). "Evaluating confidence in our memories," in *Memory and Law*, eds L. Nadel and W. P. Sinnott-Armstrong (New York: Oxford University Press), 119–141.

Chua, E. F., Hannula, D. E., and Ranganath, C. (2012). Distinguishing highly confident accurate and inaccurate memory: insights about relevant and irrelevant influences on memory confidence. *Memory* 20, 48–62.

Chua, E. F., Schacter, D. L., Rand-Giovannetti, E., and Sperling, R. A. (2006). Understanding metamemory: neural correlates of the cognitive process and subjective level of confidence in recognition memory. *Neuroimage* 29, 1150–1160.

Chua, E. F., Schacter, D. L., and Sperling, R. A. (2009). Neural correlates of metamemory: a comparison of feeling-of-knowing and retrospective confidence judgments. *J. Cogn. Neurosci.* 21, 1751–1765.

Daselaar, S. M., Rice, H. J., Greenberg, D. L., Cabeza, R., LaBar, K. S., and Rubin, D. C. (2008). The spatiotemporal dynamics of autobiographical memory: neural correlates of recall, emotional intensity, and reliving. *Cereb. Cortex* 18, 217–229.

De Mulder, R. V., van Noortwijk, K., Goldsmith, M., Pansky, A., Koriat, A., and Labin, S. K. (2010). CORMAS: a computerized tool for the analysis of eyewitness memory correspondence. *Eur. J. Law Technol.* 1. Available at: http://ejlt.org//article/view/34/72

Dennis, N. A., Bowman, C. R., and Vandekar, S. N. (2012). True and phantom recollection: an fMRI investigation of similar and distinct neural correlates and connectivity. *Neuroimage* 59, 2982–2993.

Derogatis, L. R. (1993). *BSI: Brief Symptom Inventory.* Minneapolis: National Computer Systems.

Desseilles, M., Dang-Vu, T. T., Sterpenich, V., and Schwartz, S. (2011). Cognitive and emotional processes during dreaming: a neuroimaging view. *Conscious. Cogn.* 20, 998–1008.

Dörfel, D., Werner, A., Schaefer, M., von Kummer, R., and Karl, A. (2009). Distinct brain networks in recognition memory share a defined region in the precuneus. *Eur. J. Neurosci.* 30, 1947–1959.

Düzel, E., Habib, R., Rotte, M., Guderian, S., Tulving, E., and Heinze, H. J. (2003). Human hippocampal and parahippocampal activity during visual associative recognition memory for spatial and nonspatial stimulus configurations. *J. Neurosci.* 23, 9439–9444.

Fahrenberg, J., Hampel, R., and Selg, H. (2001). *Freiburger Persönlichkeitsinventar (FPI-R) [Freiburger Personality Inventory].* Göttingen: Hogrefe.

Fan, J., McCandliss, B. D., Fossella, J., Flombaum, J. I., and Posner, M. I. (2005). The activation of attentional networks. *Neuroimage* 26, 471–479.

Fink, G. R., Markowitsch, H. J., Reinkemeier, M., Bruckbauer, T., Kessler, J., and Heiss, W.-D. (1996). Cerebral representation of one's own past: neural networks involved in autobiographical memory. *J. Neurosci.* 16, 4275–4282.

Fletcher, P. C., Frith, C. D., Baker, S. C., Shallice, T., Frackowiak, R. S., and Dolan, R. J. (1995). The mind's eye -precuneus activation in memory related imagery. *Neuroimage* 2, 195–200.

Fletcher, P. C., Shallice, T., Frith, C. D., Frackowiak, R. S., and Dolan, R. J. (1996). Brain activity during memory retrieval. The influence of imagery and semantic cueing. *Brain* 119, 1587–1596.

Frankland, P. W., and Bontempi, B. (2005). The organization of recent and remote memories. *Nat. Rev. Neurosci.* 6, 119–130.

Friedman, D., Nessler, D., Kulik, J., and Hamberger, M. (2011). The brain's orienting response (novelty P3) in patients with unilateral temporal lobe resections. *Neuropsychologia* 49, 3474–3483.

Frisk, V., and Milner, B. (1990). The role of the left hippocampal region in the acquisition and retention of story content. *Neuropsychologia* 28, 349–359.

Frith, C. D., and Frith, U. (2008). The self and its reputation in autism. *Neuron* 57, 331–332.

Gallo, D. A. (2011). "Distinctiveness and the law of false recollection suppression," in *Abstracts of the 5th International Conference on Memory S423* (York: University of York), 95.

Gallo, D. A., Meadow, N. G., Johnson, E. L., and Foster, K. T. (2008). Deep levels of processing elicit a distinctiveness heuristic: evidence from the criterial recollection task. *J. Mem. Lang.* 58, 1095–1111.

Garavan, H., Ross, T. J., and Stein, E. A. (1999). Right hemispheric dominance of inhibitory control: an event-related functional MRI study. *Proc. Natl. Acad. Sci. U.S.A.* 96, 8301–8306.

Garoff-Eaton, R. J., Kensinger, E. A., and Schacter, D. L. (2007). The neural correlates of conceptual and perceptual false recognition. *Learn. Mem* 14, 684–692.

Ghahremani, D. G., Lee, B., Robertson C. L., Tabibria, G., Morgan, A. T. De Shetler, N., et al. (2012). Striatal dopamine D_2/D_3 receptors mediate response inhibition and related activity in frontostriatal neural circuitry in humans. *J. Neurosci.* 32, 7316–7324.

Gilboa, A., Winocur, G., Grady, C. L., Hevenor, S. J., and Moscovitch, M. (2004). Remembering our past: functional neuroanatomy of recollection of recent and very remote personal events. *Cereb. Cortex* 14, 1214–1225.

Gilboa, A., Winocur, G., Rosenbaum, R. S., Poreh, A., Gao, F., Black, S. E., et al. (2006). Hippocampal contributions to recollection in retrograde and anterograde amnesia. *Hippocampus* 16, 966–980.

Goldsmith, M., Koriat, A., and Weinberg-Eliezer, A. (2002). Strategic regulation of grain size in memory reporting. *J. Exp. Psychol. Gen.* 131, 73–95.

Greenberg, D. L. (2004). President Bush's false 'flashbulb' memory of 9/11/01. *Appl. Cogn. Psychol.* 18, 363–370.

Greenberg, D. L., Rice, J. J., Cabeza, R., Rubin, D. C., and Labar, K. S. (2005). Co-activation of the amygdala, hippocampus, and inferior frontal gyrus during autobiographical memory retrieval. *Neuropsychologia* 43, 659–674.

Greenberg, D. L., and Rubin, D. C. (2003). The neuropsychology of autobiographical memory. *Cortex* 39, 687–728.

Greve, A., Doidge, A. N., Evans, C. J., and Wilding, E. L. (2010). Functional neuroanatomy supporting judgments of when events occurred. *J. Neurosci.* 30, 7099–7104.

Gruneberg, M. M., and Morris, P. (eds). (1978). *Aspects of Memory.* London: Methuen.

Habib, R., and Nyberg, L. (2008). Neural correlates of availability and accessibility in memory. *Cereb. Cortex* 18, 1720–1726.

Halamish, V., Goldsmith, M., and Jacoby, L. L. (2012). Source-constrained recall: front-end and back-end control of retrieval quality. *J. Exp. Psychol. Learn. Mem. Cogn.* 38, 1–15.

Harinck, F., Van Dijk, E., Van Beest, I., and Mersmann, P. (2007). When gains loom larger than losses: reversed loss aversion for small amounts of money. *Psychol. Sci.* 18, 1099–1105.

Härting, C., Markowitsch, H. J., Neufeld, H., Calabrese, P., Deisinger, K., and Kessler, J. (2000). *Die Wechsler-Memory-Scale Revised. Deutschsprachige Adaptation.* Bern: Huber.

Hashimoto, R., Abe, N., Ueno, A., Fujii, T., Takahashi, S., and Mori, E. (2012). Changing the criteria for old/new recognition judgments can modulate activity in the anterior hippocampus. *Hippocampus* 22, 141–148.

Hasson, U., Yang, E., Vallines, I., Heeger, D. J., and Rubin, N. (2008). A hierarchy of temporal receptive windows in human cortex. *J. Neurosci.* 28, 2539–2550.

Hayes, S. M., Buchler, N., Stokes, J., Kragel, J., and Cabeza, R. (2011). Neural correlates of confidence during item recognition and source memory retrieval: evidence for both dual-process and strength memory theories. *J. Cogn. Neurosci.* 23, 3959–3971.

Hayes, S. M., Nadel. L., and Ryan, L. (2007). The effect of scene context on episodic object recognition: parahippocampal cortex mediates memory encoding and retrieval success. *Hippocampus* 17, 873–889.

Hedden, T., and Gabrieli, J. D. E. (2010). Shared and selective neural correlates of inhibition, facilitation, and shifting processes during executive control. *Neuroimage* 51, 421–431.

Helmstaedter, C., Lendt, M., and Lux, S. (2001). *VLMT–Verbaler Lern- und Merkfähigkeitstest.* Göttingen: Beltz Test GmbH.

Henson, R. N., Rugg, M. D., Shallice, T., Josephs, O., and Dolan, R. J. (1999). Recollection and familiarity in recognition memory: an event-related functional magnetic resonance imaging study. *J. Neurosci.* 19, 3962–3972.

Herrmann, D. J., McEvoy, C., Hertzog, C., Hertel, V. J., and Johnson, M. K. (eds) (1996). *Basic and Applied Memory Research: Practical Applications.* Hillsdale: Erlbaum.

Hirshhorn, M., Grady, C., Rosenbaum, R. S., Winocur. G., and Moscovitch, M. (2012). Brain regions involved in the retrieval of spatial and episodic details associated with a familiar environment: an fMRI study. *Neuropsychologia* 50, 3094–3106.

Hofstetter, C., Achaibou, A., and Vuilleumier, P. (2012). Reactivation of visual cortex during memory retrieval: content specificity and emotional modulation. *Neuroimage* 60, 1734–1745.

Horn, W. (1983) *Leistungsprüf System*, 2nd Edn. Göttingen: Hogrefe.

Hoscheidt, S. M., Nadel, L., Payne, J., and Ryan, L. (2010). Hippocampal activation during retrieval of spatial context from episodic and semantic memory. *Behav. Brain Res.* 212, 121–132.

Huijbers, W., Pennartz, C. M., and Daselaar, S. M. (2010). Dissociating the "retrieval success" regions of the brain: effects of retrieval delay. *Neuropsychologia* 48, 491–497.

Huijbers, W., Pennartz, C. M., Rubin, D. C., and Daselaar, S. M. (2011) Imagery and retrieval of auditory and visual information: neural correlates of successful and unsuccessful performance. *Neuropsychologia* 49, 1730–1740.

Izuma, K., Saito, D. N., and Sadato N. (2008). Processing of social and monetary rewards in the human striatum. *Neuron* 58, 284–294.

Kafkas, A., and Montaldi, D. (2012). Familiarity and recollection produce distinct eye movement, pupil and medial temporal lobe responses when memory strength is matched. *Neuropsychologia* 50, 3080–3093.

Kanwisher, N. (2010). Functional specificity in the human brain: a window into the functional architecture of the mind. *Proc. Natl. Acad. Sci. U.S.A.* 107, 11163–11170.

Kelley, C. M., and Sahakyan, L. (2003). Memory, monitoring, and control in the attainment of memory accuracy. *J. Mem. Lang.* 48, 704–721.

Kensinger, E. A., and Schacter, D. L. (2006). Neural processes underlying memory attribution on a reality-monitoring task. *Cereb. Cortex* 16, 1126–1133.

Kim, H. (2013). Differential neural activity in the recognition of old versus new events: an activation likelihood estimation meta-analysis. *Hum. Brain Mapp.* 34, 814–836.

Kim, H., and Cabeza, R. (2009). Common and specific brain regions in high- versus low-confidence recognition memory. *Brain Res.* 28, 103–113.

Kim, H., Daselaar, S. H., and Cabeza, R. (2010). Overlapping brain activity between episodic memory encoding and retrieval: roles of the task-positive and task-.negative networks. *Neuroimage* 49, 145–154.

Klatzky, R. L., and Erdelyi, M. H. (1985). The response criterion problem in tests of hypnosis and memory. *Int. J. Clin. Exp. Hypn.* 33, 246–257.

Klein, T. A., Ullsperger, M., and Danielmeier, C. (2013). Error awareness and the insula: links to neurological and psychiatric diseases. *Front. Hum. Neurosci.* 7:14. doi:10.3389/fnhum.2013.00014

Konishi, S., Nakajima, K., Uchida, I., Kikyo, H., Kameyama, M., and Miyashita, Y. (1999). Common inhibitory mechanism in human inferior prefrontal cortex revealed by event-related functional MRI. *Brain* 122, 981–991.

Koriat, A., and Goldsmith, M. (1994). Memory in naturalistic and laboratory contexts: distinguishing the accuracy-oriented and quantity-oriented approaches to memory assessment. *J. Exp. Psychol. Gen.* 123, 297–315.

Koriat, A., and Goldsmith, M. (1996a). Memory metaphors and the real-life/laboratory controversy: correspondence versus storehouse conceptions of memory. *Behav. Brain Sci.* 19, 167–228.

Koriat, A., and Goldsmith, M. (1996b). Monitoring and control processes in the strategic regulation of memory accuracy. *Psychol. Rev.* 103, 490–517.

Koriat, A., Goldsmith, M., and Halamish, V. (2008). "Controlled processes in voluntary remembering," in *Cognitive Psychology of Memory*, ed. H. L. Roediger, III (Oxford: Elsevier), 307–324.

Koriat, A., Goldsmith, M., and Painsky, A. (2000). Toward a psychology of memory accuracy. *Annu. Rev. Psychol.* 51, 481–537.

Kroll, N., Markowitsch, H. J., Knight, R., and von Cramon, D. Y. (1997). Retrieval of old memories – the temporo-frontal hypothesis. *Brain* 120, 1377–1399.

Kühnel, S., Woermann, F. G., Mertens, M., and Markowitsch, H. J. (2008). Involvement of the orbitofrontal cortex during correct and false recognitions of visual stimuli. Implications for eyewitness decisions on an fMRI study using a film paradigm. *Brain Imaging Behav.* 2, 163–176.

Leding, J. K. (2012). Working memory predicts the rejection of false memories. *Memory* 20, 217–223.

LePort, A. K., Mattfeld, A. T., Dickinson-Anson, H., Fallon, J. H., Stark, C. E., Kruggel, F., et al. (2012). Behavioral and neuroanatomical investigation of Highly Superior Autobiographical Memory (HSAM). *Neurobiol. Learn. Mem.* 98, 78–92.

Leshikar, E. D., Duarte, A., and Hertzog, C. (2012). Task-selective memory effects for successfully implemented encoding strategies. *PLoS ONE* 7:e38160. doi:10.1371/journal.pone.0038160

Lezak, M. D. (1995). *Neuropsychological Assessment*, 3rd Edn. New York: Oxford University Press.

Manes, F., Paradiso, S., and Robinson, R. G. (1999). Neuropsychiatric effects of insular stroke. *J. Nerv. Ment. Dis.* 187, 707–712.

Markowitsch, H. J. (1994). The memory storehouse. *Trends Neurosci.* 17, 513–514.

Markowitsch, H. J. (2008). "Anterograde amnesia," in *Handbook of Clinical Neurology*, 3rd Edn, ed. G. M. B. L. Goldenberg (New York: Elsevier), 155–183.

Markowitsch, H. J., and Staniloiu, A. (2011a). Amygdala in action: relaying biological and social significance to autobiographic memory. *Neuropsychologia* 49, 718–733.

Markowitsch, H. J., and Staniloiu, A. (2011b). Memory, autonoetic consciousness, and the self. *Conscious. Cogn.* 20, 16–39.

Markowitsch, H. J., and Staniloiu, A. (2012). Amnesic disorders. *Lancet* 380, 1429–1440.

Markowitsch, H. J., Thiel, A., Reinkemeier, M., Kessler, J., Koyuncu, A., and Heiss, W. D. (2000). Right amygdalar and temporofrontal activation during autobiographic, but not during fictitious memory retrieval. *Behav. Neurol.* 12, 181–190.

McDonough, I. M., and Gallo, D. A. (2012). Illusory expectations can affect retrieval-monitoring accuracy. *J. Exp. Psychol. Learn. Mem. Cogn.* 38, 391–404.

Mendelsohn, A., Furman, O., and Dudai, Y. (2010). Signatures of memory: brain coactivations during retrieval distinguish correct from incorrect recollection. *Front. Behav. Neurosci.* 4:18. doi:10.3389/fnbeh.2010.00018

Mohr, P. N. C., Biele, G., and Heekeren, H. R. (2010). Neural processing of risk. *J. Neurosci.* 30, 6613–6619.

Moritz, S., Gläscher, J., Sommer, T., Büchel, C., and Braus, D. F. (2006). Neural correlates of memory confidence. *Neuroimage* 33, 1188–1193.

Moss, H. E., Abdallah, S., Fletcher, P., Bright, P., Pilgrim, L., Acres, K., et al. (2005). Selecting among competing alternatives: selection and retrieval in the left inferior frontal gyrus. *Cereb. Cortex* 15, 1723–1735.

Nieuwenhuys, R. (2012). The insular cortex. *Prog. Brain Res.* 195, 123–163.

Nieuwenhuys, R., Voogd, J., and van Hujzen, C. (2008). *The Human Central Nervous System*, 4th Edn. Berlin: Springer.

Nyberg, L., Habib, R., McIntosh, A. R., and Tulving, E. (2000). Reactivation of encoding-related brain activity during memory retrieval. *Proc. Natl. Acad. Sci. U.S.A.* 97, 11120–11124.

Oddo, S., Lux, S., Weiss, P. H., Schwab, A., Welzer, H., Markowitsch, H. J., et al. (2010). Specific role of medial prefrontal cortex in retrieving recent autobiographical memories: an fMRI study of young female subjects. *Cortex* 46, 29–39.

Oldfield, R. C. (1971). The assessment and analysis of handedness: the Edinburgh inventory. *Neuropsychologia* 9, 97–113.

Oztekin, I., Curtis, C. E., and McElree, B. (2009). The medial temporal lobe and the left inferior prefrontal cortex jointly support interference resolution in verbal working memory. *J. Cogn. Neurosci.* 21, 1967–1979.

Pansky, A., and Tenenboim, E. (2011). Inoculating against eyewitness suggestibility via interpolated verbatim vs. gist testing. *Mem. Cognit.* 39, 155–170.

Paulus, M. P., Hozack, N., Zauscher, B., McDowell, J. E., Frank, L., Brown, G. G., et al. (2001). Prefrontal, parietal, and temporal cortex networks underlie decision-making in the presence of uncertainty. *Neuroimage* 13, 91–100.

Peters, J., and Büchel, C. (2010). Episodic future thinking reduces rewards delay discounting through an enhancement of prefrontal-mediotemporal interactions. *Neuron* 65, 138–148.

Piefke, M., Weiss, P. H., Markowitsch, H. J., and Fink, G. R. (2005). Gender differences in the functional neuroanatomy of emotional episodic autobiographical memory. *Hum. Brain Mapp.* 24, 313–324.

Piefke, M., Weiss, P. H., Zilles, K., Markowitsch, H. J., and Fink, G. R. (2003). Differential remoteness and emotional tone modulate the neural correlates of autobiographical memory. *Brain* 126, 850–868.

Poppenk, J., Walia, G., McIntosh, A. R., Joanisse, M. F., Klein, D., and Kohler, S. (2008). Why is the meaning of a sentence better remembered than its form? An fMRI study on the role of novelty-encoding processes. *Hippocampus* 18, 909–918.

Poser, B. A., Koopmans, P. J., Witzel, T., Wald, L. L., and Barth, M. (2010). Three dimensional echo-planar imaging at 7 Tesla. *Neuroimage* 51, 261–266.

Poser, B. A., and Norris, D. G. (2009). Investigating the benefits of multi-echo EPI for fMRI at 7 T. *Neuroimage* 45, 1162–1172.

Ries, M. L., McLaren, D. G., Bendlin, B. B., Guanfan, X., Rowley, H. A., Birn, R., et al. (2012). Medial prefrontal functional connectivity – relation to memory self-appraisal accuracy in older adults with and without memory disorders. *Neuropsychologia* 50, 603–611.

Robbins, T. W. (2007). Shifting and stopping: fronto-striatal substrates, neurochemical modulation and clinical implications. *Philos. Trans. R. Soc. Lond. B Biol. Sci.* 362, 917–932.

Roediger, H. L. III, and McDermott, K. B. (1995). Creating false memories: remembering words not presented on lists. *J. Exp. Psychol. Learn. Mem. Cogn.* 21, 803–814.

Roediger, H. L. (1980). Memory metaphors in cognitive psychology. *Mem. Cognit.* 8, 231–246.

Ross, R. S., Brown, T. I., and Stern, C. E. (2009). The retrieval of learned sequences engages the hippocampus: evidence from fMRI. *Hippocampus* 19, 790–799.

Rutishauser, U., Schuman, E. M., and Mamelak, A. N. (2008). Activity of human hippocampal and amygdala neurons during retrieval of declarative memories. *Proc. Natl. Acad. Sci. U.S.A.* 105, 329–334.

Schacter, D. L., Israel, L., and Racine, C. (1999). Suppressing false recognition in younger and older adults:

the distinctiveness heuristic. *J. Mem. Lang.* 40, 1–24.

Schacter, D. L., and Loftus, E. F. (2013). Memory and law: what can cognitive neuroscience contribute? *Nat. Neurosci.* 16, 119–123.

Scoville, W. B., and Milner, B. (2000). Loss of recent memory after bilateral hippocampal lesions. 1957. *J. Neuropsychiatry Clin. Neurosci.* 12, 103–113.

Sharot, T., Martorella, E. A., Delgado, M. R., and Phelps, E. A. (2007). How personal experience modulates the neural circuitry of memories of September 11. *Proc. Natl. Acad. Sci. U.S.A.* 104, 389–394.

Shaw, J. S., and Zerr, T. K. (2003). Extra effort during memory retrieval may be associated with increases in eyewitness confidence. *Law Hum. Behav.* 27, 315–329.

Shergill, S., Bullmore, E. T., Brammer, M. J., Williams, S. C., Murray, R. M., and McGuire, P. K. (2001). A functional study of auditory verbal imagery. *Psychol. Med.* 31, 241–253.

Simons, J. S., Peers, P. V., Mazuz, Y. S., Berryhill, M. E., and Olson, I. R. (2010). Dissociation between memory accuracy and memory confidence following bilateral parietal lesions. *Cereb. Cortex* 20, 479–485.

Stokes, M., Thompson, R., Cusack, R., and Duncan, J. (2009). Top-down activation of shape-specific population codes in visual cortex during mental imagery. *J. Neurosci.* 29, 1565–1572.

Svoboda, E., McKinnon, M. C., and Levine, B. (2006). The functional neuroanatomy of autobiographical memory: a meta-analysis. *Neuropsychologia* 44, 2189–2208.

Swick, D., Ashley, V., and Turken, A. U. (2008). Left inferior frontal gyrus is critical for response inhibition. *BMC Neurosci.* 9:102. doi:10.1186/1471-2202-9-102

Sybirska, E., Davachi, L., and Goldman-Rakic, P. S. (2000). Prominence of direct entorhinal-CA1 pathway activation in sensorimotor and cognitive tasks revealed by 2-DG functional mapping in nonhuman primate. *J. Neurosci.* 20, 5827–5834.

Takahashi, E., Kenichi, O., and Kim, D. S. (2008). Dissociated pathways for successful memory retrieval from the human parietal cortex: anatomical and functional connectivity analyses. *Cereb. Cortex* 18, 1771–1778.

Tom, S. M., Fox, C. R., Trepel, C., and Poldrack, R. A. (2007). The neural basis of loss aversion in decision-making under risk. *Science* 315, 515–518.

Tulving, E., Markowitsch, H. J., Kapur, S., Habib, R., and Houle, S. (1994). Novelty encoding networks in the human brain: data from positron emission tomography studies. *Neuroreport* 5, 2525–2528.

Tzourio-Mazoyer, N., Landeau, B., Papathanassiou, D., Crivello, F., Etard, O., Delcroix, N., et al. (2002). Automated anatomical labeling of activations in SPM using a macroscopic anatomical parcellation of the MNI MRI single-subject brain. *Neuroimage* 2, 273–289.

van Veen, V., Krug, M. K., Schooler, J. W., and Carter, C. S. (2009). Neural activity predicts attitude change in cognitive dissonance. *Nat. Neurosci* 12, 1469–1474.

Viard, A., Desgranges, B., Eustache, F., and Piolino, P. (2012). Factors affecting medial temporal lobe engagement for past and future episodic events: an ALE meta-analysis of neuroimaging studies. *Brain Cogn.* 80, 111–125.

Visser, M., Jefferies, E., Embleton, K. V., and Lambon Ralph, M. A. (2012). Both the middle temporal gyrus and the ventral anterior temporal area are crucial for multimodal semantic processing: distortion-corrected fMRI evidence for a double gradient of information convergence in the temporal lobes. *J. Cogn. Neurosci.* 24, 1766–1778.

Vuilleumier, P., Richardson, M. P., Armony, J. L., Driver, J., and Dolan, R. J. (2004). Distant influences of amygdala lesion on visual cortical activation during emotional face processing. *Nat. Neurosci.* 7, 1271–1278.

Wagner, A. D., Shannon, B. J., Kahn, I., and Buckner, R. L. (2005). Parietal lobe contributions to episodic memory retrieval. *Trends Cogn. Sci. (Regul. Ed.)* 9, 445–453.

Walther, S., Goya-Maldonado, R., Stippich, C., Weisbrod, M., and Kaiser, S. (2010). A supramodal network for response inhibition. *Neuroreport* 21, 191–195.

Weller, J. A., Levin, I. P., Shiv, B., and Bechara, A. (2009). The effects of insula damage on decision–making for risky gains and losses. *Soc. Neurosci.* 4, 347–358.

Wheeler, M. E., Petersen, S. E., and Buckner, R. L. (2000). Memory's echo: vivid remembering reactivates sensory-specific cortex. *Proc. Natl. Acad. Sci. U.S.A.* 97, 11125–11129.

Wixted, J. T., and Squire, L. R. (2011). The familiarity/recollection distinction does not illuminate medial temporal lobe function: response to Montaldi and Mayes. *Trends Cogn. Sci. (Regul. Ed.)* 15, 340–341.

Xu, L., Liang, Z. Y., Wang, K., Li, S., and Jiang, T. (2009). Neural mechanism of intertemporal choice: from discounting future gains to future losses. *Brain Res.* 1261, 65–74.

Yonelinas, A. P. (1994). Receiver–operating characteristics in recognition memory: evidence for a dual–process model. *J. Exp. Psychol. Learn. Mem. Cogn.* 20, 1341–1354.

Zarnhofer, S., Braunstein, V., Ebner, F., Koschutnig, K., Neuper, C., Reishofer, G. et al. (2012). The influence of verbalization on the pattern of cortical activation during mental arithmetic. *Behav. Brain Funct.* 8, 13.

Zhang, J. X., Feng, C. M., Fox, P. T., Gao, J. H., and Tan, L. H. (2004). Is left inferior frontal gyrus a general mechanism for selection? *Neuroimage* 23, 596–603.

13

Shared neural substrates of emotionally enhanced perceptual and mnemonic vividness

Rebecca M. Todd[1]*, Taylor W. Schmitz[1,2], Josh Susskind[3] and Adam K. Anderson[1]

[1] *Department of Psychology, University of Toronto, Toronto, ON, Canada*
[2] *MRC Cognition and Brain Sciences Unit, University of Cambridge, Cambridge, UK*
[3] *Institute for Telecommunications and Information Technology, University of California San Diego, San Diego, CA, USA*

Correspondence:
Rebecca M. Todd, Department of Psychology, University of Toronto, 100 St. George Street, Toronto, ON M5S3G3, Canada.
e-mail: r.todd@acl.psych.toronto.edu

It is well-known that emotionally salient events are remembered more vividly than mundane ones. Our recent research has demonstrated that such memory vividness (Mviv) is due in part to the subjective experience of emotional events as more perceptually vivid, an effect we call emotionally enhanced vividness (EEV). The present study built on previously reported research in which fMRI data were collected while participants rated relative levels of visual noise overlaid on emotionally salient and neutral images. Ratings of greater EEV were associated with greater activation in the amygdala and visual cortex. In the present study, we measured BOLD activation that predicted recognition Mviv for these same images 1 week later. Results showed that, after controlling for differences between scenes in low-level objective features, hippocampus activation uniquely predicted subsequent Mviv. In contrast, amygdala and visual cortex regions that were sensitive to EEV were also modulated by subsequent ratings of Mviv. These findings suggest shared neural substrates for the influence of emotional salience on perceptual and mnemonic vividness, with amygdala and visual cortex activation at encoding contributing to the experience of both perception and subsequent memory.

Keywords: memory, emotion, amygdala, visual cortex, emotional salience, affect-biased attention, emotionally enhanced memory, fMRI

INTRODUCTION

It is well-known that emotionally important events such as the birth of a child or September 11 hold a special place in memory (e.g., Brown and Kulik, 1977). There is substantial empirical evidence that emotionally salient stimuli or events are more likely to be remembered than mundane ones (Ochsner, 2000) and are remembered more vividly (Sharot et al., 2004, 2007; Kensinger et al., 2011).

There is also abundant evidence that emotional salience influences the initial perception of events. Emotions are associated with the mutually enhancing effects of sympathetic arousal (Anderson et al., 2006b) and increased attention (Pessoa et al., 2002; Anderson et al., 2003; Talmi et al., 2008), which results in facilitated encoding of emotional events (Anderson and Phelps, 2001; Anderson, 2005; De Martino et al., 2009; Lim et al., 2009). Emotionally important stimuli are also more easily detected and identified than neutral stimuli when attentional load is high (Soares and Ohman, 1993; Anderson, 2005), or stimuli are presented at the threshold of awareness (Nielsen and Sarason, 1981). At the neural level, human fMRI studies have shown that viewing emotionally salient images, such as scenes of mutilation or erotica, is associated with enhanced engagement of regions of visual cortex (Lang et al., 1998; Bradley et al., 2003; Vuilleumier et al., 2004; Sabatinelli et al., 2005; Padmala and Pessoa, 2008).

We have previously demonstrated that emotion-enhanced memory vividness (Mviv) in part reflects a subjective richness of perceptual experience, or emotionally enhanced vividness (EEV) (Todd et al., 2012). Using a magnitude estimation task in which low levels of visual noise were overlaid on neutral and emotionally salient scenes, we demonstrated that when objective levels of noise were equated, arousing images were experientially perceived as more perceptually vivid than neutral images (Todd et al., 2012). That is, participants subjectively perceived emotionally arousing images as containing greater signal (the underlying image) relative to overlaid noise. fMRI data revealed that, after controlling for low-level features of stimuli such as contrast, color, and scene complexity, EEV ratings were positively correlated with activity in left amygdala and lateral occipital cortex (LOC). Statistical mediation analyses suggested that amygdala activation accounted for the influence of visual cortex activation on EEV (Todd et al., 2012).

We also reported behavioral data indicating that EEV predicted subsequent Mviv, measured both by cued recall 45 min after encoding and recognition memory 1 week later (Todd et al., 2012). Previous studies have shown that enhanced memory for arousing images is associated with greater amygdala and visual cortex activation during encoding (Hamann et al., 1999; Canli et al., 2000; Kensinger et al., 2007b). Since our results showed that amygdala and visual cortex were modulated by EEV, an outstanding question concerned whether activity in these same regions predicts subsequent Mviv.

The present study built on a previously reported study (Todd et al., 2012), in which to measure EEV we adapted a magnitude estimation paradigm designed to estimate human subjective estimates of graded magnitudes of sensory stimuli (Stevens, 1957). In each version of the noise estimation (NE) task, emotionally arousing (positive and negative) and neutral scenes were overlaid with sparse "visual noise," or randomly distributed pixels. Participants were asked to estimate the relative degree of "noisiness" of each picture in comparison to a standard image, which was created from scrambled versions of the scenes, matched in global luminance and contrast, overlaid with a varying levels of sparse noise (**Figure 1**). This provided a direct behavioral index of whether greater emotional salience results in greater perceptual vividness

The goal of the present study was to investigate the link between the subjective experience of perceptual vividness and mnemonic vividness. Here we examined BOLD activation predicting Mviv ratings collected from an online recognition memory task 1 week after participants were scanned during the NE procedure in relation to activation evoked by EEV (for a timeline of the procedure, see **Figure 1B**). We predicted that amygdala and LOC activation would predict Mviv, along with additional brain regions, such as the hippocampus, also implicated in episodic memory (Lepage et al., 1998; Eldridge et al., 2005).

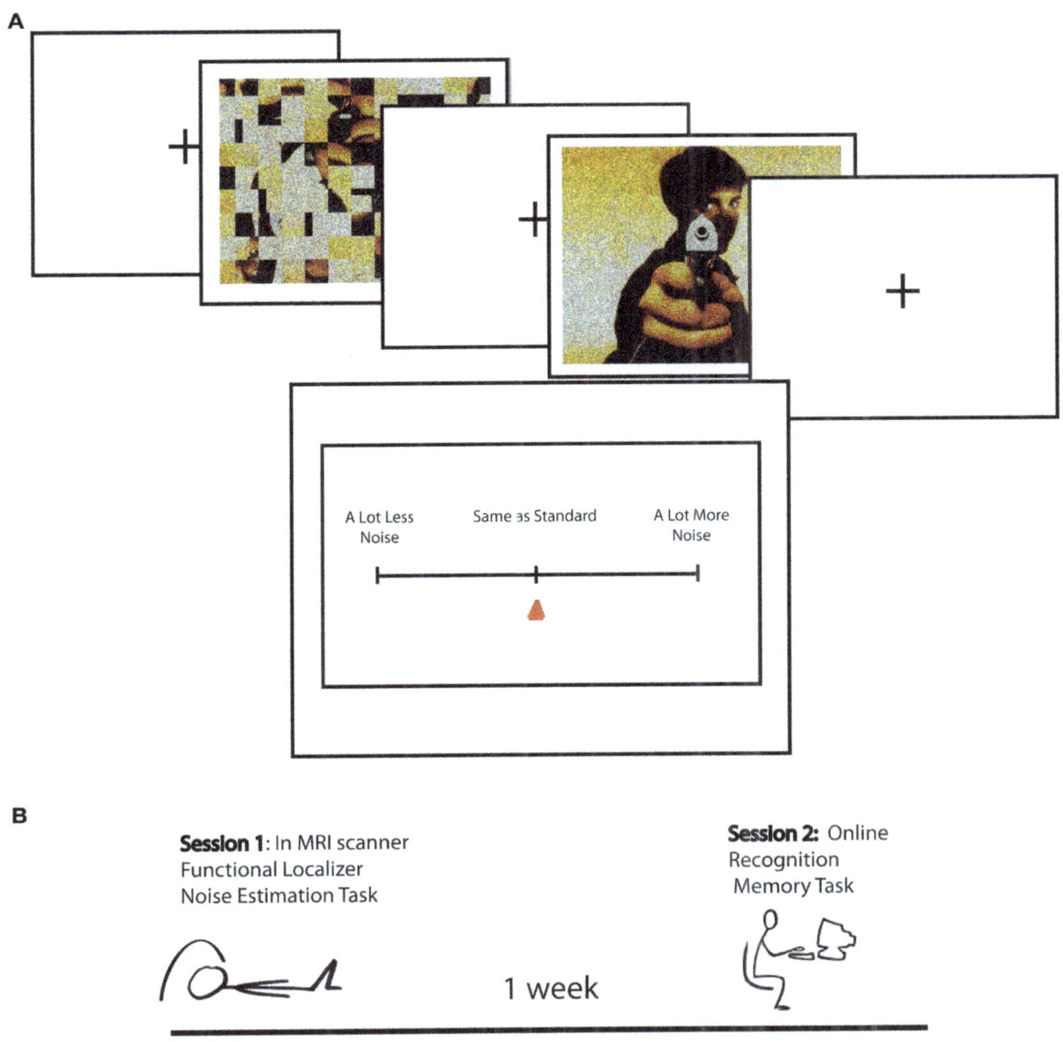

FIGURE 1 | (A) Task design for Noise Estimation fMRI experiment. A standard, created by phase scrambling the comparison image, was overlaid with 15% noise. The standard was followed by the image overlaid with 10, 15, or 20% noise. Following image offset, participants moved a cursor on a scale to indicated NE for the image relative to the standard from "a lot less noise" to "same as standard" to "a lot more noise." **(B)** Schematic of the study timeline over two sessions. In Session 1 participants performed the Noise Estimation task in the scanner. One week later they performed an online recognition memory task in which they were asked if images were old or new, and if they were old how vividly they were remembered on a scale from vague to detailed.

MATERIALS AND METHODS

fMRI STUDY

Participants

Eighteen healthy young adult volunteers from Queen's University (18–30 years) with normal or corrected to normal vision and no history of psychiatric disorders participated in this study. Two participants were removed from subsequent fMRI analysis: one had excessive movement and one misunderstood the task, leaving 16 participants (10 female).

Localizer task

In order to localize category-selective regions of visual cortex, we used a block design task that alternated blocks of line-drawings of objects and scrambled line-drawings to localize object-selective regions of the LOC. The task also included blocks of faces and houses to localize face and place selective regions of visual cortex respectively. Blocks alternated randomly to minimize category predictability and each image category was presented six times. Each 20 s block contained five images presented for 4000 ms each. In each block one of the images was repeated. To ensure that they were attending to the images presented onscreen, participants were asked to push a button with the index finger each time an image appeared if the image was not the same as the one immediately preceding it, and to press a second button with the middle finger if the image was identical to the one immediately preceding it. Because the behavioral task served merely as a vigilance task to maintain attention and maximize BOLD activation, behavioral results were not analyzed.

NOISE ESTIMATION TASK

Materials

Twenty-five negative photos and 25 positive photos were taken from the International Affective Picture System (IAPS). Twenty-five neutral photos were retrieved from the internet as well as the IAPS. A separate set of participants rated all pictures to be equal in brightness, contrast, and visual complexity, $Fs(2, 72) < 0.1$. Positive, negative, and neutral images were selected to be equivalent on basic low-level image statistics, equated in log luminance, $F(2, 72) < 1$, and RMS contrast, $F(2, 72) < 1$. One of three levels of Gaussian all-color noise (15%) was superimposed over each image using adobe Photoshop 7.0.

To minimize variance associated with differences in luminance and contrast across images, a standard was created to match each corresponding comparison image (**Figure 1**). Standards were created by phase scrambling each image and adding noise. Both standards and images subtended a visual angle of 13° × 9.5°. The level of noise on the pictures was held constant (15%) and noise level was varied in the standards (10, 15, 20%). Thus, we could measure BOLD responses related to estimations of perceptual and mnemonic vividness across images that did not vary in objective levels of noise.

Trials were presented in five separate runs of 30 trials. In order to reduce time spent into the scanner in this slow event-related design, each image was presented twice at two out of three levels of standard noise for a total of 150 trials (50 negative arousing, 50 positive arousing, and 50 neutral). Thus, each image was seen twice at 15% noise paired with a standard at two out of three possible noise levels (10, 15, and 20%). In each 12-s trial a standard was presented for 1500 ms, followed by a 500 ms ISI, followed by the picture which was presented for 1500 ms. Both standards and images subtended a visual angle of 13° × 9.5°. After a randomly jittered interval of 1500, 2000, or 2500 ms, a response meter appeared for 4000 ms, followed by a randomly jittered ITI of 2000, 2500, or 3000 ms. Participants clicked a button with the index finger to move the cursor to the left (less noisy than standard) and with the middle finger to move the cursor to the right (more noisy than standard), and a third button with the middle finger to indicate that the cursor was placed at the desired degree of noisiness. Fifty null trials (1/3), consisting of 12 s of fixation, were included at randomized intervals. After the scan participants were asked to log on to a website 1 week later.

Memory task

One week after performing the NE task, participants were instructed to log on to a website to complete a surprise memory task exactly 1 week after performing the NE task. An additional set of images, 12 positive, 12 neutral, and 12 negative, were matched with the Session 1 images for arousal, scene content, contrast, and luminance. Participants were shown the original 75 images and the 36 new images. After rating an image as new, familiar, or recollected, participants rated the vividness of the memory for recognized items on a scale of 1–7 (0 = new image), ranging from vague to detailed.

fMRI acquisition

Imaging data were collected with a 3T Siemens scanner using a 12-channel head coil. Both the localizer and experimental tasks were programed in E-prime Version 1.2 (Psychology Software Tools, Pittsburgh, PA, USA). For each subject, a three-dimensional magnetization prepared rapid-acquisition gradient-echo pulse sequence (MPRAGE) was used to acquire a high-resolution T1-weighted structural volume: repetition time (TR) = 1760 ms; echo time (TE) = 2.2 ms; FOV = 256 × 256; slice thickness = 1mm; 176 slices; total acquisition time = 7:32 min.

T2* weighted gradient-echo echo planar images were collected for two short field mapping series to correct for EPI distortion due to inhomogeneities in the magnetic field. Parameters for the field mapping series were: TR = 793 ms; TE1 = 5.19 ms, and TE2 = 7.65 ms; flip angle = 60; FOV = 211 mm. Thirty-five slices were acquired with a voxel size of 3.3 mm × 3.3 mm × 3.5 mm. EPI parameters for the two functional tasks were: TR = 2000 ms; TE = 25 ms; flip angle = 78°; FOV = 211mm. Thirty-five slices were acquired with a voxel size of 3.3 mm × 3.3 mm × 3.5 mm.

Preprocessing

Data were analyzed with Statistical Parametric Mapping software (SPM8, University College London, London, UK; http://www.fil.ion.ucl.ac.uk/spm/sofware/spm8). Slice timing correction of reconstructed images was performed after removing the first five time points from each functional run. Field maps were unwarped with the EPI time series and time series were realigned for motion and field distortion correction. T1-weighted structural images were co-registered to the EPI images, and then bias corrected and segmented using MNI template tissue probability maps. EPI images were then co-registered to the normalized segmented anatomical images. Finally, time series data were smoothed with a 6 mm full-width half maximum Gaussian kernel.

First-level statistical models

For each subject, first-level general linear models were applied to localizer data and data from the NE task. For the localizer data, boxcar stimulus functions were convolved with the canonical hemodynamic response function (HDR). Our goal was to compare regions correlated trial by trial with Mviv ratings with previously patterns of parametric modulation by emotionally enhanced perceptual vividness. We thus examined parametric modulation of the BOLD response by both perceptual and mnemonic vividness ratings for each trial across all stimulus categories (positive, negative, and neutral). For the experimental data, a delta function regressor was modeled for image onset and convolved with the canonical HRF for each trial in each analysis. For each subject, we created a first-level statistical parametric model (SPM). To capture variance due to low-level features of the images which could influence our results, we first entered four separate regressors modeling scene complexity, hue, contrast, and mean visual saliency (a measure of a combination of features that allow a part of an image to stand out from its surround) (Itti and Koch, 2001). We next entered a regressor for Mviv to interrogate regions parametrically modulated by mnemonic vividness. An additional regressor was added for perceptual vividness, or inverse NE (NE^{-1}) (for details, see Todd et al., 2012) to further interrogate effects of Mviv relative to NE^{-1}. Full results of group level analysis reported below can be found in **Tables 1** and **2**.

Second-level statistical models

For the localizer task, T contrast files for each condition (object drawings, scrambled objects, places, and faces) from each individual were entered into a one-way ANOVA, with condition as the single factor. Contrasts for (objects > scrambled objects) were used to specify category-selective activation in the LOC. An additional contrast was used to specify place-sensitive regions of parahippocampal cortex (houses > faces). Functionally defined masks were created using 10 mm spheres around maxima activations in the group maps (51, −76, 1 and −45, −79, 1) thresholded at $p < 0.05$ (FWE). Anatomical masks for right and left amygdala and right and left hippocampus were created from automated anatomical labeling (AAL) (Tzourio-Mazoyer et al., 2002) templates based on a spatially normalized high-resolution T1 single-subject data set using the MarsBaR toolbox (Brett et al., 2002). Together, these ROIs were used for small volume correction for the NE task.

To orthogonalize their comparison, contrast files for Mviv and NE^{-1} from a single first-level model were used. To enable contrasts between activation enhanced by each parametric modulator, contrast files were entered into a one-way repeated measures ANOVA (independence not assumed) at the group level. Initial SPMs were thresholded at a height threshold of $p < 0.005$, uncorrected, with a cluster extent threshold of 10 voxels (for rationale, see Lieberman and Cunningham, 2009). Primary results for hypothesized regions were corrected for family-wise error. Functionally and anatomically defined ROIs were used as masks for small volume correction based on *a priori* hypotheses. Voxels surviving a family-wise error corrected $p < 0.05$ were deemed statistically significant.

Table 1 | Regions parametrically modulated by Mviv > Pviv.

Brain region	*x*	*y*	*z*	Voxels	*t*	*p*
L lingual-parahippocampal gyrus-hippocampus/BA 37	−27	−52	−5	70	5.01	<0.001
R inf orbital gyrus/BA 47	30	29	−20	16	3.87	<0.001
L middle occipital gyrus/BA 18–19	−30	−91	19	43	3.79	<0.001
R fusiform-parahippocampal gyrus/BA 37	30	−40	11	23	3.46	0.001

Table 2 | Regions parametrically modulated by Pviv > Mviv.

Brain region	*x*	*y*	*z*	Voxels	*t*	*p*
L insula/BA 48	−36	−19	22	37	4.74	<0.001
L sup temporal gyrus/BA 48	−51	−13	−2	143	4.47	<0.001
R sup temporal gyrus-Heschl gyrus/BA 48	51	−22	1	35	3.29	0.001
R sup temporal pole/BA 38	54	8	−11	13	2.87	0.002

xyz = MNI coordinates. Cluster size as thresholded at p < 0.005, uncorrected.

RESULTS

BEHAVIORAL RESULTS

Noise estimation task

A two factor repeated measures ANOVA was performed on NE with standard noise (3) and emotion (3) as factors. Results showed a main effect of standard noise, $F(2, 28) = 28.42$, $p < 0.001$. A significant linear contrast, $F(1, 14) = 32.01$, $p < 0.001$, revealed noise ratings of the images to be relatively lower relative to the standard as standard noise levels got higher, again indicating that participants were accurate at gaging relative noise even when noise level was manipulated in the standard. There was also a main effect of emotion, $F(2, 28) = 10.32$, $p < 0.001$, with arousing images rated as less noisy – or more perceptually vivid – than neutral images, $F(1, 14) = 12.50$, $p = 0.003$. A modest standard noise × emotion interaction, $F(4, 56) = 4.26$, $p < 0.05$, revealed differences between positive and neutral images to be greater at the two lower levels of standard noise. Contrasts revealed that, as in previous studies both positive and negative images were rated as less noisy, or more vivid, than neutral images, $ps < 0.05$; unlike in previous studies, negative images were also rated as more vivid than positive images, $p < 0.05$.

Memory

A one-way ANOVA was performed on Mviv scores with emotion as a repeated measure. There was a main effect of emotion category, $F(2, 28) = 9.33$, $p = 0.001$. Contrasts revealed that negative images were remembered more vividly than neutral or positive images, $F(1, 14) = 20.82$, $p = 0.001$. There was no effect of emotion category on memory accuracy.

fMRI RESULTS

Perceptual and mnemonic vividness

As previously reported, higher levels of NE^{-1} were associated with more activation in the left amygdala ($xyz = -24, -4, -20$) and left LOC ($xyz = -51, -76, -2$). Regions where greater activation was associated with higher levels of Mviv similarly included the left amygdala ($-21, -4, -17$; $t_{1,28} = 3.21$, FWE $p = 0.02$, svc) and left LOC ($-39, -79, -5$; $t_{1,28} = 3.23$, FWE $p = 0.04$, svc). To more closely examine the relation between regions modulated by memory and perceptual vividness, the contrast for Mviv was masked inclusively by activation for NE^{-1}at a threshold of $p = 0.005$, uncorrected. All voxels activated by memory in the left amygdala and LOC fell within regions that were activated by perceptual vividness. As **Figures 2D,E** demonstrates, Mviv shows a highly similar pattern of activation to NE^{-1} in the left amygdala and left LOC. These voxels were also activated significantly in both conditions when analyzed separately.

To reveal regions uniquely recruited by Mviv, comparisons between Mviv and NE^{-1} revealed that a region of left hippocampus ($-30, -37, -8$; $t_{1,28} = 3.36$, FWE $p = 0.05$, svc) and a place-sensitive region of left parahippocampal gyrus ($-27, -52, -5$; $t_{1,14} = 5.33$, FWE $p = 0.05$, svc) were activated more for Mviv than

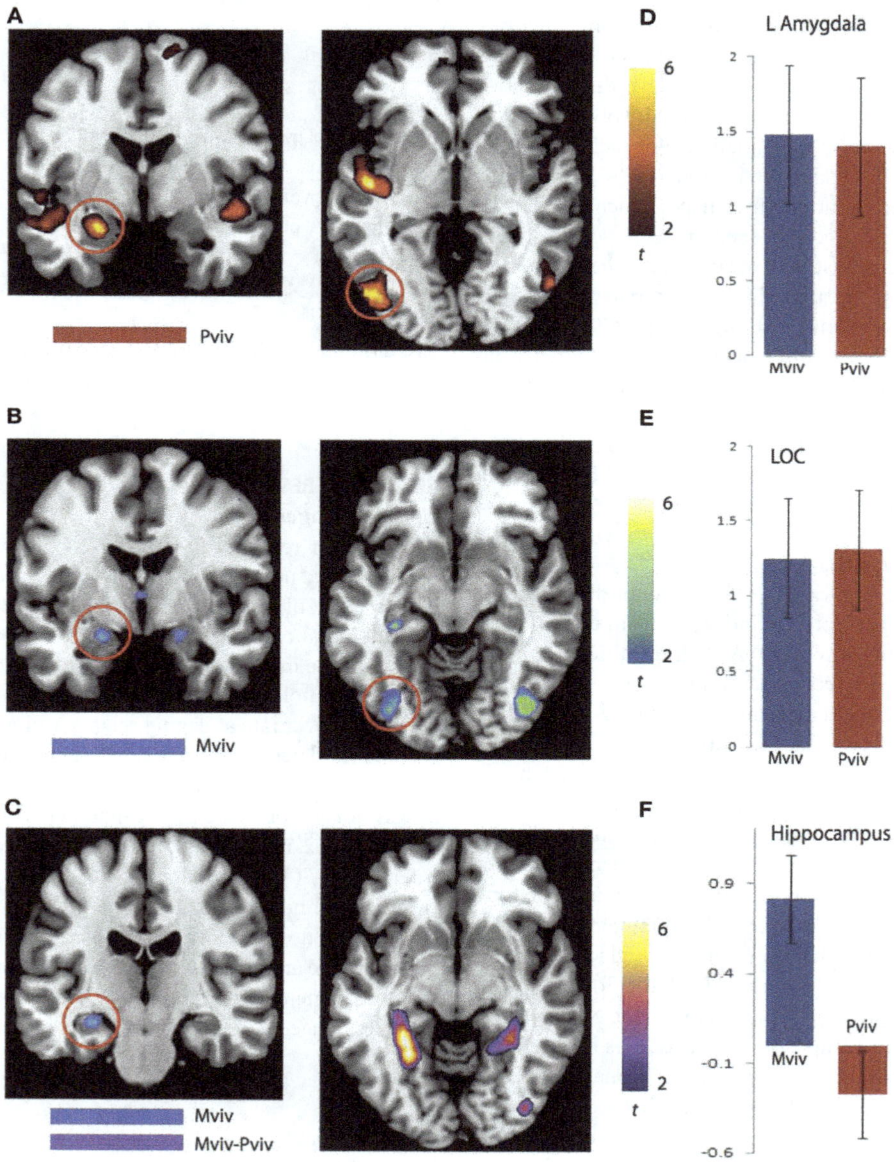

FIGURE 2 | BOLD correlates of perceptual and memory vividness. **(A)** Activation maps for regions parametrically modulated by perceptual vividness. **(B)** Activation maps for regions parametrically modulated by memory vividness. **(C)** Activation maps showing hippocampal region activated by Mviv and regions activated by the contrast Mviv > Pviv. **(D)** Contrast estimates for Pviv and Mviv for left amygdala. **(E)** Contrast estimates for Pviv and Mviv for left LOC. **(F)** Contrast estimates for Mviv and Pviv for left hippocampal region activated by Mviv.

NE^{-1} (**Figure 2**). Thus, consistent with our previously reported behavioral evidence of partial independence between EEV and Mviv, only a subset of regions activated by Mviv also reflected EEV.

DISCUSSION

Our results showed that, after controlling for differences between scenes in low-level objective features, amygdala and visual cortex regions that were sensitive to EEV were also modulated by ratings of subsequent Mviv. In contrast, hippocampus activation uniquely predicted Mviv. These findings suggest shared neural substrates for the influence of emotional salience on perceptual and mnemonic vividness, with amygdala and visual cortex regions associated with EEV at encoding contributing to the experience of emotionally enhanced memory.

Emotionally salient images (both positive and negative) are more likely to be remembered than neutral images (Ochsner, 2000). In particular, emotionally salient images have been linked to greater memory for the central, emotionally salient, or goal-relevant elements of a scene (Kensinger et al., 2007a; Levine and Edelstein, 2009). Such findings have been associated with greater amygdala activation (Hamann et al., 1999; Canli et al., 2000; Kensinger et al., 2007b) as well as high-order visual cortex activation at encoding (Kensinger et al., 2007b; Talmi et al., 2008), and suggest that perceptual processing of emotionally important events may be related to heightened memory (Kensinger et al., 2007b). Here we provide novel evidence for a direct mapping between emotion-enhanced perceptual vividness and mnemonic vividness.

Yet this finding is in contrast to a levels of processing framework (Craik and Lockhart, 1972), where it is categorization at a deeper conceptual level rather than shallower perceptual level that yields enhanced memory. Rather, our data suggest that emotional salience is associated with a unique behavioral and neural expression of memory. High levels of emotional salience, as tagged by the amygdala, may heighten the binding between objects, their meaning, and emotional significance (Nashiro and Mather, 2011), yielding a unique subjective vividness to both perception and memory.

In previous studies we found no differences between noise estimation ratings for positive and negative images (Todd et al., 2012). In the present study, although both positive and negative images were rated as less noisy than neutral images, negative images were further rated as less noisy, or more perceptually vivid, than positive images. This pattern of stronger results for negative stimuli extended to the memory findings in which negative images were more vividly remembered 1 week later than positive or negative images. Because of our parametric analysis across all trial types, we cannot report the extent to which image valence may have contributed to the pattern of results found here. Previous studies looking at emotionally enhanced memory have found amygdala activation at encoding to be associated with subsequent memory for both negative and positive stimuli (Hamann, 2001).

As previously reported, amygdala activation accounted statistically for the relation between LOC activation and EEV at the time of encoding (Todd et al., 2012). Although it is not possible to infer directionality from a mediation analysis, one hypothesis is that the enhanced visual cortex activation associated with EEV is amygdala-driven, and that a similar modulation of visual cortex by the amygdala produces subsequent Mviv. This hypothesis is consistent with a body of non-human animal research finding that emotional memory is characterized by arousal-enhanced noradrenergic activity in the basolateral amygdala, which in turn modulates activation in other brain regions implicated in memory consolidation, including the hippocampus and sensory cortices (Cahill and McGaugh, 1998; McGaugh et al., 2002; Roozendaal and McGaugh, 2011). Yet other human studies looking at emotionally enhanced perceptual activations under attentionally impoverished conditions have found a slightly different pattern of findings, with prefrontal mediation of the relation between the amygdala and visual cortex (Lim et al., 2009). Future research can use such approaches as dynamic causal modeling to investigate the directionality of amygdala influences on perceptual and mnemonic vividness.

It is important to highlight that our previously reported behavioral findings suggested that enhanced perceptual vividness contributes to, but does not entirely account for, the heightened salience of emotional memories (Todd et al., 2012). This is consistent with the current finding that the hippocampal and parahippocampal regions specifically implicated in memory formation and its emotional enhancement (Kensinger et al., 2007b; Talmi et al., 2007; Murty et al., 2010) were modulated by mnemonic – but not perceptual – vividness. Research in non-human animals (McGaugh et al., 2002) and humans (Cahill and Alkire, 2003; Anderson et al., 2006a) also indicates that arousal induced *after* encoding influences memory consolidation to alter memory retention, which by definition cannot be explained by vivid perceptual encoding. Phasic arousal related to perceptual vividness may interact with more tonic arousal extending beyond initial encoding to alter memory consolidation (Cahill and Alkire, 2003), mutually enhancing later memory. Thus, the influence of affective salience at encoding likely occurs at multiple timescales, which combine to endow emotional experiences and their associated memories with a uniquely vivid subjective character. Future research can delineate how individual differences in effects of arousal on perceptual vividness and post-encoding processes may be linked to normative differences in capacity for emotional memory as well as the prevalence of intrusively vivid memories following trauma (Nashiro and Mather, 2011; Todd et al., 2011).

REFERENCES

Anderson, A. K. (2005). Affective influences on the attentional dynamics supporting awareness. *J. Exp. Psychol. Gen.* 134, 258–281.

Anderson, A. K., Christoff, K., Panitz, D., De Rosa, E., and Gabrieli, J. D. (2003). Neural correlates of the automatic processing of threat facial signals. *J. Neurosci.* 23, 5627–5633.

Anderson, A. K., and Phelps, E. A. (2001). Lesions of the human amygdala impair enhanced perception of emotionally salient events. *Nature* 411, 305–309.

Anderson, A. K., Wais, P. E., and Gabrieli, J. D. (2006a). Emotion enhances remembrance of neutral events past. *Proc. Natl. Acad. Sci. U.S.A.* 103, 1599–1604.

Anderson, A. K., Yamaguchi, Y., Grabski, W., and Lacka, D. (2006b). Emotional memories are not all created equal: evidence for selective memory enhancement. *Learn. Mem.* 13, 711–718.

Bradley, M. M., Sabatinelli, D., Lang, P. J., Fitzsimmons, J. R., King, W., and Desai, P. (2003). Activation of the visual cortex in motivated attention. *Behav. Neurosci.* 117, 369–380.

Brett, M., Anton, J.-L., Valabregue, R., and Poiine, J.-B. (2002). Region of interest analysis using an SPM toolbox [abstract]. *Paper presented at the 8th International Conference on Functional Mapping of the Human Brain*, Sendai.

Brown, R., and Kulik, S. (1977). Flashbulb memory. *Cognition* 5, 73–99.

Cahill, L., and Alkire, M. T. (2003). Epinephrine enhancement of human memory consolidation: interaction with arousal at encoding. *Neurobiol. Learn. Mem.* 79, 194–198.

Cahill, L., and McGaugh, J. L. (1998). Mechanisms of emotional arousal and lasting declarative memory. *Trends Neurosci.* 21, 294–299.

Canli, T., Zhao, Z., Brewer, J., Gabrieli, J. D., and Cahill, L. (2000). Event-related activation in the human amygdala associates with later memory for individual emotional experience. *J. Neurosci.* 20, RC99.

Craik, F. I., and Lockhart, R. S. (1972). Levels of processing: a framework for memory research. *J. Verbal Learning Verbal Behav.* 11, 671–684.

De Martino, B., Kalisch, R., Rees, G., and Dolan, R. J. (2009). Enhanced processing of threat stimuli under limited attentional resources. *Cereb. Cortex* 19, 127–133.

Eldridge, L. L., Engel, S. A., Zeineh, M. M., Bookheimer, S. Y., and Knowlton, B. J. (2005). A dissociation of encoding and retrieval processes in the human hippocampus. *J. Neurosci.* 25, 3280–3286.

Hamann, S. (2001). Cognitive and neural mechanisms of emotional memory. *Trends Cogn. Sci. (Regul. Ed.)* 5, 394–400.

Hamann, S. B., Ely, T. D., Grafton, S. T., and Kilts, C. D. (1999). Amygdala activity related to enhanced memory for pleasant and aversive stimuli. *Nat. Neurosci.* 2, 289–293.

Itti, L., and Koch, C. (2001). Computational modelling of visual attention. *Nat. Rev. Neurosci.* 2, 194–203.

Kensinger, E. A., Addis, D. R., and Atapattu, R. K. (2011). Amygdala activity at encoding corresponds with memory vividness and with memory for select episodic details. *Neuropsychologia* 49, 663–673.

Kensinger, E. A., Garoff-Eaton, R. J., and Schacter, D. L. (2007a). Effects of emotion on memory specificity: memory trade-offs elicited by negative visually arousing stimuli. *J. Mem. Lang.* 56, 575–591.

Kensinger, E. A., Garoff-Eaton, R. J., and Schacter, D. L. (2007b). How negative emotion enhances the visual specificity of a memory. *J. Cogn. Neurosci.* 19, 1872–1887.

Lang, P. J., Bradley, M. M., Fitzsimmons, J. R., Cuthbert, B. N., Scott, J. D., Moulder, B., et al. (1998). Emotional arousal and activation of the visual cortex: an fMRI analysis. *Psychophysiology* 35, 199–210.

Lepage, M., Habib, R., and Tulving, E. (1998). Hippocampal PET activations of memory encoding and retrieval: the HIPER model. *Hippocampus* 8, 313–322. [Meta-Analysis Research Support, Non-U.S. Gov't].

Levine, L. J., and Edelstein, R. S. (2009). Emotion and memory narrowing: a review and goal relevance approach. *Cogn. Emot.* 23, 833–875.

Lieberman, M. D., and Cunningham, W. A. (2009). Type I and Type II error concerns in fMRI research: rebalancing the scale. *Soc. Cogn. Affect. Neurosci.* 4, 423–428.

Lim, S. L., Padmala, S., and Pessoa, L. (2009). Segregating the significant from the mundane on a moment-to-moment basis via direct and indirect amygdala contributions. *Proc. Natl. Acad. Sci. U.S.A.* 106, 16841–16846.

McGaugh, J. L., McIntyre, C. K., and Power, A. E. (2002). Amygdala modulation of memory consolidation: interaction with other brain systems. *Neurobiol. Learn. Mem.* 78, 539–552.

Murty, V. P., Ritchey, M., Adcock, R. A., and LaBar, K. S. (2010). fMRI studies of successful emotional memory encoding: a quantitative meta-analysis. *Neuropsychologia* 48, 3459–3469.

Nashiro, K., and Mather, M. (2011). How arousal affects younger and older adults' memory binding. *Exp. Aging Res.* 37, 108–128.

Nielsen, S. L., and Sarason, I. G. (1981). Emotion, personality, and selective attention. *J. Pers. Soc. Psychol.* 41, 945–960.

Ochsner, K. N. (2000). Are affective events richly recollected or simply familiar? The experience and process of recognizing feelings past. *J. Exp. Psychol. Gen.* 129, 242–261.

Padmala, S., and Pessoa, L. (2008). Affective learning enhances visual detection and responses in primary visual cortex. *J. Neurosci.* 28, 6202–6210.

Pessoa, L., Kastner, S., and Ungerleider, L. G. (2002). Attentional control of the processing of neural and emotional stimuli. *Brain Res. Cogn. Brain Res.* 15, 31–45.

Roozendaal, B., and McGaugh, J. L. (2011). Memory modulation. *Behav. Neurosci.* 125, 797–824.

Sabatinelli, D., Bradley, M. M., Fitzsimmons, J. R., and Lang, P. J. (2005). Parallel amygdala and inferotemporal activation reflect emotional intensity and fear relevance. *Neuroimage* 24, 1265–1270.

Sharot, T., Delgado, M. R., and Phelps, E. A. (2004). How emotion enhances the feeling of remembering. *Nat. Neurosci.* 7, 1376–1380.

Sharot, T., Martorella, E. A., Delgado, M. R., and Phelps, E. A. (2007). How personal experience modulates the neural circuitry of memories of September 11. *Proc. Natl. Acad. Sci. U.S.A.* 104, 389–394.

Soares, J. J., and Ohman, A. (1993). Backward masking and skin conductance responses after conditioning to nonfeared but fear-relevant stimuli in fearful subjects. *Psychophysiology* 30, 460–466.

Stevens, S. S. (1957). On the psychophysical law. *Psychol. Rev.* 64, 153–181.

Talmi, D., Anderson, A. K., Riggs, L., Caplan, J. B., and Moscovitch, M. (2008). Immediate memory consequences of the effect of emotion on attention to pictures. *Learn. Mem.* 15, 172–182.

Talmi, D., Schimmack, U., Paterson, T., and Moscovitch, M. (2007). The role of attention and relatedness in emotionally enhanced memory. *Emotion* 7, 89–102.

Todd, R. M., Palombo, D. J., Levine, B., and Anderson, A. K. (2011). Genetic differences in emotionally enhanced memory. *Neuropsychologia* 49, 734–744.

Todd, R. M., Talmi, D., Schmitz, T. W., Susskind, J., and Anderson, A. K. (2012). Psychophysical and neural evidence for emotion-enhanced perceptual vividness. *J. Neurosci.* 32, 11201–11212.

Tzourio-Mazoyer, N., Landeau, B., Papathanassiou, D., Crivello, F., Etard, O., Delcroix, N., et al. (2002). Automated anatomical labeling of activations in SPM using a macroscopic anatomical parcellation of the MNI MRI single-subject brain. *Neuroimage* 15, 273–289.

Vuilleumier, P., Richardson, M. P., Armony, J. L., Driver, J., and Dolan, R. J. (2004). Distant influences of amygdala lesion on visual cortical activation during emotional face processing. *Nat. Neurosci.* 7, 1271–1278.

14

Retrieval of recent autobiographical memories is associated with slow-wave sleep in early AD

Géraldine Rauchs[1,2,3,4] *, Pascale Piolino[5,6], Françoise Bertran[1,2,3,4,7], Vincent de La Sayette[1,2,3,8], Fausto Viader[1,2,3,8], Francis Eustache[1,2,3,4] and Béatrice Desgranges[1,2,3,4]

[1] U1077, INSERM, Caen, France
[2] UMR-S1077, Université de Caen Basse-Normandie, Caen, France
[3] UMR-S1077, Ecole Pratique des Hautes Etudes, Caen, France
[4] U1077, Centre Hospitalier Universitaire, Caen, France
[5] Laboratoire Mémoire et Cognition, Institut de Psychologie, Université Paris Descartes, Paris, France
[6] Centre de Psychiatrie et Neurosciences, INSERM UMR S894, Paris, France
[7] Service des Explorations Fonctionnelles Neurologiques, Centre Hospitalier Universitaire, Caen, France
[8] Service de Neurologie, Centre Hospitalier Universitaire, Caen, France

***Correspondence:**
Géraldine Rauchs, Unité de Recherche U1077, INSERM-EPHE-Université de Caen Basse-Normandie, GIP Cyceron, Bd Henri Becquerel, BP 5229, 14074 CAEN Cedex 5, France
e-mail: geraldine.rauchs@inserm.fr

Autobiographical memory is commonly impaired in Alzheimer's disease (AD). However, little is known about the very recent past which is though highly important in daily life adaptation. In addition, the impact of sleep disturbances, also frequently reported in AD, on the consolidation, and retrieval of autobiographical memories remains to be assessed. Using an adaptation of the TEMPau task, we investigated the neural substrates of autobiographical memory for recent events and the potential relationship with sleep in 14 patients with mild AD. On day 1, autobiographical memory was explored across three periods: remote (18–30 years), the last 2 years and the last month. After testing, sleep was recorded using polysomnography. The next day, AD patients benefited a resting-state ^{18}FDG-PET scan and a second exploration of autobiographical memory, focusing on the very recent past (today and yesterday). Total recall and episodic recall scores were obtained. In addition, for all events recalled, Remember responses justified by specific factual, spatial, and temporal details were measured using the Remember/Know paradigm. Retrieval of autobiographical memories was impaired in AD, but recall of young adulthood and very recent events was relatively better compared to the two intermediate periods. Recall of recent events (experienced the day and the day preceding the assessment) was correlated with brain glucose consumption in the precuneus and retrosplenial cortex, the calcarine region, the angular gyrus, and lateral temporal areas. AD patients also provided more Justified Remember responses for events experienced the previous-day than for those experienced the day of the assessment. Moreover, Justified Remember responses obtained for events experienced before sleep were positively correlated with the amount of slow-wave sleep. These data provide the first evidence of an association between the ability to retrieve recent autobiographical memories and sleep in mild AD patients.

Keywords: Alzheimer's disease, sleep, autobiographical memory, memory consolidation, PET

INTRODUCTION

Autobiographical memory is a multifaceted concept which concerns information and experiences of one's personal life and gives a sense of self-continuity (Piolino et al., 2009). Based on the observation of the amnesic patient KC, Tulving et al. (1988) proposed to distinguish within autobiographical memory an episodic component (altered in KC), containing personal specific events, situated in time and space (*'the day I had this car accident'*), and a semantic component, termed personal semantic memory (preserved in KC), storing general knowledge about our past such as the names of colleagues, generic events (*'summer holidays at Sainte Marine'*), and self-concepts. Autobiographical memory is subserved by a core neural network, mainly left-sided, including the medial and ventrolateral prefrontal cortex, medial, and lateral temporal areas, the retrosplenial/posterior cingulate cortex, the temporoparietal junction, and the cerebellum (Maguire, 2001; Conway et al., 2002; Svoboda et al., 2006; Cabeza and St Jacques, 2007; Martinelli et al., 2013a).

In the present study, we were interested in the assessment of recent episodic autobiographical memories and in the brain areas supporting their retrieval. We also investigated the impact of sleep on memory recall.

Numerous studies documented a general impairment of autobiographical memory in Alzheimer's disease (AD) (Kopelman et al., 1989; Greene and Hodges, 1996; Addis and Tippett, 2004; Ivanoiu et al., 2004; Irish et al., 2011). Most of them showed a temporally graded retrograde amnesia, with memories from the young adulthood period being better preserved than recent ones (a phenomenon well-known as the "reminiscence bump," Rubin et al., 1986). By distinguishing both components of autobiographical memory, a dissociation emerged in AD. Thus, Piolino et al. (2003), using a semi-structured questionnaire (TEMPau) assessing the ability to recollect detailed specific events situated in time and space from different periods covering the entire lifespan (from childhood/teenage to the last 12 months), they showed that retrieval of strictly episodic autobiographical memories (i.e., unique, specific in time and space, and detailed) is impaired in AD patients whatever the time period. Patients also exhibited a deficit of autonoetic consciousness, defined as the feeling of re-experiencing or reliving the past and mentally traveling back in subjective time. Contrasting with this impairment of episodic autobiographical memories, Martinelli et al. (2013b) documented a preservation of personal semantic memory assessed by asking AD patients to recall generic events memory. However, other studies reported a temporally graded deficit of personal semantic memory, with a relative preservation of the most recent information (Kopelman et al., 1989; Addis and Tippett, 2004). Greene et al. (1995) reported a similar deficit whatever the time period explored while Ivanoiu et al. (2004) observed a deficit with only a modest temporal gradient.

Several authors tried to disclose the brain areas whose atrophy or dysfunction may explain the impairment of autobiographical memory in AD. Thus, Gilboa et al. (2005) reported that episodic autobiographical memory was associated with the volume of the medial temporal lobes and the anterior lateral temporal neocortex. Interestingly, this pattern of correlation was invariant whatever the remoteness of memories suggesting that the integrity of medial temporal lobes is crucial for the retrieval of episodic autobiographical memories regardless of their age. In contrast, deficits of personal semantics were related to the atrophy of anterior and posterior lateral temporal areas bilaterally, more pronounced on the left, as well as right frontal degeneration. More recently, Philippi et al. (2012) reported positive correlations between hippocampal volume and episodic autobiographical memory for both recent and remote periods of life. Using the TEMPau task exploring autobiographical memory from three time periods (the last 5 years, middle age, teenage/childhood) and resting-state FDG-PET imaging, Eustache et al. (2004) reported a temporal gradient of recalls in favor of remote past and that right hippocampal metabolism correlated uniquely with recent memories. In addition, retrieval of recent memories was preferentially associated with right prefrontal cortex metabolism whereas remote memories relied more upon left prefrontal areas. According to the HERA model (Tulving et al., 1994), the right prefrontal cortex is more involved in episodic memory retrieval and the left in semantic memory retrieval. In this respect, the results reported by Eustache et al. (2004) support the idea that many autobiographical memories become "semanticized" over time and that preserved remote memories in AD patients are predominantly semantic by nature, even if some remote episodic memories can persist in these patients. In an fMRI study, Meulenbroek et al. (2010) contrasted the patterns of brain activity during retrieval of episodic autobiographical memories and during the processing of semantic information. They reported evidence of compensatory activations, notably within frontal areas, when AD patients retrieved episodic autobiographical memories. These compensatory activations in areas known to be involved in semantic processing, suggest that autobiographical memory would undergo an exaggerated shift from an episodic to a semantic content in AD.

Another aim of our study was to investigate the impact of sleep on the recall of autobiographical memories. Even if consolidation of freshly acquired memory traces can last months or years, it is well established that this process preferentially occurs during sleep and that the first post-learning night is crucial (Born et al., 2006). This has been demonstrated across a wide range of tasks for both procedural and episodic memories (Rauchs et al., 2005; Diekelmann and Born, 2010). In our laboratory, we have shown that both slow-wave sleep and Rapid-Eye Movement (REM) sleep are necessary for the consolidation of rich, vivid episodic memories. In particular, REM sleep favors the consolidation of the encoding context associated to the items (Rauchs et al., 2004). In addition, several studies indicate that sleep-dependent consolidation of episodic memories may be altered in older adults (Harand et al., 2012 for review) and we also reported correlations between sleep parameters and episodic memory performance in mild AD patients (Rauchs et al., 2008; Hot et al., 2011). Retention of recent personal episodic memories (e.g., memories of a recent conversation with a relative) was probed after sleep or an equivalent period of wakefulness in older adults (Aly and Moscovitch, 2010), but this issue has never been addressed in AD patients.

To sum up, episodic autobiographical memory is impaired in AD, even in the early stages of the disease (Murphy et al., 2008; Leyhe et al., 2009; Irish et al., 2010, 2011; Bastin et al., 2012). This deficit is mainly subserved by the dysfunction or degeneration of medial temporal areas. In most of the studies aforementioned, the exploration of the recent past was conducted on a period generally lasting about 1–5 years, completely neglecting the very recent past. In the present study, we explored episodic autobiographical memories experienced the day and the day preceding the assessment as well as memories dating back 2 years ago and the young adulthood period. The originality of this study also relies on the fact that our experimental design allowed us to control the events participants experienced and recalled, as they were present, most of the time, in the laboratory. A first aim of this study was therefore to precise, using resting-state ^{18}FDG-PET, the neural substrates of retrieval of recent autobiographical memories. We also aimed at investigating the impact of sleep on the recall of autobiographical memories, and expected to find significant correlations between indices of sleep quality and/or quantity (such as time spent in slow-wave sleep or REM sleep) and episodic autobiographical memories.

MATERIALS AND METHODS

PARTICIPANTS

Fourteen unmedicated, newly diagnosed AD patients (eight women, six men; mean age ± SD: 77.1 ± 4.1 years) with a MMSE score (Folstein et al., 1975) of 21 or higher (mean ± SD: 24.9 ± 2) participated in this study. Some data of most of these patients were previously published in two other studies (Rauchs et al., 2008; Hot et al., 2011). They were all recruited through a memory clinic, and all complained of memory impairment. They were selected on the basis of a neurological examination and a neuropsychological assessment, using the National Institute of Neurological and

Communicative Disorders and Stroke and the AD and Related Disorders Association criteria for probable AD (McKhann et al., 1984). At the time of the study, none of the patients was being or had been treated with specific medication, such as antiacetylcholinesterase agents. None of them suffered from sleep disorders such as periodic limb movement disorder or sleep apnea, confirmed by polysomnography.

Autobiographical memory scores of AD patients were compared to those obtained in a group of 14 age-matched healthy controls (9 women, 5 men; mean age ± SD: 75.1 ± 4.6 years) recruited in clubs for retired people. They had no neurological or psychiatric disorders. The mean score (±SD) for the MMSE was 29.4 (±0.9). These subjects were also paired according to their level of education with AD patients.

All subjects were right-handed, native French speakers and gave their written consent to the study after detailed information was provided to them and to a member of their family. The study was done in-line with the Declaration of Helsinki following approval by the Regional Ethics Committee.

GENERAL PROCEDURE

The general procedure is illustrated in **Figure 1**. Autobiographical memory for the very recent past (events experienced the day and the day preceding the assessment) was explored and compared to three other periods covering the young adulthood to the last month. On the first day, participants came to the hospital for a sleep recording. Before placement of electrodes, they performed the first part of the autobiographical memory (TEMPau) task assessing the three remote periods. Sleep was then recorded using standard polysomnography. The next morning, AD patients benefited an ^{18}FDG-PET scan to measure brain glucose consumption at the resting-state. In the evening, the second part of the TEMPau task, assessing the very recent past, was proposed to patients and controls together with other episodic memory tasks not described here but whose results have been published elsewhere (Rauchs et al., 2007, 2008; Hot et al., 2011).

MEMORY TESTING

We used an adaptation of the autobiographical memory task "TEMPau" developed by Piolino et al. (2003, 2009). This task, consisting of a semi-structured questionnaire, assesses the ability to recall detailed specific events situated in time and space from four time periods [P1: young adulthood (18–30 years), P2: the last 2 years (except the last month), P3: the last month, and P4: today and yesterday] as well as the subjective states of consciousness associated with those memories (Tulving, 1985, 2002).

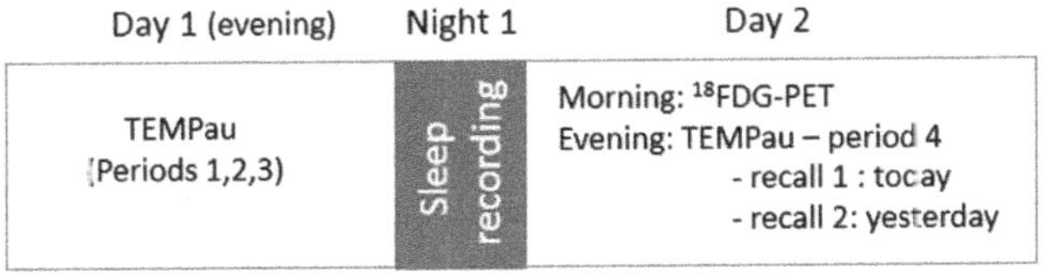

FIGURE 1 | Experimental design. Period 1: young adulthood (18–30 years), period 2: last 2 years (except the last month), period 3: last month, period 4: today and yesterday. Note that only AD patients benefited the PET examination.

For the most recent period (P4), participants had to recall what they did yesterday and today. More precisely, they were invited to relate a particular moment in the day, giving details about the chronology of the event, the place where it occurred and the people that were present.

For the three other periods, participants were invited to recall two personal events corresponding to two topics: (i) a meeting or an event associated to a person and (ii) a trip or journey. For each period, participants were invited to give details of a particular event. If a participant could not spontaneously recollect a specific event, cues were provided (for example, "on a day with a teacher or friend"), while he or she was encouraged to be specific if the memory was generic (e.g., "do you remember a particular day during this summer?"). After three cueing and/or encouragement attempts, the experimenter switched to the following topic or period.

Immediately after each recall, the participants were asked to indicate the subjective state of consciousness associated with the recall of *what* happened (i.e., the factual content), *where* (the place), and *when* (the moment). They were instructed to give a Remember, Know, or Guess response (Mäntylä, 1993) according to whether each of these three aspects of the recalled event was associated with conscious recollection, simply knowing, or guessing, respectively. A Remember response is defined as the ability to mentally relive specific aspects such as perceptions, thoughts, or feelings that occurred or were experienced at the time of the event. The participants were asked to give details aloud to ensure that they were using Remember responses properly. A Know response reflects simply knowing what happened, where and when, but this knowledge is not accompanied by any conscious recollection. A Guess response corresponds to aspects of the event that were neither consciously recollected nor simply known.

For the first three periods (P1, P2, and P3), the control of the veracity of the events recalled was made with the spouse/husband or a relative. For P4, we could perform a more stringent control of the events recalled by participants as they were present, most of the time, in the laboratory.

Each recalled event was scored on a four-point episodic scale based on that used by Baddeley and Wilson (1986). This scale takes into account the specificity of the memory (single or repeated event), the time, and spatial location, and the presence of details (perceptions, thoughts, or feelings). A specific event detailed and situated in time and space was given a score of 4 points. A specific event without any detail but located in time and space scored 3 points. A repeated or extended event scored 2 points or 1, depending on whether or not it was situated in time and space. Absence of memory or general information about the topic scored 0. The critical factor that allowed us differentiating specific events (scores 3 points) from a specific, detailed event (scored 4) was the failure, despite much encouragement, to add details concerning the source of acquisition. Recalled events scored 2 or 1 referred rather to personal semantic memory.

Two independent experts (GR and PP) rated each memory recalled and any difference of opinion between them was discussed until a consensus was reached. Two main scores were calculated for each period: (i) an overall autobiographical memory score, named hereafter "total recall score," taking into account all types of recall, both specific and generic (maximum = 8 points for each period) and (ii) a strictly episodic recall referring to the recall of a specific memory, situated in time and space and with phenomenological details (perceptions, emotions, thoughts, mental images, ...; maximum = 8 points for each period).

In addition, we also calculated a Remember score (*R*, maximum = 6 for each period) for the total number of *R* responses provided, irrespective of the kind of information (what, where, when) of each period and (iii) a justified Remember score (justified *R*, maximum = 6 for each period) for the number of *R* responses effectively associated with the recollection of a single event, with contextual details (thoughts, feelings, or perceptions for content, location for place, and time of day or temporal sequence for date).

SLEEP RECORDING

For all subjects, sleep was recorded in the sleep laboratory using a Nicolet Acquisition System, including continuous recordings of EEG, electro-oculogram, electro-myogram recorded at the chin, and electrocardiogram. EEG activity was recorded from right and left central (C3/C4), temporal (T3/T4), and occipital (O1/O2) derivations of the extended 10–20 international system (Nuwer et al., 1999), using Ag/AgCl electrodes with a vertex ground and a right ear reference. The impedance for all electrode sites was kept below 10 kΩ. The EEG filter band pass was 0.03–35 Hz and was digitized at 125 Hz.

Three additional electrodes were placed at the outer canthus and supraorbitally to the right eye with a bipolar recording for electro-oculogram activity. Sleep recordings were scored by an experienced physician (FB) according to standard criteria (Iber et al., 2007). Total sleep time, sleep onset latency, sleep efficiency, and the time and percentage of time spent in each sleep stage were determined.

PET METHODOLOGY

In the morning of day 2, all the patients underwent a resting PET examination using [^{18}F] Fluoro-2-deoxy-D-glucose (^{18}F-FDG). Data were collected using the high-resolution PET device ECAT Exact HR+ with isotropic resolution of 4.6 mm × 4.2 mm × 4.2 mm (field of view = 158 mm). The patients were fasted for at least 4 h before scanning. The head was positioned on a headrest according to the cantho-meatal line and gently restrained with straps. ^{18}F-FDG uptake was measured in the resting condition, with eyes closed, in a quiet and dark environment. A catheter was introduced in a vein of the arm for radiotracer administration. Following ^{68}Ga transmission scans, 3–5 mCi of ^{18}F-FDG were injected as a bolus at time 0, and a 10-min PET data acquisition period was begun at 50 min post-injection. Sixty-three planes were acquired with septa out (volume acquisition), using a voxel size of 2.2 mm × 2.2 mm × 2.43 mm (*x*, *y*, *z*). During PET data acquisition, head motion was monitored continuously with laser beams.

Preprocessing of FDG-PET data included (1) voxel-wise correction for partial volume effects (PVE) using the corresponding structural T1 MRI with the PMOD software (PMOD Technologies Ltd., Adliswil, Switzerland), (2) coregistration onto corresponding T1 MRI and spatial normalization to the MNI space using the parameters estimated from the corresponding T1-weighted MRI using the voxel-based morphometry 5.1 (VBM) toolbox (http://dbm.neuro.uni-jena.de) implemented in statistical parametric mapping 5 (SPM 5) software (Wellcome Trust Centre for Neuroimaging, London, UK), (3) quantitative scaling using the cerebellum gray matter as a reference to obtain standardized uptake value ratio (SUVr) images (cerebellum gray matter values were obtained for each participant using the cerebellum defined in the Automated Anatomical Labeling (AAL) atlas (Tzourio-Mazoyer et al., 2002), (4) smoothing with a 12-mm FWHM Gaussian kernel to blur individual variations in gyral anatomy and to increase signal-to-noise ratio, and (5) masking to exclude non-gray matter voxels. The resulting images were then used in the correlation analyses described below.

DATA ANALYSES

Analyses focused on the recent past (P4), the three other periods being used as control data for behavioral analyses. Memory scores obtained with the TEMPau task were analyzed using analyses of variance (ANOVA) with group (AD vs. controls) as between-subject factor and periods (P1, P2, P3, and P4) as within-subject factor. These analyses were followed by *post hoc* tests (HSD Tukey) when applicable. As the two memories of the most recent period (P4) were experienced on two different days, separated by a night during which sleep was recorded, we conducted similar analyses dividing the period P4 in two sub-periods: yesterday and today. These analyses will allow to determine whether sleep has a beneficial effect on consolidation of autobiographical in AD patients and older adults. In addition, we also looked for correlations between sleep parameters (such as the percentage of time spent in each sleep stage) measured during the night and the memory score for the event experienced the previous-day.

Then, we investigated the neural substrates of recent memories in AD patients. To do so, correlations between the total recall score obtained for period P4 and brain metabolism were searched using SPM and Pearson's correlation test. Only the positive correlations (i.e., in the neurobiologically expected direction) were assessed, using a statistical threshold (uncorrected for multiple tests) of $p < 0.001$ for the voxels, to limit the number of statistical tests and the attending risk of false positives.

RESULTS

AUTOBIOGRAPHICAL MEMORY SCORES

Here is an example of what an AD patient related for the "yesterday" sub-period, describing his arrival at the hospital, the exploration of the remote period during the TEMPau task and the preparation for the sleep recording: "*Monday, in the afternoon, I prepared my belongings and the papers you need. I ate alone. I came to this hospital in the evening with my daughter. We came by car and left the house at about 7:45 pm. I performed some tests with you and we discussed about my life when I was a young man. It lasted more than 30 minutes. Then, two nurses (a man and a woman) put electrodes on my head. During the night, I found that the bed was too high and I felt cold.*"

The total recall score for this event was 3 (as it was a specific event, located in time and space, but without sufficient details). Indeed, he could not recall any details about the specific spatial context (the places where the different examinations occurred, his position in the room . . .), giving only general information (name of the city and the hospital). Thus, while the patient provided three Remember responses, only *R* responses associated with factual and temporal were justified.

Figure 2 illustrates the results for the total recall score, the strictly episodic recall score, as well as for the number of *R* and justified *R* responses in AD patients and controls across the four time periods. An ANOVA with period (P1, P2, P3, and P4) as within-subject factor and group as between-subject factor, performed on the total recall score revealed a significant main effect of group [$F(1,25) = 31.5$, $p < 0.0001$] and time period [$F(3,75) = 10.8$, $p < 0.0001$]. The group by period interaction was not significant [$F(3,75) = 1.72, p > 0.17$]. To further investigate the effect of time period, *post hoc* comparisons (HSD Tukey) were conducted and revealed that memory scores in both groups were not different for P1 and P4 ($p > 0.97$) and higher to those obtained for P2 and P3 (all p values < 0.002), indicating the existence of a reminiscence bump (P1) and a recency effect (P4). Performance on P2 and P3 did not differ significantly ($p > 0.99$). As we hypothesized a relative preservation of the very recent past in AD, we further investigated the effect of group according to the period. Group differences were observed for P2, P3, P4 (all p values < 0.05), patients scoring lower than controls, but not for P1 ($p > 0.39$).

A similar analysis conducted on the strictly episodic recall score revealed similar main effects [group: $F(1,25) = 12.9$, $p < 0.001$; period: $F(3,75) = 4.99$, $p < 0.003$] but no group by period interaction [$F(3,75) = 1.7$, $p > 0.17$]. *Post hoc* comparisons revealed that, in the whole group of participants, scores for P1, P2, and P4 were not significantly different (all p values > 0.26) while scores for P3, corresponding to the last month, were significantly lower than those for P4 ($p < 0.006$) and P1 ($p < 0.02$). A group difference was only observed for P4 ($p < 0.05$).

An ANOVA conducted on the number of Remember responses provided during memory recall revealed significant main effects of group [$F(1,25) = 17.45$, $p < 0.001$] and time period [$F(3,75) = 5.75$, $p < 0.001$] as well as a significant interaction between both factors [$F(3,75) = 3.27$, $p = 0.026$]. The number of Remember responses was stable across periods (all p values > 0.94) in controls, while AD patients provided more Remember responses for P1 and P4 (without any difference between them) than for P2 and P3 (all p values < 0.006, no difference between P2 and P3). Only scores for the two intermediate periods (P2, P3) significantly differed between groups (all p values < 0.01).

Finally, concerning the number of Remember responses justified by phenomenological details, the ANOVA revealed significant main effects of group [$F(1,25) = 23.49$, $p < 0.001$] and period [$F(1,25) = 14.3$, $p = 0.005$], but no interaction between these factors [$F(3,75) = 0.83$, $p > 0.48$]. A *post hoc* analysis conducted to further examine the effect of period revealed exactly the same pattern of results than for Remember responses (P1 = P4 > P2 = P3). Here again, only scores for the two intermediate periods (P2, P3) differed between AD patients and controls (all p values < 0.05).

Then, we conducted similar analyses dividing P4 into two sub-periods corresponding to yesterday and today events (**Figure 3**). These analyses revealed for the total recall score, the strictly episodic score and the number of Remember responses a main effect of group (all p values < 0.03), but no effect of sub-period or interaction between both factors. In contrast, for the number of justified Remember responses, we reported a main effect of group [$F(1,25) = 9.3$, $p = 0.005$] and a main effect of sub-period [$F(1,25) = 8.7$, $p = 0.007$]. The group by sub-period interaction was not significant [$F(1,25) = 0.95$, $p > 0.33$]. These results

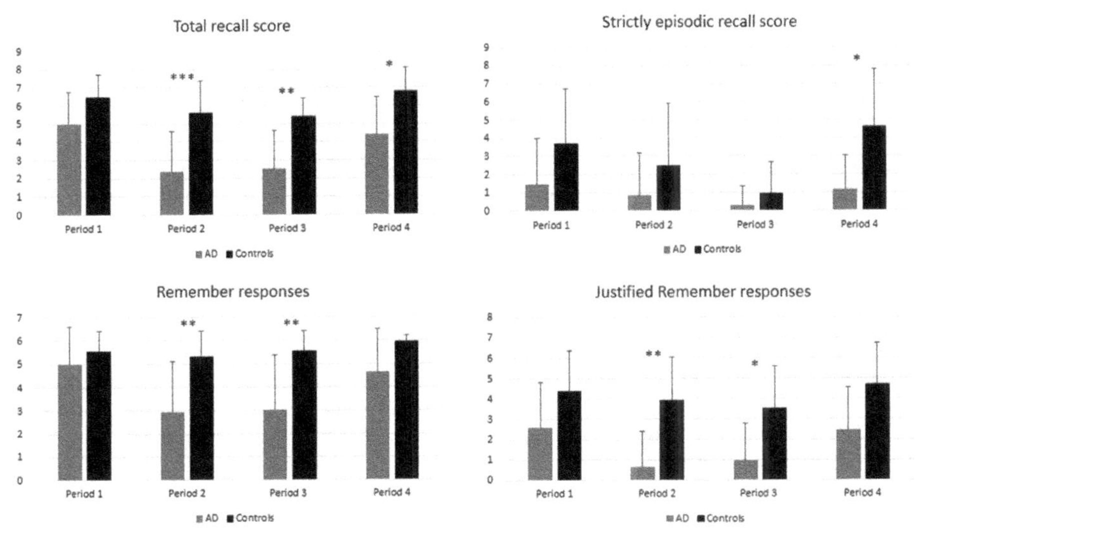

FIGURE 2 | Autobiographical memory scores in AD patients and healthy controls for the four time periods. Stars indicate between group differences. *$p < 0.05$; **$p < 0.01$; ***$p < 0.001$.

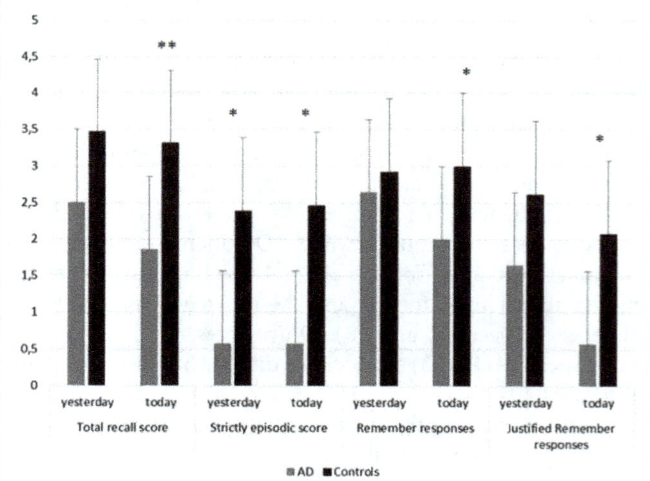

FIGURE 3 | Memory performance for yesterday and today events in AD patients and controls. This figure illustrates performance in AD patients and controls for each memory score (total recall score, strictly episodic recall score, number of Remember responses, number of justified Remember responses) for the recent period (P4), distinguishing yesterday, and today sub-periods. Stars indicate between group differences. $*p < 0.05$; $**p < 0.01$.

indicate that AD patients have lower scores than controls, and that in both groups, the number of justified Remember responses was higher for the events experienced the previous-day compared to today. These data suggest a beneficial effect of sleep on subsequent retrieval of recent autobiographical memories in mild AD patients.

SLEEP PARAMETERS

Sleep parameters in both groups are reported in **Table 1**. Group comparisons revealed that AD patients made significantly more sleep stage 1 than controls ($p < 0.01$) and tended to spent less time in slow-wave sleep ($p = 0.072$).

Table 1 | Sleep parameters in AD patients and controls.

	AD patients ($n = 13$)	Controls ($n = 14$)
GLOBAL PARAMETERS		
Time in bed (min)	531.2 ± 77.1	495.3 ± 48.7
Sleep period time (SPT, min)	504 ± 79.1	477.9 ± 46.9
Total sleep time (TST, min)	387.3 ± 91.2	385.2 ± 68.5
Sleep latency (min)	27.3 ± 33.9	17.5 ± 19.8
Sleep efficiency (%)	72.3 ± 10.9	77.7 ± 10.5
WASO (min)	23.7 ± 10.1	19.6 ± 9.3
SLEEP ARCHITECTURE (% SPT)		
Stage 1	18.2 ± 5.4^{a}	13.1 ± 4.4
Stage 2	26.7 ± 7.7	31.2 ± 7.5
SWS	18.7 ± 7.7^{b}	23.5 ± 5.5
REM sleep	12.6 ± 6.5	12.6 ± 6

Sleep period time corresponds to time in bed – sleep latency.
SWS, slow-wave sleep.
[a]$p < 0.01$;
[b]$p = 0.072$.

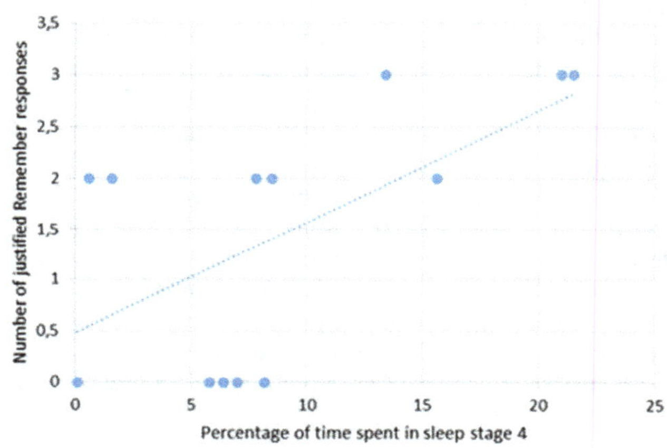

FIGURE 4 | Correlation between the number of justified Remember responses for the yesterday sub-period and the percentage of time spent in sleep stage 4 in AD patients.

CORRELATIONS BETWEEN AUTOBIOGRAPHICAL MEMORY SCORES AND SLEEP PARAMETERS

Finally, we searched for correlations, in AD patients, between sleep parameters and memory scores corresponding to events that occurred on day 1 ("yesterday" sub-period). Due to a technical recording problem, sleep scoring was not possible in one patient, which was removed from this correlation analysis.

We observed significant positive correlations between the number of justified Remember responses and the percentage of time spent in slow-wave sleep ($r = 0.55$, $p < 0.05$), especially sleep stage 4 ($r = 0.60$; $p < 0.05$; **Figure 4**).

CORRELATIONS BETWEEN AUTOBIOGRAPHICAL MEMORY AND RESTING-STATE BRAIN GLUCOSE CONSUMPTION

Correlations analyses between autobiographical memory scores and resting-state brain glucose consumption were conducted in the group of AD patients and only for the most recent period (P4). One patient did not benefit the PET examination and was excluded from these analyses. In addition, correlations were only searched for the total recall score due to a very limited inter-subject variability for the other measures. Thus, the total recall score positively correlated with brain glucose consumption in the precuneus bilaterally extending to the retrosplenial cortex, the calcarine region, the angular gyrus as well as middle temporal gyri (**Table 2** and **Figure 5**). Then, we conducted similar analyses dividing P4 in two sub-periods corresponding to "yesterday" and "today." The pattern of correlations between brain glucose consumption and memory scores for the "yesterday" period was very similar to that reported above. In contrast, for "today" events, correlations were only found in the precuneus but at a more permissive statistical threshold ($p < 0.005$).

DISCUSSION

The present study was designed to investigate autobiographical memory in patients with mild AD, focusing on the very recent past.

Table 2 | Significant correlations between brain glucose consumption and the total recall score for the recent period (P4).

Neuroanatomical region	MNI coordinates (mm)			*k*	*Z*
	x	*y*	*z*		
P4 (INCLUDING THE TWO EVENTS)					
Left precuneus	−2	−54	22	109	3.93
Right precuneus	2	−56	22	52	3.71
Left calcarine region	−10	−102	−6	74	3.66
Left angular gyrus	−52	−60	40	125	3.45
Left middle temporal gyrus	−52	−66	14	33	3.32
Right middle temporal gyrus	42	−56	14	30	3.41
P4: "YESTERDAY" EVENTS					
Right supramarginal gyrus	60	−14	28	56	3.67
Right lingual gyrus	18	−86	−14	40	3.61
Right precuneus	2	−56	20	34	3.67
Left inferior frontal gyrus	−56	20	6	18	3.54
Left calcarine region	−12	−104	−4	10	3.35
Right middle temporal gyrus	52	−66	6	27	3.29
Right inferior temporal gyrus	46	−38	−18	14	3.88
P4: "TODAY" EVENTS					
No significant correlation					

k = *cluster size > 10 voxels; correlations are reported at $p < 0.001$ (uncorrected).*

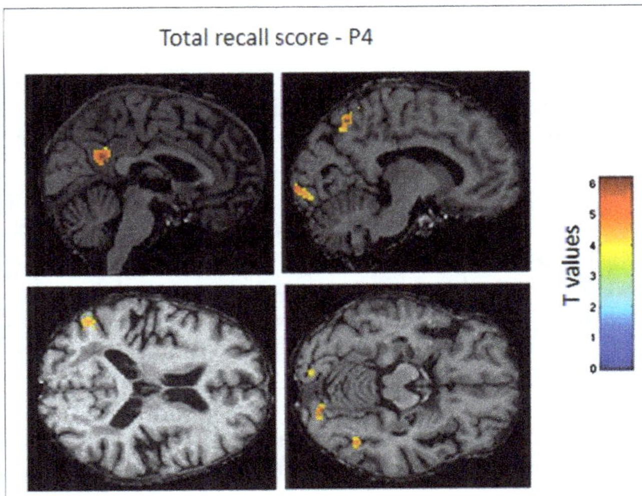

FIGURE 5 | Correlations between resting-state brain glucose consumption and autobiographical memory for recent events. Positive correlations are shown as colored voxels superimposed on sagittal sections of an individual AD patient's MRI normalized on the Montreal Neurological Institute (MNI) template ($p < 0.001$, uncorrected). The two sagittal sections (top) depict correlation with metabolism of the precuneus, calcarine region, and angular gyrus. The two axial sections (bottom) illustrate correlations with middle temporal gyri.

Compared to healthy controls, recall of autobiographical events was impaired in AD for all periods, excepted for the reminiscence bump period (P1). In addition, in AD patients, recall of very recent events (P4) was relatively better than for the periods covering the last 2 years and the last month (P2 and P3) and comparable to performance obtained for P1. Using resting-state PET imaging, we also revealed the brain areas subserving the retrieval of recent events in AD. Finally, we reported, for the first time, a correlation between the amount of slow-wave sleep and previous-day memory suggesting that the ability to consolidate episodic autobiographical memories is associated with sleep integrity.

The analysis of the total recall score revealed a temporally graded autobiographical amnesia in-line with previous reports (Kopelman, 1992; Nestor et al., 2002; Piolino et al., 2003; Hou et al., 2005). AD patients still exhibited a reminiscence bump, contrasting with a significant impairment for periods corresponding to the preclinical stages of their disease (the last 2 years). Furthermore, recall performance for the very recent past was comparable to that observed for the remote past, indicating that patients are still able to retain new personal specific information, provided the experienced events are relatively outstanding and different from typical daily events. Indeed, in the present study, patients had to recall an event that was new for them, coming to a different hospital than the one they used to visit for a sleep recording. However, when considering strictly episodic memories, patients were impaired for all periods, especially for the last month period (P3), confirming their altered capacity to recollect rich specific and unique personal episodes as reported in other studies conducted in Mild Cognitive Impairment (Tramoni et al., 2012) and in AD patients (Eustache et al., 2004; Martinelli et al., 2013b). The comparison of older adults and AD patients suggest that the content of autobiographical memories integrates more semantic, general information, and only few episodic details, as previously stated by Meulenbroek et al. (2010).

Recollective experience was also disrupted in AD patients as attested by the significant decrease in the number of Remember responses – justified or not-, fitting nicely with other studies (Piolino et al., 2003; Rauchs et al., 2007; Irish et al., 2010, 2011; Tramoni et al., 2012). However, for recent and remote memories (P4 and P1), patients still have a feeling a mentally reliving the events as attested by the lack of significant group differences for Remember and justified Remember responses. Some old memories can remain very vivid, even in AD patients, because they are particularly important for the subject's identity or are emotionally laden. For the very recent past, in this study, patients experienced events that were different from their everyday life, and therefore may be more resistant to forgetting. Our data indicate that they can have the feeling to relive these events, but cannot retrieve as much episodic details as healthy aged subjects. However, interestingly, patients provided significantly more Remember responses justified by phenomenological details for the recall of the events that occurred yesterday compared to those that occurred earlier during the day. This suggests that sleep, even if it is also disturbed in AD patients (Petit et al., 2004; Beaulieu-Bonneau and Hudon, 2009), can strengthen memory traces and reduce their sensitivity to forgetting. This point will be specifically discussed later.

Then, we looked at the brain areas subserving the recall of recent autobiographical memories in AD patients. To do so, we searched for correlations between autobiographical memory scores obtained for the period P4 and resting-state measures of brain glucose consumption. These analyses revealed that total recall score for very recent events was related to the metabolism of posterior cortical areas, including the precuneus and retrosplenial cortex and the calcarine region, the angular gyrus and lateral temporal areas, mainly on the left side. These regions play a central role in the retrieval of episodic autobiographical memories (Svoboda et al., 2006; Cabeza and St Jacques, 2007; Martinelli et al., 2013a), even in older adults (Viard et al., 2007, 2010). The retrosplenial cortex is early and severely hypometabolic in the course of AD (Nestor et al., 2003) and its activity has been related to episodic memory loss in AD (Desgranges et al., 2002). Furthermore, several studies showed greater activation of this area for recent compared to remote autobiographical memories in healthy subjects (for review, Cabeza and St Jacques, 2007). Several accounts have been suggested to explain the more important role of this region, together with the calcarine area, in recent autobiographical memories, including the construction of generic visual representations, retrieval of personally familiar information, emotional processing, and vivid recollection (Cabeza and St Jacques, 2007).

Correlations were also found in lateral temporal areas. In healthy subjects, the left middle temporal gyrus may subtend the access to general information in-line with the constructivist model of autobiographical memory proposed by Conway (Conway and Pleydell-Pearce, 2000). Indeed, according to this model, memories are not stored as a perfect record of the original event, but are rather reconstructed from our autobiographical knowledge stores. Recollecting a specific autobiographical memory therefore requires to access first general information before retrieving more precise and specific elements. Viard et al. (2007) reported, in healthy aged subjects, an activation of lateral temporal areas only for the young adult period, suggesting that the reconstruction process occurs mainly for remote memories. In AD patients, however, the correlation observed between autobiographical memory scores for the recent past and left temporal activity suggest that they use this reconstructive process even when retrieving very recent events.

This pattern of correlation was observed for events that occurred yesterday and less for those that occurred the day of the examination. It suggests that these areas play a role in the retrieval of autobiographical memories that were already remodeled and reorganized within neural networks, in particular during sleep episodes, even if the consolidation process is not necessarily completed.

Whole brain regression analyses (but also region-of-interest analyses, data not shown) failed to reveal any significant correlation between memory scores and hippocampal activity, even at a more lenient statistical threshold. Given the fact that the hippocampus is one of the primary sites of AD pathology (Baron et al., 2001) and in light of a previous study conducted in our laboratory and revealing a correlation between hippocampal metabolism and autobiographical memory scores for the recent past (Eustache et al., 2004), this finding may appear unexpected. However, the recent period in Eustache et al. (2004) study covered the last 5 years and is therefore very different from the recent past explored here (yesterday and today), making the comparison between the two studies tricky. Another study using also the TEMPau task failed to reveal significant correlations between hippocampal metabolism and autobiographical memories experienced during the last 12 months, suggesting that the decline in autobiographical memory in early stages of AD may be due to a dysfunction of other brain regions within the autobiographical core brain network (Bastin et al., 2012), such as the posterior cingulate cortex, already associated to the decline of episodic memory performance (Chételat et al., 2003; Bastin et al., 2010), and the precuneus, involved in visual imagery (Fletcher et al., 1995). In our study, correlations were observed in some of these areas, notably the precuneus but also in the temporo-parieto-occipital junction. We mentioned above that the events experienced by patients during the period P4 were different from their everyday life, probably more emotional, and therefore may be more resistant to forgetting. Amygdala atrophy is prominent in early AD (Baron et al., 2001; Basso et al., 2006; Poulin et al., 2011). However, a beneficial effect of emotion on memory was reported in AD patients in some studies (e.g., Boller et al., 2002; Nieuwenhuis-Mark et al., 2009; Borg et al., 2011, see also Klein-Koerkamp et al., 2012 for review), albeit not consistently (Abrisqueta-Gomez et al., 2002; Kensinger et al., 2002, 2004). We surmise that the emotional valence of these recently experienced events together with the fact that they were particularly self-relevant and uncommon may have favored their encoding and consolidation.

The present study also aimed at investigating, for the first time, the impact of sleep on the quality of recall of recent autobiographical events. First, the two events of the very recent past period (P4), corresponding to what the patients did today and yesterday, were compared. This analysis disclosed better memory performance in AD patients, at least for the number of justified Remember responses, for events experienced the previous-day compared to those experienced the day of the assessment. The time elapsed between the encoding of memories and retrieval was much shorter for the same day memory (<12 h) than for the previous-day memory (about 24 h, with a night of sleep in-between). Thus, the difference observed between the two sub-periods could be due either to the fact that the retention interval was longer (but which is generally supposed to induce greater forgetting) or to a genuine effect of sleep. Further studies comparing memory retrieval after equal retention intervals filled with sleep (naps for instance) and wakefulness are further needed to disentangle this issue. However, we observed a positive correlation between the number of justified Remember responses and the percentage of time spent in slow-wave sleep, especially sleep stage 4. These results indicate that patients still exhibiting high amounts of slow-wave sleep have relatively better memory recollection that those whose sleep is disrupted. It also confirms that sleep disturbances in AD are not a secondary symptom of the disease, but can really worsen the cognitive performance, in-line with previous studies (Rauchs et al., 2008; Hot et al., 2011; Westerberg et al., 2012). The positive correlation with slow-wave sleep indicates that, despite an impairment of autobiographical memory especially for the period covering the last 2 years, consolidation of episodic autobiographical mnesic traces overnight is not totally disrupted at this stage of AD. These data are likewise reminiscent and extend those reported by Aly and Moscovitch (2010) in healthy older adults, showing that brain mechanisms supporting sleep-dependent memory consolidation may be preserved when the studied material engages one's interest.

In a previous study investigating, in young adults, the effect of sleep and sleep deprivation on consolidation of episodic memories assessed by means of a word-list learning task, we showed that both slow-wave sleep and REM sleep are involved in the consolidation of rich, vivid episodic memories and that REM sleep favored preferentially the consolidation of spatial information and of details about the encoding context (Rauchs et al., 2004). This result was not replicated in the present study. Interestingly, sleep macrostructure in our group of AD patients only slightly differed compared to healthy aged controls, but both groups exhibited a marked decrease in the amount of slow-wave sleep compared to young adults. The positive correlation between justified Remember responses and time spent in slow-wave sleep suggest that the decrease in this sleep stage, classically observed in older adults, and even more in AD patients, would compromise the initial steps of memory consolidation and would prevent processes occurring normally during subsequent REM sleep to consolidate contextual details. Interestingly, Westerberg et al. (2012) also reported correlations between memory performance assessed using a word-pair recall task, and indices relative to slow-wave sleep (delta power in Non-REM sleep) in MCI patients.

To conclude, the present study shows that autobiographical memory is altered in AD patients across the entire lifespan, but with a relative preservation of memories that occurred during the very recent past. Retrieval of very recent events relies upon the functional integrity of the precuneus and retrosplenial cortex, the middle temporal cortex, and visual areas, reflecting at the same time access to general information, reconstruction, and visual imagery processes as well as recollection of specific details. Finally, we provide the first evidence of an association between the ability to recall recent autobiographical memories and preceding slow-wave sleep, highlighting the utmost importance of preserving sleep quality in older adults for optimal cognitive functioning.

ACKNOWLEDGMENTS

The authors are grateful to M. H. Noël, M. C. Onfroy, and F. Mézenge for their help in PET scanning and data analyses.

REFERENCES

Abrisqueta-Gomez, J., Bueno, O., Oliveira, M., and Bertolucci, P. (2002). Recognition memory for emotional pictures in Alzheimer's patients. *Acta Neurol. Scan.* 105, 51–54. doi:10.1034/j.1600-0404.2002.00035.x

Addis, D. R., and Tippett, L. J. (2004). Memory of myself: autobiographical memory and identity in Alzheimer's disease. *Memory* 12, 56–74. doi:10.1080/09658210244000423

Aly, M., and Moscovitch, M. (2010). The effects of sleep on episodic memory in older and younger adults. *Memory* 18, 327–334. doi:10.1080/09658211003601548

Baddeley, A. D., and Wilson, B. (1986). "Amnesia, autobiographical memory and confabulation," in *Autobiographical Memory*, ed. D. C. Rubin (Cambridge: Cambridge University Press), 225–252.

Baron, J. C., Chételat, G., Desgranges, B., Perchey, G., Landeau, B., de La Sayette, V., et al. (2001). In vivo mapping of gray matter loss with voxel-based morphometry in mild Alzheimer's disease. *Neuroimage* 14, 298–309. doi:10.1006/nimg.2001.0848

Basso, M., Yang, J., Warren, L., MacAvoy, M. G., Varma, P., Bronen, R. A., et al. (2006). Volumetry of amygdala and hippocampus and memory performance in Alzheimer's disease. *Psychiatry Res.* 146, 251–261. doi:10.1016/j.pscychresns.2006.01.007

Bastin, C., Feyers, D., Jedidi, H., Bahri, M. A., Degueldre, C., Lemaire, C., et al. (2012). Episodic autobiographical memory in amnestic mild cognitive impairment: what are the neural correlates? *Hum. Brain Mapp.* 34, 1811–1825. doi:10.1002/hbm.22032

Bastin, C., Kerrouche, N., Lekeu, F., Adam, S., Guillaume, B., Lemaire, C., et al. (2010). Controlled memory processes in questionable Alzheimer's disease: a view from neuroimaging research. *J. Alzheimer's Dis.* 20, 547–560. doi:10.3233/JAD-2010-1393

Beaulieu-Bonneau, S., and Hudon, C. (2009). Sleep disturbances in older adults with mild cognitive impairment. *Int Psychogeriatr.* 21, 654–666 doi:10.1017/S1041610209009120

Boller, F., El Massioui, F., Devouche, E., Traykov, L., Pomati, S., and Starkstein, S. E. (2002). Processing emotional information in Alzheimer's disease: effects on memory performance and neurophysiological correlates. *Dement. Geriatr. Cogn. Disord.* 14, 104–112. doi:10.1159/000064932

Borg, C., Leroy, N., Favre, E., and Laurent, B. (2011). How emotional pictures influence visuospatial binding in short-term memory in ageing and Alzheimer's disease. *Brain Cogn.* 76, 20–25. doi:10.1016/j.bandc.2011.03.008

Born, J., Rasch, B., and Gais, S. (2006). Sleep to remember. *Neuroscientist* 12, 410–424. doi:10.1177/1073858406292647

Cabeza, R., and St Jacques, P. (2007). Functional neuroimaging of autobiographical memory. *Trends Cogn. Sci.* 11, 219–227. doi:10.1016/j.tics.2007.02.005

Chételat, G., Desgranges, B., de La Sayette, V., Viader, F. Berkouk, K., Landeau, B., et al. (2003). Dissociating atrophy and hypometabolism impact on episodic memory in mild cognitive impairment. *Brain* 126, 1955–1967. doi:10.1093/brain/awg196

Conway, M. A., and Pleydell-Pearce, C. W. (2000). The construction of autobiographical memories in the self-memory system. *Psychol. Rev.* 107, 261–288. doi:10.1037/0033-295X.107.2.261

Conway, M. A., Pleydell-Pearce, C. W., Whitecross, S. E., and Sharpe, H. L. (2002). Brain imaging autobiographical memory. *Psychol. Learn. Motiv.* 41, 229–263. doi:10.1016/S0079-7421(02)80008-1

Desgranges, B., Baron, J.-C., Lalevée, C., Giffard, B., Viader, F., de La Sayette, V., et al. (2002). The neural substrates of episodic memory impairment in Alzheimer's disease as revealed by FDG-PET: relationship to degree of deterioration. *Brain* 125, 1116–1124. doi:10.1093/brain/awf097

Diekelmann, S., and Born, J. (2010). The memory function of sleep. *Nat. Rev. Neurosci.* 11, 114–126.

Eustache, F., Piolino, P., Giffard, B., Viader, F., de la Sayette, V., Baron, J.-C., et al. (2004). In the course of time: a PET study of the cerebral substrates of autobiographical amnesia in Alzheimer's disease. *Brain* 127, 1549–1560. doi:10.1093/brain/awh166

Fletcher, P. C., Frith, C. D., Baker, S. C., Shallice, T., Frackowiak, R. S. J., and Dolan, R. J. (1995). The mind's eye: precuneus activation in memory-related imagery. *Neuroimage* 2, 195–200. doi:10.1006/nimg.1995.1025

Folstein, M. F., Folstein, S. E., and McHugh, P. R. (1975). "Mini-mental state" a practical method for grading the cognitive state of patients for the clinician. *J. Psychiatr. Res.* 12, 189–198. doi:10.1016/0022-3956(75)90026-6

Gilboa, A., Ramirez, J., Köhler, S., Westmacott, R., Black, S. E., and Moscovitch, M. (2005). Retrieval of autobiographical memory in Alzheimer's disease: relation to volumes of medial temporal lobe and other structures. *Hippocampus* 15, 535–550. doi:10.1002/hipo.20090

Greene, J. D., and Hodges, J. R. (1996). The fractionation of remote memory. evidence from a longitudinal study of dementia of Alzheimer type. *Brain* 119(Pt 1), 129–142. doi:10.1093/brain/119.1.129

Greene, J. D., Hodges, J. R., and Baddeley, A. D. (1995). Autobiographical memory and executive function in early dementia of Alzheimer type. *Neuropsychologia* 12, 1647–1670. doi:10.1016/0028-3932(95)00045-1

Harand, C., Bertran, F., Doidy, F., Guénolé, F., Desgranges, B., Eustache, F., et al. (2012). How aging affects sleep-dependent memory consolidation? *Front. Neurol.* 3:8. doi:10.3389/fneur.2012.00008

Hot, P., Rauchs, G., Bertran, F., Denise, P., Desgranges, B., Clochon, P., et al. (2011). Changes in sleep theta rhythm are related to episodic memory impairment in early Alzheimer's disease. *Biol. Psychol.* 87, 334–339. doi:10.1016/j.biopsycho.2011.04.002

Hou, C. E., Miller B. L., and Kramer, J. H. (2005). Patterns of autobiographical memory loss in dementia. *Int. J. Geriatr. Psychiatry* 20, 809–815. doi:10.1002/gps.1361

Iber, C., Ancoli-Israel, S., Chesson, A., and Quan, S. F. (2007). *The AASM Manual for the Scoring of Sleep and Associated Events: Rules, Terminology and Technical Specifications.* Westchester, IL: American Academy of Sleep Medicine.

Irish, M., Hornberger, M., Lah, S., Miller, L., Pengas, G., Nestor, P. J., et al. (2011). Profiles of recent autobiographical memory retrieval in semantic dementia, behavioural-variant frontotemporal dementia, and Alzheimer's disease. *Neuropsychologia* 49, 2694–2702. doi:10.1016/j.neuropsychologia.2011.05.017

Irish, M., Lawlor, B. A., O'Mara, S. M., and Coen, R. F. (2010). Exploring the recollective experience during autobiographical memory retrieval in amnestic mild cognitive impairment. *J. Int. Neuropsychol. Soc.* 16, 546–555. doi:10.1017/S1355617710000172

Ivanoiu, A., Cooper, J. M., Shanks, M. F., and Venneri, A. (2004). Retrieval of episodic and semantic autobiographical memories in early Alzheimer's disease and semantic dementia. *Cortex* 40, 173–175. doi:10.1016/S0010-9452(08)70939-0

Kensinger, E. A., Anderson, A., Growdon, J. H., and Corkin, S. (2004). Effect of Alzheimer's disease on memory for verbal emotional information. *Neuropsychologia* 42, 791–800. doi:10.1016/j.neuropsychologia.2003.11.011

Kensinger, E. A., Brierley, B., Medford, N., Growdon, J. H., and Corkin, S. (2002). Effects of normal aging and Alzheimer's disease on emotional memory. *Emotion* 2, 118–134. doi:10.1037/1528-3542.2.2.118

Klein-Koerkamp, Y., Baciu, M., and Hot, P. (2012). Preserved and impaired emotional memory in Alzheimer's disease. *Front. Psychol.* 3:331. doi:10.3389/fpsyg.2012.00331

Kopelman, M. D. (1992). "The 'new' and the 'old': components of the anterograde and the retrograde memory loss in Korsakoff and Alzheimer patients," in *Neuropsychology of Memory*, eds L. R. Squire, and N. Butters (New York: Guilford Press), 130–146.

Kopelman, M. D., Wilson, B. A., and Baddeley, A. D. (1989). The autobiographical memory interview: a new assessment of autobiographical and personal semantic memory in amnesic patients. *J. Clin. Exp. Neuropsychol.* 11, 724–744. doi:10.1080/01688638908400928

Leyhe, T., Müller, S., Milian, M., Eschweiler, G. W., and Saur, R. (2009). Impairment of episodic and semantic autobiographical memory in patients with mild cognitive impairment and early Alzheimer's disease. *Neuropsychologia* 47, 2464–2469. doi:10.1016/j.neuropsychologia.2009.04.018

Maguire, E. A. (2001). Neuroimaging studies of autobiographical event memory. *Philos. Trans. R. Soc. Lond. B Biol. Sci.* 356, 1441–1451. doi:10.1098/rstb.2001.0944

Mäntylä, T. (1993). Knowing but not remembering: adult age differences in recollective experience. *Mem. Cognit.* 21, 379–388. doi:10.3758/BF03208271

Martinelli, P., Sperduti, M., and Piolino, P. (2013a). Neural substrates of the self memory system: new insights from a meta-analysis. *Hum. Brain Mapp.* 34, 1515–1529. doi:10.1002/hbm.22008

Martinelli, P., Anssens, A., Sperduti, M., and Piolino, P. (2013b). The influence of normal aging and Alzheimer's disease in autobiographical memory highly related to the self. *Neuropsychology* 27, 69–78. doi:10.1037/a0030453

McKhann, G., Drachman, D., Folstein, M., Katzman, R., Price, D., and Stadlan, E. M. (1984). Clinical diagnosis of Alzheimer's disease: report of the NINCDS-ADRDA work group under the auspices of Department of Health and Human Services Task Force on Alzheimer's Disease. *Neurology* 34, 939–944. doi:10.1212/WNL.34.7.939

Meulenbroek, O., Rijpkema, M., Kessels, R. P., Rikkert, M. G., and Fernández, G. (2010). Autobiographical memory retrieval in patients with Alzheimer's disease. *Neuroimage* 53, 331–340. doi:10.1016/j.neuroimage.2010.05.082

Murphy, K. J., Troyer, A. K., Levine, B., and Moscovitch, M. (2008). Episodic, but not semantic, autobiographical memory is reduced in amnestic mild cognitive impairment. *Neuropsychologia* 46, 3116–3123. doi:10.1016/j

Nestor, P. J., Fryer, T. D., Ikeda, M., and Hodges, J. R. (2003). Retrosplenial cortex (BA 29/30) hypometabolism in mild cognitive impairment (prodromal Alzheimer's disease). *Eur. J. Neurosci.* 18, 2663–2667. doi:10.1046/j.1460-9568.2003.02999.x

Nestor, P. J., Graham, K. S., Bozeat, S., Simons, J. S., and Hodges, J. R. (2002). Memory consolidation and the hippocampus: further evidence from studies of autobiographical memory in semantic dementia and frontal variant frontotemporal dementia. *Neuropsychologia* 40, 633–654. doi:10.1016/S0028-3932(01)00155-5

Nieuwenhuis-Mark, R. E., Schalk, K., and De Graaf, N. (2009). Free recall and learning of emotional word lists in very elderly people with and without dementia. *Am. J. Alzheimer Dis. Other. Demen.* 24, 155–162. doi:10.1177/1533317508330561

Nuwer, M. R., Comi, G., Emerson, R., Fuglsang-Frederiksen, A., Guerit, J. M., Hinrichs, H., et al. (1999). IFCN standards for digital recording of clinical EEG. The International Federation of Clinical Neurophysiology. *Electroencephalogr. Clin. Neurophysiol.* 52, 11–14.

Petit, D., Gagnon, J.-F., Fantini, M.-L., Ferini-Strambi, L., and Montplaisir, J. (2004). Sleep and quantitative EEG in neurodegenerative disorders. *J. Psychosom. Res.* 56, 487–496. doi:10.1016/j.jpsychores.2004.02.001

Philippi, N., Noblet, V., Botzung, A., Després, O., Renard, F., Sfikas, G., et al. (2012). MRI-based volumetry correlates of autobiographical memory in Alzheimer's disease. *PLoS ONE* 7:e46200. doi:10.1371/journal.pone.0046200

Piolino, P., Desgranges, B., Belliard, S., Matuszewski, V., Lalevée, C., De la Sayette, V., et al. (2003). Autobiographical memory and autonoetic consciousness: triple dissociation in neurodegenerative diseases. *Brain* 126, 2203–2219. doi:10.1093/brain/awg222

Piolino, P., Desgranges, B., and Eustache, F. (2009). Episodic autobiographical memories over the course of time: cognitive, neuropsychological and neuroimaging findings. *Neuropsychologia* 47, 2314–2329. doi:10.1016/j.neuropsychologia.2009.01.020

Poulin, S. P., Dautoff, R., Morris, J. C., Barrett, L. F., and Dickerson, B. C. (2011). Amygdala atrophy is prominent in Alzheimer's disease and relates to symptom severity. *Psychiatry Res.* 194, 7–13. doi:10.1016/j.pscychresns.2011.06.014

Rauchs, G., Bertran, F., Guillery-Girard, B., Desgranges, B., Kerrouche, N., Denise, P., et al. (2004). Consolidation of strictly episodic memories mainly requires rapid eye movement sleep. *Sleep* 27, 395–401.

Rauchs, G., Desgranges, B., Foret, J., and Eustache, F. (2005). The relationships between memory systems and sleep stages. *J. Sleep Res.* 14, 123–140. doi:10.1111/j.1365-2869.2005.00450.x

Rauchs, G., Piolino, P., Mézenge, F., Landeau, B., Lalevée, C., Pélerin, A., et al. (2007). Autonoetic consciousness in Alzheimer's disease: neuropsychological and PET findings using an episodic learning and recognition task. *Neurobiol. Aging* 28, 1410–1420. doi:10.1016/j.neurobiolaging.2006.06.005

Rauchs, G., Schabus, M., Parapatics, S., Bertran, F., Clochon, P., Hot, P., et al. (2008). Is there a link between sleep changes and memory in Alzheimer's disease? *Neuroreport* 19, 1159–1162. doi:10.1097/WNR.0b013e32830867c4

Rubin, D. C., Wetzler, S. E., and Nebes, R. D. (1986). "Autobiographical memory across the lifespan," in *Autobiographical Memory*, ed. D. C. Rubin (Cambridge: Cambridge University Press), 202–221.

Svoboda, E., McKinnon, M. C., and Levine, B. (2006). The functional neuroanatomy of autobiographical memory: a meta-analysis. *Neuropsychologia* 44, 2189–2208. doi:10.1016/j.neuropsychologia.2006.05.023

Tramoni, E., Felician, O., Koric, L., Balzamo, M., Joubert, S., and Ceccaldi, M. (2012). Alteration of autobiographical memory in amnestic mild cognitive impairment. *Cortex* 48, 1310–1319. doi:10.1016/j.cortex.2011.09.002

Tulving, E. (1985). How many memory systems are there? *Am. Psychol.* 40, 385–398. doi:10.1037/0003-066X.40.4.385

Tulving, E. (2002). Episodic memory: from mind to brain. *Annu. Rev. Psychol.* 53, 1–25. doi:10.1146/annurev.psych.53.100901.135114

Tulving, E., Kapur, S., Craik, F. I. M., Moscovitch, M., and Houle, S. (1994). Hemispheric encoding/retrieval asymmetry in episodic memory: positron emission tomography findings. *Proc. Natl. Acad. Sci. U.S.A.* 91, 2016–2020. doi:10.1073/pnas.91.6.2016

Tulving, E., Schacter, D. L., McLachlan, D. R., and Moscovitch, M. (1988). Priming of semantic autobiographical knowledge: a case study of retrograde amnesia. *Brain Cogn.* 8, 3–20. doi:10.1016/0278-2626(88)90035-8

Tzourio-Mazoyer, N., Landeau, B., Papathanassiou, D., Crivello, F., Etard, O., Delcroix, N., et al. (2002). Automated anatomical labeling of activations in SPM using a macroscopic anatomical parcellation of the MNI MRI single-subject brain. *Neuroimage* 15, 273–289. doi:10.1006/nimg.2001.0978

Viard, A., Lebreton, K., Chételat, G., Desgranges, B., Landeau, B., Young, A., et al. (2010). Patterns of hippocampal-neocortical interactions in the retrieval of episodic autobiographical memories across the entire life-span of aged adults. *Hippocampus* 20, 153–165. doi:10.1002/hipo.20601

Viard, A., Piolino, P., Desgranges, B., Chételat, G., Lebreton, K., Landeau, B., et al. (2007). Hippocampal activation for autobiographical memories over the entire lifetime in healthy aged subjects: an fMRI study. *Cereb. Cortex* 17, 2453–2467. doi:10.1093/cercor/bhl153

Westerberg, C. E., Mander, B. A., Florczak, S. M., Weintraub, S., Mesulam, M. M., Zee, P. C., et al. (2012). Concurrent impairments in sleep and memory in amnestic mild cognitive impairment. *J. Int. Neuropsychol. Soc.* 18, 490–500. doi:10.1017/S135561771200001X

15

Developmental trajectories of associative memory from childhood to adulthood: A behavioral and neuroimaging study

Bérengère Guillery-Girard[1,2,3,4]*, Sylvie Martins[1,2,3,4,5,6,7,8], Sebastien Deshayes[1,2,3,4], Lucie Hertz-Pannier[5,6,7,8], Catherine Chiron[5,6,7,8], Isabelle Jambaqué[5,6,7,9], Brigitte Landeau[1,2,3,4], Patrice Clochon[1,2,3,4], Gaël Chételat[1,2,3,4] and Francis Eustache[1,2,3,4]

[1] *INSERM, U1077, Caen, France*
[2] *Université de Caen Basse-Normandie, UMR-S1077, Caen, France*
[3] *Ecole Pratique des Hautes Etudes, UMR-S1077, Caen, France*
[4] *CHU de Caen, UMR-S1077, Caen, France*
[5] *INSERM, U663, Paris, France*
[6] *Université Paris Descartes, Paris, France*
[7] *CEA Saclay, Gif sur Yvette, France*
[8] *SHFJ et Neurospin, I2BM, CEA, Paris, France*
[9] *Unité de Neurochirurgie Pédiatrique, Fondation Ophtalmologique Adolphe de Rothschild, Paris, France*

Correspondence:
Bérengère Guillery-Girard, INSERM-EPHE-Université de Caen/Basse-Normandie, Unité U1077, GIP Cyceron, Bd Henri Becquerel, BP 5229 14074 Caen Cedex, France
e-mail: guillery@cyceron.fr

Episodic memory refers to the capacity to bind multimodal memories to constitute a unique personal event. Most developmental studies on episodic memory focused on one specific component, i.e., the core factual information. The present study examines the relevance of a novel episodic paradigm to assess its developmental trajectories in a more comprehensive way according to the type of association (item-feature, item-location, and item-sequence associations) with measures of both objective and subjective recollection. We conducted a behavioral study aimed at testing the effects of age in a large sample of 160 children, adolescents, and young adults (6–23 years old). We confronted the behavioral data to the neural correlates in a subgroup of 30 children using voxel-based morphometry. Behavioral data outlined differential developmental trajectories according to the type of association, with a continuous increase of factual associative memory efficiency until 10 years, a linear increase of performance in spatial associative memory that pursues until early adulthood and an abrupt increase in temporal associative memory efficiency between 9 and 10. Regarding recollection, measures showed a more pronounced enhancement from 9 to 10 years. Hence, behavioral data highlight a peculiar period in late childhood (8–10 years old) crucial for the developmental time course of episodic memory. Regarding structural data, we found that the improvement of associative memory efficiency was related to a decrease in gray matter volume in a large cerebral network including the dorsolateral and ventrolateral prefrontal cortex (and superior and anterior temporal regions), and the hippocampus bilaterally. These data suggest that multimodal integration would probably be related to the maturation of temporal regions and modulated by a fronto-parietal network. Besides, our findings emphasize the relevance of the present paradigm to assess episodic memory especially in the clinical setting.

Keywords: episodic memory, associative memory, spatial memory, sequential memory, recollection, structural imaging

INTRODUCTION

Episodic memory refers to the most complex human memory system that emerges in early childhood. It requires both the individual's self-awareness (i.e., autonoetic) of having personally experienced a past event while retrieving the overall phenomenological details (i.e., context or source) bound to that unique moment (which gives a peculiar vividness to the recall) and the ability to make sense of this recall for future experiences (Tulving, 2002). Thus, episodic memory processes rely on the binding of different types of associations, i.e., both within-domain associations such as inter-item associations (e.g., child and flower) and between-domain associations such as item-location associations (e.g., child and behind-window) (Mayes et al., 2007). These associations may be integrated into a single representation (e.g., the child standing behind the window) and may elicit a vivid sense of re-experiencing at retrieval (e.g., reliving the event with affective and perceptual information, i.e., recollection). Consequently, subjective recollection or "autonoetic" awareness would rely on a relational process (see Klein, 2013).

While several neurobehavioral models were applied to associative memory in adults (see Buchler et al., 2008), its maturation from childhood to early adulthood still needs to be explored in detail. *Within-domain* associative memory was tested in infancy in 9 months old children who were found to encode relations among two items (i.e., a face associated to a specific scenic background), and maintain this relational representation for a few seconds (Richmond and Nelson, 2009). This early developed capacity to bind information continues to improve from 4 to 6 (see Sluzenski et al., 2006; Lloyd et al., 2009 for the learning of item/background associations) and is supposed to reach adult efficiency in middle childhood. In a recent study, Thaler et al. (2013) suggested that long term associative memory, when assessed with an ordered repeated word list paradigm, may plateau from the age of 12 onward.

Other studies have focused on *between-domain* associations, either item/space or item/time respectively. As young as 2 years of age, toddlers are able to retain several item-location associations (Russell and Thompson, 2003) and performances still increase beyond the age of 10 (Barnfield, 1999; Gulya et al., 2002; Hund and Plumert, 2002). Processes of item-location memory may continue to refine until 18–20 years (Lorsbach and Reimer, 2005; see Pirogovsky et al., 2009 for odor-place associations). From 4 years on, children are able to encode temporal parameters that are knowledgeable, i.e., referring to a day. However, it is only later on, around 8 years old, that children can reliably localize multiple events extended into the past (Friedman and Lyon, 2005; Pathman et al., 2013). In sum, the developmental trajectories of associative memory seem to differ according to the component implicated (Picard et al., 2012). Within-domain associative memory dealing with factual information (item/background for instance) may plateau before between-domain associative memory. The maturation of these different types of associative memory may contribute to the development of subjective recollection. Studies that explored subjective experience with Remember/know paradigms reported slight or no modification of familiarity process with age contrary to subjective recollection (Billingsley et al., 2002; Brainerd et al., 2004; Piolino et al., 2007; Ghetti and Angelini, 2008). It is noteworthy that comparisons across developmental studies are challenging due to methodological issues with multiple paradigms and variables that may impact pediatrics behavioral data such as motivational, regulatory, and socio-educational factors.

Complex neurodevelopmental factors account for associative memory evolution from childhood to late adolescence, and can be studied by novel imaging techniques addressing various processes of cerebral maturation (Ghetti and Bunge, 2012). Looking at the cerebral maturation that supports associative memory enhancement from childhood to adolescence, two recent reviews focused on the role of both the prefrontal cortex (PFC) and the hippocampus in such associative processes (Ghetti and Bunge, 2012; Ofen et al., 2012). These two regions show distinct maturational time courses. Overall, PFC maturation appears more prolonged than in other regions (Gogtay et al., 2004). The protracted maturation of the dorsolateral PFC (Giedd, 2004) up to 20 years old seems to be associated with a progressive and late development of top-down attention modulation and strategic processes (Sander et al., 2012). The sparse structural studies that correlated children's performance in standard memory tests with anatomical data provide further evidence that maturational changes in frontal regions [decrease in either cortical thickness (Sowell et al., 2001; Østby et al., 2012) or gray matter volume (Antshel et al., 2008)], are related to increasing memory efficiency in this developmental period. Developmental trends of the hippocampus and their relations with associative memory still need to be clarified.

Because associative memory is a defining feature of episodic memory, the understanding of associative memory development needs to take into consideration the type of associations in order to better describe children's capacity to form and retrieve episodic memories. To date, no behavioral studies have explored the three associative domains (i.e., factual – WHAT, spatial – WHERE, and temporal – WHEN) with a single protocol in the same sample. Thus, the first goal of the present study is to describe the development of within-domain and inter-domain associative memory in a large sample of 160 healthy participants. We further examined our protocol's reliance by confronting these behavioral results to structural imaging data collected in a subgroup of 30 children and adolescents to identify the regions that subserve episodic memory efficiency from childhood to young adulthood. Finally, to consider the possible influence of verbalization and retrieval processes on associative memory efficiency during development, we conducted additional correlational analyses between the 30 participants' performance in verbal fluency and (1) behavioral data (the WHAT-WHERE-WHEN paradigm) and (2) volume of cerebral regions related to associative memory.

MATERIALS AND METHODS

PARTICIPANTS

We conducted the behavioral study on participants aged from 6 to 23 years old recruited among several French Schools, High Schools, and Universities. Exclusion criteria were as follows: history of previous neurological disease, head trauma, current psychoactive medication, and learning disabilities. Families were given a comprehensive description of the research. We obtained written consent from parents of minors, in line with the guidelines of the relevant ethics committees. Informed consent was also obtained from participants over the age of 18. All participants completed the WHAT-WHERE-WHEN episodic memory paradigm (Guillery-Girard et al., 2010). One hundred children from 6 to 10 years (from childhood to adolescence; Mean = 100.7 ± 17.04 months, 51 females) and 60 adolescents and young adults from 12 to 23 years (from adolescence to adulthood; Mean = 194.30 ± 49.90 months, 29 females) were involved in the behavioral study. The children sample had been equally divided among five age groups (each group $n = 20$): 6 years old group (Mean = 77.1 ± 4 months, 11 females), 7 years old group (Mean = 88.7 ± 3.54 months, 12 females), 8 years old group (Mean = 109.5 ± 3.65 months, 12 females), 9 years old group (Mean = 113.2 ± 3.05 months, 7 females), and 10 years old group (Mean = 123.55 ± 3.27 months, 9 females). Similarly, the adolescent and adult sample had been equally divided among three age groups: 11–12 years old group (Mean = 142.55 ± 6.14 months, 10 females), 14–15 years old group (Mean = 180.58 ± 6.77 months, 12 females), and 20–23 years old group (Mean = 259.5 ± 12.86 months, 9 females).

Among these participants, 30 right-handed children and adolescents underwent a morphological MRI [age range: 79–180 months (6.6–15 years), Mean = 135.77 ± 28.19 months (11.31 ± 2.35 years), 13 females]. They additionally participated in various standard neuropsychological tests among which a verbal fluency test (i.e., this French task requires the participants to generate as many words as possible, firstly in a letter fluency condition and secondly, in a category fluency condition – 60 s are provided for each condition). All 30 children and adolescents accurately performed both the behavioral and the morphological MRI investigations on the same day.

Behavioral task

The "WHAT-WHERE-WHEN" paradigm. The WHAT task relied on within-domain factual associations and required participants to learn either 10 (for children aged 6–10 years) or 13 animal-feature associations (11–23) (**Figure 1**). Different list lengths were used to prevent possible ceiling and floor effects for the different age groups (Perez et al., 1998). During the encoding phase, children were shown photographs in a special book with the animal always displayed on the left-hand side and its feature on the right-hand side. Each double page was presented for 5 s (i.e., total encoding time of 50–65 s for the all set of associations). One third of the associations had already been matched and displayed in the book prior to the presentation; another third were to be matched by the experimenter; the remaining third were to be matched by the children themselves. That is, two thirds of the feature photos were laid out in front of the experimenter and the children, at their disposal for them to complete the associations. Color frames were used to emphasize each animal-feature association and to cue children with animal-feature relationship. For instance, photograph of the vicuna displayed in the book was surrounded by a green frame which indicated that its related feature (laid out in the middle of the features set) should be matched according to this color frame. The three different ways of matching the animal and its feature represented three different sources of encoding or "objective recollection" at retrieval. In contrast with intentional encoding of the animal-feature associations, source encoding was deliberately incidental, in order to approach ecological situations as closely as possible. At testing, the children were asked to match the animals with their corresponding features. Thus, the experimenter placed all the features in front of the children, minus their color frame, and provided the animal one at a time. Once, the children matched the feature with the current animal, the experimenter added a second copy of the chosen feature in the set of feature photographs available and removed the photographs of animal-feature association to avoid potential deductions. To assess the subjective recollection that accompanied the retrieval of each animal-feature association, the children were administered the Remember-Know paradigm. This paradigm was adapted for children by using a comic strip comprising three "smiley faces" representing "I remember," "I know," and "I guess" answers. Each type of response was carefully described in order to ensure that children understood every concept. Thus, "I guess" was to be chosen when they were not sure of their answer, while "I know" and "I remember" were to be chosen when children were quite certain. "I know" was then to indicate retrieval of an animal-feature association without any specific details about the encoded episode, "I remember" indicated retrieval of an animal-feature association accompanied by a mental journey back into the past allowing the encoded episode to be relived and phenomenological details retrieved. The difference between Remember and Know was extensively explained to children. To highlight the Remember answers we used a film/video metaphor (i.e., "you remember quite well that they go together because you can see them together like at the first time, as if you were watching a film in which you are the character"). To contrast this with the Know answers, we used a computer metaphor (i.e., "you know quite well that this picture goes with this picture here because they are stored together somewhere in your head, like if they were stored together into a computer"). Specific examples were used to contrast the types of information: their date of birth to refer to personal semantic information and/or the last dance show they attended to refer to personal episodic memories. To ensure children's appropriate use of criteria, they were asked to

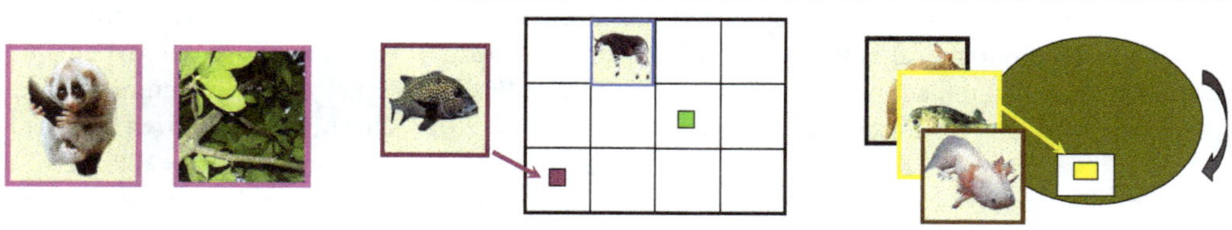

WHAT
Participants were asked to encode animal-feature associations.
At testing, children were 1- asked to match animals with their corresponding features, 2- they were administered the R/K-G paradigm and 3- asked for the source of encoding (i.e., who performed the association)?

We obtained 4 measures:
WHAT (correct associations)
Objective Recollection (correct sources)
Subjective Recollection (R responses/nb of associations)
Familiarity ((K responses/nb of associations)/1-Subjective Recollection)

WHERE
Participants were asked to encode animal- location associations.
At testing, children were asked to match animals with their corresponding locations.

We obtained 1 measure:
WHERE (correct associations)

WHEN
Participants were asked to encode the sequence of animals.
At testing, children were asked to match animals with their corresponding placement.

We obtained 1 measure:
WHEN (correct placement individually and pairs of animals in the correct temporal order)

Finally, we obtained an **Episodic score** encompassing the three associative memory tests.

FIGURE 1 | «WHAT-WHERE-WHEN»paradigm.

reformulate the instructions. This procedure was adapted to each subject and repeated until the experimenter was confident about the child's understanding of the Remember and Know judgments (see Picard et al., 2009 for a similar approach in autobiographical memory). Finally, for each association, objective recollection was assessed by asking the children to retrieve the corresponding source, in the shape of the person who performed the match (matched by the experimenter; matched by the child or matched prior to the presentation).

The WHERE task relied on between-domain spatial associations and is similar to the sub-test "Memory for designs" from the standardized battery NEPSY II (Korkman et al., 2007). Children were tested on their encoding of the exact location of each animal in an array (3 × 4 grid for children aged 6–10 years; 4 × 4 grid for children aged 11–18 years). They encoded the animal-location association by matching the colored frame surrounding the photograph of the animal to a colored marker in the center of each box of the grid. Animals were presented one at a time and the child was asked to place each animal into the correct location. The order of animals presentation was randomized across participants. Animals remained in view as the child proceeded through the task. Once all animals were placed, children were given 1 min to review the animal-location associations. In the test condition, children were again provided with the animals one at a time and were asked to place them in the array. In this condition there were no color cues. Again, animals were randomized across children.

The WHEN task investigated between-domain sequential associative memory. Children were asked to encode the animal-sequence association by placing the animals into slots in a wooden wheel. As the wheel was turned, only one slot was visible at a time. As in the other tasks, the animal-sequence association was determined by color cues that appeared in each slot. Each color corresponded to a specific animal. In the encoding condition, children were provided with the full set of animals and required to place them into the slots following the sequence determined by the color showing in the slot at each turn of the wheel. Once all animals were in place, the children were given one opportunity to review the overall sequence for a maximum of 1 min. In the test condition, children were again provided with the complete set of animals and required to retrieve the exact encoded sequence. Again, there were no color cues in this condition.

The measures derived from the WHAT-WHERE-WHEN test were then as follows:

(i) For the WHAT task: (1) total number of correct animal-feature associations (WHAT); (2) total number of sources that were correctly provided (Objective Recollection); (3) ratio of Remember judgments provided for every accurate association (Subjective Recollection, with Recollection = Remember responses/total number of associations); (4) familiarity is calculated in absence of recollection (as defined by Yonelinas and Jacoby, 1995) with Familiarity = $K/1$-R, where K = Know responses/total number of associations. This formula allows us to analyze separately Know from Recollection judgments.

(ii) For the WHERE task: total number of correct animal-location associations (WHERE).

(iii) For the WHEN task, we have taken into account both the correct placement of the animals individually and pairs of animals in the correct temporal order (see Riggins et al., 2009 for a similar approach). Thus one point was credited for each animal that was assigned to its rightful place in the sequence and 1/2 point was credited for each animals that accurately followed the original order but were inaccurately placed in the sequence [example A: animal one in first position, animal two in second position, animal three in third position = (1 + 1 + 1) = 4 points; example B: animal seven in first position, animal eight in second position, and animal nine in third position = (2 × 1/2) = 1 point] The WHEN hits thus corresponds to the sum of placement and order in the sequence. We normalized all associative memory scores and Objective Recollection scores. This transformation of these possible heterogeneous raw scores into a common domain is needed prior to combining them into an episodic score (see below) and conducting parametric statistical analysis on normal distributions.

In order to assess overall episodic memory development, we computed a composite score obtained as follow: first, we summed the three z-scores (WHAT, WHERE, and WHEN) for each participant. This score is not quite a z-score, so it has been finally divided by the square root of the sum of the variance of the three subtests (which equals 3 × 1 since we used z-score) plus twice the sum of the covariance of the three subtests. As they were z-score, their covariances equal their correlation coefficients. For detail, see "Combining different scores from tests" in "Advanced Topics" section of the Psych Assessment website. This score assesses more specifically episodic memory since it encompasses three primary components of associative memory.

$$\text{episodic score} = \frac{Z_{\text{WHAT}} + Z_{\text{WHERE}} + Z_{\text{WHEN}}}{\sqrt{(3 + 2 \times (r_{\text{WHATWHERE}} + r_{\text{WHATWHEN}} + r_{\text{WHEREWHEN}}))}}$$

Imaging data acquisition

3D T1 images were acquired at the UMR663, INSERM, in the Service Hospitalier Frédéric Joliot (CEA-I2BM, Orsay, France), on a 1.5T MRI System (Signa, LX, GEMS, USA), with the following parameters: TR = 9.9 ms; TE = 2 ms; IR-Prep-time = 600 ms flip angle = 10°; voxel size:0.9 mm × 9 mm × 1.2 mm, acquisition time: 7′56″.

Image processing

MRI data were segmented, normalized to a pediatric sample of the NIH (N = 324, age range = 4.5–18.5 years, Fonov et al., 2011), and modulated using the VBM5.1 toolbox (Ashburner and Friston, 2005) implemented in the Statistical Parametric Mapping 5 (SPM) software (Wellcome Trust Centre for Neuroimaging, London, UK) to obtain maps of local gray matter volume corrected for brain size. Finally, each image was smoothed with a Gaussian kernel (FWHM = 12 mm). Furthermore, we used a gray matter explicit mask in the voxelwise analyses so as to restrain the analyses to the gray matter. This mask was obtained by first averaging all segmented gray matter and white matter images, then thresholding the gray matter average to include voxels with a probability higher than 0.4 and the white matter average to include voxels with a probability higher than 0.2. Finally, the final GM mask used in the analyses was obtained by subtracting the WM mask from the GM mask.

Image statistical analysis

We analyzed age-related changes on brain morphometry using two statistical models entering either age (linear) or age and age2 (quadratic) as predictors using this fitting model: volume $= a0 + a1\text{score} + a2\text{score}^2 + \varepsilon$ where $a0$, $a1$, and $a2$ are polynomial parameters to be found, and error represents the residual error of the model (Büchel et al., 1998; Hu et al., 2013). Finally, we included sex as a regressor of non-interest. In a second set of analyses, each z-score (WHAT, WHERE, and WHEN) and the composite score referring to episodic memory were related to brain morphometry. These analyses were conducted first on the whole brain and second within the hippocampus only using a hippocampus delineated on a template. We performed the same regression analyses as before replacing age by the episodic score. Note that the predictor variables were first orthogonalized before being entered together in the quadratic models: age and age^2 for age-related analyses, episodic and episodic score^2 for brain-behavior relationships analyses. Because any relationship between brain volumes and memory could be driven by the common effect of age or sex, regression analyses with episodic memory were conducted with two regressors of non-interest (age and sex).

Two statistical thresholds were used, one for the whole brain and another for the hippocampus. For the whole brain where widespread effects were expected, we used a statistical threshold of uncorrected $p < 0.001$ and cluster extent $K > 500$ voxels. For analyses focusing on the hippocampus, a less stringent uncorrected p-value cut-off of $p < 0.01$ was applied with a cluster extent $K > 100$ voxels. In this latter condition, more localized effects were expected resulting from developmental differences along the longitudinal axis (DeMaster and Ghetti, 2013).

Complementary analyses

Finally, we conducted a last set of correlations between fluency z-score (which combines both letter and category fluency) and: (1) each z-score (WHAT, WHERE, and WHEN) and the composite score referring to episodic memory, (2) mean of gray matter volumes in clusters previously identified in brain-memory relationships analyses.

RESULTS

BEHAVIORAL RESULTS

Associative memory

We performed one-way ANOVA for each task with age groups as between factor and Tukey's adjustment for multiple comparisons (HSD). Those revealed three different developmental patterns (**Figure 2**).

Childhood to adolescence. First, the one-way ANOVA performed on the WHAT scores revealed a significant group effect [$F(4, 95) = 2.54$; $p = 0.04$] on performance associated with only one significant difference between 6- and 10-year-old groups ($p = 0.04$). These results illustrated a slight but significant increase from 6- to 10-year-olds. Second and considering the WHERE task, we observed a significant and linear increase in performance across age groups [$F(4, 95) = 9.51$; $p < 0.001$; $6 < 8$ and $9 - 7 < 10 - 8 < 10$-year-olds]. Finally, a significant group effect was also found for the WHEN task [$F(4, 95) = 8.33$; $p < 0.001$] with a ceiling effect until the age of 9 followed by a significant increase from 9- to 10-year-olds ($p < 0.001$, **Figure 2A**). This determining period also appeared in the analyses of the episodic scores [$F(4, 95) = 14.56$; $p < 0.001$] that combine the three associative memory tasks (**Figure 2B**). Tuckey *post hoc* tests revealed a slight increase from the age of 6 to 9 followed by a marked increase between 9- and 10-year-olds ($6 < 7, 8, 9$; $10 - 7 < 10 - 8 < 10 - 9 < 10$).

Adolescence to adulthood. The one-way ANOVAs conducted on each of the associative score revealed a significant group effect only for WHERE's performance [$F(2, 57) = 4.74$; $p = 0.01$; $11 - 12 < 21–24$ age group]. No significant developmental difference was evident for neither the two other associative memory tasks nor the episodic score.

Objective and subjective recollection

Childhood to adolescence. Simple effects analysis conducted on the child groups indicated that the group effect observed on objective recollection [$F(4, 95) = 5.10$; $p < 0.001$] resulted from a significant increase from 8- to 10-year-olds ($6, 7, 8 < 10$, **Figure 2C**). In contrast, the significant group effect on subjective recollection [$F(4, 95) = 6.44$; $p < 0.001$] was related to a slight and linear increase of the ability of remembering (**Figure 2D**).

Adolescence to adulthood. Analysis conducted on the oldest age groups revealed that only the familiarity index decreased significantly from 11–12- to 21–23-year-olds [$F(2, 57) = 3.56$; $p = 0.03$; $11 - 12 > 21–24$ age group].

IMAGING RESULTS

Age-related effects

The linear regression analysis with total gray matter volume as the dependent variable and age as the predictor variable while controlling for the effect of sex, revealed a statistically significant volume decrease from 6 to 15 years ($R^2 = 0.449$, $p < 0.001$). There was no significant contribution of age^2, when this was included in the regression. Regional analyses revealed significant structural changes mainly in fronto-temporal regions but also involving posterior parietal regions (**Figure 3**). The regression analysis focused on the hippocampus, with the volume as the dependent variable and age as the predictor variable while controlling for the effect of sex, indicate a significant reduction in the volume of the hippocampal body bilaterally extending, in the left hemisphere, to the anterior part of the hippocampus.

Relationships between brain volume and memory performances

Our analyses failed to detect any statistically significant relationship between each z-score independently (i.e., WHAT, WHERE, and WHEN) and gray matter volume. On the contrary, in both whole brain and hippocampus template-based ROI, a quadratic

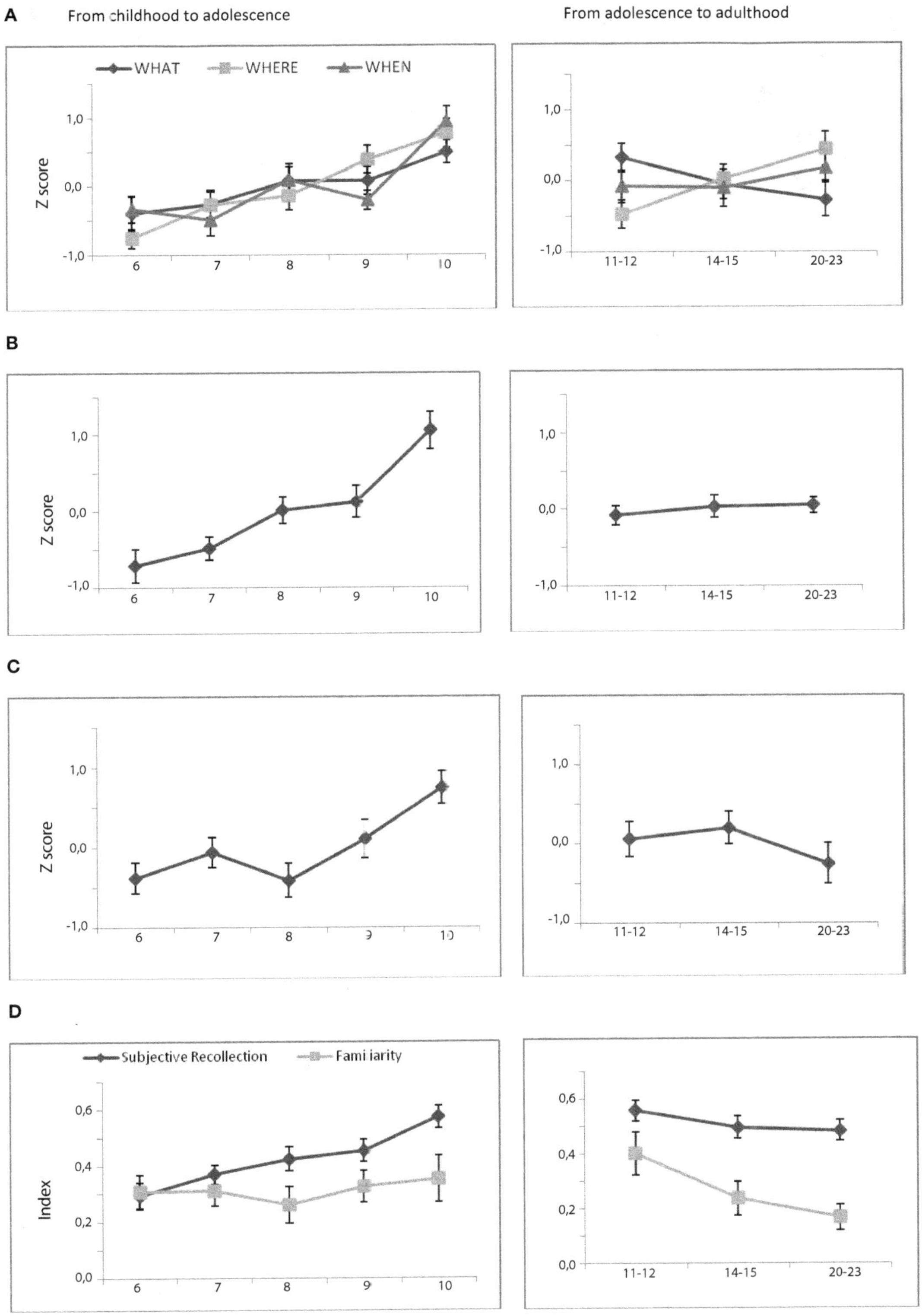

FIGURE 2 | Behavioral performances on the associative memory tasks. **(A)** Mean performance of associative cued recall (hits) for each memory task as a function of age. **(B)** Mean episodic score. **(C)** Mean objective recollection. **(D)** Mean subjective recollection and familiarity index.

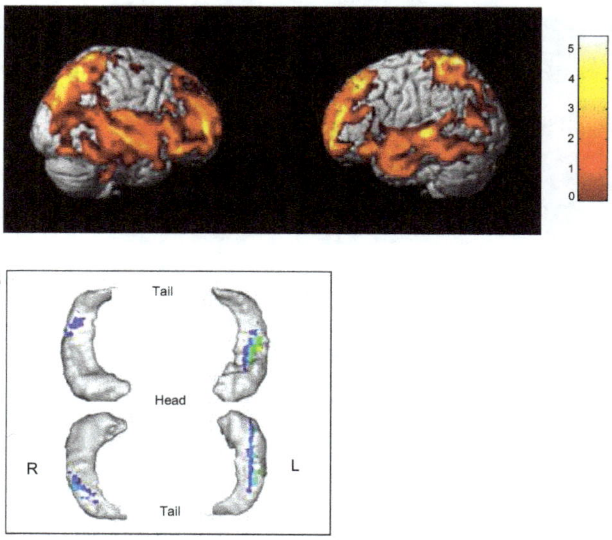

FIGURE 3 | Age-related effects on the brain. (A) Age-related changes concern fronto-temporal and posterior parietal regions bilaterally (uncorrected $p < 0.001$, $K > 500$). **(B)** A significant reduction was found in the hippocampus bilaterally, with a more extended region in the left hippocampus (uncorrected $p < 0.01$, $K > 100$).

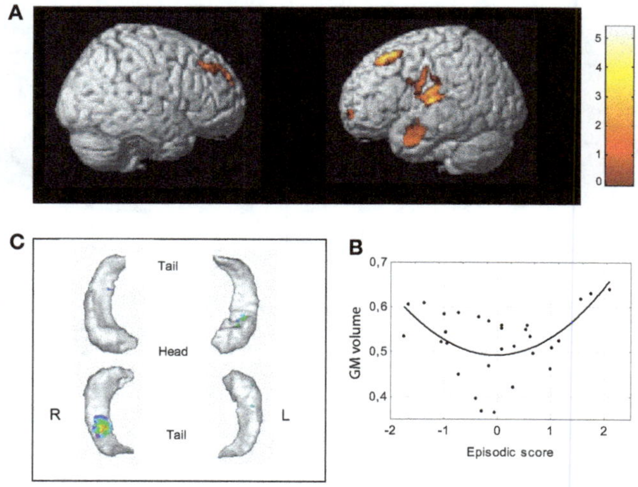

FIGURE 4 | Neural correlates of associative memory. (A) Significant positive correlation (quadratic, U-shaped) with episodic score was found with the volume of gray matter in dorsolateral frontal regions bilaterally, the superior temporal cortex, the anterior middle temporal gyrus, and the ventrolateral prefrontal cortex (upper figure, uncorrected $p < 0.001$, $K > 500$). **(B)** Scatterplots of episodic effects are shown for regions identified in whole brain analyses. **(C)** Significant positive correlation (quadratic, U-shaped) was observed between memory and right hippocampal body and the anterior part of the left hippocampus (uncorrected $p < 0.01$, $K > 100$).

positive relation (U-shaped) between volume and episodic score was found. Concerning the whole brain analysis, significant positive correlation with episodic memory was found with the volume of five brain areas in the right hemisphere (**Figure 4**; **Table 1**): (i) dorsolateral frontal regions, including the posterior part of the medial frontal gyrus, (ii) the superior temporal cortex encroaching both the transverse temporal gyrus around the lateral sulcus and the inferior parietal lobule, (iii) the anterior middle temporal gyrus, (iv) the ventrolateral prefrontal cortex (VLPFC) and, (v) the anterior part of dorsolateral PFC. Analyses performed on the hippocampus gray matter volume revealed significant relationships between memory efficiency and the body of the hippocampus on the right side and the anterior part of the hippocampus on the left side. Scatterplots of these effects showed that the enhancement of episodic performances was mainly associated with a decrease in mean volumes except for three participants with the highest scores.

Complementary analyses. Correlational behavioral analyses revealed significant positive correlation between fluency z-score and each associative memory task ($p = 0.004$ WHAT; $p = 0.026$ WHERE; $p = 0.003$ WHEN) and the episodic composite score ($p = 0.003$), indicating that better efficiency in verbal fluency was associated with better performances in associative memory. Also, we observed a significant negative correlation between the fluency z-score and two clusters previously detected, i.e., dorsolateral frontal regions bilaterally and the superior temporal cortex. Thus, a decrease in volume in these three cortical regions was associated with increased efficiency in verbal fluency. These analyses did not detect any statistical correlation with the hippocampus.

Table 1 | Brain – associative memory relationships.

	Region	*x*	*y*	*z*	No. voxels	*z*
WHOLE BRAIN ($p < 0.001$, UNCORRECTED, CLUSTER > 500)						
L	Dorsolateral PF	−17	28	48	2985	4.34
L	Sup temporal	−54	−16	23	4278	4.18
L	Middle temporal	−65	−5	−22	2277	4.14
L	Ventrolateral PF	−38	63	−5	556	3.85
R	Dorsolateral PF	20	45	39	1646	3.71
HIPPOCAMPUS ($p < 0.01$, UNCORRECTED, CLUSTER > 100)						
L	Hippocampus	−34	−17	−20	598	2.92
R	Hippocampus	30	−34	−11	323	2.92

DISCUSSION

The first aim of the present study was to describe the developmental trajectories of associative memory distinguishing within-domain (factual) and between-domain (spatial and temporal) associations by means of an original single paradigm. Results showed that these three types of associative memory follow distinct developmental trajectories: a slight but continuous increase of within-domain factual associative memory (WHAT), a linear increase of between-domain spatial associative memory (WHERE), and noticeable changes in between-domain temporal associative memory from 9 to 10 years (WHEN). Overall, the composite score that combines the three associative components of episodic memory (the "episodic score") showed a slight but significant increase up to 9 years followed by a marked increase from 9 to 10. Regarding recollection, both objective (i.e., source memory) and subjective recollection improved with age with the most important effects from 8 to 10 years. Hence, these findings highlight major changes from 8–9 to 10 years. Thereafter, adolescence is characterized by slight changes, including enhancement of spatial associative memory and noticeable decrease in familiarity. Voxel-based morphometry suggests that episodic memory performance, which thus relies on remembering WHAT, WHERE, and WHEN components, is related to gray matter volume changes (i.e., following an inverted U-curve) in temporal regions including medial structures, prefrontal, and inferior parietal regions. Although these cortical regions and medial temporal structures have been previously described in functional studies, no such morphological data have been reported in developmental studies in relation with participants' overall associative memory efficiency. Also, our results point out the relevance of using a single paradigm to assess associative memory, source memory, and recollection in order to get a more comprehensive picture of episodic memory development.

DEVELOPMENTAL TRAJECTORIES OF ASSOCIATIVE MEMORY

Consistent with the developmental literature showing a major increase in memory efficiency between 6 and 10 years of age (Jambaqué et al., 1993; Vakil et al., 1998; Waber et al., 2007; Thaler et al., 2013), we found that these three types of associative memory (WHAT, WHERE, and WHEN) jointly improved in school-age children. The associative memory for within-domain features concerning the factual component follows a slight but significant increase from 6 to 10 years. Contrary to Sluzenski et al. (2006), we thus found that associative memory efficiency pursues its developmental course beyond the age of 6. Although the "WHAT" task shares some methodological characteristics with the animal-background associative paradigm proposed by these authors, i.e., to associate an animal with a specific feature, WHAT mainly differs on: (1) the use of a cued recall task known to be more age-sensitive than a recognition task (Picard et al., 2012), (2) the type of features that we designed (i.e., animals' habitat or food), (3) the choice of unfamiliar animals to minimize putative prior semantic knowledge, and (4) the number of targets the participants were asked to remember. Furthermore, the regular increase in performance that we observed until 10 years was followed by a slight (though not significant) decrease during adolescence, which is consistent with previous studies using standard memory tests (Carey et al., 1980; Vakil et al., 1998; Waber et al., 2007). Accordingly, younger children may engage in piecemeal recording whereas older peers may deliberately organize the items to enhance memory efficiency. In adolescence, the enhancement of executive functions and verbal strategies (as assessed here by fluency tasks) may play a critical role in binding mechanisms (see by Rhodes et al., 2011; Picard et al., 2012 for recent data). The impact of the developing executive processes (in line with critical neural changes during adolescence; see Blakemore and Choudhury, 2006) on memory enhancement may explain, at least partially, the great variability in memory performance regularly discussed in the field of developmental neuropsychology (Picard et al., 2012).

In the present study, both spatial and temporal associative memories undergo specific developmental trajectories. Spatial associative memory follows a linear increase that continues from 10 onward. In contrast, we observed a large variability of temporal memory until 9 years followed by a marked increase from 9 to 10, plateauing afterward. These data are thus consistent with the idea that both spatial and temporal memory processes rely on distinct cognitive abilities subserved by distinguishable cerebral networks (Nyberg et al., 1996; Ekstrom and Bookheimer, 2007).

Spatial memory is not a unitary construct and implies per-personal and extra-personal space processing, both being progressively bound together throughout normal development. These are linked to two different referential frames: allocentric and egocentric. In object-location memory tasks, both would interact with a probable superiority of the allocentric representation allowing individuals to code the location in a relational manner to the surrounding environment (Wang et al., 2005). Previous studies have shown that the type of cues used to remember a location changes from childhood to early adulthood (Bullens et al., 2010, 2011). Allocentric spatial abilities emerge around 2 years of age (Newcombe et al., 1998; Ribordy et al., 2013). However, when experimental designs increase in complexity, performances then depend on additional cognitive functions such as working memory (Lorsbach and Reimer, 2005), mental rotation, and the capacity to understand verbal instructions (Nardini et al., 2006). All these cognitive functions develop through childhood and adolescence and may contribute to the age-related effect on spatial processes observed in the present study from six to early adulthood.

Regarding temporal memory, we observe an abrupt increase in children's performance at the age of nine followed by a plateau from 10 years onward. Memory for the temporal parameters of personal events or experimental items relies on several processes that refer to time (recency and frequency), location (labeling an event with external cues), and relative times of occurrence (sequential memory). The literature acknowledges that sequential memory needs to integrate both the relationship between an item and its position in the sequence and the relationship between two following items. To recollect the actual sequence, one needs to recreate the order in which stimuli were presented, that is to reorganize a set of items according to their temporal relationships. The ability to encode and retrieve sequences is thought to develop gradually from early childhood (McCormack and Hoerl, 1999) to adolescence in tandem with the development of language and organizational skills (Naito, 2003; Romine and Reynolds 2004). Importantly, many authors support the view that the cognitive components of executive functions are fully efficient around the age of 12 (Anderson, 2002; Huizinga et al., 2006). Effective implementation of executive functions is essential for this kind of reconstructive process to be successful (Friedman and Lyon, 2005). Unexpectedly, we observe a slight, though not significant increase of performance during adolescence. Debriefing of the participants after the test allows us to hypothesize that this results from the particular design of the task itself. Indeed, many adolescents explained that they intentionally created a script on the bases of the animal orders (i.e., "when the urodel runs after the almiqui . . ."). Thus, the use of verbal strategies to encode the sequence in a chronological and meaningful order at this age may impact subsequent retrieval. Interestingly, this is in accordance with our additional analyses showing a significant correlation between verbal fluency efficiency and the WHEN.

Taken together, the above mentioned data suggest that associative episodic memory maturation depends on the type of information to be bound and that the overall processes may differentially contribute to episodic memory enhancement. Accordingly, the evolution of the combining episodic score through childhood tends to be non-linear prompted by the time course of temporal memory. Once more, the period of late childhood (9–10 years of age) is crucial in the developmental time course of episodic memory.

SUBJECTIVE AND OBJECTIVE RECOLLECTION

Objective and subjective recollection have been distinguished in functional (Spaniol et al., 2009 for review) and clinical studies (Duarte et al., 2008) in adults and have more recently encounter an increasing interest in the developmental literature (Ghetti and Angelini, 2008; Picard et al., 2009; Friedman et al., 2010).

In the present study, remember and familiarity judgments were equally distributed in the youngest group but appeared to follow two distinct time courses thereafter. Subjective recollection (as measured by the "remember" responses) showed significant enhancement up to 10 while familiarity remained unchanged during this period. Our findings concerning recollection are thus in accordance with recent data showing that 11 years old children were able to perform like adults (Rhodes et al., 2011). However, in the present study, familiarity judgment slightly decreased during adolescence contrasting with previous published behavioral data reporting no modification of familiarity process with age (Billingsley et al., 2002; Piolino et al., 2007). Yet, functional data sets as collected in Event Related Potential's studies (Friedman et al., 2010) suggested that familiarity is unlikely to be driven by the exact same processes from childhood to late adolescence. The authors notably pointed out the relationship between familiarity and mid-frontal regions recruitment restricted to adolescents. Besides, these data argue for a comprehensive approach based on both neuroimaging and behavioral studies to understand age-related effects on episodic memory maturation.

We deliberately distinguished between subjective and objective recollection. A marked increase in "objective recollection" is reported from early childhood (4–6 years) onward (Perner and Ruffman, 1995; Welch-Ross, 1995) depending on factors such as distinctiveness, frequency, and retention interval (Parker, 1995; Ruffman et al., 2001). Recent data support the idea that objective and subjective recollection improve simultaneously from 6 to 18 years (Ghetti and Angelini, 2008; Ghetti et al., 2011). In the present study, objective (i.e., source memory) and subjective recollection followed slightly different developmental trajectories from 8 to 10 years and seemed more closely connected later on, i.e., from nine to adulthood. This developmental dissociation may be accounted for by difference in processes involved in recollection judgment with possibly preferred perceptual-based analysis in youngest participants (Ofen and Shing, 2013).

RELATIONSHIPS BETWEEN BRAIN VOLUME AND MEMORY EFFICIENCY

The present study pointed out the relationship between an increase in associative memory efficiency and a decrease in gray matter volume in a large cerebral network (including the dorsolateral and VLPFC, superior and anterior temporal regions) and the hippocampus bilaterally. In our sample, only three participants displayed a different pattern. As Shaw et al. (2006) argued in their study on global intellectual efficiency and cortical thickness, in which they reported different developmental trajectories of cortical thickness according to participants' IQs, the variability in our sample may reflect different trajectories depending on the individual level of memory performance.

Frontal regions

Structural maturational changes in frontal lobes, decrease in either cortical thickness (Sowell et al., 2001) or volume (Antshel et al., 2008), are related with enhancement of episodic memory efficiency. Greater activation of lateral PFC was associated with an intentional encoding of scenes, subjective recollection (Ofen et al., 2007; Wendelken et al., 2011), retrieval suppression (Paz-Alonso et al., 2013), contextual memory (Ghetti et al., 2010) in children. However, no functional or structural study was conducted on associative multimodal memory in this population. The only structural study conducted in children and young adults so far indicates that thinner VLPFC may support more efficient relational encoding/retrieval processes of a complex Figure (Østby et al., 2012). In the present study, increased performances were related with volume reduction in the dorsolateral and the VLPFC. Interestingly, the reduction of DLPFC was also correlated with increased performances in verbal fluency in our sample, thus suggesting a possible contribution of executive functions to memory efficiency as measured by the WHAT-WHERE-WHEN paradigm.

Hippocampal structures

Only three other studies have investigated the relationships between memory and medial temporal lobe (Sowell et al., 2001) or hippocampal volume (Yurgelun-Todd et al., 2003; Østby et al., 2012). One reported a positive correlation with consolidation processes while the two other found negative correlations with retrieval performances. Otherwise, longitudinal studies focusing on age-related effects on gray matter volume revealed that the anterior part of the hippocampus decreases in volume from ages 4–25 years (Gogtay et al., 2006). In the present study, a slight decrease in hippocampal volume restricted to the right hippocampal body and the anterior part of the left hippocampus was related to an enhancement of episodic performances. Hence, our results suggest the involvement of a more anterior region in the right hippocampus that would be consistent with a progressive specialization evocated by DeMaster and Ghetti, 2013. However, further investigations are needed to understand the contribution of the hippocampus along its longitudinal axis to the development of episodic memory.

Temporo-parietal region

High-level associative areas allowing the integration of information from several sensory modalities undergo a protracted maturation up to early adulthood (Gogtay et al., 2006). Moreover, they support cognitive processes implicated in episodic memory, working memory updates associated with episodic retrieval (Borst and Anderson, 2013) or recollection (Yonelinas et al., 2005 in adults). The superior temporal gyrus is also implicated into self generation of verbal associations at encoding (Vannest et al., 2012 in adults). In the present study, we observed that the reduced volume in the superior temporal cortex extending to the inferior parietal lobule was related to episodic enhancement in children and adolescents. This region was not reported in previous structural studies but could support the generation of verbal strategies in our three associative tasks. The negative correlation between the volume reduction in the superior temporal cortex and the increase in verbal fluency performance would be consistent with this hypothesis. Moreover, is this cortical region involved in a larger fronto-parietal network including dorsolateral PFC that would implement cognitive control functions on memory functioning, and would support the progressive development of top-down attention modulation?

METHODOLOGICAL CONSIDERATIONS AND FUTURE DIRECTIONS

Our findings bring interesting perspectives to assess episodic memory from childhood to adolescence in a more comprehensive way. To our knowledge, the present study is the first to address episodic memory maturational trajectories by investigating its main components within the same paradigm. It thus provides a more accurate picture of how episodic memory processes (i.e., binding of within/between-domain information, source memory, recollection, and familiarity) evolve.

By confronting behavioral results to structural data, we also describe the cortical regions that subserve episodic memory efficiency as a whole. Unfortunately, the present study failed to detect finer relationships between each component (factual, spatial, temporal, source memory, or recollection) and brain structures. Knowing the large inter-individual variability in both memory efficiency and cerebral maturation in children and adolescents, we assume that the lack of sensitivity in morphometric analyses could be overcome in a larger cohort.

Taken together, the behavioral and structural analyses questioned the implication of maturing executive processes that may explain, at least partially, the differential trajectories that we report according to the type of information to be encoded and recollected. This hypothesis needs to be directly addressed in a future study by using more dedicated executive tasks.

Besides its relevance to provide additional data to the research literature, the present paradigm is considered to be a sensitive and valid tool to assess episodic memory in the clinical setting. The WHAT-WHERE-WHEN paradigm has been administered to children and adolescents suffering from temporal lobe epilepsy and has successfully detected differential profiles of deficits according to epilepsy lateralization (Guillery-Girard et al., 2010). It thus can be helpful to reveal possible memory dissociations in young patients.

CONCLUSION

Episodic memory refers to the capacity to bind different components into a single representation that will promote a vivid sense of re-experiencing at retrieval. Accordingly, our findings show the differential developmental trajectories of episodic memory processes in relationship with both cortical changes and neuropsychological factors such as verbal strategies and executive functions. Specifically, the present study suggests that the multimodal integration would be related to the maturation of temporal regions and may be modulated by a fronto-parietal network. Despite a limited sample for structural analyses, this study confirms the need to combine neuroimaging and behavioral data in order to better understand the developmental trajectory of episodic memory in a research setting, and to use a single paradigm to assess episodic memory as a whole in a clinical setting.

ACKNOWLEDGMENTS

We would like to thank Valerie Gyselinck and Maud Markus for their contribution to the WHAT-WHERE-WHEN paradigm development, and Nezha Bissara, and Lionel Allirol for their assistance with data collection. We are grateful to Jane Holmes-Bernstein for her helpful comments on the manuscript. We are also indebted to the participants and institutions that took part in our research.

REFERENCES

Anderson, P. (2002). Assessment and development of executive function (EF) during childhood. *Child Neuropsychol.* 8, 71–82.

Antshel, K. M., Peebles, J., AbdulSabur, N., Higgins, A. M., Roizen, N., Shprintzen, R., et al. (2008). Associations between performance on the Rey-Osterrieth Complex Figure and regional brain volumes in children with and without velocardiofacial syndrome. *Dev. Neuropsychol.* 33, 601–622. doi:10.1080/87565640802254422

Ashburner, J., and Friston, K. J. (2005). Unified segmentation. *Neuroimage* 26, 839–851. doi:10.1016/j.neuroimage.2005.02.018

Barnfield, A. M. (1999). Development of sex differences in spatial memory. *Percept. Mot. Skills* 89, 339–350. doi:10.2466/pms.1999.89.1.339

Billingsley, R. L., Lou Smith, M., and Pat McAndrews, M. (2002). Developmental patterns in priming and familiarity in explicit recollection. *J Exp. Child Psychol.* 82, 251–277. doi 10.1016/S0022-0965(02)00007-3

Blakemore, S.-J., and Choudhury, S (2006). Development of the adolescent brain: implications for executive function and social cognition. *J. Child Psychol. Psychiatry* 47, 296–312. doi:10.1111/j.1469-7610.2006.01611.x

Borst, J. P., and Anderson, J. R. (2013). Using model-based functional MRI to locate working memory updates and declarative memory retrievals in the fronto-parietal network. *Proc. Natl. Acad. Sci. U.S.A.* 110, 1628–1633. doi:10.1073/pnas.1221572110

Brainerd, C. J., Holliday, R. E., and Reyna, V. F. (2004). Behavioral measurement of remembering phenomenologies: so simple a child can do it. *Child Dev.* 75, 505–522. doi:10.1111/j.1467-8624.2004.00689.x

Büchel, C., Holmes, A. P., Rees, G., and Friston, K. J. (1998). Characterizing stimulus-response functions using nonlinear regressors in parametric fMRI experiments. *Neuroimage* 8, 140–148. doi:10.1006/nimg.1998.0351

Buchler, N. G., Light, L. L., and Reder, L. M. (2008). Memory for items and associations: distinct representations and processes in associative recognition. *J. Mem. Lang.* 59, 183–199. doi:10.1016/j.jml.2008.04.001

Bullens, J., Klugkist, I., and Postma, A. (2011). The role of local and distal landmarks in the development of object location memory. *Dev. Psychol.* 47, 1515–1524. doi:10.1037/a0025273

Bullens, J., Nardini, M., Doeller, C. F., Braddick, O., Postma, A., and Burgess, N. (2010). The role of landmarks and boundaries in the development of spatial memory. *Dev. Sci.* 13, 170–180. doi:10.1111/j.1467-7687.2009.00870.x

Carey, S., Diamond, R., and Woods, B. (1980). Development of face recognition: a maturational component? *Dev. Psychol.* 16, 257–269. doi:10.1037/0012-1649.16.4.257

DeMaster, D. M., and Ghetti, S. (2013). Developmental differences in hippocampal and cortical contributions to episodic retrieval. *Cortex* 49, 1482–1493. doi:10.1016/j.cortex.2012.08.004

Duarte, A., Henson, R. N., and Graham, K. S. (2008). The effects of aging on the neural correlates of subjective and objective recollection. *Cereb. Cortex* 18, 2169–2180. doi:10.1093/cercor/bhm243

Ekstrom, A. D., and Bookheimer, S. Y. (2007). Spatial and temporal episodic memory retrieval recruit dissociable functional networks in the human brain. *Learn. Mem.* 14, 645–654. doi:10.1101/lm.575107

Fonov, V., Evans, A. C., Botteron, K., Almli, C. R., McKinstry, R. C., Collins, D. L., et al. (2011). Unbiased average age-appropriate atlases for pediatric studies. *Neuroimage* 54, 313–327. doi:10.1016/j.neuroimage.2010.07.033

Friedman, D., de Chastelaine, M., Nessler, D., and Malcolm, B. (2010). Changes in familiarity and recollection across the lifespan: an ERP perspective. *Brain Res.* 1310, 124–141. doi:10.1016/j.brainres.2009.11.016

Friedman, W. J., and Lyon, T. D. (2005). Development of temporal-reconstructive abilities. *Child Dev.* 76, 1202–1216. doi:10.1111/j.1467-8624.2005.00844.x-i1

Ghetti, S., and Angelini, L. (2008). The development of recollection and familiarity in childhood and adolescence: evidence from the dual-process signal detection model. *Child Dev.* 79, 339–358. doi:10.1111/j.1467-8624.2007.01129.x

Ghetti, S., and Bunge, S. A. (2012). Neural changes underlying the development of episodic memory during middle childhood. *Dev. Cogn. Neurosci.* 2, 381–395. doi:10.1016/j.dcn.2012.05.002

Ghetti, S., DeMaster, D. M., Yonelinas, A. P., and Bunge, S. A. (2010). Developmental differences in medial temporal lobe function during memory encoding. *J. Neurosci.* 30, 9548–9556. doi:10.1523/JNEUROSCI.3500-09.2010

Ghetti, S., Mirandola, C., Angelini, L., Cornoldi, C., and Ciaramelli, E. (2011). Development of subjective recollection: understanding of and introspection on memory states. *Child Dev.* 82, 1954–1969. doi:10.1111/j.1467-8624.2011.01645.x

Giedd, J. N. (2004). Structural magnetic resonance imaging of the adolescent brain. *Ann. N. Y. Acad. Sci.* 1021, 77–85. doi:10.1196/annals.1308.009

Gogtay, N., Giedd, J. N., Lusk, L., Hayashi, K. M., Greenstein, D., Vaituzis, A. C., et al. (2004). Dynamic mapping of human cortical development during childhood through early adulthood. *Proc. Natl. Acad. Sci. U.S.A.* 101, 8174–8179. doi:10.1073/pnas.0402680101

Gogtay, N., Nugent, T. F. III, Herman, D. H., Ordonez, A., Greenstein, D., Hayashi, K. M., et al. (2006). Dynamic mapping of normal human hippocampal development. *Hippocampus* 16, 664–672. doi:10.1002/hipo.20193

Guillery-Girard, B., Bon, L., Martins, S., Denaveaut, M., Fraboulet, S., and Eustache, F. (2010). "L'évaluation neuropsychologique de la mémoire chez l'enfant," in *Approche Neuropsychologique des Troubles des Apprentissages*, eds S. Chokron, J. F. Démonet, and S. Valdois (Marseille: Solal), 225–247.

Gulya, M., Rossi-George, A., Hartshorn, K., Vieira, A., Rovee-Collier, C., Johnson, M. K., et al. (2002). The development of explicit memory for basic perceptual features. *J. Exp. Child Psychol.* 81, 276–297. doi:10.1006/jecp.2001.2654

Hu, S., Pruessner, J. C., Coupé, P., and Collins, D. L. (2013). Volumetric analysis of medial temporal lobe structures in brain development from childhood to adolescence. *Neuroimage* 74, 276–287. doi:10.1016/j.neuroimage.2013.02.032

Huizinga, M., Dolan, C. V., and van der Molen, M. W. (2006). Age-related change in executive function: developmental trends and a latent variable analysis. *Neuropsychologia* 44, 2017–2036. doi:10.1016/j.neuropsychologia.2006.01.010

Hund, A. M., and Plumert, J. M. (2002). Delay-induced bias in children's memory for location. *Child Dev.* 73, 829–840. doi:10.1111/1467-8624.00441

Jambaqué, I., Dellatolas, G., Dulac, O., Ponsot, G., and Signoret, J. L. (1993). Verbal and visual memory impairment in children with epilepsy. *Neuropsychologia* 31, 1321–1337. doi:10.1016/0028-3932(93)90101-5

Klein, S. B. (2013). Making the case that episodic recollection is attributable to operations occurring at retrieval rather than to content stored in a dedicated subsystem of long-term memory. *Front. Behav. Neurosci.* 7:3. doi:10.3389/fnbeh.2013.00003

Korkman, M., Kirk, U., and Kemp, S. L. (2007). *NEPSY II. Administrative Manual.* San Antonio, TX: Psychological Corporation.

Lloyd, M. E., Doydum, A. O., and Newcombe, N. S. (2009). Memory binding in early childhood: evidence for a retrieval deficit. *Child Dev.* 80, 1321–1328. doi:10.1111/j.1467-8624.2009.01353.x

Lorsbach, T. C., and Reimer, J. F. (2005). Feature binding in children and young adults. *J. Genet. Psychol.* 166, 313–327. doi:10.3200/GNTP.166.3.313-328

Mayes, A., Montaldi, D., and Migo, E. (2007). Associative memory and the medial temporal lobes. *Trends Cogn. Sci. (Regul. Ed.)* 11, 126–135. doi:10.1016/j.tics.2006.12.003

McCormack, T., and Hoerl, C. (1999). Memory and temporal perspective: the role of temporal frameworks in memory development. *Dev. Rev.* 19, 154–182. doi:10.1006/drev.1998.0476

Naito, M. (2003). The relationship between theory of mind and episodic memory: evidence for the development of autonoetic consciousness. *J. Exp. Child Psychol.* 85, 312–336. doi:10.1016/S0022-0965(03)00075-4

Nardini, M., Burgess, N., Breckenridge, K., and Atkinson, J. (2006). Differential developmental trajectories for egocentric, environmental and intrinsic frames of reference in spatial memory. *Cognition* 101, 153–172. doi:10.1016/j.cognition.2005.09.005

Newcombe, N., Huttenlocher, J., Drummey, A. B., and Wiley, J. G. (1998). The development of spatial location coding: place learning and dead reckoning in the second and third years. *Cogn. Dev.* 13, 185–200. doi:10.1016/S0885-2014(98)90038-7

Nyberg, L., McIntosh, A. R., Cabeza, R., Habib, R., Houle, S., and Tulving, E. (1996). General and specific brain regions involved in encoding and retrieval of events: what, where, and when. *Proc. Natl. Acad. Sci. U.S.A.* 93, 11280–11285. doi:10.1073/pnas.93.20.11280

Ofen, N., Chai, X. J., Schuil, K. D. I., Whitfield-Gabrieli, S., and Gabrieli, J. D. E. (2012). The development of brain systems associated with successful memory retrieval of scenes. *J. Neurosci.* 32, 10012–10020. doi:10.1523/JNEUROSCI.1082-11.2012

Ofen, N., Kao, Y.-C., Sokol-Hessner, P., Kim, H., Whitfield-Gabrieli, S., and Gabrieli, J. D. E. (2007). Development of the declarative memory system in the human brain. *Nat. Neurosci.* 10, 1198–1205. doi:10.1038/nn1950

Ofen, N., and Shing, Y. L. (2013). From perception to memory: changes in memory systems across the lifespan. *Neurosci. Biobehav. Rev.* doi:10.1016/j.neubiorev.2013.04.006

Østby, Y., Tamnes, C. K., Fjell, A. M., and Walhovd, K. B. (2012). Dissociating memory processes in the developing brain: the role of hippocampal volume and cortical thickness in recall after minutes versus days. *Cereb. Cortex* 22, 381–390. doi:10.1093/cercor/bhr116

Parker, J. F. (1995). Age differences in source monitoring of performed and imagined actions on immediate and delayed tests. *J. Exp. Child Psychol.* 60, 84–101. doi:10.1006/jecp.1995.1032

Pathman, T., Larkina, M., Burch, M., and Bauer, P. J. (2013). Young children's memory for the times of personal past events. *J. Cogn. Dev.* 14, 120–140. doi:10.1080/15248372.2011.641185

Paz-Alonso, P. M., Bunge, S. A., Anderson, M. C., and Ghetti, S. (2013). Strength of Coupling within a mnemonic control network differentiates those who can and cannot suppress memory retrieval. *J. Neurosci.* 33, 5017–5026. doi:10.1523/JNEUROSCI.3459-12.2013

Perez, L. A., Peynircioglu, Z. F., and Blaxton, T. A. (1998). Developmental differences in implicit and explicit memory performance. *J. Exp. Child Psychol.* 70, 167–185. doi:10.1006/jecp.1998.2449

Perner, J., and Ruffman, T. (1995). Episodic memory and autonoetic consciousness: developmental evidence and a theory of childhood amnesia. *J. Exp. Child Psychol.* 59, 516–548. doi:10.1006/jecp.1995.1024

Picard, L., Cousin, S., Guillery-Girard, B., Eustache, F., and Piolino, P. (2012). How do the different components of episodic memory develop? Role of executive functions and short-term feature-binding abilities. *Child Dev.* 83, 1037–1050. doi:10.1111/j.1467-8624.2012.01736.x

Picard, L., Reffuveille, I., Eustache, F., and Piolino, P. (2009). Development of autonoetic autobiographical memory in school-age children: genuine age effect or development of basic cognitive abilities? *Conscious. Cogn.* 18, 864–876. doi:10.1016/j.concog.2009.07.008

Piolino, P., Hisland, M., Ruffeveille, I., Matuszewski, V., Jambaqué, I., and Eustache, F. (2007). Do school-age children remember or know the personal past? *Conscious. Cogn.* 16, 84–101. doi:10.1016/j.concog.2005.09.010

Pirogovsky, E., Murphy, C., and Gilbert, P. E. (2009). Developmental differences in memory for cross-modal associations. *Dev. Sci.* 12, 1054–1059. doi:10.1111/j.1467-7687.2009.00857.x

Rhodes, S. M., Murphy, D., and Hancock, P. J. B. (2011). Developmental changes in the engagement of episodic retrieval processes and their relationship with working memory during the period of middle childhood. *Br. J. Dev. Psychol.* 29, 865–882. doi:10.1111/j.2044-835X.2010.02014.x

Ribordy, F., Jabès, A., Banta Lavenex, P., and Lavenex, P. (2013). Development of allocentric spatial memory abilities in children from 18 months to 5 years of age. *Cogn. Psychol.* 66, 1–29. doi:10.1016/j.cogpsych.2012.08.001

Richmond, J., and Nelson, C. A. (2009). Relational memory during infancy: evidence from eye tracking. *Dev. Sci.* 12, 549–556. doi:10.1111/j.1467-7687.2009.00795.x

Riggins, T., Miller, N. C., Bauer, P. J., Georgieff, M. K., and Nelson, C. A. (2009). Electrophysiological indices of memory for temporal order in early childhood: implications for the development of recollection. *Dev. Sci.* 12, 209–219. doi:10.1111/j.1467-7687.2008.00757.x

Romine, C. B., and Reynolds, C. R. (2004). Sequential memory: a developmental perspective on its relation to frontal lobe functioning. *Neuropsychol. Rev.* 14, 43–64. doi:10.1023/B:NERV.0000026648.94811.32

Ruffman, T., Rustin, C., Garnham, W., and Parkin, A. J. (2001). Source monitoring and false memories in children: relation to certainty and executive functioning. *J. Exp. Child Psychol.* 80, 95–111. doi:10.1006/jecp.2001.2632

Russell, J., and Thompson, D. (2003). Memory development in the second year: for events or locations? *Cognition* 87, B97–B105. doi:10.1016/S0010-0277(02)00238-X

Sander, M. C., Werkle-Bergner, M., Gerjets, P., Shing, Y. L., and Lindenberger, U. (2012). The two-component model of memory development, and its potential implications for educational settings. *Dev. Cogn. Neurosci.* 2(Suppl. 1), S67–S77. doi:10.1016/j.dcn.2011.11.005

Shaw, P., Greenstein, D., Lerch, J., Clasen, L., Lenroot, R., Gogtay, N., et al. (2006). Intellectual ability and cortical development in children and adolescents. *Nature* 440, 676–679. doi:10.1038/nature04513

Sluzenski, J., Newcombe, N. S., and Kovacs, S. L. (2006). Binding, relational memory, and recall of naturalistic events: a developmental perspective. *J. Exp. Psychol. Learn. Mem. Cogn.* 32, 89–100. doi:10.1037/0278-7393.32.1.89

Sowell, E. R., Delis, D., Stiles, J., and Jernigan, T. L. (2001). Improved memory functioning and frontal lobe maturation between childhood and adolescence: a structural MRI study. *J. Int. Neuropsychol. Soc.* 7, 312–322. doi:10.1017/S135561770173305X

Spaniol, J., Davidson, P. S. R., Kim, A. S. N., Han, H., Moscovitch, M., and Grady, C. L. (2009). Event-related fMRI studies of episodic encoding and retrieval: meta-analyses using activation likelihood estimation. *Neuropsychologia* 47, 1765–1779. doi:10.1016/j.neuropsychologia.2009.02.028

Thaler, N. S., Goldstein, G., Pettegrew, J. W., Luther, J. F., Reynolds, C. R., and Allen, D. N. (2013). Developmental aspects of working and associative memory. *Arch. Clin. Neuropsychol.* 28, 348–355. doi:10.1093/arclin/acs114

Tulving, E. (2002). Episodic memory from mind to brain. *Annu. Rev. Psychol.* 53, 1–25. doi:10.1146/annurev.psych.53.100901.135114

Vakil, E., Blachstein, H., and Sheinman, M. (1998). Rey AVLT: developmental norms for children and the sensitivity of different memory measures to age. *Child Neuropsychol.* 4, 161–177. doi:10.1076/chin.4.3.161.3173

Vannest, J., Eaton, K. P., Henkel, D., Siegel, M., Tsevat, R. K., Allendorfer, J. B., et al. (2012). Cortical correlates of self-generation in verbal paired associate learning. *Brain Res.* 1437, 104–114. doi:10.1016/j.brainres.2011.12.020

Waber, D. P., De Moor, C., Forbes, P. W., Almli, C. R., Botteron, K. N., Leonard, G., et al. (2007). The NIH MRI study of normal brain development: performance of a population based sample of healthy children aged 6 to 18 years on a neuropsychological battery. *J. Int. Neuropsychol. Soc.* 13, 729–746.

Wang, H., Johnson, T. R., Sun, Y., and Zhang, J. (2005). Object location memory: the interplay of multiple representations. *Mem. Cognit.* 33, 1147–1159. doi:10.3758/BF03193219

Welch-Ross, M. K. (1995). An integrative model of the development of autobiographical memory. *Dev. Rev.* 15, 338–365. doi:10.1006/drev.1995.1013

Wendelken, C., Baym, C. L., Gazzaley, A., and Bunge, S. A. (2011). Neural indices of improved attentional modulation over middle childhood. *Dev. Cogn. Neurosci.* 1, 175–186. doi:10.1016/j.dcn.2010.11.001

Yonelinas, A. P., and Jacoby, L. L. (1995). Dissociating automatic and controlled processes in a memory-search task: beyond implicit memory. *Psychol. Res.* 57, 156–165. doi:10.1007/BF00431277

Yonelinas, A. P., Otten, L. J., Shaw, K. N., and Rugg, M. D. (2005). Separating the brain regions involved in recollection and familiarity in recognition memory. *J. Neurosci* 25, 3002–3008. doi:10.1523/JNEUROSCI.5295-04.2005

Yurgelun-Todd, D. A., Killgore, W. D. S., and Cintron, C. B. (2003). Cognitive correlates of medial temporal lobe development across adolescence: a magnetic resonance imaging study. *Percept. Mot. Skills* 96, 3–17. doi:10.2466/pms.2003.96.1.3

16

Making the case that episodic recollection is attributable to operations occurring at retrieval rather than to content stored in a dedicated subsystem of long-term memory

Stanley B. Klein*

Department of Psychological and Brain Sciences, University of California, Santa Barbara, CA, USA

Correspondence:
Stanley B. Klein, Department of Psychological and Brain Sciences, University of California, Santa Barbara, 551 Ucen Road, Santa Barbara, CA 93106, USA.
e-mail: klein@psych.ucsb.edu

Episodic memory often is conceptualized as a uniquely human system of long-term memory that makes available knowledge accompanied by the temporal and spatial context in which that knowledge was acquired. Retrieval from episodic memory entails a form of first–person subjectivity called autonoetic consciousness that provides a sense that a recollection was something that took place in the experiencer's personal past. In this paper I expand on this definition of episodic memory. Specifically, I suggest that (1) the core features assumed unique to episodic memory are shared by semantic memory, (2) episodic memory cannot be fully understood unless one appreciates that episodic recollection requires the coordinated function of a number of distinct, yet interacting, "enabling" systems. Although these systems—ownership, self, subjective temporality, and agency—are not traditionally viewed as memorial in nature, each is necessary for episodic recollection and jointly they may be sufficient, and (3) the type of subjective awareness provided by episodic recollection (autonoetic) is relational rather than intrinsic—i.e., it can be lost in certain patient populations, thus rendering episodic memory content indistinguishable from the content of semantic long-term memory.

Keywords: episodic memory, semantic memory, autonoetic awarness, amnesia, self, consciousness

What is episodic memory? As initially conceptualized, it is a system of long-term memory whose content provided its owner with a record of the temporal, spatial and self-referential features of the context in which the original learning transpired (e.g., Tulving, 1972, 1983). By contrast, semantic long-term memory lacked these features: Its offerings were experienced as knowledge devoid of the contextual elements in which it was acquired.

A clear implication of this distinction was the difference in subjective relations these systems of memory shared with the past. Episodic memory entailed awareness that a current recollection referred directly to, and thus was conceptualized as, an event that had transpired previously in one's life. By contrast, content from semantic memory was solely occurrent—it was present to awareness—as either thought or image—and though one could logically infer that the occurrent content must have been acquired at some time in one's past, the recollection of its acquisition was not part of its experienced presentation.

These temporal distinctions were fully appreciated by Tulving, and in 1985 he made them an explicit basis for distinguishing between episodic and semantic systems of memory (Tulving, 1985). Adopting terminology proposed originally by Husserl—"noesis" (i.e., the type of experience associated with thought and remembering; e.g., Husserl, 1964)—Tulving focused attention on the types temporal subjectivity accompanying the retrieval of episodic and semantic memory. Episodic memory was held to enable *autonoetic* awareness, while semantic memory enabled a type of awareness he termed *noetic* (e.g., Tulving, 1985, 1993, 2002; Wheeler et al., 1997; Szpunar and Tulving, 2011).

Autonoetic awareness was defined as "self-knowing": when autonoetically aware, the individual's phenomenology is characterized by "... a unique awareness of re-experiencing here and now something that happened before, at another time and in another place" (Tulving, 1993, p. 68). By contrast, noetic awareness occurs when one thinks objectively about something one knows. Individuals are said to be noetically aware when "they retrieve general information in the absence of a feeling of re-experiencing the past" (Szpunar, 2010, p. 144). Central to the proposed distinction: "Only 'autonoetic consciousness' is thought to bear a personally meaningful relation to time" (Szpunar and Tulving, 2011, p. 4).

Autnoetic and noetic awareness align naturally with episodic and semantic modes of remembering, respectively (Tulving, 1985, 1993, 2002; Wheeler et al., 1997). Only autonoetic experience is assumed capable of providing the subjective requirements for mental time travel (e.g., Suddendorf and Corballis, 1997, 2007; Wheeler et al., 1997; Tulving, 2002; but see Klein, 2013b). Accordingly, episodic memory is tied directly to temporally-rich autonoetic experience. By contrast, awareness of semantic knowledge (i.e., noetic) lacks a subjective sense that one is mentally traveling to back in time to the events and experiences in one's past that gave birth to that awareness.

Tulving's reformulation of episodic and semantic memory in terms of temporal subjectivity has been widely adopted by memory researchers and has shown to be a particularly fruitful way of generating testable hypotheses and theoretical models of the episodic and semantic division of long-term declarative memory (e.g., Perner and Ruffman, 1994; Gardiner, 2001; Piolino et al., 2003; Wheeler, 2005; Markowitsch and Staniliou, 2011; for reviews, see Wheeler et al., 1997; Dere et al., 2008). A distinction based on subjective temporality also avoids a number of untidy findings that, over the years, have chipped away at the traditional classification of episodic and semantic memory in terms of the presence or absence of the criteria of time, space and self.

For instance, the assumption that episodic, rather than semantic, memory entails a self-referential component has given way to the well-recognized fact that knowledge in semantic memory also can be self-referential (for reviews, see Klein, 2010; Klein and Gangi, 2010; Klein and Lax, 2010; Renoult et al., in press). In addition, the content of semantic memory is capable of contributing to a knowledge-based representation that includes both spatial and temporal contextual information (e.g., "I know that John Lennon was born on October 9th, 1940 in Liverpool, UK, although I do not recollect the event in which that knowledge was acquired"; e.g., Tulving et al., 1988; Kopelman et al., 1989; Klein, 2001; for recent reviews see Klein, 2004; Klein and Gangi, 2010; Klein and Lax, 2010; Martinelli et al., 2012).

Thus, the core constituents of episodic memory as initially proposed (i.e., temporal, spatial, and self-referential) also can be on display in semantic memory experience. Indeed, there appears no principled reason why the content of these two systems should differ. This is demonstrated rather dramatically in a case presented by Stuss and Guzman (1988). An individual, who, as a result of illness, suffered profound retrograde episodic amnesia, nonetheless was able to successfully re-learn specific temporal and spatial details of his personal past. However, in accord with the autonoetic/noetic distinction, the patient experienced this content as semantic fact rather than as a re-living of his personal past (since he did not suffer comparable anterograde impairment, he could, of course, mentally travel back to the experienced events in which personal knowledge was relearned).

Thus, there is no logical argument or empirical evidence supporting the assertion that only episodic memory makes reference to the "where and when" of past personal experience. While the fact that two potentially separate systems share criteria is not a "death sentence" for a taxonomy, it highlights the severe difficulties faced by those who would adopt the "time, place, and self" criteria as *the* basis for classification.

In summary, the "time, space, and self" criterion for distinguishing between semantic and episodic memory is insufficient for the task for which it originally was designed. By contrast, the autonoetic/noetic criterion for classification does good work both in capturing a fundamental feature of our memory phenomenology and in serving as fertile theoretical and empirical grounds for exploring the complexities of the types of systems subsumed under the general designator "memory" (for reviews, see Wheeler, 2000; Markowitsch, 2003; Dere et al., 2008). In the next section I discuss issues involved in identifying an occurrent mental state as a memory.

MEMORY EXPERIENCE AND ITS CONNECTION TO THE PAST

The adoption of subjective temporality as a basis for distinguishing between forms of memory trades on the notion that the criteria for classification lie not in the *form* of content experienced, but in the *manner* in which that content is received by consciousness. In one sense, all memory-based content is experienced as occurrent—it is an act of mind happening *now*. As Reid puts it, "Every man can distinguish the thing remembered from the remembrance of it. We may remember anything we have seen, or heard, or known, of done, or suffered; but the remembrance of it is a particular act of the mind which now exists, and of which we are conscious" (Reid, 1813/1969, pp 324–325). It is the attachment of the "past" to present mental experience (be it imagistic or propositional) that marks the experience as one of memory rather than, say, imagination (Reid, by the way, denied the possibility of imagistic recollection, but that need not concern us at present).

The requirement that a current mental state evoke a sense of attachment to one's past to establish it as an act of memory (rather than, say, thought or imagination) long has been recognized. And, it has been a persistent thorn in the side of psychologists and philosophers grappling with the problem of placing a current mental state in a relation to the past. And, for the relation to do good work, it must be of the "right type."

So, what is the "right type" of relation between an occurrent mental state and the past? William James (1890), as so often is the case, puts the problem in sharp relief: "A farther condition is required before the present image can be held to stand for a *past original*. That condition is the fact that the imagined be *expressly referred to the past*, thought as *in the past* . . . But even that would not be memory. Memory requires more than mere dating of a fact in the past. It must be dated in *my* past. In other words, I must think that I directly experienced its occurrence. It must have . . . 'warmth and intimacy'. . . " (James, 1890, p. 650; emphasis in original).

Over the years (both prior to and following James' remarks) numerous criteria have been proposed to do the work of differentiating memory from a non-memorial mental content.[1] Hume famously proposed that the vivacity of a mental image is a basis on which we separate an image or thought from a memory, with memory being more lively and vivacious. He also proposed that the amount of "free play" we have with our mental states serves as a useful criterion—in contrast to imagining, for example, when

[1] Although James also is clear that much of what we now call semantic knowledge would not qualify as memory in his system—lacking, as it does, obvious reference to one's past (e.g., $2 + 2 = 4$; the sun is hot)—I believe that reference to the past is overly restrictive and not a necessary criterion for a mental experience or bodily action to meet the requirements for being a memory. A memory is an occurrent mental event that can be shown to have a causal connection to past experience. On this view, the expression of learning (whether via mental state or physical act) qualifies as memorial regardless of whether its current instantiation can be consciously traced to, or felt to derive from, a previously encountered event or experience, provided the proper causal connection(s) to a past experience can be demonstrated (via inference, objective evidence, or felt experience of past). For example, intelligently coordinated movements of the body which draw on the accumulated effect of knowable past events qualify as memorial despite absence of awareness that they are causally derived from previous experience (i.e., procedural memory). Of course, a little thought reveals an obvious circularity in any criterion of memory that draws on acquaintance (direct or indirect) with the past (i.e., memory) as the evidential basis for memory (e.g., Furlong, 1951). This perplexing conundrum would take us too far from the issues at hand and thus will not be dealt with here.

we remember we have less free play with mental content, since that content is bound by the past to represent things as they actually were (Hume, 1748/2004). Russell saw things differently, proposing that to be considered a memory a mental content must be accompanied by two feelings—pastness and familiarity (Russell, 1921).

Among modern psychological investigators, the work of Johnson and her colleagues represents the most systematic attempt to tackle this vexing problem (for review, see Johnson and Raye, 1981; Johnson et al., 1993). Their research eventuated in a set of criteria—e.g., the richness of the contextual and perceptual elements contained in a mental state. Although these criteria were proposed primarily to account for discrimination between memories for thoughts and memories for perceptions, they easily are adapted for classifying mental content as a memory as opposed to an act of thought or imagination.

Unfortunately, as theorists and philosophers have discovered, none of these criteria stand the test of logical analysis or introspection (for reviews, see Furlong, 1951; Casey, 1977; Warnock, 1987; Bernecker, 2010). For example, Russell's and Hume's assumption that the content of memory experience is "bound to the past" is partly undermined by demonstrations that memorial experience is, at least to a degree, reconstructive (e.g., Bartlett, 1932). And, we all have had experiences in which an imagination is vivid and a memory faint (e.g., Warnock, 1987). As Bernecker (2010) concluded, the problem with the memory-markers thus far proposed is that "they don't offer a reliable mark" (p. 22). Each is subject to logical argument and/or empirical demonstration that makes clear that none of the proposed criteria are either necessary or sufficient for marking a memory as such.

Considered in this light, the autonoetic/noetic criterion seems encouraging. While it may not serve as a definitive basis for distinguishing semantic memory from imagination—both are, by definition, noetic—it does provide a promising conceptual and phenomenological basis for identifying present mental content as part of one's past. It thus appears to be up to the task—that is, it provides the "right type" of relation—when the issue at hand is to determine whether an occurrent mental content is an episodic memory.

IS AUTONOETIC AWARENESS INTRINSIC TO EPISODIC RECOLLECTION?

Having argued in support of Tulving's contention that temporal subjectivity can serve as a useful basis by which to classify mental content as memorial, the issue now at hand is this—does subjective temporality provide sufficient license to conclude that current mental content represents an episodic, as opposed to a semantic, memory? As noted, content alone is not sufficient to make this judgment, since the constituents of both systems of memory *can* include temporal, spatial and self-referential elements. By contrast, the mode of subjective temporality accompanying an act of memory is assumed to differ dramatically between episodic recollection and semantic retrieval.

The content retrieved from semantic memory, on Tulving's account, can (at most) be *about* the past. Retrieval from semantic memory can be taken as either temporal (Klein et al., 2002b; for review, see Klein, 2013a) or atemporal (e.g., Klein et al., 2010). What determines its stance with respect to time is not the *quality* of the experience *per se*, but rather our ability to inferentially *refer* the experience to the past on the basis of the content present in (noetic) awareness. Thus, a causal analysis is required to place an occurrent semantic memory in a relation to the past.

On the other hand, episodic memory's connection to the past is not one of logical inference. Rather, it is pre-reflective, directly *given* (e.g., Zahavi, 2005). It is a sense (i.e., a feeling) that my current mental state stands for, and thus representative of, an experience in my personal past (e.g., James, 1890). The content of episodic recollection is given as being *of* the past; it is accompanied by a feeling of mental time travel—that is, re-visiting a personal experience. This feeling, or sense of attachment, to my past (which James called "warmth and intimacy" and Russell labeled "feelings of familiarity and pastness"), is part of the subjective *quality of* the mental event. As Nagel (1974) might say, the pastness of an episodic experience is part of "the feeling of what it is like" to have such an experience. And this feeling (or qualia) accompanying episodic recollection is made possible by episodic memory's association with autonoetic awareness.

The distinction between episodic and semantic memorial experience can thus be seen as one of differences in manner of acquaintance (e.g., Russell, 1912/1999). We are acquainted with semantic pastness indirectly via inference, whereas our acquaintance with episodic pastness is directly given as the feeling that we are re-living our past. If this distinction holds, then a phenomenological state is what differentiates our experience of these two forms of long-term memory.

So what exactly is the *connection* between autonoetic awareness and episodic memory? Two possibilities present themselves. Either (as commonly assumed, though seldom stated), autonoetic awareness is (1) *intrinsic* (i.e., necessary) to episodic memory—i.e., it is a part, or constituent, of "episodic" content, or (2) it has a *relational* (i.e., contingent) connection to memory content—i.e., while under normal circumstances it is observed to be coextensive with "episodic" content, this connection is one of contingency rather than necessity.

On the relational view, the neuro-cognitive mechanisms that make possible autonoetic awareness are functionally independent of the mechanisms that make available the content of long-term memory. What makes a memory experience episodic or semantic is not the nature of the content, or the hypothesized system in which content resides while in "storage," but rather an act of temporal (or atemporal) awareness that becomes associated with the content *once* it has been retrieved.

This is the view I champion in this paper. Although evidence in support is scarce, suggestive findings have been reported in a study by Piolino and colleagues (2003). Using the remember/know paradigm (e.g., Tulving, 1985), these investigators found that patients suffering Alzhiemer's Disease and Frontotemporal Dementia report significantly fewer "remember" responses than do controls. Based on this finding, they conclude that these two forms of dementia entail impairments specific to autonoetic awareness. However, whether this impairment occurs in storage or at retrieval is indeterminate. Moreover, as I discuss in section "Conclusions," the proposed relation between remember judgments and autonoeisis is more suggestive than theoretically grounded. I present evidence that bears directly on the relation between autonoetic awareness and retrieval in section "Can Autonoetic Awareness be Separated from Episodic Content? The Case of Patient R. B."

In sum, the relational view implies that memory content is neither episodic nor semantic; rather retrieved content is classifiable as episodic or semantic by virtue of a concurrent act of autonoetic awareness, whose association (or lack thereof) is used to classify an occurrent mental state as episodic or semantic. Seen in this light, there are no systems of episodic and semantic memory *per se*. Rather, there is memory content that can, if a suitable candidate for temporal specification is present in consciousness (e.g., "where and when I learned that $2 + 2 = 4$," but not "I know that $2 + 2 = 4$") can be acted on by the autonoetic subsystem to confer a sense of temporal subjectivity on the content retrieved.[2]

EPISODIC MEMORY: A COMPONENTIAL APPROACH

Many contemporary treatments of episodic memory focus on the encoding, storage and retrieval of memory content (for discussion, see Klein, 2007). However, as Klein et al. (2004) have argued, theoretical and empirical considerations call into question the wisdom of such restrictive treatment of memory experience. Their work makes a strong case that episodic recollection entails a multiplicity of functionally independent, yet normally interacting, systems, only some of which bear an obvious a priori relation to memory taken as the encoding, storage and retrieval of content

Specifically, Klein et al. (2004) proposed that to experience memory content as episodic requires, at a minimum, four capabilities. These include (1) a capacity for self-reflection; that is, the ability to reflect on my own mental states—to know about my own knowing, (2) a sense of personal agency; that is, the belief that I am the cause of my thoughts and actions, (3) a sense of personal ownership; that is, the feeling that my thoughts and acts belong to me, and (4) the ability to think about time as an unfolding of personal happenings centered about the self. Klein and colleagues conceptualized episodic recollection as a mental state resulting from the finely tuned interplay of these four psychological capacities that, working together, transform a retrieved content into an episodic experience. It follows that breakdowns in any of these components (self-reflection, self-agency, self-ownership, and personal temporality) should produce, in varying degrees, specific, highly circumscribed impairments in episodic recollection. A review of the available evidence showed that this does indeed occur (e.g., Klein, 2001; Klein et al., 2004), leading the authors to suggest that the subsystems identified may provide a set of individually necessary and jointly sufficient conditions for enabling memory content to be experienced as episodic recollection.

I will not review the specifics of the subsystems identified by Klein et al. (2004; for a related view, see Klein, 2011). Rather, in what follows I focus on one system with direct relevance to present concerns—the system that enables a feeling of ownership of one's mental states—and I discuss its implications for autonoetic awareness and its relation to episodic memory experience.

CAN AUTONOETIC AWARENESS BE SEPARATED FROM EPISODIC CONTENT? THE CASE OF PATIENT R. B.

As noted in Section "Is Autonoetic Awareness Intrinsic to Episodic Recollection?" if autonoetic awareness is functionally independent from memory content, then temporal subjectivity and memory content should be capable of being pried apart. The case of patient R. B. (reported below), has direct bearing on this issue.

The idea that ownership of one's mental states can come loose from the states, as experienced, is not a novel observation: A substantial literature (primarily clinical) speaks to the reality of this possibility. For example, in a largely speculative treatment, Jaynes (1976) argued that prior to acquiring the capacity to confer ownership on conscious thought our ancestors were unable to accurately localize the origination of "voices heard" in their heads. Less speculative evidence comes from cases of thought insertion in schizophrenics suffering delusional symptoms (e.g., Frith, 1992; Gallagher, 2000; Northoff, 2000; Bortolotti and Broome, 2009; for review, see Stephens and Graham, 2000). However, while these cases support the realizability, and thus conceivability, of a lack of personal ownership of one's mental states, schizophrenic patients *apparent* memories, even in early stages of the disorder, likely are delusions in some sense (e.g., Northoff, 2000; Klein and Nichols, 2012), and this renders such cases less than optimal as demonstrations that memory (as opposed to, say, delusion) and ownership can come apart.

Of particular importance, then, is the case of patient R. B. (the details are summarized herein. A fuller treatment can be found in Klein and Nichols, 2012). As a result of a serious accident, R. B. suffered, in addition to severe physical injuries, a number of cognitive impairments. These included difficulty in maintaining attention, mild aphasia, and retrograde and anterograde amnesia for events in close temporal proximity to the accident. His performance on tests of verbal fluency and short-term memory span fell below the scores provided by neurologically healthy age-matched controls.

While in the hospital, R. B. was placed on morphine (IV drip, followed by pills) and Oxycontin to alleviate the considerable pain he endured. As the intensity of his pain subsided, he weaned himself off medication. Importantly, at the time of testing R. B. was not on any pain medication. In addition, his long and short-term memory impairments, aphasia and fluency deficits had resolved.

Not all cognitive function, however, had returned to normal. Of direct bearing on the question at hand—the relation of autonoetic awareness to episodic memory—R. B. was able to remember particular incidents from his life accompanied by clear temporal, spatial and self-referential content. But he did not

[2] One limitation of the present account is that I have no proven criteria for specifying when autonoetic awareness will act on retrieved content other than the trivially obvious consideration of content relevance to temporal treatment [One speculative possibility—which I develop later in this paper—trades on Nadel and Moscovitch's (1997) Mutliple Trace Theory]. However, while the lack of a clear understanding of how and when autonoetic awareness makes contact with current mental content is an obvious weakness of my proposal, I do not think the absence of research on a previously un-proposed emendation to a well-established model argues, by itself, against the potential worth of my suggested revision. Rather, it highlights the novelty of the proposal and the need for conceptual and empirical work before the ideas expressed herein can transition from plausible to likely.

feel the content experienced belonged to him. In his words, they lacked "ownership"[3] (in the descriptive language of James, Russell, and Hume, his "memories" lacked feelings of warmth, intimacy, and personal pastness). Viewed in terms of episodic criteria, his mental states presented content adhering to the original episodic criteria, but divorced from autonoetic awareness.

This particular type of memory impairment—recollection absent a sense of personal ownership—is a form of memory dissociation that, to my knowledge, has not previously been documented in the amnesic literature (Klein and Nichols, 2012). There are, however, two cases that bear similarity. One is from a study of an amnesic reported by Talland (1964). Unfortunately, the data available from that brief report, while suggesting a similar dissociation, are too limited to support strong conclusions. In the other case (touched on earlier in this paper), a patient relearned his "personal history" following a case of severe retrograde episodic amnesia spanning most of his past life (Stuss and Guzman, 1988). The patient commented that the relearned memories seemed to lack a feel of real happenings in his life. They were, to him, more like stories and facts told to him by others (which, indeed, they were!). In this sense, they were more like semantic facts about himself (e.g. Klein and Gangi, 2010; Klein and Lax, 2010) than episodic recollections: The patient knew his memories were about him, but he did not remember them as temporally and spatially acquired in the correct context (that is, when the original acts transpired). Instead, they were memories that temporally and spatially were correctly experienced as second-hand stories told to him at a particular time and place (i.e., they consisted in the recollection of information acquired following the onset of his retrograde memory loss).

So, are R. B.'s memories episodic or semantic? The reported content suggests the former, but R. B.'s reported experience suggests the latter. Almost immediately following his accident, R. B. was able to intentionally retrieve specific events temporally and spatially situated in his personal past. But, as noted, his memories were compromised in an unusual manner—retrieval of events, though fitting the standard criteria for episodic recollection (i.e., time, place, and about R. B.), were unaccompanied by a sense of personal ownership. And, absent that sense, the ability to *feel* these memories as emanating from his personal past—to mentally travel to the time in which the events represented by his current thought and images originally transpired—was lost.

Lacking the experience of personal ownership, R. B. simultaneously lost a direct, personal connection with his past. It thus appears that loss of ownership equates to an inability to draw on the resources provided by autonoetic awareness to identify the content of a current mental state as a part of one's personal history. For example, approximately 2 months following release from the hospital, R. B. offered the following description of what it is like for him to recall personal events:

". . . I did not own any memories that came before my injury. I knew things that came before my injury. In fact, it seemed that my memory was just fine for things that happened going back years in the past (the period close to the injury was more disrupted). I could answer any question about where I lived at different times in my life, who my friends were, where I went to school, activities I enjoyed. But none of it was 'me.' It was the same sort of knowledge I might have about how my parents met or the history of the Civil War or something like that."

In my review of taxonomies of long-term memory, I noted that psychologists traditionally have characterized episodic recollections as temporal, spatial, and self-referential. By these criteria, R. B.'s descriptions of his memorial experience leave little doubt that they are episodic recollections, appropriately situated in time and space, rather than factual, atemporal semantic knowledge. As I also suggested, however, there is no principled reason why a semantic fact could not contain spatial, temporal and self-referential content, or be correctly referred to a person's past—albeit a past constructed inferentially rather than autonoetically given. And therein resides a puzzle. Do R. B.'s unowned memories consist in episodic content divorced from its relational connection to autonoetic awareness, or are they rather un-categorized (i.e., as episodic or semantic) content retrieved from storage but divorced from the sense of personal ownership conferred by an act of autoneotic awareness?

R. B. addresses the question directly. When asked to recall of events from his childhood he replies:

"I was remembering scenes, not facts . . . I was recalling scenes . . . that is . . . I could clearly recall a scene of me at the beach in New London with my family as a child. But the feeling was that the scene was not my memory. As if I was looking at a photo of someone else's vacation."

All of R. B.'s memories were substantiated by third parties as valid renditions of events that actually transpired in his life. While his recollections satisfy the traditional criteria for episodic memory—time, place, and self-accompanied by clear imagistic representation of (typically) unique events (see below for additional examples)—they simultaneously exhibit an absence of experienced ownership: While he can infer that the events recalled *must* be representative of past personal experience, he does not know this by virtue of a direct, felt connection to the past. In short, he has no sense of re-living the experiences retrieved.

The absence of ownership also is evident in R. B.'s response to instructions to recall personal memories from time spent in graduate school:

"I can picture the scene perfectly clearly . . . studying with my friends in our study lounge. I can 'relive' it in the sense of re-running the experience of being there. But it has the feeling of imagining, (as if) re-running an experience that my parents described from their college days. It did not feel like it was something that really had been a part of my life. Intellectually I suppose I never doubted that it was a part of my life. Perhaps because there

[3]It is important to note that ownership of one's mental states admits to several instantiations. For example one can have "perspectival" ownership of the content of a mental state. This implies only that one is aware that the experienced state is taking place in his or her mind. R. B. clearly maintains this form of ownership. By contrast, "personal" ownership is lacking in R. B. While he understands that the memories he experiences present themselves to his consciousness, he does not feel as though they are his own. Lacking this form of ownership, he is unable to autonoetically experience the content of his mental states as expressly referring to events from his past. For detailed discussions of forms of ownership, see Albahari (2006) and Locke (1968).

was such continuity of memories that fit a pattern that lead up to the present time. But that in itself did not help change the feeling of ownership."

He continues:

"Things that were in the present, like my name, I continue to own. Having been to MIT had two different issues ... my memories of having been at MIT I did not own. Those scenes of being at MIT were vivid, but they were not mine. But I owned 'the fact that I had a degree from MIT'... that might have simply been a matter of rational acceptance of fact."

Once again, R. B.'s memory performance adheres to the traditional definition of episodic recollection: He can vividly remember where the specific event transpired, when the specific event took place, and that it directly involved him. But, autonoetic awareness is missing. In short, on the view presented here, the notions of episodic and semantic can be seen to refer not to different stores or systems of memory content, but rather to how that content, once retrieved, is acted on by mechanisms (inferential or autonoetic) to enact a reference to one's past (note: not all memory content can be mapped to the past[2]). This proposal is reflected in the way R. B. treats his perspectival, but not personally, owned pre-injury memory content, both during its separation from autonoetic awareness and following their eventual recoupling—at which point memory retrieval previously experienced as "unowned" takes on a decidedly episodic flavor:

SBK: "Can you recall personally important events from your pre-injury period?"

RB: "I remember things that came before my injury. In fact, it seems that my memory is just fine for things that happened going back years in the past. I can answer questions about where I lived at different times in my life, who my friends were, where I went to school, activities I enjoyed ... but ... to clarify ... I am remembering scenes, not facts. Since I am remembering scenes, I think this means I am dealing with exactly what you are asking about."

SBK: "Can you recall who you are? More specifically, what you were like and what you are like—that is, your trait characteristics. If so, are your traits felt as your own?"

RB: "Yes, I know what I am like ... intelligent, shy, honest, a good person, things like that? Yes, I definitely have no identity problem. And the memories created since the injury I have full ownership of."[4]

SBK: "Can you recall for me a personal event concerning your time at college that would involve knowing what happened to you as a personal experience. Or is the recall more of a factual nature?"

RB: "I can see the scene in my head. I'm studying with friends in the lounge at my residence hall. I am able to re-live it. I have a feeling ... a sense of being at there, at MIT, in the lounge. But it doesn't feel like I own it. It's like I'm imagining, re-living the experience but it was described by someone else."

SBK: "Can you recall memories whenever you desire to do so?"

RB: "I can recall memories (from the non-ownership period of his life) at will. I have normal control over remembering facts and scenes from my past. But when I remember scenes from before the injury, they do not feel as if they happened to me—though intellectually I know they did—they feel as if they happened to someone else."

With respect to the recovery of episodic ownership:

"When I did 'take ownership' of a memory, it was actually quite isolated. A single memory I might own, yet another memory connected to it I would not own. It was a startling experience to have no rhyme or reason to which memories I slowly took ownership of, one at a time at random over a period of weeks and months."

He continues:

"What happened over the coming months ... was interesting. Every once in a while, I would suddenly think about something in my past and I would 'own' it. That was indeed something 'I' had done and experienced. Over time, one by one I would come to 'own' different memories. Eventually, after perhaps 8 months or so, it seemed as if it was all owned ... as if once enough individual memories were owned, it was all owned. For example, the MIT memory, the one in the lounge ... I now own it. It's clearly part of my life, my past."

SUMMING UP: THE CASE OF PATIENT R. B. AND ITS IMPLICATIONS FOR EPISODIC MEMORY

There appears to be an intimate connection with, and possibility of separation between, the content of a memory experience and whether that experience is autonoetic. R. B.'s confusion with regard to "content ownership" highlights the intimate relation between autonoetic awareness and ownership: Absent a sense of ownership, R. B. cannot mentally travel back in time to claim as his own the re-presentation of the experience from which the occurrent content was derived. Instead he relies on inference and logical possibility to (often correctly) infer that, given the specific elements of the content retrieved, it likely represents aspects of his personal past.

The apparent paradox presented by the case of patient R. B.—episodic-like content absent the feeling of personal ownership (and thus lived pastness)—can be understood by situating episodic memory in the context of a system of interrelated memory processes, some of which provide the raw data for experience (i.e., content) and some of which enable the experience to be "mine" (for extended treatments, see Klein, 2004, 2010, 2012; Klein et al., 2004; Klein and Nichols, 2012). R. B.'s recollections during his "unowned" period can be explained in the context of the view that there is specialized neural machinery that acts on retrieved content (of the right sort; e.g., Footnote 2) to confer on it a *sense* of re-living a personal experience—i.e., episodic recollection. This neural machinery in R. B. seems to have been compromised by his injury, but only for those events that occurred in the time period preceding his injury. That is, R. B. suffered a form of retrograde amnesia that compromised his ability to experience his personal recollections as his own. During the non-ownership period, R. B. had memory of pre-injury events and could locate

[4]Note that despite his ownership/autonetic limitations, R. B.'s responses exhibit a clear sense of self both narratively and factually. Thus, it is reasonable to conclude that his memory issues are not traceable to impairments of self (Klein et al's, 2004, subsystem #1). In addition, throughout his period of impairment he exhibits a clear and precise ability to perform a requested retrieval, thus demonstrating intact agency with regard to memory (which suggests, in turn, that subsystem #2 has not unduly been impacted by his injuries). That he has an intact sense of agency also can be seen from his remarks as the interview continues.

them, via inference, in his personal past. But he lacked a sense of numerical personal identity with the experiences retrieved. The case of R. B. thus suggests that the sense of numerical personal identity is quite narrowly circumscribed: R. B. had factual self-knowledge, trait self-knowledge, and knowledge of personally experienced episodes, but he did not have a pre-reflectively given sense of continuity with his past person.

Importantly, during his "unowned" period R. B. had no trouble retrieving very specific, often one-of-a kind, personal experiences (e.g., being on a beach in New London). He presumably also had no trouble representing that his body was present for those experiences. He *knew* that the memories were about him rather than, say, his mother. And he could call up, that is, auto-cue (Donald, 1991) memories at will. So, in that sense, his memories were both agentic and involved self-reference. However, there seems to be another type of self-reference that typically accompanies episodic recollections (ownership, mineness; for discussion, see Klein, 2012) that has been impaired in his case. His apparent deficit was in representing, from the first person, "I had these experiences." That is, his impairment entailed a loss of the ability to connect personally experienced content with autonoetic awareness.

A MECHANISM: ONE PROPOSAL

Although the specifics of R. B.'s deficit are, at this point, unclear, it is worth considering the present findings in light of theoretical work by Dalla Barba and colleagues (e.g., Dalla Barba, 2002; Dalla Barba et al., 1997, 1999) on the relation between consciousness, memory, and temporal experience. These authors call attention to two modes of consciousness, which they term temporal consciousness (TC) and knowing consciousness (KC). TC is consciousness of time—it enables a person to become aware of something as part of his or her personal past, present, or future. It thus corresponds closely to what Tulving calls autonoetic awareness. KC, by contrast, does not locate objects in time. Rather, it enables a person to become aware of something as an element of knowledge without that knowledge being situated in a temporal framework. The conceptual overlap with noetic awareness is evident.

TC and KC thus conceptualized are two different ways of *addressing* the contents of memory. Long-term memory is held to contain representations that vary in terms of their stability and resistance to modification (e.g., Dalla Barba et al., 1997, 1999; Nadel and Moscovitch, 1997). The more stable, overlearned, summary representations can be thought of as roughly analogous to what *will be* experienced, on retrieval, as semantic knowledge, whereas less stable, more malleable representations—e.g., unique, one-of-a-kind-events—provide the raw material for what will subsequently become episodic recollection.

Support for these proposed distinctions in content stability can be found in Nadel and Moscovitch's (1997; Moscovitch et al., 2005) multiple trace theory (MTT) of long-term memory consolidation (see also Piolino et al., 2003). According to MTT, the hippocampal formation and related structures (primarily in the medial temporal lobes) contribute to the transformation of initially unstable and sparsely encoded content into a collection of contextually related traces—a transformative act that confers stability on represented content by virtue of its multiple instantiations. The model, developed to map the neural events and structures underlying the transition of information from episodic to semantic memory (i.e., unstable to stable), fits reasonably well with Dalla Barba's proposal that differences in representational stability determine whether a given memory content will be taken an as object by TC and KC.

But, in what sense does the relative stability (or a lack thereof) confer a temporal status on a specific content? That is, what determines if the content, as experienced, is classified as episodic or as semantic? Dalla Barba (2002) suggests that the stability of a representation is correlated with what we typically describe as episodic memory by virtue of the fact that TC takes such content as its intentional object (for a discussion of why this may be the case, see Klein et al., 2002a). In this way, temporally and representationally unique events are likely to be experienced episodically as part of one's past. By contrast, the memory content psychologists classify as semantic often, though not invariably, tends to be represented as stable, summaries of (often repeated) experiences that share features in common. While such content is acted on by KC rather than by TC (i.e., autonoetic awareness), there is nothing in Dalla Barba's model that precludes KC (i.e., noetic awareness) from recruiting an individual's logical abilities to inferentially place "stable" content in a temporal context, provided the representation being addressed contains temporally-relevant constituents. When this happens, the individual is able to locate well-learned, multiply-represented facts about the world in a temporal matrix that extends from the chronological past to the chronological future (e.g., "I know I lived in New York until I was 2 years old, even though I can't recollect any specific event from that time of my life").

Unfortunately, as the reader will have noted, Dalla Barba's "explanation" begs the question of what *causes* the observed correlation between type of temporal subjectivity and stability of content. At present, a compelling explanation is not readily at hand. Despite its conceptual limitations, however, Dalla Barba's model, in conjunction with MTT, provides a provisional (though incomplete) framework for making sense of the dissociation between the experiential and inferential forms of temporality experienced by patient R. B. As the result of a condition in which autonoetic awareness is intact, but unable to access pre-injury content in long-term memory, R. B. remains capable of describing, often in considerable detail, what happened in his pre-injury past—despite being unable to experience his present mental content as a re-living of past personal events. By contrast, autonoetic awareness still can, for reasons not clear, successfully work in conjunction with his post-injury memory content. What we see in the case of R. B. is not a failure of memory content, or a loss of the autonoetic component of recollection, but rather a dissociation between two intact, yet functionally independent, constituents of what, taken in tandem, are essential constituents of what we classify as episodic recollection.

The merit of this explanation of the relation between content and experience is further supported by R. B.'s subsequent recovery of the ability to episodically recollect the *same* memory content that lacked personal ownership during the period of his cognitive impairment. That R. B. was able to regain these functions suggests that the autoneotic aspect of his recollections was not destroyed by his injury; rather it temporarily became decoupled from memory content. The proposition that the mechanisms mediating autonoetic awareness were not lost during his amnesia also is implied by the fact that he had a sense of personal ownership of ongoing experiences that transpired *following* his accident (with the exception of temporally limited anterograde memory loss). Why his mental machinery was able to conjoin autonoetic awareness with content as memories were being built, but not when recollecting memories of pre-injury events, remains unclear.

CONCLUSIONS

The sense of a direct, pre-reflective attachment to the past given by episodic recollection is robust, indeed, it has seemed to many to be a necessary aspect of episodic memory (for reviews, see Tulving, 1985, 2002; Wheeler et al., 1997). It also gives us an "irresistible" sense of being the same person over time (e.g., Fivush and Haden, 2003; for discussion, see Klein, 2013b). But the case of R. B. indicates that this sense is dissociable from memory content. The feeling of autonoetic personal continuity (and its intimate relation to personal ownership) turns out to be a contingent feature of memory content that comes into play at retrieval.

Seen in this light, classification of content as episodic or semantic can be situated in processes that transpire once memory content is retrieved and made available for conscious experience. It is at this point that the designators episodic and semantic do the work they were developed to perform. This work is achieved via the individual's ability to connect a current mental state to a past experience via either autonoetic awareness (temporarily lost in R. B, but subsequently regained) or logical inference. The former maps to what we call episodic memory, while the latter enables temporally located semantic knowledge—i.e., the intentional placement of retrieved content in the context of one's past (provided the content has useable temporal, spatial and self-referential markers).

Of course, R. B.'s reports do not rule out the possibility that what he is reporting are inferences based on semantic memory system (as his responses make clear, he is capable of inference) rather than "un-labeled" memory content that lacks a felt connection to his past due to compromised autonoetic awareness. However, this possibility assumes that semantic memory is a system whose instantiation is a biological reality *prior to* an act of retrieval—a conceptual stance which theoretical and empirical observations presented in this paper call into question. Moreover, Occam's principle of parsimony—i.e., posit no more parameters or variables than are minimally necessary to account for the data (e.g., Ladyman, 2002)—appears to side with the view that memory content is classifiable neither as episodic or semantic while still in storage. Of the two possibilities under discussion, the retrieval-based alternative offers the simpler explanation—positing a single source of content that can be differentially acted on by autonoetic awareness. By contrast, the traditional classification of episodic and semantic memory as unique, but interacting, neuro-cognitive systems assumes two separate repositories of content (episodic *and* semantic) which *also* are differentially associated with autonoesis.

Occam's razor resonates with evolutionary considerations as well. Evolution builds on existing biological structures (e.g., Williams, 1966). Consistent with this thesis, Fuster (1995) has demonstrated a strong overlap among humans and phylogenetically older mammalian species in the cortical areas involved in memory. Accordingly, positing a pre-existing cortical network of memory content that subsequently was overlain with mechanisms that acted differentially on retrieved content to enable conscious experience to be taken as either episodic or semantic has economically favorable consequences. Specifically, it has the effect of eliminating the need to posit the evolution of separate systems of storage for episodic and semantic content, as well as separate mechanisms (i.e., autonoetic and noetic) for consciously experiencing that content as episodic recollection or semantic knowledge.

These considerations also offer an evolutionary perspective on the well-known finding that some species (e.g., scrub jays), lacking some of the structures assumed necessary for episodic recollection (e.g., personal ownership, sense of self), nonetheless behave *as though* their acts were mediated by recollection (e.g., Cheke and Clayton, 2010). Such behavior can parsimoniously be explained by assuming these species have a network for storing memory content, some which contains information about time and place, but have yet to evolve the mechanisms necessary to place that content into subjective alignment with their personal past. Thus, they can use their knowledge to appropriately guide behavior without that knowledge being experienced as part of their personal past.

The retrieval-based model of episodic and semantic memory also may help explain the well-known finding that the *experience* of remembering often is characterized by either a feeling of knowing or a feeling of remembering (for reviews, see Cohen et al., 2008 and Gardiner and Richardson-Klavehn, 2000). A popular dual systems explanation for variation in modes of retrieval experience is that feelings of remembering reflect the operation of episodic memory whereas the feelings of familiarity are associated with semantic memory (e.g., Tulving, 1985).

In contrast to dual systems analyses, a retrieval-based model proposes that whether content retrieved from memory is experienced as remembered or as known depends on whether it has been subject to autonoetic consciousness: If it has, the content is experienced as remembered; if not, it is experienced as known. This explanation has the advantage of avoiding the problem (common to dual systems models) of explaining why stimuli encoded under the *same* temporal and spatial conditions are stored in, and subsequently retrieved from, one system vs. another. A retrieval-based model posits that all stimuli are stored in the same neural system; any difference in mode of presentation pivots on whether or not content is acted on by autonoetic awareness at retrieval.

Although this model has the advantage of conceptual and phylogenetic parsimony (e.g., a single system of storage), an obvious limitation is that identification of the factors responsible for whether retrieved content will be subject to autonoetic embellishment is, at present, unknown. However, a similar indictment can be pressed against most *process*-based explanations of the remember/known phenomenon. Regardless of whether one subscribes to a dual or single process explanation (e.g., Tulving, 1985; Gardiner and Java, 1990; Donaldson, 1996; Wixted and Mickes, 2010; for review see Cohen et al., 2008), there is no compelling a priori basis for linking variations in autonoetic awareness to the potency of causally-relevant factors (such as trace strength, fluency, decision criteria, and automaticity); rather, these processes are invoked post hoc to explain observed variation in participants' retrieval phenomenology.[5]

At present, there is no conclusive theoretical or empirical evidence to select between a systems-based and retrieval-based explanation of the episodic/semantic distinction (I address the untidy nature of neural localization studies of memory in the next section). Occam's principle, while supportive of a retrieval-based view, is best treated as a logically non-binding heuristic rather than as a definitive arbiter of theoretical substantiation. Compelling empirical evidence in support of a retrieval-based interpretation comes from the fact that, on recovery of his sense ownership, the same content formerly unconnected to R. B.'s personal past re-acquired a sense of being an episodic recollection. While definitive evidence for a retrieval-based theory of episodic and semantic memory is not available at present, R. B.'s memory performance, taken in conjunction with considerations of parsimony and evolution, suggest this option should be considered a live possibility.

THE NEURAL LOCALIZATION OF EPISODIC AND SEMANTIC MEMORY

The localization of episodic (and semantic) memory in their neural substrates has been a task that has captured the interest of neuro-imagers for several decades (for reviews, see Squire, 2004; Moscovitch et al., 2006; Martinelli et al., 2012; Renoult et al., in press). However, despite guarded optimism initially expressed that the goal of localization of the relevant networks was "in sight" (e.g., Nyberg et al., 1996), the complexities underlying these early forays soon became evident. Researchers were led to conclude that the networks associated with episodic and semantic memory are widely distributed in the brain (e.g., the parietal lobes, the frontal lobes, medial temporal lobes; e.g., Nyberg and Tulving, 1998; Moscovitch et al., 2005; Wagner et al., 2005; Burianova and Grady, 2007; Squire and Bayley, 2007; Cappa, 2008; Ryan et al., 2008; Eichenbaum et al., 2012; for review, see Svoboda et al., 2006; Uttal, 2009), that their boundaries were fluid, and that their constituents varied as a function of the task performed, content retrieved, and a host of related factors such as the individual's age, handedness, gender, clinical status, and emotional state (e.g., Achim and Lepage, 2003; Bartha et al., 2003; Schwindt and Black, 2009; Smith and Squire, 2009; for review, see Dumit, 2004). Not surprisingly, even the manner in which constructs of interest were operationalized had important effects on the cortical regions activated (e.g., Renoult et al., in press). One might argue that there is as much evidence for the incoherence of the underlying constructs as there is for the complexities of the issues involved in designing studies, analyzing data and interpreting findings from brain-mapping endeavors (e.g., Uttal, 2001).

A possible reason for the diversity of imaging results is that episodic memory is not something to be neurally localized—it is not a *thing* to be found. Rather, it consists in a collection of functionally independent, but normally interacting functions (e.g., Klein, 2001; Klein et al., 2004), which, as the present study demonstrates, can differentially be impaired due to neurological damage (for reviews, see McCarthy and Warrington, 1992; Klein et al., 2004). As Polanyi (1967) cautioned "... either you know what you are looking for, and then there is no problem; or you do not know what you are looking for, and then you cannot expect to find anything" (p. 22).

Despite the difficulties of the enterprise, there are several conclusions that can provisionally be drawn from studies imaging episodic and semantic memory. Of particular relevance to present considerations, a number of labs have converged on the medial temporal lobes as a common network underlying episodic and semantic consolidation and storage (e.g., Scoville and Milner, 1957; Achim and Lepage, 2003; Bartha et al., 2003; Piolino et al., 2003; Levy et al., 2004; Moscovitch et al., 2005; Svoboda et al., 2006; Ryan et al., 2008; Smith and Squire, 2009; Naya and Suzuki, 2011; Rosenbaum et al., 2012; Eichenbaum et al., 2012). In addition, these networks also are implicated in the consolidation and storage of declarative memory content (for review, see Fuster, 1995; Squire, 2004). While highly speculative, I suggest that these regions of activation may reflect the storage of memory content prior to its subsequent demarcation as semantic and episodic via mechanisms acting at retrieval. By contrast, a number of investigators have suggested that autonoetic awareness depends on mechanisms residing primarily in the frontal lobes (e.g., Abraham et al., 2009; for reviews, see Wheeler et al., 1997; Szpunar, 2011; Tulving and Szpunar, 2012).

THE EPISODIC/SEMANTIC DICHOTOMY AND DECLARATIVE MEMORY

An implication of my proposal, in partial agreement with Squire and his colleagues, is that cortical separation of memory systems may better be captured by a declarative/procedural dichotomy (where episodic and semantic systems are folded into, rather than constituents of, declarative long-term memory; e.g., Cohen, 1984; Squire, 2004) than by a taxonomy in which episodic and semantic memory are seen as conceptually and neurologically distinct constituents of the declarative system (e.g., Schacter and Tulving, 1994; for discussion, see Foster and Jelicic, 1999).

But—and this is an important caveat—my concession to the declarative/procedural model comes at the level of the neural instantiation of memory content, not at the level of phenomenology once that content has been retrieved and made available

[5]To quote Bartlett (1932), the processes invoked "... may show us what can happen when recognition takes place, but throw no light whatever upon how any, or all, of these processes are rendered possible ... experimenters have analyzed the final stage of recognition and each has tended to claim a complete solution in terms of his particular analysis. In fact, nobody can understand recognition by confining his attention to what happens at the moment of recognition." (p. 192). Bartlett goes on to say that future experimentation focusing on the mental events that precede recognition will aid in understanding variability in the processes subsequently at work. If one substitutes retrieval (e.g., recall and recognition) for recognition, the quote from Bartlett perfectly captures my critique of process-based explanations of the remember/know phenomenon. This critique applies to my retrieval-based proposal as well: As it currently stands, a retrieval-based model cannot account for variability in the attachment of autonoetic awareness to memory content. This is not cause for dismay; rather, as Bartlett notes, it simply points out the need for further experimentation designed to clarify how the processing differences apparent at retrieval are put into place.

as an object for subjectivity. Accordingly, the episodic/semantic division of long-term memory is not subsumed by declarative memory (as Squire and colleagues might argue); rather, the episodic/semantic division of memory comes into play at the level of retrieval rather than storage.

This view can accommodate several conflicting findings in the literature. For example, while some clinical dissociations between intact and impaired memory function appear best classified in terms of a functional independence of episodic and semantic memory (for reviews, see Schacter and Tulving, 1994; Klein, 2004, 2010; Dere et al., 2008), other results do not fit as neatly into this scheme (e.g., Cohen, 1984; Squire, 1987; Kopelman et al., 1989; Klein et al., 2002c). In fact, an unambiguous sorting of spared and preserved function into the categories provided by the episodic/semantic distinction more often is the exception than the rule (e.g., Squire, 1987; Baddeley et al., 1995; Parkin, 1997; Foster and Jelicic, 1999; Klein et al., 2002c; Moscovitch et al., 2006).

However, recognition of the possibility that an episodic/semantic classification of memory impairment is attendant on contingencies acting at retrieval can accommodate the diversity of results. Specifically, impairments acting primarily on stored content may result in impairments to *both* episodic and semantic memory experience, whereas separation between these two forms of memory phenomenology is more likely to be observed when neuro-cognitive impairments act on the mechanisms operative during retrieval.

Evidence for this proposal comes from the case of patient D. B., who suffered brain damage as a result of anoxia following cardiac arrest (e.g., Klein et al., 2002b,c). Neuropsychological assessment of D. B.'s temporal orientation showed severe disorientation with respect to the present. For example, he did not know the day of the week, the current year, or even his age. Additional testing revealed that D. B. was unable to recall his past and unable to imagine what his experiences might be like in the future (for review, see Klein, 2013b). Not surprisingly, D. B.'s episodic memory was severely impaired: He could not reliably bring to mind personal experiences from any point in his past (at least within the limits of testing). By "reliably" I mean the while D. B. typically responded to requests for episodic memories with "I don't know," he occasionally did offer a specific "recollection." However, these "recollections" lacked rational placement in his past. For example, in response to the request that he remember a time he was in a car, D. B. replied "Driving down the coast with my parents." When then asked to temporally place the memory, he replied "yesterday," despite his parents having been dead for 34 years! Thus, an occurrent mental state (the content of which was verified by his daughter) appears to have broken free of its temporal moorings. That is, the content of memory, absent autonoetic temporal placement, constituted the object of D. B.'s awareness.

What I am arguing is that patients such as R. B. and D. B. may suffer from a disruption of autonoetic awareness, and that as a result of this pathology they are rendered unable to experience mental content in its proper temporal context (for a similar views, see Tulving, 1985; Dalla Barba, 2002). It is the failure to connect autonoetic awareness with retrieved content rather than the absence of such awareness, that accounts for (at least some) of the memory pathologies demonstrated by amnesic patients.

This is not to presume that all forms of episodic amnesia submit to similar analysis. Memory loss can result from failures at encoding, storage and/or retrieval. One could, for example, present symptoms consistent with episodic amnesia if s/he maintained the requisite mechanisms for temporal subjectivity, but lacked access to the content on which that awareness could be brought to bear. Content loss can be highly selective. According to MTT, less stable (and hence more autonoetically-relevant) content is likely to be under-represented in memory. It thus is more susceptible to neural insult than are the more richly distributed representations that ultimately will constitute semantic memory experience (e.g., Nadel and Moscovitch, 1997). In this way, episodic amnesia will manifest more readily than sematic amnesia (as is well-recognized to be the case)—the result of disease processes acting on content storage prior to operations taking place at retrieval. What I am suggesting, then, is that some (though certainly not all!) forms of amnesia can arise from the decoupling of temporal awareness and memory content (for a similar view, see Tulving, 1985).

Another area of research that submits to a retrieval-based analysis is the debate surrounding the mechanisms underlying false memories (for review, see Schacter, 1995; Johnson and Raye, 1998). According to the present model, memory errors can result when (1) compromised content is taken as the object of autonoteic awareness as well as (2) when autonoetic awareness is misapplied (e.g., to imagination). The phenomenon of implicit task performance also can be explained (in some cases) as the failure of autonoetic awareness to place memory content in a temporal context. While both of these phenomena (false and implicit memory) deserve considerably more attention, restrictions of space prevent further elaboration.

LIMITATIONS AND CONSIDERATIONS

An issue raised concerning the model I have presented is that it seems more a philosophical exercise that a scientific theory. Concern centers on the fact that evidence in support of my ideas derives primarily (though not exclusively: e.g., patient D. B, thought insertion) from the study of a single patient (R. B.) who now has remitted. Accordingly, it is hard to see how the ideas I have proposed can be tested via experimental manipulation. There are several things to note in this regard.

First, not all theory-based scientific enterprises admit to empirical *manipulation* (e.g., cosmology, paleontology). While the potential for refutation is essential (e.g., Popper), refutation does not mandate explicit manipulation in an experimental context (e.g., Trusted, 1987; Lipton, 1991). A good theory is one that retrodicts and predicts, both of which afford the potential for refutation in the absence of the ability to directly manipulate variables of interest.

Second, a good theory facilitates the organization of data sets that might otherwise have been viewed as collections of unrelated findings (e.g., Newell, 1973; Ladyman, 2002; Godfrey-Smith, 2003). Along these lines, the present theory has the virtue of offering a parsimonious explanation for a variety of "apparently" diverse memory phenomena, including, but not limited to, remember/know judgments, the implicit/explicit memory distinction, false memories and Déjà vu experience (to be discussed in a forthcoming paper). It also can account for the fact that some individuals suffering Dissociative Identity Disorders experience the *same* episodic content (e.g., Dorahy, 2001) despite content ownership varying as a function of the personality currently occupying awareness (e.g., Braude, 1995). The theory also accounts for the fact that episodic and semantic content evidence significant (often indistinguishable) overlap with regard the presumably differentiating features of time, place and self (e.g., Klein and Lax, 2010).

Third, the availability of theory can help to draw attention to neurological case studies whose relevance for the study (in this case, of memory) has, to date, been underappreciated. For example, Zahn et al. (2007) report the case of a patient D. P., who lost his ability experience ownership of the mental states accompanying perceived objects. In a case described by Gott et al. (1984), the patient (J. J.) was capable of holding either of two qualitatively different states of consciousness. Specifically, she was voluntarily able to switch between the feeling that her experiences belonged to her or to someone else. Finally, a patient described by Sass and Parnas (2003) reported that his feeling ownership accompanying his mental states lagged behind his initial awareness of those states. This "phenomenological delay in felt ownership" suggests that ownership is a separable component of consciousness—i.e., the patient temporarily was aware of having an experience, but only subsequently felt that his first-person perspective belonged to him.

Taken together, these studies focus attention on ownership as an aspect, or form, of consciousness that can come undone under certain conditions (e.g., Klein and Nichols, 2012; Lane, 2012). With respect to the theory of episodic memory I have proposed, these studies potentially constitute a small data-base (I suspect additional cases will appear in the literature if dysfunction of content ownership becomes a recognized issue in memory research) that, once assembled, will permit investigators to empirically test the effects of "loss of ownership" on memorial experience.

Fourth, as things currently stand, my theory also submits to empirical testing with *non*-impaired participants. Here I outline one such study (others will be discussed in a forthcoming paper). Assuming it possible to *simultaneously* achieve a high degree of temporal and spatial resolution using various brain scanning technologies (e.g., EEG, fMRI, and PET) it should be feasible to track both the chronology and localization of neural activity during performance of a "remember/know" task. If temporal resolution is sufficiently sensitive, and the constructs in play sufficiently well defined (note: "sufficiently" may require technological and conceptual refinement), it would allow us to examine the stages of memory (i.e., encoding, storage, and retrieval) activated during the process of declarative remembering. Anatomical localization—in conjunction with "stage" information provided by temporal data—would enable us to bring to focus the systems responsible for storage (which are, of logical necessity, causally prior to retrieval) followed by those involved in retrieval. If my model has merit, the activation of stored content during performance of the remember/know task will evidence comparable localization(s) regardless of whether the participant's phenomenological report turns out to be "remember" or "know." Neural separation, by contrast, should be evidenced during the retrieval phase (due to differences in the mechanisms mediating remember/know judgments—i.e., inference vs. autonoetic awareness).

Finally, the notion that single case studies have serious limitations with regard to theory construction is far from agreed on. In fact, Caramazza (1986, 1991) and Sokol et al. (1991) have argued persuasively for the importance of $N = 1$ studies in the development of neuropsychological models. Of course, not everyone shares this view: Some feel that theory construction requires inference from group performance (e.g., Shallice, 1988; Robertson et al., 1993). However, since there are no "knockdown" arguments favoring one view to the exclusion of the other, there is, at present, no logically compelling reason for conceptual closure.

The theory presented herein also offers a potential corrective on research practices that may be doing more to cloud than to illuminate the role of long-term memory in various task performances. A central idea of this paper is the episodic and semantic memories are distinguished not by their content, but rather by the way that content is phenomenologically given: The features of "episodic content" are not, in principle, distinguishable from those of "semantic content." This calls into serious question the advisability of studies attempting to document the workings of a particular type of declarative memory via analysis of reported remembered content. To take one example (and there are a multitude), a recent paper by Rasmussen and Bernsten (2012) attempts to document the episodic contributions to future-oriented thought by examining the relative proportions of episodic and semantic content present in participants' memory transcripts. Such an attempt, on present considerations, is misguided since there is no principled way in which a researcher can classify content as episodic or semantic; the episodic and semantic designationors refer to the manner in which content is experienced at retrieval.

FINAL THOUGHTS

The present emendation of the episodic/semantic memory distinction awaits the considerable work of empirical conformation and theoretical accommodation. However, despite its provisional status, it has the merit of (1) being consistent with real-world data from case studies (e.g., R. B., and D. B.), (2) helping bring some order to the debate over whether episodic and semantic memory are best construed as functionally independent neural systems, or rather two ways scientists (though not necessarily nature) have chosen to divide up declarative memory, (3) helping make sense of impairments in mental time travel (both into the past and future; for discussion, see Klein, 2013a), (4) accommodating a number of findings (e.g., the differential bases for, and forms of, episodic amnesia, memory errors, and performance on implicit memory tasks), and (5) having considerations of parsimony (both logical and evolutionary) on its side.

The decoupling of autonoetic awareness and memory content—revealed most clearly by the case of R. B. (see also the case of patient D. B)—can be taken as an "existence proof" for the proposition that the connection between autonoetic awareness and episodic memory is one of contingency rather than one of necessity. That is, R. B.'s memory phenomenology suggests that awareness is not an *intrinsic* property of episodic content; rather, the association between content and awareness may best be construed as a *relation* between two functionally independent systems that jointly contribute to the experience of episodic recollection.

Perhaps ironically, Hermann Ebbinghaus, a name typically associated with an approach to memory now discredited as being overly-influenced by logical positivism (e.g., Bartlett, 1932; Danziger, 2008), seems to have intuited (though not explored) the need to invoke acts of consciousness to explain memory phenomenology. In the introductory remarks in his book *Memory*, Ebbinghaus makes the following observation: "... in the majority of cases we at once recognize the returned mental state as one that has already been experienced; that is, we remember it. Under certain conditions, however, this *accompanying* consciousness is lacking and we know only indirectly that 'now' must be identical with 'then'... " (Ebbinghaus, 1885/1913, p. 2; emphasis mine). Put in terms of the model proposed in the present paper, Ebbinghaus is calling attention to the need to posit an autonoetic-like form of consciousness that acts on retrieved memory content to provide the experience of pastness as directly given (i.e., episodic) rather than indirectly inferred (i.e., semantic).

REFERENCES

Abraham, A., Schubotz, R. I., and von Cramon, Y. (2009). Thinking about the future versus the past in personal and non-personal contexts. *Brain Res.* 1233, 106–119.

Achim, A. M., and Lepage, M. (2003). Episodic memory-related activation in schizophrenia: a meta-analysis. *Br. J. Psychiatry* 187, 500–509.

Albahari, M. (2006). *Analytical Buddhism: The Two-Tiered Illusion of Self.* Houndsmills: Palgrave Macmillan.

Baddeley, A. D., Wilson, B. A., and Fraser, N. W. (1995). *Handbook of Memory Disorders.* New York, NY: John Wiley and Sons.

Bartha, L., Brenneis, C., Schocke, M., Trinka, E., Koylu, B., Trieb, T., et al. (2003). Medial temporal lobe activation during semantic language processing: fMRI findings in healthy left- and right-handers. *Cogn. Brain Res.* 17, 339–346.

Bartlett, F. C. (1932). *Remembering.* London: Cambridge At The University Press.

Bernecker, S. (2010). *Memory: A Philosophical Study.* Oxford: Oxford University Press.

Bortolotti, L., and Broome, M. (2009). A role for ownership and authorship in the analysis of thought insertion. *Phenomenol. Cogn. Sci.* 8, 205–224.

Braude, S. E. (1995). *First Person Plural: Multiple Personality and the Philosophy of Mind.* Lanham, MD: Rowman and Littlefield Publishers.

Burianova, H., and Grady, C. L. (2007). Common and unique neural activations in autobiographical, episodic, and semantic retrieval. *J. Cogn. Neurosci.* 19, 1520–1534.

Cappa, S. F. (2008). Imaging studies of semantic memory. *Curr. Opin. Neurobiol.* 21, 669–675.

Caramazza, A. (1986). On drawing inferences about the structure of normal cognitive systems from the analysis of patterns of impaired performance: the case for single-patient studies. *Brain Cogn.* 5, 41–66.

Caramazza, A. (1991). Data, statistics, and theory: a comment on Bates, McDonald, MacWhinney, and Applebaum's "A maximum likelihood procedure for the analysis of group and individual data in aphasia research". *Brain Lang.* 41, 43–51.

Casey, E. S. (1977). Imagining and remembering. *Rev. Metaphys.* 31, 187–209.

Cheke, L. G., and Clayton, N. S. (2010). Mental time travel in animals. *WIREs Cogn. Sci.* 1, 1–16.

Cohen, A., Rotello, C., and MacMillan, N. (2008). Evaluating models of remember-know judgments: complexity, mimicry, and discriminability. *Psychon. Bull. Rev.* 15, 906–926.

Cohen, N. J. (1984). "Preserved learning capacity in amnesia: evidence for multiple memory systems." in *Neuropsychology of Memory,* eds L R. Squire and N. Butters (New York, NY: Guilford Press), 83–103.

Dalla Barba, G. (2002). *Memory, Consciousness and Temporality.* Norwell, MA: Kluwer Academic Publishers.

Dalla Barba, G., Cappelletti, J. Y., Signorini, M., and Denes, G. (1997). Confabulation: remembering another' past, planning? another' future. *Neurocase* 3, 425–436.

Dalla Barba, G., Nedjam, Z., and Dubios, B. (1999). Confabulation, executive functions, and source memory in Alzheimer's disease. *Cogn. Neuropsychol.* 16, 385–398.

Danziger, K. (2008). *Marking the Mind: A History of Memory.* Cambridge: Cambridge University Press.

Dere, E., Easton, A., Nadel, L., and Huston, J. P. (eds.). (2008). *Handbook of Episodic Memory.* Amsterdam: Elsevier Science.

Donald, M. (1991). *Origins of the Modern Mind: Three Stages in the Evolution of Culture and Cognition.* Cambridge, MA: Harvard University Press.

Donaldson, W. (1996). The role of decision processes in remembering and knowing. *Mem. Cogn.* 24, 523–533.

Dorahy, M. (2001). Dissociative identity disorder: disorder and memory dysfunction: the current state of experimental research and its future directions. *Clin. Psychol. Rev.* 21, 771–795.

Dumit, J. (2004). *Picturing Personhood: Brain Scans and Personal Identity.* Princeton, NJ: Princeton University Press.

Ebbinghaus, H. (1885/1913). *Memory: A Contribution to Experimental Psychology.* Translated eds H. A. Ruger and C. Bussenius (New York, NY: Teacher's College, Columbia University).

Eichenbaum, H., Sauvage, M., Fortin, N., Komorowski, R., and Lipton, P. (2012). Towards a functional organization of episodic memory in the medial temporal lobe. *Neurosci. Biobehav. Rev.* 36, 1597–1608.

Fivush, R., and Haden, C. A. (eds.). (2003). *Autobiographical Memory and the Construction of a Narrative Self.* Mahwah, NJ: Lawrence Erlbaum Associates.

Foster, J. K., and Jelicic, M. (1999). *Memory: Systems, Process, or Function?* New York, NY: Oxford University Press.

Frith, C. D. (1992). *The Cognitive Neuropsychology of Schizophrenia.* East Sussex, England: Erlbaum/Taylor and Francis.

Furlong, E. J. (1951). *A Study in Memory.* New York, NY: Thomas Nelson and Sons Ltd.

Fuster, J. M. (1995). *Memory in the Cerebral Cortex: An Empirical Approach to Neural Networks in the Human and Nonhuman Primate.* Cambridge, MA: MIT Press.

Gallagher, S. (2000). Philosophical conceptions of the self: implications for cognitive science. *Trends Cogn. Sci.* 4, 14–21.

Gardiner, J., and Richardson-Klavehn, A. (2000). "Remembering and knowing," in *The Oxford Handbook of Memory*, eds E. Tulving and F. I. M. Craik (New York, NY: Oxford University Press), 229–244.

Gardiner, J. M. (2001). Episodic memory and autonoetic consciousness: a first-person approach. *Philos. Trans. R. Soc. B Biol. Sci.* 356, 1351–1361.

Gardiner, J. M., and Java, R. I. (1990). Recollective experience in word and nonword recognition. *Mem. Cogn.* 18, 23–30.

Godfrey-Smith, F. (2003). *Theory and Reality.* Chicago, IL: University of Chicago Press.

Gott, P. S., Hughes, E. C., and Whipple, K. (1984). Voluntary control of two lateralized conscious states: validation by electrical and behavioral studies. *Neuropsychologia* 22, 65–72.

Hume, D. (1748/2004). *An Enquiry Concerning Human Understanding.* New York, NY: Dover Publications.

Husserl, E. (1964) *The Phenomenology of Internal Time-Consciousness.* Bloomington, IN: Indiana University Press.

James, W. (1890). *Principles of Psychology, Vol. 1.* New York, NY: Henry Holt and Company.

Jaynes, J. (1976). *The Origin of Consciousness in the Breakdown of the Bicameral Mind.* Boston, MA: Houghton Mifflin Company.

Johnson, M., and Raye, C. (1998). False memories and confabulation *Trends Cogn. Sci.* 2, 137–145.

Johnson, M. K., and Raye, C. L. (1981) Reality monitoring. *Psychol. Rev.* 88 67–85.

Johnson, M. K., Hashtroudi, S. Lindsay, D. S. (1993). Source monitoring. *Psychol. Bull.* 114 3–28.

Klein, S. B. (2001). "A self to remember: a cognitive neuropsychological perspective on how self creates memory and memory creates self," in *Individual Self, Relational Self, and Collective Self,* eds C. Sedikides and M. B. Brewer (Philadelphia, PA: Psychology Press), 25–46.

Klein, S. B. (2004). "The cognitive neuroscience of knowing one's self," in *The Cognitive Neurosciences III*, ed M. A. Gazzaniga (Cambridge, MA: MIT Press), 1007–1089.

Klein, S. B. (2007). "Phylogeny and evolution: implications for understanding the nature of a memory system," in *Science of Memory: Concepts,* eds

H. L. Roediger, Y. Dudai, and S. Fitzgerald (New York, NY: Oxford), 377–381.

Klein, S. B. (2010). The self: as a construct in psychology and neuropsychological evidence for its multiplicity. *WIREs Cogn. Sci.* 1, 172–183.

Klein, S. B. (2011). "An evolutionary analysis of the concept of memory systems," in *Thus Spake Evolutionary Psychologists,* eds X. T. Wang and Y. J. Su (Beijing: Peking University Press), 140–157.

Klein, S. B. (2012). The self and its brain. *Soc. Cogn.* 30, 474–516.

Klein, S. B. (2013a). The complex act of projecting oneself into the future. *WIREs Cogn. Sci.* 4, 63–79.

Klein, S. B. (2013b). The sense of diachronic personal identity. *Phenomenol. Cogn. Sci.* doi: 10.1007/s11097-012-9285-8. [Epub ahead of print].

Klein, S. B., Cosmides, L., Tooby, J., and Chance, S. (2002a). Decisions and the evolution of memory: multiple systems, multiple functions. *Psychol. Rev.* 109, 306–329.

Klein, S. B., Loftus, J., and Kihlstrom, J. F. (2002b). Memory and temporal experience: the effects of episodic memory loss on an amnesic patient's ability to remember the past and imagine the future. *Soc. Cogn.* 20, 353–379.

Klein, S. B., Rozendale, K., and Cosmides, L. (2002c). A social-cognitive neuroscience analysis of the self. *Soc. Cogn.* 20, 105–135.

Klein, S. B., and Gangi, C. E. (2010). The multiplicity of self: Neuropsychological evidence and its implications for the self as a construct in psychological research. *Ann. N.Y. Acad. Sci.* 1191, 1–15.

Klein, S. B., German, T. P., Cosmides, L., and Gabriel, R. (2004). A theory of autobiographical memory: necessary components and disorders resulting from their loss. *Soc. Cogn.* 22, 460–490.

Klein, S. B., Robertson, T. E., and Delton, A. W. (2010). Facing the future: memory as an evolved system for planning future acts. *Mem. Cogn.* 38, 13–22.

Klein, S. B., and Lax, M. L. (2010). The unanticipated resilience of trait self-knowledge in the face of neural damage. *Memory* 18, 918–948.

Klein, S. B., and Nichols, S. (2012). Memory and the sense of personal identity. *Mind* 121, 677–702.

Kopelman, M. D., Wilson, B. A., and Baddeley, A. D. (1989). The autobiographical memory interview: a new assessment of autobiographical and personal semantic memory in amnesic patients. *J. Clin. Exp. Neuropsychol.* 11, 724–744.

Ladyman, J. (2002). *Understanding Philosophy of Science.* New York, NY: Routledge.

Lane, T. (2012). Toward an explanatory framework for mental ownership. *Phenomenol. Cogn. Sci.* 11, 251–286.

Levy, D. A., Bayley, P. J., and Squire, L. R. (2004). The anatomy of semantic knowledge: medial vs. lateral temporal lobe. *Proc. Natl. Acad. Sci.U.S.A.* 101, 6710–6715.

Lipton, P. (1991). *Inference to the Best Explanation, 2nd Edn.* New York, NY: Routledge.

Locke, D. (1968). *Myself and Others.* Oxford: Clarendon Press.

Markowitsch, H. J. (2003). "Autonoetic consciousness," in *The Self in Neuroscience and Psychiatry,* eds T. Kircher and A. David (Cambridge: Cambridge University Press), 180–196.

Markowitsch, H. J., and Staniliou, A. (2011). Memory, autonoetic consciousness, and the self. *Conscious. Cogn.* 20, 16–39.

Martinelli, P., Sperduti, M., and Piolino, P. (2012). Neural substrates of the self-memory system: new insights from a meta-analysis. *Hum. Brain Mapp.* doi: 10.1002/hbm.22008. [Epub ahead of print].

McCarthy, R. A., and Warrington, E. K. (1992). Actors but not scripts: the dissociation of people and events in retrograde amnesia. *Neuropsychologia* 30, 633–644.

Moscovitch, M., Nadel, L., Winocur, G., Gilboa, A., and Rosenbaum, R. S. (2006). The cognitive neuroscience of remote episodic, semantic and spatial memory. *Curr. Opin. Neurobiol.* 16, 179–190.

Moscovitch, M., Rosenbaum, R. S., Gilboa, A., Addis, D. R., Westmacott, R., Grady, C., et al. (2005). Functional neuroanatomy of remote episodic, semantic and spatial memory: a unified account based on multiple trace theory. *J. Anat.* 207, 35–66.

Nadel., L., and Moscovitch, M. (1997). Memory consolidation, retrograde amnesia and the hippocampal complex. *Curr. Opin. Neurobiol.* 7, 217–227.

Nagel, T. (1974). What is it like to be a bat? *Philos. Rev.* 83, 435–450.

Naya, Y., and Suzuki, W. A. (2011). Integrating 'what' and 'when' across the primate medial temporal lobe. *Science* 5, 773–776.

Newell, A. (1973). "You can't play 20 questions with nature and win: projective components on the papers of this symposium," in *Visual Information Processing,* ed W. G. Chase (New York, NY: Academic Press), 283–308.

Northoff, G. (2000). Are "Q-Memories" empirically realistic? A neurophilosophical approach. *Philos. Psychol.* 13, 191–211.

Nyberg, L., Cabeza, R., and Tulving, E. (1996). PET studies of encoding and retrieval: the HERA model. *Psychon. Bull. Rev.* 3, 135–148.

Nyberg, L., and Tulving, E. (1998). Functional brain imaging of episodic and semantic memory with positron emission tomography. *J. Mol. Med.* 76, 48–53.

Parkin, A. J. (1997). *Memory and Amnesia, 2nd Edn.* Oxford: Basil Blackwell.

Perner, J., and Ruffman, T. (1994). Episodic memory and autonoetic consciousness: developmental evidence and a theory of childhood amnesia. *J. Exp. Child Psychol.* 59, 516–548.

Piolino, P., Desgranges, B., Belliard, S., Matuszewski, V., Lalavee, C., De La Sayette, V., et al. (2003). Autobiographical memory and autonoteic consciousness: triple dissociation in neurogenerative diseases. *Brain* 126, 2203–2219.

Polanyi, M. (1967). *The Tacit Dimension.* Garden City, NY: Anchor Books.

Rasmussen, K. W., and Bernsten, D. (2012). Autobiographical memory and episodic future thinking after moderate to severe traumatic brain injury. *J. Neuropsychol.* doi: 10.1111/jnp.12003. [Epub ahead of print].

Reid, T. (1813/1969). *Essays on the Intellectual Powers of Man.* Cambridge, MA: MIT Press.

Renoult, L., Davidson, P. S. R., Palombo, D. J., Moscovitch, M., and Levine, B. (in press). Personal semantics: at the crossroads of semantic and episodic memory. *Trends Cogn. Sci.*

Robertson, L. C., Knight, R. T., Rafal, R., and Shimamura, A. P. (1993). Cognitive neuropsychology is more than single case studies. *J. Exp. Psychol. Learn. Mem. Cogn.* 19, 710–717.

Rosenbaum, R. S., Murphy, K. J., and Rich, J. B. (2012). The amnesias. *Wiley Interdiscip. Rev. Cogn. Sci.* 3, 47–63.

Russell, B. (1912/1999). *The Problems of Philosophy.* Mineola, NY: Dover Publications.

Russell, B. (1921). *The Analysis of Mind.* London: George Allen and Unwin Ltd.

Ryan, L., Cox, C., Hayes, S. M., and Nadel, L. (2008). Hippocampal activation during episodic and semantic memory retrieval: comparing category production and cued recall. *Neuropsychologia* 46, 2109–2121.

Sass, L. A., and Parnas, J. (2003). Schizophrenia, consciousness, and the self. *Schizophr. Bull.* 29, 427–444.

Schacter, D. L. (1995). *Memory Distortion.* Cambridge, MA: Harvard University Press.

Schacter, D. L., and Tulving, E. (eds.). (1994). *Memory Systems.* Cambridge, MA: MIT Press.

Schwindt, G., and Black, S. E. (2009). Functional imaging studies of episodic memory in Alzheimer's disease: a quantitative analysis. *Neuroimage* 45, 181–190.

Scoville, W. B., and Milner, B. (1957). Loss of recent memory after bilateral hippocampal lesions. *J. Neurol. Neurosurg. Psychiatry* 20, 11–21.

Shallice, T. (1988). *From Neuropsychology to Mental Structure.* Cambridge: Cambridge University Press.

Smith, C. N., and Squire, L. R. (2009). Medial temporal lobe activity during retrieval of semantic memory is related to the age of the memory. *J. Neurosci.* 29, 930–938.

Sokol, S. M., McCloskey, M., Cohen, N. J., and Aliminosa, D. (1991). Cognitive representations and processes in arithmetic: inferences from the performance of brain-damaged subjects. *J. Exp. Psychol. Learn. Mem. Cogn.* 17, 355–376.

Squire, L. R. (1987). *Memory and Brain.* New York, NY: Oxford University Press.

Squire, L. R. (2004). Memory systems of the brain: a brief history and current perspective. *Neurobiol. Learn. Mem.* 82, 171–177.

Squire, L. R., and Bayley, P. J. (2007). The neuroscience of remote memory. *Curr. Opin. Neurobiol.* 17, 185–196.

Stephens, G. L., and Graham, G. (2000). *When Self-Consciousness Breaks: Alien Voices and Inserted Thoughts.* Cambridge, MA: MIT Press.

Stuss, D. T., and Guzman, D. A. (1988). Severe remote memory loss with minimal anterograde amnesia: a clincial note. *Brain Cogn.* 8, 21–30.

Suddendorf, T., and Corballis, M. C. (1997). Mental time travel and the evolution of the human mind. *Genet. Soc. Gen. Psychol. Monogr.* 123, 133–167.

Suddendorf, T., and Corballis, M. C. (2007). The evolution of foresight:

what is mental time travel, and is it unique to humans? *Behav. Brain Sci.* 30, 299–313.

Svoboda, E., McKinnon, M. C., and Levince, B. L. (2006). The functional neuroanatomy of autobiographical memory: a meta-analysis. *Neuropsychologia* 44, 2189–2208.

Szpunar, K. K. (2010). Episodic future thought: an emerging concept. *Perspect. Psychol. Sci.* 5, 142–162.

Szpunar, K. K. (2011). On subjective time. *Cortex* 47, 409–411.

Szpunar, K. K., and Tulving, E. (2011). "Varieties of future experience," in *Predictions and the Brain: Using Our Past to Generate a Future,* ed M. Bar (New York, NY: Oxford University Press), 3–12.

Talland, G. A. (1964). Self-reference: a neglected component in remembering. *Am. Psychol.* 19, 351–353.

Trusted, J. (1987). *Inquiry and Understanding: An Introduction to Explanation on the Physical and Human Sciences.* Atlantic Highlands, NJ: Humanities Press.

Tulving, E. (1972). "Episodic and semantic memory," in *Organization of Memory,* eds E. Tulving and W. Donaldson (New York, NY: Academic Press), 381–403.

Tulving, E. (1983). *Elements of Episodic Memory.* New York, NY: Oxford University Press.

Tulving, E. (1985). Memory and consciousness. *Can. Psychol.* 26, 1–12.

Tulving, E. (1993). "Self-knowledge of an amnesic individual is represented abstractly," in *Advances in Social Cognition, Vol. 5,* eds T. K. Srull and R. S. Wyer (Hillsdale, NJ: Erlbaum), 147–156.

Tulving, E. (2002). Episodic memory: from mind to brain. *Ann. Rev. Psychol.* 53, 1–25.

Tulving, E., Schacter, D. L , McLachlan, D. R., and Moscovitch, M. (1988). Priming of semantic autobiographical knowledge: a case study of retrograde amnesia. *Brain Cogn.* 8, 3–20.

Tulving, E., and Szpunar, K. K. (2012). "Does the future exist?" in *Mind and the Frontal Lobes: Cognition, Behavior, and Brain Imaging,* eds B. Levince and F. I. M. Craik (New York, NY: Oxford University Press), 248–263.

Uttal, W. R. (2001). *The New Phrenology.* Cambridge, MA: MIT Press.

Uttal, W. R. (2009). *Distributed Neural Systems.* Cormwall-on-Hudson, NY: Sloan Publishing.

Wagner, A. D., Shannon, B. J., Kahn, I., and Buckner, R. L. (2005). Parietal lobe contributions to episodic memory retrieval. *Trends Cogn. Sci.* 9, 445–453.

Warnock, M. (1987). *Memory.* Boston, MA: Faber and Faber.

Wheeler, M. A. (2000). "Varieties of memory and consciousness in the developing child," in *Memory, Consciousness and the Brain: The Tallin Conference,* ed E. Tulving (Philadelphia, PA: Psychology Press), 188–199.

Wheeler, M. A. (2005). "Theories of Memory and Consciousness," in *The Oxford Handbook of Memory,* eds E. Tulving and F. I. M. Craik (Oxford: Oxford University Press), 597–608.

Wheeler, M. A., Stuss, D. T., and Tulving, E. (1997). Toward a theory of episodic memory: the frontal lobes and autonoetic consciousness. *Psychol. Bull.* 121, 331–354.

Williams, G. C. (1966). *Adaptation and Natural Selection: A Critique of Some Current Evolutionary Thought.* Princeton, NJ: Princeton University Press.

Wixted, J. T., and Mickes, L. (2010). A continuous dual-process model of remember/know Judgments. *Psychol. Rev.* 117, 1025–1054.

Zahavi, D. (2005). *Subjectivity and Selfhood: Investigating the First-Person Perspective.* Cambridge, MA: The MIT Press.

Zahn, R., Talazko, J., and Ebert, D. (2007). Loss of sense of self-ownership for perceptions of objects in a case of right inferior temporal, parieto-occipital and precentral hypometabolism. *Psychopathology* 41, 397–402.

17

Development in the organization of episodic memories in middle childhood and adolescence

Yan Chen, Helena Margaret McAnally and Elaine Reese*

Department of Psychology, University of Otago, Dunedin, New Zealand

Correspondence:
Elaine Reese, Department of Psychology, University of Otago, P.O. Box 56, Dunedin 9054, New Zealand
e-mail: ereese@psy.otago.ac.nz

The basic elements of autobiographical or episodic memory are established in early childhood, although the exact age at which memories gain episodic status is still under contention. The self-memory system proposed that adults use "lifetime periods" to group episodic memories together into chapters of the life story – an evolving and internalized account of significant life events that are self-defining. Two studies examined at what point in development children or adolescents begin to take advantage of lifetime-period chapters to organize their episodic memories. The results of Study 1 with 8- to 12-year-olds revealed that the ability to provide life story chapters began to emerge as early as 8 years of age. In Study 2 with adolescents aged 12–21, this ability continued to develop into late adolescence among New Zealand European (NZE) and New Zealand Chinese (NZC) adolescents; however, cultural differences also existed in the specificity of memories. NZC adolescents narrated fewer life story chapters containing specific memories than NZE adolescents. These findings support and extend current theories of episodic memory by specifying that pre-adolescents are starting to organize their episodic memories into lifetime periods, but this achievement is not fully realized until later in adolescence.

Keywords: episodic memory, self-memory system, culture, middle childhood, adolescence, life story

INTRODUCTION

Episodic memory requires the ability to mentally travel back in time to locate a past event and to be able to provide information about the *what, when,* and *where* aspects of that event (Tulving, 1985, 2002). An important feature that separates episodic memory from other types of memory is the experience of subjective remembering, also referred to as autonoetic consciousness. In other words, episodic memory depends on individual awareness of a continuous self over time and the ability to mentally re-experience the recalled event (Wheeler et al., 1997). Episodic memories that are self-relevant are referred to as autobiographical memories (Nelson and Fivush, 2004). The age at which true episodic/autobiographical memory emerges in development is still under debate. Some theorists claim that episodic memory emerges between the age of 4 and 6, when autonoetic consciousness is developed (Perner and Ruffman, 1995; Perner, 2001; Tulving, 2005). Tulving further proposed that episodic memory entailing autonoetic awareness is preceded by development of a generalized knowledge base (semantic memory). Other theorists assert that episodic memory is possible earlier in development, by age 3 (Scarf et al., 2013), age 2 (Howe and Courage, 1993, 1997), or even before birth (Conway, 2009). Nonetheless, all theorists agree that by the time children are of school age, they are clearly capable of episodic remembering (Piolino et al., 2007). The main aim of the present paper is to trace the continued developments in episodic remembering in middle childhood and adolescence, after episodic remembering accompanied by autonoetic awareness is possible, and specifically to explore the development of the organization of episodic memories.

Conway and colleagues proposed the *Self-Memory System* theory to describe the organization of autobiographical memory, which suggests that different memory structures co-exist in a hierarchy in the long-term memory system (see Conway and Pleydell-Pearce, 2000; Conway, 2005, 2009; for reviews). The self-memory system theory specifies that single episodic memories (i.e., memories of specific events, such as the first day of school) are placed at the lowest level, followed by general, recurring events (e.g., going to school) that are nested within different lifetime periods (e.g., primary school days), which together contribute to various themes that are part of the life story. The life story is an evolving account of the events in one's life that are currently self-defining. Note that Conway and colleagues assert that specific memories are more fundamental in the self-memory system than are general events, in the sense that general events are made up of specific instances. For example, celebrating my 21st birthday is an episodic memory that contributes to the general event of "going to parties," which is part of a lifetime period such as "my university years." Ultimately, different lifetime periods (e.g., my university years, my teenage years, and my childhood) form the outline of a person's life story. Episodic memories, general events, lifetime periods, and the life story are all part of the *autobiographical knowledge base* (Conway, 2009). The autobiographical knowledge base contains self-relevant facts (e.g., birthdate, name of school, and family members), as well as episodic memories relating to the self. In the current paper, we investigated the development of the organization of episodic memories, as defined by Tulving (1985), within the framework of the self-memory system theory. Below, we review the self-memory system theory and evidence to support this theory based on adult samples.

The different components of the self-memory system theory have been examined in terms of the structure of adults' life stories in Thomsen (2009). In this study, 30 elderly Danish adults were asked to tell their life stories, without specific instructions on the structure or content of the life story. Chapters were the most common way of structuring the life story; they were thematically organized to cover particular periods of one's life. Specific memories also featured in the chapters. However, the number of specific memories was not related to the number of chapters, suggesting that chapters and specific memories were equally important for the construction of the life story. Thomsen suggested that specific memories are the building blocks of the life story, and that chapters are organized based on a common theme extracted from various specific memories. Thomsen further argues that chapters are the preferred structure for organizing an outline for the life story, because chapters require less memory storage than specific memories. Moreover, Thomsen et al. (2011) found that specific memories tended to cluster at the beginning of chapters, indicating that chapters based on lifetime periods trigger the recall of specific autobiographical memories.

Specific autobiographical memories, which are also referred to as episodic memories, emerge in the preschool years and continue to develop in important ways during middle childhood. For instance, Piolino et al. (2007) noted that in middle childhood memories become more detailed in their inclusion of episodic elements. Other research has found that older children and adolescents require less prompting to retrieve specific memories (Willoughby et al., 2012). Middle childhood and early adolescence is also a critical time to develop the ability to organize discrete episodic memories in chronological and meaningful ways in order to construct the life story (Habermas and Bluck, 2000). For example, by age 12, autobiographical narratives within the life story become integrated with respect to time and place (i.e., chronology); however, thematic and causal integration (i.e., meaning of past events for self) develop later in adolescence (Habermas and de Silveira, 2008). Although there is evidence supporting the hierarchical structure of long-term memory in adulthood, little is known about the developmental trajectory of this process. The first goal of the current research, therefore, is to track the development of episodic memories in relation to the autobiographical knowledge base by examining when school-age children and adolescents begin to use lifetime periods to organize their episodic memories, which ultimately form the basis of their life stories.

Apart from cognitive maturation that contributes to the hierarchical structure of long-term memory, culture also influences this developmental process as autobiographical memories are constructed within a sociocultural context (Fivush and Nelson, 2004). Cultural variations in autobiographical memory are found in terms of the socialization processes that foster the development of autobiographical memory, such as parent-child joint reminiscing (Mullen and Yi, 1995; Fivush and Wang, 2005; Kulkofsky et al., 2009). Cultural differences are also present in the content and structure of the autobiographical memory. People from Western cultures, for example, recall earlier first memories, and those memories are more elaborative and emotion laden, compared to their Eastern counterparts (Mullen, 1994; MacDonald et al., 2000; Wang, 2006b). Also, people from Western cultures recall autobiographical memories that are based on specific events and are self orientated, whereas people from Eastern cultures are more likely to recall autobiographical memories that are based on generic events and are socially orientated (Wang, 2006a). Cultural differences in perceiving the self relative to others are believed to be the underlying factor causing cultural variations in the recollection of autobiographical memory (Markus and Kitayama, 1991; Wang, 2008).

Cultural differences in memory recollection are also found at the encoding phase. For example, Wang (2009a) conducted a diary study in which European American and Asian college students were asked to list specific, one-time events that happened during the day for seven consecutive days. The results showed that Asian students recorded fewer specific memories in their diaries compared to the European American students, whereas both groups showed a similar forgetting rate when they were asked to recall these events 1 and 2 weeks later. This evidence suggests that cultural variation in memory density is possibly due to cultural differences in encoding rather than the ability to retain memories in the long-term memory system. Furthermore, when asked to recall a fictional story, Asian students recalled the story with fewer segments than did the European American students. This is consistent with Nisbett and Miyamoto's (2005) claim that Asians are more likely to adopt a holistic processing style (i.e., details of the story are integrated and processed as a whole such that only the gist of the story is remembered), whereas European Americans are more likely to adopt an analytical processing style (i.e., salient features of the story are remembered separately). Given these cultural differences in the content of episodic memory, a second goal of this research was to investigate cultural differences in the structure of long-term memory among in adolescents from two cultures: New Zealand European (NZE) and New Zealand Chinese (NZC).

In Study 1, using the Emerging Life Story Interview protocol (ELSI; Reese et al., 2010), we asked 8- to 12-year-old children to tell us their life stories as if they were chapters from a book. Life story structure was assessed on two dimensions (1) for the use of lifetime-period (LP) chapters (e.g., my high school years) as opposed to single-event (SE) chapters (e.g., a family trip to Australia); and (2) for the presence of specific memories. Note that these two dimensions are not mutually exclusive. All of the LP chapters contained general memories; some of the LP chapters contained general as well as specific memories; SE chapters contained one or more specific memories. We created the following two variables to capture the structure of the life story: (1) chapters based on lifetime periods versus chapters based on single events, and (2) chapters containing specific memories. We hypothesized that there would be age-related increases in children's use of LP chapters versus SE chapters as the main structure of the life story, and potentially also in the inclusion of specific memories within chapters as episodic memory continued to develop across this age period.

In Study 2, life stories were elicited from NZE and NZC adolescents, aged between 12 and 21. Again, we hypothesized age-related increases in using LP chapters for both cultural groups. We predicted that NZE adolescents would have more chapters in the life story compared to NZC adolescents, due to the cultural differences in cognitive processes (Wang, 2009a). Based on previous research on the specificity of memory (Wang, 2006a), we also predicted more chapters containing specific memories to be present in the life stories of NZE participants.

STUDY 1

METHOD

Ethics statement

Study 1 and Study 2 were approved by the University of Otago Human Ethics Committee.

Participants

One hundred and twenty four children (69 girls and 56 boys), aged between 8 and 12 years old, and their mothers participated in the present study. Children were recruited from several local primary and intermediate public schools in Dunedin, New Zealand. The average age across the whole sample was 10.55 years, with a mean age of 10.60 years for girls (SD = 1.46) and 10.50 years for boys (SD = 1.40). The majority of the children were of NZE descent ($N = 106$); other ethnicities included Māori ($N = 2$), British ($N = 2$), Asian ($N = 1$), and mixed ($N = 12$). Most mothers had completed high school education or beyond ($N = 118$). Family socio-economic status was measured by the Elley-Irving Socio-Economic 2001 Index (Elley and Irving, 2003); the average score was 2.5 on a six-point scale, ranging from one (highly skilled professional; e.g., lawyer) to six (unskilled labor; e.g., shearing shed worker). Written parental and child consents were obtained before the interview. Each family received a small gift at the end of the interview session.

Procedure

Children and their mothers visited our lab for a single interview session, where they were greeted by two female interviewers. This research was part of a larger study (see Friedman et al., 2011 for details) and only measures pertinent to children's life stories are mentioned here. After signing the consent forms, the parent went to a separate room with one interviewer, while the child stayed in the main laboratory with another interviewer. The child and parent interviews were conducted simultaneously. Children were interviewed about their life stories and specific life-changing events.

Measures

Life story chapters. Children's life stories in this research were elicited using the Emerging Life Story Interview (ELSI, Reese et al., 2010, adapted from McAdams, 1996). In the ELSI, children were instructed to tell a story of their life as if it were a story in a book. Specifically, children were asked to divide the life story into different chapters. The interview always started with the chapter that the child was currently in. Then she or he could choose how to narrate the rest of the chapters by working backwards to the chapter that came before the current one, until reaching the first chapter. Once the child had nominated a chapter, she or he was asked to describe the important events that had happened in that chapter. They were also asked to offer a title for the chapter. There was no minimum requirement on the number of chapters, but the maximum number of chapters was kept at 10. The interviewer wrote down the structure of the life story while the interview was audiotaped, including the name and the content of each chapter on a summary sheet. Once the child had finished narrating the chapters, the interviewer recapped the entire life story starting from the earliest chapter, so that the child had a chance to correct or add new information to the life story.

Language ability. Form B of the Peabody Picture Vocabulary Test (PPVT), Fourth Edition (Dunn and Dunn, 2007) was used to assess participants' language skills because language is an important medium for the development of memory, and vocabulary is related to young children's recall of past events (Reese, 2002; Nelson and Fivush, 2004). The PPVT is an oral assessment of receptive language that is highly correlated with language ability and verbal IQ (Smith et al., 1991). Children were shown a set of four pictures and asked to indicate which picture best described the word that the experimenter had just told them. There was no time limit for the PPVT, and the test terminated when there were over eight or more errors in a set of 12 words. Standard scores were used in analyses.

Coding

The life stories were not transcribed, as we were interested in the organization rather than the content of children's autobiographical memory. Coding was conducted based on information the interviewer wrote down on the summary sheet during the interviews about the title, chapters, and memories within each chapter. Gender and other identifying information (such as the name of the child or siblings) were removed from the forms for coding.

Each chapter was coded as either *Lifetime Period* or *Single Event.* LP chapters contained several events that occurred over a certain time frame, ranging from a few months to a few years (e.g., my primary school years). These events also needed to be connected with each other in some way in order to form an overarching theme. As mentioned earlier, LP chapters contain general memories or a mixture of general and specific memories. In contrast, SE chapters contained discrete events that did not converge to an overall theme. Quite often, there was only one event listed for each chapter, typically lasting for less than a day (e.g., a trip to Movie World). Note that general event memory (i.e., semantic memory) is suggested as the developmental precursor of episodic memory (Tulving, 2005; although see Conway, 2009 for an alternative view). This claim is derived from research on cued recall and on the content of the recollection. In contrast, our investigation focused on the organization of memory, which is hierarchically constructed from episodic memories as suggested by the self-memory system theory. In line with Conway's approach, we consider LP chapters to be more developmentally advanced than SE chapters, despite the fact that LP chapters contain general event memories.

We then coded chapter specificity to capture whether each chapter contained one or more specific memories. In Conway's (2009) theory, specific episodic memories are the building blocks of general event knowledge, which ultimately develops into an abstract form of self-knowledge, namely an individual's life story. General events are also the preferred structure for long-term memory as they require less cognitive load for memory storage

(Conway et al., 2004). As a result, age-related changes were expected for the structure of life stories, such that younger children would initially organize their chapters based on specific events and older children would be more likely to use general event knowledge to represent life story chapters. Note that we did not require evidence of participants' autonoetic consciousness as a selection criterion for specific memory. Rather, all memories describing specific, one-point-in-time events were considered as specific episodic memories. This is due to the fact that true episodic/autobiographical recollection should be well developed in the age range of our participants (Perner, 2001; Piolino et al., 2007).

Two coders coded 25% of the life story chapters to reach reliability in terms of the numbers of LP chapters versus SE chapters and the number of chapters containing specific memories. Percentage agreement was calculated at above 90% for both categories. Disagreements were resolved through discussions between the coders. Once reliable, the two coders each coded 50% of the remaining life story chapters.

RESULTS

Preliminary analyses

Univariate analysis of variance (ANOVA) showed a marginal main effect of age on the proportion of LP chapters [$F(4, 119) = 2.10$, $p = 0.09$]. Fisher's LSD tests showed that children in the 8-, 9-, and 10-year-old groups reported significantly smaller proportions of life-period chapters than those in the 12-year-old group, whereas there were no significant differences between children in the 11-year old group and either the older or younger age groups. See **Figure 1** for the proportions of LP chapters reported by children from each age. Based on this finding, we decided to dichotomize the sample into two age groups, with the middle childhood group consisting of 8-, 9-, and 10-year-old children ($M = 9.62$, $SD = 0.84$, $N = 76$) and the early adolescence group consisting of 11- and 12-year-old children ($M = 12.11$, $SD = 0.59$, $N = 48$), for all further analyses.

Children's receptive language skills, as measured by the PPVT, did not differ significantly as a function of age group or gender. However, there was a significant interaction between age group and gender [$F(1, 117) = 5.15$, $p < 0.05$, partial $\eta^2 = 0.04$]. Children's PPVT scores did not differ between boys ($M = 108.03$, $SD = 11.69$) and girls ($M = 111.60$, $SD = 11.72$) in the middle childhood group. In contrast, boys scored slightly higher ($M = 114.85$, $SD = 12.81$) than did girls ($M = 107.85$, $SD = 13.82$) in the early adolescent group; however, this difference was only marginally significant [$t(45) = 1.77$, $p = 0.08$]. Higher PPVT scores among the early adolescents correlated significantly with their inclusion of a greater proportion of LP chapters ($r = 0.30$, $p < 0.05$); there were no associations between PPVT and any of the life story variables for the middle childhood group.

Main analyses

Each participant had separate scores for the number of chapters, LP chapters, SE chapters, and chapters with specific memories. Raw scores were then converted into proportions of the total number of chapters (see **Table 1**). There were no significant age or gender differences in the number of chapters or the number of chapters containing specific memories, nor were there any interactions between gender and age on the different components of life story chapters.

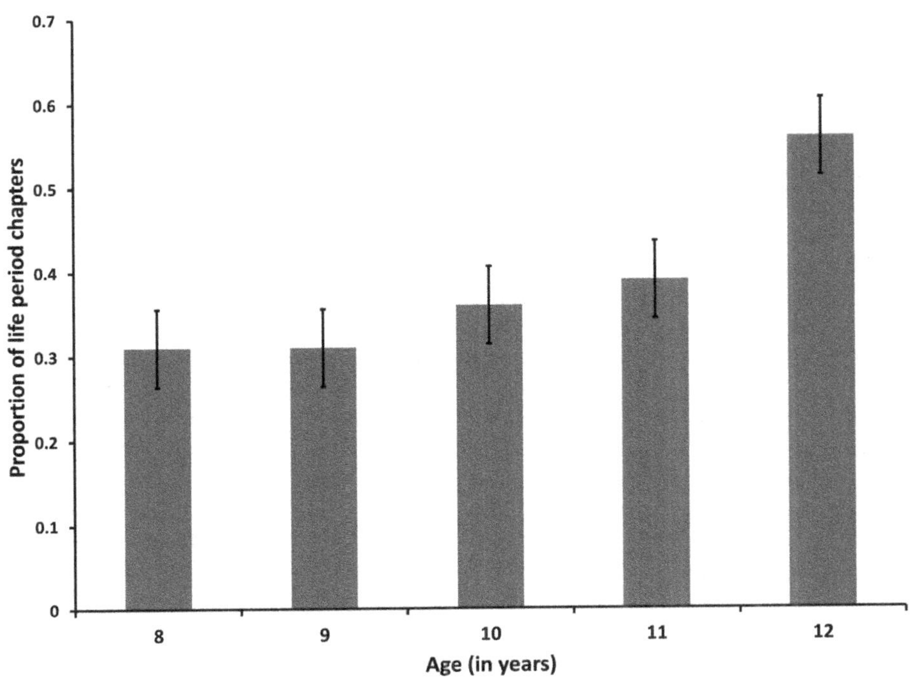

FIGURE 1 | Proportions of lifetime-period chapters across age groups (Study 1).

Table 1 | Number and types of life story chapters in middle childhood and early adolescence (Study 1).

Chapter task variables	Middle childhood ($N=76$)		Early adolescence ($N=48$)	
	M	SD	*M*	SD
Number of chapters	5.68	2.33	6.00	2.20
Proportion of LP chapters[a]	0.33	0.34	0.48	0.38
Number of SPE chapters[b]	4.75	2.46	4.67	2.18

[a] *Proportion of lifetime-period chapters.*
[b] *Number of chapters containing specific memories.*

Analyses of variance (ANOVAs) were conducted to test the effects of age and gender on the structure of life story chapters. LP and SE chapters were coded with a mutually exclusive scheme, and consequently, these codes yielded the same results (but with findings in the opposite direction). As PPVT was correlated with this variable, an ANCOVA was also conducted to test the effects of age and gender on the proportion of LP chapters when controlling for PPVT. In the interests of brevity, we only report the results for LP chapters; it can be assumed that the inverse finding was present for SE chapters.

The results showed a main effect of age on the proportion of LP chapters, such that children in the middle childhood group had smaller proportions of LP chapters in their life stories than did those in the early adolescence group [$F(1, 120)=4.99$, $p=0.03$, partial $\eta^2=0.04$]. There was also a main effect of gender, with girls reporting higher proportions of LP chapters ($M=0.46$, $\text{SD}=0.35$) than boys ($M=0.30$, $\text{SD}=0.36$), $F(1, 120)=4.53$, $p=0.04$, partial $\eta^2=0.04$. This effect remained the same when controlling for PPVT.

So far we have shown that the ability to organize autobiographical memories based on lifetime periods emerges late in middle childhood. Thus, the hierarchical structure of autobiographical memories (i.e., the integration of episodic memory and autobiographical knowledge base) begins to establish in this age range. Previous research has investigated the development of autobiographical memory in middle childhood and early adolescence in terms of autonoesis (e.g., Piolino et al., 2007) and age-related differences between episodic and semantic autobiographical memories (e.g., Willoughby et al., 2012). To our knowledge, however, Study 1 is the first to provide evidence on the developmental trajectory of the organization of episodic memory in middle childhood and early adolescence.

Given the findings so far, we wanted to explore how memory structure continues to develop beyond early adolescence in Study 2. Furthermore, given previous findings on cultural differences in the content of episodic memories (e.g., MacDonald et al., 2000; Wang, 2006a, 2008), we wanted to determine whether the organization and structure of episodic memories also differs between NZE and NZC adolescents.

STUDY 2

METHOD

Participants

One hundred and seventy-eight adolescents (96 females, 82 males) aged between 12 and 21 years ($M=16.92$ years, $\text{SD}=2.52$) took part in Study 2. All participants were part of a larger research project on identity development in adolescence (see Chen et al., 2012 for further details). Participants above the age of 18 were recruited from the local university and through a student employment agency. The remainder of the participants was recruited from secondary schools in two towns and one city in New Zealand. All participants identified themselves as either European New Zealanders (NZE, $N=90$) or as first- or second-generation immigrants with Chinese ancestry (NZC, $N=88$). Seventy-six NZE and 37 NZC adolescents were born in New Zealand, and 80% of adolescents who were born overseas (8 NZE and 41 NZC) had spent more than 5 years living in New Zealand.

Based on social and educational milestones (i.e., starting high school at age 12 or 13, getting a driver license at age 15, finishing high school, and being eligible to vote at age 18), combined with theoretical claims that the life story develops rapidly in mid to late adolescence, adolescents in Study 2 were divided into three age groups. The early adolescent group consisted of adolescents between the ages of 12 and 14 (24 girls and 25 boys), the mid-adolescent group consisted of those aged between 15 and 17 years old (37 girls and 26 boys), and the late adolescent group consisted of students aged between 18 and 21 (36 girls and 30 boys).

All participants gave their consent before being interviewed, and parental consent was also obtained for those who were younger than 16 years old at the time of the interview. One of the interviewers was bilingual (Mandarin Chinese and English) so participants could chose the language they were interviewed in; participants in this research all chose to speak in English. Among NZC adolescents who were born outside of New Zealand, the mean length of residency in New Zealand was 5.55 years. There were no differences in the number of years that they had lived in New Zealand by age group [$F(2, 48)=1.15$, $p>0.05$]. Similar to Study 1, participants' life story chapters were coded based on the interviewer's record of story structure and content.

Procedure

The interview started with the life story task, which was very similar to the procedure carried out in Study 1. However, participants were encouraged to keep the number of chapters they narrated to seven. We decided on this number based on findings from Study 1 that about 80% of children provided seven or fewer chapters, and also on McAdams' (1995) life story interview procedure. Seven chapters provided adolescents with enough space to convey the important events that happened in their lives, but constrained the time burden of the overall interview.

As in Study 1, the narrator was told to start with the chapter that she/he was in right now and to narrate backwards to the first chapter. The interviewer did not give any specific instructions on the content of the chapters. Once the narrator had reached the first chapter, the interviewer recapped all the chapters in a chronological order as in Study 1, so that the narrator had a chance to verify the content or add new information to the life story.

Coding

Coding of chapter tasks for lifetime periods and for specific memories was conducted in the same fashion as Study 1. Reliability was calculated based on 25% of the total transcripts, with an equal number of transcripts from both cultures. Percentage agreement was calculated in the same fashion as in Study 1 and ranged from 94 to 100% agreement. The remaining transcripts were coded by the main coder.

RESULTS

Multivariate analysis of variance (MANOVA) was conducted to test the effects of gender, culture, and age on the structure of life story chapters in adolescence (see **Table 2** for descriptives). Significant multivariate effects were followed up by univariate analyses. There were no significant gender differences for any of the variables related to the structure of the life story. A main effect of culture was found for the number of chapters [$F(1, 166) = 27.35$, $p < 0.001$, partial $\eta^2 = 0.14$]; NZE adolescents included more life story chapters than their NZC counterparts. This main effect was further qualified by an interaction between culture and age [$F(2, 166) = 5.70$, $p < 0.05$, partial $\eta^2 = 0.06$]; NZE adolescents in the two younger age groups (e.g., early and mid-adolescence) had more chapters than did their NZC counterparts [$t(47) = 4.50$ and $t(61) = 2.64$, respectively, $ps < 0.05$]. However, these cultural differences were not present for the late adolescence group. A main effect of culture was also found for the number of chapters with specific memories [$F(1, 166) = 7.67$, $p < 0.05$, partial $\eta^2 = 0.04$], such that NZE adolescents had more chapters with specific memories ($M = 2.49$, SD $= 2.00$) than did NZC adolescents ($M = 1.74$, SD $= 1.43$). There were no cultural differences when comparing the proportion of LP chapters and the number of chapters with specific memories.

However, there were age-related differences in the proportion of LP chapters [$F(2, 166) = 5.41$, $p < 0.05$, partial $\eta^2 = 0.06$]. *Post hoc* Bonferroni tests showed that the significant difference for the proportion of LP chapters was found between the early ($M = 0.94$, SD $= 0.14$) and the late adolescent group ($M = 1.00$, SD $= 0$), such that no-one above the age of 18 organized their life story with SE chapters.

DISCUSSION

The self-memory system theory (Conway and Pleydell-Pearce, 2000; Conway, 2005, 2009) claims that autobiographical memory is constructed in a hierarchy, which consists of episodic memories at the lowest level, general events and lifetime periods in the middle, and the life story at the highest level. Our studies investigated the development of this hierarchy from middle childhood to young adulthood by comparing the ability to use lifetime periods, as opposed to single events, as a means of organizing the life story – the most abstract structure of autobiographical memory – among 8- to 21-year-olds. In Study 1, the proportion of LP chapters in the life story increased from middle childhood to early adolescence in participants of NZE descent. In Study 2, we compared the structure of the life story between NZE and NZC adolescents aged between 12 and 21. Regardless of ethnicity, the use of LP chapters continued to increase with age, suggesting that the use of lifetime periods is still developing past age 12. By age 18, all participants organized the life story based on lifetime periods. This similarity in the organization of life stories across cultures contrasts with past findings of cultural differences in the content of autobiographical memories (Wang, 2006a). However, in line with that literature, NZC adolescents had fewer life story chapters, and fewer chapters containing specific memories, than did NZE adolescents. This finding is consistent with Wang (2009a), in which Asian participants recalled fictional stories in fewer segments than their American European counterparts.

The current studies suggest that the ability to organize episodic memories in terms of lifetime periods is generally mastered by mid-adolescence for NZE and NZC adolescents, but continues to develop in a similar fashion into late adolescence for both cultures. Moreover, despite cultural similarities in this organizational structure, culture-related differences in the volume of memories were still present in terms of the number of life story chapters and the inclusion of specific memories within those chapters. It appears that these cultural differences are in the specificity and in the quantity of memories but not in the organization of those memories.

THE CONTINUED DEVELOPMENT OF EPISODIC MEMORY IN ADOLESCENCE

Children as young as 3 years old are capable of recalling specific episodic memories (Scarf et al., 2013). By the time they reach middle childhood, most children can recall autobiographical

Table 2 | Number and types of life story chapters in early, mid, and late adolescence as a function of culture (Study 2).

	Early adolescence		Mid-adolescence		Late adolescence	
	M	SD	*M*	SD	*M*	SD
NZE	(*N*=29)		(*N*=31)		(*N*=30)	
Number of chapters	5.34	2.09	4.52	1.69	4.67	1.35
Proportion of LP chapters[a]	0.92	0.16	0.95	0.13	1.00	–
Number of SPE chapters[b]	2.76	2.37	2.45	1.73	2.27	1.91
NZC	(*N*=20)		(*N*=32)		(*N*=36)	
Number of chapters	3.1	0.91	3.56	1.13	4.28	1.03
Proportion of LP chapters[a]	0.96	0.12	0.99	0.04	1.00	–
Number of SPE chapters[b]	1.60	1.39	1.44	1.29	2.08	1.50

[a] *Proportion of lifetime-period chapters.*

[b] *Number of chapters containing specific memories.*

memories with detailed descriptions of the *what, when, where* of the events, as well as an enriched account of emotional elaborations and self reflections (e.g., Fivush et al., 2003, 2008; Piolino et al., 2007). Although the ability to recall specific details of personal experiences in an adult-like fashion may be present in middle childhood, the organization of episodic memories in the life story is still developing in middle childhood and adolescence. Note that in Study 2, children in the early adolescent group reported higher proportions of LP chapters compared to the early adolescent group in Study 1. This is most likely due to the fact that the early adolescent group in Study 2 was older on average ($M = 13.6$ years) than in Study 1 ($M = 12.1$ years). Our findings suggest that the years from 8 to 14 are particularly important for the ability to use abstract structures (such as lifetime periods and general events) to organize long-term memory. Without specific instructions, older adults automatically use lifetime periods as the basic units to organize chapters of the life story (Thomsen, 2009).

In contrast, we prompted children and adolescents to tell a life story based on chapters, and found age-related differences in the structure of those chapters. We observed an increase in the use of LP chapters and a decrease in the use of SE chapters with age. By the time they reached late adolescence, all of their life stories were based on lifetime periods. Gaining an understanding of the overarching themes of a life story may help adolescents to understand what a life story should look like and help them to organize their stories in an adult-like fashion.

CULTURE, AUTOBIOGRAPHICAL MEMORY, AND THE LIFE STORY

Cultural differences based on the content of autobiographical memory also extended to the structure of the life story. We found that NZC adolescents had fewer life story chapters compared to NZE adolescents up to the age of 18. This is consistent with the interpretation that people from Eastern cultures tend to use a holistic approach in memory encoding, such that they focus on the connections among events and recall them as general events (Nisbett and Miyamoto, 2005).

Furthermore, cultural differences in memory specificity (Wang, 2009b; Wang et al., 2011) were also shown in the content of life story chapters in Study 2. Regardless of age, NZC adolescents had fewer chapters containing specific memories than did NZE adolescents. Given this study was exploratory, further research is needed to determine what, if any, effects these cultural disparities have on aspects of the self-memory system and the self. For example, what are the consequences of having general versus specific memories as the basic elements of the life story? Would this cultural disparity in memory structure have implications for the self concept (e.g., Wang, 2008)?

Although it does appear in Study 1 that girls have a head start in organizing their memories in middle childhood, these gender differences are not apparent in adolescence. In Study 2, there were no gender differences in any of the variables relating to life story organization for any of the age groups for either culture. Willoughby et al. (2012) found that girls between the ages of 8 and 16 reported more episodic autobiographical memories than boys, and Wang et al. (in press) found similar results in a younger sample of European Americans, although this gender difference was not present among a sample of Chinese immigrants. Our findings indicate a lack of gender differences in both NZE and NZC adolescents. Thus it appears that there are some inconsistencies in the literature with regard to whether gender influences the specificity of autobiographical memories. It may be that gender differences are culturally determined, rather than common across cultures.

STRENGTHS, LIMITATIONS, AND FUTURE DIRECTIONS

The current paper provides the first developmental evidence to support the claims of the self-memory system theory that autobiographical memories can be organized in terms of the life story, lifetime periods, and episodic memories. However, we were not able to elaborate on some memory components (i.e., general events and mini-narratives) within the self-memory system framework as our coding was based on an outline of the life story, consisting of titles of story chapters and keywords for the events. Future studies could incorporate the whole range of memory structures that are included in the life story. In line with Conway's (2009) theory, we would predict that including general events would serve as an intermediary step in organizing episodic memories prior to the use of lifetime periods. We also showed that although there were some differences in the length and specificity of life stories between NZE and NZC adolescents, the organization of episodic memory developed in similar ways across the two groups. Because cultural differences in memory specificity were attenuated with age, there is a possibility that the mature self-memory system captures a memory organization that is shared across cultures. Moreover, Study 2 was based on comparisons between a sample of immigrants and their host nation; the cross-cultural differences might have been reduced due to cultural assimilation of the immigrants (Wang, 2006b). Further studies are required to compare the structure of autobiographical memories between cultures that are geographically independent in order to continue to investigate the cross-cultural validity of the self-memory system model.

Furthermore, past research has shown that the content of life story chapters is associated with cultural life scripts, which contain knowledge about the type and timing of typical events that should occur in one's life (Thomsen and Berntsen, 2008). Future studies could examine whether acquisition of a cultural life script precedes the ability to use lifetime periods to organize episodic memories.

CONCLUSION

Our studies showed that the ability to organize episodic memories based on lifetime periods develops significantly from middle childhood to mid-adolescence. This finding supports Conway's (2009) theory of the hierarchical nature of the autobiographical knowledge base. Moreover, this finding extends Conway's theory to show that episodic memories precede and support the development of higher-order structures in the autobiographical knowledge base in the form of lifetime periods (see Conway, 2009, Figure 2). This cognitive development may be the precursor to adolescents' ability to find overarching themes from discrete episodic memories. That is, this organization may be related to the ability to narrate life stories that are integrated with respect to time and place during mid- and late adolescence (Habermas and de Silveira, 2008).

ACKNOWLEDGMENTS

Study 1 was funded by the National Science Foundation under Grant No. 0241558. Study 2 was funded by the Marsden Fund of the Royal Society of New Zealand. We thank Fiona Jack, Naomi White, Sarah-Jane Robertson, Donna Anderson, and Xin Dai for their help with data collection and coding. We also thank the families who participated and are grateful to the schools for their cooperation. We would like to acknowledge Prof. William Friedman for providing us with the wording of the chapter task.

REFERENCES

Chen, Y., McAnally, H. M., Wang, Q., and Reese, E. (2012). The coherence of critical event narratives and adolescents' psychological functioning. *Memory* 20, 667–681. doi:10.1080/09658211.2012.693934

Conway, M., Singer, J. A., and Tagini, A. (2004). The self and autobiographical memory: correspondence and coherence. *Soc. Cogn.* 22, 495–537. doi:10.1521/soco.22.5.491.50768

Conway, M. A. (2005). Memory and the self. *J. Mem. Lang.* 53, 594–628. doi:10.1016/j.jml.2005.08.005

Conway, M. A. (2009). Episodic memories. *Neuropsychologia* 47, 2305–2313. doi:10.1016/j.neuropsychologia.2009.02.003

Conway, M. A., and Pleydell-Pearce, C. W. (2000). The construction of autobiographical memories in the self-memory system. *Psychol. Rev.* 107, 261–288. doi:10.1037/0033-295x.107.2.261

Dunn, L. M., and Dunn, L. M. (2007). *Peabody Picture Vocabulary Test, 4th Edn.*, Minneapolis, MN: NCS Pearson, Inc.

Elley, W. B., and Irving, J. C. (2003). The elley-irving socio-economic index: 2001 census revision. *New Zeal. J. Educ. Stud.* 38, 3–17.

Fivush, R., Hazzard, A., Sales, J. M., Sarfati, D., and Brown, T. (2003). Creating coherence out of chaos? Children's narratives of emotionally positive and negative events. *Appl. Cogn. Psychol.* 17, 1–19. doi:10.1002/Acp.854

Fivush, R., McDermott Sales, J., and Bohanek, J. G. (2008). Meaning making in mothers' and children's narratives of emotional events. *Memory* 16, 579–594. doi:10.1080/09658210802150681

Fivush, R., and Nelson, K. (2004). Culture and language in the emergence of autobiographical memory. *Psychol. Sci.* 15, 573–577. doi:10.1111/j.0956-7976.2004.00722.x

Fivush, R., and Wang, Q. (2005). Emotion talk in mother-child conversations of the shared past: the effects of culture, gender, and event valence. *J. Cogn. Dev.* 6, 489–506. doi:10.1207/s15327647jcd0604_3

Friedman, W. J., Reese, E., and Dai, X. (2011). Children's memory for the times of events from the past years. *Appl. Cogn. Psychol.* 25, 156–165. doi:10.1002/acp.1656

Habermas, T., and Bluck, S. (2000). Getting a life: the development of the life story in adolescence. *Psychol. Bull.* 126, 748–769. doi:10.1037/0033-2909.126.5.748

Habermas, T., and de Silveira, C. (2008). The development of global coherence in life narratives across adolescence: temporal, causal, and thematic aspects. *Dev. Psychol.* 44, 707–721. doi:10.1037/0012-1649.44.3.707

Howe, M. L., and Courage, M. L. (1993). On resolving the enigma of infantile amnesia. *Psychol. Bull.* 113, 305–326. doi:10.1037//0033-2909.113.2.305

Howe, M. L., and Courage, M. L. (1997). The emergence and early development of autobiographical memory. *Psychol. Rev.* 104, 499–523. doi:10.1037//0033-295X.104.3.499

Kulkofsky, S., Wang, Q., and Koh, J. B. K. (2009). Functions of memory sharing and mother-child reminiscing behaviors: individual and cultural variations. *J. Cogn. Dev.* 10, 92–114. doi:10.1080/15248370903041231

MacDonald, S., Uesiliana, K., and Hayne, H. (2000). Cross-cultural and gender differences in childhood amnesia. *Memory* 8, 365–376 doi:10.1080/09658210050156822

Markus, H. R., and Kitayama, S. (1991). Culture and the self: implications for cognition, emotion, and motivation. *Psychol. Rev.* 98, 224–253. doi:10.1037//0033-295X.98.2.224

McAdams, D. P. (1995). *The Life Story Interview.* Available at: http://www.sesp.northwestern.edu/foley/instruments/interview

McAdams, D. P. (1996). Personality, modernity, and the storied self: a contemporary framework for studying persons. *Psychol. Inq.* 7, 295–321. doi:10.1207/s15327965pli0704_1

Mullen, M. K. (1994). Earliest recollections of childhood: a demographic analysis. *Cognition* 52, 55–79. doi:10.1016/0010-0277(94)90004-3

Mullen, M. K., and Yi, S. (1995). The cultural context of talk about the past: implications for the development of autobiographical memory. *Cogn. Dev.* 10, 407–419. doi:10.1016/0885-2014(95)90004-7

Nelson, K., and Fivush, R. (2004). The emergence of autobiographical memory: a social cultural developmental theory. *Psychol. Rev.* 111, 486–511. doi:10.1037/0033-295x.111.2.486

Nisbett, R. E., and Miyamoto, Y. (2005). The influence of culture: holistic versus analytic perception. *Trends Cogn. Sci. (Regul. Ed.)* 9, 467–473. doi:10.1016/j.tics.2005.08.004

Perner, J. (2001). "Episodic memory: essential distinctions and developmental implications," in *The Self in Time: Developmental Perspectives*, eds C. Moore and K. Lemmon (Mahwah, NJ: Lawrence Erlbaum Associates), 181–202.

Perner, J., and Ruffman, T. (1995). Episodic memory and autonoetic consciousness: developmental evidence and a theory of childhood amnesia. *J. Exp. Child. Psychol.* 59, 516–548. doi:10.1006/jecp.1995.1024

Piolino, P., Hisland, M., Ruffeveille, I., Matuszewski, V., Jambaqué, I., and Eustache, F. (2007). Do school-age children remember or know the personal past? *Conscious. Cogn.* 16, 84–101. doi:10.1016/j.concog.2005.09.010

Reese, E. (2002). Social factors in the development of autobiographical memory: the state of the art. *Soc. Dev.* 11, 124–142. doi:10.1111/1467-9507.00190

Reese, E., Chen, Y., Jack, F., and Hayne, H. (2010). "Emerging identities: narrative and self from early childhood to early adolescence," in *Narrative Development in Adolescence: Creating the Storied Self*, eds K. C. McLean and M. Pasupathi (New York, NY: Springer), 23–44.

Scarf, D., Gross, J., Colombo, M., and Hayne, H. (2013). To have and to hold: episodic memory in 3- and 4-year-old children. *Dev. Psychobiol.* 55, 125–132. doi:10.1002/dev.21004

Smith, T. C., Smith, B. L., and Dobbs, K. (1991). Relationship between the peabody picture vocabulary test-revised, wide range achievement test-revised, and Weschler intelligence scale for children-revised. *J. Sch. Psychol.* 29, 53–56. doi:10.1016/0022-4405(91)90015-I

Thomsen, D. K. (2009). There is more to life stories than memories. *Memory* 17, 445–457. doi:10.1080/09658210902740878

Thomsen, D. K., and Berntsen, D. (2008). The cultural life script and life story chapters contribute to the reminiscence bump. *Memory* 16, 420–435. doi:10.1080/09658210802010497

Thomsen, D. K., Pillemer, D. E., and Ivcevic, Z. (2011). Life story chapters, specific memories and the reminiscence bump. *Memory* 19, 267–279. doi:10.1080/09658211.2011.558513

Tulving, E. (1985). Memory and consciousness. *Can. Psychol.* 26, 1–12. doi:10.1037/h0080017

Tulving, E. (2002). Episodic memory: from mind to brain. *Annu. Rev. Psychol.* 53, 1–25. doi:10.1146/annurev.psych.53.100901.135114

Tulving, E. (2005). "Episodic memory and autonoesis: uniquely human?," in *The Missing Link in Cognition: Origins of Self-Reflective Consciousness*, eds H. S. Terrace and J. Metcalfe (New York: Oxford University Press), 3–56.

Wang, Q. (2006a). Earliest recollections of self and others in European American and Taiwanese young adults. *Psychol. Sci.* 17, 708–714 doi:10.1111/j.1467-9280.2006.01770.x

Wang, Q. (2006b). Relations of maternal style and child self-concept to autobiographical memories in Chinese, Chinese immigrant, and European American 3-year-olds. *Child Dev.* 77, 1794–1809. doi:10.1111/j.1467-8624.2006.00974.x

Wang, Q. (2008). Being American being Asian: the bicultural self and autobiographical memory in Asian Americans. *Cognition* 107, 743–751. doi:10.1016/j.cognition.2007.08.005

Wang, Q. (2009a). Are Asians forgetful? Perception, retention, and recall in episodic remembering. *Cognition* 111, 123–131. doi:10.1016/j.cognition.2009.01.004

Wang, Q. (2009b). Once upon a time: explaining cultural differences in episodic specificity. *Soc. Personal. Psychol. Compass.* 3, 413–432. doi:10.1111/j.1751-9004.2009.00182.x

Wang, Q., Capous, D., Kim Koh, J. B., and Hou, Y. (in press). Past and future episodic thinking in middle childhood. *J. Cogn. Dev.* doi:10.1080/15248372.2013.784977

Wang, Q., Hou, Y., Tang, H., and Wiprovnick, A. (2011). Travelling backwards and forwards in time: culture and gender in the episodic specificity of past and future events. *Memory* 19, 103–109. doi:10.1080/09658211.2010.537279

Wheeler, M. A., Stuss, D. T., and Tulving, E. (1997). Toward a theory of episodic memory: the frontal lobes and autonoetic consciousness. *Psychol. Bull.* 121, 331–354. doi:10.1037//0033-2909.121.3.331

Willoughby, K. A., Desrocher, M., Levine, B., and Rovet, J. F. (2012). Episodic and semantic autobiographical memory and everyday memory during late childhood and early adolescence. *Front. Psychol.* 3:53. doi:10.3389/fpsyg.2012.00053

18

Perspectives on episodic-like and episodic memory

Bettina M. Pause[1]*, Armin Zlomuzica[2], Kiyoka Kinugawa[3,4,5], Jean Mariani[3,4,5], Reinhard Pietrowsky[1] and Ekrem Dere[3,4,5]

[1] *Institute of Experimental Psychology, University of Düsseldorf, Düsseldorf, Germany*
[2] *Center for the Study and Treatment of Mental Health, Ruhr-Universität Bochum, Bochum, Germany*
[3] *Neurobiologie des Processus Adaptatifs-UMR 7102, Université Pierre et Marie Curie, Paris, France*
[4] *UMR 7102, CNRS, Paris, France*
[5] *Institut de la longévité, AP-HP Hôpital Charles Foix, Ivry-sur-Seine, France*

Correspondence:
Bettina M. Pause, Institute of Experimental Psychology, University of Düsseldorf, Universitaetsstr. 1, 40225 Düsseldorf, Germany.
e-mail: bettina.pause@hhu.de

Episodic memory refers to the conscious recollection of a personal experience that contains information on what has happened and also where and when it happened. Recollection from episodic memory also implies a kind of first-person subjectivity that has been termed autonoetic consciousness. Episodic memory is extremely sensitive to cerebral aging and neurodegenerative diseases. In Alzheimer's disease deficits in episodic memory function are among the first cognitive symptoms observed. Furthermore, impaired episodic memory function is also observed in a variety of other neuropsychiatric diseases including dissociative disorders, schizophrenia, and Parkinson disease. Unfortunately, it is quite difficult to induce and measure episodic memories in the laboratory and it is even more difficult to measure it in clinical populations. Presently, the tests used to assess episodic memory function do not comply with even down-sized definitions of episodic-like memory as a memory for what happened, where, and when. They also require sophisticated verbal competences and are difficult to apply to patient populations. In this review, we will summarize the progress made in defining behavioral criteria of episodic-like memory in animals (and humans) as well as the perspectives in developing novel tests of human episodic memory which can also account for phenomenological aspects of episodic memory such as autonoetic awareness. We will also define basic behavioral, procedural, and phenomenological criteria which might be helpful for the development of a valid and reliable clinical test of human episodic memory.

Keywords: Alzheimer disease, dissociative disorders, emotional memory, episodic memory, mild cognitive impairment, spatial memory, temporal order memory, test development

INTRODUCTION

Learning and memory are indispensable capacities for humans and animals, since they permit adaptive behavior and promote the survival of the individual and the species. For example, they allow animals to revisit places where food or mating resources can be found and to avoid places where odor trails of predators were present. In general, they allow flexible and adaptive behavior in response to slow or sudden changes in the environment. The importance of learning and memory for the everyday life in humans becomes evident when one considers the decomposed personality structure in people who have lost access to information about emotionally relevant life events, such as in the case of demented patients.

Clinical studies with brain-injured patients and lesion studies in animals have revealed multiple memory systems in the brain with distinct neuroanatomical substrates and which are specialized for the learning of specific material such as how to play piano or the contents of a textbook (Squire, 2004). Accordingly, long-term memories can be divided into declarative and non-declarative memories. Declarative or explicit memories are conscious, can be voluntarily accessed and can be verbalized. In contrast non-declarative memories are not conscious and the contents of these memories cannot be verbalized. Declarative memories can be further subdivided into semantic and episodic memories. Semantic memories refer to facts and rules and basic knowledge about the world (Squire, 2004). In contrast, episodic memories refer to single events or personal experiences that also contain information about the spatial and temporal context of these events. Episodic memories also contain a blueprint of the internal state of the individual during encoding, e.g., its emotions, perceptions, and thoughts (Dere et al., 2008, 2010).

Due to its complexity of being a multi-dimensional memory trace that is distributed across the central nervous system and since it is established on a single occasion, episodic memory is highly vulnerable to disease conditions and easily disturbed (Aggleton and Brown, 1999; Aggleton and Pearce, 2001) Impairments in episodic memory function are observed in individuals with Mild Cognitive Impairment (MCI), in neurodegenerative diseases such as Alzheimer's Disease (AD), Huntington's Disease (HD), and Parkinson's Disease (PD) and also in a number of psychiatric diseases including Schizophrenia, Major Depression (MD), and dissociative disorders.

In this review we will describe the concept of episodic memory, and present human disease conditions that are associated with episodic memory impairment. In the main part of this review, we will describe currently used tests of episodic memory function and discuss their validity. Hereby, we will discuss the implications of animal research on episodic-like memory for the theory and measurement of episodic memory. We will also describe a new concept of episodic memory that addresses the important questions of what is actually triggering episodic memory formation and its retrieval, and why some events are stored only transiently and others permanently. Finally, we will define basic criteria for the development of valid tests of episodic-like memory.

ENDEL TULVING'S CONCEPT OF EPISODIC MEMORY

The concept of episodic memory was developed by Endel Tulving in the early 70s (Tulving, 1972, 1983). At this time Tulving defined episodic memory rather technically as a memory system specialized to store specific idiosyncratic experiences in terms of what happened and where and when it happened. This initial definition is amenable to operationalization using a pure behaviorist approach to measure learning and memory performance (Dere et al., 2008, 2010) and has stimulated the development of what, where, and when paradigms for testing whether animals have the capacity to form episodic memories (Clayton and Dickinson, 1998; Dere et al., 2005a; Roberts et al., 2008).

In later work, Tulving widened the concept of episodic memory to include prerequisites of a fully developed episodic memory system (Tulving, 2001, 2002). Additionally, he described phenomenological processes that are specifically associated with the retrieval of episodic but not semantic memories. According to Tulving, episodic memory depends on a *self* (the awareness of the own existence) that goes along with *autonoetic awareness* (the awareness that remembered personal experiences have happened to oneself, are not happening now, and are part of one's personal history). Furthermore, Tulving proposed that humans have a *sense of subjective time* which enables them to distinguish between mental representations of the *self* in the past, present, and future (Tulving, 2001, 2002). Recently, the definition of episodic memory has been expanded by Klein (2013; this issue) by postulating that the core features of episodic memory in terms of a memory for what, happened, where and when are also shared by semantic memory and that episodic recollection requires the coordinated function of a number of distinct, but interacting, "enabling" systems. As enabling systems Klein postulates the para-mnestic constructs "ownership," "self," "subjective temporality," and "agency" that are necessary for episodic or autonoetic recollection in the sense of Tulving (2001, 2002).

It is further assumed that the type of subjective awareness provided by episodic or autonoetic recollection is relational rather than intrinsic in nature. Klein also assumes that the latter would imply that in some patient populations autonoetic recollection can be disturbed while core elements of episodic-like memory remain intact and are indistinguishable from the content of semantic long-term memory (Klein, 2013).

Nevertheless, it is obvious that the assessment of these phenomenological aspects during the retrieval of episodic memories is difficult to obtain by objective methods (Pennartz, 2009; Tagini and Raffone, 2010; Aleksander and Gamez, 2011). The possibilities to develop tests of autonoetic awareness and episodic recollection will be discussed later in this article. In the second part of this review we will outline the advantages of a behavioral definition of episodic-like memory for the development of a test that can be used for diagnostic purposes in healthy and patient populations and that allows to measure whether at least episodic-like memory is intact. We will also discuss the possibilities to combine a test of episodic-like memory with a second test that measures phenomenological aspects of episodic memory including autonoetic awareness to capture all elements of human episodic memory.

IMPAIRMENTS OF HUMAN EPISODIC MEMORY

Episodic memory deficits are observed after medial temporal lobe injury (Nyberg et al., 1996) which includes important memory structures such as the hippocampus (Burgess et al., 2002) and amygdala (Markowitsch and Staniloiu, 2011), but also after lesions to the frontal cortex (Kirchhoff et al., 2000) and diencephalic structures, such as the mediodorsal thalamus and the mammillary bodies (Tsivilis et al., 2008; Wolff et al., 2008).

Episodic memory impairments have also been demonstrated in the course of healthy aging (Tulving, 1983; Shing et al., 2010), the acute phase following mild traumatic brain injury (Dickerson and Eichenbaum, 2010; Tsirka et al., 2010), and in a variety of neuropsychiatric diseases (Butters et al., 1987; Dere et al., 2010). Furthermore, it seems that episodic memory deficits usually precede more global cognitive impairments associated with neurodegenerative diseases such as AD or PD (Williams-Gray et al., 2006; Dubois et al., 2007). Therefore, one can view episodic memory functioning as a highly sensitive indicator or seismograph of incipient brain pathology which manifests well before the full dimension of the disease becomes evident at the psychological and behavioral level.

MILD COGNITIVE IMPAIRMENT AND ALZHEIMER'S DISEASE

Presently, more than 24 million individuals across the world suffer from dementia and the majority of these cases is likely to be caused by AD. This high prevalence is predicted to double every 20 years because of the unprecedented level of aging in developed countries and the increased life-expectancy in the fast developing threshold countries (Ballard et al., 2011). The major histopathological hallmarks of AD include the loss of synapses, neurodegeneration, extracellular amyloid plaque deposits, and intracellular neurofibrillary tangles (Yankner, 1996a,b; Ballard et al., 2011), affecting brain areas within the medial temporal lobe, such as the entorhinal cortex and the hippocampus (Schwindt and Black, 2009). AD is a progressive, irreversible, and severely disabling disorder of memory and cognition that inevitably results in the need of intensive care and death. Accordingly, the health-care costs associated with the disease are exceptional high. There is a preclinical period covering several years in both AD and other dementias, called MCI, during which early and mild cognitive deficits can be identified (Brand et al., 2003; Galluzzi and Frisoni, 2008; Bordet et al., 2010). On average 50% of the individuals with MCI will develop AD within a few years (Trojanowski et al., 2010). Cognitive decline in early stages of AD typically begins with deficits in episodic memory (Bäckman et al., 2004; Ringman, 2005; Sarazin and Dubois, 2005; Thomas-Anterion and Laurent, 2006; Bäckman and Small, 2007; Dubois et al., 2007; Small and Bäckman, 2007; Schwindt and Black, 2009).

Until to date, there is no definite diagnostic test available which could identify AD in living patients (Reitz et al., 2010). Furthermore, the establishment of diagnostic tools for AD is time-consuming and expensive. Imaging tests include the measurement of amyloid-beta burden with PET (Nordberg et al., 2010) or measurements of hippocampal and frontal cortex volume with MRI (Wagner, 2000). Other tests include the analysis of cerebrospinal fluid biomarkers, e.g., the concentration of Aβ-oligomerization, Aβ-fragments, or phosphorylated-Tau (Blennow, 2010a,b; van Rossum et al., 2010). Although, these measurements have a high predictive value for identifying individuals in the prodromal stage of AD among patients with MCI (Hampel et al., 2010), these tests are too time-consuming, invasive, and expensive for being adopted as a routine screening. Therefore, AD is often unrecognized or misdiagnosed in its early stages.

Currently, the patient populations used to test the efficiency of drugs to ameliorate AD symptoms or its pathology in clinical trials are either very heterogeneous, as in the case of individuals with MCI, or patients are in a progressed stadium of AD where the effect of the drug is limited by extensive neurodegeneration. In fact, the potential of pharmacotherapy to ameliorate symptoms and/or pathology in AD has not yet been fully explored because of the difficulty to identify patients in a prodromal stage of AD (Blennow, 2010a,b).

The cognitive tests currently used for the diagnosis of AD are unspecific and cannot exclude cognitive impairments induced by other diseases. Furthermore, these tests are not sensitive to very mild forms of cognitive impairment (Pike and Savage, 2008). Thus, the main problem is that by the time the patient is diagnosed with AD, the disease had been progressed to a stadium in which pharmacological, immuno- (Weiner and Frenkel, 2006), and gene-therapy treatments (Urbaniak-Hunter et al., 2010) have only limited effects because of the advanced neurodegeneration in the target structures such as the frontal cortex or the hippocampus.

Therefore, there is a need for the development of a new cognitive marker of the presymptomatic stage of AD based on a test of episodic memory functioning. With such a diagnostic episodic memory test at hand it might be possible to identify individuals with a presymptomatic stage of AD among individuals with MCI. It might then be possible to delay the onset of the disease or to decelerate its progression with the currently available anti-Alzheimer disease treatments (Di Stefano et al., 2011; Pettersson et al., 2011).

DISSOCIATIVE AMNESIA

Dissociative amnesia also known as functional or psychogenic amnesia is a disease condition characterized by a transient and selective inability to retrieve episodic and autobiographical memories after experiencing traumatic events that have been associated with intolerable high levels of enduring stress (Brand and Van Gorp, 2006; Reinhold and Markowitsch, 2009). Patients with dissociative amnesia have generally no impairment in the formation and retrieval of new memories as in the case of organic anterograde amnesia. The transient episodic memory retrieval deficit can be confined to episodic memories of a certain age and usually includes the memory for the traumatic event. It is assumed that the inability to retrieve traumatic events serves as a protective mechanism that inhibits the conscious recollection of self-endangering memories (Kapur, 1991).

Imaging studies have revealed functional changes in the activity of the right temporal-frontal region and in the inferior-lateral prefrontal cortex in brains of patients with dissociative amnesia during the resting state (Brand et al., 2009). Furthermore, it has been proposed that the inability to retrieve episodic memories in patients with dissociative amnesia might be related to functional disturbances in the activity of the precuneus, the lateral parietal, the right dorsolateral, and polar prefrontal cortex (Markowitsch et al., 1997). There is also recent evidence suggesting that the inability to retrieve episodic memories in dissociative amnesia is correlated with functional alterations of left posterior parietal cortex (Arzy et al., 2011).

Dissociative amnesia is an example for the disruption of episodic memory function induced by extreme levels of emotional activation or stress that is enduring and uncontrollable. The case of dissociative amnesia suggests that extreme levels of emotional activation or stress do not interfere with the formation of durable episodic memories but rather with their accessibility during attempts of retrieval. With regard to the findings with dissociative amnesia, the relationship between emotional activation and the formation of durable episodic memories could be precised as follows: Too low levels of emotional activation are not suited to consolidate episodic memories into long-term memory, while extreme levels of emotional activation or stress (transiently) impair the retrieval of durable episodic memories. This hypothesis will be outlined in detail below.

ASSESSING EPISODIC MEMORY

CONVENTIONAL MEASURES

The pertinent literature indicates that even the measurement of human episodic-like memory (without an explicit test of episodic or autonoetic recollection) based on the rather narrow (initial) definition of Tulving (1972) as a memory system that receives and stores personal experiences in terms of what, where, and when information was and is a daunting task, with only very few successful approaches available (Dere et al., 2004, 2010). For example, due to the lack of a valid test, the utility of subtests of the Mini Mental Status Examination Test (Carcaillon et al., 2009) or the Wechsler Memory Scale (Humphreys et al., 2010) have been evaluated as tools to measure episodic memory or episodic-like memory. The subtests of the Wechsler Memory Scale only measures verbal and visual memory and not episodic memory or episodic-like memory as defined above. The Mini Mental Status Examination Test is used for assessing the severity of dementia, comprising items on semantic memory and executive functions. Thus, both tests are not suited to detect selective episodic memory or episodic-like memory impairments that are associated with, e.g., MCI.

Currently used more specific tests of episodic memory or episodic-like memory function either measure the learning and reproduction of study list items such as the California Verbal Learning Test (Woodard et al., 1999; Fine et al., 2008; Lekeu et al., 2010) or are based on verbal or written reports of autobiographical events, such as in the Autobiographical Interview (Gilboa et al., 2005; Dreyfus et al., 2010; Irish et al., 2011).

VERBAL LEARNING TESTS

In the recognition test studies, healthy participants or patients are requested to discriminate previously studied word or picture items from novel items (e.g., California Verbal Learning Test, Grober and Buschke, 1987). In some studies the maintenance of the learned material due to rehearsal in-between the encoding and retrieval sessions is prevented by an intervening and distracting task. The Rey Auditory Verbal Learning Task is based on the interference induced by the consecutive learning of two word lists and the immediate and delayed recall of the first list (Lezak, 1995).

The problem with verbal learning tests is that they do not explicitly measure whether the spatial and temporal context of the learning event is indeed recalled and often there is no spatial and temporal component implicated in the way the verbal memory is tested. Although, one can certainly assume that healthy adults are potentially able to remember where and when the recognized items have been presented, this is not sure in patient populations so that this ability has to be measured directly. Therefore, simple recognition tests cannot be used for episodic memory or episodic-like memory assessment in patient populations. Another problem associated with simple word list or picture recognition tests is that the participant or patient is instructed to memorize the learning material. This instruction is very likely to activate semantic instead of episodic memory systems for learning and consolidation of the learning material.

THE AUTOBIOGRAPHICAL INTERVIEW

Questionnaires for autobiographical or important life events have also been used to asses episodic memory function (Levine et al., 2002; Piolino et al., 2009; Dreyfus et al., 2010). Kopelman et al. (1989), have developed a semi-structured interview schedule, that assesses the recall of autobiographical incidents and of "personal semantic" memory across three broad time periods termed: "childhood," "early adult life," and "recent" events/information. With the term "personal semantic" memory, they refer to factual knowledge about a person's own past (e.g., addresses where lived, names of teachers/friend, colleagues at work, etc.). Thus, individuals are asked to recall a number of events from different periods of their life such as early childhood etc. or to recall a series of positive, negative, and neutral episodes from their lives. Usually, the participants or patients are asked to describe complete episodes that happened at a certain time and place. The verbal or written reports on events are then scored according to the frequency of episodic and non-episodic detail categories given. Episodic details refer to event, time, place, perceptual, thought, and emotion information (Kopelman et al., 1989). The general idea is that the fewer episodic details remembered for a given life event, the stronger the impairment in episodic memory functioning. However, there are a number of problems associated with this form of episodic memory assessment.

Generally, autobiographical memories are likely to be retrieved and narrated many times and due to their constructive and dynamic nature there might be changes in the contents and stability of a memory across time (e.g., due to reconsolidation and interference phenomena) (Schacter et al., 1998; Walker et al., 2003; Earles et al., 2008). Therefore, it is not always clear what type of memory (e.g., episodic or semantic memory) is actually measured by autobiographical memory tests. To account for this problem, tests have been designed that aim to distinguish between episodic and semantic components of autobiographical memory by scoring the spatio-temporal uniqueness of events (Levine et al., 2002; Piolino et al., 2009). Another problem is that episodic memory or episodic-like memory function is obviously judged by the assessment of the episodic memories that *can* be retrieved.

In early stages of neurodegenerative diseases such as MCI and AD autobiographical memories for personal life events which have been established decades before the onset of memory complaints are, although still accessible (Squire and Alvarez, 1995), possibly not completely normal. It has been shown that such autobiographical memories are overgeneralized, contain less specificity, and are less vivid (Murphy et al., 2008; Donix et al., 2010; Martinelli et al., 2013). Nevertheless, it is reasonable to assume that any impairment in episodic memory or episodic-like memory function should also impair the ability to encode and consolidate new or more recently formed episodic memories. These difficulties should manifest themselves as an inability to form novel episodic memories possibly independent of, or in addition to, changes in the ability retrieve episodic memories. Although the recollection of overgeneralized autobiographical memories for personal life events might be a hint for disturbed episodic memory function, reports on more recent events are probably more valid measures of the current status of episodic memory function.

Furthermore, the performance is also dependent on factors such as verbal competence, the ability and disposition to express feelings and emotions, the level of education, and pre-morbid verbal intelligence.

In conclusion, there is still a need for a valid standardized test to induce episodic-like memories and measure their retrieval. The arguments raised above suggest that it might be better to measure novel episodic memories rather than just ask the participant to elaborate on memories from the individual's personal history, without having the option to control the exact circumstances and the time of episodic memory formation.

ANIMAL RESEARCH ON EPISODIC-LIKE MEMORY

Animal research with rats and mice allows the study of the neurobiological mechanisms that might underlie episodic-like memory formation and retrieval with methods that are not available in human research. The animal research on episodic-like memory has its origins in now classic experiments on food-hoarding behavior in birds performed by Nicola Clayton and Anthony Dickinson (Salwiczek et al., 2009, for review). This line of research will be briefly discussed in the following paragraph. Thereafter we will discuss the importance of using one-trial memory paradigms (contextual fear conditioning and novelty-preference) which bear the unique capacity of being translatable to human episodic-like memory research.

FOOD-HOARDING PARADIGMS

The first evidence for episodic-like memory in animals was provided by Clayton and Dickinson (1998) showing that birds (scrub jays) are able to remember where and when they have cached a particular food item. In the studies that followed, it was reported that corvids are also able to use tools (Cheke et al., 2011), show object permanence (Salwiczek et al., 2009), plan for the future (Raby et al., 2007), and might have a theory of mind (Emery and Clayton, 2004; Dally et al., 2006; Grodzinski and Clayton, 2010; but see Roberts, 2002; Dere et al., 2008; Rattenborg and Martinez-Gonzalez, 2011 for critical discussion).

In fact, all these remarkable abilities of corvids have been demonstrated with behavioral paradigms that are in one or the other way related to food caching and retrieval behavior which is very likely to be a genetically fixed instinctive behavior. In other words, all of these abilities might be restricted to a narrow class of content or what information. In contrast, the human episodic memory is not restricted to a specific type of events or stimuli. Therefore, it is indispensable to show that these birds are also able to perform all of these sophisticated tasks with stimuli other than food, such as the objects which do not have a biologically significant meaning to the animals (despite being of course novel stimuli) used in the episodic-like memory task developed by Dere et al. (2005a).

CONTEXTUAL FEAR CONDITIONING

In the one-trial contextual fear paradigm, the animal receives a food shock upon the transition from a brightly lit large chamber into a smaller dark one (Sara et al., 1975; Ebenezer, 1988; Rudy and Sutherland, 1995; Rudy et al., 2004). If the animal is reintroduced to the big chamber, e.g., after a delay of 24 h, one finds that the animal avoids the normally preferred dark chamber. Thus, one-trial contextual fear conditioning can be described as a type of associative learning that is associated with a strong emotional arousal due to the sudden application of a painful stimulus in a specific spatial context. The formation of this memory seems to depend on hippocampal NMDA-receptors in the CA3 region (Cravens et al., 2006). It can be acquired in one trial, leads to a memory that is quite long-lasting (up to months), and is sensitive to hippocampal lesions (Anagnostaras et al., 2001; Lehmann et al., 2007). Therefore, there are some similarities between one-trial contextual fear conditioning and human episodic-like memory.

However, concerning the formation of episodic memory, the main problem that is associated with the contextual fear paradigm is that it does not measure whether the animals remember the temporal context of the aversive event (when information). Furthermore, human episodic memories are not restricted to fearful events, but also cover pleasant events (Ehrlichman and Halpern, 1988; Hamann et al., 1999). Nevertheless, the contextual fear conditioning paradigm has been useful to study the neurobiological mechanisms that might underlie one-trial spatial memory formation in rodents (Tronche et al., 2010; Li et al., 2011).

THE NOVELTY-PREFERENCE PARADIGM

The novelty-preference paradigm is based on the attraction of rats and mice by novel objects (Dere et al., 2007; Ennaceur, 2010; for a review see Dere et al., 2007). If rodents have the choice between an old and novel object they spent more time exploring the more interesting novel object suggesting that they remember the physical characteristics of the old object. The exploration of a novel object reflects approach behavior and likely to be motivated by an emotional activation that is rather pleasant to the animal and triggers episodic-like memory formation (reviewed in Dere et al., 2010). However, rodents prefer old objects when they have been placed in novel locations which render these objects more interesting as compared to old objects that are placed in a familiar location, which is taken as evidence for spatial object memory (Assini et al., 2009). In addition, rodents prefer objects which they have not seen very recently over those they have investigated more recently, which is taken as a measure for temporal order memory (Mitchell and Laiacona, 1998). By combining these different versions of the novelty-preference paradigm Dere et al. (2005a,b) tested whether rodents are able to remember specific events in terms of what happened where and when.

THE EPISODIC-LIKE MEMORY TEST

The episodic-like memory test for rats and mice (Dere et al., 2005a; Kart-Teke et al., 2006) allows the simultaneous measurement of the memory for the temporal order of objects presented within an open-field as well as the spatial positions in which these objects have been encountered. The test is also able to detect whether what, where, and when information has been integrated into a unified multi-dimensional episodic memory (Kart-Teke et al., 2006; Zlomuzica et al., 2007). In brief, each animal receives two sample trials with four identical copies of a novel object and an inter-trial interval of 50 min followed by a test trial in which two objects from the first sample trial (old objects) are presented together with two objects known from the second sample trial (recent objects). During the test trial one of the old and one of the recent objects are displaced to a novel location. It has been demonstrated that rats and mice are able to associate object-, spatial-, and temporal information after a single exposure to such stimulus constellations (Dere et al., 2005a,b, 2007). This remarkable ability is in accord with the concept of episodic-like memory and can be further classified as a kind of one-trial contextual learning (Kart-Teke et al., 2006; Zlomuzica et al., 2008).

BEHAVIORAL CRITERIA FOR THE MEASUREMENT OF EPISODIC-LIKE MEMORY

Findings from animal research were useful for the better understanding and definition of the conditions that might lead to episodic-like memory formation and its retrieval as well as for the generation of objective behavioral criteria by which the different features of episodic-like memory can be operationalized experimentally and can be assessed in both animals and humans (Clayton and Dickinson, 1998; Dere et al., 2005a,b, 2006). Accordingly, it has been proposed that episodic-like memory and episodic memory formation is an automatic, one-trial learning process based on the principles of one-trial contextual conditioning that is induced by a strong pleasant or aversive emotional activation (Dere et al., 2010). The generation of an episodic-like memory itself can be inferred from behavioral expressions referring to the content (what happened), place (where did it happen), and temporal context (in terms of the sequence of events attended) of personally experienced emotional events (Dere et al., 2006, 2008, 2010). Based on this behavioral definition of episodic-like memory a novel paradigm to induce and measure this type of memory non-verbally via quantifiable and reproducible motor responses in humans has been devised that will be presented below (Pause et al., 2010).

EMOTIONS TRIGGER EPISODIC MEMORY FORMATION

In order to measure novel episodic or episodic-like memories in the laboratory for research and diagnostic purposes it is necessary to define the properties of the events which induce episodic memory formation. Usually, only a subset of events that have occurred in the course of a day can be recalled after a few hours and the percentage of events that can be recalled decreases further if the delay between encoding and recall is extended to days, weeks, months, and years. The important question here is why are some events only stored for a few hours in the episodic memory system while others are stored permanently.

According to a distinction in memory duration, the classic test of episodic memory "please describe your breakfast this morning" would be a test of short-durable episodic memory, because it is obvious that the question "please describe your breakfast on Monday the week before last" will not yield a vivid description of this event. In contrast, the event of a car accident that occurred later on that particular Monday morning when the person was for example driving to its work place will be permanently remembered in great detail. It has been proposed that the impact of the trigger for episodic memory formation that decides for how long an event is stored in episodic memory is dependent on the emotional arousal that is associated with that event (Libkuman et al., 2004; Dere et al., 2010). Here, the rule might be that the stronger the emotional activation, the longer the durability of the episodic memory. Of course, this does not affect the fact that the durability and content of memories can also be modulated by factors such as rehearsal or the number of previous recalls of the memory (Zimmer et al., 2003; McKenzie and Eichenbaum, 2011). Furthermore, it is important to note that extreme emotional activation (e.g., stress) can disrupt episodic memory function similar to other types of memory. An example for such stress-induced impairment of episodic memory function is discussed under the section dealing with dissociative amnesia.

Furthermore, it is possible that the relationship between episodic memory performance and the degree of emotional activation during the encoding of episodic information has the form of an inverted U-shaped curve as it has been described for the dose-response function between orally administered cortisol and explicit memory performance in humans (Abercrombie et al., 2003; Baldi and Bucherelli, 2005). This assumption implicates that excessive emotional activation similar to insufficient emotional activation would impair episodic memory formation. One example for impaired episodic memory formation after excessive emotional activation is that of a trauma memory which can be either fragmentarily or incorrectly remembered (Bower and Sivers, 1998; van der Hart and Nijenhuis, 2001; Brewin, 2011). Moreover, emotional arousal might not be only a trigger for episodic memory formation but might also play a role in binding of different features of an event into a unified episodic memory (Nashiro and Mather, 2011).

One prediction of the necessity of emotional arousal for the establishment of long-durable episodic memories would be that bilateral amygdala damage impairs episodic memory function. In this regard, it has been proposed that the amygdala contributes to the integration of emotion, perception, and the memory for past autobiographical events, plays an integral part in the establishment and maintenance of an integrated self, and provides retrieval cues during the memory search for emotionally significant events (Markowitsch and Staniloiu, 2011). Evidence for an implication of the amygdala for the encoding and retrieval of episodic memories has been provided by the examination of patients with Urbach–Wiethe syndrome who suffer from relatively selective bilateral lesions of the amygdala (Hurlemann et al., 2007). In fact, it has been reported that Urbach–Wiethe patients show an impairment of the memory for autobiographic episodes but not for autobiographic facts (Wiest et al., 2006). Furthermore, it has been reported that a 54-year-old woman with bilateral damage to the amygdala showed impaired episodic memory performance for stimuli that elicited an arousal response (taboo words) but not for emotional stimuli which did not elicit an arousal response (Phelps et al., 1998).

THE TEMPORAL COMPONENT OF EPISODIC MEMORY

A main difference between episodic and semantic memory is that the episodic memories have also a temporal connotation are time-dated or endowed with time-tags such as that something has happened "this morning" or "last summer" (Tulving, 2001, but see also Klein, 2013 this issue for a different view). However, in humans the perception of time and the assessment of the duration of events are not represented on a linear time scale (Pöppel, 1997; Roberts, 2002). In this regard, Friedman (1996) speaks of a "chronological illusion," and proposes that the memory for time is rather reconstructive and inferential in nature.

We have proposed that temporal information is either stored as succession or order information relative to other events already stored in episodic memory or is reconstructed during the recall processes using anchor events (events for which an episodic memory exists) (Dere et al., 2006). It is reasonable to assume that the temporal context of a particular event is either encoded in relation to, or inferred from its occurrence before or after, other "anchor events." One of which is proximal in terms of just preceding or following the event to be temporally specified, whereas the other is more distal that is the anchor event stands at the beginning or end of a larger sequence of events centered by the event to be temporally specified. The when component of an episodic memory can thus be operationalized by successively presenting two or more distinct events and by probing whether the participants are able to remember their order of occurrence (Dere et al., 2006, 2008).

THE RETRIEVAL OF EPISODIC MEMORY

One difficulty that is associated with the traditional concept of episodic memory is that they do not specify the circumstances that lead to the retrieval of episodic memories besides postulating that it should be a "free recall" instead of a "cued" recall (Yonelinas, 2002). This assumption might not be correct since it is unlikely that any memory retrieval either episodic or semantic occurs without a cue stimulus which triggers memory retrieval (Dere et al., 2004; McCabe et al., 2011; Unsworth et al., 2011). There must be a cue stimulus present either produced internally (e.g., a thought) or externally, within the environment that triggers the memory retrieval (Light and Albertson, 1989). Otherwise our episodic and semantic memories would be retrieved in an uncontrolled and highly disturbing manner.

Recently, it could be demonstrated that odors are highly valid stimuli cuing episodic or autobiographic memory contents (Aggleton and Waskett, 1999; Saive et al., 2013). Odor evoked memories are experienced as more emotional and are associated with feelings of being brought back in time to the occurrence of the event (Masaoka et al., 2012; Arshamian et al., 2013). The potency of odors to evoke highly vivid episodic memories has been discussed to be due to the emotional nature of olfactory stimuli (Pause et al., 2008; see Laudien et al., 2008; Adolph and Pause, 2012).

The new concept of episodic memory presented here holds that episodic memory formation is based on principles similar to one-trial contextual conditioning and that its retrieval depends on the presence of a cue or conditioned stimulus. This concept is at variance with the traditional distinction between declarative and non-declarative memory (Squire, 2004) in which episodic memory is generally attributed to declarative memory, while classical conditioning, including contextual conditioning, is attributed to non-declarative memory. It seems that it is time to revise this useful nomenclature of long-term memory systems to better reflect the novel insights gained into the nature of episodic memory.

PROMISING NOVEL PARADIGMS

SPATIAL AND TEMPORAL ORDER MEMORY FOR EMOTIONAL PICTURES

In a reverse translational approach by Pause et al. the rationale and principles of the episodic-like memory test for rodents (Dere et al., 2005a,b; Kart-Teke et al., 2006) have been adapted to humans. Pause et al. (2010) developed a paradigm which measures the spatio-temporal memory for emotional and neutral pictures presented on an eight-quadrant computer-screen task. Visual stimuli were hidden in four out of eight quadrants on a computer-screen. Each of these quadrants could be highlighted by pushing a corresponding button on a keyboard which either revealed a visual stimulus for 100 ms or remained black. Participants had to remember on which occasion (when) and at which position (where) a specific picture (what) has been encountered. It was investigated whether exploratory button presses can be used as a non-verbal behavioral expression of what, where, and when memory. Verbal what, where, and when memory performance was measured by a standardized interview.

Pause et al. (2010) also examined whether the variation of the visual stimuli in terms of concreteness and emotional content would have an effect on what, where, and when memory performance or quadrants exploration. In the verbal test, healthy adult participants were able to recollect the details and the spatio-temporal context of visual stimuli with combinations of high or low concreteness and neutral or emotional content after retention delays up to 72 h. The number of button presses to each of the four quadrants containing visual stimuli was positively correlated with verbal what, where, and when memory performance.

These results demonstrate that what, where, and when memory can be induced experimentally and can be measured by motor behavior which can serve as a non-verbal correlate of episodic memory performance (Pause et al., 2010). Compared to classical methods this novel paradigm is certainly an improvement as it measures novel long-term memories for what, where, and when information. However, since the participants were instructed to memorize the learning material, the task might not only have involved episodic memory mechanisms. Therefore, a slightly different version of this paradigm has been applied in young and elderly participants (Kinugawa et al., 2013, this issue). Here, the participants were not informed to memorize the test items and the memory retrieval was not foreseeable for the participants. Furthermore, explicit memory performance was tested already 2.5 h after the initial learning phase. It was found that the young group (age: 21–45) had significantly higher episodic memory scores as compared to both the middle (age: 48–62) and aged group (age: 71–83). The latter two groups performed not significantly different from each other. The results suggest that this novel test of what, where, and when memory that measures the core components of an memory for event, spatial, and temporal information and in addition is likely to probe the ability to form new episodic memories is suited to detect age-related impairments in what, where, and when memory performance. Due to its simplicity, its one-trial nature and the option of a non-verbal measurement this task could be probably adapted to clinical populations.

THE KENSINGER EPISODIC-LIKE MEMORY TASK

In a recent fMRI study by Kensinger et al. (2011) on the role of the amygdala for the encoding of episodic-like memories the participants studied four sets of emotional pictures. It was found that amygdala activity was correlated with item-specific details of the learning material used and the subjective assessment of memory vividness, but not with the diversity of episodic details remembered (Kensinger et al., 2011). In this study, each picture was presented in one out of four quadrants of a monitor screen. On the retention test performed 30 min after the presentation of a total of four picture sets, verbal labels corresponding to the pictures viewed were presented. This approach aims to induce and measure a memory for what, where, and when. The what and where components have been operationalized by different pictures presented in different quadrants on a monitor screen. The temporal component of episodic-like memory was operationalized by the four different sets of pictures. In general the task was associated with a rather high memory load. The participants had to memorize four sets with a total of 30 pictures and as well as their positions on the screen. Furthermore, the task performance certainly depended on pre-morbid learning abilities and the susceptibility to interference. For these reasons the task might be too complicated to be performed with individuals suffering, e.g., from MCI. Furthermore, a retention delay of only 30 min might not fall into the range of long-term episodic memory and retention performance might involve short-term memory phenomena such as recency effects. The combination of emotional pictures with spatial and temporal information is certainly a useful approach to identify the neuroanatomical substrates of episodic-like memory in humans.

VIRTUAL REALITY-BASED TASKS

Another reverse translational approach aims to induce and measure core elements of episodic-like memory such as spatial and temporal order memory in humans with a navigational "starmaze" task, initially developed to measure egocentric and allocentric spatial orientation in rodents (Rondi-Reig et al., 2006; Fouquet et al. 2011). Here the individual's ability to remember a sequential order of choices during spatial navigation in a virtual reality environment is measured (Fouquet et al., 2010). The participant has to learn to reach a goal using the most direct path. During the multiple acquisition trials, the individuals can use allocentric (spatial reference memory) or egocentric (temporal order based) strategies to solve the task. Fouquet et al. (2010) propose that the use of the egocentric strategy to perform this task involves an "active, flexible, and complex integration of past and current states" which is a feature shared by episodic memory. Following this rationale it can be predicted that an individual with impaired episodic memory function would be forced to choose the allocentric strategy to learn the path through the virtual environment.

Allocentric orientation in a novel environment is a function which is critically dependent on the integrity of the hippocampal formation in rodents and humans. Furthermore, the hippocampus is also indispensable for the integration of spatial and temporal information into a unified episodic memory (Ranganath, 2010). In fact, animal studies have shown that rodents with hippocampal lesions shift to egocentric striatum-based strategies to solve spatial tasks and that healthy controls spontaneously use allocentric strategies and only shift to egocentric strategies if the former is not successful (Oliveira et al., 1997; DeCoteau and Kesner, 2000; Dere et al., 2001). Nevertheless, this approach is interesting and certainly worth of being evaluated with patient populations.

Yet another approach to measure episodic memory function using virtual reality technology has been recently communicated by Plancher et al. (2012a). In this study the authors argue that virtual reality-based tests allow to investigate episodic memory profiles in an ecological fashion, including the assessment of the memory for central and perceptual details, spatio-temporal contextual elements, and binding of these multi-dimensional information. The authors tested older individuals, patients with MCI as well as patients with early stages of AD. These groups were tested under active and passive exploration conditions and were instructed to memorize as many information as possible as well as all spatio-temporal information that was associated with detail information. As expected the performance of patients with AD was inferior to that of the patients with MCI and healthy older individuals. The authors found that spatial allocentric memory assessments discriminated between patients with MCI from controls and that active exploration was associated with better performance in all of the three groups.

Additional studies by this and other groups have further substantiated the important influence of enactment, exercise, and active engagement of subjects in the encoding phase (Madan and Singhal, 2012; Plancher et al., 2012b). The theoretical background of this line of research is derived from the concept of embodied cognition that holds that physical properties of the human body, particularly the perceptual and motor systems, modulate learning and memory formation (Madan and Singhal, 2012).

In conclusion virtual reality and enactment-based tests of episodic-like memory might allow measuring this function in a more ecological fashion. However, it is also important to avoid explicit instructions asking the participants to memorize the information presented, including precise instructions on what kind of information should be memorized. This kind of instruction might prompt the participants to use semantic learning strategies rather than incidental episodic memory encoding. It is important to note that although the recollection of episodic memories is associated with autonoetic awareness, its encoding is rather automatic and effortless (Zentall et al., 2008; Dere et al., 2010). Generally, any assessment of episodic-like and episodic memory should be unexpected.

BASIC CRITERIA FOR EPISODIC-LIKE MEMORY TEST DEVELOPMENT

Although, the above reviewed novel approaches to measure episodic-like memory have moved the field forward toward a valid and reliable test of episodic memory (besides of not probing autonoetic recollection) all of them have their pitfalls and are not easily applicable to patient populations. Similarly, animal research has led to the definition of behavioral criteria that are considered important for the measurement of episodic-like memory in animals and also for the measurement of episodic-like memory in humans (Griffiths and Clayton, 2001; Dere et al., 2008).

In the following we will outline seven basic criteria which should be met by a test of episodic-like memory. These seven criteria might facilitate the development of routine diagnostic tests of episodic-like memory for patient populations and tests to be utilized for the investigation of the neurobiological and electrophysiological substrates of episodic memory in healthy individuals.

First criterion, in order to be able to control the correctness of the episodic-like memory retrieved and also to control the time of encoding of these events, as well as to have the option to manipulate experimental variables that would affect episodic memory formation in healthy and patient populations differently, it is necessary to induce the episodic memories in the laboratory.

Second criterion, the participants of an experimental investigation or patients to be tested for episodic-like memory integrity should not receive any explicit instruction to memorize the episodic information. Otherwise, the episodic information might be acquired and retained by semantic memory systems, e.g., by rehearsing the episodic information until it is consolidated using a semantic memory system.

Third criterion, since long-durable episodic-like memory which are permanently stored are generally related to important life events which have been accompanied and probably induced by a relatively strong (but not excess, see above) emotional activation, the episodic information to be retained needs to have an emotional valence and should be associated with emotional arousal to be demonstrated at the level of physiological stress responses or autonomic activation associated with pleasant events.

Fourth criterion, the induction of the episodic-like memory must be per definition a one-trial learning event. The acquisition of episodic information presented repeatedly is always mediated through a semantic memory system.

Fifth criterion, the episodic information to be induced, retained and retrieved must include what, where, and when information. Episodic-like memory assessment has to include the measurement of the ability to remember what, where, and when information.

Sixth criterion, the memory test has to be unexpected and only the first recall is a valid measure of episodic-like memory performance. Generally, the possibility to perform re-tests or multiple assessments of the same individual with the same episodic memory test is therefore very limited.

Seventh criterion, the storage of long-durable episodic-like memories requires memory consolidation which requires the activation of specific genes and *de novo* synthesis of proteins (Abel and Lattal, 2001; Igaz et al., 2002). Drugs that block protein synthesis such as antibiotics have amnesic effects when administered immediately after the acquisition of new information (Schafe et al., 1999; Díaz-Trujillo et al., 2009) but not after delays of 60 min or more (Fulton et al., 2005; Rossato et al., 2007; Lima et al., 2009). Therefore, the memory test has to be performed after a retention interval of at least 60 min after presentation of the episodic information to be considered a fully consolidated long-term memory. Tests which adhere to these requirements can be considered as measuring episodic-like memory in a valid and reliable way.

BASIC CRITERIA FOR A TEST OF EPISODIC MEMORY

A valid test of human episodic memory should include the seven criteria defined above to qualify as a test of episodic-like memory and should also measure phenomenological aspects of episodic memory such as autonoetic awareness, self, subjective sense of time. This could be potentially done with a separate tests performed after the episodic-like memory test. In the past it has been attempted to measure autonoetic awareness with the remember/know procedure derived from the dual-process signal-detection theory (Yonelinas, 2002). With this method individuals are asked to learn a list of items and thereafter presented with items form the list and novel items. If the subject recognizes an item the participant is asked to state whether it "remembers" that the item was on the list or whether he/or she just "knows" that the item was on the list because of a feeling of familiarity. It is obvious that this procedure is not suited to capture the richness and complexity of Tulving's understanding of episodic memory (Tulving, 2002)

"*Episodic memory is a recently evolved, late-developing, and early-deteriorating past-oriented memory system, more vulnerable than other memory systems to neuronal dysfunction, and probably unique to humans. It makes possible mental time travel through subjective time, from the present to the past, thus allowing one to re-experience, through autonoetic awareness, one's own previous experiences. Its operations require, but go beyond, the semantic memory system. Retrieving information from episodic memory (remembering or conscious recollection) is contingent on the establishment of a special mental set, dubbed episodic "retrieval mode." Episodic memory is subserved by a widely distributed network of cortical and subcortical brain regions that overlaps with but also extends beyond the networks subserving other memory systems. The essence of episodic memory lies in the conjunction of three concepts – self, autonoetic awareness, and subjectively sensed time.*"

CONCLUSION

Although, one can note some progress toward the goal of a valid and reliable test of episodic-like memory that can be utilized in clinical settings for diagnostic purposes the currently available approaches still have to be optimized and modified before they can be possibly adapted for patient populations. A valid test of episodic memory that also includes the phenomenological aspects of episodic memory is still lacking. The above criteria should help to approach the optimal solution more directly. It is hoped that this review will sensitize clinicians and researchers in the field of episodic memory to critically re-evaluate their current methods and tools to measure episodic-like or episodic memory and will induce a lively discussion concerning the urgent need to develop novel and better paradigms to measure episodic memory.

ACKNOWLEDGMENTS

Supported by the German Science Foundation (Deutsche Forschungsgemeinschaft) through Grant No. DFG-DE 1149/6-1 and the CNRS «Programme Interdisciplinaire Vieillissement et Longévité» to Ekrem Dere.

REFERENCES

Abel, T., and Lattal, K. M. (2001). Molecular mechanisms of memory acquisition, consolidation and retrieval. *Curr. Opin. Neurobiol.* 11, 180–187.

Abercrombie, H. C., Kalin, N. H., Thurow, M. E., Rosenkranz, M. A., and Davidson, R. J. (2003). Cortisol variation in humans affects memory for emotionally laden and neutral information. *Behav. Neurosci.* 117, 505–516.

Adolph, D., and Pause, B. M. (2012). Different time course of emotion regulation towards odors and pictures: are odors more potent than pictures? *Biol. Psychol.* 91, 65–73.

Aggleton, J. P., and Brown, M. W. (1999). Episodic memory, amnesia, and the hippocampal-anterior thalamic axis. *Behav. Brain Sci.* 22, 425–444.

Aggleton, J. P., and Pearce, J. M. (2001). Neural systems underlying episodic memory: insights from animal research. *Philos. Trans. R. Soc. Lond. B Biol. Sci.* 356, 1467–1482.

Aggleton, J. P., and Waskett, L. (1999). The ability of odours to serve as state-dependent cues for real-world memories: can Viking smells aid the recall of Viking experiences? *Br. J. Psychol.* 90, 1–7.

Aleksander, I., and Gamez, D. (2011). Informational theories of consciousness: a review and extension. *Adv. Exp. Med. Biol.* 718, 139–147.

Anagnostaras, S. G., Gale, G. D., and Fanselow, M. S. (2001). Hippocampus and contextual fear conditioning: recent controversies and advances. *Hippocampus* 11, 8–17.

Arshamian, A., Iannilli, E., Gerber, J. C., Willander, J., Persson, J., Seo, H. S., et al. (2013). The functional neuroanatomy of odor evoked autobiographical memories cued by odors and words. *Neuropsychologia* 51, 123–131.

Arzy, S., Collette, S., Wissmeyer, M., Lazeyras, F., Kaplan, P. W., and Blanke, O. (2011). Psychogenic amnesia and self-identity: a multimodal functional investigation. *Eur. J. Neurol.* 18, 1422–1425.

Assini, F. L., Duzzioni, M., and Takahashi, R. N. (2009). Object location memory in mice: pharmacological validation and further evidence of hippocampal CA1 participation. *Behav. Brain Res.* 204, 206–211.

Bäckman, L., Jones, S., Berger, A. K., Laukka, E. J., and Small, B. J. (2004). Multiple cognitive deficits during the transition to Alzheimer's disease. *J. Intern. Med.* 256, 195–204.

Bäckman, L., and Small, B. J. (2007) Cognitive deficits in preclinical Alzheimer's disease and vascular dementia: patterns of findings from the Kungsholmen Project. *Physiol. Behav.* 10, 80–86.

Baldi, E., and Bucherelli, C. (2005). The inverted "u-shaped" dose-effect relationships in learning and memory: modulation of arousal and consolidation. *Nonlinearity Biol. Toxicol. Med.* 3, 9–21.

Ballard, C., Gauthier, S., Corbett, A., Brayne, C., Aarsland, D., and Jones, E. (2011). Alzheimer's disease. *Lancet* 377, 1019–1031.

Blennow, K. (2010a). Dementia in 2010: paving the way for Alzheimer disease drug development. *Nat. Rev. Neurol.* 7, 65–66.

Blennow, K. (2010b). Biomarkers in Alzheimer's disease drug development. *Nat. Med.* 16, 1218–1222.

Bordet, R., Dartigues, J. F., Dubois, B., Goehrs, J. M., Vernoux, L., Semah, F., et al. (2010). Biomarkers for the early stages of clinical development in Alzheimer's disease. *Therapie* 65, 285–290.

Bower, G. H., and Sivers, H. (1998). Cognitive impact of traumatic events. *Dev. Psychopathol.* 10, 625–653.

Brand, M., Eggers, C., Reinhold, N., Fujiwara, E., Kessler, J., Heiss, W. D., et al. (2009). Functional brain imaging in 14 patients with dissociative amnesia reveals right inferolateral prefrontal hypometabolism. *Psychiatry Res.* 174, 32–39.

Brand, M., Kalbe, E., Fujiwara, E., Huber, M., and Markowitsch, H. J. (2003). Cognitive estimation in patients with probable Alzheimer's disease and alcoholic Korsakoff patients. *Neuropsychologia* 41, 575–584.

Brandt, J., and Van Gorp, W. G. (2006). Functional ("psychogenic") amnesia. *Semin. Neurol.* 26, 331–340.

Brewin, C. R. (2011). The nature and significance of memory disturbance in posttraumatic stress disorder. *Annu. Rev. Clin. Psychol.* 7, 203–227.

Burgess, N., Maguire, E. A., and O'Keefe, J. (2002). The human hippocampus and spatial and episodic memory. *Neuron* 35, 625–641.

Butters, N., Granholm, E., Salmon, D. P., Grant, I., and Wolfe, J. (1987). Episodic and semantic memory: a comparison of amnesic and demented patients. *J. Clin. Exp. Neuropsychol.* 9, 479–497.

Carcaillon, L., Amievaa, H., Auriacombea, S., Helmera, C., and Dartiguesa, J.-F. (2009). A subtest of the MMSE as a valid test of episodic memory? Comparison with the free and cued reminding test. *Dement. Geriatr. Cogn. Disord.* 27, 429–438.

Cheke, L. G., Bird, C. D., and Clayton, N. S. (2011). Tool-use and instrumental learning in the Eurasian jay (*Garrulus glandarius*). *Anim. Cogn.* 14, 441–455.

Clayton, N. S., and Dickinson, A. (1998). Episodic-like memory during cache recovery by scrub jays. *Nature* 395, 272–274.

Cravens, C. J., Vargas-Pinto, N., Christian, K. M., and Nakazawa, K. (2006). CA3 NMDA receptors are crucial for rapid and automatic representation of context memory. *Eur. J. Neurosci.* 24, 1771–1780.

Dally, J. M., Emery, N. J., and Clayton, N. S. (2006). Food-caching western scrub-jays keep track of who was watching when. *Science* 312, 1662–1665.

DeCoteau, W. E., and Kesner, R. P. (2000). A double dissociation between the rat hippocampus and medial caudoputamen in processing two forms of knowledge. *Behav. Neurosci.* 114, 1096–1108.

Dere, E., De Souza Silva, M. A., and Huston, J. P. (2004). Higher order memories for objects encountered in different spatio-temporal contexts in mice: evidence for episodic memory. *Rev. Neurosci.* 15, 231–240.

Dere, E., Frisch, C., De Souza Silva, M. A., Gödecke, A., Schrader, J., and Huston, J. P. (2001). Unaltered radial maze performance and brain acetylcholine of the endothelial nitric oxide synthase knockout mouse. *Neuroscience* 107, 561–570.

Dere, E., Huston, J. P., and De Souza Silva, M. A. (2005a). Integrated memory for objects, places and temporal order: evidence for episodic-like memory in mice. *Neurobiol. Learn. Mem.* 84, 214–221.

Dere, E., Huston, J. P., and De Souza Silva, M. A. (2005b). Protocol: episodic-like memory in mice: simultaneous assessment of object, place and temporal order memory. *Brain Res. Brain Res. Protoc.* 16, 10–19.

Dere, E., Huston, J. P., and De Souza Silva, M. A. (2007). The pharmacology, neuroanatomy and neurogenetics of one-trial object recognition in rodents. *Neurosci. Biobehav. Rev.* 31, 673–704.

Dere, E., Kart-Teke, E., Huston, J. P., and De Souza Silva, M. A. (2006). The case for episodic memory in animals. *Neurosci. Biobehav. Rev.* 30, 1206–1224.

Dere, E., Pause, B., and Pietrowsky, R. (2010). Emotion and episodic memory in neuropsychiatric disorders. *Behav. Brain Res.* 215, 162–171.

Dere, E., Zlomuzica, A., Huston, J. P., and De Souza Silva, M. A. (2008). "Chapter 2.2: animal episodic memory," in *Handbook of Episodic Memory*, Vol. 18, eds E. Dere, A. Easton, L. Nadel, and J. P. Huston (Amsterdam: Elsevier Science), 155–184.

Di Stefano, A., Iannitelli, A., Laserra, S., and Sozio, P. (2011). Drug delivery strategies for Alzheimer's disease treatment. *Expert Opin. Drug Deliv.* 8, 581–603.

Díaz-Trujillo, A., Contreras, J., Medina, A. C., Silveyra-Leon, G. A., Antaramian, A., Quirarte, G. L., et al. (2009). Enhanced inhibitory avoidance learning prevents the long-term memory-impairing effects of cycloheximide, a protein synthesis inhibitor. *Neurobiol. Learn. Mem.* 91, 310–314.

Dickerson, B. C., and Eichenbaum, H. (2010). The episodic memory system: neurocircuitry and disorders. *Neuropsychopharmacology* 35, 86–104.

Donix, M., Brons, C., Jurjanz, L., Poettrich, K., Winiecki, P., and Holthoff, V. A. (2010). Overgenerality of autobiographical memory in people with amnestic mild cognitive impairement and early Alzheimer's disease. *Arch. Clin. Neuropsychol.* 25, 22–27.

Dreyfus, D. M., Roe, C. M., and Morris, J. C. (2010). Autobiographical memory task in assessing dementia. *Arch. Neurol.* 67, 862–866.

Dubois, B., Feldman, H. H., Jacova, C., Dekosky, S. T., Barberger-Gateau, P., Cummings, J., et al. (2007). Research criteria for the diagnosis of Alzheimer's disease: revising the NINCDS-ADRDA criteria. *Lancet Neurol.* 6, 734–746.

Earles, J. L., Kersten, A. W., Curtayne, E. S., and Perle, J. G. (2008). That's the man who did it, or was it a woman? Actor similarity and binding errors in event memory. *Psychon. Bull. Rev.* 15, 1185–1189.

Ebenezer, I. S. (1988). Can vasopressin alone act as an unconditioned stimulus to produce passive avoidance behaviour in rats in a typical memory experiment? *Neuropharmacology* 27, 903–907.

Ehrlichman, H., and Halpern, J. N. (1988). Affect and memory: effects of pleasant and unpleasant odors on retrieval of happy and unhappy memories. *J. Pers. Soc. Psychol.* 55, 769–779.

Emery, N. J., and Clayton, N. S. (2004). The mentality of crows: convergent evolution of intelligence in corvids and apes. *Science* 306, 1903–1907.

Ennaceur, A. (2010). One-trial object recognition in rats and mice: methodological and theoretical issues. *Behav. Brain Res.* 215, 244–254.

Fine, E. M., Delis, D. C., Wetter, S. R., Jacobson, M. W., Hamilton, J. M., Peavy, G., et al. (2008). Identifying the "source" of recognition memory deficits in patients with Huntington's disease or Alzheimer's disease: evidence from the CVLT-II. *J. Clin. Exp. Neuropsychol.* 30, 463–470.

Friedman, W. J. (1996). "Distance and location processes in the memory for the times of past events," in *The Psychology of Learning and Motivation*, Vol. 35, ed. D. L. Medin (San Diego: Academic Press), 1–41.

Fouquet, C., Petit, G. H., Auffret, A., Gaillard, E., Rovira, C., Mariani, J., et al. (2011). Early detection of age-related memory deficits in individual mice. *Neurobiol. Aging* 32, 1881–1895.

Fouquet, C., Tobin, C., and Rondi-Reig, L. (2010). A new approach for modeling episodic memory from rodents to humans: the temporal order memory. *Behav. Brain Res.* 215, 172–179.

Fulton, D., Kemenes, I., Andrew, R. J., and Benjamin, P. R. (2005). A single time-window for protein synthesis-dependent long-term memory formation after one-trial appetitive conditioning. *Eur. J. Neurosci.* 21, 1347–1358.

Galluzzi, S., and Frisoni, G. B. (2008). Imaging, subjective complaints, and MCI: 30 years before. *J. Nutr. Health Aging* 12, 80S–83S.

Gilboa, A., Ramirez, J., Köhler, S., Westmacott, R., Black, S. E., and Moscovitch, M. (2005). Retrieval of autobiographical memory in Alzheimer's disease: relation to volumes of medial temporal lobe and other structures. *Hippocampus* 15, 535–550.

Griffiths, D. P., and Clayton, N. S. (2001). Testing episodic memory in animals: a new approach. *Physiol. Behav.* 73, 755–762.

Grober, E., and Buschke, H. (1987). Genuine memory deficits in dementia. *Dev. Neuropsychol.* 3, 13–36.

Grodzinski, U., and Clayton, N. S. (2010). Problems faced by food-caching corvids and the evolution of cognitive solutions. *Philos. Trans. R. Soc. Lond. B Biol. Sci.* 365, 977–987.

Hamann, S. B., Ely, T. D., Grafton, S. T., and Kilts, C. D. (1999). Amygdala activity related to enhanced memory for pleasant and aversive stimuli. *Nat. Neurosci.* 2, 289–293.

Hampel, H., Frank, R., Broich, K., Teipel, S. J., Katz, R. G., Hardy, J., et al. (2010). Biomarkers for Alzheimer's disease: academic, industry and regulatory perspectives. *Nat. Rev. Drug Discov.* 9, 560–574.

Humphreys, M. S., Smith, S., Pachana, N. A., Tehan, G., and Byrne, G. J. (2010). Measuring episodic memory: a novel approach with an indefinite number of alternative forms. *Appl. Cogn. Psychol.* 24, 1080–1094.

Hurlemann, R., Wagner, M., Hawellek, B., Reich, H., Pieperhoff, P., Amunts, K., et al. (2007). Amygdala control of emotion-induced forgetting and remembering: evidence from Urbach-Wiethe disease. *Neuropsychologia* 45, 877–884.

Igaz, L. M., Vianna, M. R., Medina, J. H., and Izquierdo, I. (2002). Two time periods of hippocampal mRNA synthesis are required for memory consolidation of fear-motivated learning. J. Neurosci. 22, 6781–6789.

Irish, M., Lawlor, B. A., O'Mara, S. M., and Coen, R. F. (2011). Impaired capacity for autonoetic reliving during autobiographical event recall in mild Alzheimer's disease. Cortex 47, 236–249.

Kapur, N. (1991). Amnesia in relation to fugue states – distinguishing a neurological from a psychogenic basis. Br. J. Psychiatry 159, 872–877.

Kart-Teke, E., De Souza Silva, M. A., Huston, J. P., and Dere, E. (2006). Wistar rats show episodic-like memory for unique experiences. Neurobiol. Learn. Mem. 85, 173–182.

Kensinger, E. A., Addis, D. R., and Atapattu, R. K. (2011). Amygdala activity at encoding corresponds with memory vividness and with memory for select episodic details. Neuropsychologia 49, 663–673.

Kinugawa, K., Schumm, S., Pollina, M., Depre, M., Jungbluth, C., Doulazmi, M., et al. (2013). Aging-related episodic memory decline: are emotions the key? Front. Behav. Neurosci. 7:2. doi:10.3389/fnbeh.2013.00002

Kirchhoff, B. A., Wagner, A. D., Maril, A., and Stern, C. E. (2000). Prefrontal-temporal circuitry for episodic encoding and subsequent memory. J. Neurosci. 20, 6173–6180.

Klein, S. B. (2013). Making the case that episodic recollection is attributable to operations occurring at retrieval rather than to content stored in a dedicated subsystem of long-term memory. Front. Behav. Neurosci. 7:3. doi:10.3389/fnbeh.2013.00003

Kopelman, M. D., Wilson, B. A., and Baddeley, A. D. (1989). The autobiographical memory interview: a new assessment of autobiographical and personal semantic memory in amnesic patients. J. Clin. Exp. Neuropsychol. 11, 724–744.

Laudien, J. H., Wencker, S., Ferstl, R., and Pause, B. M. (2008). Context effects on odor processing: an event-related potential study. Neuroimage 41, 1426–1436.

Lehmann, H., Lacanilao, S., and Sutherland, R. J. (2007). Complete or partial hippocampal damage produces equivalent retrograde amnesia for remote contextual fear memories. Eur. J. Neurosci. 25, 1278–1286.

Lekeu, F., Magis, D., Marique, P., Delbeuck, X., Bechet, S., Guillaume, B., et al. (2010). The California Verbal Learning Test and other standard clinical neuropsychological tests to predict conversion from mild memory impairment to dementia. J. Clin. Exp. Neuropsychol. 32, 164–173.

Levine, B., Svoboda, E., Hay, J. F., Winocur, G., and Moscovitch, M. (2002). Aging and autobiographical memory: dissociating episodic from semantic retrieval. Psychol. Aging 17, 677–689.

Lezak, M. D. (1995). Neuropsychological Assessment, 3rd Edn. New York: Oxford University Press.

Li, J. S., Hsiao, K. Y., and Chen, W. M. (2011). Effects of medial prefrontal cortex lesions in rats on the what-where-when memory of a fear conditioning event. Behav. Brain Res. 218, 94–98.

Libkuman, T. M., Stabler, C. L., and Otani, H. (2004). Arousal, valence, and memory for detail. Memory 12, 237–247.

Light, L. L., and Albertson, S. A. (1989). Direct and indirect tests of memory for category exemplars in young and older adults. Psychol. Aging 4, 487–492.

Lima, R. H., Rossato, J. I., Furini, C. R., Bevilaqua, L. R., Izquierdo, I., and Cammarota, M. (2009). Infusion of protein synthesis inhibitors in the entorhinal cortex blocks consolidation but not reconsolidation of object recognition memory. Neurobiol. Learn. Mem. 91, 466–472.

Madan, C. R., and Singhal, A. (2012) Using actions to enhance memory: effects of enactment, gestures, and exercise on human memory. Front. Psychol. 3:507. doi:10.3389/fpsyg.2012.00507

Markowitsch, H. J., Calabrese, P., Fink, G. R., Durwen, H. F., Kessler, J., Härting, C., et al. (1997). Impaired episodic memory retrieval in a case of probable psychogenic amnesia. Psychiatry Res. 74, 119–126.

Markowitsch, H. J., and Staniloiu, A. (2011). Amygdala in action: relaying biological and social significance to autobiographical memory. Neuropsychologia 49, 718–733.

Martinelli, P., Anssens, A., Sperduti, M., and Piolino, P. (2013). The influence of normal aging and Alzheimer's disease in autobiographical memory highly related to the self. Neuropsychology 27, 69–78.

Masaoka, Y., Sugiyama, H., Katayama, A., Kashiwagi, M., and Homma, I. (2012). Slow breathing and emotions associated with odor-induced autobiographical memories. Chem. Senses 37, 379–388.

McCabe, D. P., Roediger, H. L. III, and Karpicke, J. D. (2011). Automatic processing influences free recall: converging evidence from the process dissociation procedure and remember-know judgments. Mem. Cognit. 39, 389–402.

McKenzie, S., and Eichenbaum, H. (2011). Consolidation and reconsolidation: two lives of memories? Neuron 71, 224–233.

Mitchell, J. B., and Laiacona, J. (1998). The medial frontal cortex and temporal memory: tests using spontaneous exploratory behaviour in the rat. Behav. Brain Res. 97, 107–113.

Murphy, K. J., Troyer, A. K., Levine, B., and Moscovitch, M. (2008). Episodic, but not semantic, autobiographical memory is reduced in amnestic mild cognitive impairment. Neuropsychologia 46, 3116–3123.

Nashiro, K., and Mather, M. (2011). How arousal affects younger and older adults' memory binding. Exp. Aging Res. 37, 108–128.

Nordberg, A., Rinne, J. O., Kadir, A., and Långström, B. (2010). The use of PET in Alzheimer disease. Nat. Rev. Neurol. 6, 78–87.

Nyberg, L., McIntosh, A. R., Houle, S., Nilsson, L. G., and Tulving, E. (1996). Activation of medial temporal structures during episodic memory retrieval. Nature 380, 715–717.

Oliveira, M. G., Bueno, O. F., Pomarico, A. C., and Gugliano, E. B. (1997). Strategies used by hippocampal- and caudate-putamen-lesioned rats in a learning task. Neurobiol. Learn. Mem. 68, 32–41.

Pause, B., Jungbluth, C., Adolph, D., Pietrowsky, R., and Dere, E. (2010). Induction and measurement of episodic memories in healthy adults. J. Neurosci. Methods 189, 88–96.

Pause, B. M., Hellmann, G., Göder, R., Aldenhoff, J. B., and Ferstl, R. (2008). Increased processing speed for emotionally negative odors in schizophrenia. Int. J. Psychophysiol. 70, 16–22.

Pennartz, C. M. (2009). Identification and integration of sensory modalities: neural basis and relation to consciousness. Conscious. Cogn. 18, 718–739.

Pettersson, M., Kauffman, G. W., Ende, C. W., Patel, N. C., Stiff, C., Tran, T. P., et al. (2011). Novel γ-secretase modulators: a review of patents from 2008 to 2010. Expert Opin. Ther. Pat. 21, 205–226.

Phelps, E. A., Labar, K. S., Anderson, A. K., O'Connor, K. J., Fulbright, R. K., and Spencer, D. D. (1998). Specifying the contributions of the human amygdala to emotional memory: a case study. Neurocase 6, 527–540.

Pike, K. E., and Savage, G. (2008). Memory profiling in mild cognitive impairment: can we determine risk for Alzheimer's disease? J. Neuropsychol. 2, 361–372.

Piolino, P., Desgranges, B., and Eustache, F. (2009). Episodic autobiographical memories over the course of time: cognitive, neuropsychological and neuroimaging findings. Neuropsychologia 47, 2314–2329.

Plancher, G., Tirard, A., Gyselinck, V., Nicolas, S., and Piolino, P. (2012a). Using virtual reality to characterize episodic memory profiles in amnestic mild cognitive impairment and Alzheimer's disease: influence of active and passive encoding. Neuropsychologia 50, 592–602.

Plancher, G., Barra, J., Orriols, E., and Piolino, P. (2012b). The influence of action on episodic memory: a virtual reality study. Q. J. Exp. Psychol. (Hove). (in press).

Pöppel, E. (1997). A hierarchical model of temporal perception. Trends Cogn. Sci. (Regul. Ed.) 1, 56–61.

Raby, C. R., Alexis, D. M., Dickinson, A., and Clayton, N. S. (2007). Planning for the future by western scrub-jays. Nature 445, 919–921.

Ranganath, C. (2010). A unified framework for the functional organization of the medial temporal lobes and the phenomenology of episodic memory. Hippocampus 20, 1263–1290.

Rattenborg, N. C., and Martinez-Gonzalez, D. (2011). A bird-brain view of episodic memory. Behav. Brain Res. 222, 236–245.

Reinhold, N., and Markowitsch, H. J. (2009). Retrograde episodic memory and emotion: a perspective from patients with dissociative amnesia. Neuropsychologia 47, 2197–2206.

Reitz, C., Tang, M. X., Schupf, N., Manly J. J., Mayeux, R., and Luchsinger, J. A. (2010). A summary risk score for the prediction of Alzheimer disease in elderly persons. Arch. Neurol. 67, 835–841.

Ringman, J. M. (2005). What the study of persons at risk for familial Alzheimer's disease can tell us about the earliest stages of the disorder: a review. J. Geriatr. Psychiatry Neurol. 18, 228–233.

Roberts, W. A. (2002). Are animals stuck in time? Psychol. Bull. 128, 473–489.

Roberts, W. A., Feeney, M. C., MacPherson, K., Petter, M., McMillan, N., and Musolino, E. (2008). Episodic-like memory in rats: is it based on when or how long ago? *Science* 320, 113–115.

Rondi-Reig, L., Petit, G. H., Tobin, C., Tonegawa, S., Mariani, J., and Berthoz, A. (2006). Impaired sequential egocentric and allocentric memories in forebrain-specific-NMDA receptor knock-out mice during a new task dissociating strategies of navigation. *J. Neurosci.* 26, 4071–4081.

Rossato, J. I., Bevilaqua, L. R., Myskiw, J. C., Medina, J. H., Izquierdo, I., and Cammarota, M. (2007). On the role of hippocampal protein synthesis in the consolidation and reconsolidation of object recognition memory. *Learn. Mem.* 14, 36–46.

Rudy, J. W., Huff, N. C., and Matus-Amat, P. (2004). Understanding contextual fear conditioning: insights from a two-process model. *Neurosci. Biobehav. Rev.* 28, 675–685.

Rudy, J. W., and Sutherland, R. J. (1995). Configural association theory and the hippocampal formation: an appraisal and reconfiguration. *Hippocampus* 5, 375–389.

Saive, A.-L., Ravel, N., Thévenet, M., Royet, J.-P., and Plailly, J. (2013). A novel experimental approach to episodic memory in humans based on the privileged access of odors to memories. *J. Neurosci. Methods* 213, 22–31.

Salwiczek, L. H., Emery, N. J., Schlinger, B., and Clayton, N. S. (2009). The development of caching and object permanence in Western scrub-jays (*Aphelocoma californica*): which emerges first? *J. Comp. Psychol.* 123, 295–303.

Sara, S. J., David-Remacle, M., and Lefevre, D. (1975). Passive avoidance behavior in rats after electroconvulsive shock: facilitative effect of response retardation. *J. Comp. Physiol. Psychol.* 89, 489–497.

Sarazin, M., and Dubois, B. (2005). A guide to diagnosis of Alzheimer's disease. *Rev. Prat.* 55, 1879–1890.

Schacter, D. L., Norman, K. A., and Koutstaal, W. (1998). The cognitive neuroscience of constructive memory. *Annu. Rev. Psychol.* 49, 289–318.

Schafe, G. E., Nadel, N. V., Sullivan, G. M., Harris, A., and LeDoux, J. E. (1999). Memory consolidation for contextual and auditory fear conditioning is dependent on protein synthesis, PKA, and MAP kinase activity. *Learn. Mem.* 6, 97–110.

Schwindt, G. C., and Black, S. E. (2009). Functional imaging studies of episodic memory in Alzheimer's disease: a quantitative meta-analysis. *Neuroimage* 45, 181–190.

Shing, Y. L., Werkle-Bergner, M., Brehmer, Y., Müller, V., Li, S. C., and Lindenberger, U. (2010). Episodic memory across the lifespan: the contributions of associative and strategic components. *Neurosci. Biobehav. Rev.* 34, 1080–1091.

Small, B. J., and Bäckman, L. (2007). Longitudinal trajectories of cognitive change in preclinical Alzheimer's disease: a growth mixture modeling analysis. *Cortex* 43, 826–834.

Squire, L. R. (2004). Memory systems of the brain: a brief history and current perspective. *Neurobiol. Learn. Mem.* 82, 171–177.

Squire, L. R., and Alvarez, P. (1995). Retrograde amnesia and memory consolidation: a neurobiological perspective. *Curr. Opin. Neurobiol.* 5, 169–177.

Tagini, A., and Raffone, A. (2010). The 'I' and the 'Me' in self-referential awareness: a neurocognitive hypothesis. *Cogn. Process.* 11, 9–20.

Thomas-Anterion, C., and Laurent, B. (2006). Neuropsychological markers for the diagnosis of Alzheimer's disease. *Rev. Neurol. (Paris)* 162, 913–920.

Trojanowski, J. Q., Vandeerstichele, H., Korecka, M., Clark, C. M., Aisen, P. S., Petersen, R. C., et al. (2010). Update on the biomarker core of the Alzheimer's disease neuroimaging initiative subjects. *Alzheimers Dement.* 6, 230–238.

Tronche, C., Lestage, P., Louis, C., Carrie, I., and Béracochéa, D. (2010). Pharmacological modulation of contextual "episodic-like" memory in aged mice. *Behav. Brain Res.* 215, 255–260.

Tsirka, P., Simos, A., Vakis, M., Vourkas, V., Arzoglou, N., Syrmos, S., et al. (2010). Material-specific difficulties in episodic memory tasks in mild traumatic brain injury. *Int. J. Neurosci.* 120, 184–191.

Tsivilis, D., Vann, S. D., Denby, C., Roberts, N., Mayes, A. R., Montaldi, D., et al. (2008). A disproportionate role for the fornix and mammillary bodies in recall versus recognition memory. *Nat. Neurosci.* 11, 834–842.

Tulving, E. (1972). "Episodic and semantic memory," in *Organization of Memory*, eds E. Tulving and W. Donaldson (New York: Academic Press), 381–403.

Tulving, E. (1983). *Elements of Episodic Memory*. London: Oxford University Press.

Tulving, E. (2001). Episodic memory and common sense: how far apart? *Philos. Trans. R. Soc. Lond. B Biol. Sci.* 356, 1505–1515.

Tulving, E. (2002). Episodic memory: from mind to brain. *Annu. Rev. Psychol.* 53, 1–25.

Unsworth, N., Brewer, G. A., and Spillers, G. J. (2011). Inter- and intra-individual variation in immediate free recall: an examination of serial position functions and recall initiation strategies. *Memory* 19, 67–82.

Urbaniak-Hunter, K., Yarbrough, C., and Ciacci, J. (2010). Gene- and cell-based approaches for neurodegenerative disease. *Adv. Exp. Med. Biol.* 671, 117–130.

van der Hart, O., and Nijenhuis, E. (2001). Generalized dissociative amnesia: episodic, semantic and procedural memories lost and found. *Aust. N. Z. J. Psychiatry* 35, 589–600.

van Rossum, I. A., Vos, S., Handels, R., and Visser, P. J. (2010). Biomarkers as predictors for conversion from mild cognitive impairment to Alzheimer-type dementia: implications for trial design. *J. Alzheimers Dis.* 20, 881–891.

Wagner, A. D. (2000). Early detection of Alzheimer's disease: an fMRI marker for people at risk? *Nat. Neurosci.* 3, 973–974.

Walker, M. P., Brakefield, T., Hobson, J. A., and Stickgold, R. (2003). Dissociable stages of human memory consolidation and reconsolidation. *Nature* 425, 616–620.

Weiner, H. L., and Frenkel, D. (2006). Immunology and immunotherapy of Alzheimer's disease. *Nat. Rev. Immunol.* 6, 404–416.

Wiest, G., Lehner-Baumgartner, E., and Baumgartner, C. (2006). Panic attacks in an individual with bilateral selective lesions of the amygdala. *Arch. Neurol.* 63, 1798–1801.

Williams-Gray, C. H., Foltynie, T., Lewis, S. J., and Barker, R. A. (2006). Cognitive deficits and psychosis in Parkinson's disease: a review of pathophysiology and therapeutic options. *CNS Drugs* 20, 477–505.

Wolff, M., Loukavenko, E. A., Will, B. E., and Dalrymple-Alford, J. C. (2008). The extended hippocampal-diencephalic memory system: enriched housing promotes recovery of the flexible use of spatial representations after anterior thalamic lesions. *Hippocampus* 18, 996–1007.

Woodard, J. L., Goldstein, F. C., Roberts, V. J., and McGuire, C. (1999). Convergent and discriminant validity of the CVLT (dementia version). California Verbal Learning Test. *J. Clin. Exp. Neuropsychol.* 21, 553–558.

Yankner, B. A. (1996a). New clues to Alzheimer's disease: unraveling the roles of amyloid and tau. *Nat. Med.* 2, 850–852.

Yankner, B. A. (1996b). Mechanisms of neuronal degeneration in Alzheimer's disease. *Neuron* 16, 921–932.

Yonelinas, A. P. (2002). The nature of recollection and familiarity: a review of 30 years of research. *J. Mem. Lang.* 46, 441–517.

Zentall, T. R., Singer, R. A., and Stagner, J. P. (2008). Episodic-like memory: pigeons can report location pecked when unexpectedly asked. *Behav. Processes* 79, 93–98.

Zimmer, H. D., Speiser, H. R., and Seidler, B. (2003). Spatio-temporal working-memory and short-term object-location tasks use different memory mechanisms. *Acta Psychol. (Amst.)* 114, 41–65.

Zlomuzica, A., De Souza Silva, M. A., Huston, J. P., and Dere, E. (2007). NMDA receptor modulation by D-cycloserine promotes episodic-like memory in mice. *Psychopharmacology* 193, 503–509.

Zlomuzica, A., Dere, E., Huston, J. P., and de Souza Silva, M. A. (2008). NK(3) receptor agonism promotes episodic-like memory in mice. *Neurobiol. Learn. Mem.* 90, 420–425.

19

Episodic memories and their relevance for psychoactive drug use and addiction

Christian P. Müller*

Section of Addiction Medicine, Department of Psychiatry and Psychotherapy, Friedrich-Alexander-University of Erlangen-Nuremberg, Erlangen, Germany

***Correspondence:**
Christian P. Müller, Section of Addiction Medicine, Department of Psychiatry and Psychotherapy, Friedrich-Alexander-University of Erlangen-Nuremberg, Schwabachanlage 6, Erlangen 91054, Germany.
e-mail: christian.mueller@uk-erlangen.de

The majority of adult people in western societies regularly consume psychoactive drugs. While this consumption is integrated in everyday life activities and controlled in most consumers, it may escalate and result in drug addiction. Non-addicted drug use requires the systematic establishment of highly organized behaviors, such as drug-seeking and -taking. While a significant role for classical and instrumental learning processes is well established in drug use and abuse, declarative drug memories have largely been neglected in research. Episodic memories are an important part of the declarative memories. Here a role of *episodic drug memories* in the establishment of non-addicted drug use and its transition to addiction is suggested. In relation to psychoactive drug consumption, episodic drug memories are formed when a person prepares for consumption, when the drug is consumed and, most important, when acute effects, withdrawal, craving, and relapse are experienced. Episodic drug memories are one-trial memories with emotional components that can be much stronger than "normal" episodic memories. Their establishment coincides with drug-induced neuronal activation and plasticity. These memories may be highly extinction resistant and influence psychoactive drug consumption, in particular during initial establishment and at the transition to "drug instrumentalization." In that, understanding how addictive drugs interact with episodic memory circuits in the brain may provide crucial information for how drug use and addiction are established.

Keywords: episodic drug memory, experimental consumption, drug instrumentalization, addiction

INTRODUCTION

> *"I smoked my first cigarette when I was 12 years old – behind the house, together with a few friends and some older guys who had provided it for trying. It was incredibly cool, not allowed of course, and it tasted awful. Despite persistent peer pressure, the memory of this one event still accompanies me until present day. It forms part of my personality and prevents me from trying cigarettes again. My first experience with alcohol a little later at the retirement party of my much beloved grand dad was quite bad as well. I felt sick and abstained from any countable consumption of alcohol for a few years. However, when I was a student I felt forced to social drinking which I tentatively did. At one occasion, however, I learned from rather unexpected feedback that my constitutively restricted social skills were tremendously enhanced after a few glasses of wine. This one episode, again vividly remembered to the present day, has shaped my drug consumption behaviour into another direction. After establishing a working dose window, I can now "instrumentalize" a controlled consumption for just this one purpose: "socializing on demand."*
>
> *(personal communication)*

These admittedly very personal example may illustrate that the availability of a psychoactive drug may lead to very different behavioral patterns in the long run after having established episodic memory of the first (few) drug consumption episodes. But do episodic memories just orchestrate other, more important learning processes at consciously accessible level or do they play a causal role in the establishment of regular drug consumption and addiction?

Psychoactive drugs are chemical compounds which influence our subjective perception and/or our behavior. Human beings consume psychoactive drugs voluntarily (Abel, 1980; Waldorf et al., 1991; Heath, 2000; Amendt, 2003). The consumption may range from a one-trial experience, after which the consummatory behavior is never repeated up to a stage of drug addiction when virtually all behavioral activity is directed toward the consumption of one or more psychoactive drugs. What starts with a single episode, remembered as an episodic memory, may finally control the complete behavioral repertoire of an individual.

Drug addiction is a now regarded a major psychiatric disorder which carries a considerable burden for individuals and their social environment (American Psychiatric Association, 1994). Much like other psychiatric disorders it compromises life quality of affected individuals and their families and has profound economic consequences. There is still no effective treatment available which may reverse the rather complex set of behaviors regarded as addiction, to a condition of either controlled drug use or abstinence. Understanding how drug addiction develops is, therefore, a major quest for behavioral neuroscience and psychiatry. While early views on addiction development were based on the action of psychoactive drugs as pharmacological reinforcers (Koob, 1992; Wise, 1994, 2002; Koob et al., 1998) and addiction as an aberrant learning mediated by the reinforcement system (Di Chiara, 1995), more recent views have acknowledged the role of various memory systems in the establishment of drug use and addiction (Nestler, 2002; Kelley, 2004; Hyman et al., 2006). A recent analysis suggests that virtually all memory systems that humans are capable of might contribute to addiction development (Müller and Schumann, 2011a).

Importantly, not every individual who tries a psychoactive drug and establishes an episodic memory of the subsequent consummatory occasion with its aftermath becomes addicted to the drug. Inter-individual differences based on genetic (Stacey et al., 2009, 2012; Schumann et al., 2011; Easton et al., 2013a) and developmental factors (Campbell et al., 2009; Dong et al., 2011), accentuated personality traits (Piazza et al., 1989; Belin et al., 2008), or comorbid psychiatric disorders (Robbins and Everitt, 1999) appear to predispose individuals differently to the risk of fast establishment of drug consumption and/or the transition from controlled to compulsive drug use. However, most regular consumers of psychoactive drugs do never become addicts. Large consumer surveys in the US (SAMHSA, 2011) and Europe (EMCDDA, 2012) reveal that the majority of the regular consumers of legal drugs like alcohol or illicit drugs like cannabis or cocaine may exert a lifelong control over their consumption (Ahmed, 2010; Müller and Schumann, 2011a). However, a significant minority of those humans and animals, who have established drug-seeking and consumption behaviors lose control and develop a compulsive pattern of consumption (Gawin, 1991; Deroche-Gamonet et al., 2004; Vanderschuren and Everitt, 2004).

While it is currently under debate whether the controlled use of psychoactive drugs might under certain circumstances have beneficial effects for behavioral performance, the achievement of life goals, or wellbeing (Lende and Smith, 2002; Lende et al., 2007; Hagen et al., 2009; Müller and Schumann, 2011a,b), it has to be acknowledged that the behavior of psychoactive drug consumption is established by the majority of humans in the western world and forms a rather stable trait. Since neither humans nor drug consuming animals are developmentally determined to automatically establish drug consumption, it may be assumed that the stability of this trait over generations is based on the capability to learn it by social learning or *de novo* (Müller and Schumann, 2011a). The ability to modify food consumption according to non-nutritional needs may be seen as the phylogenetic origin of psychoactive drug consumption. This capability is already present in various animal species (Rodriguez and Wrangham, 1993; Lozano, 1998; Huffman, 2003). The learning of consummatory behaviors may then involve either a learning by trial-and-error (e.g., for newly emerging substances; Hassan et al., 2013), or by cultural inheritance/learning (Dean et al., 2012). Importantly, any way to acquire drug consumption related behaviors involves learning and memory processes. The high persistence of the behavior after long periods of abstinence suggests high stability and extinction resistance of related memories.

The goal of this paper was to review the role of episodic memories in non-addicted psychoactive drug use and in drug addiction. While there is no such role acknowledged yet, this is to my knowledge the first attempt to make a case for episodic drug memories and their function. I will first consider the role of learning and memories in the establishment of drug use behaviors and review the history of drug- and addiction memory concepts. Then a recently suggested concept of drug memories is discussed which includes for the first time also episodic drug memories. An attempt is made to further refine a potential definition of episodic drug memories. It is discussed when in the time course of establishing drug use and abuse behaviors, they might play a role. Finally I review some of the neuropharmacological evidence for brain processes, potentially related to episodic drug memories. This discussion is meant to introduce episodic drug memories into the frame of relevant memory systems for drug use and addiction. As such it may not be complete and cannot deliver final conclusions, but should be understood as a first suggestion for subsequent debate.

DRUG USE REQUIRES MEMORIES

According to current diagnostic manuals, drug addiction is diagnosed by the incidence of a number of rather complex behaviors which involve, e.g., mental occupation with the drug, active seeking of the drug, and active drug consumption. Most important, it also involves compulsive drug use and relapse long after the drug has left the organism and even long after compensatory processes in the brain have subsided. Thus, it was suggested that drug addiction may be based on memory formation and voluntary and involuntary retrieval.

Although still poorly defined in psychological terms, the concept of a *drug-* or *addiction memory* is not new (Boening, 2001). Mello (1972) introduced the term "memory of addiction" in a discussion of addiction-related behaviors. However, the dominating concept of drug action at that time and later on assumed that the reinforcing effects of psychoactive drugs were mostly dissociated from their interaction with memory systems (White and Milner, 1992). Nevertheless, several lines of evidence suggested important interactions of psychoactive drugs with memory systems. It was shown in animals and humans that drug-associated cues can work as a classically conditioned stimulus and induce either drug-related effects or withdrawal symptoms (Wikler and Pescor, 1967; Siegel, 1975; O'Brien et al., 1977; Siegel et al., 1982). The conditioned withdrawal symptoms, which can be ameliorated almost immediately by new drug consumption, were assumed to contribute significantly to the continuation of the drug use (Siegel, 1988; O'Brien et al., 1998; but, see Drummond et al., 1990). Another line of evidence showed that psychoactive drugs applied post trial can also enhance memory for non-drug-related behaviors (Huston et al., 1974, 1977), thus indicating that drugs do not just shape memories to acute drug-effects, but also of preceding events and behaviors. White (1996), when summarizing the evidence, suggested that the reinforcing effects of addictive drugs may at least in part be brought about by their interaction with multiple memory systems of the brain. He suggested three general types of memory that are influenced independently by psychoactive drugs. These systems would be involved in conditioned incentive learning, declarative learning, and habit or stimulus-response learning. Conditioned incentive learning described the learning of stimulus-incentive associations, after which a neutral cue would become a conditioned reward that is able to elicit conditioned approach behavior (Squire et al., 1993; Milner et al., 1998). Major brain structures mediating the influence of psychoactive drugs on conditioned incentive learning are the amygdala, the nucleus accumbens, and the tegmental pedunculopontine nucleus (White, 1996). Declarative learning describes the learning of relationships among cues which can be neutral in their consequences, also known as stimulus–stimulus learning (Squire et al., 1993; Milner et al., 1998). In contrast to non-declarative memories, the content of declarative memories should be consciously accessible (Squire et al., 1993; Milner et al., 1998). In terms of addiction memory, it contains information on the relationships among external cues and events relevant for drug taking (White, 1996). Brain structures that are involved are the hippocampus network and the neocortex (Milner et al., 1998; Bast, 2007). Habit learning described the learning of stimulus-response associations, which are strengthened by the occurrence of reinforcement. The neural correlate for habit learning is the caudate-putamen (Knowlton et al., 1996; Milner et al., 1998). An important role of habit learning for drug addiction was early recognized in particular for drug self-administration behavior (White, 1989, 1996). This view received important support from more recent studies demonstrating not only the neuroanatomical preconditions (Haber et al., 2000), but also their functional relevance for a transfer of information between stimulus-outcome learning and stimulus-response learning systems (Porrino et al., 2004; Belin and Everitt, 2008). White (1996) argued that the addictive properties of drugs have multiple causes based on their multiple independent interactions with those memory systems which store different aspects of the drug experience and of drug taking behaviors. Another classification of addiction memories was proposed by Heyne et al. (2000). They suggested distinguishing at least three different memory types in relation to drug consumption: a memory of drug-effects, a memory of drug use, and a memory of addiction (Heyne et al., 2000; Boening, 2001).

A more recent view considered the hypothesis that drug addiction may be understood in terms of recruitment of neural systems that normally mediate learning and memory (Robbins et al., 2008). Thereby, drugs are assumed to always work as unconditioned reinforcers which support emotional learning, encompassing Pavlovian as well as instrumental conditioning. The amygdala, nucleus accumbens, and orbitofrontal cortex play important roles in the acquisition and retrieval of emotional memories related to the drug (Kilts et al., 2001; Everitt et al., 2007). For the procedural (habit) learning system, a cascading loop transfer of cue-controlled drug-related behavior from the ventral to the dorsal striatum was suggested (Robbins et al., 2008). It was concluded that "addiction is a product of aberrant associative learning" which might also involve other pathological changes in behavior. A significant part of its aberrant nature might be its compulsive impact on drug-seeking and -taking behavior, which was suggested to be mediated by a loss of prefrontal cortex control over drug-related habits in the dorsal striatum (Belin et al., 2009). Although this model acknowledges important roles of memory circuits in drug addiction, the view on potential types of memories involved in drug use remains somewhat incomplete and limited to the concept of addiction. It should be noted that there appeared a conceptual gap between the concepts of addiction and the supportive literature on brain mechanisms. Virtually all evidence derived from the host of animal studies did actually not measure the syndrome of addiction, but only single drug-associated behaviors which were not established up to the level of compulsiveness (but, see Deroche-Gamonet et al., 2004; Vanderschuren and Everitt, 2004). In that, conclusions on brain mechanisms might predominantly apply to non-addicted drug use and only serve as a starting point for neuronal adaptations related to addiction.

To allow for a more focused research in the subtypes of a drug memory, a nomenclature for different subtypes of memories was recently suggested by Müller and Schumann (2011a). Research in the neuronal mechanisms of non-drug memories has shown that there are different memories with distinct neuronal mechanism (Eichenbaum, 1997; Milner et al., 1998; McGaugh, 2000). It was suggested that a similar differentiation might also help to segregate single types of drug-related memories and elucidate crucial neuronal mechanism. Accordingly, the drug memory nomenclature was expanded to the types of memories originally identified for non-drug-related experiences (Squire et al., 1993; Milner et al., 1998).

For drug memory it is suggested to distinguish two major categories: a *declarative drug memory* and a *non-declarative drug memory* (**Figure 1**). The declarative drug memory contains information that is consciously accessible, i.e., it can be reported verbally by humans. The declarative drug memory should comprise a *semantic memory* for drug facts and one for *drug episodes*. The semantic memory for drugs contains all impersonal facts, rules, and concepts involving drugs, e.g., their names, where they come from, recommended doses, what others report about its effects, and what the rules of their consumption are (Müller and Schumann, 2011a). The establishment of this type of drug memory usually starts before a person is engaged in the first episode of consumption by learning facts from others about the drug (Miller et al., 1990; Leigh and Stacy, 2004). By that way an early semantic drug memory shapes the first expectations of drug-effects, which is then constantly adapted after actual consumption started (Kidorf et al., 1995). It was suggested to conceptualize the expectation of drug-effects (Leigh, 1989; Del Boca et al., 2002) as a retrieval process from different types of memories (Goldman et al., 1991). Also in experienced users, it was shown that the expectation of the drug-effects can still shape the physiological effects of the drug as well as its subjective perception (Volkow et al., 2003, 2006), and thus, influence the establishment of episodic drug memories.

The *episodic drug memory* comprises the memories of all personally experienced episodes with the drug. It is an autobiographical memory of the "What," "Where," and "When" of the personal drug encounters. It involves an "autonoetic awareness" of single drug experiences in the continuity of ones subjectively apprehended time. It involves a remembering of the drug episodes as well as "thinking about" the drug when planning for future behavior (Tulving, 2001; Dere et al., 2006, 2008). This may include automatically formed memories of subjectively experienced acute drug-effects, e.g., the mental states the drug induced. The episodic drug memory also comprises aversive withdrawal episodes and periods during subsequent abstinence. These episodes are either characterized by the feeling of drug craving or mental preoccupation with the drug. Clearly, relapse episodes also have episodic memory components. The episodic drug memory system can also contain memories of what was done during a particular drug-induced mental state, and even what effects it had in terms of the environmental feedback (Boening, 2001). In accordance with Tulving's definition (Tulving, 2002), also episodic

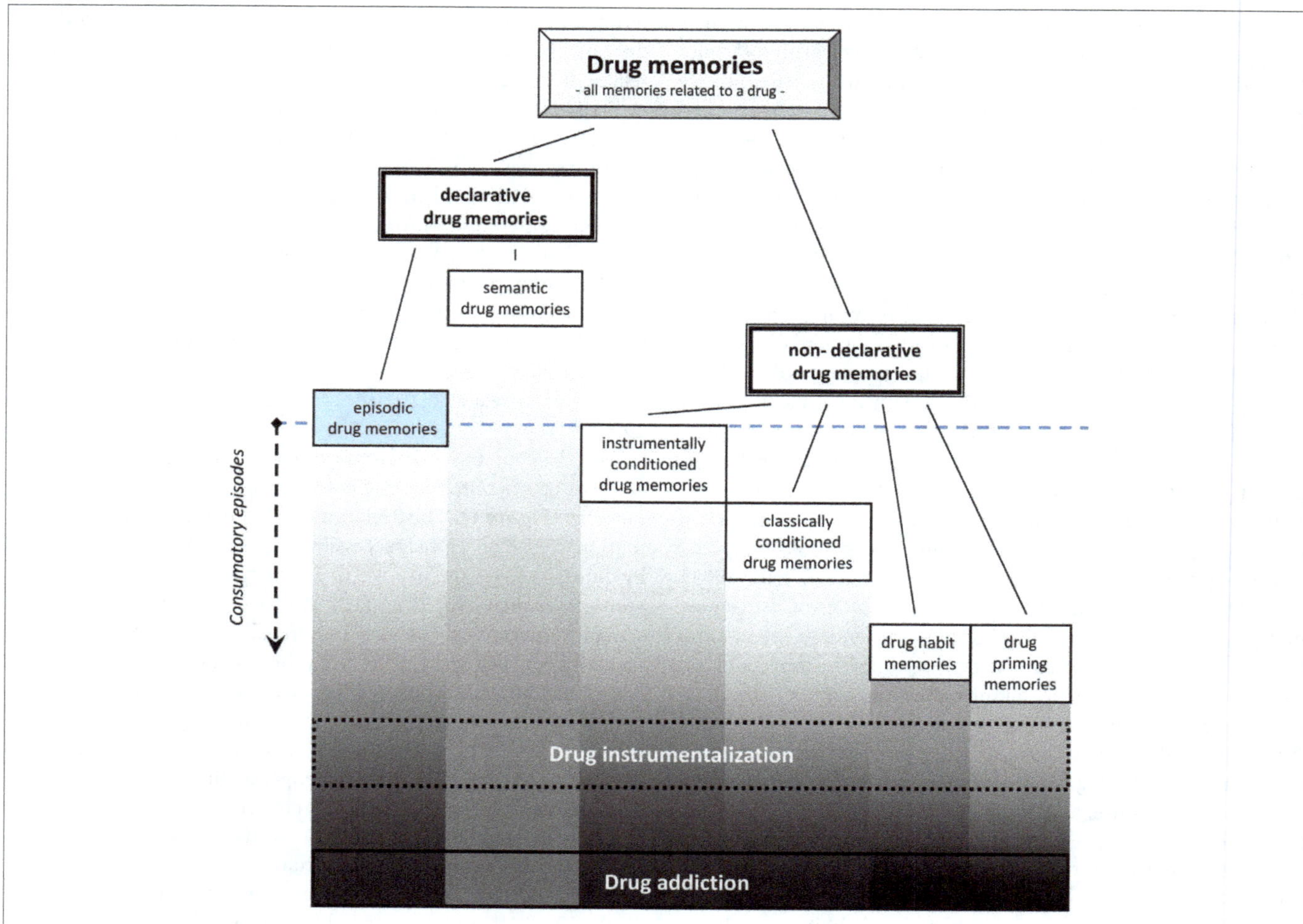

FIGURE 1 | Episodic and other drug memory systems as they are established during drug consumption. Note that semantic drug memories may already establish before first drug consumption, while episodic drug memories require only single consumption episode [modified from Müller and Schumann (2011a)].

drug memories involve the ability for "mental time travel" and "conscious recollection."

While the experience of "euphoria" or a "high" is often the sought after mental state, it is not the only one occurring on the time scale of a drug consumption episode. A single drug episode may better be considered as a sequence of several distinct mental states. This can be measured as the discriminative stimulus properties of a drug. The discriminative stimulus properties are directly reflecting the mental state induced by a psychoactive drug (Overton, 1968; Stolerman, 1992). As such, this type of memory appears to be crucial for "drug instrumentalization" (Müller and Schumann, 2011a,b). An episodic drug memory requires only a single learning trial, but may be extinction resistant up to a whole life span. Its retrieval may trigger psychoactive drug-seeking and taking, but also passive avoidance of the drug (Eissenberg and Balster, 2000; Miller, 2001).

The *non-declarative drug memory*, in contrast, is not consciously accessible and can only be inferred from behavioral changes in animals and humans. The non-declarative drug memories contain engrams of the classically conditioned drug memory, instrumentally conditioned drug memory, habit memory, procedural drug memories, and drug priming memories.

Classically conditioned drug memories may contain all drug-effects that refer to the process of Pavlovian conditioning (Bouton and Moody, 2004). These may include, e.g., the sensitization of the acute drug-effects (Kalivas et al., 1993; Vanderschuren and Kalivas, 2000), drug tolerance, conditioned locomotor activity, conditioned emotional and physiological responses (Foltin and Haney, 2000), conditioned place preference (Bardo and Bevins, 2000; Tzschentke, 2007), and conditioned withdrawal effects (Goldberg, 1975; Siegel, 1988; O'Brien et al., 1998).

Instrumentally conditioned drug memories comprise engrams established by instrumental conditioning. Major behaviors induced by the retrieval of those engrams are drug-seeking behaviors and drug self-administration (Spealman and Goldberg, 1978; Richardson and Roberts, 1996). These memories also include drug-cues which are rewarding by themself, as shown in conditioned place preference (Huston et al., 2013), or which can re-instate drug-seeking and drug self-administration behavior (de Wit and Stewart, 1981; Shaham et al., 2003).

Drug habit memories refer to instrumental behavior that is no longer goal directed, but stimulus controlled, i.e., a behavioral response that is triggered by a cue, but independent from its behavioral consequences (Everitt and Robbins, 2005). This type of memory is not only important for the transition from controlled to compulsive drug use and addiction (Porrino et al., 2004; Belin and Everitt, 2008), but may already in non-addicted drug users play a role in stimulus driven drug instrumentalization.

Procedural drug memories comprise all memories for skills involved in handling a drug. This may range from its production (e.g., cooking up heroin; rolling a joint with marijuana) to the actual way of self-administration (e.g., snorting cocaine; setting a needle for an i.v. heroin injection).

The *Drug priming memories* refer to those engrams whose activation by a small amounts of the drug, which would not induce major subjective and behavioral effects in drug naïve individuals, may in an experienced user induce drug-related behavior (e.g., re-instate drug-seeking, conditioned place preference, or self-administration) and subjective effects (**Figure 1**).

It was recently suggested that the majority of non-addicted humans, who consume psychoactive drugs as an integral part of their lives (O'Malley and Johnston, 2002; Skogen et al., 2009) take drugs because the subsequent effects can be used for their personal goals in a systematic way. Evidence reviewed by Müller and Schumann (2011a,b) suggests that psychoactive drugs can be "*instrumentalized*," i.e., used like an instrument. Thereby, "*drug instrumentalization*" was defined as a two-step behavioral complex of two interconnected processes: (a) the seeking and consumption of a psychoactive drug in order to change the present mental state into a previously learned mental state, which then allows for (b) a better performance of other, previously established behaviors and a better goal achievement by these behaviors. It was suggested that drug instrumentalization requires the interplay of various, if not all, types of drug memories which need to be established during different stages of experimental consumption (Müller and Schumann, 2011a).

It was suggested that drug-related behaviors, including self-administration, can be learned and maintained in several ways, which may also involve contributions of several memory systems to what appears as one behavioral output, but may in fact contain many different sequences (White, 1996). Externally induced or spontaneous retrieval from certain types of the drug memories allows for a systematic instrumentalization of the drug's psychotropic effects. Thereby, episodic and instrumentally conditioned drug memories may be considered as the most important memories for drug instrumentalization.

It should be noted that the occurrence of these memories does not automatically implicate a transition to addition. In fact, most people with drug experience are able to manage drug use and instrumentalization in order to gain a fitness benefit within socially approved limits during their entire life. A drug memory is, therefore, not an indicator for drug addiction. Learning and memory research in relation to psychoactive drugs aimed mostly at defining the memory in relation to addiction as an *addiction memory*, although animal models depicted mostly non-addicted consumption; Olmstead, 2006; Sanchis-Segura and Spanagel, 2006). In line with White (1996) and Heyne et al. (2000), a distinction between *drug memory* and *addiction memory* is suggested, based on the degree of elaboration and the compulsive nature that the retrieval of memories has in addiction (**Figure 1**). In that, the drug memory should comprise all information about psychoactive drugs as defined above, whereas an addiction memory contains quantitatively more of this information with stronger engrams that are more powerful to suppress non-drug memories. Considering the compulsive nature of drug addiction, it cannot be ruled out that there will also be some sort of qualitative differences in the engrams and/or the retrieval of the memories.

THE SPECIFIC NATURE OF EPISODIC DRUG MEMORIES

Episodic memories are major constituents of an individual personality. The encoding and later retrieval of episodes and experiences shapes individual biographies and makes memories accessible for individuals later in live. This also comprises the psychoactive drug biography, i.e., the consumer history of an individual. In that single consummatory episodes may be the substrate of what is remembered in an episodic drug memory. In contrast to non-drug episodes, there are some specific properties to the "What," "Where," and "When" criteria of episodic drug memories. The classical concept of episodic memory refers to three external dimensions; the "What" refers to an event or series of external stimuli, the "Where" is an external place, and the "When" describes subjectively anchored time referenced to an individual's life (Tulving, 2001). Episodic drug memories may expand all three components by a subjective and social cognitive component:

What: the "*What*" may be best defined as the drug-effect on the mental state of an individual, in fact being a series of introspectively perceived mental state changes. This usually happens parallel to perceived changes in autonomous system activity (e.g., sickness after a heroin injection) and is influenced by external events (e.g., dance music during an ecstasy episode). One drug episode may involve several different mental states. As, for example, an alcohol episode may involve the sequence of "sobriety – slight disinhibition – emotional high – sedation – hangover with headaches."

Where: drug-effects do not only depend on the dose of a particular substance but also on the *set* and *setting* of the individual (Zinberg, 1984). As such the "Where" component may comprise not only a spatial environment, but the overall setting of a consummatory episode. Thereby the *setting* involves social parameters such as peers present and psychological factors like peer group pressure. The *setting* also involves expectations on the subjective effects of the drug that is about to be consumed, and on emotional arousal derived there from Volkow et al. (2003, 2006).

When: the "When" refers to a temporal localization of an event in the individuals own biography. However, this may also include the *set* of a person at this time point, i.e., the physical constitution and mental state a person was in at the moment of drug-seeking and consumption.

The earliest episodic drug memories of an individual are established upon the first encounter with a drug when the experimental consumption has no other goal than to experience the mental state change and other physiological effects induced by a psychoactive drug. In its simplest form, episodic drug memories may be a compound percept of a time in personal history with a particular mental state (When), a spatial location with all present social influences (Where), and the mental (and physiological) state change that the drug induced (What). This may for instance be the memory of an episode when a slightly anxious and aroused adolescent person tries alcohol for the first time in a group of friends following social pressure to do so and experiencing a burning taste with some dizziness afterward.

Once drug consumption has been initially established, but is not at the level of a habit yet, there is another important occasion when episodic drug memories come into play: the establishment of "drug instrumentalization." It was argued before that during experimental consumption, humans and animals do not only learn the set and setting of drug-effects, but also the instrumentalization of a drug (Müller and Schumann, 2011b). Thus, it is postulated that a particular type of episodic drug memories will include additional components related to the drug's instrumentalization, such as:

What: the beneficial effects on non-drug-related behavior by a drug-induced change of mental state.

Where: a place or situation where both are available/possible, a particular psychoactive drug and a chance to perform a goal-directed instrumental behavior.

When: a given situation, where the present mental state of an individual appears to be a suboptimal state for a desired goal-directed behavior, so that a mental state change is desirable.

The components of a drug-instrumentalization episodic memory may for example include engrams of a pub with alcohol and potential sex partners available as chance for rewarded behavior (Where). It may include the memory of a date and time but also of a stressed and tired mental state with the wish to change this to a relaxed and slightly disinhibited mental state (When). Finally it may comprise the memory of having a few drinks that changed the initial to the desired mental state with a subsequent successful social interaction and securing a partner for life (What).

Evidence for these types of compound drug memories may be derived from numerous verbal reports of drug users that are able to consciously retrieve rather complex "What-Where-When" information of their drug-instrumentalization episodes (Waldorf et al., 1991; Heath, 2000; Boys et al., 2001; Boys and Marsden, 2003; Boyd et al., 2006; Frederiksen et al., 2012). One may argue that these are conscious self-analyses of one's own instrumentally conditioned behavior. However, it is well known that instrumental conditioning, in particular of complex behavioral sequences, requires numerous learning trials. Many drug users, however, can report single events as crucial and sometimes life-changing episodes. This might favor the view that there are persistent one-trial drug memories which are very complex and extinction resistant.

While there is no doubt on whether there are episodic drug memories, it is not entirely clear which causal role they might play in the course of establishing drug consumption, instrumentalization and, possibly, addiction. Here it is suggested that episodic drug memories play important roles at least at two different stages in the etiology of drug use: during the initiation of consumption and at the transition to drug instrumentalization.

Drug use behaviors start with experimental consumption usually during adolescence (Sher et al., 2005) with a rather undifferentiated consumption (Spear, 2000; Kuntsche et al., 2005). Experimental consumption, in contrast to instrumentalization and compulsive consumption, refers to a consummatory behavior of which the consequences are initially unknown to the individual. The introduction to the drug in appropriate settings is usually done by older and/or more experienced members of the peer group (e.g., Friedman et al., 1985; Eissenberg and Balster, 2000). However, given inter-individual differences in drug pharmacokinetics and -dynamics, in personality, and in life circumstances, each person has to customize the drug use. It should be noted that although there are expectancies of the drug-effects in drug naïve consumers (Miller et al., 1990), the individual response profile after first consumption is often unpredictable (e.g., Waskow et al., 1970; Jones, 1971). Importantly, during experimental consumption not only the effects of a drug are explored at usually different doses and settings (Patrick and Maggs, 2008). At the same time it is also experimented with how the drug-effects on mental states can be "used" in relation to different settings (Zinberg, 1984; Simons et al., 2000). Thereby numerous episodic drug memories are formed which guide later parameters of consumption. Evidence for a systematic knowledge about drugs and drug-effects is provided by the elaborate expectancies that people develop toward the drug-effects before and during consumption (e.g., Brown et al., 1980; Brown, 1985; Gustafson, 1991; Peele and Brodsky, 2000). As such, an individual dose titration can be the consequence of a series of episodes with either too low or too high doses and perceived subjective and behavioral consequences.

The other important time when episodic memories guide future consumption is the establishment of drug instrumentalization. This occurs usually not after first consumption, but requires already some experience with the drug including the knowledge of an individual dose-effect relationship. The learning of drug-instrumentalization involves an extension of the episodic drug memory components in terms of the preconditions and consequences of behavior. However, it can still be a one-trial experience by which future drug use is shaped. Several reports from drug users show that the perceived and reported "usefulness" of the drug-effects was found to predict future use of the drugs (Boys et al., 1999; Boys and Marsden, 2003; Leigh and Stacy, 2004). For instance, a certain dose of alcohol can be a boring experience when consumed alone at home by a teenager, i.e., when no instrumentalization is possible, while the disinhibitory effects of the same dose may be found highly entertaining and rewarding at a party with peers and the opposite sex. In this case, an episodic drug memory is established which contributes to later drug instrumentalization. It can be retrieved at a future occasion to facilitate socializing and mating approaches.

It was argued that one pathway into addiction is by an attempted over-instrumentalization of drug-effects, e.g., under stressed conditions (Kippin, 2011; Müller and Schumann, 2011b). While episodic memories may contribute to it, important processes most likely involve classical and instrumental conditioning and habit learning (Everitt and Robbins, 2005). At present one cannot say if there is a role of episodic memories in the transition from regular drug use and instrumentalization to compulsive use and addiction.

ACUTE PHYSIOLOGICAL EFFECTS OF DRUGS IN MEMORY SYSTEMS OF THE BRAIN

One way to investigate the neuronal mechanisms of episodic drug memories may be to look at the first encounter with an addictive drug. At this time, no conditioned drug-effects are established, and no adaptive or neurotoxic drug-effects have occurred in the brain. In this section I look at those acute drug-effects which might serve or influence episodic drug memories in drug naïve individuals.

DOPAMINE AND SEROTONIN

Psychotropic drugs exert profound effects on extracellular neurotransmitter activity. A significant increase in dopaminergic (DA) activity was reported, which is particularly well documented in the mesolimbic system for alcohol (McBride et al., 2002; Tupala and Tiihonen, 2004; Spanagel, 2009), nicotine (Markou, 2008), cocaine (Di Chiara and Imperato, 1988; Johanson and Fischman, 1989; Müller et al., 2002), amphetamines (Seiden et al., 1993; Green et al., 2003; Müller et al., 2007a), opiates (Di Chiara and North, 1992; McBride et al., 1999), cannabis/marijuana (Ameri, 1999; Iversen, 2000), and caffeine (Cauli and Morelli, 2005). However, activation of DA activity was also described for, e.g., cocaine and amphetamine in the neocortex and the hippocampus and related cortical structures (Müller and Huston, 2007; Pum et al., 2007). There is now good evidence for a functional role of the DA effects in the mesolimbic system for the establishment of various addiction-related behaviors (Koob et al., 1998; Wise, 2002; Pierce and Kumaresan, 2006). The functional role in most memory-associated structures still has to be determined. Importantly, DA activation plays also an important functional role in various types of memory, such as working memory (Williams and Goldman-Rakic, 1995; Wang et al., 2004) and reward learning (Schultz, 2000; Willuhn et al., 2012). It may be speculated that a drug-induced DA activation is an early step in amplifying learning processes. Although DA is a central mechanism for addiction and learning and memory, it is by far not the only transmitter which is acutely activated. Various psychoactive drugs enhance also serotonergic activity (5-HT; Müller et al., 2004, 2007b, 2010). Animal studies showed that psychoactive drugs like cocaine and amphetamine induce strong 5-HT responses in several neocortical and hippocampus-associated regions (Müller et al., 2004, 2007b; Pum et al., 2007) which play important roles in components of the episodic memory (Aggleton and Brown, 1999; Dere et al., 2006, 2007).

Formation of an episodic memory depends on emotional valence of the perceived episode. The higher the emotional valence, the more likely it appears for the event to be remembered. High emotional impact is characterized by strong activation of emotion processing systems, such as serotonin responses in the amygdala for negative emotions (Rex et al., 1993; Pum et al., 2009) or dopamine responses in the nucleus accumbens for unexpected positive valence (Schultz, 2000; Willuhn et al., 2012). The neurochemical acute effects of psychoactive drugs in emotion processing brain areas usually exaggerate the activation by natural stimuli (Rueter et al., 1997; Müller et al., 2007a). This may result in a mock signal of emotional importance of the preceding events and behavior (Nesse and Berridge, 1997), but a very real episodic memory thereof.

ACETYLCHOLINE

The acetylcholinergic (ACh) system plays an important role in attentional and memory processes (Blokland, 1995; Sarter et al., 2005) and is crucially involved in consciousness (Perry et al., 1999; Müller et al., 2011; Woolf and Butcher, 2011) and episodic memory (Dere et al., 2007). Acute application of cocaine was shown to activate cholinergic interneurons in the nucleus accumbens (Witten et al., 2010). Several drugs have been shown to increase extracellular ACh levels after acute application, such as cocaine, amphetamine, morphine, alcohol, and nicotine. It was observed in the ventral striatum, caudate nucleus, cortex, and ventral tegmental area (VTA), but most pronounced in the hippocampus (Imperato et al., 1992, 1993a, 1996; Quirion et al., 1994; Zocchi and Pert, 1994; Summers and Giacobini, 1995; Henn et al., 1998; Consolo et al., 1999; Larsson et al., 2005). The later effect was suggested to be a potential base for drug-effects on declarative memories (Williams and Adinoff, 2008). The nicotine-induced ACh increase is mediated by local nicotinergic ACh receptors (Summers and Giacobini, 1995; Tani et al., 1998). It was shown that the psychostimulant-induced ACh increase was not mediated by direct interaction with muscarinergic or nicotinergic ACh receptors, but depends mainly on DA-induced D1 receptor activation (Imperato et al., 1992, 1993a,b; Consolo et al., 1999). While a crucial role of the ACh system in addiction-related behaviors which require instrumental and classical conditioning is now evident (Bardo, 1998; McBride et al., 1999; Williams and Adinoff, 2008), a functional role of acute drug-effects in the ACh system for episodic drug memories still needs to be investigated.

GLUTAMATE

An important finding was that major drugs of addiction, such as cocaine, amphetamine, morphine, ethanol, and nicotine can enhance synaptic plasticity at excitatory synapses in VTA DA neurons, as measured by the ratio of alpha-amino-3-hydroxy-5-methyl-4-isoxazolepropionic acid receptor (AMPA)- and *N*-methyl-D-aspartate receptor (NMDA) dependent excitatory postsynaptic currents (EPSCs; Ungless et al., 2001; Saal et al., 2003; Faleiro et al., 2004). This plasticity is persistent for several days during which it may be the base for behavioral hypersensitivity (Borgland et al., 2004; Wanat and Bonci, 2008; Zweifel et al., 2008). Downstream mechanisms for this fast plasticity include protein synthesis, a reduced NMDA receptor function, and the active insertion of GluR2-lacking AMPA receptors, such as GluR1-containing AMPA receptors (Dong et al., 2004; Argilli et al., 2008; Mameli et al., 2011). GluR2-lacking AMPA receptors have a greater channel conductance and are Ca^{2+} permeable, which allows them to trigger also Ca^{2+} dependent signaling cascades (Bowers et al., 2010). It should be noted, however, that none of the investigated drugs induces addiction after a single administration in humans or animals. However, there is some learning involved already after a single drug exposure, which may in animals include a one-trial conditioned place preference (Zweifel et al., 2008), and also the memory of the self-administration episode. As such, early synaptic plasticity after acute drug exposure may be an important substrate of one-trial episodic drug memory. Neurophysiological studies have so far focused mainly on DA neurons in the VTA. Given the omnipresence of neuroplasticity at glutamatergic synapses in the brain and the dopamine-independent effects of some addictive drugs (Pierce and Kumaresan, 2006), it would be important to investigate the potential of addictive drugs to cause this early plasticity also in other memory-related synapses.

INTRACELLULAR SIGNALING CASCADES

The concept of drug memory proofed to be useful when animal studies revealed that many of the molecular changes at cellular level, which occurred after single and chronic drug administration, were similar to those observed during normal learning. Drugs of addiction, for example, acutely increased the levels the second messenger, cyclic adenosine monophosphate (cAMP), and activated the protein kinase A – cAMP-response element binding protein (CREB) cascade, which regulates gene transcription and protein synthesis. This leads, among others, to changes in the expression of NMDA and AMPA glutamate receptors (Nestler and Aghajanian, 1997; Hyman and Malenka, 2001; Nestler, 2002; Hyman et al., 2006; Kauer and Malenka, 2007). In particular CREB-regulated gene transcription and protein synthesis are believed to be essential mechanisms for long lasting cellular and behavioral plasticity (Kandel and Pittenger, 1999; Kandel, 2001). Another important pathway activated by drugs of addiction involves the second messenger Ca^{2+}, calmodulin, and Ca^{2+}/Calmodulin-dependent-kinases. Activation of this pathway is essential for various types of learning (Giese et al., 1998; Irvine et al., 2006; Easton et al., 2013b) as well as for several drug-related behaviors (Licata and Pierce, 2003; Liu et al., 2006; Anderson et al., 2008; Bilbao et al., 2008; Easton et al., 2013a). A series of functional studies showed that antisense oligodeoxynucleotides for the immediate early gene, Zif268, in the basolateral amygdala could disrupt different memories for cocaine and heroin (Lee et al., 2005, 2006; Hellemans et al., 2006). Altogether, drugs of addiction were shown to be very efficient in activating gene transcription factors (Nestler, 2008) and cellular plasticity after only a single drug exposure for several days (Hyman et al., 2006; Ungless et al., 2010). Both are indicators of cellular processes underlying fast learning (Morris et al., 1986; Aggleton and Brown, 2005).

NEURONAL MORPHOLOGY

There is a growing physiological base for drug-related memories in particular in structures of the brain's reinforcement system (Kelley, 2004). However, the neurophysiological adaptations were not only observed in the reward system, but also in other structures of the brain. A series of studies in animals by Robinson and Kolb (Robinson and Kolb, 1997, 1999, 2004; Robinson et al., 2001; Li et al., 2003; Ferrario et al., 2005) showed that psychoactive drugs, such as cocaine, amphetamine, nicotine, and morphine can cause a number of morphological changes in neocortical neurons, i.e., in areas not considered to be part of the reward system, but rather part of other memory circuits (Eichenbaum, 1997; Milner et al., 1998). These changes, which comprise an increase in neuronal spine density and axonal sprouting, were normally observed during normal, i.e., drug free, learning (Moser et al., 1994). Furthermore, when induced by psychoactive drugs, normal environmental enrichment, was no longer able to induce it (Kolb et al., 2003).

NEUROIMAGING

An activation of cortical memory areas was also shown in various imaging studies in humans during drug exposure or presentation of craving-eliciting cues (Grant et al., 1996; Bonson et al., 2002; Goldstein et al., 2007). Thereby, the brain areas activated during actual drug exposure often overlap with those areas activated during presentation of drug-associated cues (e.g., Breiter et al., 1997; Childress et al., 1999). These findings support the view that psychoactive drugs do not only functionally interact with the brain reward system, but also with other memory systems – if not with the whole brain (Tretter et al., 2009), thus causing acute responses and plastic changes which are similar to those observed during normal learning (Kelley, 2004).

While the review of neurophysiological drug-effects is far from complete, it shows several mechanisms of how an acute drug-induced activation of memory systems may result in fast plasticity which can shape future behavioral responses to drug-cues and the drug itself. How each of them relates specifically to episodic drug memories still has to be shown. It should also be noted, that these effects might reflect merely functional correlates of episodic drug memories during initial/early drug exposure. There are also consummatory episodes remembered during chronic consumption and addiction. However, after repeated drug exposition, many more drug memories are formed, which control future drug directed behaviors (**Figure 1**). Furthermore, episodic memories of a single consummatory episode may consist of rather different components, such as an initial euphoria episode later followed by an aversive withdrawal episode. Both are characterized by quite different neurochemical profiles (I have only discussed the initial effects here), but may result in equally well remembered episodes. Currently this may only suggest that quite different mechanisms may shape episodic drug memories, e.g., in their affective value, which clearly awaits further research.

Another limitation in the interpretation of neurophysiological drug-effects arises from a lack of proper models for episodic drug memories. Virtually all animal models of addiction, such as operant self-administration or conditioned place preference, focus on addiction-related behaviors which all require multiple drug expositions (Olmstead, 2006; Sanchis-Segura and Spanagel, 2006). Coinciding neuronal and functional adaptations in the brain may, thus, reflect more than one type of learning and memory (e.g., Huston et al., 2013). For future research in the episodic memories of drug-effects, a specific animal model would be useful.

CONCLUSION

Here a potential role of episodic drug memories in psychoactive drug use and drug instrumentalization is suggested. Easily accessible verbal reports from human drug users suggest that there are episodic memories with specific drug-related content. These memories are, especially when involving strong emotional responses, one-trial memories with a particularly high extinction resistance. Neurophysiological analyses of drug-effects in the brain provide evidence for strong neurochemical effects of psychoactive drugs in memory processing systems, which outreach those of non-drug stimuli/events. As such, there emerges also a neurophysiological base for episodic drug memories which may influence later consummatory behaviors. A more in depth analysis of the concept suggests that the "What-Where-When" characteristic of episodic memories can be applied equally well to the analysis of episodic drug memories. Altogether, it is suggested to consider episodic drug memories as an important mediator in the establishment of early drug consumption and the transition to drug instrumentalization which should warrant further exploration.

ACKNOWLEDGMENTS

This work was supported by funds of the University of Erlangen-Nuremberg (Germany). The author wishes to thank Dr. Davide Amato for his comments on a previous version of the paper and acknowledges the support by Deutsche Forschungsgemeinschaft (DFG) and Friedrich-Alexander-University Erlangen-Nuremberg within the funding programme Open Access Publishing.

REFERENCES

Abel, E. L. (1980). *Marihuana: The First Twelve Thousand Years.* New York: Plenum Press.

Aggleton, J. P., and Brown, M. W. (1999). Episodic memory, amnesia, and the hippocampal-anterior thalamic axis. *Behav. Brain Sci.* 22, 425–444.

Aggleton, J. P., and Brown, M. W. (2005). Contrasting hippocampal and perirhinal cortex function using immediate early gene imaging. *Q. J. Exp. Psychol. B* 58, 218–233.

Ahmed, S. H. (2010). Validation crisis in animal models of drug addiction: beyond non-disordered drug use toward drug addiction. *Neurosci. Biobehav. Rev.* 35, 172–184.

Amendt, G. (2003). *No Drugs No Future.* Hamburg: Europa Verlag.

Ameri, A. (1999). The effects of cannabinoids on the brain. *Prog. Neurobiol.* 58, 315–348.

American Psychiatric Association. (1994). *Diagnostic Statistical Manual of Mental Disorders,* 4th Edn. (Washington: American Psychiatric Association).

Anderson, S. M., Famous, K. R., Sadri-Vakili, G., Kumaresan, V., Schmidt, H. D., Bass, C. E., et al. (2008). CaMKII: a biochemical bridge linking accumbens dopamine and glutamate systems in cocaine seeking. *Nat. Neurosci.* 11, 344–353.

Argilli, E., Sibley, D. R., Malenka, R. C., England, P. M., and Bonci, A. (2008). Mechanism and time course of cocaine-induced long-term potentiation in the ventral tegmental area. *J. Neurosci.* 28, 9092–9100.

Bardo, M. T. (1998). Neuropharmacological mechanisms of drug reward: beyond dopamine in the nucleus accumbens. *Crit. Rev. Neurobiol.* 12, 37–67.

Bardo, M. T., and Bevins, R. A. (2000). Conditioned place preference: what does it add to our preclinical understanding of drug reward? *Psychopharmacology (Berl.)* 153, 31–43.

Bast, T. (2007). Toward an integrative perspective on hippocampal function: from the rapid encoding of experience to adaptive behavior. *Rev. Neurosci.* 18, 253–281.

Belin, D., and Everitt, B. J. (2008). Cocaine seeking habits depend upon dopamine-dependent serial connectivity linking the ventral with the dorsal striatum. *Neuron* 57, 432–441.

Belin, D., Jonkman, S., Dickinson, A., Robbins, T. W., and Everitt, B J. (2009). Parallel and interactive learning processes within the basal ganglia: relevance for the understanding of addiction. *Behav. Brain Res.* 199, 89–102.

Belin, D., Mar, A. C., Dalley, J. W., Robbins, T. W., and Everitt, B. J. (2008). High impulsivity predicts the switch to compulsive cocaine-taking. *Science* 320, 1352–1355.

Bilbao, A., Parkitna, J. R., Engblom, D., Perreau-Lenz, S., Sanchis-Segura, C., Schneider, M., et al. (2008). Loss of the Ca2+/calmodulin-dependent protein kinase type IV in dopaminoceptive neurons enhances behavioral effects of cocaine. *Proc. Natl. Acad. Sci. U.S.A.* 105, 17549–17554.

Blokland, A. (1995). Acetylcholine: a neurotransmitter for learning and memory? *Brain Res. Brain Res. Rev.* 21, 285–300.

Boening, J. A. (2001). Neurobiology of an addiction memory. *J. Neural Transm.* 108, 755–765.

Bonson, K. R., Grant, S. J., Contoreggi, C. S., Links, J. M., Metcalfe, J., Weyl, H. L., et al. (2002). Neural systems and cue-induced cocaine craving. *Neuropsychopharmacology* 26, 376–386.

Borgland, S. L., Malenka, R. C., and Bonci, A. (2004). Acute and chronic cocaine-induced potentiation of synaptic strength in the ventral tegmental area: electrophysiological and behavioral correlates in individual rats. *J. Neurosci.* 24, 7482–7490.

Bouton, M. E., and Moody, E. W. (2004). Memory processes in classical conditioning. *Neurosci. Biobehav. Rev.* 28, 663–674.

Bowers, M. S., Chen, B. T., and Bonci, A. (2010). AMPA receptor synaptic plasticity induced by psychostimulants: the past, present, and therapeutic future. *Neuron* 67, 11–24.

Boyd, C. J., McCabe, S. E., Cranford, J. A., and Young, A. (2006). Adolescents' motivations to abuse prescription medications. *Pediatrics* 118, 2472–2480.

Boys, A., and Marsden, J. (2003). Perceived functions predict intensity of use and problems in young polysubstance users. *Addiction* 98, 951–963.

Boys, A., Marsden, J., Griffiths, P., Fountain, J., Stillwell, G., and Strang, J. (1999). Substance use among young people: the relationship between perceived functions and intentions. *Addiction* 94, 1043–1050.

Boys, A., Marsden, J., and Strang, J. (2001). Understanding reasons for drug use amongst young people: a functional perspective. *Health Educ. Res.* 16, 457–469.

Breiter, H. C., Gollub, R. L., Weisskoff, R. M., Kennedy, D. N., Makris, N., Berke, J. D., et al. (1997). Acute effects of cocaine on human brain activity and emotion. *Neuron* 19, 591–611.

Brown, S. A. (1985). Expectancies versus background in the prediction of college drinking patterns. *J. Consult. Clin. Psychol.* 53, 123–130.

Brown, S. A., Goldman, M. S., Inn, A., and Anderson, L. R. (1980). Expectations of reinforcement from alcohol: their domain and relation to drinking patterns. *J. Consult. Clin. Psychol.* 48, 419–426.

Campbell, J. C., Szumlinski, K. K., and Kippin, T. E. (2009). Contribution of early environmental stress to alcoholism vulnerability. *Alcohol* 43, 547–554.

Cauli, O., and Morelli, M. (2005). Caffeine and the dopaminergic system. *Behav. Pharmacol.* 16, 63–77.

Childress, A. R., Mozley, P. D., McElgin, W., Fitzgerald, J., Reivich, M., and O'Brien, C. P. (1999). Limbic activation during cue-induced cocaine craving. *Am. J. Psychiatry* 156, 11–18.

Consolo, S., Caltavuturo, C., Colli, E., Recchia, M., and Di Chiara, G. (1999). Different sensitivity of in vivo acetylcholine transmission to D1 receptor stimulation in shell and core of nucleus accumbens. *Neuroscience* 89, 1209–1217.

de Wit, H., and Stewart, J. (1981) Reinstatement of cocaine-reinforced responding in the rat. *Psychopharmacology (Berl.)* 75, 134–143.

Dean, L. G., Kendal, R. L., Schapiro S. J., Thierry, B., and Laland, K. N. (2012). Identification of the social and cognitive processes underlying human cumulative culture. *Science* 335, 1114–1118.

Del Boca, F. K., Darkes, J., Goldman, M. S., and Smith, G. T. (2002). Advancing the expectancy concept via the interplay between theory and research. *Alcohol. Clin. Exp. Res.* 26, 926–935.

Dere, E., Easton, A., Nadel, L., and Huston, J. P. (2008). *Handbook of Episodic Memory.* New York: Elsevier.

Dere, E., Huston, J. P., and De Souza Silva, M. A. (2007). The pharmacology, neuroanatomy and neurogenetics of one-trial object recognition in rodents. *Neurosci. Biobehav. Rev.* 31, 673–704.

Dere, E., Kart-Teke, E., Huston, J. P., and De Souza Silva, M. A. (2006). The case for episodic memory in animals. *Neurosci. Biobehav. Rev.* 30, 1206–1224.

Deroche-Gamonet, V., Belin, D., and Piazza, P. V. (2004). Evidence for addiction-like behavior in the rat. *Science* 305, 1014–1017.

Di Chiara, G. (1995). The role of dopamine in drug abuse viewed from the perspective of its role in motivation. *Drug Alcohol. Depend.* 38, 95–137.

Di Chiara, G., and Imperato, A. (1988). Drugs abused by humans preferentially increase synaptic dopamine concentrations in the mesolimbic system of freely moving rats. *Proc. Natl. Acad. Sci. U.S.A.* 85, 5274–5278.

Di Chiara, G., and North, R. A. (1992). Neurobiology of opiate abuse. *Trends Pharmacol. Sci.* 13, 185–193.

Dong, L., Bilbao, A., Laucht, M., Henriksson, R., Yakovleva, T., Ridinger, M., et al. (2011). Effects of the circadian rhythm gene period 1 (per1) on psychosocial stress-induced alcohol drinking. *Am. J. Psychiatry* 168, 1090–1098.

Dong, Y., Saal, D., Thomas, M., Faust, R., Bonci, A., Robinson, T., et al. (2004). Cocaine-induced potentiation of synaptic strength in dopamine neurons: behavioral correlates in GluRA(-/-) mice. *Proc. Natl. Acad. Sci. U.S.A.* 101, 14282–14287.

Drummond, D. C., Cooper, T., and Glautier, S. P. (1990). Conditioned learning in alcohol dependence: implications for cue exposure treatment. *Br. J. Addict.* 85, 725–743.

Easton, A. C., Lucchesi, W., Lourdusamy, A., Lenz, B., Solati, J., Golub, Y., et al. (2013a). αCaMKII autophosphorylation controls the establishment of alcohol reinforcement by altering dopamine-serotonin balance. *Neuropsychopharmacology* (in press).

Easton, A. C., Lourdusamy, A., Loth, E., Toro, R., Giese, K. P., Kornhuber, J., et al. (2013b). alphaCaMKII gene (CAMK2A) polymorphisms predict spatial working memory performance in humans. *Mol. Psychiatry* (in press).

Eichenbaum, H. (1997). How does the brain organize memories? *Science* 277, 330–332.

Eissenberg, T., and Balster, R. L. (2000). Initial tobacco use episodes in children and adolescents: current knowledge, future directions. *Drug Alcohol. Depend.* 59(Suppl. 1), S41–S60.

EMCDDA. (2012). *European Monitoring Center for Addictive Drugs. State of the Drug Problem 2009.* Available at: http://www.emcdda.europa.eu/publications/annual-report/2012

Everitt, B. J., Hutcheson, D. M., Ersche, K. D., Pelloux, Y., Dalley, J. W., and Robbins, T. W. (2007). The orbital prefrontal cortex and drug addiction in laboratory animals and humans. *Ann. N. Y. Acad. Sci.* 1121, 576–597.

Everitt, B. J., and Robbins, T. W. (2005). Neural systems of reinforcement for drug addiction: from actions to habits to compulsion. *Nat. Neurosci.* 8, 1481–1489.

Faleiro, L. J., Jones, S., and Kauer, J. A. (2004). Rapid synaptic plasticity of glutamatergic synapses on dopamine neurons in the ventral tegmental area in response to acute amphetamine injection. *Neuropsychopharmacology* 29, 2115–2125.

Ferrario, C. R., Gorny, G., Crombag, H. S., Li, Y., Kolb, B., and Robinson, T. E. (2005). Neural and behavioral plasticity associated with the transition from controlled to escalated cocaine use. *Biol. Psychiatry* 58, 751–759.

Foltin, R. W., and Haney, M. (2000). Conditioned effects of environmental stimuli paired with smoked cocaine in humans. *Psychopharmacology (Berl.)* 149, 24–33.

Frederiksen, N. J., Bakke, S. L., and Dalum, P. (2012). "No alcohol, no party": an explorative study of young Danish moderate drinkers. *Scand. J. Public Health* 40, 585–590.

Friedman, L. S., Lichtenstein, E., and Biglan, A. (1985). Smoking onset among teens: an empirical analysis of initial situations. *Addict. Behav.* 10, 1–13.

Gawin, F. H. (1991). Cocaine addiction: psychology and neurophysiology. *Science* 251, 1580–1586.

Giese, K. P., Fedorov, N. B., Filipkowski, R. K., and Silva, A. J. (1998). Autophosphorylation at Thr286 of the alpha calcium-calmodulin kinase II in LTP and learning. *Science* 279, 870–873.

Goldberg, S. R. (1975). Stimuli associated with drug injections as events that control behavior. *Pharmacol. Rev.* 27, 325–340.

Goldman, M. S., Brown, S. A., Christiansen, B. A., and Smith, G. T. (1991). Alcoholism and memory: broadening the scope of alcohol-expectancy research. *Psychol. Bull.* 110, 137–146.

Goldstein, R. Z., Tomasi, D., Rajaram, S., Cottone, L. A., Zhang, L., Maloney, T., et al. (2007). Role of the anterior cingulate and medial orbitofrontal cortex in processing drug cues in cocaine addiction. *Neuroscience* 144, 1153–1159.

Grant, S., London, E. D., Newlin, D. B., Villemagne, V. L., Liu, X., Contoreggi, C., et al. (1996). Activation of memory circuits during cue-elicited cocaine craving. *Proc. Natl. Acad. Sci. U.S.A.* 93, 12040–12045.

Green, A. R., Mechan, A. O., Elliott, J. M., O'Shea, E., and Colado, M. I. (2003). The pharmacology and clinical pharmacology of 3,4-methylenedioxymethamphetamine (MDMA, "ecstasy"). *Pharmacol. Rev.* 55, 463–508.

Gustafson, R. (1991). Is the strength and the desirability of alcohol-related expectancies positively related? A test with an adult Swedish sample. *Drug Alcohol. Depend.* 28, 145–150.

Haber, S. N., Fudge, J. L., and McFarland, N. R. (2000). Striatonigrostriatal pathways in primates form an ascending spiral from the shell to the dorsolateral striatum. *J. Neurosci.* 20, 2369–2382.

Hagen, E. H., Sullivan, R. J., Schmidt, R., Morris, G., Kempter, R., and Hammerstein, P. (2009). Ecology and neurobiology of toxin avoidance and the paradox of drug reward. *Neuroscience* 160, 69–84.

Hassan, Z., Muzaimi, M., Navaratnam, V., Yusoff, N. H., Suhaimi, F. W., Vadivelu, R., et al. (2013). From Kratom to mitragynine and its derivatives: physiological and behavioural effects related to use, abuse, and addiction. *Neurosci. Biobehav. Rev.* 37, 138–151.

Heath, D. B. (2000). *Drinking Occasions: Comparative Perspectives on Alcohol and Culture.* New York: Brunner/Mazel.

Hellemans, K. G., Everitt, B. J., and Lee, J. L. (2006). Disrupting reconsolidation of conditioned withdrawal memories in the basolateral amygdala reduces suppression of heroin seeking in rats. *J. Neurosci.* 26, 12694–12699.

Henn, C., Loffelholz, K., and Klein, J. (1998). Stimulatory and inhibitory effects of ethanol on hippocampal acetylcholine release. *Naunyn Schmiedebergs Arch. Pharmacol.* 357, 640–647.

Heyne, A., May, T., Goll, P., and Wolffgramm, J. (2000). Persisting consequences of drug intake: towards a memory of addiction. *J. Neural Transm.* 107, 613–638.

Huffman, M. A. (2003). Animal self-medication and ethno-medicine: exploration and exploitation of the medicinal properties of plants. *Proc. Nutr. Soc.* 62, 371–381.

Huston, J. P., de Souza Silva, M. A., Topic, B., and Müller, C. P. (2013). What's conditioned in conditioned place preference? *Trends Pharmacol. Sci.* 34, 162–166.

Huston, J. P., Mondadori, C., and Waser, P. G. (1974). Facilitation of learning by reward of post-trial memory processes. *Experientia* 30, 1038–1040.

Huston, J. P., Mueller, C. C., and Mondadori, C. (1977). Memory facilitation by posttrial hypothalamic stimulation and other reinforcers: a central theory of reinforcement. *Neurosci. Biobehav. Rev.* 1, 143–150.

Hyman, S. E., and Malenka, R. C. (2001). Addiction and the brain: the neurobiology of compulsion and its persistence. *Nat. Rev. Neurosci.* 2, 695–703.

Hyman, S. E., Malenka, R. C., and Nestler, E. J. (2006). Neural mechanisms of addiction: the role of reward-related learning and memory. *Annu. Rev. Neurosci.* 29, 565–598.

Imperato, A., Obinu, M. C., Demontis, M. V., and Gessa, G. L. (1992). Cocaine releases limbic acetylcholine through endogenous dopamine action on D1 receptors. *Eur. J. Pharmacol.* 229, 265–267.

Imperato, A., Obinu, M. C., and Gessa, G. L. (1993a). Effects of cocaine and amphetamine on acetylcholine release in the hippocampus and caudate nucleus. *Eur. J. Pharmacol.* 238, 377–381.

Imperato, A., Obinu, M. C., and Gessa, G. L. (1993b). Stimulation of both dopamine D1 and D2 receptors facilitates in vivo acetylcholine release in the hippocampus. *Brain Res.* 618, 341–345.

Imperato, A., Obinu, M. C., Mascia, M. S., Casu, M. A., Zocchi, A., Cabib, S., et al. (1996). Strain-dependent effects of dopamine agonists on acetylcholine release in the hippocampus: an in vivo study in mice. *Neuroscience* 70, 653–660.

Irvine, E. E., von Hertzen, L. S., Plattner, F., and Giese, K. P. (2006). alphaCaMKII autophosphorylation: a fast track to memory. *Trends Neurosci.* 29, 459–465.

Iversen, L. L. (2000). *The Science of Marihuana.* Oxford: Oxford University Press.

Johanson, C. E., and Fischman, M. W. (1989). The pharmacology of cocaine related to its abuse. *Pharmacol. Rev.* 41, 3–52.

Jones, R. T. (1971). Marihuana-induced "high": influence of expectation, setting and previous drug experience. *Pharmacol. Rev.* 23, 359–369.

Kalivas, P. W., Sorg, B. A., and Hooks, M. S. (1993). The pharmacology and neural circuitry of sensitization to psychostimulants. *Behav. Pharmacol.* 4, 315–334.

Kandel, E. R. (2001). The molecular biology of memory storage: a dialogue between genes and synapses. *Science* 294, 1030–1038.

Kandel, E. R., and Pittenger, C. (1999). The past, the future and the biology of memory storage. *Philos. Trans. R. Soc. Lond. B Biol. Sci.* 354, 2027–2052.

Kauer, J. A., and Malenka, R. C. (2007). Synaptic plasticity and addiction. *Nat. Rev. Neurosci.* 8, 844–858.

Kelley, A. E. (2004). Memory and addiction: shared neural circuitry and molecular mechanisms. *Neuron* 44, 161–179.

Kidorf, M., Sherman, M. F., Johnson, J. G., and Bigelow, G. E. (1995). Alcohol expectancies and changes in beer consumption of first-year college students. *Addict. Behav.* 20, 225–231.

Kilts, C. D., Schweitzer, J. B., Quinn, C. K., Gross, R. E., Faber, T. L., Muhammad, F., et al. (2001). Neural activity related to drug craving in cocaine addiction. *Arch. Gen. Psychiatry* 58, 334–341.

Kippin, T. E. (2011). Does drug mis-instrumentalization lead to drug abuse? *Behav. Brain Sci.* 34, 316–317.

Knowlton, B. J., Mangels, J. A., and Squire, L. R. (1996). A neostriatal habit learning system in humans. *Science* 273, 1399–1402.

Kolb, B., Gorny, G., Li, Y. L., Samaha, A. N., and Robinson, T. E. (2003). Amphetamine or cocaine limits the ability of later experience to promote structural plasticity in the neocortex and nucleus accumbens. *Proc. Natl. Acad. Sci. U.S.A.* 100, 10523–10528.

Koob, G. F. (1992). Drugs of abuse: anatomy, pharmacology and function of reward pathways. *Trends Pharmacol. Sci.* 13, 177–184.

Koob, G. F., Sanna, P. P., and Bloom, F. E. (1998). Neuroscience of addiction. *Neuron* 21, 467–476.

Kuntsche, E., Knibbe, R., Gmel, G., and Engels, R. (2005). Why do young people drink? A review of drinking motives. *Clin. Psychol. Rev.* 25, 841–861.

Larsson, A., Edstrom, L., Svensson, L., Soderpalm, B., and Engel, J. A. (2005). Voluntary ethanol intake increases extracellular acetylcholine levels in the ventral tegmental area in the rat. *Alcohol Alcohol.* 40, 349–358.

Lee, J. L., Di Ciano, P., Thomas, K. L., and Everitt, B. J. (2005). Disrupting reconsolidation of drug memories reduces cocaine-seeking behavior. *Neuron* 47, 795–801.

Lee, J. L., Milton, A. L., and Everitt, B. J. (2006). Cue-induced cocaine seeking and relapse are reduced by disruption of drug memory reconsolidation. *J. Neurosci.* 26, 5881–5887.

Leigh, B. C. (1989). In search of the Seven Dwarves: issues of measurement and meaning in alcohol expectancy research. *Psychol. Bull.* 105, 361–373.

Leigh, B. C., and Stacy, A. W. (2004). Alcohol expectancies and drinking in different age groups. *Addiction* 99, 215–227.

Lende, D. H., and Smith, E. O. (2002). Evolution meets biopsychosociality: an analysis of addictive behavior. *Addiction* 97, 447–458.

Lende, D. H., Leonard, T., Sterk, C. E., and Elifson, K. (2007). Functional methamphetamine use: the insider's perspective. *Addict. Res. Theory* 15, 465–477.

Li, Y. L., Kolb, B., and Robinson, T. E. (2003). The location of persistent amphetamine-induced changes in the density of dendritic spines on medium spiny neurons in the nucleus accumbens and caudate-putamen. *Neuropsychopharmacology* 28, 1082–1085.

Licata, S. C., and Pierce, R. C. (2003). The roles of calcium/calmodulin-dependent and Ras/mitogen-activated protein kinases in the development of psychostimulant-induced behavioral sensitization. *J. Neurochem.* 85, 14–22.

Liu, J., Suncion-Chin, M., Liu, P., and Dopico, A. M. (2006). CaM kinase II phosphorylation of slo Thr107 regulates activity and ethanol responses of BK channels. *Nat. Neurosci.* 9, 41–49.

Lozano, G. A. (1998) Parasitic stress and self-medication in wild animals. *Adv. Stud. Behav.* 27, 291–317.

Mameli, M., Bellone, C., Brown, M. T., and Lüscher, C. (2011). Cocaine inverts rules for synaptic plasticity of glutamate transmission in the ventral tegmental area. *Nat. Neurosci.* 14, 414–416.

Markou, A. (2008). Neurobiology of nicotine dependence. *Philos. Trans. R. Soc. Lond. B Biol. Sci.* 363, 3159–3168.

McBride, W. J., Le, A. D., and Noronha, A. (2002). Central nervous system mechanisms in alcohol relapse. *Alcohol. Clin. Exp. Res.* 26, 280–286.

McBride, W. J., Murphy, J. M., and Ikemoto, S. (1999). Localization of brain reinforcement mechanisms: intracranial self-administration and intracranial place-conditioning studies. *Behav. Brain Res.* 101, 129–152.

McGaugh, J. L. (2000). Memory – a century of consolidation. *Science* 287, 248–251.

Mello, N. K. (1972). "Behavioral studies of alcoholism," in *Biology of Alcoholism*, eds B. Kissin and H. Begleiter (New York: Plenum Press), 210–219.

Miller, C. S. (2001). Toxicant-induced loss of tolerance. *Addiction* 96, 115–137.

Miller, P. M., Smith, G. T., and Goldman, M. S. (1990). Emergence of alcohol expectancies in childhood: a possible critical period. *J. Stud. Alcohol* 51, 343–349.

Milner, B., Squire, L. R., and Kandel, E. R. (1998). Cognitive neuroscience and the study of memory. *Neuron* 20, 445–468.

Morris, R. G., Anderson, E., Lynch, G. S., and Baudry, M. (1986). Selective impairment of learning and blockade of long-term potentiation by an N-methyl-D-aspartate receptor antagonist, AP5. *Nature* 319, 774–776.

Moser, M. B., Trommald, M., and Andersen, P. (1994). An increase in dendritic spine density on hippocampal Ca1 pyramidal cells following spatial-learning in adult-rats suggests the formation of new synapses. *Proc. Natl. Acad. Sci. U.S.A.* 91, 12673–12675.

Müller, C. P., Carey, R. J., Huston, J. P., and De Souza Silva, M. A. (2007a). Serotonin and psychostimulant addiction: focus on 5-HT1A-receptors. *Prog. Neurobiol.* 81, 133–178.

Müller, C. P., De Souza Silva, M. A., and Huston, J. P. (2007b). Double dissociating effects of sensory stimulation and cocaine on serotonin activity in the occipital and temporal cortices. *Neuropharmacology* 52, 854–862.

Müller, C. P., Pum, M. E., Amato, D., Schüttler, J., Huston, J. P., and de Souza Silva, M. A. (2011). The in-vivo neurochemistry of the brain during general anesthesia. *J. Neurochem.* 119, 419–446.

Müller, C. P., De Souza Silva, M. A., DePalma, G., Tomaz, C., Carey, R. J., and Huston, J. P. (2002). The selective serotonin(1A)-receptor antagonist WAY 100635 blocks behavioral stimulating effects of cocaine but not ventral striatal dopamine increase. *Behav. Brain Res.* 134, 337–346.

Müller, C. P., and Huston, J. P. (2007). Dopamine activity in the occipital and temporal cortices of rats: dissociating effects of sensory but not pharmacological stimulation. *Synapse* 61, 254–258.

Müller, C. P., and Schumann, G. (2011a). Drugs as an instrument: a new framework for non-addictive psychoactive drug use. *Behav. Brain Sci.* 34, 293–310.

Müller, C. P., and Schumann, G. (2011b). To use or not to use: expanding the view on non-addictive psychoactive drug consumption and its implications. *Behav. Brain Sci.* 34, 328–347.

Müller, C. P., Thönnessen, H., Barros, M., Tomaz, C., Carey, R. J., and Huston, J. P. (2004). Hippocampus 5-HT(1A)-receptors attenuate cocaine-induced hyperlocomotion and the increase in hippocampal but not nucleus accumbens 5-HT. *Hipppocampus* 14, 710–721.

Müller, C. P., Pum, M. E., Schumann, G., and Huston, J. P. (2010). "The role of serotonin in drug addiction" in *The Behavioral Neurobiology of Serotonin*, eds C. P. Müller and B. L. Jacobs (London: Academic Press), 507–546.

Nesse, R. M., and Berridge, K. C. (1997). Psychoactive drug use in evolutionary perspective. *Science* 278, 63–66.

Nestler, E. J. (2002). Common molecular and cellular substrates of addiction and memory. *Neurobiol. Learn. Mem.* 78, 637–647.

Nestler, E. J. (2008). Review. Transcriptional mechanisms of addiction: role of DeltaFosB. *Philos. Trans. R. Soc. Lond. B Biol. Sci.* 363, 3245–3255.

Nestler, E. J., and Aghajanian, G. K (1997). Molecular and cellular basis of addiction. *Science* 278, 58–63.

O'Brien, C. P., Childress, A. R., Ehrman R., and Robbins, S. J. (1998). Conditioning factors in drug abuse: can they explain compulsion? *J. Psychopharmacol.* 12, 15–22.

O'Brien, C. P., Testa, T., O'Brien, T. J., Brady, J. P., and Wells, B. (1977). Conditioned narcotic withdrawal in humans. *Science* 195, 1000–1002.

Olmstead, M. C. (2006). Animal models of drug addiction: where do we go from here? *Q. J. Exp. Psychol. (Hove)* 59, 625–653.

O'Malley, P. M., and Johnston, L. D. (2002). Epidemiology of alcohol and other drug use among American college students. *J. Stud. Alc.* 14, 23–39.

Overton, D. A. (1968). Visual cues and shock sensitivity in the control of

T-maze choice by drug conditions. *J. Comp. Physiol. Psychol.* 66, 216–219.

Patrick, M. E., and Maggs, J. L. (2008). Short-term changes in plans to drink and importance of positive and negative alcohol consequences. *J. Adolesc.* 31, 307–321.

Peele, S., and Brodsky, A. (2000). Exploring psychological benefits associated with moderate alcohol use: a necessary corrective to assessments of drinking outcomes? *Drug Alcohol. Depend.* 60, 221–247.

Perry, E., Walker, M., Grace, J., and Perry, R. (1999). Acetylcholine in mind: a neurotransmitter correlate of consciousness? *Trends Neurosci.* 22, 273–280.

Piazza, P. V., Deminiere, J. M., Le, M. M., and Simon, H. (1989). Factors that predict individual vulnerability to amphetamine self-administration. *Science* 245, 1511–1513.

Pierce, R. C., and Kumaresan, V. (2006). The mesolimbic dopamine system: the final common pathway for the reinforcing effect of drugs of abuse? *Neurosci. Biobehav. Rev.* 30, 215–238.

Porrino, L. J., Lyons, D., Smith, H. R., Daunais, J. B., and Nader, M. A. (2004). Cocaine self-administration produces a progressive involvement of limbic, association, and sensorimotor striatal domains. *J. Neurosci.* 24, 3554–3562.

Pum, M., Carey, R. J., Huston, J. P., and Müller, C. P. (2007). Dissociating effects of cocaine and d-amphetamine on dopamine and serotonin in the perirhinal, entorhinal, and prefrontal cortex of freely moving rats. *Psychopharmacology (Berl.)* 193, 375–390.

Pum, M. E., Huston, J. P., and Müller, C. P. (2009). The role of cortical serotonin in anxiety and locomotor activity in Wistar rats. *Behav. Neurosci.* 123, 449–454.

Quirion, R., Richard, J., and Wilson, A. (1994). Muscarinic and nicotinic modulation of cortical acetylcholine release monitored by in vivo microdialysis in freely moving adult rats. *Synapse* 17, 92–100.

Rex, A., Marsden, C. A., and Fink, H. (1993). Effect of diazepam on cortical 5-HT release and behaviour in the guinea-pig on exposure to the elevated plus maze. *Psychopharmacology (Berl.)* 110, 490–496.

Richardson, N. R., and Roberts, D. C. S. (1996). Progressive ratio schedules in drug self-administration studies in rats: a method to evaluate reinforcing efficacy. *J. Neurosci. Methods* 66, 1–11.

Robbins, T. W., Ersche, K. D., and Everitt, B. J. (2008). Drug addiction and the memory systems of the brain. *Ann. N. Y. Acad. Sci.* 1141, 1–21.

Robbins, T. W., and Everitt, B. J. (1999). Drug addiction: bad habits add up. *Nature* 398, 567–570.

Robinson, T. E., Gorny, G., Mitton, E., and Kolb, B. (2001). Cocaine self-administration alters the morphology of dendrites and dendritic spines in the nucleus accumbens and neocortex. *Synapse* 39, 257–266.

Robinson, T. E., and Kolb, B. (1997). Persistent structural modifications in nucleus accumbens and prefrontal cortex neurons produced by previous experience with amphetamine. *J. Neurosci.* 17, 8491–8497.

Robinson, T. E., and Kolb, B. (1999). Alterations in the morphology of dendrites and dendritic spines in the nucleus accumbens and prefrontal cortex following repeated treatment with amphetamine or cocaine. *Eur. J. Neurosci.* 11, 1598–1604.

Robinson, T. E., and Kolb, B. (2004). Structural plasticity associated with exposure to drugs of abuse. *Neuropharmacology* 47, 33–46.

Rodriguez, E., and Wrangham, R. (1993). Zoopharmacognosy: the use of medicinal plants by animals. *Recent Adv. Phytochem.* 27, 89–105.

Rueter, L. E., Fornal, C. A., and Jacobs, B. L. (1997). A critical review of 5-HT brain microdialysis and behavior. *Rev. Neurosci.* 8, 117–137.

Saal, D., Dong, Y., Bonci, A., and Malenka, R. C. (2003). Drugs of abuse and stress trigger a common synaptic adaptation in dopamine neurons. *Neuron* 37, 577–582.

SAMHSA. (2011). *National Survey on Drug Use and Health.* Rockville: Substance Abuse and Mental Health Services Administration. Available at: http://www.samhsa.gov/data/NSDUH/2011SummNatFindDetTables/Index.aspx

Sanchis-Segura, C., and Spanagel, R. (2006). Behavioural assessment of drug reinforcement and addictive features in rodents: an overview. *Addict. Biol.* 11, 2–38.

Sarter, M., Hasselmo, M. E., Bruno, J. P., and Givens, B. (2005). Unraveling the attentional functions of cortical cholinergic inputs: interactions between signal-driven and cognitive modulation of signal detection. *Brain Res. Brain Res. Rev.* 48, 98–111.

Schultz, W. (2000). Multiple reward signals in the brain. *Nat. Rev. Neurosci.* 1, 199–207.

Schumann, G., Coin, L. J., Lourdusamy, A., Charoen, P., Berger, K. H., Stacey, D., et al. (2011). Genome-wide association and genetic functional studies identify autism susceptibility candidate 2 gene (AUTS2) in the regulation of alcohol consumption. *Proc. Natl. Acad. Sci. U.S.A.* 108, 7119–7124.

Seiden, L. S., Sabol, K. E., and Ricaurte, G. A. (1993). Amphetamine – effects on catecholamine systems and behavior. *Annu. Rev. Pharmacol. Toxicol.* 33, 639–677.

Shaham, Y., Shalev, U., Lu, L., de Wit, H., and Stewart, J. (2003). The reinstatement model of drug relapse: history, methodology and major findings. *Psychopharmacology (Berl.)* 168, 3–20.

Sher, K. J., Grekin, E. R., and Williams, N. A. (2005). The development of alcohol use disorders. *Annu. Rev. Clin. Psychol.* 1, 493–523.

Siegel, S. (1975). Evidence from rats that morphine tolerance is a learned response. *J. Comp. Physiol. Psychol.* 89, 498–506.

Siegel, S. (1988). Drug anticipation and the treatment of dependence. *NIDA Res. Monogr.* 84, 1–24.

Siegel, S., Hinson, R. E., Krank, M. D., and McCully, J. (1982). Heroin "overdose" death: contribution of drug-associated environmental cues. *Science* 216, 436–437.

Simons, J., Correia, C. J., and Carey, K. B. (2000). A comparison of motives for marihuana and alcohol use among experienced users. *Addict. Behav.* 25, 153–160.

Skogen, J. C., Harvey, S. B., Henderson, M., Stordal, E., and Mykletun, A. (2009). Anxiety and depression among abstainers and low-level alcohol consumers. The Nord-Trondelag Health Study. *Addiction* 104, 1519–1529.

Spanagel, R. (2009). Alcoholism: a systems approach from molecular physiology to addictive behavior. *Physiol. Rev.* 89, 649–705.

Spealman, R. D., and Goldberg, S. R. (1978). Drug self-administration by laboratory animals: control by schedules of reinforcement. *Annu. Rev. Pharmacol. Toxicol.* 18, 313–339.

Spear, L. P. (2000). The adolescent brain and age-related behavioral manifestations. *Neurosci. Biobehav. Rev.* 24, 417–463.

Squire, L. R., Knowlton, B., and Musen, G. (1993). The structure and organization of memory. *Annu. Rev. Psychol.* 44, 453–495.

Stacey, D., Bilbao, A., Maroteaux, M., Jia, T., Easton, A. C., Longueville, S., et al. (2012). RASGRF2 regulates alcohol-induced reinforcement by influencing mesolimbic dopamine neuron activity and dopamine release. *Proc. Natl. Acad. Sci. U.S.A.* 109, 21128–21133.

Stacey, D., Clarke, T. K., and Schumann, G. (2009). The genetics of alcoholism. *Curr. Psychiatry Rep.* 11, 364–369.

Stolerman, I. (1992). Drugs of abuse: behavioural principles, methods and terms. *Trends Pharmacol. Sci.* 13, 170–176.

Summers, K. L., and Giacobini, E. (1995). Effects of local and repeated systemic administration of (-)nicotine on extracellular levels of acetylcholine, norepinephrine, dopamine, and serotonin in rat cortex. *Neurochem. Res.* 20, 753–759.

Tani, Y., Saito, K., Imoto, M., and Ohno, T. (1998). Pharmacological characterization of nicotinic receptor-mediated acetylcholine release in rat brain – an in vivo microdialysis study. *Eur. J. Pharmacol.* 351, 181–188.

Tretter, F., Gebicke-Haerter, P. J., Albus, M., an der Heiden, U., and Schwegler, H. (2009). Systems biology and addiction. *Pharmacopsychiatry* 42(Suppl. 1), S11–S31.

Tulving, E. (2001). Episodic memory and common sense: how far apart? *Philos. Trans. R. Soc. Lond. B Biol. Sci.* 356, 1505–1515.

Tulving, E. (2002). Episodic memory: from mind to brain. *Annu. Rev. Psychol.* 53, 1–25.

Tupala, E., and Tiihonen, J. (2004). Dopamine and alcoholism: neurobiological basis of ethanol abuse. *Prog. Neuropsychopharmacol. Biol. Psychiatry* 28, 1221–1247.

Tzschentke, T. M. (2007). Measuring reward with the conditioned place preference (CPP) paradigm: update of the last decade. *Addict. Biol.* 12, 227–462.

Ungless, M. A., Argilli, E., and Bonci, A. (2010). Effects of stress and aversion on dopamine neurons: implications for addiction. *Neurosci. Biobehav. Rev.* 35, 151–156.

Ungless, M. A., Whistler, J. L., Malenka, R. C., and Bonci, A. (2001). Single cocaine exposure in vivo induces long-term potentiation in dopamine neurons. *Nature* 411, 583–587.

Vanderschuren, L. J., and Everitt, B. J. (2004). Drug seeking becomes compulsive after prolonged cocaine self-administration. *Science* 305, 1017–1019.

Vanderschuren, L. J., and Kalivas, P. W. (2000). Alterations in dopaminergic and glutamatergic transmission in the induction and expression of behavioral sensitization: a critical review of preclinical studies. *Psychopharmacology (Berl.)* 151, 99–120.

Volkow, N. D., Wang, G. J., Ma, Y. M., Fowler, J. S., Wong, C., Jayne, M., et al. (2006). Effects of expectation on the brain metabolic responses to methylphenidate and to its placebo in non-drug abusing subjects. *Neuroimage* 32, 1782–1792.

Volkow, N. D., Wang, G. J., Ma, Y. M., Fowler, J. S., Zhu, W., Maynard, L., et al. (2003). Expectation enhances the regional brain metabolic and the reinforcing effects of stimulants in cocaine abusers. *J. Neurosci.* 23, 11461–11468.

Waldorf, D., Reinarman, C., and Murphy, S. (1991). *Cocaine Changes: The Experience of Using and Quitting.* Philadelphia: Temple University Press.

Wanat, M. J., and Bonci, A. (2008). Dose-dependent changes in the synaptic strength on dopamine neurons and locomotor activity after cocaine exposure. *Synapse* 62, 790–795.

Wang, M., Vijayraghavan, S., and Goldman-Rakic, P. S. (2004). Selective D2 receptor actions on the functional circuitry of working memory. *Science* 303, 853–856.

Waskow, I. E., Olsson, J. E., Salzman, C., and Katz, M. M. (1970). Psychological effects of tetrahydrocannabinol. *Arch. Gen. Psychiatry* 22, 97–107.

White, N. M. (1989). Reward or reinforcement: what's the difference? *Neurosci. Biobehav. Rev.* 13, 181–186.

White, N. M. (1996). Addictive drugs as reinforcers: multiple partial actions on memory systems. *Addiction* 91, 921–949.

White, N. M., and Milner, P. M. (1992). The psychobiology of reinforcers. *Annu. Rev. Psychol.* 43, 443–471.

Wikler, A., and Pescor, F. T. (1967). Classical conditioning of a morphine abstinence phenomenon, reinforcement of opioid-drinking behavior and "relapse" in morphine-addicted rats. *Psychopharmacologia* 10, 255–284.

Williams, G. V., and Goldman-Rakic, P. S. (1995). Modulation of memory fields by dopamine D1 receptors in prefrontal cortex. *Nature* 376, 572–575.

Williams, M. J., and Adinoff, B. (2008). The role of acetylcholine in cocaine addiction. *Neuropsychopharmacology* 33, 1779–1797.

Willuhn, I., Burgeno, L. M., Everitt, B. J., and Phillips, P. E. (2012). Hierarchical recruitment of phasic dopamine signaling in the striatum during the progression of cocaine use. *Proc. Natl. Acad. Sci. U.S.A.* 109, 20703–20708.

Wise, R. A. (2002). Brain reward circuitry: insights from unsensed incentives. *Neuron* 36, 229–240.

Wise, R. A. (1994). "A brief history of the anhedonia hypothesis," in *Appetite: Neural and Behavioural Base*, eds C. R. Legg and D. A. Both (Oxford: Oxford University Press), 234–263.

Witten, I. B., Lin, S. C., Brodsky, M., Prakash, R., Diester, I., Anikeeva, P., et al. (2010). Cholinergic interneurons control local circuit activity and cocaine conditioning. *Science* 330, 1677–1681.

Woolf, N. J., and Butcher, L. L. (2011). Cholinergic systems mediate action from movement to higher consciousness. *Behav. Brain Res.* 221, 488–498.

Zinberg, N. E. (1984). *Drug, Set, and Setting: The Basis for Controlled Intoxicant Use.* New Haven: Yale University Press.

Zocchi, A., and Pert, A. (1994). Alterations in striatal acetylcholine overflow by cocaine, morphine, and MK-801: relationship to locomotor output. *Psychopharmacology (Berl.)* 115, 297–304.

Zweifel, L. S., Argilli, E., Bonci, A., and Palmiter, R. D. (2008). Role of NMDA receptors in dopamine neurons for plasticity and addictive behaviors. *Neuron* 59, 486–496.

20

The effect of retrieval focus and emotional valence on the medial temporal lobe activity during autobiographical recollection

Ekaterina Denkova[1]*, Sanda Dolcos[2] and Florin Dolcos[2,3,4]*

[1] Alberta Cognitive Neuroscience Group, University of Alberta, Edmonton, AB, Canada
[2] Psychology Department, University of Illinois at Urbana-Champaign, Urbana, IL, USA
[3] Neuroscience Program, University of Illinois at Urbana-Champaign, Urbana, IL, USA
[4] Beckman Institute for Advanced Science and Technology, University of Illinois at Urbana-Champaign, Urbana, IL, USA

Correspondence:
Ekaterina Denkova and Florin Dolcos, Affective, Cognitive, and Clinical Neuroscience Lab, The Neuroscience Program, Department of Psychology, Beckman Institute for Advanced Science and Technology, University of Illinois at Urbana-Champaign, 405 North Mathews Avenue, Room 2057, Urbana, IL 61801, USA
e-mail: ekaterina.denkova@yahoo.ca; fdolcos@illinois.edu

Laboratory-based episodic memory studies, using micro-events (pictures/words), point to a role of the amygdala (AMY), an emotion-based region, in the encoding and retrieval of emotionally valenced memories. However, autobiographical memory (AM) studies, using real-life personal events, do not conclusively support AMY's involvement in AM recollection. This could be due to differences in instructions across the AM studies – i.e., whether emotional aspects were explicitly emphasized or not. The present study investigated the effect of retrieval focus on activity in emotion (AMY) and memory (hippocampus – HC) based regions of the medial temporal lobe in 17 subjects, who remembered emotional AMs while event-related fMRI data were recorded. The retrieval focus was manipulated by instructions to focus either on emotional (*Emotion* condition) or on other contextual (*Context* condition) details of the recollected AMs. The effect of retrieval focus according to the valence of AMs was also investigated by involving an equal proportion of positive and negative AMs. There were four main findings, showing both similarities and differences in retrieving positive and negative AMs. Regarding similarities, (1) focusing on Emotion was associated with increased scores of subjective re-experience of emotion and increased activity in the left AMY, for both positive and negative AMs, compared to focusing on Context; (2) the subjective emotional ratings were also positively correlated with bilateral AMY activity for both positive and negative AMs. Regarding differences, (3) focusing on Emotion was associated with increased activity for positive but not for negative AMs in the right AMY, and with (4) opposing patterns of activity linked to the valence of AMs in the left HC – i.e., increased activity for positive and decreased activity for negative AMs. These findings shed light on the role of AMY and HC in emotional AM recollection, linked to the retrieval focus and the valence of memories.

Keywords: personal memories, retrieval goal, fMRI, MTL, valence

INTRODUCTION

Remembering emotional autobiographical memories (AMs) is an integral part of everyday life that may influence personal well-being and psychological health. Thinking about emotional personal experiences can be used to re-experience positive affect (Bluck and Alea, 2009a) or to reverse negative mood (Josephson et al., 1996; Joormann et al., 2007). However, empirical research has mainly focused on the consequences of reflecting on negative experiences, and has produced contradictory findings. Reflecting on negative events has been found either to reduce the intensity of those experiences (Pennebaker and Graybeal, 2001; Wilson and Gilbert, 2008) or to increase negative affect (Mor and Winquist, 2002; Nolen-Hoeksema et al., 2008; Smith and Alloy, 2009), which may lead to depression. These inconsistent findings might be due, in part, to the type of focus people adopt when recollecting personal experiences, such as focusing on the emotional aspects or on other non-emotional details of the experience (e.g., when and where personal events occurred).

Neuroimaging evidence from "emotional" AM studies[1] (Svoboda et al., 2006) has associated the retrieval of emotional AMs with activity in emotion (amygdala – AMY) and memory (hippocampus – HC) related medial temporal lobe (MTL) regions (Markowitsch et al., 2000; Piefke et al., 2003). Moreover, activity in the AMY and HC was associated with the emotional intensity of memories (e.g., Botzung et al., 2010). This evidence is consistent with findings from laboratory-based episodic memory studies, which have demonstrated greater engagement of both emotion

[1] Referring to AM studies specifically eliciting the recall of emotional memories, as opposed to "standard" AM studies, referring to studies without explicit instructions to retrieve emotional aspects of memories (see meta-analysis by Svoboda et al., 2006).

and memory MTL systems during encoding (Dolcos et al., 2004; Kensinger and Corkin, 2004; Kensinger and Schacter, 2006; Sergerie et al., 2006), consolidation (Ritchey et al., 2008), and retrieval (Hamann et al., 1999; Dolcos et al., 2005; Sergerie et al., 2006) of emotional items (reviewed in Dolcos et al., 2012). However, the majority of the "standard" AM studies have not identified AMY involvement during retrieval of personal events or its modulation by emotional intensity (Maguire and Frith, 2003; Addis et al., 2004; but see Daselaar et al., 2008).

The inconsistencies in the AMY engagement during retrieval of AMs could be due to several factors (Greenberg et al., 2005; Denkova et al., 2006; Markowitsch and Staniloiu, 2011). First, it is possible that differences in image acquisition parameters and in statistical analyses (whole-brain vs. ROI analysis) could, at least partially, account for the inconsistencies in AMY activation across these studies (Greenberg et al., 2005). Second, AMY may be involved only in recollections that are sufficiently vivid and strong to elicit a re-experience of the associated emotion (Ochsner and Schacter, 2000). Third, because of the complexity and multifaceted nature of autobiographical events, it is possible that more elaborative processing and cognitive resources needed for their constructive retrieval may attenuate AMY's involvement during the "standard" AM studies (Denkova et al., 2006; Dolcos et al., 2012). Finally, given that the "standard" AM studies commonly ask participants to retrieve a specific event without a clear and explicit focus on emotional aspects of recollections (Svoboda et al., 2006), and that the episodic laboratory-based memory studies suggest a goal-modulated involvement of the AMY (Smith et al., 2006), it is reasonable to infer that the retrieval instructions given to the participants may influence the AMY engagement during the recollection of personal events. However, this possibility has never been tested and clarified in the AM neuroimaging literature.

The main goal of the present study was to investigate the effect of manipulating the retrieval focus (on emotional vs. on non-emotional, contextual, aspects) on the involvement of emotion (AMY) and memory (HC) related MTL regions during remembering of emotional AMs. In addition, the role of *valence* (positive or negative), which is an important and understudied aspect of AMs, was also investigated. Available evidence suggests that positive and negative AMs may be governed by different mechanisms and lead to different outcomes. Specifically, positive or negative affective biases in AM recollection are closely linked to personal well-being or impaired mental health, respectively. For instance, a positive memory bias in recollections of past personal events and in simulations of future personal events is reported in normal population and healthy aging (Bluck and Alea, 2009b; Denkova et al., 2012; Finnbogadottir and Berntsen, 2012; Szpunar et al., 2012; Rasmussen and Berntsen, 2013), while a negative memory bias is reported in people with/or susceptible to affective disorders, such as depression and post-traumatic stress disorder (PTSD) (MacLeod and Byrne, 1996; Brewin et al., 1999; Nolen-Hoeksema et al., 2008). The valence of AMs can also modulate brain activity. For example, across the few AMs neuroimaging studies considering the valence of memories, recollection of positive personal events has been shown to engage MTL regions linked to greater re-experience of positive events, and orbito-frontal regions, which are involved in the representation of rewarding experiences; on the other hand, recollection of negative AMs engages lateral temporal regions, linked to the processing of negative emotions (Markowitsch et al., 2003; Piefke et al., 2003, but see Vandekerckhove et al., 2005, which failed to observe such an effect).

To investigate these issues, fMRI data were recorded while participants focused either on emotional (*Emotion* condition) or on other contextual (*Context* condition) details during elaboration of recollected positive and negative AMs. In the Emotion condition, participants were instructed to remember past events by focusing on the emotional aspects of their recollections, whereas in the Context condition participants were instructed to remember past events by focusing on other, non-emotional, contextual details (e.g., details about the time and place of personal events). Based on the extant evidence, we made the following predictions. Concerning the behavioral results, we predicted increased emotional ratings for both positive and negative AMs when focusing on emotional details of the recollected AMs. Concerning the fMRI results, we predicted both similar and dissociable effects in the MTL regions, linked to the retrieval focus and the emotional valence of the AMs. Specifically, we expected overall similar greater engagement of MTL activity during AMs recollection in the *Emotion* condition than in the *Context* condition, for both positive and negative memories. We also expected a link between increased emotional ratings and AMY activity in the *Emotion* condition. Finally, based on evidence that positive and negative AMs may be governed by different mechanisms, we also expected a dissociable engagement of MTL regions according to the valence of memories, possibly with positive memories leading to greater MTL engagement, particularly in the *Emotion* condition.

MATERIALS AND METHODS

PARTICIPANTS

Eighteen right-handed native English speaking young adults with no history of neurological, psychological, or psychiatric illness participated in this study (six men; age range 18–46, mean = 26 years SD = 7.02). One subject dropped out the study after the first run of the fMRI session, hence, data from 17 subjects (six men, mean age = 26.06 years; SD = 7.20) were analyzed. The experimental protocol was approved by the Institutional Health Research Ethics Board, and all participants provided written informed consent and received payment for their participation.

COLLECTION AND SELECTION OF EMOTIONAL AUTOBIOGRAPHICAL MEMORIES

Personal memories were elicited from each participant during an interview performed ~5 weeks prior to the fMRI session, similar to other AM neuroimaging studies (Markowitsch et al., 2000; Maguire and Frith, 2003; Piefke et al., 2003; Addis et al., 2004; Botzung et al., 2008). This procedure allows increased control over the properties of the memories to be used in different trial types, as compared to involving AM retrieval directly in the scanning session (Maguire, 2001; Cabeza and St Jacques, 2007; St Jacques, 2012). In addition, it attenuates the disadvantage of reactivation by interposing sufficient time between the pre-scan interview and the subsequent scanning session (Maguire and Mummery, 1999). We used an autobiographical memory questionnaire (AMQ) specifically constructed to target the assessment of emotional personal episodes and their recollective properties (Denkova et al., 2012). The AMQ comprised a list of 115 verbal cues for distinct life events (e.g., "the birth of a family member," "being hospitalized"), resulted from a combination and extension of lists employed by other authors (Levine et al., 2002; Markowitsch et al., 2003; Sharot et al., 2007). For each cue, participants were asked to remember a unique episode from their life, that occurred in a specific place and time (e.g., one instance when s/he played in a specific basketball game), rather than remembering general or repeated events (e.g., playing basketball in high school). Importantly, the memories had to be accompanied by the recollection of being personally involved, rather than hearing about them from others. Upon recollection, participants were asked to provide a brief description of the memory, which was then used as a personalized memory cue during the fMRI scanning; at the time of collecting the AMs, participants were naïve to the specific purpose of the pre-scanning interview. To assess phenomenological characteristics of each event, participants dated the memory and rated it on several Likert scales, similar to those used in other AM studies (Addis et al., 2004; Greenberg et al., 2005), as follows: Emotional Valence (using a 7-point scale: −3 = very negative, 0 = neutral, and +3 = very positive), Emotional Intensity, Personal Significance, Vividness (i.e., the amount of visuo-perceptual details), the amount of Contextual Details, and the Frequency of Retrieval (all of the latter used a 7-point scale: 1 = not at all, 7 = extremely).

For each participant, we selected the 40 most emotional memories (20 positive and 20 negative), based on the ratings provided on the AMQ (i.e., rated 2 or 3 and −2 or −3, respectively). Half of the selected memories, with an equal proportion of positive and negative AMs, were assigned to an *Emotion* Retrieval Focus AM condition (10 positive and 10 negative), and the other half of AMs were assigned to a *Context* Retrieval Focus AM condition (10 positive and 10 negative). This resulted in four AM event types: Emotion Focus Positive, Emotion Focus Negative, Context Focus Positive, and Context Focus Negative Memories. To ensure that any differences between the two retrieval foci/goals during the fMRI session would not be due to initial differences in the properties of the memories assigned to the Emotion and Context conditions, the positive and negative memories of the two conditions were matched as closely as possible in terms of phenomenological properties (see **Table 1**). The descriptions provided by the participants were used to create memory cues specific for each participant. If necessary, the descriptions were slightly adapted to be matched as closely as possible in terms of length and grammatical complexity. Four other memories were also selected and used in practice trials before the fMRI session.

fMRI TASKS

The fMRI session comprised two AM tasks, according to retrieval focus (*Emotion* and *Context*), and a semantic memory (SM) control task. Given the goal of the present investigation, in each AM task, half of the memories were positive and the other half were negative. Just before performing the fMRI tasks, participants were given detailed instructions and examples for the tasks they had to perform in the scanner. In addition, participants performed practice trials in order to familiarize themselves with the tasks and to ensure that they understood the instructions.

The autobiographical memory tasks

Participants were asked to retrieve the memories associated with each personalized memory cue by either focusing on emotional (*Emotion* condition) or focusing on other contextual (*Context* condition) aspects of their positive and negative memories. For the *Emotion* condition, participants were instructed to remember the specific event and focus on the emotional aspects of their memories, including associated sensations and feelings that they may have triggered (e.g., butterflies in the stomach, palpitations). For the *Context* condition, participants were instructed to remember the specific event and focus on other, non-emotional, contextual aspects of their memories, by retrieving as many contextual details as possible (e.g., about where and when the event occurred, who else was involved, etc.). Each memory cue was preceded by an instruction cue, as follows: "Remember Emotion," for the Emotion condition, and "Remember Context," for the Context condition, respectively. Once the memory cue appeared on the screen, participants had to indicate by a button press that they recognized the cue as belonging to them, and then continued remembering details of the event until cued to rate the recollected memory. Each recollection was rated on three five-point Likert scales including Emotional Intensity, Vividness, and Reliving (1 = very low; 5 = very high). The participants were instructed to make quick (spontaneous) and accurate responses and to use the whole scale.

The semantic memory control task

In line with other AM functional neuroimaging studies (Greenberg et al., 2005; Young et al., 2012), we used a control

Table 1 | Phenomenological properties of the selected autobiographical memories.

	Negative		*t* test, *p*	Positive		*t* test, *p*
	Emotion	**Context**		**Emotion**	**Context**	
Emotional intensity	5.68 (0.51)	5.70 (0.52)	0.60	5.25 (0.83)	5.29 (0.82)	0.20
Vividness	5.19 (0.80)	5.15 (0.67)	0.47	5.54 (0.61)	5.49 (0.73)	0.52
Contextual details	4.94 (1.06)	4.92 (1.12)	0.72	5.38 (1.17)	5.30 (1.25)	0.32
Personal significance	4.42 (1.02)	4.32 (1.08)	0.09	4.69 (1.01)	4.73 (0.93)	0.61
Frequency of rehearsal	3.33 (1.04)	3.32 (0.96)	0.87	3.64 (0.96)	3.54 (0.95)	0.20

Standard deviations are given in parentheses. There were no significant differences between memories assigned to the Emotion condition and those assigned to the Context condition.

condition involving SM retrieval. Specifically, the SM task involved generation of exemplars from 20 different semantic categories (e.g., musical instruments, sports, vegetables) (Battig and Montague, 1969), which like the AM retrieval involves search in memory and extended retrieval time. The participants were presented with a semantic category name cue (e.g., fruits, vegetables) and instructed to recall as many exemplars as possible for each category. Each semantic category cue was preceded by an instruction cue ("Generate Examples"). Once the category cue appeared on the screen, participants had to indicate by a button press that they started recalling exemplars from the category, and then they continued recalling until cued again for memory ratings. To be consistent with AM conditions, each exemplar generation was rated on three five-point Likert scales appropriate for SM generation – i.e., Vividness, Difficulty of the task (1 = very low; 5 = very high), and approximate Number of the recalled items (1 = 1 to 3 items; 5 = 15 or more items).

fMRI DESIGN AND PROCEDURE

The AM conditions and the SM control condition had the same general structure (see **Figure 1**). Each trial began with an instruction screen for 2 s, immediately followed by a memory cue for 4 s. After the cue offset, a fixation screen was presented for 10 s during which participants elaborated their personal memories or generated exemplars. The end of the retrieval period was marked by the presentation of an instructions screen for upcoming ratings, for 1.5 s. Then, each of the three ratings was presented for 2.5 s and in a counterbalanced order across trials. The ratings were followed by an inter-trial interval of variable duration (2–9 s, average = 6 s), before the beginning of the next trial.

The scanning session was divided into two parts of four runs. Each run started with a 6-s fixation, to allow stabilization of the fMRI signal, and comprised five trials from each condition (Emotion, Context, and Semantic). To avoid induction of longer-lasting effects, the trials within each run were pseudo-randomized, so that no more than two consecutive trials of the same type were presented. To prevent possible biases resulted from using the same run order, participants were assigned different run orders. Similar to other AM neuroimaging studies (Greenberg et al., 2005), in order to increase statistical power, the four runs from the first part were immediately repeated in the second part of the scanning session, and the order of the runs was counterbalanced across participants. Stimuli were projected on a screen directly behind the subjects' heads within the scanner, which they viewed through a mirror.

All stimuli appeared in white letters against a black background created in Adobe Photoshop. The CIGAL software (http://www.nitrc.org/projects/cigal/) was used for stimulus presentation and collection of behavioral responses during the fMRI session. All responses were made on a four-button MRI-compatible response box placed under the subject's right hand; the fifth rating was indicated by the participants with a double click on button #1.

MRI DATA COLLECTION

MRI data were recorded using a 1.5-T Siemens Sonata scanner. The anatomical images were 3D MPRAGE anatomical series (repetition time [TR] = 1600 ms, echo time [TE] = 3.82 ms, field of view [FOV] = 256 mm × 256 mm, number of slices = 112, voxel size = 1 mm × 1 mm × 1 mm). The functional images consisted of series of images acquired axially using an echoplanar sequence (TR = 2000 ms, TE = 40 ms, FOV = 256 mm × 256 mm, number of slices = 28, voxel size = 4 mm × 4 mm × 4 mm).

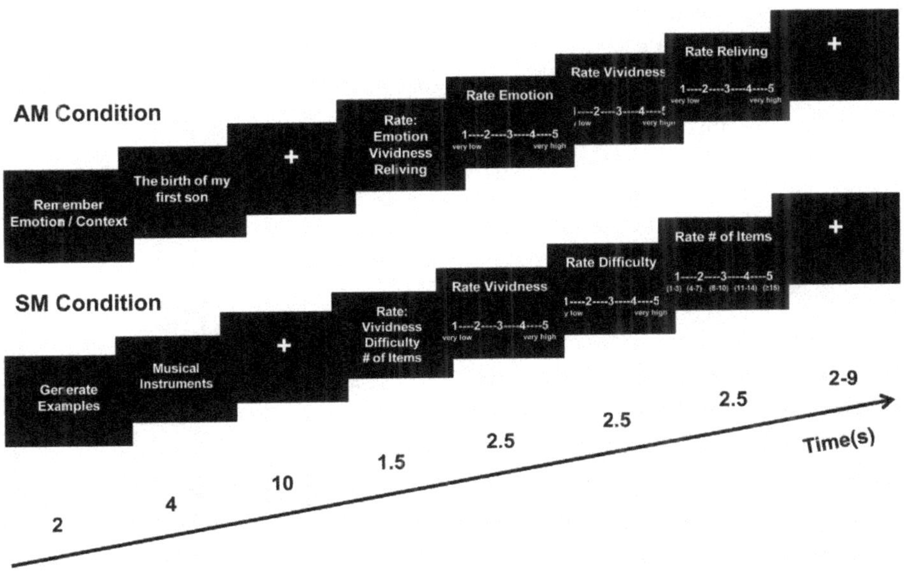

FIGURE 1 | Diagram of the task. During the Autobiographical Memory (AM) conditions, participants remembered highly emotional personal memories by focusing either on emotional (Emotion) or on other contextual (Context) aspects of their recollections, and then rated each AM for Emotional Intensity, Vividness, and Reliving on five-point scales. During the control Semantic Memory (SM) condition, participants generated as many exemplars as possible from a given semantic category, and then rated each of them for Vividness, Difficulty, and Number of Items on five-point scales.

BEHAVIORAL DATA ANALYSIS

To investigate the effect of retrieval focus on the qualities of the negative and positive remembered memories, we performed repeated-measures ANOVA with three factors: Focus (Emotion, Context), Valence (Negative, Positive), and Ratings (Emotional Intensity, Reliving, Vividness).

fMRI DATA ANALYSIS

Statistical analyses, performed with SPM2 (Statistical Parametric Mapping), were preceded by the following pre-processing steps: Quality Assurance, TR Alignment, Motion Correction, Coregistration, Normalization, and Smoothing (8 mm full-width half maximum isotropic Kernel). At the individual level, each event was modeled by the canonical hemodynamic response function (*hrf*) and its temporal derivate. Movement parameters calculated during the realignment were included as parameters of no interest to control for movement artifacts. According to previous AM neuroimaging studies (Addis et al., 2007), to allow for reading the cue, the *hrf* was time-locked to 2 s (1TR) following the onset of the memory cues, in the Emotion and Context AM conditions, and 1 s (0.5TR) after the onset of the category cue, in the SM condition. Consistent with these, investigation of the RT data showed that the recognition of the AM cues occurred at an average RT of 1.67 s (±0.44), and the beginning of exemplar generation in the SM condition occurred at an average RT of 1.03 s (±0.40). For the fMRI analysis according to focus and valence, we selected randomly only 10 SM events to match the numbers of each of the four AM event types. Individual contrasts were computed directly between the different AM event types (e.g., Emotion Positive vs. Context Positive, Emotion Negative vs. Context Negative). These individual contrasts were then entered into group-level t tests, to perform random-effects analyses. The SPM analyses were complemented by analyses performed with in-house MATLAB tools (Dolcos and McCarthy, 2006; Denkova et al., 2010), which allowed extraction of the fMRI signal and examination of the time course of activity related to different conditions, across the whole length of the trials.

To investigate the effects of retrieval focus on positive memories in MTL regions, we compared positive AMs with Emotion focus and positive AMs with Context focus (Emotion Positive > Context Positive and Context Positive > Emotion Positive). Similarly, to investigate the effects of retrieval focus on negative memories, we performed the following comparisons: Emotion Negative > Context Negative and Context Negative > Emotion Negative. Additionally, to also investigate the effect of valence within each retrieval focus, we compared positive and negative AMs with Emotion focus (Emotion Positive > Emotion Negative and Emotion Negative > Emotion Positive) and positive and negative AMs with Context focus (Context Positive > Context Negative and Context Negative > Context Positive).

The common effects of the retrieval focus on both positive and negative memories were investigated through conjunction analyses [e.g. (Emotion Positive vs. Context Positive) ∩ (Emotion Negative vs. Context Negative)]. The dissociating effects of the retrieval focus and valence were investigated through interaction analyses using paired t tests [e.g., (Emotion Positive vs. Context Positive) vs. (Emotion Negative vs. Context Negative)], whose outputs were inclusively masked with the corresponding direct effect (e.g., Emotion Positive vs. Context Positive) to ensure that the interaction difference is due to an existing increased difference in the comparisons/contrasts of interest. Finally, to investigate whether differential activity in the MTL according to the focus of retrieval is linked to differences in the subjective feeling of emotion, linear regression analyses were performed between difference scores in self-reported emotion ratings (Emotion ratings minus Context ratings) and MTL activity for Emotion > Context contrasts, for positive and negative AMs, respectively.

As the main goal of the study was to investigate the effects of retrieval focus and valence of AMs on emotion- and memory-related MTL regions, we used anatomical masks of the AMY and HC, based on the Wake Forest University Pick Atlas toolbox. Overall, for all ROI analyses in the AMY and HC, identified as regions of *a priori* interest, we used a statistical threshold of $p < 0.05$ and an extent threshold of five contiguous voxels. For completeness, we also report results of whole-brain analyses for regions outside of the MTL. For these analyses, an intensity threshold of $p < 0.001$ was used for the specific direct contrasts and a threshold of $p < 0.005$ was used for the interactions; the extent threshold was of 10 contiguous voxels.

RESULTS

BEHAVIORAL RESULTS

Increased re-experiencing of emotion for both positive and negative AMs in the Emotion condition

Repeated-measures ANOVA revealed a main effect of focus [$F_{(1,16)} = 6.33$, $p = 0.02$], indicating higher ratings for the memories retrieved with the Emotion focus. This effect was qualified by a focus x ratings interaction [$F_{(1,16)} = 4.12$, $p = 0.03$], driven by an increase only for the emotional intensity ratings of AMs retrieved with an emotional focus (Emotion condition); no significant increase was observed in the Reliving and Vividness ratings. The increase was significant for both positive (3.21 vs. 3.03, $p = 0.02$) and negative (3.38 vs. 3.07, $p = 0.003$) AMs (see **Figure 2**), thus

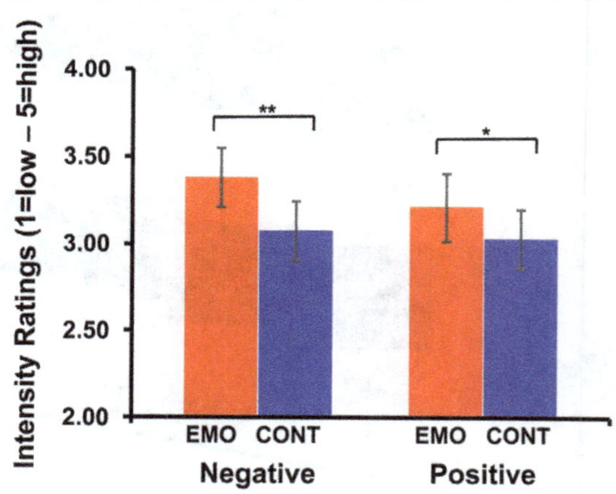

FIGURE 2 | Increased subjective re-experiencing of emotion during Emotion focus retrieval. Self-reported ratings for emotional intensity were higher in the Emotion (EMO) than in the Context (CONT) condition, for both negative (**$p < 0.005$) and positive (*$p < 0.05$) autobiographical memories.

precluding a significant focus x valence x ratings interaction [$F_{(1, 16)} = 1.30$, $p = 0.29$]. Overall, the ratings assessed immediately after recollecting AMs during the scanning sessions showed that the manipulation of the retrieval focus (Emotion vs. Context) dissociated the subjective re-experience of emotion for both positive and negative memories, without affecting significantly the subjectively reported ratings for Reliving and Vividness.

fMRI RESULTS

The present fMRI results revealed both common and dissociable effects of retrieval focus (Emotion vs. Context), linked to the valence of AMs, in emotion (AMY) and memory (HC) related MTL regions.

COMMON EFFECTS OF RETRIEVAL FOCUS ON POSITIVE AND NEGATIVE AM RETRIEVAL IN AMY

Increased activity in left AMY for both positive and negative memories in the Emotion condition

Manipulation of the retrieval focus was associated with increased activity in the left AMY for both positive and negative memories, in the Emotion compared to the Context condition (Emotion > Context) (see **Figure 3** and **Table 2**). Common engagement of this left AMY area during retrieval of both positive and negative AMs was revealed by the following conjunction analysis: [(Emotion Positive > Context Positive) ∩ (Emotion Negative > Context Negative)].

AMY activity linked to subjective re-experiencing of emotion for both positive and negative memories

The difference in AMY activity between Emotion and Context (Emotion > Context) was positively correlated with the difference in emotional intensity ratings between Emotion and Context (intensity ratings in Emotion condition minus intensity ratings in Context condition) (see **Figure 4**). This effect was observed in both left and right AMY and for both positive and negative AMs. For negative memories, the AMY areas showing the correlation with the ratings also overlapped with the area showing greater activity in the Emotion than in the Context condition, in the left ($x = -28$, $y = -1$, $z = -10$; $R = 0.72$, $p = 0.001$), but not in the right ($x = 24$, $y = -1$, $z = -13$; $R = 0.53$, $p = 0.03$) hemisphere. For positive memories, the areas of left and right AMY showing the correlations with emotional ratings ($x = -28$, $y = 7$, $z = -17$; $R = 0.62$, $p = 0.004$, and $x = 24$, $y = 7$, $z = -21$; $R = 0.62$, $p = 0.004$, respectively) showed only very little overlaps with the areas showing increased activity for Emotion compared to the Context condition.

DISSOCIABLE EFFECTS OF RETRIEVAL FOCUS ON POSITIVE AND NEGATIVE AM RETRIEVAL IN AMY AND HC

Increased right AMY activity for positive but not for negative memories in the Emotion condition

Focusing on Emotion compared to Context led to a dissociable pattern of activity in the right AMY for positive and negative AMs (see **Figure 3** and **Table 2**). Specifically, retrieval of positive memories was associated with greater activity in the Emotion than in the Context condition (Emotion Positive > Context Positive), while retrieval of negative memories produced similar effects in the Emotion and Context conditions (Emotion Negative = Context Negative). These effects were confirmed by a repeated-measures ANOVA, performed on the extracted signal, which revealed a significant valence x focus interaction [$F_{(1, 16)} = 6.84$, $p = 0.02$]

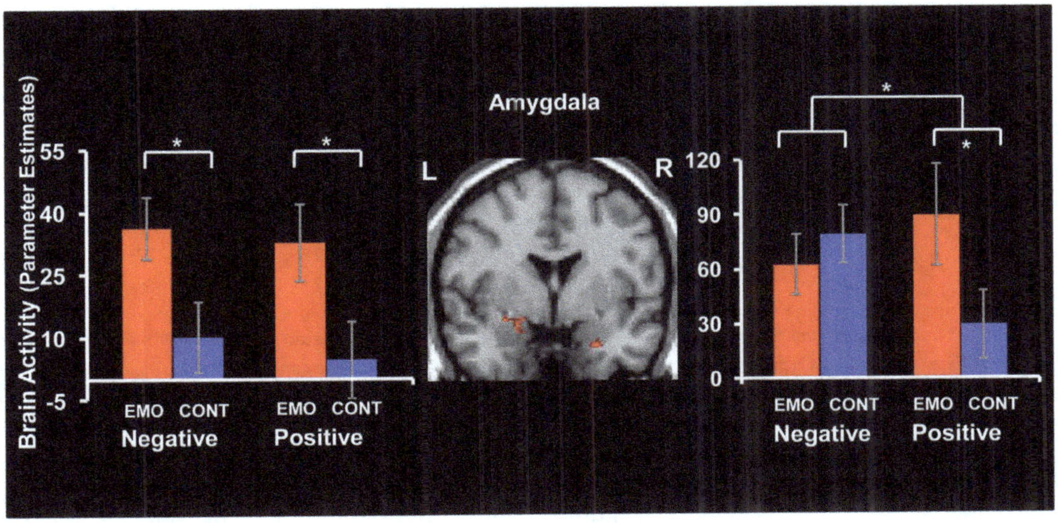

FIGURE 3 | Common and dissociable effects of retrieval focus in the amygdala (AMY), for positive and negative memories. Focusing on Emotion (EMO) compared to focusing on Context (CONT) led to similar increases of activity in the left AMY (left panel) for both positive and negative memories; dissociable patterns of activity linked to valence were observed in the right AMY (right panel). The conjunction and interaction maps for the left and right AMY, respectively, are superimposed on a high resolution brain image displayed in a coronal view. The bar graphs represent the contrasts estimates extracted from representative voxels in the left and right AMY, respectively. The error bars correspond to the standard errors of the means. L = Left, R = Right.

Table 2 | Activations in MTL ROIs linked to the retrieval focus and emotional valence of memories.

MTL regions	Side	Talairach coordinates			*T* score	Cluster size
		x	*y*	*z*		
A. DIRECT CONTRASTS						
Emotion Negative vs. Context Negative						
Amygdala	L	−20	−4	−10	2.76	13
	L	−32	−1	−10	2.43	
Emotion Positive vs. Context Positive						
Amygdala	L	−32	−1	−10	3.56	32
	R	20	3	−24	3.57	35
Hippocampus	L	−32	−16	−16	3.99	67
	R	32	−27	−5	3.24	52
Context Negative vs. Emotion Negative						
Hippocampus	L	−32	−39	−1	3.56	8
	L	−40	−16	−20	2.32	8
Emotion Positive vs. Emotion Negative						
Hippocampus	L	−36	−24	−9	3.39	21
Context Negative vs. Context Positive						
Amygdala	L	−32	−8	−13	3.59	5
	R	24	−1	−20	3.33	35
Hippocampus	L	−32	−12	−9	4.33	67
	R	32	−12	−13	4.47	59
B. CONJUNCTION						
(Emotion Negative vs. Context Negative) ∩ (Emotion Positive vs. Context Positive)						
Amygdala	L	−32	−1	−10	3.56	12
	L	−24	−1	−13	2.79	
C. INTERACTIONS						
(Emotion Positive vs. Context Positive) vs. (Emotion Negative vs. Context Negative)						
Amygdala	R	24	3	−24	2.66	11
Hippocampus	L	−32	−16	−16	5.06	41
Hippocampus	R	32	−31	−5	2.97	24
(Context Negative vs. Emotion Negative) vs. (Context Positive vs. Emotion Positive)						
Hippocampus	L	−36	−16	−16	3.60	7
	L	−32	−27	−5	2.70	8
(Emotion Positive vs. Emotion Negative) vs. (Context Positive vs. Context Negative)						
Hippocampus	L	−32	−16	−16	5.06	19
(Context Negative vs. Context Positive) vs. (Emotion Negative vs. Emotion Positive)						
Amygdala	R	24	−1	−23	2.61	8
Hippocampus	L	−32	−16	−16	5.06	46
Hippocampus	R	32	−32	−9	3.20	32

Significant activations resulting from direct contrasts, conjunctions, and interactions analyses in a priori targeted MTL ROIs (AMY and HC) are reported. An intensity threshold of $p < 0.05$ and an extent threshold of 5 contiguous voxels were used for all ROI analyses. For the conjunction analyses, a threshold of $p < 0.05$ was used in each of the contributing contrast, and for the interaction analyses the interaction contrast was inclusively masked with the corresponding direct contrast set up at $p < 0.05$ (see Materials and Methods for details). MTL = Medial Temporal Lobe; L = left, R = right.

This interaction was driven by a significant increase in the Emotion condition compared to the Context condition for positive ($p = 0.01$) but not for negative ($p = 0.44$) AMs.

Opposing patterns of activity in the left hippocampus for positive and negative memories

Comparison of the effect of retrieval focus also identified increased activity for positive (Emotion Positive > Context Positive) and decreased activity for negative (Emotion Negative < Context Negative) AMs in the left HC, in the Emotion condition (see **Figure 5** and **Table 2**). The decreased activity observed for the negative AMs in the left HC extended more posteriorly to the parahippocampal gyrus. Although similar overall patterns of activity were observed in the right HC, only the increased response for positive AMs when focusing on Emotion compared to Context was significant (Emotion Positive > Context Positive).

These effects were confirmed by repeated-measures ANOVAs performed on the extracted signal from peak voxels, which, in the left HC, revealed a significant valence x focus interaction [$F_{(1,16)} = 12.94$, $p = 0.002$]. This interaction was driven by a significant increase for positive memories ($p = 0.009$) and a significant decrease for negative memories ($p = 0.048$) in the Emotion compared to the Context condition. Similarly, the effect in the right HC was confirmed by a repeated-measures ANOVA revealing a significant valence x focus interaction [$F_{(1,16)} = 6.66$, $p = 0.02$], which was driven by a significant increase for positive memories ($p = 0.03$) in the Emotion compared to the Context condition.

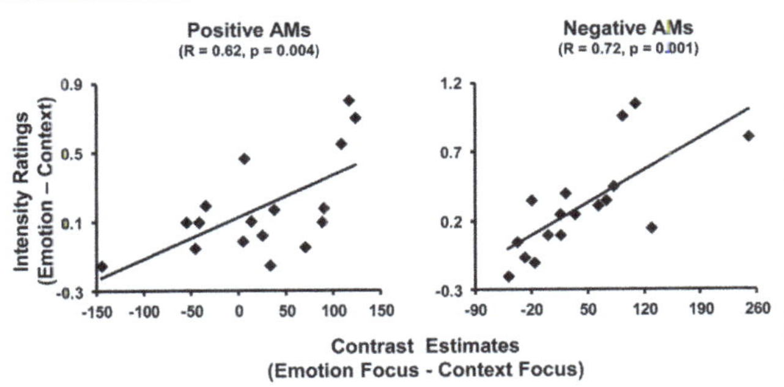

FIGURE 4 | Positive correlation between activity in the AMY and self-reported emotional ratings. Differential activity in the AMY for Emotion and Context focuses was positively related to the difference in emotion intensity ratings between Emotion and Context conditions during recollection of positive (left panel) and negative (right panel) memories. The scatter plots are based on contrast estimates for Emotion – Context conditions extracted from the peak voxel of the areas showing the co-variation with the differences in ratings, in the left AMY. Similar co-variations were also identified in right AMY (not shown).

EFFECTS OF RETRIEVAL FOCUS ON BRAIN REGIONS OUTSIDE OF THE MTL

While the primary focus in the present report concerns the effects of retrieval focus on the MTL activity during retrieving positive and negative AMs, for completeness, results of whole-brain analyses are also reported (see **Table 3**).

DISCUSSION

The present study investigated the behavioral and brain imaging effects of retrieval instructions, linked to the valence of memories, on AM recollection. There were four main findings, showing both similarities and differences in retrieving positive and negative AMs. Regarding similarities, (1) the behavioral data showed that focusing on Emotion was associated with increased scores of subjective re-experience of emotion, and the fMRI data identified increased activity in the left AMY, for both positive and negative AMs, compared to focusing on the Context; (2) the subjective emotional ratings were also positively correlated with bilateral AMY activity for both positive and negative AMs. Regarding differences, (3) focusing on Emotion was associated with increased activity for positive but not for negative AMs in the right AMY, and with (4) opposing patterns of activity linked to the valence of AMs in the left HC – i.e., increased activity for positive AMs and decreased activity for negative AMs. These findings will be discussed in turn below.

COMMON EFFECTS OF RETRIEVAL FOCUS ON POSITIVE AND NEGATIVE AM RETRIEVAL IN AMY

(1) Manipulation of the retrieval focus was associated with increased activity in the left AMY for both positive and negative memories in the Emotion compared to the Context condition

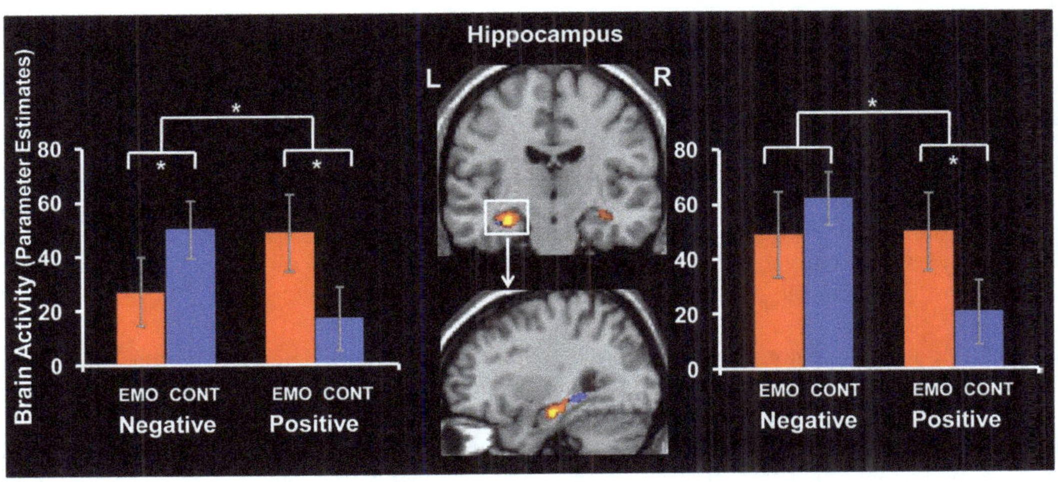

FIGURE 5 | Dissociable effects of retrieval focus in the hippocampus (HC) for positive and negative memories. Focusing on Emotion (EMO) compared to focusing on Context (CONT) led to increased activity for positive and decreased activity for negative memories in the left hippocampus (HC) (left panel). Although, overall, a similar effect was observed in the right HC (right panel), only the increased activity for positive memories was statistically significant. The interaction map for the left and right HC is superimposed on a high resolution brain image displayed in a coronal view (top panel). The sagittal view (bottom panel) illustrates the posterior extension of activity in the left HC (blue blob), for negative memories (Context Negative > Emotion Negative). The bar graphs represent the contrasts estimates extracted from representative voxels of the interaction effects in left and right HC. The error bars correspond to the standard errors of the means. L = Left, R = Right.

Table 3 | Whole-brain activations linked to retrieval focus and valence of memories.

Brain regions	BA	Side	Talairach coordinates			*T* score	Cluster size
			x	*y*	*z*		
A. DIRECT CONTRASTS							
Emotion Positive vs. Context Positive							
Inferior frontal gyrus	47	R	28	35	−5	6.08	54
Anterior cingulate	10	R	20	47	1	5.37	
Middle temporal gyrus	21	L	−56	0	−7	5.63	26
Superior temporal gyrus	38	L	−56	11	−7	4.83	
Precuneus	7	L	−4	−59	62	4.97	10
Inferior frontal gyrus	44	L	−55	12	10	4.91	10
Inferior frontal gyrus	47	L	−36	19	−8	4.85	41
Emotion Positive vs. Emotion Negative							
Precentral gyrus	4	L	−44	−18	34	4.68	11
Context Negative vs. Context Positive							
Inferior frontal gyrus	47	L	−36	19	−14	4.84	13
Hippocampus		L	−32	−12	−9	4.40	5
Hippocampus		R	32	−12	−13	4.47	5
B. INTERACTIONS							
(Emotion Positive vs. Context Positive) vs. (Emotion Negative vs. Context Negative)							
Middle temporal gyrus	21	L	−60	−4	−3	6.20	13
Hippocampus		L	−32	−16	−16	5.06	17
Caudate (tail)		L	−24	−42	13	4.98	24
Postcentral gyrus	3	L	−48	−18	34	4.51	28
Middle frontal gyrus	10	R	44	42	−5	4.40	14
(Context Negative vs. Emotion Negative) vs. (Context Positive vs. Emotion Positive)							
Caudate (tail)		L	−24	−42	13	4.98	13
Hippocampus		L	−36	−16	−16	3.60	7
(Emotion Positive vs. Emotion Negative) vs. (Context Positive vs. Context Negative):							
Hippocampus		L	−32	−16	−16	5.06	10
Cingulate gyrus	31	L	−24	−46	13	4.64	17
Postcentral gyrus	3	L	−48	−18	34	4.51	28
(Context Negative vs. Context Positive) vs. (Emotion Negative vs. Emotion Positive):							
Hippocampus		L	−32	−16	−16	5.06	19
Caudate (tail)		L	−24	−42	13	4.98	13
Postcentral gyrus	3	L	−48	−18	34	4.51	15
Middle frontal gyrus	10	R	40	42	−5	4.32	11

Significant activations resulting from whole-brain analyses investigating direct contrasts and interactions are reported. For direct contrasts, a threshold of $p < 0.001$ was used, and for interactions a threshold of $p < 0.005$ was used. For the interaction analyses, the interaction contrast was inclusively masked with the corresponding direct contrast set up at $p < 0.05$. A cluster size of 10 contiguous voxels was used in all analyses, except for the MTL, where a cluster size of 5 contiguous voxels was used. BA = Brodmann's area; L = left, R = right.

This finding is consistent with the emotion research suggesting that the AMY's engagement can be modulated by attention, current goals, and task demands (Blair et al., 2007; Lieberman et al., 2007; Shafer et al., 2012). Moreover, this finding extends the available evidence by revealing that this effect also applies to the retrieval of positive and negative AMs. This is important because the evidence that left AMY activity is susceptible to and acts in accordance with the current retrieval goals clarifies inconsistent findings regarding its involvement in previous AM studies. Typically, these studies emphasize the effortful reconstruction of personal episodes that occurred at a specific time and place (Maguire, 2001; Svoboda et al., 2006), and do not systematically or explicitly probe the emotionality of the recollected memories.

(2) The AMY activity was also positively correlated with the emotional intensity ratings in the Emotion vs. Context condition, so that greater engagement of the AMY when focusing on emotional compared to the contextual details was associated with greater subjective re-experience of emotion of the recollected AMs. This finding provides, therefore, a direct link between AMY activity and subjective affective re-experience, which was not observed in previous "standard" AM studies (Maguire and Frith, 2003; Addis et al., 2004) probably due to the absence of a clear emotional focus during retrieval.

DISSOCIABLE EFFECTS OF RETRIEVAL FOCUS ON POSITIVE AND NEGATIVE AM RETRIEVAL IN AMY AND HC

(3) Retrieval of positive AMs was associated with increased right AMY activity in the Emotion compared to the Context condition, while retrieval of negative AMs produced similar effects in the right AMY. The latter finding suggests that the right AMY activity is not modulated by the current retrieval goals in the case of negative AMs. This is in contrast to the left AMY activity, which is sensitive to the current retrieval goals in the case of both positive and negative AMs, and altogether these findings suggest a hemispheric dissociation in the AMY regarding to the retrieval focus during AM recollection. Available evidence points to various factors that may influence hemispheric asymmetries in emotion processing that may also affect AMY activity, including emotional valence (negative vs. positive) (Canli et al., 1998), memory processes (encoding vs. retrieval) (Sergerie et al., 2006), and level of processing (automatic vs. elaborated) (Morris et al., 1998; Glascher and Adolphs, 2003; Dyck et al., 2011; Ritchey et al., 2011).

The present AMY lateralization cannot be fully explained by valence effects alone, but could be linked to Glascher's and Adolphs' (2003) suggestion that the right AMY is involved in initial, automatic detection of emotions, whereas the left AMY is involved in more elaborated cognitive representation of emotions (see also Morris et al., 1999; Phelps et al., 2001). In the present study, it might be the case that because of its more automatic engagement in emotion detection and processing, and possibly because of different prioritization of processing negative emotions, the right AMY may be less susceptible to modulations of the retrieval focus during recollection of negative AMs. Hence, its response was similarly high regardless of whether the focus was on Emotion or on Context, which was not the case for positive AMs. This interpretation is also consistent with evidence of fast processing of negative stimuli in the AMY (Morris et al., 1999; Vuilleumier et al., 2001).

The absence of significant differences in AMY activity between positive and negative AMs retrieved with an Emotion focus is in line with a valence-independent role of the AMY in the detection and evaluation of relevant and salient emotions (Wager et al., 2008; Lindquist et al., 2012) and with evidence of its involvement in emotional personal recollections (Botzung et al., 2010; Staniloiu and Markowitsch, 2012). Overall, the present data are consistent with both a stronger left AMY engagement for positive and negative AMs, when there is an explicit emphasis on emotional aspects, and a differential right AMY engagement for positive and negative AMs, when emotional processing is not overtly demanded. These findings point to the interplay between emotional valence and retrieval focus, which if not considered together can lead to incomplete conclusions.

(4) Manipulation of the retrieval focus was associated with increased activity for positive and decreased activity for negative AMs in the left HC, in the Emotion condition. Given the evidence linking left hippocampal activity to more detailed recollections (Addis et al., 2004), a possible interpretation is that negative AMs in the Emotion condition are less detailed than the negative AMs in the Context condition. However, this interpretation is not consistent with the present behavioral results, which did not show differences in the scores for Vividness in the Emotion and Context conditions (3.37 and 3.32, respectively). A slightly more nuanced interpretation can be proposed if the effects observed in the HC are considered in the context of evidence regarding its role in processing visual landmarks (Berthoz, 1997) and in binding together contextual and scene-related details (Davachi et al., 2003; Davachi, 2006). Specifically, it could be speculated that greater involvement of the posterior portion of the HC may be solicited to bind contextual details that are detached from emotional aspects (i.e., negative AMs with Context focus). Therefore, the decrease in the left HC for negative memories in the Emotion condition (which had the highest intensity ratings) could be due to an automatic binding of details by arousal (Mather and Sutherland, 2011), which probably required less hippocampal involvement. However, in the case of positive AMs, probably attaining similar level of recollection required increased left hippocampal involvement when the retrieval focus was on Emotion.

Caveats

One limitation of the present study is the absence of a Neutral control condition, which limits the interpretation of the findings. This was mainly dictated by the difficulty in identifying enough neutral memories that could be equated with the emotional AMs in terms of their phenomenological properties. The inclusion of neutral memories in future studies could be used as an additional baseline to complement the present findings. Another limitation is that the number of subjects did not allow proper investigation of sex-related differences, which have been addressed in only a handful of AM neuroimaging studies (e.g., Piefke et al., 2005; St Jacques et al., 2011). Future studies should examine whether the effects of retrieval focus and valence are differently affected in women and men.

CONCLUSION

In summary, the present study reveals similar and differential involvement of the AMY and HC during the recollection of emotional personal memories, linked to the current retrieval goals and the valence of memories. By shedding light on the role of AMY and HC in these effects, the present findings clarify mixed or inconclusive findings of previous AMs studies in healthy participants, and have the potential to contribute to a better understanding and prevention of affective disorders, which are characterized by an excessive focus on negative AMs.

ACKNOWLEDGMENTS

This research was supported by funds from NARSAD (currently the Brain & Behavior Research Foundation), CPRF (currently Healthy Minds Canada), and the University of Illinois (to FD). ED was supported by a Wyeth-CIHR Post-Doctoral Fellowship. The authors wish to thank Trisha Chakrabarty and Kristina Suen for assistance with data collection and analysis.

REFERENCES

Addis, D. R., Moscovitch, M., Crawley, A. P., and McAndrews, M. P. (2004). Recollective qualities modulate hippocampal activation during autobiographical memory retrieval. *Hippocampus* 14, 752–762. doi:10.1002/hipo.10215

Addis, D. R., Wong, A. T., and Schacter, D. L. (2007). Remembering the past and imagining the future: common and distinct neural substrates during event construction and elaboration. *Neuropsychologia* 45, 1363–1377. doi:10.1016/j.neuropsychologia.2006.10.016

Battig, W. F., and Montague, W. E. (1969). Category norms of verbal items in 56 categories a replication and extension of the connecticut category norms. *J. Exp. Psychol.* 80, 1–46. doi:10.1037/h0027577

Berthoz, A. (1997). Parietal and hippocampal contribution to topokinetic and topographic memory. *Philos. Trans. R. Soc. Lond. B Biol. Sci.* 352, 1437–1448. doi:10.1098/rstb.1997.0130

Blair, K. S., Smith, B. W., Mitchell, D. G., Morton, J., Vythilingam, M., Pessoa, L., et al. (2007). Modulation of emotion by cognition and cognition by emotion. *Neuroimage* 35, 430–440. doi:10.1016/j.neuroimage.2006.11.048

Bluck, S., and Alea, N. (2009a). Thinking and talking about the past: why remember? *Appl. Cogn. Psychol.* 23, 1089–1104. doi:10.1002/acp.1612

Bluck, S., and Alea, N. (2009b). Characteristics of positive autobiographical memories in adulthood. *Int. J. Aging Hum. Dev.* 69, 247–265. doi:10.2190/AG.69.4.a

Botzung, A., Denkova, E., Ciuciu, P., Scheiber, C., and Manning, L. (2008). The neural bases of the constructive nature of autobiographical memories studied with a self-paced fMRI design. *Memory* 16, 351–363. doi:10.1080/09658210801931222

Botzung, A., Rubin, D. C., Miles, A., Cabeza, R., and Labar, K. S. (2010). Mental hoop diaries: emotional memories of a college basketball game in rival fans. *J. Neurosci.* 30, 2130–2137. doi:10.1523/JNEUROSCI.2481-09.2010

Brewin, C. R., Reynolds, M., and Tata, P. (1999). Autobiographical memory processes and the course of depression. *J. Abnorm. Psychol.* 108, 511–517. doi:10.1037/0021-843X.108.3.511

Cabeza, R., and St Jacques, P. (2007). Functional neuroimaging of autobiographical memory. *Trends Cogn. Sci.* 11, 219–227. doi:10.1016/j.tics.2007.02.005

Canli, T., Desmond, J. E., Zhao, Z., Glover, G., and Gabrieli, J. D. (1998). Hemispheric asymmetry for emotional stimuli detected with fMRI. *Neuroreport* 9, 3233–3239. doi:10.1097/00001756-199810050-00019

Daselaar, S. M., Rice, H. J., Greenberg, D. L., Cabeza, R., LaBar, K. S., and Rubin, D. C. (2008). The spatiotemporal dynamics of autobiographical memory: neural correlates of recall, emotional intensity, and reliving. *Cereb. Cortex* 18, 217–229. doi:10.1093/cercor/bhm048

Davachi, L. (2006). Item, context and relational episodic encoding in humans. *Curr. Opin. Neurobiol.* 16, 693–700. doi:10.1016/j.conb.2006.10.012

Davachi, L., Mitchell, J. P., and Wagner, A. D. (2003). Multiple routes to memory: distinct medial temporal lobe processes build item and source memories. *Proc. Natl. Acad. Sci. U.S.A.* 100, 2157–2162. doi:10.1073/pnas.0337195100

Denkova, E., Botzung, A., Scheiber, C., and Manning, L. (2006). Implicit emotion during recollection of past events: a nonverbal fMRI study. *Brain Res.* 1078, 143–150. doi:10.1016/j.brainres.2006.01.061

Denkova, E., Dolcos, S., and Dolcos, F. (2012). Reliving emotional personal memories: affective biases linked to personality and sex-related differences. *Emotion* 12, 515–528. doi:10.1037/a0026809

Denkova, E., Wong, G., Dolcos, S., Sung, K., Wang, L., Coupland, N., et al. (2010). The impact of anxiety-inducing distraction on cognitive performance: a combined brain imaging and personality investigation. *PLoS ONE* 5:e14150. doi:10.1371/journal.pone.0014150

Dolcos, F., Denkova, E., and Dolcos, S. (2012). Neural correlates of emotional memories: a review of evidence from brain imaging studies. Special issue on recent advances of functional neuroimaging studies on episodic memories. *Psychologia* 55, 80–111. doi:10.2117/psysoc.2012.80

Dolcos, F., LaBar, K. S., and Cabeza, R. (2004). Interaction between the amygdala and the medial temporal lobe memory system predicts better memory for emotional events. *Neuron* 42, 855–863. doi:10.1016/S0896-6273(04)00289-2

Dolcos, F., LaBar, K. S., and Cabeza, R. (2005). Remembering one year later: role of the amygdala and the medial temporal lobe memory system in retrieving emotional memories. *Proc. Natl. Acad. Sci. U.S.A.* 102, 2626–2631. doi:10.1073/pnas.0409848102

Dolcos, F., and McCarthy, G. (2006). Brain systems mediating cognitive interference by emotional distraction. *J. Neurosci.* 26, 2072–2079. doi:10.1523/JNEUROSCI.5042-05.2006

Dyck, M., Loughead, J., Kellermann, T., Boers, F., Gur, R. C., and Mathiak, K. (2011). Cognitive versus automatic mechanisms of mood induction differentially activate left and right amygdala. *Neuroimage* 54, 2503–2513. doi:10.1016/j.neuroimage.2010.10.013

Finnbogadottir, H., and Berntsen, D. (2012). Involuntary future projections are as frequent as involuntary memories, but more positive. *Conscious. Cogn.* 22, 272–280. doi:10.1016/j.concog.2012.06.014

Glascher, J., and Adolphs, R. (2003). Processing of the arousal of subliminal and supraliminal emotional stimuli by the human amygdala. *J. Neurosci.* 23, 10274–10282.

Greenberg, D. L., Rice, H. J., Cooper, J. J., Cabeza, R., Rubin, D. C., and Labar, K. S. (2005). Co-activation of the amygdala, hippocampus and inferior frontal gyrus during autobiographical memory retrieval. *Neuropsychologia* 43, 659–674. doi:10.1016/j.neuropsychologia.2004.09.002

Hamann, S. B., Ely, T. D., Grafton, S. T., and Kilts, C. D. (1999). Amygdala activity related to enhanced memory for pleasant and aversive stimuli. *Nat. Neurosci.* 2, 289–293. doi:10.1038/6404

Joormann, J., Siemer, M., and Gotlib, I. H. (2007). Mood regulation in depression: differential effects of distraction and recall of happy memories on sad mood. *J. Abnorm. Psychol.* 116, 484–490. doi:10.1037/0021-843X.116.3.484

Josephson, B. R., Singer, J. A., and Salovey, P. (1996). Mood regulation and memory: repairing sad moods with happy memories. *Cogn. Emot.* 10, 437–444. doi:10.1080/026999396380222

Kensinger, E. A., and Corkin, S. (2004). Two routes to emotional memory: distinct neural processes for valence and arousal. *Proc. Natl. Acad. Sci. U.S.A.* 101, 3310–3315. doi:10.1073/pnas.0306408101

Kensinger, E. A., and Schacter, D. L. (2006). Amygdala activity is associated with the successful encoding of item, but not source, information for positive and negative stimuli. *J. Neurosci.* 26, 2564–2570. doi:10.1523/JNEUROSCI.5241-05.2006

Levine, B., Svoboda, E., Hay, J. F., Winocur, G., and Moscovitch, M. (2002). Aging and autobiographical memory: dissociating episodic from semantic retrieval. *Psychol. Aging* 17, 677–689. doi:10.1037/0882-7974.17.4.677

Lieberman, M. D., Eisenberger, N. I., Crockett, M. J., Tom, S. M., Pfeifer, J. H., and Way, B. M. (2007). Putting feelings into words: affect labeling disrupts amygdala activity in response to affective stimuli. *Psychol. Sci.* 18, 421–428. doi:10.1111/j.1467-9280.2007.01916.x

Lindquist, K. A., Wager, T. D., Kober, H., Bliss-Moreau, E., and Barrett, L. F. (2012). The brain basis of emotion: a meta-analytic review. *Behav. Brain Sci.* 35, 121–143. doi:10.1017/S0140525X11000446

MacLeod, A. K., and Byrne, A. (1996). Anxiety, depression, and the anticipation of future positive and negative experiences. *J. Abnorm. Psychol.* 105, 286–289. doi:10.1037/0021-843X.105.2.286

Maguire, E. A. (2001). Neuroimaging studies of autobiographical event memory. *Philos. Trans. R. Soc. Lond. B Biol. Sci.* 356, 1441–1451. doi:10.1098/rstb.2001.0944

Maguire, E. A., and Frith, C. D. (2003). Lateral asymmetry in the hippocampal response to the remoteness of autobiographical memories. *J. Neurosci.* 23, 5302–5307.

Maguire, E. A., and Mummery, C. J. (1999). Differential modulation of a common memory retrieval network revealed by positron emission tomography. *Hippocampus* 9, 54–61. doi:10.1002/(SICI)1098-1063(1999)9:1<54::AID-HIPO6>3.0.CO;2-O

Markowitsch, H. J., and Staniloiu, A. (2011). Amygdala in action: relaying biological and social significance to autobiographical memory. *Neuropsychologia* 49, 718–733. doi:10.1016/j.neuropsychologia.2010.10.007

Markowitsch, H. J., Thiel, A., Reinkemeier, M., Kessler, J., Koyuncu, A., and Heiss, W. D. (2000). Right amygdalar and temporofrontal activation during autobiographic, but not during fictitious memory retrieval. *Behav. Neurol.* 12, 181–190.

Markowitsch, H. J., Vandekerckhove, M. M., Lanfermann, H., and Russ, M. O. (2003). Engagement of lateral and medial prefrontal areas in the ecphory of sad and happy autobiographical memories. *Cortex* 39, 643–665. doi:10.1016/S0010-9452(08)70858-X

Mather, M., and Sutherland, M. R. (2011). Arousal-biased competition in perception and memory. *Perspect. Psychol. Sci.* 6, 114–133. doi:10.1177/1745691611400234

Mor, N., and Winquist, J. (2002). Self-focused attention and negative affect: a meta-analysis. *Psychol. Bull.* 128, 638–662. doi:10.1037/0033-2909.128.4.638

Morris, J. S., Ohman, A., and Dolan, R. J. (1998). Conscious and unconscious emotional learning in the human amygdala. *Nature* 393, 467–470. doi:10.1038/30976

Morris, J. S., Ohman, A., and Dolan, R. J. (1999). A subcortical pathway to the right amygdala mediating "unseen" fear. *Proc. Natl. Acad. Sci. U.S.A.* 96, 1680–1685. doi:10.1073/pnas.96.4.1680

Nolen-Hoeksema, S., Wisco, B. E., and Lyubomirsky, S. (2008). Rethinking rumination. *Perspect. Psychol. Sci.* 3, 400–424. doi:10.1111/j.1745-6924.2008.00088.x

Ochsner, K. N., and Schacter, D. L. (2000). "A social cognitive neuroscience approach to emotion and memory," in *The Neuropsychology of Emotion*, ed. J. C. Borod (New York: Oxford University Press), 163–193.

Pennebaker, J. W., and Graybeal, A. (2001). Patterns of natural language use: disclosure, personality, and social integration. *Curr. Dir. Psychol. Sci.* 10, 90–93. doi:10.1111/1467-8721.00123

Phelps, E. A., O'Connor, K. J., Gatenby, J. C., Grillon, C., Gore, J. C., and Davis, M. (2001). Activation of the left amygdala to a cognitive representation of fear. *Nat. Neurosci.* 4, 437–441. doi:10.1038/86110

Piefke, M., Weiss, P. H., Markowitsch, H. J., and Fink, G. R. (2005). Gender differences in the functional neuroanatomy of emotional episodic autobiographical memory. *Hum. Brain Mapp.* 24, 313–324. doi:10.1002/hbm.20092

Piefke, M., Weiss, P. H., Zilles, K., Markowitsch, H. J., and Fink, G. R. (2003). Differential remoteness and emotional tone modulate the neural correlates of autobiographical memory. *Brain* 126(Pt 3), 650–668. doi:10.1093/brain/awg064

Rasmussen, A. S., and Berntsen, D. (2013). The reality of the past versus the ideality of the future: emotional valence and functional differences between past and future mental time travel. *Mem Cognit.* 41, 187–200. doi:10.3758/s13421-012-0260-y

Ritchey, M., Dolcos, F., and Cabeza, R. (2008). Role of amygdala connectivity in the persistence of emotional memories over time: an event-related FMRI investigation. *Cereb. Cortex* 18, 2494–2504. doi:10.1093/cercor/bhm262

Ritchey, M., LaBar, K. S., and Cabeza, R. (2011). Level of processing modulates the neural correlates of emotional memory formation. *J. Cogn. Neurosci.* 23, 757–771. doi:10.1162/jocn.2010.21487

Sergerie, K., Lepage, M., and Armony, J. L. (2006). A process-specific functional dissociation of the amygdala in emotional memory. *J. Cogn. Neurosci.* 18, 1359–1367. doi:10.1162/jocn.2006.18.8.1359

Shafer, A. T., Matveychuk, D., Penney, T., O'Hare, A. J., Stokes, J., and Dolcos, F. (2012). Processing of emotional distraction is both automatic and modulated by attention: evidence from an event-related fMRI investigation. *J. Cogn. Neurosci.* 24, 1233–1252. doi:10.1162/jocn_a_00206

Sharot, T., Riccardi, A. M., Raio, C. M., and Phelps, E. A. (2007). Neural mechanisms mediating optimism bias. *Nature* 450, 102–105. doi:10.1038/nature06280

Smith, A. P., Stephan, K. E., Rugg, M. D., and Dolan, R. J. (2006). Task and content modulate amygdala-hippocampal connectivity in emotional retrieval. *Neuron* 49, 631–638. doi:10.1016/j.neuron.2005.12.025

Smith, J. M., and Alloy, L. B. (2009). A roadmap to rumination: a review of the definition, assessment, and conceptualization of this multifaceted construct. *Clin. Psychol. Rev.* 29, 116–128. doi:10.1016/j.cpr.2008.10.003

St Jacques, P. L. (2012). "Functional neuroimaging of autobiographical memory," in *Understanding Autobiographical Memory: Theories and Approaches*, eds D. Bernsten, and D. C. Rubin (Cambridge: Cambridge University Press), 114–138.

St Jacques, P. L., Conway, M. A., and Cabeza, R. (2011). Gender differences in autobiographical memory for everyday events: retrieval elicited by SenseCam images versus verbal cues. *Memory* 19, 723–732. doi:10.1080/09658211.2010.516266

Staniloiu, A., and Markowitsch, H. J. (2012). A rapprochement between emotion and cognition: amygdala, emotion, and self-relevance in episodic-autobiographical memory. *Behav. Brain Sci.* 35, 164–166. doi:10.1017/S0140525X11001543

Svoboda, E., McKinnon, M. C., and Levine, B. (2006). The functional neuroanatomy of autobiographical memory: a meta-analysis. *Neuropsychologia* 44, 2189–2208. doi:10.1016/j.neuropsychologia.2006.05.023

Szpunar, K. K., Addis, D. R., and Schacter, D. L. (2012). Memory for emotional simulations: remembering a rosy future. *Psychol. Sci.* 23, 24–29. doi:10.1177/0956797611422237

Vandekerckhove, M. M., Markowitsch, H. J., Mertens, M., and Woermann, F. G. (2005). Bi-hemispheric engagement in the retrieval of autobiographical episodes. *Behav. Neurol.* 16, 203–210.

Vuilleumier, P., Armony, J. L., Driver, J., and Dolan, R. J. (2001). Effects of attention and emotion on face processing in the human brain: an event-related fMRI study. *Neuron* 30, 829–841. doi:10.1016/S0896-6273(01)00328-2

Wager, T. D., Barrett, L. F., Bliss-Moreau, E., Lindquist, K., Duncan, S., Kober, H., et al. (2008). "The neuroimaging of emotion," in *The Handbook of Emotion*, eds M. Lewis, J. M. Haviland-Jones, and L. F. Barrett, 3rd Edn. (New York: Guilford), 249–271.

Wilson, T. D., and Gilbert, D. T. (2008). Explaining away: a model of affective adaptation. *Perspect. Psychol. Sci.* 3, 370–386. doi:10.1111/j.1745-6924.2008.00085.x

Young, K. D., Bellgowan, P. S., Bodurka, J., and Drevets, W. C. (2012). Functional neuroimaging of sex differences in autobiographical memory recall. *Hum. Brain Mapp.* doi:10.1002/hbm.22144

Permissions

All chapters in this book were first published by Frontiers; hereby published with permission under the Creative Commons Attribution License or equivalent. Every chapter published in this book has been scrutinized by our experts. Their significance has been extensively debated. The topics covered herein carry significant findings which will fuel the growth of the discipline. They may even be implemented as practical applications or may be referred to as a beginning point for another development.

The contributors of this book come from diverse backgrounds, making this book a truly international effort. This book will bring forth new frontiers with its revolutionizing research information and detailed analysis of the nascent developments around the world.

We would like to thank all the contributing authors for lending their expertise to make the book truly unique. They have played a crucial role in the development of this book. Without their invaluable contributions this book wouldn't have been possible. They have made vital efforts to compile up to date information on the varied aspects of this subject to make this book a valuable addition to the collection of many professionals and students.

This book was conceptualized with the vision of imparting up-to-date information and advanced data in this field. To ensure the same, a matchless editorial board was set up. Every individual on the board went through rigorous rounds of assessment to prove their worth. After which they invested a large part of their time researching and compiling the most relevant data for our readers.

The editorial board has been involved in producing this book since its inception. They have spent rigorous hours researching and exploring the diverse topics which have resulted in the successful publishing of this book. They have passed on their knowledge of decades through this book. To expedite this challenging task, the publisher supported the team at every step. A small team of assistant editors was also appointed to further simplify the editing procedure and attain best results for the readers.

Apart from the editorial board, the designing team has also invested a significant amount of their time in understanding the subject and creating the most relevant covers. They scrutinized every image to scout for the most suitable representation of the subject and create an appropriate cover for the book.

The publishing team has been an ardent support to the editorial, designing and production team. Their endless efforts to recruit the best for this project, has resulted in the accomplishment of this book. They are a veteran in the field of academics and their pool of knowledge is as vast as their experience in printing. Their expertise and guidance has proved useful at every step. Their uncompromising quality standards have made this book an exceptional effort. Their encouragement from time to time has been an inspiration for everyone.

The publisher and the editorial board hope that this book will prove to be a valuable piece of knowledge for researchers, students, practitioners and scholars across the globe.

List of Contributors

Michael A. Yassa and Zachariah M. Reagh
Department of Psychological and Brain Sciences, Johns Hopkins University, Baltimore, MD, USA

Armin Schnider
Division of Neurorehabilitation, Department of Clinical Neurosciences, University Hospital, University of Geneva, Geneva, Switzerland

Muireann Irish
School of Psychology, University of New South Wales, Sydney, NSW, Australia
Neuroscience Research Australia, Randwick, NSW, Australia
Australian Research Council Centre of Excellence in Cognition and its Disorders, Sydney, NSW, Australia

Olivier Piguet
Neuroscience Research Australia, Randwick, NSW, Australia
Australian Research Council Centre of Excellence in Cognition and its Disorders, Sydney, NSW, Australia
School of Medical Sciences, University of New South Wales, Sydney, NSW, Australia

Patric Meyer, Hanna Feldkamp, Michael Hoppstädter, Andrea V. King and Herta Flor
Department of Cognitive and Clinical Neuroscience, Central Institute of Mental Health, Medical Faculty Mannheim, Heidelberg University, Mannheim, Germany

Lutz Frölich
Division of Gerontopsychiatry, Central Institute of Mental Health, Medical Faculty Mannheim, Heidelberg University, Mannheim, Germany

Michèle Wessa
Section for Experimental Psychopathology and Neuroimaging, Department of General Psychiatry, Center for Psychosocial Medicine, Heidelberg University, Heidelberg, Germany

Katharina Henke, Thomas P. Reber and Simone B. Duss
Division of Experimental Psychology and Neuropsychology, Department of Psychology, University of Bern, Bern, Switzerland
Center for Cognition, Learning and Memory, University of Bern, Bern, Switzerland

Amy L. Griffin and Henry L. Hallock
Department of Psychology, University of Delaware, Newark, DE, USA

Brendan D. Murray and Elizabeth A. Kensinger
Department of Psychology, Boston College, Chestnut Hill, MA, USA

Sheri J. Y. Mizumori
Laboratory of Neural Systems, Decision Science, Learning and Memory, Department of Psychology, University of Washington, Seattle, WA, USA

Michaela Baumann
Department of Psychology, University of Konstanz, Konstanz, Germany

Bastian Zwissler
Department of Psychology, University of Konstanz, Konstanz, Germany
Department of Psychiatry, University of Tuebingen, Tuebingen, Germany

Inga Schalinski, Martina Ruf-Leuschner and Maggie Schauer
Department of Psychology, University of Konstanz, Konstanz, Germany
Center of Excellence for Psychotraumatology, University of Konstanz, Konstanz, Germany

Johanna Kissler
Department of Psychology, University of Konstanz, Konstanz, Germany
Department of Psychology, University of Bielefeld, Bielefeld, Germany

Mohamed Doulazmi
Neurobiologie des Processus Adaptatifs, UMR 7102, Université Pierre et Marie Curie, Paris 6, Paris, France
CNRS, UMR 7102, Paris, France

Kiyoka Kinugawa, Monica Pollina, Marion Depre, Claude Sebban, Jean Mariani and Ekrem Dere
Neurobiologie des Processus Adaptatifs, UMR 7102, Université Pierre et Marie Curie, Paris 6, Paris, France
CNRS, UMR 7102, Paris, France
Institut de la longévité, AP-HP Hôpital Charles Foix, Ivry-sur-Seine, Paris, France

Sophie Schumm
Institut de la longévité, AP-HP Hôpital Charles Foix, Ivry-sur-Seine, Paris, France

Carolin Jungbluth, Reinhard Pietrowsky and Bettina Pause
Institute of Experimental Psychology, University of Düsseldorf, Düsseldorf, Germany

Armin Zlomuzica
Center for the Study and Treatment of Mental Health, Ruhr-Universität Bochum, Bochum, Germany

Marco Sperduti, Pénélope Martinelli and Sandrine Kalenzaga
Laboratoire Mémoire et Cognition, Institut de Psychologie, Université Paris Descartes, Boulogne-Billancourt, France
INSERM U894, Centre de Psychiatrie et Neurosciences, Université Paris Descartes, Paris, France

Anne-Dominique Devauchelle, Stéphanie Lion, Caroline Malherbe and Catherine Oppenheim
INSERM U894, Service d'Imagerie, Université Paris Descartes Sorbonne Paris Cité, Paris, France

Thierry Gallarda, Isabelle Amado and Marie-Odile Krebs
INSERM U894, Centre de Psychiatrie et Neurosciences, Université Paris Descartes, Paris, France
Faculté de Médecine, Centre Hospitalier Sainte-Anne, Service Hospitalier Universitaire, Université Paris Descartes, Paris, France

Pascale Piolino
Laboratoire Mémoire et Cognition, Institut de Psychologie, Université Paris Descartes, Boulogne-Billancourt, France
INSERM U894, Centre de Psychiatrie et Neurosciences, Université Paris Descartes, Paris, France
Institut Universitaire de France, Paris, France

Uda-Mareke Risius and Angelica Staniloiu
Physiological Psychology, University of Bielefeld, Bielefeld, Germany

Martina Piefke
Physiological Psychology, University of Bielefeld, Bielefeld, Germany
Neurobiology and Behavioral Genetics, University Witten-Herdecke, Witten, Germany

StefanMaderwald
Erwin L.Hahn Institute for Magnetic Resonance Imaging, Essen, Germany

Frank P. Schulte and Matthias Brand
Erwin L. Hahn Institute for Magnetic Resonance Imaging, Essen, Germany
General Psychology: Cognition, University of Duisburg-Essen, Duisburg, Germany

Hans J. Markowitsch
Physiological Psychology, University of Bielefeld, Bielefeld, Germany
Institute for Advanced Science, Delmenhorst, Germany
Center of Excellence Cognitive Interaction Technology, University of Bielefeld, Bielefeld, Germany

Rebecca M. Todd and Adam K. Anderson
Department of Psychology, University of Toronto, Toronto, ON, Canada

Taylor W. Schmitz
Department of Psychology, University of Toronto, Toronto, ON, Canada
MRC Cognition and Brain Sciences Unit, University of Cambridge, Cambridge, UK

Josh Susskind
Institute for Telecommunications and Information Technology, University of California San Diego, San Diego, CA, USA

Géraldine Rauchs, Francis Eustache and Béatrice Desgranges
U1077, INSERM, Caen, France
UMR-S1077, Université de Caen Basse-Normandie, Caen, France
UMR-S1077, Ecole Pratique des Hautes Etudes, Caen, France
U1077, Centre Hospitalier Universitaire, Caen, France

Françoise Bertran
U1077, INSERM, Caen, France
UMR-S1077, Université de Caen Basse-Normandie, Caen, France
UMR-S1077, Ecole Pratique des Hautes Etudes, Caen, France
U1077, Centre Hospitalier Universitaire, Caen, France
Service des Explorations Fonctionnelles Neurologiques, Centre Hospitalier Universitaire, Caen, France

Vincent de La Sayette and Fausto Viader
U1077, INSERM, Caen, France
UMR-S1077, Université de Caen Basse-Normandie, Caen, France
UMR-S1077, Ecole Pratique des Hautes Etudes, Caen, France
Service de Neurologie, Centre Hospitalier Universitaire, Caen, France

Bérengère Guillery-Girard, Sebastien Deshayes, Brigitte Landeau, Patrice Clochon, Gaël Chételat and Francis Eustache
INSERM, U1077, Caen, France Université de Caen Basse-Normandie, UMR-S1077, Caen, France
Ecole Pratique des Hautes Etudes, UMR-S1077, Caen, France
CHU de Caen, UMR-S1077, Caen, France

Brendan D. Murray and Elizabeth A. Kensinger
Department of Psychology, Boston College, Chestnut Hill, MA, USA

Sylvie Martins
INSERM, U1077, Caen, France
Université de Caen Basse-Normandie, UMR-S1077, Caen, France
Ecole Pratique des Hautes Etudes, UMR-S1077, Caen, France
CHU de Caen, UMR-S1077, Caen, France
INSERM, U663, Paris, France
Université Paris Descartes, Paris, France
CEA Saclay, Gif sur Yvette, France
SHFJ et Neurospin, I2BM, CEA, Paris, France

Lucie Hertz-Pannier and Catherine Chiron
INSERM, U663, Paris, France
Université Paris Descartes, Paris, France
CEA Saclay, Gif sur Yvette, France
SHFJ et Neurospin, I2BM, CEA, Paris, France
Isabelle Jambaqué
INSERM, U663, Paris, France
Université Paris Descartes, Paris, France
CEA Saclay, Gif sur Yvette, France
Unité de Neurochirurgie Pédiatrique, Fondation Ophtalmologique Adolphe de Rothschild, Paris, France

Stanley B. Klein
Department of Psychological and Brain Sciences, University of California, Santa Barbara, CA, USA

Yan Chen, Helena Margaret McAnally and Elaine Reese
Department of Psychology, University of Otago, Dunedin, New Zealand

Bettina M. Pause
Institute of Experimental Psychology, University of Düsseldorf, Düsseldorf, Germany

Christian P. Müller
Section of Addiction Medicine, Department of Psychiatry and Psychotherapy, Friedrich-Alexander-University of Erlangen-Nuremberg, Erlangen, Germany

Ekaterina Denkova
Alberta Cognitive Neuroscience Group, University of Alberta, Edmonton, AB, Canada

Sanda Dolcos
Psychology Department, University of Illinois at Urbana-Champaign, Urbana, IL, USA

Florin Dolcos
Psychology Department, University of Illinois at Urbana-Champaign, Urbana, IL, USA
Neuroscience Program, University of Illinois at Urbana-Champaign, Urbana, IL, USA
Beckman Institute for Advanced Science and Technology, University of Illinois at Urbana-Champaign, Urbana, IL, USA

Index